INQUIRY JOURNAL

WORLD
HISTORY AND GEOGRAPHY

Mc
Graw
Hill
Education

About the Cover: View of the Jinshanling and Simatai sections of the Great Wall of China, located in Luanping County, northeast of Beijing, at sunrise.

Cover Photo Credits: Shutterstock/Sofiaworld

mheducation.com/prek-12

Send all inquiries to:
McGraw-Hill Education
8787 Orion Place
Columbus, OH 43240

ISBN: 978-0-07-692760-9
MHID: 0-07-692760-1

Printed in the United States of America.

1 2 3 4 5 6 7 8 9 QVS 23 22 21 20 19 18

Table of Contents

Dear Student,

Many of us are curious, and we have questions about many things. We have the more personal questions, such as, "What type of job or career might I be suited for?" or "How do I learn the best way to save money to buy the things I want or need?" to questions of a larger nature about the world around us. These might include questions such as the following: "What does being treated like an adult mean? Why do nations go to war with one another? How do I understand what I see or read about in history or online or in the news? Why do political parties clash with one another so frequently?"

Asking good questions helps us take charge of our own learning. Learning to ask good questions is a process, as "yes" or "no" types of questions do not get us very far in discovering why events happened or why people feel as they do. Once we master this process, however, we become better thinkers and researchers and can find out more about subjects that interest us. Asking good questions is also important if we want to understand and affect the world around us.

In this book, as in other parts of the program, there will be "Essential Questions" that you will research. These are universal questions. Examples of such questions include: "How do new ideas change the way people live?" and "What makes a culture unique?" and "What characteristics make a good leader?" and "Why does conflict develop?" You will choose some of your own supporting questions to help you answer the Essential Question.

As you move through the study of history, you will be reading primary and secondary sources about a specific time period. **Primary sources**—whether they are diaries, poetry, letters, or artwork—were created by people who saw or experienced the event they are describing. **Secondary sources**—whether they are biographies, or history books, or your student text, are created after an event, by people who were not part of the original event.

Once you have completed the readings and the text notes, there is a "Report Your Findings" project in which you answer the Essential Question. You will work on some parts of the project by yourself, and you will work on other parts of the project with your classmates. You will be given many opportunities to take informed action. This means that you will use what you have learned and apply it to a current issue in a way that interests you. You will share this information with other students or with people in your community.

The Rise of Civilization: Prehistory—c. 2300 B.C.

ESSENTIAL QUESTION

What do archaeology and anthropology teach us about prehistoric humans? What is a civilization, and how does one form?

Think about how artifacts provide evidence to anthropologists that civilizations may have formed a permanent settlement in an area.

TALK ABOUT IT

With a partner, brainstorm artifacts that might help anthropologists learn about prehistoric humans and the beginnings of civilizations. For example, what artifacts cannot easily be moved? What artifacts are meant to be used over time in the same place?

DIRECTIONS: Now write down three additional questions that will help you explain what kind of evidence anthropologists might look for to indicate that a permanent settlement or civilization has formed in a place. For example, you might ask, "What artifacts of our own time show that we have permanent settlements?"

MY RESEARCH QUESTIONS

Supporting Question 1:

_____

_____

Supporting Question 2:

_____

_____

Supporting Question 3:

_____

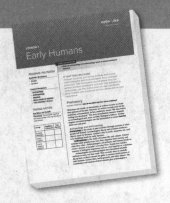

Early Humans

DIRECTIONS Search for evidence in the lesson to help you answer the following questions.

1 **COMPARING AND CONTRASTING** What is the difference between archaeology and anthropology?

_____

_____

_____

_____

_____

2 **SUMMARIZING** What were some of the major characteristics of the Paleolithic Age?

Paleolithic Age

ESSENTIAL QUESTION

What do archaeology and anthropology teach us about prehistoric humans?

As you gather evidence to answer the Essential Question, think about:

- how evidence of prehistoric early humans differs from evidence gathered after writing was developed.

- how the earliest humans developed during the early stages of human history.

- what characteristics define the Paleolithic Age.

My Notes

_____

_____

_____

_____

_____

_____

_____

3 **UNDERSTANDING CONTEXT** Why are the ideas that archaeologists and anthropologists have about the earliest humans considered theories?

_____

_____

_____

_____

4 **ANALYZING** What can we learn about early humans by knowing that they only had tools made of stone, and that their stone weapons improved over time?

_____

_____

_____

_____

_____

_____

5 **IDENTIFYING CAUSE AND EFFECT** How did brain development in hominids allow for the emergence of modern humans?

_____

_____

_____

_____

_____

_____

6 **EXPLAINING EFFECTS** What effect did the mastery of fire have on the migration of early humans?

_____

_____

_____

_____

_____

_____

VOCABULARY

innovation: advancement

oblivion: nothingness

bipedal: having two legs or feet

bestowed: gave

Richard Leakey on Human Origins

DIRECTIONS: Study the excerpt. Then respond to the questions that follow.

EXPLORE THE CONTEXT: Richard Leakey is the son of Mary and Louis Leakey, archaeologists famous for their work on early humans. Like his parents, Leakey studies human origins. Through his own archaeology work and his study of the work of others, he has expanded our understanding of how the first humans developed. In this excerpt, Leakey explores the role of the environment in evolution.

SECONDARY SOURCE: BOOK

❝ Biologists have come to realize that mosaic environments of this kind, which offer many different kinds of habitat, drive evolutionary innovation. Populations of a species that once were widespread and continuous may become isolated and exposed to new forces of natural selection. Such is the recipe for evolutionary change. Sometimes that change is toward oblivion, if favorable environments disappear. This, clearly, was the fate of most of the African apes: just three species exist today—the gorilla, the common chimpanzee, and the pygmy chimpanzee. But while most ape species suffered because of the environmental shift, one of them was blessed with a new adaptation that allowed it to survive and prosper. This was the first bipedal ape. Being bipedal clearly bestowed important survival advantages in the changing conditions. ❞

—Richard Leakey, *The Origin of Humankind*

1 **IDENTIFYING CAUSES** According to the excerpt, what is "the recipe for evolutionary change"?

_____

_____

_____

_____

2 **INTERPRETING** What feature of the African apes allowed for an adaptive advantage over the others? Why?

_____

_____

_____

_____

3 **EXPLAINING EFFECTS** According to Leakey, what is the effect of a "mosaic environment"?

_____

_____

_____

_____

4 **INTERPRETING** How does Leakey describe the changes that occurred to the three African ape species still living today?

_____

_____

_____

_____

5 **DRAWING CONCLUSIONS** What environmental changes do you think species will be affected by in the future, continuing the process of natural selection?

_____

_____

_____

_____

ESSENTIAL QUESTION

What do archaeology and anthropology teach us about prehistoric humans?

Paleolithic Cave Painting

DIRECTIONS: Study the image. Then respond to the questions that follow.

EXPLORE THE CONTEXT: This photo of a cave painting found in Europe shows bison, horses, and human hand prints. The paintings are among the earliest known art, dating back about 35,000 years.

PRIMARY SOURCE: PHOTO

—Paleolithic cave painting, found in Europe

1 **INTERPRETING** The cave painting is typical of many others done at the same time. What does the painting suggest about life in the Paleolithic Era?

_____

_____

_____

_____

2 **UNDERSTANDING CONTEXT** Anthropologists suggest that the paintings tell stories about life during the Paleolithic Era. Why do you think the hand prints were included in the paintings?

_____

_____

_____

_____

3 **INTERPRETING** Why do you think the paintings were done on cave walls?

_____

_____

_____

_____

4 **COMPARING AND CONTRASTING** What questions do you think anthropologists would ask as they compare and contrast paintings from different caves that were done around the same time? Give an example.

_____

_____

_____

_____

5 **DRAWING CONCLUSIONS** Because the paintings lasted on the walls for a long time, what role do you think they played for children growing up at the time?

_____

_____

_____

The Neolithic Revolution

DIRECTIONS Search for evidence in the lesson to help you answer the following questions.

ESSENTIAL QUESTIONS

What do archaeology and anthropology teach us about prehistoric humans? What is a civilization, and how does one form?

As you gather evidence to answer the Essential Questions, think about:

- how the Neolithic Revolution saw a shift away from hunting and gathering to systematic agriculture in places around the world.

- how changes in human society during the Neolithic Revolution brought about the development of civilization.

- what kinds of characteristics people share in a distinct culture or civilization.

My Notes

_____

_____

_____

_____

_____

1 **DETERMINING CENTRAL IDEAS** In your own words, provide a definition of the Neolithic Revolution.

_____

_____

_____

_____

_____

_____

2 **IDENTIFYING CAUSE AND EFFECT** What were some of the major causes and effects of the Neolithic Revolution?

Cause	Effect

3 **INTERPRETING** How did increased trade in the Neolithic Age lead to the rise of artisans? What kinds of tools became popular at this time?

_____

_____

_____

_____

_____

_____

4 **COMPARING AND CONTRASTING** How is life in a nomadic group different from life in a permanent settlement?

_____

_____

_____

_____

_____

_____

_____

_____

5 **ANALYZING INFORMATION** How did priests fit into the Neolithic social structure? Why?

_____

_____

_____

_____

_____

_____

_____

_____

_____

Copyright © McGraw-Hill Education   Mihelic Pulsipher, Lydia and Pulsipher, Alex. World Regional Geography: Global Patterns, Local Lives - Fifth Edition. New York: W.H. Freeman and Company, 2011.

ESSENTIAL QUESTION

What do archaeology and anthropology teach us about prehistoric humans?

VOCABULARY

husbandry: care of plants and animals

"day job": familiar term for work that a person needs to play everyday bills

sustenance: food needed for survival

Agriculture and Trade

DIRECTIONS: Study the excerpt. Then respond to the questions that follow.

EXPLORE THE CONTEXT: Geographer Lydia Mihelic Pulsipher is a cultural-historical geographer. She studies how people and geography affect each other in the present and the past. In this excerpt, she discusses the development of farming.

SECONDARY SOURCE: BOOK

❝Why did agriculture and animal husbandry develop in the first place? Certainly the desire for more secure food resources played a role, but the opportunity to trade may have been just as important. Many of the known locations of agricultural innovation lie near early trade centers. There, people would have had access to new information and new plants and animals brought by traders, and would have needed products to trade. Perhaps, then, agriculture was at first a profitable hobby for hunters and gatherers that eventually, because of the desire for food security and market demands, grew into a "day job" for some—their primary source of sustenance.❞

—Lydia Milhelic Pulsipher, *World Regional Geography: Global Patterns, Local Lives*

1 **SUMMARIZING** What reasons does Lydia Mihelic Pulsipher give for the development of farming?

_____

_____

_____

_____

_____

_____

_____

_____

2 **INTERPRETING** How did one reason for farming overtake the other and become more prominent in developing societies?

_____

_____

_____

_____

3 **ANALYZING POINT OF VIEW** According to Pulsipher's ideas, why did trade centers develop near ports over time?

_____

_____

_____

_____

4 **INFERRING** Why did this pattern of farming for sustenance develop in many regions around the globe, instead of just in those with the best agricultural resources?

_____

_____

_____

_____

5 GEOGRAPHY What role do you think weather and climate may have played in the success of the earliest farmers? Explain.

_____

_____

_____

_____

_____

_____

_____

ESSENTIAL QUESTION
What do archaeology and anthropology teach us about prehistoric humans?

Neolithic Archeological Site: Skara Brae

DIRECTIONS: Study the image. Then respond to the questions that follow.

EXPLORE THE CONTEXT: This photo shows an ancient Neolithic archeological site in Scotland. The Skara Brae was a series of eight dwellings linked together, and inhabited for about 600 years between around 3200 B.C. and 2200 B.C. The site was eventually covered in sand and preserved until its discovery in the 1800s.

PRIMARY SOURCE: PHOTO

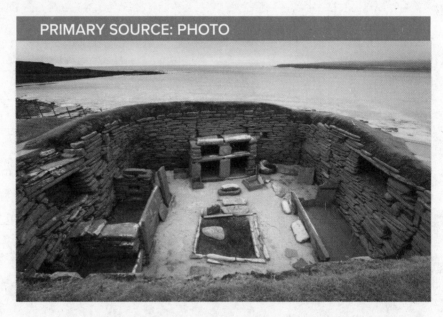

—Neolithic Archeological Site: Skara Brae, located in Orkney, Scotland

1 **INTERPRETING** What can you tell about the craftsmanship of the people who lived in the dwellings?

_____

_____

_____

_____

_____

_____

2 UNDERSTANDING CONTEXT What does the fact that the dwellings are connected tell about the way the people lived?

_____

_____

_____

_____

3 GEOGRAPHY Based on what you know about geology, what do you think the landscape looked like when the structures were inhabited 4,000 years ago?

_____

_____

_____

_____

4 ASKING QUESTIONS What questions do you think anthropologists might ask about the people who lived in these dwellings?

_____

_____

_____

_____

5 DRAWING CONCLUSIONS What benefits and drawbacks did the residents have for being in this location?

_____

_____

_____

_____

ESSENTIAL QUESTION

What is a civilization, and how does one form?

As you gather evidence to answer the Essential Question, think about:

- what the Mesopotamian civilization taught archaeologists about the past.
- how the Mesopotamians affected later civilizations.
- how the Mesopotamians used the land to help their society thrive.

My Notes

_____

_____

_____

_____

_____

Mesopotamia

DIRECTIONS Search for evidence in the lesson to help you answer the following questions.

1 **DETERMINING CENTRAL IDEAS** Why was Mesopotamia considered one of the first civilizations?

_____

_____

_____

_____

_____

_____

2 **COMPARING AND CONTRASTING** How did the location of the Mesopotamian civilization make the Sumerians different from people who came before them?

_____

_____

_____

_____

3 **EXPLAINING EFFECTS** Choose one of the inventions of the Sumerians. How did it affect people who came after?

_____

_____

_____

4 **SUMMARIZING** What were some of the major characteristics of the Mesopotamian civilization?

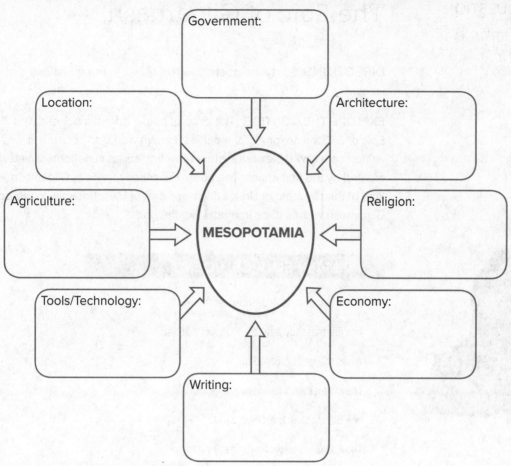

5 **COMPARING AND CONTRASTING** What does the difference between city dwellings and ziggurats tell about the priorities of the Sumerians?

_____
_____
_____

6 **ANALYZING** What made the development of metalwork possible for Sumerians?

_____
_____
_____

7 **UNDERSTANDING CONTEXT** Why was the work of scribes so important to modern anthropologists?

_____
_____
_____

ESSENTIAL QUESTION

What is a civilization, and how does one form?

VOCABULARY

whither: where; wherever

whither hurriest thou?: Where are you hurrying to?

The Epic of Gilgamesh

DIRECTIONS: Study the poem. Then respond to the questions that follow.

EXPLORE THE CONTEXT: The excerpt below is from a poem called *The Epic of Gilgamesh,* one of the earliest known works of literature. It was written on a clay tablet in a system of writing called cuneiform, which was created by the Sumerians. The poem describes the life of Gilgamesh, a king of the city state of Uruk, which was part of Mesopotamia. In the poem, Gilgamesh wishes to be immortal like the gods.

PRIMARY SOURCE: POEM

“Gilgamesh, whither hurriest thou?

The life that thou seekest thou wilt not find.

When the gods created man

They fixed death for mankind.

Life they took in their own hand.

Thou, O Gilgamesh, let thy belly be filled!

Day and night be merry,

Daily celebrate a feast,

Day and night dance and make merry!

Clean be thy clothes,

Thy head be washed, bathe in water!

Look joyfully on the child that grasps thy hand,

Be happy with the wife in thine arms!”

—*The Epic of Gilgamesh*

1 SUMMARIZING What message is the narrator trying to give Gilgamesh in the excerpt?

_____

_____

_____

2 ANALYZING POINT OF VIEW How do you think Gilgamesh's position as a king affects his point of view about death?

_____

_____

_____

3 INTERPRETING Based on Gilgamesh's obsession to find the secrets of immortality, what might be his likely personality and ruling style?

_____

_____

_____

_____

4 INTERPRETING How can you describe the types of activities the narrator is suggesting for Gilgamesh?

_____

_____

_____

5 DRAWING CONCLUSIONS What possible outcomes might Gilgamesh face going forward in his life?

_____

_____

_____

_____

ESSENTIAL QUESTION

What do archaeology and anthropology teach us about prehistoric humans?

Ancient Ziggurat

DIRECTIONS: Study the image. Then respond to the questions that follow.

EXPLORE THE CONTEXT: This photo shows a ziggurat, a Sumerian stepped tower that had a temple on top built for gods and goddesses. It is located in modern-day Iraq and was built by King Ur-Nammu around 2,100 B.C. for the moon goddess Nanna, patron of Ur. Citizens of Ur would likely go to the temple for worship and to receive food rations.

PRIMARY SOURCE: PHOTO

—Restored ziggurat in Ancient Ur

1 **INTERPRETING** What can you tell about the amount of time it likely took people to build the temple?

_____

_____

_____

2 **UNDERSTANDING CONTEXT** Why is it likely that the civilization that built this temple understood mathematics?

_____

_____

_____

3 **INTERPRETING** What does the size of the structure suggest about its purpose and function?

_____

_____

_____

_____

4 **ANALYZING CENTRAL IDEAS** What questions do you think anthropologists would ask about the ancient structure?

_____

_____

_____

_____

5 **DRAWING CONCLUSIONS** The structure has gone through two restorations. Why do you think it is considered an important structure to maintain?

_____

_____

_____

ESSENTIAL QUESTIONS

What do archaeology and anthropology teach us about prehistoric humans?

What is a civilization, and how does one form?

My Notes

_____

_____

_____

_____

_____

_____

_____

_____

_____

_____

_____

_____

_____

_____

1 Think About It

Review the evidence you gathered throughout the chapter to help you answer the Supporting Questions. Were you able to answer each of the Supporting Questions? If not, what additional evidence do you think you need to consider to answer those questions?

_____

_____

_____

2 Organize Your Evidence

Complete the chart below with information you learned about the earliest humans, settlements, and civilizations.

Earliest Humans	Earliest Settlements	Earliest Civilizations
	The Neolithic Age introduced systematic agriculture.	
Homo sapiens had rapid brain growth and mastered fire.		City-states allowed for the spread of ideas, religion, and culture.
The Paleolithic Age was characterized by hunter and gatherers who used simple stone and wooden tools.	The Neolithic Revolution introduced food storage, the division of labor, and societal roles.	
		Sumerian technology included the wagon wheel, sundial, bronze, and discoveries in math and astronomy.

3 Talk About It

Work in small groups. With your group, discuss the various methods anthropologists and archaeologists use to learn about artifacts, cultures, and people from the earliest civilizations. Consider information from each lesson in the chapter. Take notes about your discussion below.

_____

_____

_____

4 Write About It

Choose one of the human groups, settlements, or civilizations covered in the chapter. Write a summary of the group, its skills, technologies, and cultures, if any, its impact on civilizations that came after it.

_____

_____

_____

5 Connect to the Essential Question

Work in pairs to conduct and record a fictional interview with an anthropologist about his or her discoveries of prehistoric humans or early civilizations. Be sure to include information from the chapter as well as your own reasoning about the significance of anthropological findings about the past.

_____

_____

_____

TAKE ACTION

MAKE CONNECTIONS Modern communities learn about the past by reading, and also through the entertainment they see in the forms of nonfiction, fiction, graphic novels, and movies. Interpretations of historic events and fictional stories in historical settings provide details about our collective past as humans. Novels such as Jean Auel's *Clan of the Cave Bear* and *Valley of the Horses* shed light on the complex lives of early people in an entertaining way. Showing history in a different format helps people feel connected to the past and shows how we are similar to the people and cultures that came before us.

DIRECTIONS: Create storyboards for a movie that shows how two groups of people you learned about in the chapter lived and interacted with each other and their environment. Make one storyboard for act one of the movie about an earlier group and the storyboard for act two of the movie about a group that came later. Use information from the chapter to help you write your story as accurately as possible, bringing tools, culture, agriculture, or other appropriate characteristics into the storyline.

Your storyboards can use later descendants of your earlier characters to help emphasize the progression over time, or you may use different characters for each act. Work with your group to write, research, and illustrate the storyboards for your movie. Present your storyboards to the class.

_____

_____

_____

_____

_____

_____

_____

_____

_____

The Spread of Civilization

How does geography affect the development of civilizations?

In what ways do civilizations influence each other?

Think about why people settle in a particular region. What are some ways people modify their environments to create distinctive places and cultures? Under what conditions do those cultures spread elsewhere?

TALK ABOUT IT

With a partner, discuss what you would need to know to answer these questions. For example, one question might be: *What factors are most important to establishing and maintaining a civilization?*

DIRECTIONS: Now write down three additional questions that will help you explain why civilizations emerge in particular places and which characteristics of a complex society might enable that culture to influence other places. For example, you might ask, "What makes a place culturally unique? Why might one culture adopt the practices of another?"

MY RESEARCH QUESTIONS

Supporting Question 1:

_____

_____

Supporting Question 2:

_____

_____

Supporting Question 3:

_____

_____

Copyright © McGraw Hill Education

The Rise of Egypt

DIRECTIONS: Search for evidence in the lesson to help you answer the following questions.

1A **EVALUATING** What were Egypt's natural barriers, and how did they help Egypt thrive?

_____

_____

_____

_____

1B GEOGRAPHY Use the graphic organizer below to describe the Nile River's impact on the development of ancient Egypt.

_____

_____

ESSENTIAL QUESTION

How does geography affect the development of civilizations?

As you gather evidence to answer the Essential Question, think about:

- how the Nile River influenced Egypt's early history.
- the characteristics of Egypt's Old and Middle Kingdoms.
- how Egyptians lived and contributed to culture.

My Notes

_____

_____

_____

_____

_____

_____

_____

Nile River

```
  ┌────┐  ┌────┐  ┌────┐  ┌────┐
  │    │  │    │  │    │  │    │
  └────┘  └────┘  └────┘  └────┘
```

2 IDENTIFYING CONNECTIONS How did geography influence the Egyptians' beliefs and world view?

_____

_____

_____

_____

_____

3 SUMMARIZING How did the pharaohs and other features of Egyptian life contribute to stability in the Middle and Old Kingdoms?

_____

_____

_____

_____

_____

4 DESCRIBING What role did social class play in Egyptian daily life?

_____

_____

_____

_____

_____

5 EVALUATING EVIDENCE What evidence is there of Egyptian contributions to the arts and sciences?

_____

_____

_____

_____

_____

Education in Ancient Egypt

ESSENTIAL QUESTION

How does geography affect the development of civilizations?

DIRECTIONS: Read the excerpt. Then respond to the questions that follow.

EXPLORE THE CONTEXT: In this excerpt, James Baikie describes a privileged Egyptian child who was being tutored, unlike most children of the early Egyptian times.

SECONDARY SOURCE: BOOK

66 When Tahuti grew a little older, and had fairly mastered the rudiments of writing, his teacher set him to write out copies of different passages from the best known Egyptian books, partly to keep up his hand-writing, and partly to teach him to know good Egyptian and to use correct language. Sometimes it was a piece of a religious book that he was set to copy, sometimes a poem, sometimes a fairy-tale. For the Egyptians were very fond of fairy-tales, and later on, perhaps, we may hear some of their stories, the oldest fairy-stories in the world. But generally the piece that was chosen was one which would not only exercise the boy's hand, and teach him a good style, but would also help to teach him good manners, and fill his mind with right ideas. Very often Tahuti's teacher would dictate to him a passage from the wise advice which a great King of long ago left to his son, the Crown Prince, or from some other book of the same kind. And sometimes the exercises would be in the form of letters which the master and his pupils wrote as though they had been friends far away from one another. Tahuti's letters, you may be sure, were full of wisdom and of good resolutions, and I dare say he was just about as fond of writing them as you are of writing the letters that your teacher sometimes sets as a task for you. 99

—James Baikie, *Peeps at Many Lands: Ancient Egypt*

VOCABULARY

rudiments: basics

hand: refers to handwriting

dictate: to read aloud something for another person to transcribe, or write down

resolutions: deciding to take a certain action

1 **DESCRIBING** What subjects or topics is Tahuti's teacher including in Tahuti's education?

_____

_____

_____

_____

2 **INFERRING** Think about the social structure of ancient Egypt. What kinds of careers might Tahuti have qualified for? Cite evidence from the excerpt to support your answer.

_____

_____

_____

_____

3 **ANALYZING CENTRAL IDEAS** What were the purposes of ancient Egyptian education?

_____

_____

_____

_____

_____

_____

4 **CIVICS** Based on this excerpt, what civic virtues were valued in ancient Egypt?

_____

_____

_____

_____

_____

_____

5 **COMPARING AND CONTRASTING** How were the methods used by Tahuti's tutor different from the methods your instructors use today? Are there any similarities?

_____

_____

_____

_____

_____

_____

An Egyptian Book of the Dead

DIRECTIONS: Study the image. Then respond to the questions that follow.

EXPLORE THE CONTEXT: Egyptian Books of the Dead were illustrated texts buried in the tombs of those whose families could afford them. Written on papyrus, the books were popular in the Egyptian New Kingdom, from around 1550 B.C. to 50 B.C. These books contained spells meant to guide the deceased's journey to the afterlife. This illustration is a detail from the Book of the Dead of the priest Aha-Mer, from the Egyptian 21st Dynasty (around 1069–945 B.C.). In such images, the god Anubis (associated with the afterlife), weighs the deceased's heart against a feather to determine whether he was worthy of entering the underworld. This feather was meant to represent Ma'at, meaning "truth," sometimes represented as a goddess. If found too heavy, or unworthy, the soul would be devoured by Ammit, a female demon known as the "Devourer of the Dead" and represented as a combination of a lion, a hippopotamus, and a crocodile.

PRIMARY SOURCE: PAINTING AND HIEROGLYPHICS ON PAPYRUS

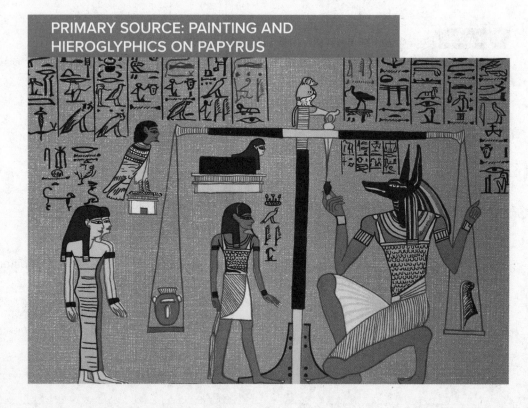

1 IDENTIFYING What is the subject of this illustration?

_____

_____

_____

2 INTERPRETING During this period of ancient Egypt, the heart—unlike other parts of the human body—was preserved through mummification. Given the scene depicted in this illustration, what might be the significance of this practice?

_____

_____

_____

_____

3A DRAWING CONCLUSIONS How does the image illustrate social beliefs of the ancient Egyptian civilization?

_____

_____

_____

3B IDENTIFYING CONNECTIONS What does the presence of this illustration in Aha-Mer's tomb tell us about religious beliefs of the civilization?

_____

_____

4 INFERRING What virtue does this illustration imply was significant in Egyptian society?

_____

_____

_____

5 ECONOMICS What does the presence of this illustration and the survival of the priest's tomb tell us about social hierarchies in ancient Egypt?

_____

_____

_____

_____

Peoples in the Eastern Mediterranean

ESSENTIAL QUESTION

In what ways do civilizations influence each other?

As you gather evidence to answer the Essential Question, think about:

- how Indo-Europeans spread goods and technological advances.
- the cultural and economic achievements of the Phoenicians.
- how religious beliefs of the Israelites had a lasting influence.

My Notes

DIRECTIONS: Search for evidence in the lesson to help you answer the following questions.

1 **EVALUATING INFORMATION** In what ways did Indo-Europeans contribute to the development of civilization?

2 **RELATING EVENTS** How did the movement of Indo-Europeans eventually result in the rise of the Phoenicians?

3A ECONOMICS What was the primary economic activity of the Phoenicians, and why was this so? What can you infer from this about the natural resources of the Phoenician empire?

3B **CITING TEXT EVIDENCE** Use the graphic organizer to show how the Phoenicians contributed to the development of civilization.

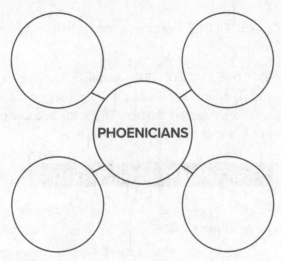

PHOENICIANS

4 **ANALYZING IDEAS** How do monotheism and the religious beliefs of the Israelites influence the world today?

_____

_____

_____

_____

_____

5 **INFERRING** What helped Jews maintain their identify after the loss of Jewish independence?

_____

_____

6 **EVALUATING EVIDENCE** Which aspects of the palace at Knossos are related to the Minoans' extensive trading networks and culture? Explain.

_____

_____

_____

_____

_____

_____

Copyright © McGraw-Hill Education; Genesis 21:1-7 from New Revised Standard Version Bible: Catholic Edition, copyright © 1989, 1993 National Council of the Churches of Christ in the United States of America. Used by permission. All rights reserved worldwide.

ESSENTIAL QUESTION

In what ways do civilizations influence each other?

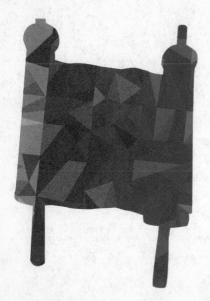

VOCABULARY

conceived: became pregnant

bore: gave birth

The Birth of Isaac

DIRECTIONS: Read the excerpt. Then respond to the questions that follow.

EXPLORE THE CONTEXT: Abraham is considered to be the father of Judaism and Sarah its mother. According to the Hebrew Bible, Abraham and Sarah wanted children. This is the account of the beginning of their family and of the Israelites' family tree.

SECONDARY SOURCE: BOOK

❝1 The Lord dealt with Sarah as he had said, and the Lord did for Sarah as he had promised.

2 Sarah conceived and bore Abraham a son in his old age, at the time of which God had spoken to him.

3 Abraham gave the name Isaac to his son whom Sarah bore to him . . . .

5 Abraham was a hundred years old when his son Isaac was born to him.

6 Now Sarah said: 'God has brought laughter for me; everyone who hears will laugh with me.'

7 And she said: 'Who would ever have said to Abraham that Sarah would nurse children? Yet I have borne him a son in his old age.'❞

—Genesis 21:1–7

1 **DETERMINING CENTRAL IDEAS** What is the main idea of this passage from the Hebrew Bible?

_____

_____

_____

_____

_____

2 **ANALYZING STRUCTURE** What is the purpose of the repetition of certain words, names, and phrases in this passage?

_____

_____

_____

_____

_____

3 **INFERRING** In the text, what does Sarah mean by "God has brought laughter for me"?

_____

_____

_____

_____

4 **ANALYZING TEXTS** What line in the text indicates that Sarah believed it was unlikely she would ever have children?

_____

_____

_____

_____

5 **CIVICS** How does the Israelites' concept of God differ from that of the ancient Egyptians? How might this have influenced the different social roles people played in these two cultures?

_____

_____

_____

_____

_____

In what ways do civilizations influence each other?

The Phaistos Disk

DIRECTIONS: Study the image. Then respond to the questions that follow.

EXPLORE THE CONTEXT: Likely of Minoan origin, the nearly 4,000-year-old Phaistos Disk was discovered in Crete in 1908. The circular clay disk is about six inches in diameter and is covered on both sides with 45 different characters, which have been stamped into the object. Several of the characters appear numerous times in different locations, and many depict easily identifiable objects such as a fish or a boat. There is little to no variation between different copies of the same symbol. However, the meaning and significance of the disk remains a mystery. Some scholars believe the disk is written in Minoan script that records the Minoan language, with each symbol representing a syllable and each group of syllables representing a word. Others believe each symbol represents a whole word. They might even represent letters of an alphabet. Dashes and dotted lines on the disk may indicate punctuation marks, prefixes or suffixes, or markers at the start of a word.

PRIMARY SOURCE: PHOTO

—Clay disc with inscribed symbols

1 **IDENTIFYING** What is this object? Why is it important?

_____

_____

_____

_____

2 **INFERRING** Why is it significant that the symbols were stamped into the clay rather than individually carved and that there is essentially no variation between different copies of the same symbol?

_____

_____

_____

_____

_____

_____

3 **HISTORY** How might the Phaistos Disk indicate that the Minoan language was similar to the language of the Phoenicians? How might the disk indicate that the Minoan language was similar to Egyptian hieroglyphics?

_____

_____

_____

_____

4 **IDENTIFYING CONNECTIONS** Why do you think historians know more about the ancient Israelites, Phoenicians, and Egyptians than about the Minoans? What conclusion can you draw from this?

_____

_____

_____

The Indus Valley Civilization

DIRECTIONS: Search for evidence in the lesson to help you answer the following questions.

ESSENTIAL QUESTION

How does geography affect the development of civilizations?

As you gather evidence to answer the Essential Question, think about:

- how geography and climate influenced civilizations in the Indus River Valley.

- the features of Indus Valley civilizations.

- why India's culture changed as the Indus Valley civilization declined.

1 **SUMMARIZING** Explain how the geography and climate of India influenced settlements in the Indian subcontinent.

_____

_____

_____

_____

_____

_____

2 **UNDERSTANDING CHANGE** How might changes in the characteristics of the Indus River valley have influenced the development of civilization in India?

_____

_____

_____

_____

_____

My Notes

_____

_____

_____

_____

_____

3A **EVALUATING EVIDENCE** What does the design of the cities of Harappa and Mohenjo Daro tell us about the values of the Indus Valley peoples?

_____

_____

_____

_____

_____

_____

3B **COMPARING AND CONTRASTING** Use the graphic organizer to compare early Egyptian civilization with that of the Indus Valley.

	Egypt	Indus Valley
Geography		
Power and Authority		
Cultural/Scientific Accomplishments		

4 **TESTING HYPOTHESES** Scholars are divided in their opinions on whether the Indus Valley civilization was a single society or a collection of independent city-states. What evidence suggests that a single authority was in control?

_____

_____

_____

5 **ANALYZING ISSUES** What accounts for the change in Indian culture after the decline of the Indus Valley civilization—migration or interaction? Explain.

_____

_____

_____

_____

_____

_____

6 **ANALYZING** Identify the main source of our knowledge about both the Indus Valley and Aryan civilizations. Then identify an aspect of each civilization that remains unknown and explain why.

_____

_____

_____

_____

_____

ESSENTIAL QUESTION

How does geography affect the development of civilizations?

Life in Harappa and Mohenjo-Daro

DIRECTIONS: Read the excerpt. Then respond to the questions that follow.

EXPLORE THE CONTEXT: This excerpt is from a study on the ancient cities of Harappa and Mohenjo-Daro. It takes a look at the archaeological evidence and provides insights into what life might have been like when the cities thrived.

VOCABULARY

archaeologists: people who study earlier cultures by examining their artifacts and writings

excavated: dug holes in the earth to find remains of cultures

granaries: storage buildings for harvested grain

extensive: wide and broad in size

surveying: figuring the exact size and form of something using mathematics, geometry, and trigonometry

uniform: all the same; consistent

dwindled: decreased

SECONDARY SOURCE: BOOK EXCERPT

66 The ruins of Harappa and Mohenjo-Daro reveal that they were the products of the first city planning in history. Wide, straight streets divide residential areas into square city blocks. Archaeologists have excavated houses, granaries, public halls, and shops. Both cities had extensive sewer systems. Walled fortresses with towers provided protection. To create such well-planned cities, the people needed a knowledge of surveying and geometry. Furthermore, only a strong central government in each city could have supervised the planning and construction. Scholars are not sure who ruled the Indus Valley cities, but they think that a priest-king probably headed the government of each city. The rulers must have had considerable power because the governments exercised strict control. For example, they controlled construction of new buildings and established standards of weight and measures. Because of the tight control, writing, building styles, street plans, and even the size of bricks remained unchanged for nearly 1,000 years. . . . Evidence from the diggings shows that the Indus Valley civilization began to decline many years before it finally ended about 1500 B.C. Builders abandoned the uniform standards of earlier times, and quality of work declined. The arts showed less creativity, and trade with Mesopotamia dwindled. 99

—from *World History: Patterns of Civilization* by Burton Beers, quoted in *Ancient India: The Asiatic Ethiopians* by Carolyn McPherson Scott

1 **SUMMARIZING** Why was the discovery of the ruins of Harappa and Mohenjo-Daro important?

_____

_____

_____

2 **EVALUATING ARGUMENTS** In the excerpt, the author claims that Harappa and Mohenjo-Daro must have had strong central governments. What evidence is presented to support that conclusion?

_____

_____

_____

_____

_____

3 **CONSTRUCTING HYPOTHESES** Why would the people of Harappa and Mohenjo-Daro have needed a granary for their produce? What does this tell us about agriculture in the Indus Valley?

_____

_____

_____

_____

_____

_____

_____

4 **CITING TEXT EVIDENCE** What do the ruins of Harappa and Mohenjo-Daro reveal about the scientific knowledge possessed by the people of the Indus Valley civilization?

_____

_____

_____

_____

_____

5 **GEOGRAPHY** Identify the reasons for the flourishing of civilization in the Indus Valley.

_____

_____

_____

_____

_____

_____

ESSENTIAL QUESTION

How does geography affect the development of civilizations?

Indus Valley Seals

DIRECTIONS: Study the image. Then respond to the questions that follow.

EXPLORE THE CONTEXT: Archaeologists have found more than 3,500 carved stone seals in the Indus Valley, similar to the one shown here (beside a clay impression of the seal). The seals are small and usually square with symbols along the top, an animal in the center, and more symbols along the bottom. Various animals are depicted on the seals, such as elephants, rhinoceros, bulls, and even mythological creatures such as unicorns. Most scholars believe the symbols are script from the Indus Valley language, though they have not been deciphered. The seals were designed to leave an impression when they were pressed into wet clay. The imprint would then be attached to bundles of merchandise as merchants' marks. They could also have been worn as amulets. Indus Valley seals have been found at the Mesopotamian city of Ur and other sites in the region.

VOCABULARY

amulet: an ornament or small piece of jewelry thought to give protection against evil, danger, or disease

PRIMARY SOURCE: CARVED SEAL AND IMPRESSION

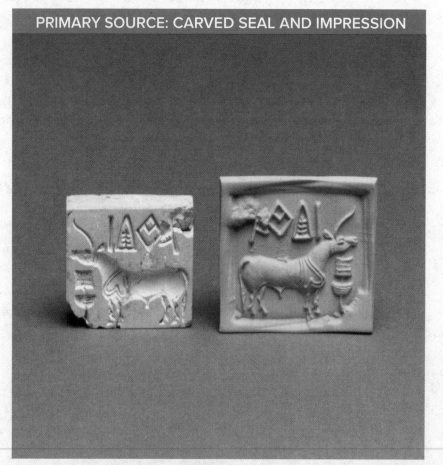

—Carved stone Indus Valley seal and it clay impression

Copyright © McGraw-Hill Education; ©The Metropolitan Museum of Art, New York, Dodge Fund, 1949

1 **DESCRIBING** What was the purpose of the Indus Valley seals?

_____

_____

2 **INTEGRATING VISUAL INFORMATION** What elements of an advanced civilization can you find in the image of the seal?

_____

_____

_____

_____

3 **CONSTRUCTING HYPOTHESES** Why might the seals contain writing? Why might they contain an image of an animal?

_____

_____

_____

_____

4 **DRAWING CONCLUSIONS** What conclusions can you draw from these seals about contacts between the people of Mesopotamia and the Indus Valley? Support your ideas.

_____

_____

_____

_____

5 GEOGRAPHY In what ways are Indus Valley seals similar to the Minoan Phaistos Disk? How are they different?

_____

_____

_____

_____

_____

The Rise of China

DIRECTIONS: Search for evidence in the lesson to help you answer the following questions.

ESSENTIAL QUESTION

In what ways do civilizations influence each other?

As you gather evidence to answer the Essential Question, think about:

- how the geographic isolation of China affected its development.
- how ruling dynasties gained and maintained power.
- the importance of filial piety in everyday life.

My Notes

_____

_____

_____

_____

_____

_____

_____

1   **IDENTIFYING CONNECTIONS** What natural features isolated China from other parts of Asia? How might Chinese civilization have developed differently without these features?

_____

_____

_____

_____

_____

_____

2   **SUMMARIZING** What were the characteristics of Shang society and government, and how did the government maintain order in such a large area?

_____

_____

_____

_____

_____

3A   **EXPLAINING ISSUES** When the Zhou overthrew the Shang and established a new dynasty, what did they do to gain acceptance of their rule?

_____

_____

_____

_____

3B **DESCRIBING** Use the graphic organizer to illustrate the dynastic cycle.

_____

_____

_____

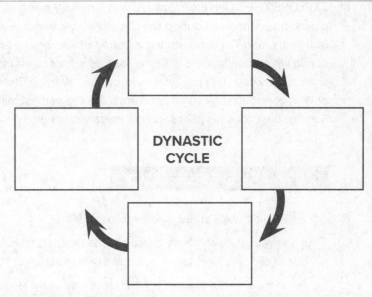

4 **DETERMING CENTRAL IDEAS** What was the basic social and economic unit in ancient China, and how did the principle of filial piety influence social roles?

_____

_____

_____

_____

_____

_____

_____

5 HISTORY What were the characteristics of ancient Chinese written language, and how does it differ from that developed by cultures such as the Phoenicians?

_____

_____

_____

_____

_____

ESSENTIAL QUESTION

In what ways do civilizations influence each other?

Military Strategy in Ancient China

DIRECTIONS: Read the excerpt. Then respond to the questions.

EXPLORE THE CONTEXT: Sun Tzu was a military general, strategist, and philosopher who lived during the Zhou Dynasty, which lasted for almost 800 years. Sun Tzu wrote during a period of war among aristocrats, during which clan leaders in China rose up against the king in rebellion against the Zhou. This period was known as "Warring States." In *The Art of War*, considered by some scholars to be the earliest military treatise, Sun Tzu describes his philosophy of military strategy.

PRIMARY SOURCE: BOOK

66 The art of war is of vital importance to the State.

It is a matter of life and death, a road either to safety or to ruin. Hence it is a subject of inquiry which can on no account be neglected.

The art of war, then, is governed by five constant factors, to be taken into account in one's deliberations, when seeking to determine the conditions obtaining in the field.

These are:

1. The Moral Law   4. The Commander

2. Heaven   5. Method and discipline.

3. Earth

The Moral Law causes the people to be in complete accord with their ruler, so that they will follow him regardless of their lives, undismayed by any danger.

Heaven signifies night and day, cold and heat, times and seasons.

Earth comprises distances, great and small; danger and security; open ground and narrow passes; the chances of life and death.

The Commander stands for the virtues of wisdom, sincerity, benevolence, courage and strictness.

By method and discipline are to be understood the marshaling of the army in its proper subdivisions, the graduations of rank among the officers, the maintenance of roads by which supplies may reach the army, and the control of military expenditure.

These five heads should be familiar to every general: he who knows them will be victorious; he who knows them not will fail.

Therefore, in your deliberations, when seeking to determine the military conditions, let them be made the basis of a comparison, in this way:

1. Which of the two sovereigns is imbued with the Moral law?

2. Which of the two generals has most ability?

3. With whom lie the advantages derived from Heaven and Earth?

VOCABULARY

vital: essential

deliberation: careful contemplation or discussion

accord: agreement, sometimes formally announced

undismayed: not distressed

marshal: arrange in order

4. On which side is discipline most rigorously enforced?

5. Which army is stronger?

6. On which side are officers and men more highly trained?

7. In which army is there the greater constancy both in reward and punishment?

By means of these seven considerations I can forecast victory or defeat.

The general that hearkens to my counsel and acts upon it, will conquer—let such a one be retained in command! The general that hearkens not to my counsel nor acts upon it, will suffer defeat—let such a one be dismissed! 🙶

—Sun Tzu, "The Art of War," 512 B.C.

1 HISTORY Sun Tzu begins by declaring that the art of war is of vital importance to the State. Connect this statement to the Chinese concept of dynastic cycles.

_____

_____

_____

_____

2 **COMPARING** According to Sun Tzu, what are the attributes of a good commander, and how might they relate to the Dao?

_____

_____

_____

_____

3 **EVALUATING** How does Sun Tzu's concept of the moral law reflect the Chinese concept of filial piety?

_____

_____

_____

4 **UNDERSTANDING CONTEXT** How might the events occurring in China during Sun Tzu's time have influenced the writing of *The Art of War*?

_____

_____

_____

_____

In what ways do civilizations influence each other?

The Common Possession of Pure Virtue

DIRECTIONS: Read the excerpt. Then respond to the questions that follow.

EXPLORE THE CONTEXT: The Common Possession of Pure Virtue is part of a longer work known as the Book of Documents (Shujing, or "Classic of History"). Traditionally attributed to Confucius—although likely a compilation of many sources—the Book of Documents is a collection of writings about ancient China. Its principles were the foundation of Chinese political philosophy for over 2,000 years. In this excerpt, the narrator (Yin) discusses "pure virtue" and its importance to China's rulers. He describes the fall of the Hsiâ [Xia] dynasty and the elevation of a new king, Thang, who founded the Shang dynasty.

PRIMARY SOURCE: BOOK

He said, 'Oh! it is difficult to rely on Heaven;—its appointments are not constant. (But if the sovereign see to it that) his virtue be constant, he will preserve his throne; if his virtue be not constant, the nine provinces will be lost by him. The king of Hsiâ could not maintain the virtue (of his ancestors) unchanged, but contemned the spirits and oppressed the people. Great Heaven no (longer) extended its protection to him. It looked out among the myriad regions to give its guidance to one who should receive its favoring appointment, fondly seeking (a possessor of) pure virtue; whom it might make lord of all the spirits. Then there were I, Yin, and Thang, both possessed of pure virtue, and able to satisfy the mind of Heaven. He received (in consequence) the bright favor of Heaven, so as to become possessor of the multitudes of the nine provinces, and proceeded to change Hsiâ's commencement of the year. It was not that Heaven had any private partiality for the lord of Shang;—it simply gave its favor to pure virtue. It was not that Shang sought (the allegiance of) the lower people;—the people simply turned to pure virtue. Where (the sovereign's) virtue is pure, his enterprises are all fortunate; where his virtue is wavering and uncertain, his enterprises are all unfortunate. Good and evil do not wrongly befall men, but Heaven sends down misery or happiness according to their conduct.'

—"The Common Possession of Pure Virtue"

VOCABULARY

appointments: arrangements

constant: continuous, unbroken

contemned: scorned, treated with contempt

myriad: many

favor: approval

commencement: beginning

enterprises: projects, tasks

1A **DETERMINING CENTRAL IDEAS** According to the excerpt, why did the king of Hsiâ lose power and Thang of Shang become the new king?

_____

_____

_____

1B **MAKING CONNECTIONS** Which political and religious doctrine, introduced by the Zhou dynasty, is illustrated in this excerpt? Explain.

_____

_____

_____

2 **INFERRING** Based on this excerpt, what do you think Confucius taught about the obligation of subordinates to be loyal and obedient to their superiors? Explain.

_____

_____

_____

3 **CONTRASTING** How does the Chinese conception of a sovereign and of the subjects' relationship to their sovereign differ from the Egyptian view?

_____

_____

_____

_____

4 CIVICS What does this excerpt tell us about the Confucian teaching on good governance and its use of force or the threat of punishment to maintain power?

_____

_____

_____

_____

Civilizations in the Americas

DIRECTIONS: Search for evidence in the lesson to help you answer the following questions.

1A **DESCRIBING** What name did archaeologists give to the first Mesoamerican civilization and why?

_____

_____

_____

_____

1B **COMPARING AND CONTRASTING** Use the Venn diagram to compare and contrast aspects of Olmec and Zapotec culture.

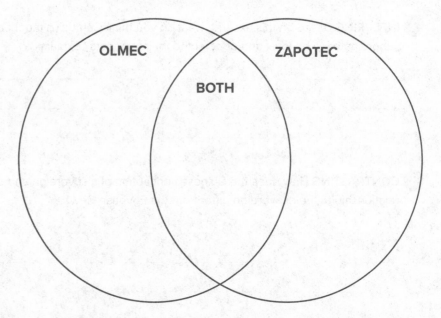

ESSENTIAL QUESTION

In what ways do civilizations influence each other?

As you gather evidence to answer the Essential Question, think about:

- the characteristics of early Mesoamerican peoples.
- how Mesoamerican cities were organized.
- the features of early civilizations in South America.

My Notes

_____

_____

_____

_____

_____

_____

_____

2 **EVALUATING EVIDENCE** What is the archaeological evidence that the Zapotec city of Monte Alban was the center of a complex civilization?

_____

_____

_____

_____

3 ECONOMICS How could the city of Teotihuacán support a population of up to 200,000 people?

_____

_____

_____

4 **INFERRING** How do we know that the people of Teotihuacán traveled throughout—and beyond—Mesoamerica?

_____

_____

_____

5 **COMPARING** What do inhabitants of Caral and the people of the Chavin culture in South America have in common with the peoples of Monte Alban and Teotihuacán?

_____

_____

_____

ESSENTIAL QUESTION

In what ways do civilizations influence each other?

Ancient Mesoamerican City of Teotihuacán

DIRECTIONS: Study the image. Then respond to the questions that follow.

EXPLORE THE CONTEXT: Teotihuacán was the first major city in Mesoamerica. Archaeologists believe Teotihuacán arose around 250 B.C. and reached its peak by A.D. 400 with as many as 200,000 residents. Located in central Mexico, the city is laid out in a grid pattern dominated by two large pyramids and the wide Avenue of the Dead. The Pyramid of the Moon sits at the northern end of this avenue, and the larger Pyramid of the Sun is situated about half a mile south. At the far end of the Avenue of the Dead lies the Ciudadela (or Citadel), a courtyard with living quarters for the city's elite along with the Temple of Quetzalcoatl, which is decorated with stone heads of this feathered serpent god. The city contains additional pyramids, temples, workshops, and plazas as well as about 2,000 apartment compounds. The builders of Teotihuacán are unknown, but features of numerous cultures, including the Maya and Zapotec peoples, are evident. Around A.D. 600 many government buildings in Teotihuacán were burned and artwork and religious artifacts were destroyed. Within another 150 to 200 years the city had been abandoned. The city had been in ruins for centuries when it was rediscovered by the Aztecs, who named the site Teotihuacán, or "birthplace of the gods." Aztec leaders regularly made pilgrimages there.

PRIMARY SOURCE: ILLUSTRATION

—panoramic view of Teotihuacán

1 **INTEGRATING VISUAL INFORMATION** Which features of Teotihuacán can you identify?

_____

_____

_____

_____

2 **COMPARING AND CONTRASTING** How does Teotihuacán compare to the Indus Valley cities of Harappa and Mohenjo-Daro?

_____

_____

_____

_____

_____

3 **CONSTRUCTING HYPOTHESES** Based on the evidence, why might Teotihuacán have been deliberately set afire?

_____

_____

_____

_____

4 HISTORY How did Teotihuacán reflect Mesoamerican civilizations that came before it and influence the further development of Mesoamerica?

_____

_____

_____

_____

_____

_____

_____

_____

In what ways do civilizations influence each other?

24-Ton Olmec head

DIRECTIONS: Study the image. Then respond to the questions that follow.

EXPLORE THE CONTEXT: The Olmec, who lived along Mexico's gulf coast from about 1200 to 400 B.C., were talented artists. Their most famous creations are the colossal stone heads they sculpted. Weighing as much as 40 tons, the sculptures depict the head and face of a man wearing a headdress. The back of the heads are flat and unfinished. Seventeen heads have been discovered. Each is carved from a single basalt boulder that was transported as far as 50 miles to a workshop, where Olmec artisans used stone tools to create the sculptures. Each of the 17 faces has a unique expression and a distinctive headdress.

PRIMARY SOURCE: PHOTO

—24-Ton Olmec head

1 **DESCRIBING** What does the fact that the stones were moved before they were carved tell you about Olmec society?

_____

_____

2 GEOGRAPHY In what way are the Olmec colossal heads similar to the pyramids constructed in Egypt's Old Kingdom?

_____

_____

_____

_____

3 **ANALYZING POINTS OF VIEW** Some scholars believe the Olmec colossal heads represent gods; others think they are rulers. Give a brief argument in support of each theory.

_____

_____

_____

_____

4 **CONSTRUCTING HYPOTHESES** What do you think is the significance of depicting only the heads rather than the entire body?

_____

_____

_____

_____

_____

5 **INFERRING** What does the ability to produce these sculptures imply about Olmec civilization?

_____

_____

_____

_____

_____

ESSENTIAL QUESTIONS

How does geography affect the development of civilizations?

In what ways do civilizations influence each other?

1 Think About It

Review the supporting questions you developed at the beginning of the chapter. Review the evidence you gathered in the chapter. Were you able to answer each Supporting Question? If there was not enough evidence to answer your Supporting Questions, what additional evidence do you need to consider?

_____

_____

_____

2 Organize Your Evidence

Complete the chart below with information you learned about ancient civilizations, where they developed, and the notable characteristics of each. As you complete the chart, think about core elements of civilization and how they were expressed in these different places.

Civilization	Location	Notable Characteristics
Ancient Egypt		
Phoenicians		
Israelites		
Indus Valley Civilization		
Ancient China		
Olmec and Zapotec Civilizations		
Teotihuacán Civilization		

3 Write About It

In the space below, explain why location is important in the development of a civilization. Give some examples of how civilizations have adapted to and modified their environments to meet the needs of their people.

_____

_____

_____

_____

4 Talk About It

Work in small groups. With your group, discuss the different ways an ancient civilization might influence the culture of other places. Which characteristics must one complex society possess before it can influence another? Take notes about your discussion below.

_____

_____

_____

_____

_____

5 Connect to the Essential Question

Following your work in steps 3 and 4, choose an ancient civilization that you believe strongly influenced the culture of other places. Then write a visual essay that explains (1) how geography played a role in that civilization's development and (2) which characteristics that civilization developed that enabled it to influence other places. Include maps, images, illustrations, or infographics to enhance the information in your essay. Use historical evidence and sound reasoning to support your ideas.

CITIZENSHIP
TAKE ACTION

MAKE CONNECTIONS Just as ancient cultures and civilizations influenced and learned from one another, different cultures continue to influence one another today. The spread of culture from one place, population, or society to another is called *cultural diffusion*. Every culture develops through internal improvement as well as by borrowing from others. However, an increasing number of people are beginning to make a distinction between cultural borrowing and what is termed *cultural appropriation*—the adoption of elements of minority culture by members of the majority culture, sometimes in a disrespectful way. There is sometimes a fine line between cultural diffusion and cultural appropriation, but as members of a modern, multicultural society, it is a distinction worth discussing.

DIRECTIONS: Use what you have learned in the chapter—along with additional research—to create a pamphlet discussing the interplay between cultures and explaining the differences between cultural diffusion and cultural appropriation. In your pamphlet, provide examples of acceptable and unacceptable cultural borrowing and address common misconceptions about cultural appropriation.

_____

_____

_____

_____

_____

_____

_____

_____

_____

_____

_____

Early Empires in the Ancient Near East

ESSENTIAL QUESTION

How do empires rise, how are they maintained, and what causes them to fall?

Think about the great empires that arose in the Near East in ancient times. What types of government did these early peoples invent? What made these empires possible? How did they continue to control vast areas from their capitals? Each empire eventually fell victim to another rising empire. What were the causes that led to the decline and ultimate collapse of each empire?

TALK ABOUT IT

With a partner, discuss the sort of information you would need to know to answer these questions. For example, one question might be: *What developments made the rise of empires in the ancient Near East possible?*

DIRECTIONS: Now write down three additional questions that will help you analyze the conditions that made the rise, maintenance, and eventual fall of the empires of the early Near East possible. For example, you might ask, "How did these early peoples learn to form governments? How were these governments able to conquer and control vast areas?"

MY RESEARCH QUESTIONS

Supporting Question 1:

_____

_____

Supporting Question 2:

_____

_____

Supporting Question 3:

_____

Akkad and Babylon

DIRECTIONS: Search for evidence in this lesson to help you answer the following questions.

1A **ANALYZING INDIVIDUALS** Why is Sargon an important figure in world history?

_____

_____

1B **DRAWING CONCLUSIONS** How were both Sargon and his grandson Naram-Sin able to effectively control and govern such a large empire?

_____

_____

_____

_____

2 **IDENTIFYING CAUSES** What led to the decline and fall of the Akkadian empire?

_____

_____

_____

_____

3 **DISTINGUISHING FACT FROM OPINION** Hammurabi said that he was "the sun of Babylon, . . . the king who caused the four quarters of the world to render obedience." Was this statement a fact or an opinion? Give reasons to support your answer.

_____

_____

_____

_____

ESSENTIAL QUESTION

How do empires rise, how are they maintained, and what causes them to fall?

As you gather evidence to answer the Essential Question, think about:

- the Akkadian Empire and its accomplishments.
- why we consider the Code of Hammurabi to be one of the key developments of civilization.

My Notes

_____

_____

_____

_____

_____

_____

4 CIVICS The Code of Hammurabi was a comprehensive set of laws that were written down and enforced throughout the empire. Use the table below to list the consequence of each action described.

Action	Consequence Under the Code
You steal your neighbor's horse	
A woman is unable to have children	
Your new house collapses	
You slap your father	
You borrow your best friend's boat and it sinks	
You accuse your cousin of robbing you but you have no proof	
You get in a fight that blinds your opponent 's left eye	
You are a married woman who starts her own business	
You have small children, but your husband divorces you	

5 EVALUATING INFORMATION In what ways might the Code of Hammurabi have provided stability in the empire?

_____

_____

_____

_____

ESSENTIAL QUESTION

How do empires rise, how are they maintained, and what causes them to fall?

Herodotus on Babylon

DIRECTIONS: Read the excerpt. Then respond to the questions that follow.

EXPLORE THE CONTEXT: Herodotus was an early Greek historian who traveled and described the actions and sights he witnessed. This excerpt gives us a view of the defense system as well as the largest temple of the great city of Babylon.

PRIMARY SOURCE: HISTORICAL ACCOUNT

❝I.181: The outer wall is the main defense of the city. There is, however, a second inner wall, of less thickness than the first, but very little inferior to it in strength. The center of each division of the town was occupied by a fortress. In the one stood the palace of the kings, surrounded by a wall of great strength and size; in the other was the sacred precinct of Jupiter Belus [Bel], a square enclosure two furlongs each way, with gates of solid brass; which was also remaining in my time. In the middle of the precinct there was a tower of solid masonry, a furlong in length and breadth, upon which was raised a second tower, and on that a third, and so on up to eight. The ascent to the top is on the outside, by a path which winds round all the towers. When one is about halfway up, one finds a resting place and seats, where persons are wont to sit some time on their way to the summit. On the topmost tower there is a spacious temple, and inside the temple stands a couch of unusual size, richly adorned [decorated], with a golden table by its side. There is no statue of any kind set up in the place, nor is the chamber occupied of nights by any one but a single native woman, who, as the Chaldaeans, the priests of this god, affirm, is chosen for himself by the deity out of all the women of the land. ❞

—The History of Herodotus

VOCABULARY

furlong: a distance of approximately one-eighth of a mile, or 220 yards

enclosure: an area shut in by walls or fences

masonry: something built with bricks or stones

precinct: a district or area

Jupiter Belus: reference to Akkadian god Bel

breadth: width

chamber: a private room

wont: a habit or something a person is used to doing

1 HISTORY In what ways does Herodotus show admiration for the defense system that the Babylonians constructed?

_____

_____

_____

_____

_____

2 **INFERRING** What can we learn about Babylonian society by studying its defenses?

_____

_____

_____

_____

_____

3 **CITING TEXT EVIDENCE** What does the source tell us about the religious beliefs of the early Babylonians?

_____

_____

_____

_____

_____

_____

4 **IDENTIFYING PERSPECTIVES** What does Herodotus find remarkable about the temple of Jupiter Belus?

_____

_____

_____

_____

_____

5 **DRAWING CONCLUSIONS** What role does the lone occupant of the temple play in the Babylonian religion?

_____

_____

_____

_____

ESSENTIAL QUESTION

How do empires rise, how are they maintained, and what causes them to fall?

The Law Code Of Hammurabi

DIRECTIONS: Read the excerpt. Then respond to the questions that follow.

EXPLORE THE CONTEXT: The Code of Hammurabi consists of 282 laws carved into a giant black stone pillar in what was the city of Babylon and the capital of his empire. The pillar also includes a carving of Hammurabi receiving the code from Shamash, the Babylonian god of justice. The code also provides the origin of the English phrase "*an eye for an eye*." While we use the phrase metaphorically, it was literal for the Babylonians. If you put someone's eye out, your punishment was to have one of your eyes put out.

PRIMARY SOURCE: LAW CODE

1. If any one ensnare another, putting a ban upon him, but he can not prove it, then he that ensnared him shall be put to death.

2   If any one bring an accusation against a man, and the accused go to the river and leap into the river, if he sink in the river his accuser shall take possession of his house. But if the river prove that the accused is not guilty, and he escape unhurt, then he who had brought the accusation shall be put to death, while he who leaped into the river shall take possession of the house that had belonged to his accuser.

3. If any one bring an accusation of any crime before the elders, and does not prove what he has charged, he shall, if it be a capital offense charged, be put to death.

4. If he satisfy the elders to impose a fine of grain or money, he shall receive the fine that the action produces.

5. If a judge try a case, reach a decision, and present his judgment in writing; if later error shall appear in his decision, and it be through his own fault, then he shall pay twelve times the fine set by him in the case, and he shall be publicly removed from the judge's bench, and never again shall he sit there to render judgement.

6. If any one steal the property of a temple or of the court, he shall be put to death, and also the one who receives the stolen thing from him shall be put to death.

7. If any one buy from the son or the slave of another man, without witnesses or a contract, silver or gold, a male or female slave, an ox or a sheep, an ass or anything, or if he take it in charge, he is considered a thief and shall be put to death.

8. If any one steal cattle or sheep, or an ass, or a pig or a goat, if it belong to a god or to the court, the thief shall pay thirtyfold therefor; if they belonged to a freed man of the king he shall pay tenfold; if the thief has nothing with which to pay he shall be put to death.

VOCABULARY

ensnare: capture or trap

elder: high-ranking leader

capital offense: crime punishable by death

thirtyfold: thirty times

tenfold: ten times

1 **SUMMARIZING** What happens to an accuser if the accused jumps into a river and swims to the other side?

_____

2A **COMPARING** In what ways are the laws in the code similar to the laws in the United States today?

_____

_____

_____

_____

2B **CONTRASTING** In what ways are the laws in the code different from the laws in the United States today?

_____

_____

_____

_____

_____

3 CIVICS In American courts today, people can ask that an appeals court review a decision made by a lower court. In many instances, the appellate court overturns the verdict of the lower court. How did the Code of Hammurabi deal with judges whose decisions are overturned?

_____

_____

4 **CITING TEXT EVIDENCE** One of the fundamental principles of the American justice system is that it treats everyone equally. Cite details from the Code of Hammurabi that show that the Babylonian system did not treat everyone equally.

_____

_____

_____

_____

Egypt and Kush

DIRECTIONS: Search for evidence in this lesson to help you answer the following questions.

1 **IDENTIFYING EFFECTS** What impact did the Hyksos have on Egyptian civilization?

_____

_____

_____

2 **ANALYZING INFORMATION** How was the New Kingdom in Egypt able to become the most powerful state in the ancient Near East?

_____

_____

_____

_____

_____

3 **EVALUATING EVIDENCE** What led to the decline and fall of the New Kingdom?

_____

_____

_____

_____

_____

_____

_____

ESSENTIAL QUESTION

How do empires rise, how are they maintained, and what causes them to fall?

As you gather evidence to answer the Essential Question, think about:

- the contributions that the ancient Egyptians made to civilization.
- the achievements of Kush and Axum.

My Notes

_____

_____

_____

_____

_____

4 RELATING EVENTS Use the flow chart below to list factors that led to the rise of Kush until the Assyrians forced the Kushites out of Egypt.

Factors Leading to the Fall of Kush

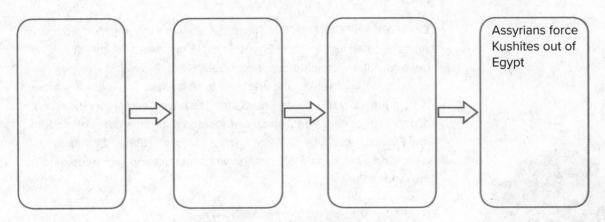

Assyrians force Kushites out of Egypt

5 ANALYZING CHANGE What role did technology play in the Assyrian defeat of Kush?

_____
_____
_____
_____
_____
_____

6 ECONOMICS How did the economy of Kush change over time?

_____
_____
_____
_____
_____
_____
_____
_____
_____

Copyright © McGraw-Hill Education   Tappan, Eva March. Translated by W. K. Flinders Petrie. Tales Of Ancient Egypt, from The World's Story: A History Of The World In Story, Song And Art. Volume III: Egypt, Africa, And Arabia. Boston: Houghton Mifflin, 1914.

ESSENTIAL QUESTION

How do empires rise, how are they maintained, and what causes them to fall?

VOCABULARY

contrary: hostile, causing problems

cubits: a cubit was the length of the forearm, 17–21 inches

thicket: underbrush, bushes

withal: with it all

burnt offering: a ritual to honor the gods

Nubia and Kush

DIRECTIONS: Read the excerpt. Then respond to the questions that follow.

EXPLORE THE CONTEXT: Nubia and Kush were thriving civilizations in Africa, located just south of Egypt. These kingdoms near the Nile became natural candidates for conquest. Kush and Nubia were prosperous, with fertile land and gold to be mined. The following excerpt is from the story of a sailor who claimed to have been shipwrecked on an island in or near Punt, which was located along the coast of modern-day Ethiopia and Djibouti. Although this story is fictional, the resources described were items Egypt traded with Nubians and with people from the land of Punt.

SECONDARY SOURCE: BOOK

&&Let thy heart be satisfied, O my lord, for that we have come back to the country... Moreover, we have come back in good health, and not a man is lacking; although we have been to the ends of Wawat [Nubia], and gone through the land of Senmut [Kush], we have returned in peace, and our land—behold, we have come back to it. ... They had said that the wind would not be contrary, or that there would be none. But as we approached the land, the wind arose, and threw up waves eight cubits high. As for me, I seized a piece of wood; but those who were in the vessel perished, without one remaining. A wave threw me on an island, after that I had been three days alone, without a companion beside my own heart. I laid me in a thicket, and the shadow covered me. Then stretched I my limbs to try to find something for my mouth. I found there figs and grain, melons of all kinds, fishes, and birds. Nothing was lacking. And I satisfied myself; and left on the ground that which was over, of what my arms had been filled withal. I dug a pit, I lighted a fire, and I made a burnt offering unto the gods... Then I bowed myself before [a serpent calling himself the Prince of Punt], and held my arms low before him, and he, he gave me gifts of precious perfumes, of cassia, of sweet woods, of kohl, of cypress, an abundance of incense, of ivory tusks, of baboons, of apes, and all kinds of precious things. 99

—Eva March Tappan, *Tales of Ancient Egypt*

1 **CITING TEXT EVIDENCE** What phrases in the text show that the writer was thankful for the experiences he discusses?

_____

_____

_____

_____

2 **INFERRING** What does the excerpt tell us about Egyptian religious beliefs?

_____

_____

_____

_____

_____

3 **ANALYZING** What about the expedition came unexpectedly and found the writer totally unprepared?

_____

_____

_____

_____

4 **HISTORY** Does the writer respect the civilizations of Nubia and Kush? How do you know?

_____

_____

_____

_____

_____

_____

Copyright © McGraw-Hill Education   Tappan, Eva March, ed. The world's story: A History of the World in Story, Song and Art, Volume III. Boston & New York: Houghton Mifflin Company, 1914.

ESSENTIAL QUESTION

How do empires rise, how are they maintained, and what causes them to fall?

The Victory of Ramses II

DIRECTIONS: Read the excerpt. Then respond to the questions that follow.

EXPLORE THE CONTEXT: Ramses II ruled Egypt from 1279 B.C. to 1213 B.C., the second longest reign of any pharaoh. Ramses reconquered territories that had been lost during the tumultuous reigns of Akhenaton and Tutankhamen. He also was known for his ambitious building program. The poem excerpted below, along with war scenes celebrating the Battle of Kadesh against the Hittites in 1275 B.C., was carved into the walls of five temples in Egypt and Nubia. Although the Egyptians were not able to conquer the city of Kadesh, the pharaoh and a tiny force of his soldiers were able to fight off a much larger Hittite force until Egyptian reinforcements arrived. The Egyptians then signed a truce agreement with the Hittites and withdrew their forces. The poem celebrates the pharaoh's seemingly miraculous survival against all odds.

PRIMARY SOURCE: POETRY

Then spake Pharaoh, and he cried: "Father Ammon, where art thou?

Shall a sire forget his son?

Is there aught without thy knowledge I have done?

From the judgments of thy mount when have I gone?

Have I e'er transgressed thy word?

Disobeyed, or broke a vow?

Is it right, who rules in Egypt, Egypt's lord,

Should e'er before the foreign peoples bow,

Or own their rod?

Whate'er may be the mind of this Hittite herdsman-horde?

Sure Ammon should stand higher than the wretch who knows no God?

Father Ammon, is it nought

That to thee I dedicated noble monuments, and filled

Thy temples with the prisoners of war?

That for thee a thousand years shall stand the shrines I dared to build?

That to thee my palace-substance I have brought,

That tribute unto thee from afar

A whole land comes to pay,

That to thee ten thousand oxen for sacrifice I fell,

And burn upon thine altars the sweetest woods that smell;

That all thy heart required, my hand did ne'er gainsay?

VOCABULARY

spake: spoke

sire: father

aught: anything

transgress: infringe or go beyond the bounds of an accepted behavior

thine: your

1 **CITING TEXT EVIDENCE** When during the battle do you think the pharaoh spoke these words? Cite specific text to support your answer.

_____

_____

_____

2 **SUMMARIZING** How has the pharaoh honored and worshipped Ammon?

_____

_____

3 **HISTORY** What prediction does Ramses make in the poem? Is the prediction correct? How do you know?

_____

_____

4 **IDENTIFYING BIAS** A Hittite version of the Battle of Kadesh has also survived and tells a very different story of the battle, which historians believe is more accurate than the poem of Ramses. Why would the two stories be so different?

_____

_____

_____

_____

_____

_____

5 **INFERRING** What in the poem shows that Ramses considered himself a god?

_____

_____

_____

Assyria and Persia

DIRECTIONS: Search for evidence in this lesson to help you answer the following questions.

1 CIVICS How did the Assyrians govern such a large empire?

_____

_____

_____

_____

_____

_____

_____

_____

_____

ESSENTIAL QUESTION

How do empires rise, how are they maintained, and what causes them to fall?

As you gather evidence to answer the Essential Question, think about:

- the factors that allowed the Assyrians to capture such a large empire.
- the achievements of the Persian Empire.

2 **IDENTIFYING CAUSES** Complete the web diagram below to examine the factors that allowed the Assyrians to capture such a large empire.

Factors Leading to the Rise of Assyria

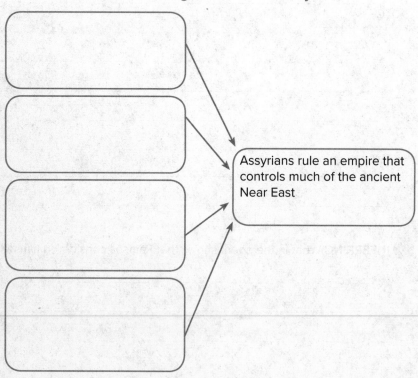

Assyrians rule an empire that controls much of the ancient Near East

My Notes

_____

_____

_____

_____

_____

_____

3 **ANALYZING INDIVIDUALS** Who was Nebuchadnezzar and why is he important in the history of the ancient Near East?

_____

_____

_____

_____

4 **USING MAPS** Study the map of the Persian Empire in 500 B.C. Through what modern-day countries did the Royal Road pass?

_____

_____

5 **CONTRASTING** How were the governing strategies of the Persians, particularly under the rule of Cyrus, different from those of Assyria?

_____

_____

_____

_____

_____

_____

6 **EVALUATING EVIDENCE** What were the major religious beliefs of the Persians?

_____

_____

_____

_____

_____

_____

_____

_____

ESSENTIAL QUESTION

How do empires rise, how are they maintained, and what causes them to fall?

The Struggle Between Good and Evil

DIRECTIONS: Read the excerpt. Then respond to the questions that follow.

EXPLORE THE CONTEXT: The following excerpt is taken from *The Divine Songs of Zarathushtra* [Zoroaster]. The reading describes some of the major teachings of the Persian religion—Zoroastrianism. The religion was one of Persia's greatest cultural legacies. Unlike the Persian Empire of ancient times, Zoroastrianism remains very much alive today, with its followers concentrated in Iran.

PRIMARY SOURCE: RELIGIOUS SCRIPTURE

" In the beginning, there were two Primal Spirits, Twins spontaneously active;
These are the Good and the Evil, in thought, and in word, and in deed;
Between these two, let the wise choose aright;
Be good, not base.

And when these Twin Spirits came together at first,
They established Life and Non-Life,
And so shall it be as long as the world shall last;
The worst existence shall be the lot of the followers of evil,
And the Good Mind shall be the reward of the followers of good,

Of these Twin Spirits, the Evil One chose to do the worst;
While the bountiful Holy Spirit of Goodness,
Clothing itself with the massy heavens for a garment, chose the Truth;
And so will those would fain please Ahura Mazda with righteous deeds,
performed with faith in Truth.

Let him that knows tell him that would know, which of the two creeds is better,
The belief of the righteous, or of the liar?
Let not the unenlightened deceive you any more!
Be Thou to us, O Ahura Mazda, the bestower of Good Thought.

So may we be like those making the world progress towards perfection;
May the Lord and His Angels help us and guide our efforts through Truth;
For a thinking man is where Wisdom is at home. "

—*The Divine Songs of Zarathushtra*

VOCABULARY

aright: correctly

base: evil

fain: gladly or with pleasure

creed: way of living

Irani, D. J. Yasna 30 in The Divine Songs of Zarathushtra - Volume 21. London & New York: Routledge Taylor & Francis Group, 1924.

1. **ANALYZING** What are the two "Primal Spirits" that the text discusses? How do you know?

_____

_____

2. **COMPARING** What do the beliefs of Zoroastrianism have in common with those of Judaism, Islam, and Christianity?

_____

_____

_____

3. **CITING TEXT EVIDENCE** What does the term _Good Mind_ mean as used in the excerpt? Give evidence from the text to support your answer.

_____

_____

_____

_____

4. **DETERMINING MEANING** Was Ahuramazda a vengeful or a forgiving god? Provide evidence from the text to support your case.

_____

_____

_____

_____

_____

5. **HISTORY** How does the excerpt reflect a basic belief that in turn influenced other cultures that developed throughout the world?

_____

_____

_____

_____

ESSENTIAL QUESTION

How do empires rise, how are they maintained, and what causes them to fall?

Darius and his Views on Government

DIRECTIONS: Read the excerpt. Then respond to the questions that follow.

EXPLORE THE CONTEXT: Known as "the father of history," Herodotus was the first writer in history to systematically study the past. *The Histories* was completed about 425 B.C. and detailed the wars between the Greek city-states and the Persian Empire from 499 B.C. and 479 B.C. Herodotus spent most of his life travelling throughout the Persian Empire and Egypt. The excerpt below tells of a speech that the Persian emperor Darius gave after one of his generals, Megabyzus, gave his ideas on what form of government was best for Persia.

PRIMARY SOURCE: HISTORIAN'S ACCOUNT

> This was the advice which Megabyzus gave, and after him Darius came forward, and spoke as follows:
>
> 'All that Megabyzus said against democracy was well said, I think; but about oligarchy he did not speak advisedly; for take these three forms of government, democracy, oligarchy, and monarchy, and let them each be at their best, I maintain that monarchy far surpasses the other two. What government can possibly be better than that of the very best man in the whole state? The counsels of such a man are like himself, and so he governs the mass of the people to their heart's content; while at the same time his measures against evil-doers are kept more secret than in other states. Contrariwise, in oligarchies, where men vie with each other in the service of the commonwealth, fierce enmities are apt to arise between man and man, each wishing to be leader, and to carry his own measures; whence violent quarrels come, which lead to open strife, often ending in bloodshed. Then monarchy is sure to follow; and this too shows how far that rule surpasses all others. Again, in a democracy, it is impossible but that there will be malpractices; these malpractices, however, do not lead to enmities, but to close friendships, which are formed among those engaged in them, who must hold well together to carry on their villanies. And so things go on until a man stands forth as champion of the commonalty, and puts down the evil-doers. Straightway the author of so great a service is admired by all, and from being admired soon comes to be appointed king; so that here too it is plain that monarchy is the best government. Lastly, to sum up all in a word, whence, I ask, was it that we got the freedom which we enjoy?—did democracy give it us, or oligarchy, or a monarch? As a single man recovered our freedom for us, my sentence is that we keep to the rule of one.

VOCABULARY

surpass: exceed

counsels: advice or leadership

commonwealth: independent country or state

whence: from which or from where

malpractice: improper action

1 **CITING TEXT EVIDENCE** What is Darius's opinion of democracy? Why do you think he had this opinion? Cite specific text examples to support your answers.

_____

_____

_____

_____

2 **CIVICS** Use the following table to list the three forms of government that Darius discusses. Give a brief description of each form.

Form of Government	Description/Definition

3 **IDENTIFYING BIAS** What bias does Darius show toward oligarchies?

_____

_____

4 **INFERRING** What in the excerpt shows that Darius holds himself in high regard?

_____

_____

5 **IDENTIFYING PERSPECTIVES** Herodotus was a Greek historian writing about comments made by the leader of Persia, the traditional enemy of the Greek city-states. The long Persian Wars that had started in 492 B.C. were still raging while Herodotus was travelling and writing his history. How might this fact have influenced what Herodotus wrote about the Persian leader? Give reasons to defend your answer.

_____

_____

_____

_____

_____

ESSENTIAL QUESTION

How do empires rise, how are they maintained, and what causes them to fall?

My Notes

_____

_____

_____

_____

_____

_____

_____

_____

_____

_____

_____

_____

_____

1 Think About It

Review the supporting questions you developed at the beginning of the chapter. Review the evidence on the rise, and ultimate fall of each empire you studied in the chapter. Also make certain that you have information on how each empire was able to maintain control over large territories. Were you able to answer each Supporting Question? If there was not enough evidence to answer your Supporting Questions, what additional evidence do you think you need to consider?

_____

2 Organize Your Evidence

Complete the chart below with information you learned about how empires of the ancient Near East rose and what caused each to fall.

Empire	Conditions Leading to its Rise	Why the Empire Collapsed
Akkad		
Babylon		
New Kingdom Egypt		The "Sea Peoples" invaded and forced Egyptians back to their boundaries.
Kush		A new power, Axum, became more powerful.
Assyria	Exploited the use of iron weapons	
Persia		

③ Write About It

Artifacts help archaeologists and historians learn about how a particular people or group of peoples lived during the past. What was the ancient Near East is filled with archaeological sites and the ruins of great civilizations. Choose one of the great empires that you studied in the chapter. Then use Internet and print resources to find information about archaeological sites of that civilization. What do we know about these people? What remains a mystery? Use what you learn to write a Facebook post, taking the role of an archaeologist and describing some of the highlights of the site you have just visited. If possible add photos to your post.

_____

_____

_____

④ Talk About It

Work in small groups. With your group, choose one of the empires that you studied in this chapter. Then discuss with the group the cultural, political, religious, or economic legacy that made this empire important in world history. Consider whether the civilization being discussed had a positive or a negative impact both on people living at that time and on future people of the Near East and of the world. Take notes about your discussion below.

_____

_____

_____

⑤ Connect to the Essential Question

The "father of history," Herodotus was a man in motion. From an early age, he travelled throughout the known world in search of information and data to use in his history of the Persian Wars. But, he wrote this history from a Greek perspective. We know this because he starts his masterpiece by stating his purpose: "in order that the deeds of men not be erased by time, and that the great and miraculous works—both of the Greeks and the barbarians—not go unrecorded." In other words, if you were not Greek, you were a barbarian! Choose one of the great civilizations studied in the chapter. Then take the role of Herodotus and write a history of your chosen empire. How did it rise? How did it maintain power? Why did it collapse? Remember that you are Greek and that the empire you are exploring, no matter how wealthy or sophisticated, is the product of barbarians.

_____

_____

TAKE ACTION

MAKE CONNECTIONS The ruins of what were once mighty civilizations lie scattered across the modern Middle East. The United Nations Educational, Scientific and Cultural Organization (UNESCO) has declared many of the sites to be World Heritage sites. UNESCO seeks to find and protect all such sites, whether they be cultural or natural. UNESCO representatives work with local and national governments and people to identify sites and then to provide resources to protect them so that future generations can enjoy and continue to learn from them. As of May 2018, UNESCO had identified 1,073 sites throughout the world. Of these, 867 were cultural or mixed-use sites, including 83 in what had been the ancient Near East. The United States also has its share with 10 cultural, 1 mixed-use, and 12 natural sites.

DIRECTIONS: Think about your own community and the various natural or cultural sites or locations that should be protected to make certain that whatever they offer or provide for the community is preserved. It might, for example, be a natural site such as a forest or a waterfall. On the other hand, it might be a cultural site such as the old town railroad station or an old ornate movie theater from the 1920s. After you have chosen a site, take notes to organize your thoughts about what needs to be done to protect the site. Note its cultural legacy or its sheer physical beauty. What about the site do you find interesting? What will future generations lose if the site is destroyed or altered?

After you have chosen your site and organized your plan of action to preserve the site, plan a fundraiser to attract businesses and individuals to donate to the preservation. You might decide to also interview local history buffs or town or city officials to find out if your community has an official program to preserve natural and cultural sites. They might be able to suggest what has been done in the past to raise funds for preservation projects. You might also want to include either a Twitter account or a Facebook page for your preservation fundraiser.

_____

_____

_____

_____

The Ancient Greeks

ESSENTIAL QUESTIONS

How can geography influence political organization?

How can cultural and political difference lead to conflict and change?

Think about the Olympic games that bring athletes from all over the world to compete in sporting events every four years. In doing so the nations of today's world are following many of the traditions that the ancient Greeks began. Modern world civilization can trace many institutions and ideas back to ancient Greece, whose civilization began about 1600 B.C. in Mycenae. Through conquest and persuasion, the Greeks spread these ideas and institutions throughout the known world of their time.

TALK ABOUT IT

With a partner, discuss the sort of information you would need to know to answer these questions. For example, one question might be: *What developments made the rise of city-states in Greece possible?*

DIRECTIONS: Now write down three additional questions that will help you analyze the conditions that made the rise, accomplishments, and long-lasting contributions of the early Greeks possible. For example you might ask: "What institutions and practices to we have in the United States today that can trace their origins to ancient Greece?

MY RESEARCH QUESTIONS

Supporting Question 1:

_____

_____

Supporting Question 2:

_____

_____

Supporting Question 3:

_____

_____

Poets and Heroes

DIRECTIONS: Search for evidence in this lesson to help you answer the following questions.

1 **GEOGRAPHY** What role did geography play in both helping and hindering the development of the Greek city states?

_____

_____

_____

_____

_____

2 **INTERPRETING** What negative impact did the growth of independent city states have on Greek civilization?

_____

_____

_____

_____

_____

_____

3 **DRAWING CONCLUSIONS** What role did the Mycenaean civilization play in the ancient world? Why did their civilization collapse?

_____

_____

_____

_____

_____

_____

ESSENTIAL QUESTIONS

How can geography influence political organization?

How can cultural and political differences lead to conflict and change?

As you gather evidence to answer the Essential Questions, think about:

- how the geography of the Greek Peninsula influenced the development of independent city-states, particularly that of the Mycenae.

- how Greek civilization suffered during the Dark Age.

- the ways that Homer provided a record of Greek accomplishments during the Dark Age.

My Notes

_____

_____

_____

_____

4 EVALUATING INFORMATION How did Homer immortalize Mycenaean civilization? Was the story of their exploits true?

_____

_____

_____

_____

_____

5 RELATING EVENTS Complete a web diagram similar to the one below to help you understand what regions the Greeks began colonizing during the difficult times of the Dark Age?

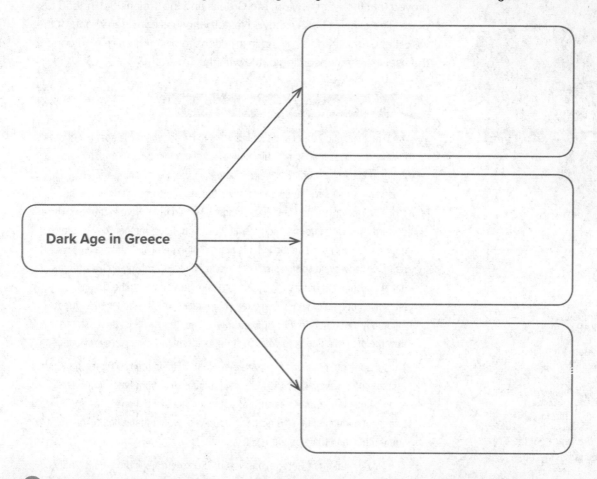

6 ANALYZING INFORMATION In what ways did Homer help safeguard the traditions of ancient Greece?

_____

_____

_____

ESSENTIAL QUESTION

How can cultural and political differences lead to conflict and change?

Nestor Organizes the Greek Forces at Troy

DIRECTIONS: Read the excerpt from Homer's *The Iliad*. Then respond to the questions that follow.

EXPLORE THE CONTEXT: Homer's epic poem, *The Iliad*, told the heroic story of the Greeks' long and ultimately victorious campaign against the city of Troy, in what is today Turkey. For many years, later peoples thought the story was a fictional one designed to inspire the ancient Greeks. No trace of the alleged Troy existed. But the archaeologist Heinrich Schliemann began excavating a site in Anatolia in 1870. The extensive site proved that the war between the Greeks and the Trojans did indeed take place. The excerpt below shows Nestor, who was considered one of the wisest of Greek leaders, giving instructions to his men on how to conduct themselves in an upcoming battle with the Trojans.

PRIMARY SOURCE: EPIC POETRY

❝With this he left them and went onward to Nestor, the facile speaker of the Pylians, who was marshalling his men and urging them on, in company with Pelagon, Alastor, Chromius, Haemon, and Bias shepherd of his people. He placed his knights with their chariots and horses in the front rank, while the foot-soldiers, brave men and many, whom he could trust, were in the rear. The cowards he drove into the middle, that they might fight whether they would or no. He gave his orders to the knights first, bidding them hold their horses well in hand, so as to avoid confusion. "Let no man," he said, "relying on his strength or horsemanship, get before the others and engage singly with the Trojans, nor yet let him lag behind or you will weaken your attack; but let each when he meets an enemy's chariot throw his spear from his own; this be much the best; this is how the men of old took towns and strongholds; in this wise were they minded."

Thus did the old man charge them, for he had been in many a fight, and King Agamemnon was glad. "I wish," he said to him, "that your limbs were as supple and your strength as sure as your judgment is; but age, the common enemy of mankind, has laid his hand upon you; would that it had fallen upon some other, and that you were still young."

And Nestor, knight of Gerene, answered, "Son of Atreus, I too would gladly be the man I was when I slew mighty Ereuthalion; but the gods will not give us everything at one and the same time. I was then young, and now I am old; still I can go with my knights and give them that counsel which old men have a right to give. The wielding of the spear I leave to those who are younger and stronger than myself."❞

—Homer, *The Iliad*

VOCABULARY

Pylians: people from the Greek city of Pylius

facile: easily achieved, effortless

marshalling: gathering

Agamemnon: Leader of the Greek forces and king of Mycenae

1 GEOGRAPHY Was Troy's location an advantage or a disadvantage for the Trojans? Explain your answer.

_____

_____

_____

_____

_____

2 CITING TEXT EVIDENCE Why did Nestor place the cowards in the middle? Cite specific evidence from the text to support your answer.

_____

_____

_____

3 DETERMINING MEANING Is Nestor going to lead the men he is organizing into battle? How do you know this?

_____

_____

_____

4 DRAWING CONCLUSIONS Why did Nestor organize the troops the way that he did?

_____

_____

_____

_____

5 SUMMARIZING What battle strategies does Nestor tell his men to use? Why?

_____

_____

_____

_____

How can cultural and political differences lead to conflict and change?

Advice to Greek Farmers

DIRECTIONS: Read the excerpt from Hesiod's *Works and Days*. Then respond to the questions that follow.

EXPLORE THE CONTEXT: Writing about 700 B.C., the Greek poet Hesiod was one of the earliest Greek poets. Two of his major epic works have survived. One, the *Theogony,* gives the story of all of the gods and the myths associated with them. The other, *Works and Days,* provides advice on daily living throughout ancient Greece. The excerpt below is from the latter.

PRIMARY SOURCE: EPIC POETRY

"A bad neighbour is as great a plague as a good one is a great blessing; he who enjoys a good neighbour has a precious possession. Not even an ox would die but for a bad neighbour. Take fair measure from your neighbour and pay him back fairly with the same measure, or better, if you can; so that if you are in need afterwards, you may find him sure.

. . .

Be friends with the friendly, and visit him who visits you. Give to one who gives, but do not give to one who does not give.

. . .

For the man who gives willingly, even though he gives a great thing, rejoices in his gift and is glad in heart; but whoever gives way to shamelessness and takes something himself, even though it be a small thing, it freezes his heart. He who adds to what he has, will keep off bright-eyed hunger; for if you add only a little to a little and do this often, soon that little will become great.

. . .

Let the wage promised to a friend be fixed; even with your brother smile – and get a witness; for trust and mistrust, alike ruin men.

. . .

There should be an only son, to feed his father's house, for so wealth will increase in the home; but if you leave a second son you should die old. Yet Zeus can easily give great wealth to a greater number. More hands mean more work and more increase.

If your heart within you desires wealth, do these things and work with work upon work."

—Hesiod, *Works and Days*

VOCABULARY

neighbour: old spelling for neighbor

fair measure: moderate amount of money or goods

glad in heart: happy

wage: earnings

Zeus: chief Greek god

Hesiod. Translated by Hugh G. Evelyn-White. "Works and Days." In Hesiod - The Homeric Hymns and Homerica. London: William Heinemann; New York: G. P. Putnam's Sons, 1920.

1 ECONOMICS What does Hesiod advise about repaying debts and about charitable giving?

_____

_____

_____

_____

2 IDENTIFYING CONNECTIONS How does the advice that Hesiod gives apply to life in the modern United States?

_____

_____

_____

3 IDENTIFYING BIAS How would Hesiod view a modern-day unemployed 30-year-old man who lives alone, who lets his dog (who often bites) wander the neighborhood, and who is losing his house to foreclosure? What advice would he give him?

_____

_____

_____

_____

_____

_____

4 CITING TEXT EVIDENCE Modern Americans often refer to someone as having a "strong work ethic." What does the phrase mean? How did Hesiod address this topic? Cite text evidence to support your answer.

_____

_____

_____

5 ANALYZING POINT OF VIEW How would Hesiod view today's 401K plans? Cite evidence from the text to support your answer.

_____

_____

_____

The Greek City-States

DIRECTIONS: Search for evidence in this lesson to help you answer the following questions.

1 **ANALYZING** What role did the polis play in ancient Greek life?

_____

_____

_____

_____

_____

2 **SUMMARIZING** What different types of residents did each polis include?

_____

_____

_____

_____

3 CIVICS What were the positives and the negatives of the Greek ideal of the rights and responsibilities of citizens?

_____

_____

_____

_____

_____

4 **IDENTIFYING CONNECTIONS** How were the tyrants who ruled in Greek city-states different from rulers called tyrants today?

_____

_____

_____

_____

ESSENTIAL QUESTIONS

How can cultural and political differences lead to conflict and change?

How can cultural and political differences lead to conflict and change?

As you gather evidence to answer the Essential Questions, think about:

- how the polis served as the center of Greek life.
- what led the Greeks to found colonies.
- the basic differences between Sparta and Athens.

My Notes

_____

_____

_____

_____

_____

_____

5 RELATING EVENTS How did the results of Greek colonization of other lands differ from the goal the Greeks had for the colonization?

_____

_____

_____

_____

_____

_____

6 DRAWING CONCLUSIONS What role did tyrants play in governing ancient Greece and how were they able to maintain control?

_____

_____

_____

_____

_____

7 COMPARING AND CONTRASTING Use the table below to list the major similarities and differences between Athens and Sparta.

	Athens	Sparta
Methods of Adding Territory		
Role of Government		
Type of Government		
Role of the Individual		
Foreign Policy		

ESSENTIAL QUESTION

How can cultural and political differences lead to conflict and change?

Spartan Sayings

DIRECTIONS: Read the excerpt. Then respond to the questions that follow.

EXPLORE THE CONTEXT: Plutarch was a Greek biographer and author who wrote about 227 works. Living in the first century A.D., Plutarch studied philosophy and mathematics in Athens and later travelled to Rome several times. During his trips to Rome he lectured on philosophy and was awarded Roman citizenship. He also travelled throughout Greece and Egypt. Plutarch also collected quotations from the people of Sparta. These quotes help explain the ideas and attitudes of the citizens of ancient Sparta.

PRIMARY SOURCE: BOOK

66 ANAXANDRIDAS

When another person asked why the Spartans, in their wars, ventured boldly into danger, he said, 'Because we train ourselves to have regard for life and not, like others, to be timid about it.'

ANDROCLEIDAS

Androcleidas the Spartan, who had a crippled leg, enrolled himself among the fighting-men. And when some persons were insistent that he be not accepted because he was crippled, he said, 'But I do not have to run away, but to stay where I am when I fight the opposing foe.'

ARISTON

1 When someone inquired how many Spartans there were in all, he said, 'Enough to keep away our enemies.'

2 When one of the Athenians read a memorial oration in praise of those who fell at the hands of the Spartans, he said, 'What kind of men, then, do you think ours must be who vanquished these?'

ZEUXIDAMUS

3 When someone inquired why they kept the laws in regard to bravery unwritten, and did not have them written down and thus give them to the young men to read, Zeuxidamus said, 'Because the young ought to accustom themselves to deeds of manly valour, a better thing than to apply their mind to writings. 99

— Plutarch, *Apophthegmata Laconica*, c. A.D. 96-98

VOCABULARY

vertured: took a risk

valour: courage, bravery

memorial: a time or event set aside to remember

oration: speech

vanquished: conquered

1 **CITING TEXT EVIDENCE** Would Androcleidas have proven himself a valuable fighter? Cite text evidence to support your answer.

_____

_____

_____

_____

_____

_____

2 **INFERRING** What does the excerpt show us about the value that the Spartans put on education?

_____

_____

_____

_____

3 **CIVICS** Compare this reading with the one from Pericles at the opening of your textbook chapter. What does each tell you about the rights and responsibilities of citizens of Sparta and of Athens?

_____

_____

_____

_____

_____

4 **EVALUATING TEXT EVIDENCE** What is Ariston's opinion of Athenians? Was he correct in his assessment? Use examples from the text to support your answer.

_____

_____

_____

_____

_____

6 **ANALYZING** What character traits did the Spartans value the most? How does the reading show you this information?

_____

_____

_____

_____

Copyright © McGraw-Hill Education   Plutarch. Translated by Bernadette Perrin. Plutarch's Lives. Vol. 1. Cambridge, Massachusetts: Harvard University Press; London: William Heinemann, Ltd., 1914.

ESSENTIAL QUESTION

How can cultural and political differences lead to conflict and change?

Democratic Reforms

DIRECTIONS: Read the excerpt. Then respond to the questions that follow.

EXPLORE THE CONTEXT: Perhaps the best known work by Plutarch is *Parallel Lives,* in which he records the deeds and words of famous Greeks and Romans. In *Parallel Lives* he wrote about some of the people he had met or heard about during his travels throughout Greece and Egypt. In the excerpt, Plutarch is describing the reforms that the Athenian statesman Solon made when he led the city-state.

PRIMARY SOURCE: BOOK

❝[W]ishing to leave all the magistracies in the hands of the well-to-do, as they were, but to give the common people a share in the rest of the government, of which they had hitherto [so far] been deprived, Solon made an appraisement of the property of the citizens. Those who enjoyed a yearly increase of five hundred measures (wet and dry), he placed in the first class, and called them Pentakosiomedimnoi; the second class was composed of those who were able to keep a horse, or had a yearly increase of three hundred measures, and they were called Hippada Telountes, since they paid a Knight's tax; the members of the third class, whose yearly increase amounted to two hundred measures (wet and dry together), were called Zeugitai. All the rest were called Thetes; they were not allowed to hold any office, but took part in the administration only as members of the assembly and as jurors. This last privilege seemed at first of no moment [importance], but afterwards proved to be of the very highest importance, since most disputes finally came into the hands of these jurors. ❞

—from Plutarch's *Parallel Lives,* c. A.D. 96–98

VOCABULARY

magistracies: control of territory

appraisement: a statement of the value of something

measures: a standard unit used to measure quantity

administration: the people who manage the government

disputes: an argument or difference of opinion

deprived: lacking something considered necessary

① **CONTRASTING** Contrast this excerpt with the one about Sparta that you read earlier. How were the governments of each city-state different? How was the individual in each state regarded differently?

_____

_____

_____

_____

_____

2 **EVALUATING TEXT EVIDENCE** What in the text shows that Solon did not want a completely democratic government for Athens? How is this at odds with the ideal Greek democracy? Use examples from the text to support your answer.

_____

_____

_____

_____

_____

_____

3 **CITING TEXT EVIDENCE** What in the excerpt shows that the people of the time considered Solon's reforms to be democratic?

_____

_____

_____

_____

_____

4 ECONOMICS What elements of Solon's reforms to you see reflected in the way that the national and state governments of the United States levy income taxes?

_____

_____

_____

_____

5 **IDENTIFYING CONNECTIONS** What elements of Solon's reforms do you see reflected in the American system of government? Which reforms are radically different?

_____

_____

_____

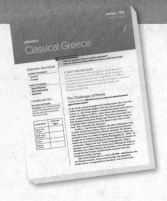

Classical Greece

DIRECTIONS: Search for evidence in this lesson to help you answer the following questions.

ESSENTIAL QUESTION

How can cultural and political differences lead to conflict and change?

As you gather evidence to answer the Essential Questions, think about:

- the impact that the Persians had on Greek civilization..
- how the Age of Pericles proved the height of Athenian power and brilliance.
- what impact Athenian democracy had on later generations.
- How the Peloponnesian War destroyed much of Greek civilization.

① ANALYZING POINTS OF VIEW What did Persia hope to gain by conquering the Greek city-states?

_____

_____

_____

_____

_____

② IDENTIFYING CONNECTIONS What enduring legacy did the battle of Marathon leave for future generations?

_____

_____

_____

_____

_____

③ DETERMINING POINTS OF VIEW The Persians viewed the defeat at Marathon as a minor setback. The Athenians, however, viewed it as a major victory. How do you account for the different points of view?

_____

_____

_____

_____

_____

My Notes

_____

_____

_____

_____

_____

4 CIVICS Why were the governmental developments under Pericles so important to world history?

_____

_____

_____

_____

_____

_____

5 ECONOMICS What were the major features of the Athenian economy that allowed it to support a population of more than 300,000?

_____

_____

_____

_____

6A IDENTIFYING CAUSES What were the major causes of the Peloponnesian War?

_____

_____

_____

_____

_____

6B IDENTIFYING EFFECTS Complete a web diagram similar to the one below to help you understand the impact that the Peloponnesian War had on Greece.

Peloponnesian War

Pericles's Funerary Address

DIRECTIONS: Read the excerpt. Then respond to the questions that follow.

EXPLORE THE CONTEXT: As Athens battled Sparta in the Great Peloponnesian War, the famous Athenian leader Pericles gave a public oration at the funeral of one of the first soldiers on his side to fall. Though it was not unusual for leaders to mark such occasions with speeches, Pericles's focus on democracy and the wonders of Athens made his speech famous for centuries to come. Pericles (495–429 B.C.) was an Athenian general and politician, known as a supporter of the arts and public speaker. However, he also played a role in sparking the Great Peloponnesian War, which eventually led to the downfall of the Greek Empire that, as evidenced in this speech, he so cherished.

PRIMARY SOURCE: SPEECH

VOCABULARY

extravagance: an excessive use of resources, particularly money

indispensable: necessary

adjudged: decided to be true

conferring: bestowing; giving

expediency: quick and convenient, though perhaps immoral

❝ Nor are these the only points in which our city is worthy of admiration. We cultivate refinement without extravagance and knowledge without effeminacy; wealth we employ more for use than for show, and place the real disgrace of poverty not in owning to the fact but in declining the struggle against it. Our public men have, besides politics, their private affairs to attend to, and our ordinary citizens, though occupied with the pursuits of industry, are still fair judges of public matters; for, unlike any other nation, regarding him who takes no part in these duties not as unambitious but as useless, we Athenians are able to judge at all events if we cannot originate, and, instead of looking on discussion as a stumbling-block in the way of action, we think it an indispensable preliminary to any wise action at all. Again, in our enterprises we present the singular spectacle of daring and deliberation, each carried to its highest point, and both united in the same persons; although usually decision is the fruit of ignorance, hesitation of reflection. But the palm of courage will surely be adjudged most justly to those, who best know the difference between hardship and pleasure and yet are never tempted to shrink from danger. In generosity we are equally singular, acquiring our friends by conferring, not by receiving, favours. Yet, of course, the doer of the favour is the firmer friend of the two, in order by continued kindness to keep the recipient in his debt; while the debtor feels less keenly from the very consciousness that the return he makes will be a payment, not a free gift. And it is only the Athenians, who, fearless of consequences, confer their benefits not from calculations of expediency, but in the confidence of liberality. ❞

— Pericles as quoted in *The History of the Peloponnesian War, Book 1,* by Thucydides, 431 B.C.

1 **ANALYZING** How does Pericles characterize Athens? Explain your answer.

_____

_____

_____

2 **IDENTIFYING CONNECTIONS** What does this speech demonstrate about the unity of Greece?

_____

_____

_____

3 **UNDERSTANDING CONTEXT** How does the subject matter of this speech support or contradict the occasion at which it was given?

_____

_____

_____

4 **COMPARING AND CONTRASTING** How does the speech differentiate between Athens and other city-states?

_____

_____

_____

5 **IDENTIFYING BIAS** How might the speaker be demonstrating political bias?

_____

_____

_____

6 **HISTORY** Why might giving this speech have been politically expedient for Pericles?

_____

_____

_____

The Peloponnesian War

ESSENTIAL QUESTION

How can cultural and political differences lead to conflict and change?

DIRECTIONS: Read the excerpt. Then respond to the questions that follow.

EXPLORE THE CONTEXT: Historians know little about the Athenian historian Thucydides who was born about 460 B.C. and died some time after 404 B.C. They do, however, have his most important work, *History of the Peloponnesian War*. This comprehensive history gives an account of the disastrous war between democratic Athens and authoritarian Sparta. Thucydides was the first historian to systematically analyze a government's war policies.

PRIMARY SOURCE: BOOK

❝ The Peloponnesian War was prolonged to an immense length, and, long as it was, it was short without parallel for the misfortunes that it brought upon Hellas. Never had so many cities been taken and laid desolate, here by the barbarians, here by the parties contending (the old inhabitants being sometimes removed to make room for others); never was there so much banishing and blood-shedding, now on the field of battle, now in the strife of faction. Old stories of occurrences handed down by tradition, but scantily confirmed by experience, suddenly ceased to be incredible; there were earthquakes of unparalleled extent and violence; eclipses of the sun occurred with a frequency unrecorded in previous history; there were great droughts in sundry places and consequent famines, and that most calamitous and awfully fatal visitation, the plague.

. . .

The real cause I consider to be the one which was formally most kept out of sight. The growth of the power of Athens, and the alarm which this inspired in Lacedaemon, made war inevitable. Still it is well to give the grounds alleged by either side which led to the dissolution of the treaty and the breaking out of the war. ❞

—Thucydides, *The History of the Peloponnesian War*

VOCABULARY

parallel: equal

Hellas: Greece

barbarians: uncivilized people

banishing: making someone leave their home permanently and against their will

faction: disputes: state of conflict within a group

Lacedaemon: Sparta

1 **CITING TEXT EVIDENCE** What did Thucydides believe was the real reason for the war? Cite examples from the text to support your answer.

_____

_____

_____

_____

2 **EVALUATING TEXT EVIDENCE** In what ways was the war unprecedented in Greek history? From what you have learned, was Thucydides' account accurate? Why or why not?

_____

_____

_____

_____

_____

_____

_____

3 GEOGRAPHY What impact did Thucydides believe the war had on weather events and health on the Greek peninsula?

_____

_____

4 **IDENTIFYING BIAS** What in the reading shows Thucydides' pro-Athenian bias?

_____

5 **COMPARING AND CONTRASTING** Think about the sources from Herodotus that you studied. Note that Thucydides and Herodotus lived at about the same time and might even have met. How were the works of these two historians the same? How were they different?

_____

_____

_____

_____

6 **IDENITFYING EFFECTS** What impact did the war have on civilians?

_____

_____

ESSENTIAL QUESTION

How can cultural and political differences lead to conflict and change?

As you gather evidence to answer the Essential Question, think about:

- the impact that religious beliefs had on Greek culture.
- the ways in which the Greeks excelled in art and literature.
- how Greek philosophy influenced Western philosophy through the ages.

My Notes

_____

_____

_____

_____

_____

_____

Classical Greek Culture

DIRECTIONS: Search for evidence in this lesson to help you answer the following questions.

1 **ANALYZING POINTS OF VIEW** What impact did Greek religious beliefs have on the daily life of the Greeks?

_____

_____

_____

_____

_____

_____

2 **IDENTIFYING CONNECTIONS** In what ways did Greek architecture and sculpture reflect their ideals of reason, moderation, balance, harmony, and beauty?

_____

_____

_____

_____

_____

3 **SUMMARIZING** What were the major themes of early Greek dramas?

_____

_____

_____

_____

_____

4 HISTORY What contributions did the ancient Greeks make to the study of history as a discipline?

_____
_____
_____
_____
_____
_____

5 **DETERMINING MEANING** What is the origin of the term _philosophy_?

_____
_____

6 **EVALUATING EVIDENCE** In the table below, note the major influence that each philosopher listed had on the development of philosophy.

Philosopher	Legacy
Socrates	
Plato	
Aristotle	

Greek Pottery

DIRECTIONS: Study the photos. Then respond to the questions that follow.

EXPLORE THE CONTEXT: As Greek civilization arose and established stable governments that valued the roles of individuals, art as a form of expression also flourished. The vases shown below are arranged in chronological order to help you see the developing artistic skills that the ancient Greeks were fine tuning as they became more sophisticated. Vase A was made in Mycenae about between about 1250 B.C. and 1225 B.C. Vase B was painted in the mid-700s B.C., while Vase C is attributed to the Euphiletos Painter who was actively working on his art between 530 B.C. and 520 B.C. The final vase is the newest. It is a mixing bowl that dates to about 400 B.C.

PRIMARY SOURCE: POTTERY

1 HISTORY What elements in Vase A show that it was definitely made during the Mycenaean period, probably on what is today Crete?

_____

_____

2 CONSTRUCTING HYPOTHESES What can you hypothesize about the painter who worked on Vase B? What types of scenes is the vase showing?

_____

_____

_____

_____

3 COMPARING AND CONTRASTING In what ways is Vase C different from and similar to Vases A and B.

_____

_____

_____

4 IDENTIFYING CONNECTIONS Historians use artifacts such as these vases to learn about how a specific people lived. Take the role of a historian or archaeologist in A.D. 3500. You discover a cellphone buried in the ruins of a site that you are helping investigate. What would the cellphone tell you about the people who lived in the 21st century?

_____

_____

_____

_____

5 ANALYZING What do all four vases tell us about life in ancient Greece?

_____

_____

_____

_____

_____

Copyright © McGraw-Hill Education   Martin, Thomas R. with Neel Smith & Jennifer F. Stuart. "Democracy in the Politics of Aristotle." in C.W. Blackwell, ed., Dēmos: Classical Athenian Democracy. A. Mahoney and R. Scaife, ed. The Stoa: A Consortium for Electronic Publication in the Humanities. July 26, 2003.

ESSENTIAL QUESTION

How can cultural and political differences lead to conflict and change?

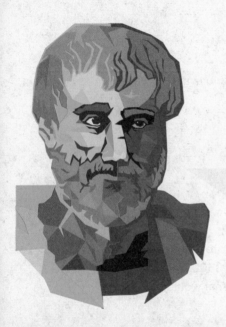

VOCABULARY

measures: actions

multitude: entire population

revenues: income

conferring: bestowing; giving

expediency: quick and convenient, though perhaps immoral

Aristotle's Views on Democracy

DIRECTIONS: Read the excerpt. Then respond to the questions that follow.

EXPLORE THE CONTEXT: The ancient Greek philosopher and writer Aristotle was born about 384 B.C. and died about 322 B.C. A great intellectual, Aristotle originated a system of philosophical and scientific inquiry that formed the basis of later systems in both the Christian and Islamic worlds. He was also a close friend and student of Plato in Athens. Aristotle wrote down his political theories in what was perhaps his most famous works, *Politics*. The excerpt shows a little about what Aristotle had to say about democracy.

PRIMARY SOURCE: BOOK

❝To preserve a democracy, one should strive not for measures that will make it absolutely as democratic as possible but rather that will preserve it for the longest time. The following measures are recommended: any confiscations of property imposed as punishment in a legal judgment should become property of the gods, not of the public, to prevent corrupt court judgments meant to secure a distribution to the population from the confiscated property; large penalties should be imposed for frivolous prosecutions to prevent harassment of the rich; if there are no [additional] sources of public revenues besides taxes [on individuals], confiscations, and corrupt court judgments to pay subsidies to the multitude for attending the assembly, then only infrequent assembly meetings and brief court sessions should be held [to minimize the need to take money from the rich to pay the subsidies]; if there are [additional] public revenues, no surplus from them should be distributed to the poor, for this practice stimulates more demand for this sort of distribution; at the same time, the multitude should be kept from becoming overly poor, since this development creates wretched [and thus excess] democracy; money should be provided from public revenues to the poor so that they can acquire land for farming or learn a craft and become better off over time; the rich should be taxed to provide pay [to ordinary citizens to enable them to attend] necessary meetings, but the rich should be released from unnecessary public service; the rich should divide the poor citizens among themselves and then give them enough money [for necessary tools, etc.] so that they can start to work; magistracies should be chosen some by election and some by lot.❞

— Aristotle, *Politics*

1 **CITING TEXT EVIDENCE** What is Aristotle's purpose for this paragraph? Cite text evidence to support your answer.

_____

_____

_____

2 **IDENTIFYING BIAS** What parts of the text show that Aristotle is biased toward the rich? Why do you think he had this bias?

_____

_____

_____

_____

_____

_____

3 **IDENTIFYING CONNECTIONS** In the United States today, does the government follow Aristotle's advice about providing aid to the poor? Why or why not?

_____

_____

_____

_____

_____

4 **CIVICS** How do Aristotle's views of the role of the poor in government contrast with those of Pericles that you read at the beginning of the chapter in your textbook?

_____

_____

_____

Alexander and the Hellenistic Era

DIRECTIONS: Search for evidence in this lesson to help you answer the following questions.

1 **ANALYZING INDIVIDUALS** How was Alexander the Great able to unite with the Greeks to defeat the mighty Persian Empire?

_____

_____

_____

_____

_____

_____

_____

ESSENTIAL QUESTION

How can cultural and political differences lead to conflict and change?

As you gather evidence to answer the Essential Question, think about:

- how Alexander was able to defeat the mighty Persian Empire.
- the political, economic, and cultural legacy of Alexander the Great.
- what the Hellenistic kingdoms did to preserve Greek culture.
- the scientific developments made during the Hellenistic Age.

2 **HISTORY** What enduring political and cultural legacy did Alexander the Great leave?

_____

_____

_____

_____

_____

_____

My Notes

_____

_____

_____

_____

_____

3 **INFERRING** Alexander hoped to fuse Macedonians, Greeks, and Persians into his new empire by using all three groups as part of his government. Why did he want to be certain to include all three groups in his administration?

_____

_____

_____

4 **EVALUATING EVIDENCE** In what sense did the Hellenistic kingdoms prove to be worthy successors to Alexander the Great? In what sense were they unworthy?

_____

_____

_____

_____

5 **SUMMARIZING** How did Hellenistic cities evolve into centers of culture?

_____

_____

_____

_____

_____

6 **ANALYZING INFORMATION** Use the web diagram below to list the various scientific and philosophical developments of the Hellenistic Age.

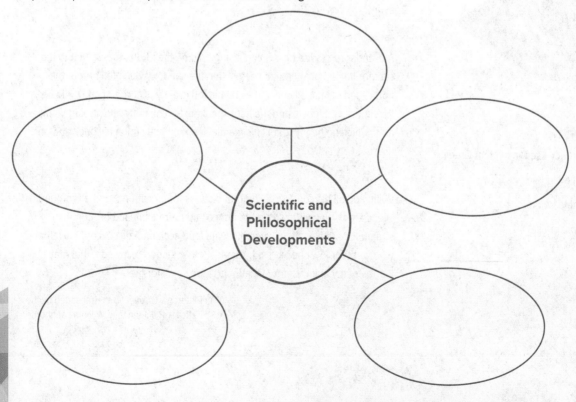

Scientific and Philosophical Developments

ESSENTIAL QUESTION

How can cultural and political differences lead to conflict and change?

Alexander Tames a Horse

DIRECTIONS: Read the excerpt. Then respond to the questions that follow.

EXPLORE THE CONTEXT: Plutarch wrote his famed *Parallel Lives* years after Alexander the Great had ruled the known world and died, yet we consider his accounts to be accurate portrayals of life at the time. Plutarch undoubtedly visited Macedonia on his many travels. The story of Bucephalus was already legendary. Plutarch recounted it, making it even more famous. It also helped serve Plutarch's purpose in writing the book. He hoped that it would foster respect and admiration for both Greek and Roman culture.

PRIMARY SOURCE: BOOK

" When Philonicus, the Thessalian, offered the horse named Bucephalus in sale to Philip, for the price of thirteen talents . . . the king with the prince [Alexander] and many others, went into the field to see some trial made of him. The horse appeared extremely vicious and unmanageable, and was so far from suffering himself to be mounted, that he would not bear to be spoken to, but turned fiercely upon all the grooms. Philip was displeased at their bringing him so wild and ungovernable a horse, and bade them take him away.

. . .

Alexander ran to the horse, and laying hold on the bridle, turned him to the sun; for he had observed, it seems, that the shadow which fell before the horse, and continually moved as he moved greatly disturbed him. While his fierceness and fury lasted, he kept speaking to him softly and stroking him; after which he gently let fall his mantle, leaped lightly upon his back and got his seat very safe.

. . .

Philip and all his court were in great distress for him at first, and a profound silence took place. But when the prince had turned him and brought him straight back, they all received him with loud acclamations, except his father, who wept for joy, and . . . said, "Seek another kingdom, my son, that may be worthy of thy abilities; for Macedonia is too small for thee. "

— from Plutarch's *Parallel Lives,* translated by the Reverend John and William Langhorne

VOCABULARY

talents: currency used in ancient Greece

suffering: allowing

grooms: stable workers

acclamations: praise

Plutarch. Lives of Romulus, Lycurgus, Solon, Pericles, Cato, Pompey, Alexander the Great, Julius Caesar, Demosthenes, Cicero, Mark Antony, Brutus, and Others, and His Comparisons: With Notes, Critical and Historical. John and William Langhorne, Tr. W.L. Allison Company, 1889.

1 **ANALYZING** Why was Bucephalus behaving so wildly?

_____

_____

_____

2 `ECONOMICS` Bucephalus is one of the most famous horses in history. He accompanied the young Alexander as he conquered many territories when horses made a difference in battle. Today, human inventions have replaced horses on the battlefield. Yet they remain a part of life in many areas of the United States. In what ways do horses benefit the U.S. economy?

_____

_____

_____

3 **UNDERSTANDING CONTEXT** At the time of Philip and Alexander, Macedonia was a relatively obscure kingdom in the north of Greece,. What in the excerpt acknowledges that fact?

_____

_____

_____

4 **EVALUATING TEXT EVIDENCE** How does the excerpt help accomplish Plutarch's goal of fostering respect and admiration for Greek and Roman culture?

_____

_____

_____

_____

_____

5 **DISTINGUISHING FACT FROM OPINION** Was Plutarch's account factual? Give reasons to justify your answer.

_____

_____

_____

_____

_____

_____

ESSENTIAL QUESTION

How can cultural and political differences lead to conflict and change?

Epicurus Explains his Philosophy

DIRECTIONS: Read the excerpt. Then respond to the questions that follow.

EXPLORE THE CONTEXT: The ancient Greek philosopher Epicurus believed that everyone should look for happiness in life. To do so, he taught, people must seek the absence of physical and spiritual pain. He valued friendship and thought that people could achieve more happiness by retiring from public life. He also thought that the gods did not really care what happened to people and that there was no life after death. The following excerpt is taken from a letter that Epicurus wrote to a friend.

PRIMARY SOURCE: LETTER

❝When we say, then, that pleasure is the end and aim, we do not mean the pleasures of the prodigal or the pleasures of sensuality, as we are understood to do by some through ignorance, prejudice, or willful misrepresentation. By pleasure we mean the absence of pain in the body and of trouble in the soul. It is not an unbroken succession of drinking-bouts and of merrymaking . . . not the enjoyment of the fish and other delicacies of a luxurious table, which produce a pleasant life; it is sober reasoning, searching out the grounds of every choice and avoidance, and banishing those beliefs through which the greatest disturbances take possession of the soul. Of all this the [foundation] is prudence. For this reason prudence is a more precious thing even than the other virtues, for [as] a life of pleasure which is not also a life of prudence, honor, and justice; nor lead a life of prudence, honor, and justice, which is not also a life of pleasure. For the virtues have grown into one with a pleasant life, and a pleasant life is inseparable from them. ❞

— Epicurus, *Letter to Menoeceus*

VOCABULARY

prodigal: wastefully extravagant

sensuality: physical pleasure

banishing: forcing away

prudence: cautiousness

1 **IDENTIFYING CONNECTIONS** What does the word *epicurean* mean in modern English. How is this different from what it meant in the world of ancient Greece?

_____

_____

_____

_____

_____

_____

2 **EVALUATING TEXT EVIDENCE** According to Epicurus what is the foundation of pleasure?

_____

_____

_____

_____

3 **INFERRING** How did people of the time misinterpret the philosophy? How do you know?

_____

_____

_____

_____

_____

_____

_____

4A **CONTRASTING** How did Epicureanism differ from Stoicism?

_____

_____

_____

_____

_____

_____

_____

_____

4B **COMPARING** How were Epicuranism and Stoicism alike?

_____

_____

_____

ESSENTIAL QUESTIONS

How can geography influence political organization?

How can cultural and political differences lead to conflict and change?

My Notes

_____

_____

_____

_____

_____

_____

_____

_____

_____

_____

_____

_____

_____

1 Think About It

Review the supporting questions you developed at the beginning of the chapter. Review the evidence on the Greek city-states you studied in the chapter. Also make certain that you have information on the many contributions that these city-states provided to world civilization. Do you have enough information on the role that geography played in the formation of these cities as independent and often isolated states? Then review the information that you gathered on Alexander the Great and his legacy. Were you able to answer each Supporting Question? If there was not enough evidence to answer your Supporting Questions, what additional evidence do you think you need to consider?

_____

_____

_____

2 Organize Your Evidence

Complete the chart below with information you learned about the Greek city-states as well as Alexander the Great and his legacy.

City-State or Ruler	Role of Geography in State	Contributions and Legacy
Mycenae		
Athens	Mountains isolated it from other states and allowed it to develop independently	
Sparta		
Alexander the Great		

③ Write About It

The influence of the early Greek city-states continues to be a prominent force in architecture throughout the world today. Think about one of the major monuments either in your city or state or in Washington, D.C. Then use Internet or print resources to learn more about your chosen structure. Write a two-paragraph informative essay in which you discuss the elements in the modern monument that are derived from the ancient Greeks.

④ Talk About It

Work in small groups. With your group, choose one of the philosophers or scientists that you learned about in the chapter. Then discuss with the group the impact that your chosen person had on future generations and future thinkers. Did any of the ideas put forth by your subject lead to conflict? Did any make people change their minds about a particular subject and therefore lead to change in how people viewed a particular event or state of being? For example, the Hellenistic scientist Aristarchus theorized that the sun was the center of the universe and that the planets revolved around it. But later, during the early Christian era, scientists believed that the planets and the sun revolved around the Earth. In this case, Aristarchus did not have a lasting impact on science, at least not until later thinkers revisited and reinterpreted the information. Take notes about your discussion of a specific philosopher or scientist below.

_____

_____

_____

_____

_____

_____

⑤ Connect to the Essential Question

Use the information about the influence of geography on the formation of the early Greek city-states as well as how political and cultural differences among these states led to conflict and change. Choose one of the major city-states or kingdoms studied to set up an interview with one of the leaders or philosophers about whom you read. Take the role of an investigative reporter who is trying to uncover the truth about a specific situation or action. For example, you might choose to interview Paris of Troy to learn why he took Helen of Sparta back to Troy when he knew that such an action would have consequences. Or you might choose Pericles and try to learn why he favored so many democratic reforms for Athens. Then, working with a classmate, conduct and record an interview in which you try to gather the information you want. Remember that your interview will air on cable channels, so your time will be limited. Use a time frame of about two to four minutes as a guide.

CITIZENSHIP
TAKE ACTION

MAKE CONNECTIONS One of the greatest legacies that the ancient Greek city-states, particularly Athens, bequeathed to later generations was the concept of a direct democracy in which all citizens, no matter their educational, class, or financial background, played a role. All citizens were allowed to vote during assembly meetings. While Athenian democracy was far from perfect—many people, including women, did not have equal rights, it was the first time that so many people had been granted so many rights. Nor was Athens the only city-state to practice democracy. Others, such as Argos, Syracuse, Rhodes, and Erythrai, all chose democracies as their form of government.

DIRECTIONS: Think about your own community and the type of government it has. It undoubtedly includes a democratic form of government. But is it as democratic as it could be? Brainstorm ways in which more people of the city could be able to take a more direct role in the government. Do research to find out whether the city or town government excludes any specific groups from taking part in government, holding office, and even voting. According to American law, all citizens who are 18 or older must have the right to vote, but should that right be extended to people younger than 18? Use what you have learned to begin a poster campaign or a telephone survey to find out whether there might be support for lowering the voting age in local elections to 16. After all, 16 year-olds are in school where they study voting requirements in their civics and history classes. In many ways they know more about current politics than do many people who are allowed to vote.

Gather your information to use as the basis for a petition that you can circulate throughout your community. The petition can ask that the issue of giving 16-year-olds the vote be placed on the ballot in the next local election. Be certain to check with your city or county government to find out how many signatures you will need in order for the petition to be valid. In most localities all signatures must be those of registered voters, so you should be certain to ask whether a signer is registered before collecting the signature. After you have gathered the required number of signatures, submit it to the appropriate city or county office. Conclude the activity by writing a brief paragraph detailing what the experience has taught you about individual citizens in the United States can make a difference. Would you do it again for another cause?

_____

_____

_____

India's First Empires

ESSENTIAL QUESTION

How was early Indian culture influenced by religion and social structure?

How did ideas and events during the Mauryan and Gupta Empires affect India's development?

Think about two of the world's great religions—Hinduism and Buddhism—that can trace their origins to ancient India and which became a vital part of the emergence of Indian civilization.

TALK ABOUT IT

With a partner, discuss the sort of information you would need to know to answer these questions. For example, one question might be: How did Hindu teachings influence the social structure of early India?

DIRECTIONS: Now write down three additional questions that will help you evaluate the role that early Indian religious teachings played in the rise of Indian civilization as well as help you analyze how the Mauryan and Gupta Empires affected India's development: the conditions that made the rise, accomplishments, and long-lasting contributions of the early Indians possible. For example, you might ask: "What are the major beliefs of Hinduism?"

MY RESEARCH QUESTIONS

Supporting Question 1:

_____

_____

Supporting Question 2:

_____

_____

Supporting Question 3:

_____

_____

Origins of Hindu India

DIRECTIONS: Search for evidence in this lesson to help you answer the following questions.

ESSENTIAL QUESTION

How was early Indian culture influenced by religion and social structure?

As you gather evidence to answer the Essential Questions, think about:

- the four varnas and how membership in each was determined.
- the origins and beliefs of Hinduism.
- the principles that underlay Hinduism.

1 **DESCRIBING** Use the table below to write a description of each of the four varnas of early Indian society.

Varna	Description
Brahmin	
Kshatriya	
Vaisya	
Sudra	

2 **SUMMARIZING** Who are the three chief gods in Hinduism?

_____

_____

_____

3 **DRAWING CONCLUSIONS** What was the ultimate goal that Hindus sought to achieve? Explain your answer.

_____

_____

_____

My Notes

_____

_____

_____

_____

_____

_____

4 SUMMARIZING What were the four types of yoga that Hindus developed and the purpose of each?

_____
_____
_____
_____
_____
_____

5 EVALUATING INFORMATION How did the forms taken by the Hindu gods and goddesses help believers relate to them?

_____
_____
_____
_____
_____

6 ANALYZING CENTRAL IDEAS What roles do the principles of reincarnation and karma play in the Hindu religion?

_____
_____
_____
_____
_____
_____

7 IDENTIFYING CONNECTIONS How does the concept of dharma relate to karma?

_____
_____
_____

The Bhagavad Gita

Copyright © McGraw-Hill Education   From The Bhagavad Gita, Translated by Eknath Easwaran, Founder of the Blue Mountain Center of Meditation, Copyright 1985, 2007, Reprinted by Permission of Nilgiri Press, P. O. Box 256, Tomales, CA 94971, www.bmcm.org.

ESSENTIAL QUESTION

How was early Indian culture influenced by religion and social structure?

VOCABULARY

acquire: to gain

pierced: go into or through

infinite: limitless or endless

unmanifested: secret or difficult to detect

inevitable: impossible to avoid

manifestation: clearly shown

lament: to be sad

DIRECTIONS: Read the excerpt. Then respond to the questions that follow.

EXPLORE THE CONTEXT: *The Bhagavad Gita,* which means the "Song of God," is an episode in the Sanskrit poem, the *Mahabharata*. Historians believe *The Bhagavad Gita* was recorded in writing between 400 B.C. and A.D. 200. Sections are set into numbered lines, often called verses. Much of it consists of a dialogue between Prince Arjuna and Krishna, an incarnation of the god Vishnu. Just before a great battle between warring members of the same family is to take place, Arjuna is worried that killing so many people, particularly members of his own family, is immoral. He says as much to Krishna, who persuades Arjuna to do his duty as a warrior and fight. The excerpt details how killing qwarriors in battle does not really bring about their death because they will be reborn.

PRIMARY SOURCE: POETRY

"22 As one abandons worn-out clothes and acquires new ones, so when the body is worn out a new one is acquired by the Self, who lives within. 23 The Self cannot be pierced by weapons or burned by fire; water cannot wet it, nor can the wind dry it. 24 The Self cannot be pierced or burned, made wet or dry. It is everlasting and infinite, standing on the motionless foundations of eternity. 25 The Self is unmanifested, beyond all thought, beyond all change. Knowing this, you should not grieve. 26 O mighty Arjuna, even if you believe the Self to be subject to birth and death, you should not grieve. 27 Death is inevitable for the living; birth is inevitable for the dead. Since these are unavoidable, you should not sorrow. 28 Every creature is unmanifested at first and then attains manifestation. When its end has come, it once again becomes unmanifested. What is there to lament in this? 29 The glory of the Self is beheld by a few, and a few describe it; a few listen, but many without understanding. 30 The Self of all beings, living within the body, is eternal and cannot be harmed. Therefore, do not grieve."

—from *The Bhagavad Gita*

1 HISTORY How do the beliefs expressed in this excerpt match what you have read in the chapter about Hinduism?

_____

_____

2 **CITING TEXT EVIDENCE** What does the text tell us about proving that the Self does indeed exist? Cite examples from the excerpt to support your answer.

_____

_____

_____

_____

3 **DETERMINING CENTRAL IDEAS** What is the central idea of this excerpt? Explain your reasoning.

_____

_____

_____

_____

4 **ANALYZING** How does the text make the idea of reincarnation and of the Self easier to understand?

_____

_____

_____

5 **DETERMINING MEANING** Can the Self be destroyed? What in the excerpt supports your answer?

_____

_____

_____

6 **DETERMINING POINT OF VIEW** Why does the text say not to grieve death?

_____

_____

Copyright © McGraw-Hill Education   From The Upanishads, Translated by Eknath Easwaran, Founder of the Blue Mountain Center of Meditation, Copyright 1987, 2007; Reprinted by Permission of Nilgiri Press, P. O. Box 256, Tomales, Ca 94971, www.bmcm.org.

ESSENTIAL QUESTION
How was early Indian culture influenced by religion and social structure?

The Upanishads

DIRECTIONS: Read the excerpt. Then respond to the questions that follow.

EXPLORE THE CONTEXT: The Upanishads are the concluding portions of the Vedas—the sacred books of Hinduism. The Upanishads are also known as Vedanta, which means "conclusion." They served as the religion's foundation, and much of the later Hindu theological discussions of the interconnectedness of life on Earth were based on their arguments.

PRIMARY SOURCE: POETRY

"Place this salt in water and bring it here tomorrow morning."

The boy did.

"Where is that salt?" his father asked.

"I do not see it."

"Sip here. How does it taste?"

"Salty, Father."

"And here? And there?"

"I taste salt everywhere."

"It is everywhere, though we see it not. Just so, dear one, the Self is everywhere, within all things, although we see him not. There is nothing that does not come from him. Of everything he is the inmost Self. He is the truth; he is the Self supreme. You are that, Shvetaketu; you are that."

—The Updanishads

VOCABULARY

inmost: something that is most private

supreme: superior to everything else

1 **ANALYZING** Why does the father have his son place the salt in the water?

_____

_____

_____

_____

_____

2 `HISTORY` How does the salt represent the Self?

_____

_____

_____

_____

3 **EXPLAINING** Who or what is Svetaketu in the text?

_____

_____

_____

_____

4 **DETERMINING MEANING** What did the writer hope to gain by telling such a simple story? What was the motivation for telling it so simply?

_____

_____

_____

_____

_____

_____

_____

5 **UNDERSTANDING CONTEXT** What does the father mean by subtile essence?

_____

_____

_____

_____

_____

_____

_____

_____

Buddhism

DIRECTIONS: Search for evidence in this lesson to help you answer the following questions.

1 **HISTORY** What do we know about the life of Siddhārtha Gautama?

_____

_____

_____

_____

_____

_____

_____

_____

_____

_____

_____

_____

_____

_____

_____

_____

ESSENTIAL QUESTION

How was early Indian culture influenced by religion and social structure?

As you gather evidence to answer the Essential Question, think about:

- who the Buddha was and how he was able to found such a large religion.
- the central ideas of Buddhism.
- the impact that Buddhism had on Indian society.

My Notes

_____

_____

_____

_____

_____

_____

_____

2 **EVALUATING** How was Siddhārtha Gautama able to reach enlightenment, according to the text?

_____

_____

3 **DETERMINING MEANING** What paths did Siddhārtha Gautama attempt to follow before reaching enlightenment?

_____

_____

_____

4 COMPARING AND CONTRASTING Complete the table below to show what beliefs the Hindus and Buddhists share and which they do not. Place an **X** in each row as it applies.

Belief	Buddhism	Hinduism
Reincarnation		
Nirvana, or ultimate reality		
Unity with Brahman		
Four noble truths		
Eightfold path		
Karma		
Series of lives needed to reach unity with Brahman		
Goal of oneness with god		

5 UNDERSTANDING CONTEXT What were Siddhārtha's views on suffering?

_____

_____

_____

6 DETERMINING CENTRAL IDEAS Siddārtha provided his followers with the Four Noble Truths. What is the central idea behind these truths?

_____

_____

_____

7 SUMMARIZING What is the Middle Path?

_____

_____

_____

ESSENTIAL QUESTION

How was early Indian culture influenced by religion and social structure?

The Brahma-Gâla Sutta

DIRECTIONS: Read the excerpt. Then respond to the questions that follow.

EXPLORE THE CONTEXT: The Brahma-Gâla Sutta, or the Perfect Net, is a dialogue between the Buddha and his followers. It begins with a conversation between man named Suppiya and Brahmadatta, a student of Buddha. Suppiya argues against the Buddha and his teachings while Brahmadatta praising Buddha and his teachings. As the Buddha's followers were discussing their conversation, the Buddha overhears and delivers this response.

PRIMARY SOURCE: POETRY

❝Now the Blessed One, on realising what was the drift of their talk, went to the pavilion, and took his seat on the mat spread out for him. And when he had sat down he said: 'What is the talk on which you are engaged sitting here, and what is the subject of the conversation between you?' And they told him all. And he said:

'Brethren, if outsiders should speak against me, or against the Doctrine, or against the Order, you should not on that account either bear malice, or suffer heart-burning, or feel illwill. If you, on that account, should be angry and hurt, that would stand in the way of your own self-conquest. If, when others speak against us, you feel angry at that, and displeased, would you then be able to judge how far that speech of theirs is well said or ill?'

'That would not be so, Sir.'

'But when outsiders speak in dispraise of me, or of the Doctrine, or of the Order, you should unravel what is false and point it out as wrong, saying: "For this or that reason this is not the fact, that is not so, such a thing is not found among us, is not in us."

'But also, brethren, if outsiders should speak in praise of me, in praise of the Doctrine, in praise of the Order, you should not, on that account, be filled with pleasure or gladness, or be lifted up in heart. Were you to be so that also would stand in the way of your self-conquest. When outsiders speak in praise of me, or of the Doctrine, or of the Order, you should acknowledge what is right to be the fact, saying: "For this or that reason this is the fact, that is so, such a thing is found among us, is in us."

'It is in respect only of trifling things, of matters of little value, of mere morality, that an unconverted man, when praising the Tathâgata, would speak. And what are such trifling, minor details of mere morality that he would praise?' ❞

—*Brahma-Gâla Sutta*

VOCABULARY

quitted: released or let go

mortal frames: human bodies

indivisible: incapable of being divided or separated

incorruptible: unable to be spoiled or corrupted

inconceivable: unable to be understood

unalterable: unchanging

behove: fit or suit a person

1 HISTORY Who is speaking in the excerpt? How do you know? Was the role he was playing here religious or secular? Defend your answer.

_____

_____

_____

_____

2 **CITING TEXT EVIDENCE** What does the Buddha instruct his followers to do when others criticize their beliefs? Cite text evidence to support your answer.

_____

_____

_____

_____

_____

3 **DETERMINING CENTRAL IDEAS** What is the central idea of this excerpt? Provide your reasoning in determining this central idea.

_____

_____

_____

_____

4 **ANALYZING** What role does logic play in the advice that the Buddha is providing his followers?

_____

_____

_____

5 **UNDERSTANDING CONTEXT** How can you tell the Buddha is referring to himself when he uses the term Tathâgata?

_____

_____

_____

Copyright © McGraw-Hill Education

Chapter 5   **123**

ESSENTIAL QUESTION

How was early Indian culture influenced by religion and social structure?

Three Different Buddhas

DIRECTIONS: Study the photos. Then respond to the questions.

EXPLORE THE CONTEXT: There are many different cultural interpretations of the Buddha. The hand position, or *mudra,* is significant in interpreting the message of an image. *Abhaya*, with an upraised hand, symbolizes blessing or protection. *Dhyani* has both hands in the lap with palms facing upward and indicates meditation. *Bhumisparsha* has one hand in the lap and the other resting on the knee and shows the victory of enlighten ment over the powers of illusion.

SECONDARY SOURCE: PHOTOS

1 HISTORY   What in photo A shows that people are viewing Buddha as a god?

_____

_____

_____

2 HISTORY   The pose of the Buddha in photo A shows the "Protection Buddha" with the raised hand representing a shield that is designed to overcome fear? Why is such a pose fitting in the sculpture shown?

_____

_____

3 EXPLAINING   Photo B shows the Buddha in what is called the "Meditation Buddha"? What do you suppose is meant by this terminology?

_____

_____

_____

4 DETERMINING MEANING   Photo B shows the great Kamakura Buddha at Kotokuin Temple in Japan. It is the second largest statue of Buddha in the world. Devout Buddhists often come here to pray. How are the ways that Christians pray similar to the ways that Buddhists pray?

_____

_____

_____

_____

5 EVALUATING ISSUES   How is the pose shown in Photo C different from the other poses in the photographs? Why might this be a different pose? What might it signify?

_____

_____

_____

_____

The Mauryans and the Guptas

DIRECTIONS: Search for evidence in this lesson to help you answer the following questions.

1   CIVICS   What were the key elements of the Mauryan government?

_____

_____

_____

2   **ANALYZING INDIVIDUALS**   What led to an increase in prosperity in India during Aśoka's rule?

_____

_____

_____

3   **USING MAPS**   Study the map in your textbook. Of the three empires shown, which controlled the largest territory?

_____

_____

4   **IDENTIFYING EFFECTS**   Although many cultures contributed to the rise of the Kushan Empire, it was able to maintain its own distinct culture. How was it able to do so?

_____

_____

_____

_____

_____

_____

_____

ESSENTIAL QUESTION

How did ideas and events during the Mauryan and Gupta Empires affect the development of India?

As you gather evidence to answer the Essential Question, think about:

- the factors that led to the rise and fall of the Mauryan, Kushan, and Gupta Empires.
- the cultural contributions of ancient India.
- Indian contributions to literature, architecture, science, and mathematics.

My Notes

_____

_____

_____

_____

_____

_____

5 ECONOMICS What policies did the Gupta rulers follow in order to achieve a prosperous economy and a vibrant culture?

_____

_____

_____

_____

6 INTEGRATING INFORMATION Use the web diagram below to provide examples of some of the Gupta's contributions to world architecture, literature, and science.

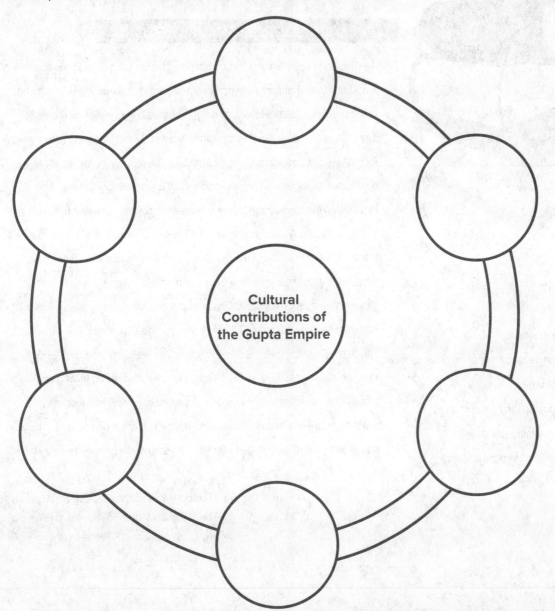

Cultural Contributions of the Gupta Empire

A Record of Buddhist Kingdoms

ESSENTIAL QUESTION

How was early Indian culture influenced by religion and social structure?

DIRECTIONS: Read the excerpt. Then respond to the questions that follow.

EXPLORE THE CONTEXT: The Chinese Monk Faxian embarked on a journey through Central Asia to India between 399 and 414 A.D. He went on this journey to find copies of Buddhist texts and monastic rules. Faxian's writings provide an important firsthand account of Buddhist sites and practices during this time period in northern India. In this excerpt, Faxian has arrived at Pataliputra, the seat of power in the Gupta Empire.

PRIMARY SOURCE: TRAVEL RECORD

❝The cities and towns of this country are the greatest of all in the Middle Kingdom. The inhabitants are rich and prosperous, and vie with one another in the practice of benevolence and righteousness. Every year on the eighth day of the second month they celebrate a procession of images. They make a four-wheeled car, and on it erect a structure five storeys by means of bamboos tied together. This is supported by a king-post, with poles and lances slanting from it, and is rather more than twenty cubits high, having the shape of a tope. White and silk-like cloth of hair is wrapped all round it, which is then painted in various colours. They make figures of devas, with gold, silver, and lapis lazuli grandly blended and having silken streamers and canopies hung out over them. On the four sides are niches [nooks], with a Buddha seated in each, and a Bodhisattva standing in attendance on him. . . . This is the practice in all the other kingdoms as well. The Heads of Vaisya families in them establish in the cities houses for dispensing [giving out] charity and medicines. All the poor and destitute [needy] in the country, orphans, widowers and childless men, maimed [injured] people and cripples, and all who are diseased, go to those houses, and are provided every kind of help. . . . ❞

—from *A Record of Buddhist Kingdoms, Being an Account by The Chinese Monk Fâ-hien of his Travels in India and Ceylon* (A.D. 399-414)

VOCABULARY

vie: compete

benevolence: goodwill

righteousness: decency

procession: parade

king-post: a post in the center of a roof

cubit: unit of measurement

tope: dome-shaped structure

devas: divine beings

Legge, James. A Record of Buddhist Kingdoms, Being an Account by The Chinese Monk Fâ-hien of His Travels in India and Ceylon (A.D. 399-414) in Search of the Buddhist Books of Discipline. Oxford: Clarendon Press, Translated 1886.

1 HISTORY According to Faxian, what was life like for the residents of the city? Defend your answer.

_____

_____

2 DETERMINING MEANING What does Faxian mean when he refers to the region as the *Middle Kingdom?*

_____

_____

3 DETERMINING CENTRAL IDEAS What in the text shows that the people of the city as well as the surrounding areas are very religious?

_____

_____

_____

4 CITING TEXT EVIDENCE What parts of the text show that Faxian admires the people of the Gupta Empire?

_____

_____

_____

5 IDENTIFYING CONNECTIONS Religious institutions as well as government agencies in the United States today help provide aid to the poor and the unemployed. In what ways did Gupta society provide for the poor? Which type of aid, that of the Guptas or that in the United States today, was more effective in addressing the issues. Give reasons to support your answer.

_____

_____

_____

_____

_____

_____

ESSENTIAL QUESTION

How was early Indian culture influenced by religion and social structure?

The Ramayana

DIRECTIONS: Read the excerpt. Then respond to the questions that follow.

EXPLORE THE CONTEXT: Two great epic poems have come down to us from ancient India. One, *The Ramayana,* was probably written about 300 B.C. and includes about 24,000 couplets organized into seven books. The poem describes the early life of the god Rama, who is banished to the forest. The stories examine Rama as he tries to reenter the chief god's good graces. Valmiki was the alleged writer of the epic, and the epic provides part of a conversation he has with one of the spirits, Narada Muni.

PRIMARY SOURCE: EPIC POETRY

The Sage Valmiki... enquired of Shri Narada:

"Who is there in the world to-day, endowed with excellent and heroic qualities, who is versed in all the duties of life, grateful, truthful, firm in his vows, an actor of many parts, benevolent to all beings, learned, eloquent, handsome, patient, slow to anger, one who is truly great; who is free from envy and when excited to wrath can strike terror into the hearts of celestial beings? O Sage, I would hear of such a man from thee, who art able to describe him to me."

Narada, acquainted with the past, the present and the future, pleased with the words of the Sage Valmiki, answered him saying:"Rare indeed are those, endowed with the qualities thou has enumerated, yet I can tell thee of one. Born in the family of Ikshwaku, he is named Rama... "

—from *The Ramayana*

VOCABULARY

sage: a wise person or thinker

endowed: given or provided

benevolent: kind behavior

celestial beings: deities or gods

enumerated: listed or named

1 **ANALYZING INDIVIDUALS** Who is the only figure who has all of the characteristics mentioned? Why is he important?

_____

_____

_____

2 **HISTORY** What does the existence of this poem tell us about life under the Guptas?

_____

_____

_____

_____

_____

3 **EVALUATING** _The Ramayana_ is one of the great pieces of Hindu literature. In what ways was it important to preserve the Hindu legacy in writing such as this?

_____

_____

_____

_____

4 **UNDERSTANDING CONTEXT** Based on the excerpt, what do you think the phrase _free from envy_ means in the pararaph describing "excellent and heroic qualities"?

_____

_____

_____

5 **INTERPRETING** What might the description of Narada as being "acquainted with the past, the present and the future" mean?

_____

_____

_____

ESSENTIAL QUESTIONS

How was early Indian culture influenced by religion and social structure?

How did ideas and events during the Mauryan and Gupta Empires affect the development of India?

My Notes

_____

_____

_____

_____

_____

_____

_____

_____

_____

_____

_____

_____

_____

_____

1 Think About It

Review the supporting questions you developed at the beginning of the chapter. Review the evidence on early Indian civilizations as well as on Hinduism and Buddhism that you studied in the chapter. Also make certain that you have information on the many contributions of the Gupta and Mauryan societies as well as the beliefs of Hindus and Buddhists. Do you have enough information on how religion and social structure influenced early Indian culture? Did you learn enough about how the Mauryan and Gupta Empires affected the development of India? Then review the information that you gathered on the empires and on the religions. Were you able to answer each Supporting Question? If there was not enough evidence to answer your Supporting Questions, what additional evidence do you think you need to consider?

_____

_____

_____

_____

2 Organize Your Evidence

Complete the chart below with information you learned about how religion, ideas, and events during the Mauryan and the Gupta Empires affected the development of India.

Impact on:	Mauryan Empire	Gupta Empire
Religion		
Ideas	Centralized government divided into provinces directly responsible to the emperor; great builders of pillars, stupas, and rock chambers	
Events		

Copyright © McGraw-Hill Education

3 Write About It

India provided the world with two of its greatest religions—Hinduism and Buddhism. Both had an impact on India's culture and its social system. Think about one of these religions and its impact not only in India but throughout the world. Then use Internet or print resources to learn more about your chosen religion. Write a two-paragraph informative essay in which you discuss the religion as it is today. How has it changed over the centuries? What region or nation includes followers of the religion? Be certain to use information from the textbook as a starting point since the narrative provides much of the historical background that you will need as you begin your research.

4 Talk About It

Work in small groups. With your group, choose one of the three empires discussed in the textbook—Mauryan, Kushan, and Gupta. Then discuss with the group the impact that your chosen empire had on the culture of India. Did any of the empires have long lasting effects on life in India? Did any help improve the lives of people under their rule? For example, the Gupta rulers engaged in widespread trade that brought goods from all over the world into India. How would such trade have benefited the people of the time? Would it have continued to benefit the people after the empire collapsed? Why or why not? Take notes about your discussion of an empire below.

_____

_____

_____

_____

_____

_____

_____

_____

5 Connect to the Essential Question

Think about what you have learned about the basic beliefs of Hinduism and Buddhism as well as the events and legacies of the Mauryan and Gupta Empires. Choose one of these religions or one of the two empires to study in more detail. Your task is to bridge the span of history—from the times examined in the textbook to the modern day. For example, if you choose Hinduism, use Internet and print resources to learn about the religion today. If you choose the Gupta Empire, focus your research on finding the cultural legacies that the empire left for us today. Then use what you learn to create a multimedia presentation that links the past—as noted in your textbook and in some of your research—with the present—what your sources teach you. If possible, try to include some video as part of your presentation.

CITIZENSHIP
TAKE ACTION

MAKE CONNECTIONS Our country, the state we live in, and the local areas or communities we call home each have their own cultures. A culture is not just things like art, lierature, or music, but it can also be our ways of life. This includes our holidays or the way we celebrate other important events or people in our past or in our present. Culture impacts the way in which you and your family live in and interact with the world around you. Think about how the culture of your community impacts the life of you and your family. What are the most important influences in your local area that shape your personal culture?

DIRECTIONS: What is a belief you hold that is also central to your community's culture? How can you become involved in promoting this belief? Promote either what you feel should be changed to improve your community or to encourage more growth in the area you think is positive. Promote your idea by choosing one of these methods: write and gather signatures for a petition, organize a community rally, or create promotional posters decribing your idea. If these methods do not work for you you may also create your own. Use the space below to explain the aspect of your community's culture that you hope to change or promote, the method you will use to do so, and how you would go about implementing your plan.

The First Chinese Empires, 221 B.C. – A.D. 220

ESSENTIAL QUESTIONS

How can differing philosophies influence a culture?

What factors can help a dynasty stay in power?

Think about how these two questions might overlap. How might a philosophy help a dynasty stay in power?

TALK ABOUT IT

With a partner, discuss what information you would need to know to answer this question as it relates to the first Chinese empires. For example, what philosophies were influential during this time in China? Did certain dynasties follow certain philosophies? Did those philosophies influence how they governed?

DIRECTIONS: Now write down three additional questions that you need to answer to explain how different philosophies influenced Chinese culture and helped the early Chinese dynasties stay in power.

MY RESEARCH QUESTIONS

Supporting Question 1:

_____

_____

Supporting Question 2:

_____

_____

Supporting Question 3:

_____

_____

Schools of Thought in Ancient China

DIRECTIONS: Search for evidence in the lesson to help you answer the following questions.

ESSENTIAL QUESTION

How can differing philosophies influence a culture?

As you gather evidence to answer the Essential Question, think about:

- how Chinese philosophers focused on worldly matters and society.
- how the teachings of Confucius were focused on duty and humanity.
- how the philosophy of Daoism presents proper forms of human behavior.
- how Legalism proposed that society needed a strong ruler to keep people serving his interests.

My Notes

---

1 **CONTRASTING** How was the focus of Chinese philosophers different from that of Hindus and Buddhists?

_____

_____

_____

_____

2 **HISTORY** How were Confucius's ideas a product of the time in which he lived?

_____

_____

_____

3 **DRAWING CONCLUSIONS** Why might aristocrats have resisted some of Confucius's ideas?

_____

_____

_____

_____

4 **CONTRASTING** What is the primary way that Daoism differs from Confucianism?

_____

_____

_____

5 **IDENTIFYING CONNECTIONS** How is Legalism's view of human nature related to its beliefs about government?

_____

_____

6 **PREDICTING** Legalism was strictly followed during the Qin dynasty. Based on what you know about Legalism, how do you think the Qin rulers likely treated the common people?

_____

7 **COMPARING AND CONTRASTING** Use the following chart to compare and contrast the philosophies of Confucianism, Daoism, and Legalism.

	Confucianism	Daoism	Legalism
Founder			Unknown
View of Human Nature			
Beliefs About Government			
Other Basic Beliefs			

Copyright © McGraw-Hill Education   Confucius. Translated by William Jennings, John Francis Davis, and Epiphanus Wilson. Chinese Literature Comprising The Analects of Confucius, The Sayings of Mencius, The Shi-King, The Travels of Fä-Hien, and The Sorrows of Han, and The Travels of Fä-Hien. London & New York: The Colonial Press, 1900.

ESSENTIAL QUESTION

How can differing philosophies influence a culture?

Teachings of Confucius

DIRECTIONS: Read the excerpt. Then respond to the questions that follow.

EXPLORE THE CONTEXT: This excerpt from an anonymous collection of quotations (compiled c. 475 B.C.—221 B.C.) provides insight into the mind of Confucius and his teachings.

PRIMARY SOURCE: BOOK EXCERPT

" 'One should not be greatly concerned at not being in office; but rather about the requirements in one's self for such a standing. Neither should one be so much concerned at being unknown; but rather with seeking to become worthy of being known.'

Addressing his disciple Tsang Sin, the Master said, 'Tsang Sin, the principles which I inculcate have one main idea upon which they all hang.' 'Aye, surely,' he replied.

When the Master was gone out the other disciples asked what was the purport of this remark. Tsang's answer was, 'The principles of our Master's teaching are these—whole-heartedness and kindly forbearance; these and nothing more.' "

—from Chinese Literature Comprising The Analects of Confucius, The Sayings of Mencius, The Shi-King, The Travels of Fâ-Hien, and The Sorrows of Han

VOCABULARY

standing: rank or position; how others regard you

disciple: follower, student, learner

inculcate: consistently teach

aye: a word that shows agreement

purport: meaning or sense

whole-heartedness: dedication or commitment

forbearance: patience or self-control

1 **ANALYZING** What does Confucius believe should be the highest concern of those who wish they could hold office?

_____

_____

_____

_____

_____

2 ANALYZING STRUCTURE How do the first two sentences of the excerpt demonstrate a parallel structure?

_____

_____

_____

_____

3 CIVICS Based on what you have read about Confucius's ideas, what did Confucius likely believe were the "requirements in one's self" for being in office?

_____

_____

_____

_____

_____

4 UNDERSTANDING CONTEXT Based on what you have read about Confucius's life, how does the first paragraph of this excerpt relate to Confucius's own experiences?

_____

_____

_____

_____

_____

_____

5 IDENTIFYING CONNECTIONS How do the two principles mentioned in the last paragraph of the excerpt relate to the key elements of Confucianism described in the lesson?

_____

_____

_____

_____

_____

Copyright © McGraw-Hill Education   Lao-Tzu. Tao Te Ching. Legge, J., Tr. In The Sacred Books Of The East Vol.39. Muller, F. Max, ed. Clarendon Press, 1891.

ESSENTIAL QUESTION

How can differing philosophies influence a culture?

Tao Te Ching

DIRECTIONS: Study the excerpt. Then respond to the questions that follow.

EXPLORE THE CONTEXT: The *Tao Te Ching*, or *The Way of the Dao*, contains the main ideas of Daoism. It has been attributed to Laozi, traditionally considered the founder of Daosim, although this authorship (and even Laozi's very existence) has been disputed. The date that it was written is also uncertain, as there is no mention of events or people in the text that would help assign a date to it. Many scholars now believe that it was actually written by multiple authors over an extended period of time.

PRIMARY SOURCE: BOOK EXCERPT

"The highest excellence is like (that of) water. The excellence of water appears in its benefiting all things, and in its occupying, without striving (to the contrary), the low place which all men dislike. Hence (its way) is near to (that of) the Tao.

The excellence of a residence is in (the suitability of) the place; that of the mind is in abysmal stillness; that of associations is in their being with the virtuous; that of government is in its securing good order; that of (the conduct of) affairs is in its ability; and that of (the initiation of) any movement is in its timeliness.

And when (one with the highest excellence) does not wrangle (about his low position), no one finds fault with him. "

—Laozi, from the *Tao Te Ching*

VOCABULARY

abysmal: very great or deep

associations: friendships or associating with people

virtuous: those with high moral standards

initiation: beginning or start

wrangle: argue or dispute

1 **ANALYZING IDEAS** According to this excerpt, how is water similar to the way of the Dao?

_____

_____

_____

_____

_____

_____

2 ANALYZING STRUCTURE How does the second paragraph use repetition to make its point?

_____

_____

_____

_____

3 `CIVICS` According to this excerpt, what is the sign of excellence in government?

_____

_____

_____

_____

4 ANALYZING CENTRAL IDEAS According to this excerpt, how can a person show that he is of the highest excellence?

_____

_____

_____

_____

5 CITING TEXT EVIDENCE What words or phrases in this excerpt convey the idea of inaction, which is a key concept in Daoism?

_____

_____

_____

_____

6 COMPARING AND CONTRASTING TEXTS How does this excerpt and the excerpt from the teachings of Confucius both address man's concern with his position in society?

_____

_____

_____

_____

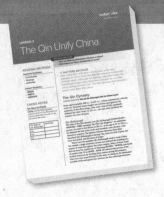

The Qin Unify China

DIRECTIONS: Search for evidence in the lesson to help you answer the following questions.

1 **SUMMARIZING** Complete the web diagram below to indicate how Qin Shihuangdi united China.

ESSENTIAL QUESTIONS

How can differing philosophies influence a culture?

What factors can help a dynasty stay in power?

As you gather evidence to answer the Essential Questions, think about:

- how Qin Shihuangdi worked to unify China economically and geographically.

- how Qin Shihuangdi initiated a large-scale building project to keep out invaders near China's northern frontier.

- how the Qin dynasty made many administrative and political changes in China.

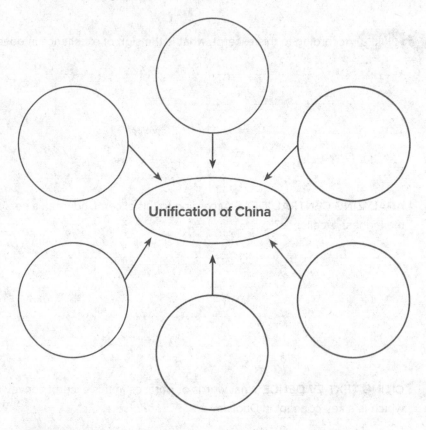

Unification of China

My Notes

_____

_____

_____

_____

_____

_____

2 **IDENTIFYING EFFECTS** What two benefits did Qin Shihuangdi achieve by dividing the estates of landed aristocrats among the peasants?

_____

_____

_____

3 **IDENTIFYING CONNECTIONS** How are the terra-cotta army and the taxation of peasants related?

_____

_____

_____

4 IDENTIFYING CAUSES What problem led to the creation of the Great Wall of China?

_____

_____

_____

_____

5 IDENTIFYING EFFECTS How did the philosophy of Legalism affect Chinese politics?

_____

_____

_____

_____

_____

_____

6 CIVICS What was the role of the censorate in the Chinese bureaucracy?

_____

_____

_____

_____

_____

7 ASSESSING How was Qin Shihuangdi able to gather control of the empire into his own hands?

_____

_____

_____

_____

_____

_____

_____

ESSENTIAL QUESTIONS

How can differing philosophies influence a culture?

What factors can help a dynasty stay in power?

Records of the Grand Historian

DIRECTIONS: Read the excerpt. Then respond to the questions that follow.

EXPLORE THE CONTEXT: The *Shiji*, or Records of the *Grand Historian*, was written by Sima Qian, the first great Chinese historian, about 85 B.C. It covers events and people in China over a 2,000-year period and took 18 years to complete. Like his father before him, Sima Qian was the grand historian at the Han court. This position included keeping a daily record of important events, as well as maintaining the Chinese calendar and making astronomical observations. In writing the *Shiji*, Sima Qian drew on earlier court records as well as various historical sources and philosophical writings. In this excerpt, he describes actions taken by Qin Shihuangdi (the "First Emperor").

PRIMARY SOURCE: BOOK EXCERPT

66 An edict was issued, saying: "We have heard that in high antiquity there were titles but no posthumous names. In middle antiquity there were titles, and posthumous names were assigned after the death of a person on the basis of his actions. This results in the son passing judgment on the father, and subjects passing judgment on the ruler. Such a procedure is highly improper and we will have none of it! From now on, this manner of assigning posthumous names shall be abolished. We ourselves shall be called First Emperor, and successive generations of rulers shall be numbered consecutively, Second, Third, and so on for 1,000 or 10,000 generations, the succession passing down without end."

The First Emperor believed that the Five Powers succeed each other in unending cycle, and he held that the Zhou dynasty had ruled by the power of fire. Since the Qin had replaced the Zhou, its power should therefore proceed from that which fire cannot overcome; the power of water had now begun its era of dominance. He changed the time for the court celebrations marking the beginning of the year, holding them all on the first day of the tenth month, and all clothing, flags, and pennants honoured the colour black. Among numbers, six was the standard, so that tallies and official caps were six inches, carriages were six feet, six feet were taken to make up one pace, and carriages were drawn by six horses. He also changed the name of the Yellow River, calling it "Powerful Water" to indicate that the era of the power of water had begun. Only by being stern and severe, by settling all affairs in the light of the law, by cutting and slashing without mercy or gentleness, he believed, could he comply with the destiny decreed by the Five Powers. Hence he assiduously applied the law and refused to pardon even crimes committed far in the past. 99

—Sima Qian, from *Records of the Grand Historian*,
translated by Burton Watson

VOCABULARY

edict: a decree or command issued by a ruler

posthumous: occurring after someone's death

succession: the order or line of persons who follow one another as king, emperor, etc.

assiduously: persistently, continuously, or zealously

1 DRAWING CONCLUSIONS In the first paragraph of this excerpt, Sima Qian quotes Qin Shihuangdi. What practice does Qin Shighuandi find objectionable? Why?

_____

_____

_____

_____

2 SUMMARIZING According to Sima Qian, what changes did Qin Shihuangdi initiate?

_____

_____

_____

3 UNDERSTANDING CONTEXT According to Sima Qian, why did Qin Shihuangdi change the name of the Yellow River?

_____

_____

_____

_____

4 CIVICS Which sentences in this excerpt indicate that Qin Shihuangdi was ruling according to the philosophy of Legalism?

_____

_____

_____

_____

5 DETERMINING POINT OF VIEW How does Sima Qian view Qin Shihuangdi? Cite evidence from the excerpt to support your answer.

_____

_____

_____

Army of the Terracotta Warriors

DIRECTIONS: Study the image. Then respond to the questions that follow.

EXPLORE THE CONTEXT: This photograph shows a portion of the burial place of the First Qin Emperor, Shihuangdi. The entire burial compound covers 20 square miles and contains an army of thousands of terra-cotta soldiers, as well as horses, chariots, and weapons. The terra-cotta figures were originally painted with bright colors and were arranged as if ready to go into battle. The actual tomb of the emperor has not been excavated but was described by the historian Sima Qian as a huge underground palace with mechanical inventions, including crossbows that were rigged to automatically shoot intruders and re-creations of rivers and the ocean that were designed to flow with mercury.

PRIMARY SOURCE: PHOTOGRAPH

—photograph of the Army of Terracotta Warriors

1 **DRAWING CONCLUSIONS** What do the terra-cotta figures in this image indicate about Qin Shihuangdi's beliefs about the afterlife?

_____

_____

_____

_____

_____

2 **IDENTIFYING CONNECTIONS** What connection do you see between this image and Qin Shihuangdi's edict in the excerpt from the _Records of the Grand Historian_?

_____

_____

_____

_____

_____

3 **DRAWING CONCLUSIONS** Assuming that the terra-cotta figures were a re-creation of Qin Shihuangdi's imperial guard, what does this image indicate about Qin Shihuangdi's power?

_____

_____

_____

_____

_____

4 **ECONOMICS** Based on what you have read about Qin Shihuangdi, how did he likely pay for the terra-cotta army?

_____

_____

_____

_____

_____

The Han Dynasty

DIRECTIONS: Search for evidence in the lesson to help you answer the following questions.

1 **COMPARING AND CONTRASTING** Complete the Venn diagram below to compare and contrast political structures during the Qin and Han dynasties.

ESSENTIAL QUESTIONS

How can differing philosophies influence a culture?

What factors can help a dynasty stay in power?

As you gather evidence to answer the Essential Questions, think about:

- how the first Han emperor adopted Confucianism as the new state philosophy but kept the Qin system of a merit-based bureaucracy.

- how under the Han emperors the Chinese Empire expanded.

- how the new technologies developed during the Han dynasty contributed to its economic success.

My Notes

_____

_____

_____

_____

_____

_____

_____

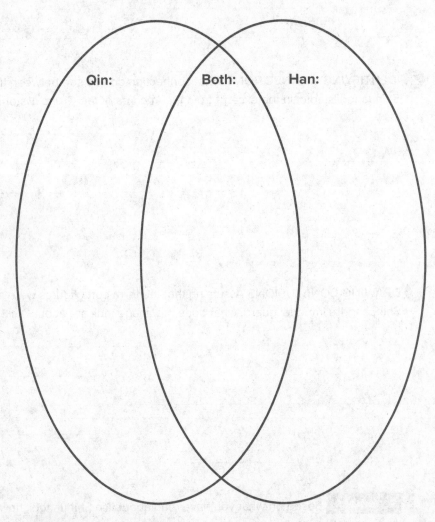

Qin: Both: Han:

2 **CIVICS** How did the civil service system ensure the influence of Confucianism on government?

_____

_____

_____

_____

3 **SUMMARIZING** In what ways did the Chinese Empire expand under the Han dynasty?

_____

_____

_____

4 **IDENTIFYING EFFECTS** How did the adoption of Confucianism as the basis of the state philosophy affect society in the Han Empire?

_____

_____

_____

5 **ECONOMICS** What was the Chinese economy like during the Han era?

_____

_____

_____

6 **SUMMARIZING** Complete the web diagram below to identify four technologies that were invented during the Han era.

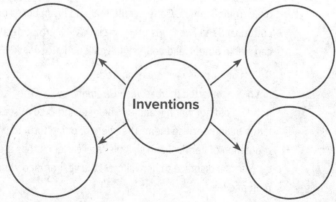

7 **IDENTIFYING CAUSES** How did noble families once again amass huge estates, and how did this contribute to the fall of the Han dynasty?

_____

_____

_____

_____

ESSENTIAL QUESTION

How can differing philosophies influence a culture?

VOCABULARY

distinguish: recognize the differences

diligent: untiring, hardworking

cross threads: the crosswise or horizontal threads in weaving

gauze: lightweight woven fabric, usually of cotton or silk

idle: lacking in effort; lazy

exhort: caution; encourage to do something

Instruction on Conduct for Chinese Women and Girls

DIRECTIONS: Read the excerpt. Then respond to the questions that follow.

EXPLORE THE CONTEXT: The author of this instruction manual for women and girls in early China was a daughter of a high official living during the Han dynasty. She was well known for her literary achievements at the time. Here she offers advice to young women regarding the roles of women in China at this time.

PRIMARY SOURCE: BOOK EXCERPT

Woman's Work.—Weaving Silk, etc.

❝ All girls, everywhere, should learn woman's work. In weaving cloth, distinguish between the coarse and fine; When sitting at the loom, work carefully; when boiling the silk cocoons, collecting for them the mulberry and chia leaves, in all be very diligent. Protect the worms from wind and rain. If cold, warm them by the fire; keep them in a clean place. As the young ones grow, transfer them to baskets, but crowd them not; provide them leaves, not too many nor too few. Making silk, be careful of the straight and cross threads, so you will make a perfect piece. When finished remove the gauze at once from the loom. Cotton cloth, fold and lay in boxes or baskets. Silk, cotton, and the two kinds of grass cloth, all learn perfectly to make, then you can sell to others, and yourself have clothing to wear. . . .

Do not imitate lazy women who from youth to womanhood have been stupid; not having exerted themselves in woman's work. They are prepared for neither cold nor warm weather. Their sewing is so miserable, people both laugh at and despise them. The idle girl, going forth to be married, injures the reputation of her husband's whole family. Her clothes are ragged and dirty. . . . She is a disgrace to her village. I thus exhort and warn the girls, let them hear and learn. ❞

—from The Chinese Book of Etiquette and Conduct for Women and Girls, c. 49 C.E.—120 C.E.

1 **SUMMARIZING** What specific instructions does the author give about caring for silk worms?

_____

_____

_____

_____

2 **ANALYZING IDEAS** According to the author, what should be the goal in making cloth?

_____

_____

3A **IDENTIFYING PERSPECTIVES** What character trait does the author find particularly blameworthy?

_____

3B **CITING TEXT EVIDENCE** What words and phrases does she use to describe women or girls with this trait?

_____

_____

_____

4 CIVICS The author says that the "idle girl, going forth to be married, injures the reputation of her husband's whole family." How does this sentence reflect the concerns of Confucianism?

_____

_____

_____

5 **ASSESSING** How would you describe the overall tone of this excerpt?

_____

ESSENTIAL QUESTIONS

How can differing philosophies influence a culture?

What factors can help a dynasty stay in power?

Han Dynasty Seismograph

DIRECTIONS: Study the image. Then respond to the questions that follow.

EXPLORE THE CONTEXT: An early seismograph, or seismoscope, like the one pictured below, was invented by a Chinese scholar, Zhang Heng, during the Han era. It had eight dragons or dragon heads attached to it, each pointed in a different direction, and a frog with an open mouth directly below each of the dragon heads. When an earthquake took place, a ball dropped from a dragon's mouth into the mouth of the frog below to indicate that an earthquake had occurred and the direction of the earthquake. This was likely accomplished through a pendulum on the inside of the seismograph that detected and moved with the vibration. The seismograph would have allowed the emperor to know that an earthquake had taken place and where he needed to send aid.

PRIMARY SOURCE: PHOTOGRAPH

—photograph of Han Dynasty seismograph

1 **IDENTIFYING STEPS** Briefly list the steps that would have taken place when a Han seismograph responded to an earthquake.

_____

_____

_____

_____

_____

_____

_____

2 **EVALUATING** The Han seismograph did not measure earthquakes, as modern seismographs do. What two pieces of information was it able to provide?

_____

_____

_____

_____

3 GEOGRAPHY What does the invention of the seismograph indicate about China's geography during the Han era?

_____

_____

_____

_____

_____

4 **DRAWING CONCLUSIONS** What does the invention of the seismograph indicate about technological development during the Han era?

_____

_____

_____

_____

ESSENTIAL QUESTIONS

How can differing philosophies influence a culture?

What factors can help a dynasty stay in power?

1 Think About It

What were the policies of the Qin dynasty? Review the supporting questions you developed at the beginning of the chapter and the evidence you gathered. Were you able to find information to answer each supporting question? If not, what additional evidence do you think you need to gather?

_____

_____

_____

_____

2 Organize Your Evidence

Complete the chart below with information you learned about the Qin and Han dynasties and the philosophies they followed.

Dynasty	Founder	Philosophy Followed	How Philosophy Influenced Government

3 Talk About It

Work in small groups. With your group, discuss the chart you created in the Organize Your Evidence activity. Compare notes and add information from your group members to your chart. Then talk about the principles of Legalism and Confucianism and how those principles influenced government during the Qin and Han dynasties. Take notes about your discussion below.

_____

_____

_____

_____

4 Write About It

Using information from your chart and the discussion with your small group, write a paragraph comparing and contrasting the Qin and Han dynasties. In your paragraph, focus on how the principles of Legalism and Confucianism influenced the Qin and Han governments.

_____

_____

_____

5 Connect to the Essential Question

Now imagine that Qin Shihuangdi and Han Gaozu are in the same room. Write a dialogue between the two rulers, in which they debate the merits of Legalism and Confucianism. As they debate, have them emphasize why they think their respective philosophies are the best for governing and staying in power. Then, with another member of your small group, present the dialogue to your class as a two-person play.

_____

_____

_____

_____

CITIZENSHIP
TAKE ACTION

MAKE CONNECTIONS In this chapter, you have read about different philosophies and how they influenced governments in China. In the modern world, different philosophies have continued to influence governments. For example, in the 20th century, the philosophy of communism influenced the government of many countries, including the former Soviet Union. Within the United States, political parties are often influenced by different philosophies. These philosophies are generally reflected in the platforms of the parties. A *platform* is a statement of the principles and goals of a political party or other organization.

DIRECTIONS: Use the Internet to find the platform of a political party at the national or state level. Study the platform and analyze the philosophies that have influenced it. Decide whether or not you agree with those philosophies. You may find that you agree with some of the planks, or parts, of the platform, but not all.

Once you have analyzed the party platform, write a platform that reflects your own beliefs. If you found that you did not agree with some of the planks in the platform you analyzed, you may wish to read the platforms of other parties to see if any of their planks are more closely aligned with your own beliefs. Then use what you learn to help you write your own platform.

_____

_____

_____

_____

_____

_____

_____

_____

_____

The Romans, 600 B.C.— A.D. 500

ESSENTIAL QUESTIONS

How do different types of political organizations emerge?
How can new ideas lead to social and political change?

Think about how these two questions might relate to government and politics in ancient Rome.

TALK ABOUT IT

Discuss with a partner what information you would need to know to answer these questions. For example, one question might be, "What types of political organizations emerged in ancient Rome?" Another might be, "What social and political changes took place in Rome?"

DIRECTIONS: Now write down three additional questions that you need to answer to be able to describe social and political change in ancient Rome.

MY RESEARCH QUESTIONS

Supporting Question 1:

_____

_____

Supporting Question 2:

_____

_____

Supporting Question 3:

_____

_____

The Rise of Rome

DIRECTIONS: Search for evidence in the lesson to help you answer the following questions.

1 **GEOGRAPHY** How did Rome's location contribute to its development and expansion?

_____

_____

_____

_____

_____

_____

_____

_____

_____

_____

2 **ANALYZING EVENTS** In what way did the Etruscans help Rome develop?

_____

_____

_____

3 **EVALUATING** Why were the Romans so successful in gaining control of the Italian Peninsula?

_____

_____

_____

_____

_____

_____

_____

ESSENTIAL QUESTIONS

How do different types of political organizations emerge?

How can new ideas lead to social and political change?

As you gather evidence to answer the Essential Questions, think about:

- how the Etruscans influenced the early development of Rome.

- how the Roman Republic was highly structured into political groups.

- how Rome contributed a system of law, which still influences legal systems today.

My Notes

_____

_____

_____

_____

_____

_____

4 IDENTIFYING CAUSES Why did the Romans establish a republic instead of a monarchy?

_____

_____

_____

5 SUMMARIZING Complete the chart below to summarize the political structure of the Roman Republic.

	Number of Members	Responsibilities
Consuls		
Praetors		
Senate		
Centuriate Assembly	Number Varied	
Council of the Plebs	Number Varied	

6 CIVICS How does Roman law still influence legal systems today?

_____

_____

_____

_____

7 IDENTIFYING EFFECTS How did the Punic Wars help Rome gain control of the Mediterranean region?

_____

_____

_____

_____

ESSENTIAL QUESTIONS

ESSENTIAL QUESTIONS

How do different types of political organizations emerge?

How can new ideas lead to social and political change?

Polybius on the Roman Senate

DIRECTIONS: Read the excerpt. Then respond to the questions that follow.

EXPLORE THE CONTEXT: Polybius was a Greek historian who lived during the time of the Roman Republic. He was a friend of the general Scipio and traveled extensively with him. Polybius's *Histories* presented the history of Rome from the beginning of the First Punic War to the destruction of Carthage. His goal was to show how the Roman state had developed and how it had managed to conquer so much of the world in so short a time. He compared the Roman and Greek political systems and argued that the Roman system was superior. In the excerpt below, he describes the powers and responsibilities of the Roman Senate.

PRIMARY SOURCE: BOOK EXCERPT

66 The senate has first of all control of the treasury, and regulates the receipts and disbursements alike. For the quaestors cannot issue any public money for the various departments of the state without a decree of the senate, except for the service of the consuls. The senate controls also what is by far the largest and most important expenditure [in time of peace], that made by the censors in every term of their office for the repair or construction of public buildings; this money cannot be obtained by the censors except by the grant of the senate. Similarly all crimes committed in Italy requiring a public investigation, such as treason, conspiracy, poisoning, or wilful murder, are in the hands of the senate. Besides, if any individual or state among the Italian allies requires a controversy to be settled, a penalty to be assessed, help or protection to be afforded, —all this is the province of the senate. Or again, outside Italy, if it is necessary to send an embassy to reconcile warring communities, or to remind them of their duty, or sometimes to impose requisitions upon them, or to receive their submission, or finally to proclaim war against them, —this too is the business of the senate. 99

—from Polybius, *Histories*

VOCABULARY

receipts: money received

disbursements: money paid out

quaestors: Roman officials who handled financial affairs

embassy: a group of people entrusted with a mission to another country

requisitions: formal demands for something to be done or given

Polybius. Quoted by George Willis Botsford. A History of Rome for High Schools and Academies. New York: The Macmillan Company, London: Macmillan and Co., 1901.

1 **EVALUATING** Originally, the Senate's only role was to advise government officials. By the time that Polybius wrote this excerpt, did the Senate have more or less power? Explain.

_____

_____

_____

_____

2 **ECONOMICS** What financial affairs did Polybius say the Senate controlled?

_____

_____

_____

_____

3 **CIVICS** What judicial responsibilities did the Senate have?

_____

_____

_____

_____

4 **SUMMARIZING** In what ways was the Senate involved in foreign policy?

_____

_____

_____

_____

5 **ANALYZING TEXT** How does the structure of this passage emphasize the power of the Senate?

_____

_____

_____

_____

ESSENTIAL QUESTIONS

How do different types of political organizations emerge?

How can new ideas lead to social and political change?

Comparing the Governments of Rome and Carthage

DIRECTIONS: Read the excerpt. Then respond to the questions that follow.

EXPLORE THE CONTEXT: The Greek historian Polybius was present at the siege and destruction of Carthage in 146 B.C. In this excerpt from his *Histories*, he seeks to explain why Rome was more successful than Carthage.

PRIMARY SOURCE: BOOK EXCERPT

❝ But at the time of the war of Hannibal the Carthaginian constitution was worse in its condition than the Roman. For as nature has assigned to every body, every government, and every action, three successive periods; the first, of growth; the second, of perfection; and that which follows, of decay; and as the period of perfection is the time in which they severally display their greatest strength; from hence arose the difference that was then found between the two republics. For the government of Carthage, having reached the highest point of vigor and perfection much sooner than that of Rome, had now declined from it in the same proportion: whereas the Romans, at this very time, had just raised their constitution to the most flourishing and perfect state. The effect of this difference was, that among the Carthaginians the people possessed the greatest sway in all deliberations, but the senate among the Romans. And as, in the one republic, all measures were determined by the multitude; and, in the other, by the most eminent citizens; of so great force was this advantage in the conduct of affairs, that the Romans, though brought by repeated losses in the greatest danger, became, through the wisdom of their counsels, superior to the Carthaginians in the war. ❞

—from Polybius, *Histories, in The Library of Original Sources: The Roman World,* edited *by* Oliver Joseph Thatcher

VOCABULARY

successive: following in order or sequence

severally: separately, or each in turn

vigor: strength or power

flourishing: thriving, prospering

eminent: distinguished or highest in rank

1A CIVICS What cycle does Polybius believe every government goes through?

_____

_____

_____

_____

1B **ANALYZING CENTRAL IDEAS** How does this cycle explain the Romans' success against Carthage, according to Polybius?

_____

_____

_____

_____

2A **CONTRASTING** What difference does Polybius see between the way the Carthaginians and the Romans made governmental decisions?

_____

_____

_____

_____

2B HISTORY How did this difference affect the outcome of the war between the Carthaginians and the Romans, according to Polybius?

_____

_____

_____

_____

3 **CITING TEXT EVIDENCE** How does Polybius's word choice show his admiration for the Roman constitution and the Roman Senate?

_____

_____

_____

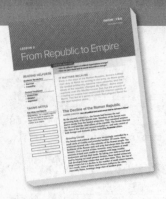

From Republic to Empire

DIRECTIONS: Search for evidence in the lesson to help you answer the following questions.

1A **IDENTIFYING CAUSES** What were the Gracchi trying to achieve by passing land-reform bills?

_____

_____

_____

_____

_____

_____

1B **IDENTIFYING EFFECTS** What was the actual result of their efforts?

_____

_____

_____

_____

_____

2 **IDENTIFYING EFFECTS** What unintended consequence did the change in military recruitment initiated by Marius bring about?

_____

_____

_____

_____

_____

_____

_____

ESSENTIAL QUESTIONS

How do different types of political organizations emerge?

How can new ideas lead to social and political change?

As you gather evidence to answer the Essential Questions, think about:

- how the attempts at reform by the Gracchi brought instability to the Roman Republic.

- how a new system of military recruitment gave individual generals a great deal of power.

- how Crassus, Pompey, and Julius Caesar formed the First Triumvirate.

- how Julius Caesar became dictator of Rome.

- how Octavian and Antony fought over control of Rome, culminating in Octavian's victory and the end of the Republic.

- how Caesar Augustus began a new system for governing the provinces.

My Notes

_____

_____

_____

_____

3 IDENTIFYING CAUSES How did the actions of General Sulla eventually lead to the establishment of the First Triumvirate?

_____

_____

_____

_____

_____

4 ANALYZING CHANGE Julius Caesar was not the first dictator that Rome had had. Why was his dictatorship different?

_____

_____

_____

5 SUMMARIZING Use the graphic organizer below to trace the developments that led from the assassination of Julius Caesar to the end of the Roman Republic.

```
┌─────────────────────────┐        ┌─────────────────────────┐
│ Julius Caesar assassinated │        │                         │
└─────────────────────────┘        └─────────────────────────┘
            ↓                                   ↓
┌─────────────────────────┐        ┌─────────────────────────┐
│                         │        │                         │
└─────────────────────────┘        └─────────────────────────┘
            ↓                ↗                  ↓
┌─────────────────────────┐        ┌─────────────────────────┐
│                         │        │ Octavian becomes first Roman │
│                         │        │        emperor          │
└─────────────────────────┘        └─────────────────────────┘
```

6 EVALUATING How did Augustus's system for governing the provinces reduce the Senate's power?

_____

_____

_____

_____

_____

ESSENTIAL QUESTIONS

How do different types of political organizations emerge?

How can new ideas lead to social and political change?

VOCABULARY

consular: annually elected chief magistrate

ovation: a ceremony attending the entering of Rome

curule: a high-ranking dignitary

imperator: a commander-in-chief or emperor

laurels: a crown awarded as an honor

legates: official emissaries

auspices: kindly patronage and guidance

tribunician: resembling a Roman tribune or his office

The Ancyra Inscription

DIRECTIONS: Read the excerpt. Then respond to the questions that follow.

EXPLORE THE CONTEXT: Caesar Augustus was the founder of the Roman Principate and considered the first Roman emperor, controlling the empire from 27 B.C. until his death in A.D. 14. Written by Caesar Augustus about his own reign, the Ancyra Inscription was carved on a temple shortly after Augustus's death.

PRIMARY SOURCE: HISTORICAL ACCOUNT

"When I was nineteen I collected an army on my own account and at my own expense, by the help of which I restored the republic to liberty, . . . for which services the Senate, in complimentary decrees, added my name to the roll of their House. . . , giving me at the same time consular precedence [priority] in voting; and gave me imperium [supreme civil and military power]. It ordered me as proprietor [highest judicial authority] "to see along with the consuls that the republic suffered no damage." . . . I had to undertake wars by land and sea, civil and foreign, all over the world, and when victorious I spared all citizens who asked for pardon. Those foreign nations, who could safely be pardoned, I preferred to preserve rather than exterminate. . . . I twice celebrated an ovation, three times curule triumphs, and was twenty-one times greeted as imperator. Though the Senate afterwards voted me several triumphs I declined them. I frequently also deposited laurels in the Capitol after performing the vows which I had taken in each war. For successful operations performed by myself or by my legates under my auspices by land and sea, the Senate fifty-three times decreed a supplication [prayer] to the immortal gods. . . . I had been consul thirteen times at the writing of this, and am in the course of the thirty-seventh year of my tribunician power [13–14 A.D.]."

—Caesar Augustus, from *Augustus: The Life and Times of the Founder of the Roman Empire*

1 **IDENTIFYING CAUSES** According to Augustus, why did the Senate grant him imperium?

_____

_____

_____

2 **CITING TEXT EVIDENCE** What examples does Augustus use to portray himself as merciful?

_____

_____

_____

3 **DRAWING CONCLUSIONS** Augustus says, "Though the Senate afterwards voted me several triumphs I declined them," and "I frequently also deposited laurels in the Capitol." What impression of his character do you think Augustus is trying to create?

_____

_____

_____

_____

4 **EVALUATING** What is the overall tone of the excerpt? Cite evidence to explain your answer.

_____

_____

_____

5 CIVICS Augustus considered public religion a pillar of a strong state. How is this reflected in this excerpt?

_____

_____

_____

_____

_____

ESSENTIAL QUESTIONS

How do different types of political organizations emerge?

How can new ideas lead to social and political change?

VOCABULARY

compensate: offset or make up for

novi homines: Latin for "new men"; refers to men, like Cicero, who had no ancestors who had held the upper offices

syndicate: a group of individuals organized to undertake a project

equestrian order: a privileged class, derived from the ancient Roman cavalry, ranking just below the senators

trade guilds: organizations of merchants or craftsmen

Quintus Cicero's Letter to His Brother Marcus Cicero, 64 B.C.

DIRECTIONS: Read the excerpt. Then respond to the questions that follow.

EXPLORE THE CONTEXT: Marcus Tullius Cicero was a Roman politician, lawyer, and writer who lived during the First and Second Triumvirates. He is generally considered Rome's greatest orator. After serving first as a quaestor and then as a praetor, he won election as consul in 63 B.C. The excerpt below is from a letter supposedly written by Marcus's younger brother Quintus, also a Roman politician, while Marcus was campaigning for the consulate. (Many scholars now question whether Quintus actually wrote the letter.)

PRIMARY SOURCE: LETTER

" Almost every day as you go down to the Forum you must say to yourself, I am without noble ancestry. "I am a candidate for the consulship." "This is Rome." For the "newness" of your name you will best compensate by the brilliance of your oratory. This has ever carried with it great political distinction. A man who is held worthy of defending ex-consuls, cannot be deemed unworthy of the consulship itself. Wherefore approach each individual case with the persuasion that on it depends as a whole your entire reputation. See that all those aids to natural ability, which I know are your special gifts are ready for use. . . and finally take care that both the number and rank of your friends are unmistakable. For you have, as few *novi homines* have had, —all the tax-syndicate promoters, nearly the whole equestrian order, and many municipal towns, especially devoted to you, many people who have been defended by you, many trade guilds, and beside these a large number of the rising generation, who have become attached to you in their enthusiasm for public speaking, and who visit you daily in swarms, and with such constant regularity! "

—attributed to Quintus Cicero

1A **ANALYZING INDIVIDUALS** According to Quintus, what is Marcus's main *disadvantage* politically?

_____

_____

1B **ANALYZING INDIVIDUALS** What is Marcus's main *advantage* politically?

_____

_____

2 **EVALUATING ARGUMENTS** What logic does Quintus use to argue that Marcus must be considered worthy of being consul?

_____

_____

3 **IDENTIFYING CONNECTIONS** The Roman historian Sallust wrote of the time period in which Cicero lived: "Ambition drove many men to become false; to have one thought locked in the breast, another ready on the tongue; to value friendships and enmities not on their merits but by the standard of self-interest." How does this quote relate to what Quintus says about friendship?

_____

_____

_____

_____

4 **SUMMARIZING** Which groups does Quintus believe Marcus can count on for support?

_____

_____

_____

_____

5 CIVICS What connections do you see between Quintus's advice and the actions of politicians today?

_____

_____

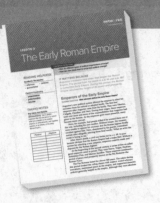

The Early Roman Empire

DIRECTIONS: Search for evidence in the lesson to help you answer the following questions.

1 **ANALYZING EVENTS** What weakness in the Roman Empire did the civil war after the death of Nero reveal?

_____

_____

_____

_____

_____

_____

_____

2 **EVALUATING** Why are the emperors who ruled during the Pax Romana considered "good emperors"?

_____

_____

_____

_____

_____

_____

_____

3 **ECONOMICS** What was the Roman economy like during the Early Empire?

_____

_____

_____

_____

_____

ESSENTIAL QUESTIONS

How do different types of political organizations emerge?

How can new ideas lead to social and political change?

As you gather evidence to answer the Essential Questions, think about:

- the elements that defined the early Roman Empire.

- how the Romans spread Greco-Roman culture throughout the empire.

- what the family life, social structure, and religion of the ancient Romans were like.

My Notes

_____

_____

_____

_____

_____

4 SUMMARIZING Complete the web diagram below to describe features of Greco-Roman civilization.

GRECO-ROMAN CIVILIZATION	
Architecture	
Art	
Literature	
Mathematics	
Science	

5 ANALYZING CHANGE How did family life change during the Early Empire?

6 DESCRIBING How was Rome a city of contradictions during the Early Empire?

7 IDENTIFYING CAUSES Why did the Romans emphasize religious observances?

ESSENTIAL QUESTIONS

How do different types of political organizations emerge?

How can new ideas lead to social and political change?

VOCABULARY

vilest: most evil

coerce: force

forsooth: in truth, implies contempt or doubt

embellished: decorated

The Annals of Tacitus

DIRECTIONS: Read the excerpt. Then respond to the questions that follow.

EXPLORE THE CONTEXT: Publius Cornelius Tacitus was a senator and a historian of the Roman Empire. In his two major works of writing, the Annals and the Histories, he examined the reigns of several Roman emperors. He is considered to be one of the greatest Roman historians and is known for his serious examinations of politics.

PRIMARY SOURCE: BOOK

❝On the day of the funeral soldiers stood round as a guard, amid much ridicule [scorn] from those who had either themselves witnessed or who had heard from their parents of the famous day when slavery was still something fresh, and freedom had been resought [attempted again] in vain [hopelessly], when the slaying [killing] of [Julius] Caesar, the Dictator, seemed to some the vilest, to others, the most glorious of deeds. "Now," they said, "an aged sovereign [ruler], whose power had lasted long, who had provided his heirs with abundant means to coerce the State, requires forsooth the defence of soldiers that his burial may be undisturbed." . . .

. . . the State had been organized under the name neither of a kingdom nor a dictatorship, but under that of a prince. The ocean and remote rivers were the boundaries of the empire; the legions, provinces, fleets, all things were linked together; there was law for the citizens; there was respect shown to the allies. The capital had been embellished on a grand scale; only in a few instances had he resorted to force, simply to secure general tranquility [peace]. . . . No doubt, there was peace after all this, but it was a peace stained with blood. . .❞

—Tacitus, Annals, Book 1, 109 C.E.

Tacitus. Translated by Alfred John Church, and William Jackson Brodribb. Annals of Tacitus: Translated into English, With Notes and Maps. London: Macmillan and Co., 1876.

1 **IDENTIFYING CAUSES** According to Tacitus, why was there "much ridicule" on the day of Augustus's funeral?

_____

_____

_____

2 CIVICS How does Tacitus describe the organization of the Roman state under Augustus?

_____

_____

_____

3 **SUMMARIZING** What accomplishments of Augustus's reign does Tacitus find noteworthy?

_____

_____

_____

_____

_____

4 **EVALUATING** According to Tacitus, why was the peace during Augustus's reign a flawed accomplishment?

_____

5 **COMPARING AND CONTRASTING** Compare this excerpt to the one from the Ancyra Inscription, which Augustus wrote about his own reign. In what ways are they similar? What differences do you see?

_____

_____

_____

_____

ESSENTIAL QUESTION

How can new ideas lead to social and political change?

A Gathering Place for the Masses

DIRECTIONS: Study the image. Then respond to the questions that follow.

EXPLORE THE CONTEXT: Emperor Vespasian commissioned the Roman Coliseum in the early first century. Known at the time as the "Flavian Amphitheater" due to Vespasian's dynasty, the Coliseum could seat up to 80,000 spectators. Initially, the Romans used the Coliseum for events such as gladiator fights. Animal fighting was also popular, and tunnels under the building held 32 spaces for animals, with complex systems by which to move them quickly into the arena. Above ground, 76 separate entrances and other features helped control crowds. Over four centuries, the Romans used the Coliseum for everything from sporting events to battle reenactments.

PHOTOGRAPH: ARCHITECTURE

—The ruins of the ancient Coliseum in the modern city of Rome

1 **UNDERSTANDING CONTEXT** Why might the Coliseum have been an important investment for the state?

_____

_____

_____

_____

2 INTERPRETING Why is the size of the Coliseum significant?

_____

_____

3 DRAWING CONCLUSIONS How was the Coliseum used to reinforce the state's power among its people?

_____

_____

_____

_____

4 DRAWING CONCLUSIONS How was the Coliseum used to reinforce the state's power among other nations?

_____

_____

_____

5 IDENTIFYING CONNECTIONS How does the design of the Coliseum relate to other Roman advances in infrastructure and architecture?

_____

_____

_____

_____

_____

6 CIVICS What can we infer about official Roman attitudes towards the people from the construction of the Coliseum?

_____

_____

_____

_____

_____

ESSENTIAL QUESTIONS

How do different types of political organizations emerge?

How can new ideas lead to social and political change?

My Notes

_____

_____

_____

_____

_____

_____

_____

_____

_____

_____

_____

_____

1 Think About It

Review the supporting questions you developed at the beginning of the chapter and the evidence you gathered. Were you able to answer each supporting question? If there was not enough evidence to answer your supporting questions, what additional evidence do you think you need to gather?

_____

_____

2 Organize Your Evidence

Complete the chart below to organize the causes and effects of significant events in Rome's political development from the founding of the Roman Republic to the beginning of the Roman Empire.

CAUSE(S)	EVENT	EFFECT(S)
Romans distrust kingship	Romans overthrow the last Etruscan king	
Romans conquer virtually all of Italy		Conquered people feel they have a real stake in Rome's success
	The Gracchi have the council of the plebs pass land-reform bills	
A Roman general named Marius becomes consul		
		Example of using an army to seize power has been set
Crassus, Pompey, and Julius Caesar come to hold enormous military power		
	Caesar marches on Rome and defeats Pompey's forces	
Leading senators resent Caesar's growing power		
Octavian, Antony, and Lepidus join forces		Soon Octavian and Antony divide the Roman world between them
		Octavian becomes first Roman emperor

③ Write About It

Using information from your chart, identify two historical figures that you feel had the greatest impact on Rome's political development. In the space below, briefly explain why you chose these individuals.

_____

_____

_____

_____

④ Talk About It

Work in a small group. With your group, discuss the major events that led to political changes in Rome, as well as the historical figures most responsible for those changes. Did everyone in your group identify the same causal relationships? Did everyone agree on the most significant historical figures? Take notes about your discussion below.

_____

_____

_____

_____

⑤ Connect to the Essential Question

Choose one of the historical figures that you identified in the Write About it and Talk About It activities, and write an obituary for this person. An obituary is a notice about the death of a person that often includes biographical information. In your obituary, highlight the significant achievements of this person, emphasizing the person's impact on the political development of Rome. Include quotes by or about this person, if possible.

_____

_____

_____

_____

_____

CITIZENSHIP
TAKE ACTION

MAKE CONNECTIONS Romans campaigned for public office, just as our politicians do today. In fact, the English word *candidate* comes from the Latin word *candidatus* meaning "white-robed" because candidates for political office in ancient Rome wore white togas. Campaign strategies were important, as they are today. As you have read, when Marcus Tullius Cicero ran for election as consul, his brother, Quintus, offered political advice on how to run a successful campaign.

DIRECTIONS: Even if you're too young to vote, you can still help out with and participate in a political campaign. Candidates at every level—local, county, state, and national—need volunteers. If there is a particular candidate for whom you would like to campaign, contact that person's office and tell them you would like to volunteer. If you don't have a particular candidate in mind, contact the local office of a political party whose platform you support to see how you can get involved. Then in the space below, list the steps you took, what volunteer opportunities you learned about, and how you plan to be involved in a particular campaign.

_____

_____

_____

_____

_____

_____

_____

_____

_____

_____

_____

_____

The Byzantine Empire and Emerging Europe

ESSENTIAL QUESTIONS

How can religion impact a culture?

What factors led to the rise and fall of empires?

Think about the decline and fall of the Roman Empire. What factors weakened the empire? How and why did other empires and kingdoms emerge in the wake of Rome's fall? What was Christianity's relationship with these emerging empires and kingdoms?

TALK ABOUT IT

With a partner, discuss what you would need to know to answer these questions. For example, one question might be: "How did the Roman Empire change as Christianity spread?"

DIRECTIONS: Write down three additional questions that will help you explain how religions impact a culture and why empires rise and fall. For example, you might ask, "Do empires share similar strengths and weaknesses? How have rulers used religion to seize and maintain power?"

MY RESEARCH QUESTIONS

Supporting Question 1:

_____

_____

Supporting Question 2:

_____

_____

Supporting Question 3:

_____

_____

The First Christians

DIRECTIONS: Search for evidence in the lesson to help you answer the following questions.

1 **COMPARING AND CONTRASTING** Compare and contrast the ways Jews reacted to Roman rule.

_____

_____

_____

_____

_____

_____

_____

_____

2 **SUMMARIZING** What was the main message of Jesus's teaching? Why did some authorities believe he was a Zealot?

_____

_____

_____

_____

_____

3A **DETERMINING CENTRAL IDEAS** Use the graphic organizer to identify the main teachings of the apostle Paul.

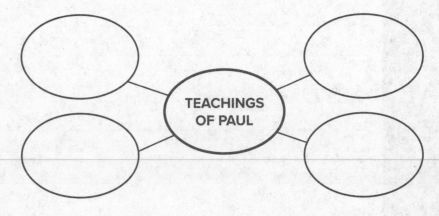

ESSENTIAL QUESTION

How can religion impact a culture?

As you gather evidence to answer the Essential Question, think about:

- how Jews reacted to Roman rule.
- what Jesus and early Christian leaders taught.
- the factors related to the spread of Christianity.

My Notes

_____

_____

_____

_____

_____

_____

_____

3B **EVALUATING** Which of Paul's actions and teachings do you think was most influential in making Christianity a universal religion? Why?

_____

_____

_____

_____

4 **INFERRING** Who was considered the leader of the apostles? Why do you think he and the other apostles traveled so widely to spread the teachings of Jesus despite Roman persecution?

_____

_____

_____

_____

5 **EXPLAINING ISSUES** How did Christianity's message help it attract followers and permit it to spread throughout the Roman Empire? Which Roman tradition further contributed to Christianity's spread?

_____

_____

_____

_____

_____

_____

_____

6 CIVICS How did Rome's leaders react to the spread of Christianity? How did this reaction change over time?

_____

_____

_____

_____

_____

ESSENTIAL QUESTION
How can religion impact a culture?

Pilate's Letter to Herod

DIRECTIONS: Read the excerpt. Then respond to the questions that follow.

EXPLORE THE CONTEXT: In the New Testament (Luke 23:1-25), Jewish priests bring Jesus before Roman governor Pontius Pilate for trial, claiming that Jesus had been inciting rebellion. Pilate sent him on to Herod, ruler of the Judean province of Galilee, for further questioning. Herod then returned Jesus to Pilate, and although neither found Jesus guilty, Pilate had Jesus crucified at the request of the people. This letter, considered fictitious by some scholars, is from a collection that dates to the 500s or 600s A.D. They were not written by Pilate himself and are best read as a dramatic recounting of his life.

PRIMARY SOURCE: LETTER

❝ LETTER OF PILATE TO HEROD.

Pilate to Herod the Tetrarch: Peace.

KNOW and see, that in the day when thou didst deliver Jesus unto me, I took pity on myself, and testified by washing my hands (that I was innocent), concerning him who rose from the grave after three days, and had performed thy pleasure in him, for thou didst desire me to be associated with thee in his crucifixion. But I now learn from the executioners and from the soldiers who watched his sepulchre that he rose from the dead. And I have especially confirmed what was told me, that he appeared bodily in Galilee, to the same form, and with the same voice, and with the same doctrine, and with the same disciples, not having changed in anything, but preaching with boldness his resurrection, and an everlasting kingdom. . . .

Now when Procla, my wife, heard that Jesus was risen, and had appeared in Galilee, she took with her Longinus the centurion and twelve soldiers, the same that had watched at the sepulcher, and went to greet the face of Christ, as if to a great spectacle, and saw him with his disciples.

Now while they were standing, and wondering, and gazing at him, he looked at them, and said to them, What is it? Do ye believe in me? Procla, know that in the covenant which God gave to the fathers, it is said that every body which had perished should live by means of my death, which ye have seen. And now, ye see that I live, whom ye crucified. And I suffered many things, till that I was laid in the sepulchre. But now, hear me, and believe in my Father—God who is in me. For I loosed the cords of death, and brake the gates of Sheol; and my coming shall be hereafter. . . . ❞

—The Lost Books of the Bible, 1926

VOCABULARY

sepulchre: tomb

doctrine: teachings

resurrection: rising from the dead

covenant: promise

perished: died

Sheol: the underworld

1 **SUMMARIZING** Briefly summarize the contents of the letter from Pilate to Herod.

_____

_____

_____

_____

2 **IDENTIFYING CONNECTIONS** Which Christian doctrines preached by the apostle Paul are echoed in the letter?

_____

_____

_____

_____

3 **DRAWING CONCLUSIONS** Why do you think arrangements were made to post soldiers at the sepulchre where Jesus's body was placed?

_____

_____

_____

_____

_____

4 **INTERPRETING** What message does the writer say Jesus conveyed to those who witnessed his appearance after being crucified?

_____

_____

_____

_____

_____

_____

_____

_____

ESSENTIAL QUESTION

How can religion impact a culture?

Nero's Persecution of Christians

DIRECTIONS: Read the excerpt. Then respond to the questions that follow.

EXPLORE THE CONTEXT: Tacitus (A.D. 56–c. 120) was a Roman historian who wrote about various periods of the empire. His *Annals* cover the period from A.D. 14 to 68, from the death of Augustus to the end of the reign of Nero. In this excerpt from the *Annals,* Tacitus discusses the Great Fire of Rome, which occurred in A.D. 64, and his persecution of Roman Christians.

PRIMARY SOURCE: BOOK

❝ But neither human aid, nor imperial bounty, nor atoning-offerings to the Gods, could remove the sinister suspicion that the fire had been brought about by Nero's order. To put an end therefore to this rumor, he shifted the charge on to others, and inflicted the most cruel tortures upon a body of men detested for their abominations, and popularly known by the name of Christians. This name came from one Christus, who was put to death in the reign of origin of Tiberius by the Procurator Pontius Pilate; but though checked for the time, the detestable superstition broke out again, not in Judaea only, where the mischief began, but even in Rome, where every horrible and shameful iniquity, from every quarter of the world, pours in and finds a welcome. First those who acknowledged themselves of this persuasion were arrested; and upon their testimony a vast number were condemned, not so much on the charge of incendiarism as for their hatred of the human race. Their death was turned into a diversion. They were clothed in the skins of wild beasts, and torn to pieces by dogs; they were fastened to crosses, or set up to be burned, so as to serve the purpose of lamps when daylight failed. Nero gave up his own gardens for this spectacle; he provided also Circensian games, during which he mingled with the populace, or took his stand upon a chariot, in the garb of a charioteer. But guilty as these men were and worthy of direst punishment, the fact that they were being sacrificed for no public good, but only to glut the cruelty of one man, aroused a feeling of pity on their behalf. ❞

—The *Annals* of Tacitus

VOCABULARY

Imperial bounty: gifts from the ruler

detested: hated

abominations: horrible crimes

iniquity: evil, sin

incendiarism: arson, setting fires

Circensian: relating to the Circus, a stadium in ancient Rome

garb: clothing

glut: satisfy

1 **EXPLAINING ISSUES** According to Tacitus, what was Nero's motivation for persecuting the Christians?

_____

_____

_____

2 **IDENTIFYING STEPS** Describe the sequence of events Christians faced from the point of their arrest to their execution. How does Tacitus describe Nero's behavior?

_____

_____

_____

_____

_____

3 HISTORY What is Tacitus's view of Christians? Ultimately, do his sympathies lie with them or with Nero? Support your answer with evidence from the text.

_____

_____

_____

_____

4 **ANALYZING TEXT** Why do you think Tacitus describes the executions of Christians in such explicit detail?

_____

_____

5 **INTEGRATING INFORMATION** In what way does Tacitus corroborate parts of the letter from Pilate to Herod? What can we learn about the spread of Christianity from this excerpt from the _Annals_?

_____

_____

_____

Decline and Fall of Rome

DIRECTIONS: Search for evidence in the lesson to help you answer the following questions.

ESSENTIAL QUESTION

What factors lead to the rise and fall of empires?

As you gather evidence to answer the Essential Question, think about:

- factors that led to the decline of the Roman Empire.
- how emperors Diocletian and Constantine changed the Roman Empire.
- why the Western Roman Empire collapsed.

1A **DESCRIBING** Which problems weakened the Roman Empire in the 200s?

_____

_____

_____

1B **IDENTIFYING CAUSES AND EFFECTS** Complete the cause-and-effect organizer to explain why Rome had trouble recruiting soldiers and the subsequent effects.

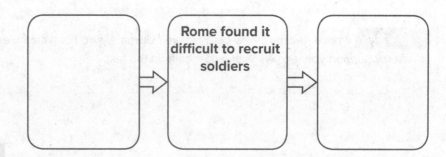

Rome found it difficult to recruit soldiers

2 **PREDICTING** How did the Roman Empire choose to deal with Christianity at the beginning of the fourth century? What do you think might have happened had this not occurred?

_____

_____

_____

My Notes

_____

_____

_____

_____

_____

_____

_____

3 **EVALUATING** Do you believe the economic and social policies of Diocletian and Constantine were worthwhile? Explain.

_____

_____

_____

4 **HISTORY** How was Constantine's choice of location for his new capital city influenced by the Roman Empire's weaknesses, and how might his decision have further weakened the Western Empire?

_____

_____

_____

_____

_____

5 **RELATING EVENTS** How did invaders from Central Asia contribute to the fall of the Western Roman Empire?

_____

_____

_____

_____

6 **ANALYZING EVENTS** Identify the five factors you think were the most responsible for the ultimate fall of the Western Roman Empire. Rank them in order from most to least important, then explain the reasons behind your first choice.

_____

_____

_____

_____

_____

_____

_____

ESSENTIAL QUESTION

What factors lead to the rise and fall of empires?

VOCABULARY

licentiousness: wickedness

extol: brag about

forsooth: indeed

torpid indolence: extreme laziness

dearth was apprehended: shortage [of food] became evident

1 **INTERPRETING** What does Marcellinus mean by Romans thinking "that they can be handed down to immortality by means of statues"?

_____

_____

_____

_____

_____

Rome Before the Fall

DIRECTIONS: Read the excerpt. Then respond to the questions that follow.

EXPLORE THE CONTEXT: Ammianus Marcellinus (c. 330–395) was a professional soldier and historian who wrote about the Roman Empire in *The Chronicles of Events.* The parts that survived describe events in Rome from 353 to 378—not long before the Visigoths sacked Rome.

PRIMARY SOURCE: BOOK

❝ [Despite the changes of the times] Rome is still looked upon as the queen of the earth, and the name of the Roman people is respected and venerated. But the [magnificence of Rome] is defaced by the inconsiderate levity of a few, who never recollect where they are born, but fall away into error and licentiousness as if a perfect immunity were granted to vice. Of these men, some, thinking that they can be handed down to immortality by means of statues, are eager after them, as if they would obtain a higher reward from brazen figures unendowed with sense than from a consciousness of upright and honorable actions ; and they are even anxious to have them plated over with gold!

Others place the summit of glory in having a couch higher than usual, or splendid apparel; and so toil and sweat under a vast burden of cloaks which are fastened to their necks by many clasps, and blow about by the excessive fineness of the material, showing a desire by the continual wriggling of their bodies, and especially by the waving of the left hand, to make more conspicuous their long fringes and tunics, which are embroidered in multiform figures of animals with threads of divers colors.

Others again, put on a feigned severity of countenance, and extol their patrimonial estates in a boundless degree, exaggerating the yearly produce of their fruitful fields, which they boast of possessing in numbers, from east and west, being forsooth ignorant that their ancestors, who won greatness for Rome, were not eminent in riches; but through many a direful war overpowered their foes by valor, though little above the common privates in riches, or luxury, or costliness of garments. . . .

Those few mansions which were once celebrated for the serious cultivation of liberal studies, now are filled with ridiculous amusements of torpid indolence, reechoing with the sound of singing, and the tinkle of flutes and lyres. You find a singer instead of a philosopher; a teacher of silly arts is summoned in place of an orator, the libraries are shut up like tombs, [but] organs played by water-power are built, and lyres so big that they look like wagons! and flutes, and huge machines suitable for the theater.

[The Romans] have even sunk so far, that not long ago, when a dearth was apprehended, and the foreigners were driven from the city, those who

Ammianus, Marcellinus. "The Luxury and Arrogance of the Rich in Rome." In Readings in Ancient History - II. Rome and the West. Reprinted by William Stearns Davis. Boston: Allyn and Bacon, 1913.

practiced liberal accomplishments were expelled instantly, yet the followers of actresses and all their ilk were suffered to stay. . . .

[On account of the frequency of epidemics in Rome, rich men take absurd precautions to avoid contagion, but. even] when these rules are observed thus stringently, some persons, if they be invited to a wedding, though the vigor of their limbs be vastly diminished, yet when gold is pressed in their palm they will go with all activity as far as Spoletum! So much for the nobles.

As for the lower and poorer classes some spend the whole night in the wine shops, some lie concealed in the shady arcades of the theaters. They play at dice so eagerly as to quarrel over them, snuffing up their nostrils, and making unseemly noises by drawing back their breath into their noses : — or (and this is their favorite amusement by far) from sunrise till evening, through sunshine or rain, they stay gaping and examining the charioteers and their horses; and their good and bad qualities. . . . **99**

—from "The Luxury and Arrogance of the Rich in Rome"

2 **CONTRASTING** How does Marcellinus contrast the Romans of his day to their ancestors?

_____

_____

_____

_____

3 **IDENTIFYING PERSPECTIVES** Does Marcellinus seem to believe that the final decline of Rome is inevitable? What changes do you think he would recommend? Explain your answer.

_____

_____

_____

_____

_____

4 HISTORY How does Marcellinus's depiction of Rome in this excerpt compare with Tacitus's description of Nero and his persecution of Christians? Does Tacitus's account predict any of the events Marcellinus discusses?

_____

_____

_____

_____

ESSENTIAL QUESTION

What factors lead to the rise and fall of empires?

The Sack of Rome

DIRECTIONS: Read the excerpt. Then respond to the questions that follow.

EXPLORE THE CONTEXT: Jordanes, who lived in the 6th century A.D. was a Goth historian who wrote several works about various Germanic tribes. This excerpt from his "The Origin and Deeds of the Getae" is about the sack of Rome in 410.

PRIMARY SOURCE: BOOK

"But as I was saying, when the army of the Visigoths had come into the neighborhood of this city, they sent an embassy to the Emperor Honorius, who dwelt within. They said that if he would permit the Goths to settle peaceably in Italy, they would so live with the Roman people that men might believe them both to be of one race; but if not, whoever prevailed in war should drive out the other, and the victor should henceforth rule unmolested. But the Emperor Honorius feared to make either promise. So he took counsel with his senate and considered how he might drive them from the Italian borders.

He finally decided that Alaric and his race, if they were able to do so, should be allowed to seize for their own home the provinces farthest away, namely Gaul and Spain. For at this time he had almost lost them, and moreover they had been devasted by the invasion of Gaiseric, king of the Vandals. The grant was confirmed by an imperial rescript, and the Goths, consenting to the arrangement, set out for the country given them.

When they had gone away without doing any harm in Italy, Stilicho, the Patrician and father-in-law of the Emperor Honorius. . . . treacherously hurried to Pollentia, a city in the Cottian Alps. There he fell upon the unsuspecting Goths in battle, to the ruin of all Italy and his own disgrace.

When the Goths suddenly beheld him, at first they were terrified. Soon regaining their courage and arousing each other by brave shouting, as is their custom, they turned to flight the entire army of Stilicho and almost exterminated it. Then forsaking the journey they had undertaken, the Goths with hearts full of rage returned again to Liguria whence they had set out. When they had plundered and spoiled it, they also laid waste Aemilia, and then hastened toward the city of Rome along the Flaminian Way, which runs between Picenum and Tuscia, taking as booty whatever they found on either hand.

When they finally entered Rome, by Alaric's express command they merely sacked it and did not set the city on fire, as wild peoples usually do, nor did they permit serious damage to be done to the holy places. Thence they departed to bring like ruin upon Campania and Lucania, and then came to Bruttii. Here they remained a long time and planned to go to Sicily and thence to the countries of Africa. . . .

When Athavulf became king, he returned again to Rome, and whatever had escaped the first sack his Goths stripped bare like locusts, not merely despoiling Italy of its private wealth, but even of its public resources. The Emperor Honorius was powerless to resist. . . ."

—from "On the Origins and Deeds of the Getae"

VOCABULARY

embassy: a group of political representatives

prevailed: succeeded, triumphed

henceforth: from this time forward

devasted: devastated, destroyed

consenting: agreeing

turned to flight: caused them to retreat

1 **SUMMARIZING** Summarize the events described in the excerpt in correct chronological order.

_____

_____

_____

_____

_____

_____

_____

2 **HISTORY** What was Rome like in the early 400s? Use information from the text and the account of Ammianus Marcellinus to answer. How did this contribute to the events described by Jordanes?

_____

_____

_____

_____

_____

3 **ANALYZING STRUCTURE** Why does Jordanes include the detail that the Goths "merely sacked [Rome] and did not set the city on fire, as wild peoples usually do"?

_____

_____

_____

_____

_____

4 **IDENTIFYING BIAS** Do you think Jordanes has written an accurate account of the events surrounding the sack of Rome? Why or why not?

_____

_____

_____

_____

_____

The Early Christian Church

DIRECTIONS: Search for evidence in the lesson to help you answer the following questions.

ESSENTIAL QUESTION

How can religion impact a culture?

As you gather evidence to answer the Essential Question, think about:

- how the early Christian Church was organized.
- how the ascendency of the bishop of Rome (the pope) impacted the Church.
- the role monasticism played in the development of the early Church.

1A **DESCRIBING** In the early Church, what was a parish? Who led parishes and what were their roles?

_____

_____

_____

1B **SUMMARIZING** Use the graphic organizer to illustrate the hierarchy of Church organization as it had developed by the fourth century.

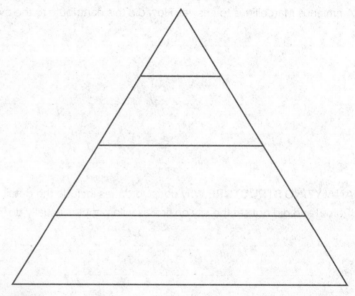

2 **HISTORY** How did the work of Gregory I win respect and influence for the papacy?

_____

_____

_____

_____

_____

_____

My Notes

_____

_____

_____

_____

_____

_____

3 **EXPLAINING ISSUES** In what way were the bishops of Rome, Jerusalem, Alexandria, and Antioch similar? Why did the bishop of Rome claim to have greater authority over all other bishops?

_____

_____

_____

_____

_____

_____

_____

4 **DRAWING CONCLUSIONS** Why do you think Gregory I is known as Gregory the Great?

_____

_____

5 **CITING TEXT EVIDENCE** What contributions did monks make to Europe? Which do you believe to be the most significant? Support your answer.

_____

_____

_____

_____

_____

6 **INFERRING** What purposes did gardens serve in the Benedictine monastic life?

_____

_____

_____

_____

ESSENTIAL QUESTION

How can religion impact a culture?

Benedictine Rule

DIRECTIONS: Read the excerpt. Then respond to the questions that follow.

EXPLORE THE CONTEXT: *The Rule of St. Benedict* was written by St. Benedict of Nursia (c. 480–547) as a book of spiritual and administrative precepts for monks living under an abbot's authority. These excepts provide some instructions for monks living in a Benedictine monastery.

Copyright © McGraw-Hill Education   St. Benedict. The Rule of Our Most Holy Father St. Benedict, Patriarch of Monks. Translated by One of the Benedictine Fathers of St. Michael's, Near Hereford. London: R. Washbourne, 1875.

PRIMARY SOURCE: BOOK

"OF SILENCE.

Let us act in accordance with that saying of the Prophet "I have said: I will keep my ways, that I offend not with my tongue. I have been watchful over my mouth: I held my peace and humbled myself, and was silent from speaking even good things." If, therefore, according to this saying of the Prophet we are at times to abstain, for silence sake, even from good talk, how much more ought we to refrain from evil words, on account of the guilt and penalty of sin! Therefore, because of the importance of silence, let leave to speak be seldom given, even to perfect disciples, although their words be of good and holy matters, tending unto edification; because it is written: "In much speaking, thou shalt not escape sin." And in another place: "Death and life are in the hands of the tongue." For it behoveth a master to speak and teach; and it beseemeth a disciple to hold his peace and listen. If, therefore, anything must be asked of the Prior, let it be done with all humility, subjection, and reverence, that he who asks may not seem to speak more than is necessary. But as for buffoonery, idle words, or such as move to laughter, we utterly condemn and forbid them in all places, nor do we allow a disciple to open his mouth to give them utterance.

WHETHER MONKS OUGHT TO HAVE ANYTHING OF THEIR OWN.

Especially let this vice be cut away from the Monastery by the very roots, that no one presume, without leave of the Abbot, to give, or receive, or hold as his own, anything whatsoever, either book, or tablets, or pen, or anything at all; because they are men whose very bodies and wills are not in their own power. But all that is necessary they may hope for from the Father of the Monastery; nor can they keep anything which the Abbot has not given or allowed. Let all things be common to all, as it is written: "Neither did any one say or think that aught was his own." If any one shall be found given to this most wicked vice, let him be admonished once or twice, and if he do not amend, let him be subjected to correction. "

—from *The Rule of St. Benedict* (c. 6th century)

VOCABULARY

accordance: agreement

abstain: give up

edification: improvement, education

behoveth/beseemeth: to be appropriate for

subjection: submission, compliance

Prior: title for a monastic superior, usually ranking just below an abbot

buffoonery: silliness

without leave: without permission

1 DESCRIBING Based on these excerpts, describe the values a Benedictine monk was expected to embody.

_____

_____

_____

_____

_____

2 EXPLAINING ISSUES Why did Benedict emphasize the importance of silence?

_____

_____

_____

_____

3 COMPARING AND CONTRASTING TEXTS In the New Testament (Matthew 19:21), Jesus says to a rich young man, "If you want to be perfect, go, sell your possessions and give to the poor, and you will have treasure in heaven. Then come, follow me." In what way do the excerpts from _The Rule of St. Benedict_ reflect Jesus's call?

_____

_____

_____

4 IDENTIFYING CONNECTIONS What is the proper relationship of a monk to an abbot or prior? How does this resemble the relationship a Christian is to have with God?

_____

_____

_____

_____

5 EXPLANATORY WRITING Do you think it is practical or even necessary for all Christians to live as the Benedictine monks lived? Explain your answer.

_____

_____

_____

_____

ESSENTIAL QUESTION

How can religion impact a culture?

Illuminated Manuscript

DIRECTIONS: Study the image. Then respond to the questions that follow.

EXPLORE THE CONTEXT: An illuminated manuscript is a handwritten and intricately decorated book. In addition to brilliant colors, gold and silver leaf were often used in the designs or illustrations, creating the impression that the pages are "illuminated," or lit up. Most illuminated manuscripts were written on parchment, or vellum—specially treated animal skins—before paper was widely used. Typically, the illustration in an illuminated manuscript supports or amplifies the accompanying text. In this example, possibly from a wealthy person's prayer book, the illustration depicts the event known as the Annunciation—the announcement to the Virgin Mary by the angel Gabriel that she is to give birth to Jesus.

PRIMARY SOURCE: ILLUMINATED MANUSCRIPT

1 **INTEGRATING VISUAL INFORMATION** In this scene, which figure is the angel Gabriel and which is Mary? How do you know?

_____

_____

_____

2 **IDENTIFYING CAUSES** Much of the visual art during the medieval period dealt with religious themes. Why do you think this was so?

_____

_____

_____

3 **DRAWING CONCLUSIONS** Who most likely would have owned the illuminated prayer book containing these pages? Explain your answer.

_____

_____

_____

_____

_____

4 **EVALUATING** Why were illuminated manuscripts created?

_____

_____

_____

5 ECONOMICS What can we learn about the distribution of wealth in medieval Europe from illuminated manuscripts?

_____

_____

_____

_____

ESSENTIAL QUESTION

What factors lead to the rise and fall of empires?

As you gather evidence to answer the Essential Question, think about:

- how the Germanic kingdoms influenced Europe after the fall of Rome.

- why and how the Carolingian Renaissance took place.

My Notes

_____

_____

_____

_____

_____

_____

_____

The Age of Charlemagne

DIRECTIONS: Search for evidence in the lesson to help you answer the following questions.

1A SUMMARIZING Use the graphic organizer to identify the various Germanic kingdoms that arose in Western Europe after the fall of Rome.

Name of Germanic Tribe	Location

1B EXPLAINING ISSUES Why do you think Western Europe was divided among several small kingdoms after the fall of Rome, rather than being more unified? Which kingdoms retained the Roman structure of government?

_____

_____

_____

_____

_____

2 ANALYZING EVENTS What is the significance of Clovis's conversion to Christianity?

_____

_____

_____

_____

_____

3 CIVICS How did social status and the social bond of extended family impact the way Germanic law treated the problem of crime and punishment?

_____

_____

_____

_____

4 **PREDICTING** What does the coronation of Charlemagne in 800 suggest about the future relationship between secular European rulers and the Church?

_____

_____

_____

_____

5 **EVALUATING** Why is Charlemagne sometimes referred to as the "Father of Europe"?

_____

_____

_____

_____

6 **ANALYZING EVENTS** What was the Carolingian Renaissance? Why was Charlemagne's support of education so important?

_____

_____

_____

_____

ESSENTIAL QUESTION

What factors lead to the rise and fall of empires?

The Battle of Tours

DIRECTIONS: Read the excerpt. Then respond to the questions that follow.

EXPLORE THE CONTEXT: It is not known who wrote the *Chronicle of 754*, a history of Muslim Spain from the years 610 to 754 A.D. It is attributed to Isidore of Beja, in present day Portugal, but most scholars agree its author is an anonymous Christian who lived under Arab rule in eighth-century Spain. The *Chronicle* contains an account of the Battle of Tours, fought in 732 between forces led by Frankish leader Charles Martel and Muslim invaders from Spain near the city of Tours, France.

PRIMARY SOURCE: BOOK

" Then Abderrahman, [the Muslim emir] seeing the land filled with the multitude of his army, crossed the Pyrenees, and traversed the defiles [in the mountains] and the plains, so that he penetrated ravaging and slaying clear into the lands of the Franks. He gave battle to Duke Eudes (of Aquitaine) beyond the Garonne and the Dordogne, and put him to flight---so utterly [was he beaten] that God alone knew the number of the slain and wounded. Whereupon Abderrahman set in pursuit of Eudes; he destroyed palaces, burned churches, and imagined he could pillage the basilica of St. Martin of Tours. It is then that he found himself face to face with the lord of Austrasia, Charles, a mighty warrior from his youth, and trained in all the occasions of arms.

For almost seven days the two armies watched one another, waiting anxiously the moment for joining the struggle. Finally they made ready for combat. And in the shock of the battle the men of the North seemed like a sea that cannot be moved. Firmly they stood, one close to another, forming as it were a bulwark of ice; and with great blows of their swords they hewed down the Arabs. Drawn up in a band around their chief, the people of the Austrasians carried all before them. Their tireless hands drove their swords down to the breasts [of the foe].

At last night sundered the combatants. The Franks with misgivings lowered their blades, and beholding the numberless tents of the Arabs, prepared themselves for another battle the next day. Very early, when they issued from their retreat, the men of Europe saw the Arab tents ranged still in order, in the same place where they had set up their camp. Unaware that they were utterly empty, and fearful lest within the phalanxes of the Saracens were drawn up for combat, they sent out spies to ascertain the facts. These spies discovered that all the squadrons of the [Muslims] had vanished. In fact, during the night they had fled with the greatest silence, seeking with all speed their home land. The Europeans, uncertain and fearful, lest they were merely hidden in order to come back [to fall upon them] by ambushments, sent scouting parties everywhere, but to their great amazement found nothing. Then without troubling to pursue the fugitives, they contented themselves with sharing the spoils and returned right gladly to their own country. **"**

—from *Chronicle of 754*, in *Readings in Ancient History*, ed. W. S. Davis

VOCABULARY

multitude: crowd

traversed the defiles: crossed the valleys

put him to flight: caused him to retreat

phalanxes: groups

sundered: separated

misgivings: doubts

1 **DESCRIBING** Describe the events that led up to the Battle of Tours.

_____

_____

_____

_____

_____

2 **ANALYZING TEXT** According to this account, how long did the battle last? Cite evidence from the text to support your answer.

_____

_____

_____

3 **EXPLAINING ISSUES** Why were the Franks "uncertain and fearful" even after they discovered that the Muslim soldiers had gone away? What did the Franks do to ease their uncertainty?

_____

_____

_____

4 **IDENTIFYING BIAS** Scholars agree that the author of the _Chronicle of 754_ was a Christian. Do you see any signs of religious bias in this account of the Battle of Tours?

_____

_____

_____

_____

5 HISTORY How might Europe be different today if the outcome of the Battle of Tours had been different?

_____

_____

_____

Copyright © McGraw-Hill Education   Eginhard. "The Wars of Charlemagne - The Great Saxon War." In Readings in Ancient History - II. Rome and the West, Reprinted by William Stearns Davis. Boston: Allyn and Bacon, 1913.

ESSENTIAL QUESTION

What factors lead to the rise and fall of empires?

The Saxon War

DIRECTIONS: Read the excerpt. Then respond to the questions that follow.

EXPLORE THE CONTENT: Einhard was a Frankish historian who wrote his *Life of Charlemagne* around 830. A trusted advisor to Charlemagne for more than 20 years, his history examines the king's family, accomplishments, and governing style and supplies numerous personal details of Charlemagne's life. This excerpt discusses Charlemagne's military campaigns against the Saxons of northwestern Germany, who resisted conquest for more than 30 years until finally being defeated in 804.

PRIMARY SOURCE: BOOK

❝[As to the Saxon War] no war ever undertaken by the Franks was waged with such persistence and bitterness, or cost so much labor, because the Saxons, like almost all Germans, were a ferocious folk, given over to devil-worship, hostile to our Faith, and they did not consider it dishonorable to transgress and violate all law—be it human or divine. Then, too, special circumstances caused a breach of the peace daily.

Accordingly, war was begun against the Saxons and was waged furiously for thirty-three consecutive years [772–804] on the whole to the disadvantage of the Saxons. Much earlier surely it would have terminated but for the perfidy of the Saxons. It is hard to tell how often they were conquered, humbly submitted to the King and promised to do what was commanded, gave the required hostages and received the royal officers. Sometimes they were so abased that they promised to renounce "devil-worship '' and adopt Christianity. Nevertheless, they were as prone to repudiate these terms as to accept them. It was actually impossible to tell which came easier for them to do. Hardly a year passed from the beginning of the war without such changes on their part.

[The King, however, pressed them with unvarying purpose despite great difficulties] and either took the field against them himself, or sent his counts against them with a host to wreak vengeance and exact due satisfaction, [Many of the prisoners he settled as colonists in Gaul and the obedient parts of Germany.] The war that had lasted so many years at last terminated when the Saxons gave way to the terms proffered by the King; namely, the renunciation of their native religious cults and devil-worship, the acceptance of the Christian sacraments, and union with the Franks into one people.

The Saxon war began two years before the Italian war, but although it went on continuously, business elsewhere was not neglected, nor did the King hesitate to enter on other equally severe contests. Excelling, as he did, all the princes of his time in wisdom and magnanimity, he did not suffer difficulty to turn him back, nor danger to daunt him, from any task to be assumed or carried to a conclusion. ❞

—from *Life of Charlemagne*

VOCABULARY

transgress: to misbehave, to sin

perfidy: treachery

abased: lowered

renounce: to give up

repudiate: to retract, to go back upon

proffered: offered

magnanimity: fairness, generosity

1 **DESCRIBING** What is Einhard's opinion of the Saxons?

_____

_____

_____

2 **IDENTIFYING CAUSES** According to Einhard, why did the Saxon War last so long?

_____

_____

_____

_____

3 **CIVICS** What terms were the Saxons forced to accept upon their defeat?

_____

_____

_____

_____

4 **ANALYZING EVENTS** Comment on the religious nature of the Saxon War.

_____

_____

_____

_____

_____

5 **DETERMINNG THEMES** How does Einhard describe Charlemagne in the last paragraph of this passage? How does this fit in with the overall theme of the passage?

_____

_____

_____

_____

_____

_____

The Byzantine Empire

DIRECTIONS: Search for evidence in the lesson to help you answer the following questions.

1 **ANALYZING EVENTS** Why did Justinian want to revise Roman law? Why might he have wished to have a well-organized code of laws?

_____

_____

_____

_____

2A **IDENTIFYING CONNECTIONS** Explain the connection between the rise of Islam and the weakening of the Eastern Roman Empire during the seventh century.

_____

_____

_____

_____

2B **SUMMARIZING** Use the graphic organizer to identify other groups that posed threats to the security of the Eastern Roman Empire during this period.

Name of Group	Location of Threat to Empire

ESSENTIAL QUESTION

What factors lead to the rise and fall of empires?

As you gather evidence to answer the Essential Question, think about:

- how Justinian impacted Roman law.
- why Islam created a challenge for the Eastern Roman Empire.
- the factors that led to schisms between the Roman Catholic and Eastern Orthodox churches.

My Notes

_____

_____

_____

_____

_____

_____

_____

3 ECONOMY How did Constantinople's location impact its economy and culture?

_____

_____

_____

_____

_____

_____

4 **EXPLAINING ISSUES** Under which emperors did the Byzantine Empire reach its greatest height? Why are these years considered a "golden age" in the history of the empire?

_____

_____

_____

_____

_____

_____

5 **ANALYZING EVENTS** How did the use of religious icons create controversy in the eighth century? How did this controversy relate to a larger issue?

_____

_____

_____

_____

_____

_____

_____

_____

6 **DIFFERENTIATING** How do members of the Eastern Orthodox Church and Roman Catholic Church view the power of the pope? What has been the result?

_____

_____

_____

Procopius on the Emperor Justinian

ESSENTIAL QUESTION

What factors lead to the rise and fall of empires?

DIRECTIONS: Read the excerpt. Then respond to the questions that follow.

EXPLORE THE CONTEXT: Procopius was a Byzantine historian who lived during the reign of Justinian. His *Wars* and *The Buildings of Justinian* were flattering accounts of Justinian's military successes and public works projects. His *Secret History* provides a more personal portrait of the emperor. Procopius is often considered by scholars to be the last major historian of the ancient world.

PRIMARY SOURCE: BOOK

66 This Emperor [Justinian], then, was deceitful, devious, false, hypocritical, two-faced, cruel, skilled in dissembling his thought, never moved to tears by either joy or pain, though he could summon them artfully at will when the occasion demanded, a liar always, not only offhand, but in writing, and when he swore sacred oaths to his subjects in their very hearing. Then he would immediately break his agreements and pledges, like the vilest of slaves, whom indeed only the fear of torture drives to confess their perjury. A faithless friend, he was a treacherous enemy, insane for murder and plunder, quarrelsome and revolutionary, easily led to anything, but never willing to listen to good counsel, quick to plan mischief and carry it out, but finding even the hearing of anything good distasteful to his ears. . . .

He had no scruples about appropriating other people's property, and did not even think any excuse necessary, legal or illegal, for confiscating what did not belong to him. And when it was his, he was more than ready to squander it in insane display, or give it as an unnecessary bribe to the barbarians. In short, he neither held on to any money himself nor let anyone else keep any: as if his reason were not avarice, but jealousy of those who had riches. Driving all wealth from the country of the Romans in this manner, he became the cause of universal poverty. 99

—from *Secret History* (c. 550–560)

VOCABULARY

dissembling: misleading

perjury: lies

scruples: pangs of conscience

appropriating: taking

squander: to waste

avarice: greed

1 **DETERMINING POINT OF VIEW** What does Procopius think of Justinian? What characteristics does he stress in this excerpt?

_____

_____

_____

2 **IDENTIFYING BIAS** Do you think Procopius is a reliable source of information about the private life of Justinian? Explain.

_____

_____

_____

_____

3 **INFERRING** What can we infer about Procopius's views on government and good leadership from his characterization of Justinian?

_____

_____

_____

_____

_____

4 **EXPLAINING ISSUES** What might account for the difference in the opinions expressed in _Secret History_ and Procopius's other works about Justinian?

_____

_____

_____

5 **HISTORY** How does Procopius's characterization of Justinian influence your opinion about him?

_____

_____

_____

ESSENTIAL QUESTION

What factors lead to the rise and fall of empires?

Hagia Sophia

DIRECTIONS: Study the photograph. Then respond to the questions that follow.

EXPLORE THE CONTEXT: Hagia Sophia was built as a cathedral by the Byzantine emperor Justinian in the sixth century. It is considered the most important example of Byzantine architecture and one of the most beautiful structures in the world. It is filled with mosaics, tall arches and columns, and features a high, window-pierced dome that on sunny days appears to float on the light. Construction on Hagia Sophia lasted from 532 to 537, taking only five years. After the Turks conquered Constantinople in 1453, Hagia Sophia was used as a mosque. The Turkish government converted the building into a museum in 1935.

PRIMARY SOURCE: PHOTOGRAPH

—Hagia Sophia, Istanbul, Turkey

1 **UNDERSTANDING CONTEXT** Why did Justinian order construction projects such as the building of Hagia Sophia?

_____

_____

_____

_____

2 **INTEGRATING VISUAL INFORMATION** What are the distinctive characteristics of Hagia Sophia? Why was such care given to the creation of the main dome?

_____

_____

_____

3 **DRAWING CONCLUSIONS** The interior of Hagia Sophia has two levels—a ground floor and a gallery above. Why might the building have been constructed in this way?

_____

_____

4 **HISTORY** Which elements of Hagia Sophia shown in the photograph are not part of the original church's Byzantine design? How do you know?

_____

_____

_____

_____

_____

_____

_____

_____

ESSENTIAL QUESTIONS

How can religion impact a culture?

What factors lead to the rise and fall of empires?

My Notes

_____

_____

_____

_____

_____

_____

_____

_____

_____

_____

_____

_____

1 Think About It

Review the supporting questions you developed at the beginning of the chapter. Review the evidence you gathered in the chapter. Were you able to answer each Supporting Question? If there was not enough evidence to answer your Supporting Questions, what additional evidence do you need to consider?

_____

_____

_____

2 Organize Your Evidence

Complete the chart below with information you learned about the rise and fall of various empires between A.D. 50 to A.D. 800 and the ways the rulers of these empires began to develop close relationships with Christianity.

Cause	Effect
Paul made several missionary journeys in the years following Jesus's crucifixion.	
	Constantine proclaims Christianity as the official religion of the Roman Empire.
Constantine constructs a new capital city, Constantinople, in the east.	
	Western Christians come to accept the bishop of Rome as the head of the Church.
Charlemagne begins to build power and influence as king of the Franks.	
	Eastern Roman Empire transforms into the Byzantine Empire.

3 Write About It

In the space below, discuss the growth of the Christian Church's political power after the fall of Rome. Give some examples of how the Church expressed political as well as religious power.

_____

_____

_____

_____

4 Talk About It

Work in small groups. With your groups, discus the various ways Christianity impacted the power of rulers such as Clovis, Charlemagne, and Justinian. Why might these rulers want to be closely identified with the Church? Are there any disadvantages? Take notes about your discussion below.

_____

_____

_____

_____

5 Connect to the Essential Question

It is A.D. 650 and you are the ruler of a small Germanic kingdom in Western Europe. Your power has been growing and you have attracted the attention of the pope, who offers you his support. Write a series of "text messages" between yourself and the pope. The conversation should reveal the pope's motivations and your responses. Will the pope's support strengthen your rule? What does the pope want in return?
Limit each message to 200 characters.

_____

_____

_____

_____

_____

_____

TAKE ACTION

MAKE CONNECTIONS In the United States, the principle of separation of church and state prohibits the government from promoting any particular religion. This is very different from medieval Europe, when political and religious power were tightly connected. Some people in the United States believe that America has become too secular (not affiliated with religion) and blame many of society's problems on a lack of religion in the public sphere. Sometimes they promote actions such as placing the Ten Commandments in front of government buildings or allowing a "moment of silence" for voluntary prayer at the beginning of the school day.

DIRECTIONS: Contact an organization that promotes public expressions of religious faith such as those described above or an organization that works on issues related to the separation of church and state. Ask what that organization believes the relationship between faith and government should be. Summarize your discussion for the class.

_____

_____

_____

_____

_____

_____

_____

_____

_____

_____

_____

_____

_____

Islam and the Arab Empire

ESSENTIAL QUESTIONS

How can religion influence the development of an empire?

How might religious beliefs affect society, culture, and politics?

Think about what effect the religion of Islam had on the Arab Empire, including the effects on society, culture, and politics.

TALK ABOUT IT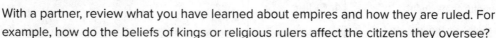

With a partner, review what you have learned about empires and how they are ruled. For example, how do the beliefs of kings or religious rulers affect the citizens they oversee?

DIRECTIONS: Now write down three additional questions that will help you explain how religion can affect a society and its culture, or politics. For example, you might ask, "Are societies or empires with more than one religion different than those that encourage just one main religion?"

MY RESEARCH QUESTIONS

Supporting Question 1:

_____

_____

Supporting Question 2:

_____

_____

Supporting Question 3:

_____

_____

The First Muslims

DIRECTIONS: Search for evidence in the lesson to help you answer the following questions.

ESSENTIAL QUESTIONS

How can religion influence the development of an empire?

How might religious beliefs affect society, culture, and politics?

As you gather evidence to answer the Essential Questions, think about:

- how trade routes on the Arabian peninsula were influenced by the domestication of the camel and political discord in the religion.
- how the revelations to Muhammad led to the foundation of Islam.
- how Islamic beliefs influenced law and culture in Southwest Asia.

My Notes

_____

_____

_____

_____

_____

_____

_____

1. **SUMMARIZING** What influence did the camel have on trade in the Arabian Peninsula?

_____

_____

_____

_____

2. **DETERMINING CENTRAL IDEAS** Name the five pillars of Islam and describe how they are practiced by Muslims.

1. Belief	
2. Prayer	
3. Charity	
4. Fasting	
5. Pilgrimage	

3 **UNDERSTANDING CONTEXT** What was the role of sheikhs in the Arabian Peninsula?

_____

_____

_____

4 **ANALYZING CHANGE** How did Islam shape life in the Arabian Peninsula from the first teachings of Muhammad to the development of shari'ah law?

_____

_____

_____

5 **USING MAPS** Describe the location and direction of the route that Muhammad took in 622 to Makkah. Why is Makkah an important location for Muslims today?

_____

_____

_____

6 **ANALYZING INDIVIDUALS** How do Muslims view Muhammad and his role in the Islamic religion?

_____

_____

_____

_____

How can religion influence the development of an empire?

How might religious beliefs affect society, culture, and politics?

Islam and Charity

DIRECTIONS: Read the excerpt. Then respond to the questions that follow.

EXPLORE THE CONTEXT: The following text is from "The Five Principles of Islam and their Significance." It specifically explains Islam's final principle, zakat, or the giving of alms.

SECONDARY SOURCE: PERIODICAL

"Now I come to the last and fifth principle of Islam, which has been promulgated [declared] by the Holy Qur-an in the terms of Zakat (poor-rates) or Sadaquat (alms). Every Muslim is expected to take a stock of his savings every year and to disburse [hand out] $2\text{-}\frac{1}{2}$ per cent. of this as "alms." Charity in Islam takes two different forms: one is optional and the other compulsory [required], which is also called zakat. When asked as to what was the ultimate object of zakat, the Holy Prophet replied that it was a means whereby the rich had to give something out of their wealth for the help of those who are in need. The Holy Qur-an has laid down eight different purposes for the expenditure [spending] of this zakat money. It says: 'Alms are only for the poor, the needy, the officials appointed over them, those whose hearts are made inclined to truth, the ransoming of captives, those in debt, in the way of Allah and the wayfarer.'

It is Islam that has given charity the prestige [respect] and form of an institution. Before the advent [founding] of Islam the followers of other religions used to do charitable deeds on their own personal fancies and had no organization. But the Holy Prophet, whose aim was to systemize the religion and make it a living force in the civilization of mankind, laid down rules and regulations for charity, so that the general welfare of the society may be achieved."

—from "The Five Principles of Islam and their Significance"
by Maulvi Mustafakhan

Maulvi, Mustafkhan. "The Five Principles of Islam and Their Significance." In The Islamic Review. Vol. IX, No. 6 (June-July). 1921.

VOCABULARY

optional: voluntary

ultimate: essential

inclined: tend to take a particular action

fancies: desires or whims

institution: organization or society

systemize: to develop a method, order, or regularity

1 **ANALYZING STRUCTURE** Is the text written for someone who is familiar with Islam or unfamiliar with it? Explain how the structure of the excerpt reveals the audience it is meant for.

_____

_____

_____

2 **INTERPRETING** What evidence does the author give that shows the idea of the zakat was declared part of the principles of Islam by Muhammad?

_____

_____

_____

_____

3 **COMPARING AND CONTRASTING** According to the excerpt, how does the Islamic idea of charity differ from those of other religions or cultures?

_____

_____

_____

4 **INTERPRETING** According to the excerpt, what was the intention of making charity within society one of the pillars of the religion of Islam?

_____

_____

_____

5 **DRAWING CONCLUSIONS** Why do you think there are two kinds of charity named in the Quran: Zakat (poor-rates) and Sadaquat (alms)?

_____

_____

_____

How can religion influence the development of an empire?

How might religious beliefs affect society, culture, and politics?

Hadith on Fasting

DIRECTIONS: Read the excerpt. Then respond to the questions that follow.

EXPLORE THE CONTEXT: This excerpt about fasting comes from the Hadith, a sacred text for Muslims. It is a collection of sayings and guidance for Muslims from Muhammad's life. It provides guidance about how to live beyond the words in the Quran.

PRIMARY SOURCE: SACRED TEXT

" Fasting is an armour with which one protects oneself; so let not him (who fasts) utter immodest (or foul) speech, nor let him act in an ignorant manner; and if a man quarrels with him or abuses him, he should say twice, I am fasting. And by Him in Whose hand is my soul, the odour of the mouth of one fasting is sweeter in the estimation of Allāh than the odour of muskh—gives up his food and his drink and his . . . desire for MY sake; fasting is for Me and I will grant its reward; and a virtue brings reward ten times like it. "

—from *A Manual of Hadith*, Maulana Muhammad Ali

1 **IDENTIFYING PERSPECTIVES** Why might religious practices that involve self-sacrifice such as fasting be an important spiritual experience for people of faith?

_____

_____

_____

_____

_____

_____

_____

2 **INTERPRETING** Why does the Hadith state fasting is virtuous?

_____

_____

_____

_____

_____

3 **UNDERSTANDING CONTEXT** According to the Hadith how are those who are fasting obligated to act?

_____

_____

_____

_____

_____

4 **INTERPRETING** What kind of influence do you think fasting had on communities in the Arabian Peninsula?

_____

_____

_____

_____

_____

5 **IDENTIFYING PERSPECTIVES** Why do you think Muslims read from sacred texts like this one to understand Muhammad's advice about fasting?

_____

_____

_____

_____

_____

The Arab Empire and the Caliphates

DIRECTIONS: Search for evidence in the lesson to help you answer the following questions.

1 **COMPARING AND CONTRASTING** What are the basic differences in beliefs and practices between Sunni and Shia Muslims?

_____

_____

_____

_____

2 **SUMMARIZING** Use the organizer to describe the role of caliphs in the Arab Empire.

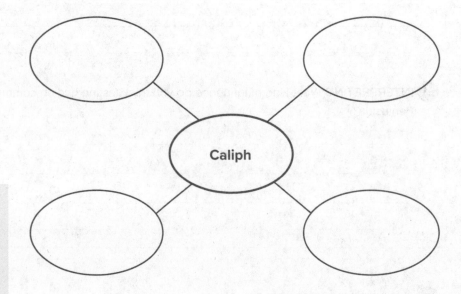

ESSENTIAL QUESTIONS

How can religion influence the development of an empire?

How might religious beliefs affect society, culture, and politics?

As you gather evidence to answer the Essential Questions, think about:

- how the death of Muhammad left his followers without an heir or a chosen successor.

- how the leadership of Abū Bakr expanded the Islamic movement and united the Muslim world.

- how the Arab Empire made many conquests under the rule of the Umayyad dynasty.

My Notes

_____

_____

_____

_____

_____

_____

3 **UNDERSTANDING CONTEXT** How did Muslims view engaging in battles to spread their empire?

_____

_____

_____

_____

_____

4 **ANALYZING CHANGE** How was Abū Bakr's leadership different from Muhammad's?

_____

_____

_____

_____

_____

5 **USING MAPS** How did the Abbasid Dynasty differ from the Umayyad Dynasty?

_____

_____

_____

_____

_____

6 **ANALYZING EVENTS** What caused a revolt during the Umayyad Dynasty that caused a split in Islam?

_____

_____

_____

_____

_____

ESSENTIAL QUESTIONS

How can religion influence the development of an empire?

How might religious beliefs affect society, culture, and politics?

Rome and the West

DIRECTIONS: Read the excerpt. Then respond to the questions that follow.

EXPLORE THE CONTEXT: The following excerpt is from the book *Rome and the West*, which describes ancient civilizations.

SECONDARY SOURCE: BOOK

Baghdad Under the Abbasid Caliphs

“The city of Bagdad formed two vast semi-circles on the right and left banks of the Tigris, twelve miles in diameter. The numerous suburbs, covered with parks, gardens, villas, and beautiful promenades, and plentifully supplied with rich bazaars, and finely built mosques and baths, stretched for a considerable distance on both sides of the river. In the days of its prosperity the population of Bagdad and its suburbs amounted to over two millions! The palaces of the [Caliph] stood in the midst of a vast park "several hours in circumference" which beside a menagerie and aviary comprise an inclosure for wild animals reserved for the chaste. The palace grounds were laid out with gardens, and adorned with exquisite taste with plants, flowers, and trees, reservoirs and fountains, surrounded by sculpted figures. On this side of the river stood the palaces of the great nobles. Immense streets, none less than forty cubits wide, traversed the city from one end to the other, dividing it into blocks or quarters, each under the control of an overseer or supervisor, who looked after the cleanliness, sanitation and the comfort of the inhabitants. ”

—from *Rome and the West* by William Stearns Davis

VOCABULARY

promenade: walkway

mosque: place of worship for Muslims

menagerie: collection kept for view

1 **ANALYZING INFORMATION** Without knowledge of the title of the excerpt, what clues does the author give that the Abbasid Caliph is being described?

_____

_____

_____

_____

_____

2 INTERPRETING What does "in the days of its prosperity" imply about the mosques and baths?

_____

_____

_____

_____

3 ANALYZING INFORMATION Who do you think the book was written for?

_____

_____

_____

_____

_____

4 INTERPRETING What do you think the author meant by "several hours in circumference" when referring to the palaces of the caliph, and why is the information in quotations?

_____

_____

_____

_____

_____

5 DRAWING CONCLUSIONS What kind of statement do you think the palaces, with gardens and enclosures for wild animals, makes about the Empire?

_____

_____

_____

_____

_____

ESSENTIAL QUESTIONS

How can religion influence the development of an empire?

How might religious beliefs affect society, culture, and politics?

VOCABULARY

lance: a long weapon designed to be used by a fighter on horseback

onslaught: a fierce attack

Warfare in the Medieval World/ The Alexiad

DIRECTIONS: Read the excerpt. Then respond to the questions that follow.

EXPLORE THE CONTEXT: This excerpt comes from the book *Warfare in the Medieval World* by Brian Todd Carey. It describes the methods of war of various civilizations and empires throughout history.

> ### SECONDARY SOURCE: BOOK

Turkish Tactics

66 He [Alexius Comnenus] knew from long experience that the Turkish battle-line differs from that of other peoples . . . but their right and left wings and their center formed separate groups with the ranks cut off, as it were, from one another; whenever an attack was made on right or left, the center leapt into action and all the rest of the army behind, in a whirlwind onslaught that threw into confusion the accepted tradition of battle. As for weapons they use in war, unlike the [Franks] they do not fight with lances, but completely surround the enemy and shoot him with arrows; they also defend themselves with arrows from a distance. In hot pursuit the Turk makes prisoners by using his bow; in flight he overwhelms his pursue with the same weapon and when he shoots, the arrow in its course strikers either rider or horse, fired with such a tremendous force that it passes clean through the body. So skilled are the Turkish archers. 99

—from *Warfare in the Medieval World* by Brian Todd Carey

1 **INTERPRETING** What is the author's general assessment of the way the Turks fought?

_____

_____

_____

_____

_____

_____

2 **UNDERSTANDING CONTEXT** How is an arrow more powerful than a lance in battle?

_____

_____

_____

_____

_____

_____

3 **INTERPRETING** In battle, what is the benefit of shooting a horse but missing the rider?

_____

_____

_____

_____

_____

_____

4 **IDENTIFYING PERSPECTIVES** Why do you think historians look back at the battle techniques of earlier civilizations?

_____

_____

_____

_____

_____

_____

5 **COMPARING AND CONTRASTING** How do the battle methods of the Turks differ from methods used today?

_____

_____

_____

_____

_____

_____

Islamic Civilization

DIRECTIONS: Search for evidence in the lesson to help you answer the following questions.

1 **ANALYZING CHANGE** How did trade across the Arab world affect both the economy and agricultural of the region?

_____

_____

_____

_____

_____

_____

2 **ANALYZING CENTRAL IDEAS** Use the organizer to describe aspects of Islamic society.

Class Structure	Treatment of Non-Muslims	Rights of Women

ESSENTIAL QUESTIONS

How can religion influence the development of an empire?

How might religious beliefs affect society, culture, and politics?

As you gather evidence to answer the Essential Questions, think about:

- how trade resulted in the growth of cities and helped expand the reach of Islam.

- how the Islamic teaching of equality in the eyes of Allah was not translated into social reality.

- what Islamic advancements in philosophy, science, and history contributed to the world's knowledge.

- how Islam brought major changes to the culture of Southwest Asia, including its literature, art, and architecture.

My Notes

_____

_____

_____

3 ANALYZING CENTRAL IDEAS How did the growth of agriculture in the Islamic World contribute to population growth and urbanization?

_____

_____

_____

_____

4 EXPLAINING ISSUES How was the social structure of Arab societies different from the way it was intended in the Quran?

_____

_____

_____

_____

_____

5 DESCRIBING What contributions did Islamic scholars make to the world of astronomy?

_____

_____

_____

_____

_____

6 IDENTIFYING CONNECTIONS How does Islamic architecture and art use mathematics?

_____

_____

_____

_____

_____

The Poetry of Omar Khayyam

ESSENTIAL QUESTIONS

How can religion influence the development of an empire?

How might religious beliefs affect society, culture, and politics?

DIRECTIONS: Read the poem. Then respond to the questions that follow.

EXPLORE THE CONTEXT: Omar Khayyam is one of the most famous authors of early Islam. In this poem, Khayyam explores a large topic—life—in very few sentences.

VOCABULARY

vanity: pride, conceit

avail: benefit

shrouded: covered

allure: attract

depart: leave

PRIMARY SOURCE: POEM

66 Nothing in this world of ours

Flows as we would have it flow;

What avail, then, careful hours,

Thought and trouble, tears and woe?

Through the shrouded veil of earth,

Life's rich colors gleaming bright,

Though in truth of little worth,

Yet allure with meteor light.

Life is torture and suspense;

Thought is sorrow—drive it hence!

With no will of mine I came,

With no will depart the same. 99

—Omar Khayyam, "The Vanity of Regret," c. 1100

Copyright © McGraw-Hill Education   Horne, Charles F., ed. The Sacred Books and Early Literature of the East, Volume VIII, New York: Parke, Austin, & Lipscomb, 1917.

1 **DRAWING CONCLUSIONS** How would you describe the author's outlook on life?

_____

_____

_____

_____

2 **EVALUATING** Who would be reading the poem at the time it was written?

_____

_____

_____

_____

3 **UNDERSTANDING CONTEXT** What do you think the poem means to historians who study this period of history?

_____

_____

_____

_____

4 **INTERPRETING** Which line in the poem indicates that the author knows that life has good moments that make people feel good?

_____

_____

_____

_____

5 **DRAWING CONCLUSIONS** What statement do you think the poem makes about the time in which the author lived? Explain.

_____

_____

_____

_____

ESSENTIAL QUESTIONS

How can religion influence the development of an empire?

How might religious beliefs affect society, culture, and politics?

Medieval Chemistry

DIRECTIONS: Read the passage. Then respond to the questions that follow.

EXPLORE THE CONTEXT: During the Middle Ages, Muslim Arabs not only adapted scientific and technological advances of the people in regions they conquered, they also made significant achievements of their own. This was particularly true in mathematics and the natural sciences. Jabir ibn Hayyan was a chemist, astronomer, engineer, and physicist, among other occupations, in eighth-century Persia. He is particularly known for his work with metals. Some of his writings about that work were translated and dispersed throughout Europe, where his name was Latinized as "Gerber." In the following passage, Jabir explains how the process of calcination, or exposing elements to heat, can be used to purify metals.

PRIMARY SOURCE: WRITTEN TEXT

❝Souls and spirits [i.e., volatile substances like sulphur and salammoniac] will not sustain calcination, since the latter can be effected only with a very hot fire; now spirits will not sustain a very hot fire as they are volatile and fly away from it. Moreover, the aim of calcination is nothing more than the removal of impurities from metals and their complete combustion, so that the metals may be purified and remain unadulterated and unsullied; in a spirit, however, there is no necessity for the same treatment as in a metal, and all that is needed is the first process in calcination [i.e. gentle heating], when the same effect is produced on the spirit as [complete] calcination effects on the metals, namely, full purification. As for the process which is to spirits what calcination is to metals . . . thou wilt find it to be sublimation. As I have now made clear the aim of calcination I will next speak of its various forms, for each metal is calcined in a different way from the others. This is because among the metals are found some which are already pure, such as gold; in this case the object of calcination is to convert the metal into a fine powder so that it may be enabled to combine and enter into union with the sublimed spirits, and also to dissolve. The same applies to silver, but silver is slightly impure, so that it needs purification as well as conversion into a fine powder. As for the rest of the metals, that is excluding the two above-mentioned, they indeed all require calcination both for purification and also for converting them into powder; and the same is true for those minerals which are infusible, according to their degree of purity. ❞

—Quoted in *Makers of Chemistry,* John Eric Holmyard, 1931

VOCABULARY

volatile: easily evaporated

calcination: to reduce, oxidize, or dry by exposing to strong heat

combustion: burning

unsullied: pure

sublimation: the transformation of a solid directly to gas, without passing through a liquid stage

1 **DETERMINING CENTRAL IDEAS** What is the main idea of the text? Explain your answer.

_____

_____

_____

2 **UNDERSTANDING CONTEXT** What do these discoveries and their publication tell us about scientific exploration in the medieval Muslim world?

_____

_____

_____

3 **IDENTIFYING CONNECTIONS** How does calcination apply to metals and spirits, according to the text? Explain your answer.

_____

_____

_____

4 **INFERRING** How does calcification work differently on metals like gold?

_____

_____

_____

5 **ECONOMICS** Why is it significant that Jabir was working on the purification of metals?

_____

_____

_____

6 **DETERMINING MEANING** What does the term "souls and spirits" mean in the context of the first sentence?

_____

_____

_____

ESSENTIAL QUESTIONS

How can religion influence the development of an empire?

How might religious beliefs affect society, culture, and politics?

My Notes

_____

_____

_____

_____

_____

_____

_____

_____

_____

_____

_____

_____

_____

_____

_____

1 Think About It

Review the evidence you gathered as you read the chapter that helped you answer the Supporting Questions. Were you able to answer each Supporting Question? If not, what additional evidence do you think you need to gather to prepare your answers?

_____

_____

_____

_____

2 Organize Your Evidence

Complete the chart below with information you learned about Islam and the Arab Empire.

The First Muslims	The Arab Empire and the Caliphates	Islamic Civilization

3 Talk About It

Work in small groups. With your group, discuss the various contributions of Muslims throughout the Arab Empire. Consider information from each lesson in the chapter. Take notes about your discussion below.

_____

_____

_____

_____

4 Write About It

Choose one of the Islamic caliphates covered in the chapter. Write a summary of the general ideals of the caliphate, the regions it conquered, and any major changes or growth it brought to the Arab Empire.

_____

_____

_____

_____

5 Connect to the Essential Question

Work in pairs to write an article for the school newspaper about the history of the Arab Empire. In the article, address both Essential Questions about the influence the Islamic religion had on the development of the empire and its society, culture, and politics.

_____

_____

_____

_____

_____

_____

_____

CITIZENSHIP
TAKE ACTION

MAKE CONNECTIONS Some Muslim communities have struggled over the past decades to assimilate and feel part of American culture. Misinformation about the religion and culture of Islam has caused unnecessary conflict among community members. Sometimes education and awareness is all that is needed to improve relations within a community.

DIRECTIONS: Organize and create a community education pamphlet about the history of Islam, including its origins and the way it views its most important ideas, such as the life and teachings of Muhammad, the Five Pillars, and the contributions to art, architecture, math, and astronomy.

Distribute the pamphlets throughout the school and to local community organizations.

_____

_____

_____

_____

_____

_____

_____

_____

_____

_____

_____

_____

_____

_____

Medieval Kingdoms in Europe

ESSENTIAL QUESTIONS

How can changes to political systems impact economic activities?

How is society influenced by changes in political and economic systems?

Think about how changes to political systems of Medieval Europe affected the economic systems of the time. What could make a political system change? How could those political developments affect economies?

TALK ABOUT IT

With a partner, discuss the sort of information that could help you answer these questions. For example, one question might be: *What political changes occurred in the Carolingian Empire after Charlemagne's death? Why?*

DIRECTIONS: Now write down three additional questions that will help you explain how changes in political and economic systems influence a society. For example, you might ask, "How could invasions and the conquering of lands change economic systems?"

MY RESEARCH QUESTIONS

Supporting Question 1:

_____

_____

Supporting Question 2:

_____

_____

Supporting Question 3:

_____

Feudalism

DIRECTIONS: Search for evidence in the lesson to help you answer the following questions.

1 **IDENTIFYING EFFECTS** Why did the system of feudalism develop after Viking invasions?

_____

_____

_____

_____

2 **SUMMARIZING** Use the following chart to identify important details about vassals, including their obligations and benefits in the feudal system.

	Vassal	

3 **ANALYZING CHANGE** What ideal developed among the nobility in the eleventh and twelfth centuries? Explain.

_____

_____

_____

_____

_____

ESSENTIAL QUESTIONS

How can changes to political systems impact economic activities?

How is society influenced by changes in political and economic systems?

As you gather evidence to answer the Essential Questions, think about:

- how the collapse of central authority led to feudalism.

- the political and social relationships that developed under feudalism.

- how feudalism determined the functions of society and the economy.

My Notes

_____

_____

_____

_____

_____

_____

_____

_____

4 **UNDERSTANDING CONTEXT** How did the introduction of larger horses change the way battles were fought?

_____

_____

_____

_____

_____

5 **EXPLAINING ISSUES** What role did women play in the feudal system?

_____

_____

_____

_____

_____

6 **INTERPRETING** How would you describe the relationship between a lord and his vassal?

_____

_____

_____

_____

_____

ESSENTIAL QUESTIONS

How can changes to political systems impact economic activities?

How is society influenced by changes in political and economic systems?

VOCABULARY

Gemot: a meeting

Both: debt

Burh-gemot: a town council meeting

Oferhyrnes: penalties for disobedience

Burh: a town or city

Shire-gemot: a county meeting

Anglo-Saxon Early Law

DIRECTIONS: Read the excerpt. Then respond to the questions that follow.

EXPLORE THE CONTEXT: This passage was written around the year 930 C.E. It comes from a collection of laws created by the Anglo-Saxon government officials. These two paragraphs represent two of the laws that people of England were required to follow.

PRIMARY SOURCE: LAW

66 If any one [when summoned] fail to attend the gemot thrice [three times], let him pay the king's 'oferhyrnes,' and let it be announced seven days before the gemot is to be. But if he will not do right, nor pay the 'oferhyrnes,' then let all the chief men belonging to the 'burh' ride to him, and take all that he has, and put him in 'both.' But if any one will not ride with his fellows, let him pay the king's 'oferhyrnes.' . . .

And let the hundred gemot be attended as it was before fixed; and thrice in the year let a burh-gemot be held; and twice, a shire-gemot; and let there be present the bishop of the shire and the ealdorman, and there both expound as well the law of God as the secular law from Select Charters and Other Illustrations of English Constitutional History from the Earliest Times to the Reign of Edward the First. 99

—from *Select Charters and Other Illustrations of English Constitutional History from the Earliest Times to the Reign of Edward the First*, c. 930 C.E.

1 **INFERRING** Why do you think such specific laws existed during the reign of Edward the First?

_____

_____

_____

_____

_____

_____

William, Stubbs. Select Charters and Other Illustrations of English Constitutional History From the Earliest Times to the Reign of Edward the First. London: MacMillan and Co., 1900.

2 **INTERPRETING** What does the law suggest about the importance of the town council and county meetings?

_____

_____

_____

_____

_____

3 **DRAWING CONCLUSIONS** What benefit would there be to having the bishop of the shire and the ealdorman contribute to the meetings?

_____

_____

_____

_____

_____

4 **INTERPRETING** Why would announcements be made seven days in advance for urgent town meetings?

_____

_____

_____

_____

_____

5 **DRAWING CONCLUSIONS** What issues do you think were discussed at town council meetings?

_____

_____

_____

_____

_____

ESSENTIAL QUESTIONS

How can changes to political systems impact economic activities?

How is society influenced by changes in political and economic systems?

The Oseberg Ship

DIRECTIONS: Study the image. Then respond to the questions that follow.

EXPLORE THE CONTEXT: The oak vessel in this image is an actual Viking ship now displayed in a museum. It was used by the Vikings in the 700s to 800s C.E. The ship has oar holes for oarsmen so that it can be rowed. It also has a mast for a sail so that it can use wind power to navigate. The prows, or fronts, of many of these ships were carved with ornate decorations, one of the most common of which was a curled serpent. These beautiful carvings were likely the work of skilled artists, making them very expensive to create.

PRIMARY SOURCE: ARTIFACT

1 **INTEGRATING VISUAL INFORMATION** What does the number and placement of the oar holes on the ship suggest about the way the ship was operated?

_____

_____

_____

_____

2 **COMPARING AND CONTRASTING** How does the size and structure of the ship compare to transportation vessels used today?

_____

_____

_____

3 **INTERPRETING** Why do you think the decoration at the front of the ship is the most ornate detail about it?

_____

_____

_____

_____

4 ECONOMICS **IDENTIFYING POINT OF VIEW** Why is the mention of the expense of the ship an important detail for the viewer to know?

_____

_____

_____

_____

5 **DRAWING CONCLUSIONS** What might it have been like to use this ship on the open ocean, and what does this suggest about the Vikings?

_____

_____

_____

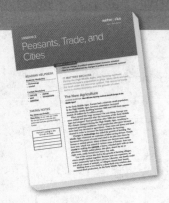

Peasants, Trade, and Cities

DIRECTIONS: Search for evidence in the lesson to help you answer the following questions.

1 **ANALYZING CHANGE** How did changes in farming support population growth?

_____

_____

_____

_____

_____

2 **SUMMARIZING** Use the following chart to describe the major elements of the manorial system.

Manorial System	
Lords	
Serfs	
Peasants	
Manor tasks	

ESSENTIAL QUESTIONS

How can changes to political systems impact economic activities?

How is society influenced by changes in political and economic systems?

As you gather evidence to answer the Essential Question, think about:

- how new farming inventions and practices supported population growth.

- how serfs contributed to the manorial system.

- why increases in trade led to a money-based economy and the rise of cities.

My Notes

_____

_____

_____

_____

_____

_____

3 IDENTIFYING EFFECTS How did the growth of trade affect the social systems in the Middle Ages?

_____

_____

_____

_____

_____

4 COMPARING AND CONTRASTING What was different about the location of cities in medieval Europe than in previous empires?

_____

_____

_____

_____

_____

_____

5 ANALYZING CHANGE What caused the need for towns to have their own systems of law?

_____

_____

_____

_____

_____

_____

6 INTERPRETING How did craft guilds add to the power of medieval economies?

_____

_____

_____

_____

_____

ESSENTIAL QUESTIONS

How can changes to political systems impact economic activities?

How is society influenced by changes in political and economic systems?

VOCABULARY

hae: have

decree: order

edict: official order

denar: payment

Otto III Forbids the Unfree Classes to Attempt to Free Themselves, ca. 1000

DIRECTIONS: Read the excerpt. Then respond to the questions that follow.

EXPLORE THE CONTEXT: This passage was written around the year 930 C.E. It comes from a collection of laws created by the Anglo-Saxon government officials.

PRIMARY SOURCE: LAW

Otto III Forbids The Unfree Classes To Attempt To Free Themselves, Ca. 1000

❝There is need of careful legislation because the princes of the empire, both lay and clerical, rich and poor, the higher as well as the lower, make frequent complaints that they are not able to obtain from their unfree subjects those services to which they have a right. For some falsely declare that they are free because their lords, in many cases, cannot prove the servitude which they [their unfree subjects] are trying in a dishonest way to escape. Others are trying to rise to the honor of freedom because their lords hae, for a long time, been hindered from knowing anything about their unfree subjects, and hence the latter have not been kept in their accustomed state of servitude, nor are they forced to pay a tax as proof of their unfree state. So on this account they declare that they are free and boast that they have lived in freedom, because for a short time they have not fulfilled their servile duties. Therefore we have issued this imperial law: (1) If a serf, led by his desire for liberty, says that he is free, his lord may settle the case by a duel with him, fighting either in person or by his champion [representative], as he may wish. The lord is given this privilege because of the great difficulty there is in proving such things in the regular way. The unfree man may secure a champion for himself if, because of age or disease, he is unable to fight. (2) In order that the unfree may not hide his real condition by avoiding his duties for a time, we decree by this our edict, which, with the help of God, shall be valid forever, that hereafter each one shall show his servile condition by paying a denar of the ordinary currency every year on the first of December to his lord or to the agent whom he shall appoint for this purpose. (3) The children of the free shall begin to pay this tax as a proof of their servile condition in their twenty-fifth ear and at the appointed time. And no matter how long they may avoid paying this tax, they shall not thereby become free. (4) If any unfree man belonging to the church shall disobey this edict, he shall be fined one-half of all his goods and he shall be reduced to his former unfree condition. For an unfree man of the church may never become free. We strictly forbid the unfree of the churches to be set free, and we order all those who have, by any device, been freed to be reduced to servitude again. ❞

—from *A Source Book for Medieval History* by Oliver J. Thatcher, Edgar H. McNeal

Copyright © McGraw-Hill Education   Otto III. A Source Book for Mediaeval History. Reprinted 1905 by Oliver J. Thatcher and Edgar H. McNeal. New York: C. Scribner's Sons, 1000.

1 CIVICS **ANALYZING CENTRAL IDEAS** What does the detailed explanation about free subjects suggest about the laws of medieval Europe?

_____

_____

_____

2 **CITING TEXT EVIDENCE** What part of the text explains that a serf may not necessarily have to spend his time in servitude to be free of a tax?

_____

_____

_____

3 **ANALYZING TEXTS** Does the child of a freed serf become free as well? What affect does this have on the society?

_____

_____

_____

_____

4 **INTERPRETING** What indication does the text give that the church has heavy political power?

_____

_____

_____

5 **DRAWING CONCLUSIONS** What problem do the laws mentioned in the passage try to prevent?

_____

_____

_____

_____

_____

ESSENTIAL QUESTIONS

How can changes to political systems impact economic activities?

How is society influenced by changes in political and economic systems?

Medieval Bologna

DIRECTIONS: Study the image. Then respond to the questions that follow.

EXPLORE THE CONTEXT: The photo shows the Bologna Cathedral, also known as the Metropolitan Cathedral of Saint Peter in Bologna, Italy. The Baroque style building was completed in the 18th century. The two towers of the cathedral are among only 22 towers remaining of as many as 180 vertical towers built around medieval Bologna. The tall structures were likely a symbol of wealth and meant to guard and defend the city.

PRIMARY SOURCE: PHOTO

—Metropolitan Cathedral of Saint Peter and the Towers of Bologna, in Bologna, Italy

1 **INTEGRATING VISUAL INFORMATION** What evidence in the photo shows that the towers were likely used as defense?

_____

_____

_____

_____

2 **IDENTIFYING CONNECTIONS** What do the buildings and streets around the church reveal about life in a medieval city?

_____

_____

_____

_____

3 **IDENTIFYING POINT OF VIEW** Why do you think medieval merchants would gather in an area like this city center in Bologna?

_____

_____

_____

_____

4 **ECONOMICS** **COMPARING AND CONTRASTING** What modern structures compare to the Towers of Bologna, and how is their function similar to that of these medieval towers?

_____

_____

_____

_____

5 **DRAWING CONCLUSIONS** How do you think the church and towers are viewed by people in modern Bologna?

_____

_____

_____

The Growth of European Kingdoms

DIRECTIONS: Search for evidence in the lesson to help you answer the following questions.

1 **ANALYZING SOURCES** Why was the Magna Carta such an important document for the growth of European kingdoms?

_____

_____

_____

_____

_____

2 **SUMMARIZING** Use the following chart to describe the major characteristics of Slavic Europe.

Slavic Europe

ESSENTIAL QUESTIONS

How can changes to political systems impact economic activities?

How is society influenced by changes in political and economic systems?

As you gather evidence to answer the Essential Questions, think about:

- how English society and legal systems changed after 1066.

- how political changes in France, Germany, and Spain influenced their societies.

- how the Slavic peoples formed new kingdoms in eastern and central Europe.

My Notes

_____

_____

_____

_____

_____

3 IDENTIFYING EFFECTS What effects did the Norman conquest have on England?

_____

_____

_____

_____

_____

_____

4 SUMMARIZING How did England's government and Church change during King Henry II's rule?

_____

_____

_____

_____

_____

_____

5 ANALYZING EVENTS How did France change during Phillip II Augustus's rule?

_____

_____

_____

_____

6 UNDERSTANDING CHANGE What changes occurred in Spain as a result of Muslim rule?

_____

_____

_____

_____

_____

_____

How can changes to political systems impact economic activities?

How is society influenced by changes in political and economic systems?

The Excommunication of Frederick II, 1239

DIRECTIONS: Read the excerpt and answer the questions that follow.

EXPLORE THE CONTEXT: The excerpts from this document explain the reasons for the excommunication of Frederick II, who was the King of Italy and Holy Roman Emperor after Otto IV from 1220 to 1250. He was excommunicated from the church four times during his reign.

PRIMARY SOURCE: CHURCH DOCUMENT

The Excommunication of Frederick II, 1239

1. By the authority of the Father, Son, and Holy Spirit, and of the blessed apostles Peter and Paul, and by our own authority, we excommunicate and anathematize Frederick the so-called emperor, because he has incited rebellion in Rome against the Roman church, for the purpose of driving the pope and his brothers [the cardinals] from the apostolic seat, thus violating the dignity and honor of the apostolic seat, the liberty of the church, and the oath which he swore to the church.

3. We excommunicate and anathematize him because he has not allowed the vacancies in certain bishoprics and churches to be filled, thereby imperiling the liberty of the church, and destroying the true faith, because in the absence of the pastor there is no one to declare unto the people the word of God or to care for their souls . . .

9. We excommunicate and anathematize him because he has occupied and wasted the lands of some of the nobles of his kingdom which were held by the church.

13. Because he has extorted taxes and other payments from the churches and monasteries of his kingdom contrary to the treaty of peace.

16. We excommunicate and anathematize him because he has hindered the recovery of the Holy Land and the restoration of the Roman empire.

We absolve all his subjects from their oaths of fidelity to him, forbidding them to show him fidelity as long as he is under excommunication. We shall admonish him again to give up oppressing and injuring the nobles, the poor, the widows and orphans, and others of his land, and then we shall proceed to act ourselves in the matter. For all and each of these causes, in regard to which we have frequently admonished him to no purpose, we excommunicate and anathematize him. In regard to the accusation of heresy which is made against Frederick, we shall consider and act upon this in the proper place and time.

—from *A Source Book for Medieval History* by Oliver J. Thatcher and Edgar H. McNeal

VOCABULARY

excommunicate: to exclude from church membership and rights

anathematize: condemn

apostolic: relating to the succession of spiritual authority from the twelve apostles

bishoprics: the rank of bishop

absolve: to pardon a sin

heresy: opinions contrary to church doctrine

1 **ANALYZING CENTRAL IDEAS** What is the central purpose of the document?

_____

_____

_____

2 CIVICS **CITING TEXT EVIDENCE** Frederick II had attempted to establish a strong centralized state in Italy. What evidence best shows that his attempts contributed to his excommunication?

_____

_____

_____

3 **DRAWING CONCLUSIONS** Because the state and church were a centralized power during this time, how might Frederick II have been able to prove whether he did or did not do the things he was accused of?

_____

_____

_____

_____

4 **INTERPRETING** If Frederick II was the Holy Roman Emperor, who is the "we" writing the document?

_____

_____

_____

5 **DRAWING CONCLUSIONS** Frederick II was excommunicated four times. What does that suggest about the claims in the document?

_____

_____

_____

_____

ESSENTIAL QUESTIONS

How can changes to political systems impact economic activities?

How is society influenced by changes in political and economic systems?

Magna Carta of England

DIRECTIONS: Read the document. Then respond to the questions that follow.

EXPLORE THE CONTEXT: In the thirteenth century, British nobles turned against monarchical authority and forced the king to sign the Magna Carta ("Great Charter"). This document set forth feudal customs, based on the rights and obligations of both the king and his knights, in a written form. King John signed the original document at Runnymede, near Windsor, in 1215 C.E. Later monarchs, as evidenced by the text below, also agreed to the provisions of the charter.

VOCABULARY

realm: kingdom

in perpetuity: for a period with no fixed end date

heir: a person entitled to the property or title of another after the latter's death

bailiff: a legal official

PRIMARY SOURCE: WRITTEN DECLARATION

"Edward by the grace of God King of England, lord of Ireland and duke of Aquitaine sends greetings to all to whom the present letters come. We have inspected the great charter of the lord Henry, late King of England, our father, concerning the liberties of England in these words:

Henry by the grace of God King of England, lord of Ireland, duke of Normandy and Aquitaine and count of Anjou sends greetings to his archbishops, bishops, abbots, priors, earls, barons, sheriffs, reeves, ministers and all his bailiffs and faithful men inspecting the present charter. Know that we, at the prompting of God and for the health of our soul and the souls of our ancestors and successors, for the glory of holy Church and the improvement of our realm, freely and out of our good will have given and granted to the archbishops, bishops, abbots, priors, earls, barons and all of our realm these liberties written below to hold in our realm of England in perpetuity.

(1) In the first place we grant to God and confirm by this our present charter for ourselves and our heirs in perpetuity that the English Church is to be free and to have all its rights fully and its liberties entirely. We furthermore grant and give to all the freemen of our realm for ourselves and our heirs in perpetuity the liberties written below to have and to hold to them and their heirs from us and our heirs in perpetuity. . . .

(8) Neither we nor our bailiffs will seize any land or rent for any debt, as long as the existing chattels of the debtor suffice for the payment of the debt and as long as the debtor is ready to pay the debt, nor will the debtor's guarantors be distrained for so long as the principal debtor is able to pay the debt; and should the principal debtor default in his payment of the debt, not having the means to repay it, or should he refuse to pay it despite being able to do so, the guarantors will answer for the debt and, if they wish, they are to have the lands and rents of the debtor until they are repaid the debt that previously they paid on behalf of the debtor, unless the principal debtor can show that he is quit in respect to these guarantors.

(9) The city of London is to have all its ancient liberties and customs. Moreover we wish and grant that all other cities and boroughs and vills and the barons of the Cinque Ports and all ports are to have all their liberties and free customs.

(10) No-one is to be distrained to do more service for a knight's fee or for any other free tenement than is due from it.

(11) Common pleas are not to follow our court but are to be held in a certain fixed place."

—Magna Carta, 1297

1 **ANALYZING CENTRAL IDEAS** Is the text arguing for or against extending a monarch's powers? Explain your answer.

_____

_____

_____

_____

_____

2 **IDENTIFYING CONNECTIONS** Who would the provisions in this text primarily benefit? Explain your answer.

_____

_____

_____

_____

3 **IDENTIFYING BIAS** How might the writers of this document be demonstrating class bias?

_____

_____

_____

_____

4 **UNDERSTANDING CONTEXT** What events led to writing of the document?

_____

_____

_____

_____

5 **CIVICS** What was the significance of a fixed court as set forth in Article 11?

_____

_____

_____

ESSENTIAL QUESTIONS

How can changes to political systems impact economic activities?

How is society influenced by changes in political and economic systems?

My Notes

_____

_____

_____

_____

_____

_____

_____

_____

_____

_____

_____

_____

_____

1 Think About It

Review the evidence you gathered as you read the chapter that helped you answer the Supporting Questions. Were you able to answer each Supporting Question? If not, what additional evidence do you think you need to gather to prepare your answers?

_____

_____

_____

2 Organize Your Evidence

Complete the chart below with information you learned about medieval kingdoms in Europe.

Feudalism	Peasants, Trades, and Cities	The Growth of European Kingdoms

3 Talk About It

Work in small groups. With your group discuss how at least one change to a political system in medieval Europe affected the economics of the region.

_____

_____

_____

_____

_____

_____

_____

4 Write About It

Choose one of the medieval kingdoms of Europe and explain how changes in the political and economic systems influenced the society.

_____

_____

_____

_____

_____

_____

_____

5 Connect to the Essential Question

Following your work in steps 3 and 4, choose one of the medieval kingdoms that you identified as either having an economy changed by a political system or having a society influenced by political and economic systems. Then write and design a graphic novel to describe the changes, their origins, and their effects. Include information on both the places and the people involved. Be sure to include the historical context as well as factual support for your viewpoint.

CITIZENSHIP
TAKE ACTION

MAKE CONNECTIONS Many people today do not realize the influence that medieval Europe has had on our modern society. The work of artisans and craftsmen of the era continue to be part of our everyday life, culture, and even our entertainment.

DIRECTIONS: Work in groups to create a video advertisement for an artisan product or craft that was invented or made popular in one of the medieval kingdoms.

Record and play the advertisement for the class.

Civilizations of East Asia, 220–1500

ESSENTIAL QUESTIONS

What qualities define power struggles and stable periods of rule?

How can invasion change the lives of people in conquered lands?

Think about how these two questions might relate to a region like East Asia.

TALK ABOUT IT

With a partner, discuss what information you would need to know to answer these two questions as they relate to East Asia during the medieval period. For example, what power struggles took place in East Asia during this time? Which lands were conquered, and by whom?

DIRECTIONS: Now write down three additional questions that you need to answer to describe the effects of power struggles, stable periods of rule, and invasions on people in East Asia.

MY RESEARCH QUESTIONS

Supporting Question 1:

_____

_____

Supporting Question 2:

_____

_____

Supporting Question 3:

_____

_____

_____

China Reunified

DIRECTIONS: Search for evidence in the lesson to help you answer the following questions.

1 **COMPARING** Complete the chart below to compare the Sui, Tang, and Song dynasties.

Dynasty	Time Period	Accomplishments	Weaknesses	Reason for Fall
Sui				
Tang				
Song				

ESSENTIAL QUESTIONS

What qualities define power struggles and stable periods of rule?

How can invasion change the lives of people in conquered lands?

As you gather evidence to answer the Essential Question, think about:

- how the Sui, Tang, and Song dynasties brought progress, stability, and a mature political system to China.

- how trade expanded during this period, stimulated by new technological developments.

- how rebellions and unrest brought an end to the Sui and Tang dynasties and Mongol invasions ended the Song dynasty.

My Notes

_____

_____

_____

_____

_____

2 IDENTIFYING CAUSES Why did the Chinese rebel against Sui Yangdi, the second Sui emperor?

_____

_____

3 ECONOMICS How did the Tang create a more stable economy in China?

_____

_____

4 IDENTIFYING EFFECTS What effects did China's northern neighbors have on the Song dynasty?

_____

_____

_____

5 SUMMARIZING Complete the web diagram below to identify technological developments that stimulated trade during the Tang and Song dynasties.

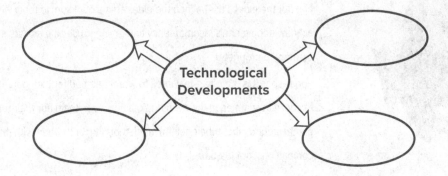

6 ECONOMICS How did trade change during the Tang and Song dynasties?

_____

_____

_____

7 IDENTIFYING CONNECTIONS How was the rise of the scholar-gentry related to the development of a mature political system in China?

_____

_____

_____

_____

_____

Confucius. The Sacred Books of China - The Texts of Confucianism. Part III - The Li Kî, I-X. Translated by James Legge. In The Sacred Books of the East - Translated by Various Oriental Scholars. Vol. XXVII. Edited by F. Max Müller. Oxford: The Clarendon Press, 1885.

ESSENTIAL QUESTION

What qualities define power struggles and stable periods of rule?

The Rules of Propriety

DIRECTIONS: Read the excerpts. Then answer the questions that follow.

EXPLORE THE CONTEXT: As you have read, Confucian principles became the basis for Chinese government during the Han dynasty, which introduced the civil service examination as the main method of recruiting officials for the government bureaucracy. The Tang restored the civil service examination, and young men prepared to take the examination by memorizing all the Confucian classics. One of these classics is the *Lî Kî*, or *Liji*, usually translated as "The Book of Rites" or "Record of Rites." Often attributed to Confucius himself, it is a collection of various texts that describe religious practices and appropriate behaviors.

PRIMARY SOURCE: BOOK EXCERPT

1. In going to take counsel with an elder, one must carry a stool and a staff with him (for the elder's use). When the elder asks a question, to reply without acknowledging one's incompetency and (trying to) decline answering, is contrary to propriety.

2. For all sons it is the rule: --In winter, to warm (the bed for their parents), and to cool it in summer; in the evening, to adjust everything (for their repose), and to inquire (about their health) in the morning; and, when with their companions, not to quarrel. . . .

5. A son, when he is going abroad, must inform (his parents where he is going); when he returns, he must present himself before them. Where he travels must be in some fixed (region); what he engages in must be some (reputable) occupation.

6. In ordinary conversation (with his parents), he does not use the term 'old' (with reference to them).

7. He should serve one twice as old as himself as he serves his father, one ten years older than himself as an elder brother; with one five years older he should walk shoulder to shoulder, but (a little) behind him. . . .

12. He should be (as if he were) hearing (his parents) when there is no voice from them, and as seeing them when they are not actually there.

— from *The Lî Kî: A Collection of Treatises on the Rules of Propriety or Ceremonial Usages,* edited by Max F. Müller, 1885.

VOCABULARY

propriety: proper behavior or manners

elder: an older person

repose: rest or sleep

reputable: respectable or honorable

1 **ANALYZING CENTRAL IDEAS** What relationship is the main focus of these excerpts?

_____

_____

2 **IDENTIFYING CONNECTIONS** A well-known saying of Confucius is: "The duty of children to their parents is the fountains, whence all other virtues spring." How do these excerpts develop this idea?

_____

_____

_____

3 **SUMMARIZING** What specific behaviors is a son supposed to do (or not do)?

_____

_____

_____

_____

_____

_____

4 **DETERMINING MEANING** What does rMaybe ule 12 mean by "He should be (as if he were) hearing (his parents) when there is no voice from them, and as seeing them when they are not actually there"?

_____

_____

5 **CIVICS** Why might the government have included texts such as these in the training of candidates for government positions?

_____

_____

_____

_____

_____

ESSENTIAL QUESTION

What qualities define power struggles and stable periods of rule?

Military Might

DIRECTIONS: Study the image. Then respond to the questions that follow.

EXPLORE THE CONTEXT: During the Tang dynasty (618–907 A.D.), China progressed on many fronts: industrial, agricultural, economic, and technological. In particular, the country made significant advances in military technology. The Chinese began making steel, which they used to craft swords and sickles. They also invented gunpowder. Initially, they used gunpowder for explosives, though its use in firearms would lead to the later development of the "gunpowder empires."

PRIMARY SOURCE: CAVE PAINTING

1 **IDENTIFYING** What is the subject of this cave painting, and what is its significance?

_____

_____

_____

2 **INTREPRETING** What scene does this painting depict?

_____

_____

_____

3 **INTEGRATING VISUAL INFORMATION** Based on the colors and other elements of this painting, how did the artist likely feel about the subject of the painting?

_____

_____

_____

4 **INFERRING** What does this image tell us about Tang military strategies during this time?

_____

_____

_____

_____

5 CIVICS How could this painting be interpreted as a political statement?

_____

_____

_____

_____

ESSENTIAL QUESTIONS

What qualities define power struggles and stable periods of rule?

How can invasion change the lives of people in conquered lands?

As you gather evidence to answer the Essential Questions, think about:

- how the ruler Kublai Khan completed the Mongol conquest of the Song and established the Yuan dynasty.
- how the Mongol dynasty won the support of many Chinese people.
- how Mongol rulers increased trade.
- how cultural advancements in the arts reached their height during the Tang, Song, and Mongol dynasties.

My Notes

_____

_____

_____

_____

_____

The Mongols and Chinese Culture

DIRECTIONS: Search for evidence in the lesson to help you answer the following questions.

1 **ANALYZING INFORMATION** What strengths allowed the Mongols to conquer much of the Eurasian landmass?

_____

_____

_____

2 **ANALYZING EVENTS** Why were the Mongols less successful in conquering Vietnam and Japan?

_____

_____

_____

_____

_____

3 **DRAWING CONCLUSIONS** Why was the Mongol dynasty that was established by Kublai Khan successful in ruling China?

_____

_____

_____

_____

_____

4 **ECONOMICS** How were the Mongols able to increase trade?

_____

_____

_____

5 IDENTIFYING CAUSES Why did Buddhism and Daoism gain support following the Han dynasty?

_____

_____

_____

_____

_____

_____

6 EVALUATING INFORMATION Why did the Song dynasty give official support to neo-Confucianism?

_____

_____

_____

_____

_____

_____

_____

7 SUMMARIZING Complete the chart below to describe the cultural advancements in China in printing, poetry, porcelain, and landscape painting.

	Advancements
Printing	
Poetry	
Porcelain	
Landscape Painting	

ESSENTIAL QUESTION

What qualities define power struggles and stable periods of rule?

VOCABULARY

inauguration: the act of placing someone in an official job

nominally: in name only

Tartars: nomadic people of northeastern Mongolia

pastoral: related to grazing sheep or cattle

grandeur: greatness

confined: limited

toil: hard work

roam: wander, travel

Genghis Khan

DIRECTIONS: Read the excerpt. Then respond to the questions that follow.

EXPLORE THE CONTEXT: Genghis Khan, or "strong ruler," was the title given to the Mongol leader Temüjin. After conquering much of Eurasia, he set up his capital at Karakorum in what is now north-central Mongolia. However, as this excerpt explains, the Mongols were a pastoral, nomadic people, so they looked down upon city-dwellers.

SECONDARY SOURCE: BOOK EXCERPT

66 After the ceremonies of the inauguration were concluded, Genghis Khan returned, with the officers of his court and his immediate followers, to Karakorom. This town, though nominally the capital of the empire, was, after all, quite an insignificant place. . . . The Monguls and Tartars led almost exclusively a wandering and pastoral life, and all their ideas of wealth and grandeur were associated with great flocks and herds of cattle, and handsome tents, and long trains of wagons loaded with stores of clothing, arms, and other movables, and vast encampments in the neighborhood of rich and extended pasture-grounds. Those who lived permanently in fixed houses they looked down upon as an inferior class, confined to one spot by their poverty or their toil, while they themselves could roam at liberty with their flocks. 99

—from *Genghis Khan, Makers of History,* 1901

Abbott, Jacob. 1901. Genghis Khan. New York, London: Harper & Brothers Publishers.

1 **INTERPRETING** Based on this excerpt, why was Karakorum "quite an insignificant place" even though it was Genghis Khan's capital?

_____

_____

_____

_____

2 ECONOMICS According to this excerpt, what did the Mongols and Tartars consider signs of wealth?

_____

_____

_____

_____

3 ANALYZING TEXT Why did the Mongols looked down upon city-dwellers?

_____

_____

_____

_____

_____

4A COMPARING Genghis Khan's grandson Kublai Khan established his capital at Khanbalik in China. Based on what you have read about Khanbalik, how did it compare to Karakorum?

_____

_____

_____

_____

_____

4B DRAWING CONCLUSIONS What does this indicate about the change in Mongol attitudes from the time of Genghis Khan to that of Kublai Khan?

_____

_____

_____

_____

_____

_____

ESSENTIAL QUESTION

What qualities define power struggles and stable periods of rule?

Clearing Up At Dawn/Spring Morning

DIRECTIONS: Read the following poems from the Tang era. Then respond to the questions that follow.

EXPLORE THE CONTEXT: As you have read, the Tang era is viewed as the golden age of poetry in China. Two of the most important poets during this era were Li Bo and Du Fu. The first poem below, "Clearing Up At Dawn," was written by Li Bo, while the second, "Spring Morning," was written by Du Fu. Like many poems of this era, these two poems celebrate the beauty of nature.

VOCABULARY

sparse: scattered or infrequent

teem: are abundant

thrushes: medium-sized songbirds that are usually brown with a spotted breast

dabbled: splashed, smeared, or mottled

swallows: small, long-winged birds that fly swiftly and gracefully

lulls: soothes or puts to sleep

PRIMARY SOURCE: POETRY

The fields are chill; the sparse rain has stopped;

The colours of Spring teem on every side.

With leaping fish the blue pond is full;

With singing thrushes the green boughs droop.

The flowers of the field have dabbled their powdered cheeks;

The mountain grasses are bent level at the waist.

By the bamboo stream the last fragments of cloud

Blown by the wind slowly scatter away.

—Li Bo, "Clearing Up At Dawn"

Slowly—the sun!

Light—high, low.

Gently the winds,

Perfumes, trees, flowers, blow.

Soft mud makes the swallows sweep.

Warm sand lulls the swans to sleep.

Water is white.

But the birds are whiter.

Mountains are purple,

Petals burn.

Time—*Spring. Spring—and the old delight!*

Will there ever be one when I, too, may return?

—Du Fu, "Spring Morning"

1 **ANALYZING TEXTS** Personification is attributing human characteristics to non-human things. What examples of personification do you see in "Clearing Up At Dawn"?

_____

_____

_____

_____

2 **GEOGRAPHY** If you did not already know that "Clearing Up At Dawn" was written by a Chinese poet, what phrase in the poem might provide a clue that the poem is describing a scene in China or another part of Asia?

_____

_____

_____

3 **UNDERSTANDING CONTEXT** In "Spring Morning," what does the line "Slowly—the sun!" indicate about the time of day this poem is describing?

_____

_____

_____

_____

4 **CITING TEXT EVIDENCE** In "Spring Morning," what words express a feeling of gentleness?

_____

_____

_____

5 **COMPARING** What similarities do you see between the two poems?

_____

_____

_____

_____

Early Japan and Korea

DIRECTIONS: Search for evidence in the lesson to help you answer the following questions.

1 **DESCRIBING** What steps did Shōtoku Taishi take to try to unify the Japanese clans?

_____

_____

_____

_____

2 **SUMMARIZING** Complete the chart below to describe three periods in Japanese history.

	Nara Period	**Heian Period**	**Kamakura Shogunate**
Time Period			
Location of Capital			
Role of Emperor			
Features of Government			

ESSENTIAL QUESTIONS

What qualities define power struggles and stable periods of rule?

How can invasion change the lives of people in conquered lands?

As you gather evidence to answer the Essential Question, think about:

- how a Yamato prince tried to unify early Japan by creating a centralized government based on the Chinese model.

- how power struggles between Japan's central government and aristocrats resulted in the collapse of central rule.

- how a new class of military servants—the samurai—emerged.

- why Minamoto Yoritomo set up a new system of government known as the shogunate.

- how a civil war brought an end to centralized power in Japan.

- how Korea struggled for independence against the Chinese.

My Notes

_____

_____

_____

3 COMPARING How were the samurai similar to knights in Europe?

_____

_____

4 ANALYZING INFORMATION Why did Minamoto Yoritomo set up the shogunate?

_____

_____

_____

5 IDENTIFYING EFFECTS What was the ultimate outcome of the power struggles between the central government and aristocrats during the fourteenth and fifteenth centuries?

_____

_____

_____

6 ECONOMICS Why was trade slow to develop in early Japan, and why did it begin to develop in the Kamakura period?

_____

_____

7 CONTRASTING How were the origins of Shinto and Buddhism in Japan different?

_____

_____

8 IDENTIFYING CAUSES Why were women the main writers of prose fiction in early Japan?

_____

_____

9 ANALYZING EVENTS How did the Mongol invasion affect Korea?

_____

_____

_____

Copyright © McGraw-Hill Education   Sansom, George. 1958. A History of Japan to 1334. Stanford, California: Stanford University Press.

ESSENTIAL QUESTION

What qualities define power struggles and stable periods of rule?

VOCABULARY

subordinates: those of lower rank

obvious: easy to see

distinction: difference

misdeeds: errors

circumstances: situations

provocation: baiting

haste: speed

remorse: regret, sorrow

Hojo Shigetoki's Letter of Instruction to His Son Nagatoki

DIRECTIONS: Read the excerpt. Then respond to the questions that follow.

EXPLORE THE CONTEXT: Hojo Shigetoki was a leading samurai in Japan. In 1247, the Kamakura shoguns appointed his 18-year-old son to a key position. Shigetoki then wrote his son a letter instructing him in the ways of the warrior.

PRIMARY SOURCE: LETTER

❝. . . In dealing with subordinates do not make an obvious distinction between good and not-good. Use the same kind of language, give the same kind of treatment to all, and thus you will get the best out of the worst. But you yourself must not lose sight of the distinction between good character and bad character, between capable and incapable. You must be fair, but in practice you must not forget the difference between men who are useful and men who are not. Remember that the key to discipline is fair treatment in rewards and in punishments. But make allowances for minor misdeeds in young soldiers and others, if their conduct is usually good . . . Remember, however, that there are times when a commander must exercise his power of deciding questions of life or death. In those circumstances since human life is at stake you must give most careful thought to your action. Never kill or wound a man in anger, however great the provocation. Better get somebody else to administer the proper punishment. Decisions made in haste before your feelings are calm can only lead to remorse. Close your eyes and reflect carefully when you have a difficult decision to make. When accusations are brought to you, always remember that there must be another side to the question. Do not merely indulge in anger. To give fair decisions is the most important thing not only in commanding soldiers but also in governing a country. ❞

1A **ANALYZING TEXTS** Based on the information in the Explore the Context paragraph and the advice that Shigetoki gives in this excerpt, what is his purpose in writing the letter?

_____

_____

_____

1B **DRAWING CONCLUSIONS** Based on the excerpt, what kind of position will Shigetoki's son likely be assuming? How do you know this?

_____

_____

_____

_____

2 **DETERMINING CENTRAL IDEAS** What is the main idea of this excerpt?

_____

_____

_____

_____

3 **DETERMINING MEANING** What does Shigetoki mean when he says "thus you will get the best out of the worst"?

_____

_____

_____

_____

4 **HISTORY** Based on the advice that Shigetoki gives, what conclusions can you draw about Bushido, the samurai's code of conduct?

_____

_____

_____

The Tale of Genji

Copyright © McGraw-Hill Education   Lady Shikib, Murasaki. Genji Monogatari (The Tale of Genji). Tr. by Suematsu Kencho, Penguin, 1900.

ESSENTIAL QUESTION

What qualities define power struggles and stable periods of rule?

VOCABULARY

disdainfully: with contempt or scorn

malignant: showing hatred, evil

indignant: angry or resentful

diffident: lacking confidence in one's own worth

animadversion: criticism or blame

improbable: unlikely

allude: refer

DIRECTIONS: Read the excerpt. Then respond to the questions that follow.

EXPLORE THE CONTEXT: *The Tale of Genji* is one of the world's first great novels and is often considered to be the greatest work in Japanese literature. It was written in the 11th century by Murasaki Shikibu, who was a lady-in-waiting at the Japanese court. While much of it deals with a fictional prince named Genji and his love life, it also provides a great deal of information about life at the Japanese court during the Heian period.

PRIMARY SOURCE: BOOK EXCERPT

❝ In the reign of a certain Emperor, whose name is unknown to us, there was, among the Niogo and Kôyi [official titles held by Court ladies] of the Imperial Court, *one* who, though she was not of high birth, enjoyed the full tide of Royal favor. Hence her superiors, each one of whom had always been thinking—"I shall be the one," gazed upon her disdainfully with malignant eyes, and her equals and inferiors were more indignant still.

Such being the state of affairs, the anxiety which she had to endure was great and constant, and this was probably the reason why her health was at last so much affected, that she was often compelled to absent herself from Court, and to retire to the residence of her mother.

Her father, who was a Dainagon [the name of a Court office], was dead; but her mother, being a woman of good sense, gave her every possible guidance in the due performance of Court ceremony, so that in this respect she seemed but little different from those whose fathers and mothers were still alive to bring them before public notice, yet, nevertheless, her friendliness made her oftentimes feel very diffident from the want of any patron of influence.

These circumstances, however, only tended to make the favor shown to her by the Emperor wax warmer and warmer, and it was even shown to such an extent as to become a warning to after-generations. There had been instances in China in which favoritism such as this had caused national disturbance and disaster; and thus the matter became a subject of public animadversion, and it seemed not improbable that people would begin to allude even to the example of Yô-ki-hi [a celebrated and beautiful favorite of an emperor of the Tang dynasty in China, whose administration was disturbed by a rebellion, said to have been caused by the neglect of his duties for her sake]. ❞

— from Murasaki Shikibu, *The Tale of Genji*, translated by Suematsu Kencho, 1900

1 **DRAWING CONCLUSIONS** What does this excerpt indicate about relationships at the Imperial Court?

_____

_____

_____

2 **DESCRIBING** How would you describe the character who is the focus of this excerpt?

_____

_____

_____

_____

3 **IDENTIFYING CAUSES** What is the reason for the intense anxiety that the girl feels?

_____

_____

_____

_____

4A HISTORY Based on what you know about Tang history, what is the writer referring to when she says "there had been instances in China in which favoritism such as this had caused national disturbance and disaster"?

_____

_____

_____

_____

4B **INFERRING** Based on what you know about this event in Chinese history, why would people have wanted to allude to the example of Yô-ki-hi (or Yang Guifei)?

_____

_____

_____

_____

India and Southeast Asia

DIRECTIONS: Search for evidence in the lesson to help you answer the following questions.

1 HISTORY How did the influence of Buddhism in India change over time?

_____

_____

_____

_____

_____

_____

_____

_____

2 **ANALYZING EVENTS** How did Islam expand in the Indian subcontinent?

_____

_____

_____

_____

_____

_____

_____

_____

_____

_____

ESSENTIAL QUESTIONS

What qualities define power struggles and stable periods of rule?

How can invasion change the lives of people in conquered lands?

As you gather evidence to answer the Essential Question, think about:

- how political disunity led to the expansion of Islam but Islamic rule created tension in Indian society.

- why Southeast Asia was never unified under a single government.

- how the Chinese influenced Vietnamese government.

- how Angkor and Thai culture blended to create modern Thailand.

My Notes

_____

_____

_____

_____

_____

3 EVALUATING What impact did Timur Lenk's invasion have on India?

_____

4 IDENTIFYING EFFECTS What effect did Islamic rule have on Indian society?

_____
_____
_____
_____
_____

5 GEOGRAPHY Why was Southeast Asia never unified under a single government?

_____
_____
_____

6 COMPARING Complete the chart below to compare the cultures of Southeast Asia.

	Government	Religion	Primary Economic Activity
Dai Viet (Vietnam)			
Angkor/Cambodia		Hinduism and later Buddhism	
Thai			
Pagan (Burma)			
Majapahit (Malay)			
Melaka (Malay)			

7 SUMMARIZING How were societies in Southeast Asia organized?

_____
_____
_____
_____

ESSENTIAL QUESTION

What qualities define power struggles and stable periods of rule?

VOCABULARY

contrived: planned or plotted

pervaded: filled, or affected strongly

mutual: shared or reciprocal

brahman: a member of the Hindu priestly class

appeased: soothed or pacified

The Adventures of Ten Princes

DIRECTIONS: Read the excerpt. Then respond to the questions that follow.

EXPLORE THE CONTEXT: Dandin was a writer who lived in India in the 6th and 7th centuries. He wrote both prose romances and literary criticism. His *Dasakumaracharitam,* often translated as *The Adventures of Ten Princes,* tells the stories of 10 different princes as they search for love. The excerpt below is from a story about a prince named Râjavâhana.

PRIMARY SOURCE: SHORT STORY

❝On the day of the festival, the parks and gardens were crowded with people, some engaged in various sports, some walking about or sitting under the trees, looking at the players.

Among them was the Princess Avantisundari, who was sitting on a sandy spot, under a large tree, attended by her women, especially by her dear friend Bâlachandrika, and making offerings to the god of various perfumes and flowers. The prince [Râjavâhana] also walked in the park with his friend Pushpodbhava; and wishing to see the princess, of whose grace and beauty he had already heard, contrived to approach; and being encouraged by Bâlachandrika with a gesture of the hand, came and stood very near her.

Then, indeed, having an opportunity of observing her, he was struck by her exceeding beauty. She seemed to him as if formed by the god of love with everything most beautiful in the world; and, as he gazed, he felt more and more entranced, till almost unconsciously he was deeply in love.

She . . . was almost equally affected, and, pervaded by strong feeling, trembled like the branch of a creeping plant agitated by a gentle wind. . . .

Then Râjavâhana, more deeply in love even than the princess, thought to himself, "There surely must be some reason for this very sudden attraction which I feel towards her. She must have been my beloved wife in a former existence. Perhaps a curse was laid upon us; and now that is removed. If so, the recognition ought to be mutual; at all events I will try what I can do to produce the same feeling in her which exists in my mind."

While he was considering how this might be accomplished, a swan approached the princess, as if expecting to be fed or caressed; and in sport, she desired Bâlachandrika to catch it.

Inspired by this circumstance with a happy thought, Râjavâhana said to the princess, "Will you allow me to tell you a short story? There was formerly a king called Samba. When walking one day together with his beloved wife at the side of a small lake in the pleasure-grounds, he saw a swan asleep, just under the bank. Having caught it, he tied its legs together, put it down again on the ground, and . . . amused himself with laughing at its awkward attempts to walk. Then the swan suddenly spoke: 'O king, though in the form of a swan, I am a devout brahman; and since you have thus, without cause, ill-treated me while sitting quiet here, engaged in meditation, I lay my curse upon you, and you shall endure the pain of separation from your beloved wife.'

"Hearing this, the king, alarmed and distressed, bowed respectfully to the ground, and said, 'O mighty sage, forgive an act done through ignorance.'

"Then that holy person, having his anger appeased, answered, 'My words cannot be made of no effect. I will, however, so far modify the curse that it will not take place during your present existence; but in a future birth, when you are united to the same lady in another body, you must endure the misery of separation from her for two months, though you will afterwards enjoy very great happiness with her; and I will also confer on you both the power of recognising each other in your next existence,'—I beg of you therefore not to tie this bird which you were wishing to catch."

The princess, hearing this story, was quite ready to believe it; and from her own feelings was convinced that it really referred to a previous existence of herself, now brought to her recollection; and that the love which she felt springing up in her heart was directed towards one who had formerly been her husband. With a sweet smile, she answered: "Doubtless Samba tied the bird in that way on purpose to obtain the power of recognition in another birth; and it was very cleverly managed by him." 99

— from Dandin, *The Adventures of Ten Princes*

1A **EVALUATING INFORMATION** To what does Râjavâhana attribute the sudden attraction he feels for the Princess Avantisundari?

_____

1B HISTORY What does this indicate about his religious beliefs?

_____

2A **SUMMARIZING** What strategy does the prince use to convince the princess that they are destined for each other?

_____
_____

2B **CITING TEXT EVIDENCE** Was his strategy successful? Cite evidence from the excerpt to support your answer.

_____
_____
_____

3 **ANALYZING TEXT** What supernatural or fantastic elements are found in the prince's story?

_____
_____

4 **DRAWING CONCLUSIONS** If the prince's story is true, then who was he in a previous life?

_____

ESSENTIAL QUESTION

What qualities define power struggles and stable periods of rule?

Khajuraho Temple

DIRECTIONS: Study the image. Then respond to the questions that follow.

EXPLORE THE CONTEXT: Some of the best examples of Hindu temple art are found in Khajuraho in the northern Madhya Pradesh state of central India. Khajuraho was one of the capitals of the Chandela kings who ruled in north-central India from the 9th to the 11th centuries. The temples at Khajuraho were built from the mid-10th to the mid-11th centuries and were made of sandstone, ornately carved with sculptures that were often sensual in nature. After the 14th century, Khajuraho was forgotten, which likely saved it from damage by Muslim conquerors. It was rediscovered in 1838 by a British army captain.

PRIMARY SOURCE: PHOTOGRAPH/HINDU TEMPLE

1 IDENTIFYING CONNECTIONS Read the description of Hindu temples in this lesson. What features do you see in this image?

_____

_____

_____

_____

2 DESCRIBING How else would you describe this temple?

_____

_____

_____

3 CONSTRUCTING HYPOTHESES Why might a lion-type figure have been placed prominently at the front of the shrine?

_____

_____

_____

4A COMPARING Compare this image to the picture of Angkor Wat in this lesson. What similarities do you see?

_____

_____

_____

_____

4B HISTORY What does this comparison indicate about the influence of Indian culture in Southeast Asia?

_____

_____

_____

_____

ESSENTIAL QUESTIONS

What qualities define power struggles and stable periods of rule?

How can invasion change the lives of people in conquered lands?

My Notes

_____

_____

_____

_____

_____

_____

_____

_____

_____

_____

_____

_____

_____

① Think About It

Review the supporting questions you developed at the beginning of the chapter and the evidence you gathered. Were you able to find information to answer each supporting question? If not, what additional evidence do you need to gather?

_____

_____

_____

② Organize Your Evidence

On a separate paper complete the chart below with information you learned about how invasions, power struggles, and stable periods of rule affected people in East Asia.

Invasions	Power Struggles	Stable Periods of Rule

3 Talk About It

In a small group, discuss the effects of invasions, power struggles, and stable periods you noted in your charts. Did you note the same effects as you? If not, add information that the others shared to your own chart. Overall, what benefits do you see from stable periods of rule?

_____

_____

4 Write About It

Choose one country and write about the benefits stable periods had on that country. Describe the achievements that the people of that country were able to make during stable periods.

_____

_____

_____

5 Connect to the Essential Question

Choose one country and create a visual compare-and-contrast essay to show the difference between that country during invasions and/or power struggles and during stable periods of rule. Contrast the economy, politics, and cultural achievements during these different periods. Use pictures and other images to illustrate your points.

Invasions	China:
	Korea:
	India:
Power Struggles	China:
	Japan:
	India:
Stable Periods of Rule	China:
	Japan:

CITIZENSHIP
TAKE ACTION

MAKE CONNECTIONS As you have read, the Tang dynasty restored the civil service examination as the chief method of recruiting officials for the Chinese bureaucracy. Although there is no longer a single civil service exam for all federal jobs in the United States, written exams are still required for some jobs, such as certain jobs with the postal service. However, other requirements have replaced exams for many federal jobs.

Students who think they might be interested in a job in the civil service may want to consider applying for an internship. Some internships are open to high school students. Students who complete these internships may be eligible to convert the internship into a permanent position.

DIRECTIONS: Conduct research to learn more about the federal Internship Program. Find out how to locate possible internships and how to apply for them. Then prepare a brochure to explain what you have learned to other students. Design the brochure to be eye-catching, and proofread it carefully. Ask if you can make copies available in your school's guidance office.

_____
_____
_____
_____
_____
_____
_____
_____
_____
_____
_____
_____

Crusades and Culture in the Middle Ages

ESSENTIAL QUESTIONS

How did the Church influence political and cultural changes in medieval Europe?

How did both innovations and disruptive forces affect people during the Middle Ages?

Think about the different ways Europe changed and developed during the Middle Ages. How did power struggles both within the Church and between religious and secular leaders influence medieval Europe? Why did an intellectual and artistic revival blossom in Europe beginning in the 11th century? What were the lasting consequences of the disastrous forces that overwhelmed 14th century Europe?

TALK ABOUT IT

With a partner, discuss what you would need to know to answer these questions. For example, one question might be: "How did the Crusades reflect the power of the Church in medieval Europe?"

DIRECTIONS: Now write down three additional questions that will help you understand the factors that influenced political and cultural changes in medieval Europe. For example, you might ask, "Why was the Church such an important part of everyday life in medieval England? How did the Black Death and the Hundred Years' War impact religious, economic, and social life in Europe?"

MY RESEARCH QUESTIONS

Supporting Question 1:

_____

_____

Supporting Question 2:

_____

_____

Supporting Question 3:

_____

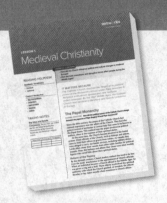

Medieval Christianity

DIRECTIONS: Search for evidence in the lesson to help you answer the following questions.

1A **DIFFERENTIATING** What was lay investiture? How did the view of Pope Gregory VII on lay investiture differ from that of King Henry IV?

_____

_____

_____

_____

_____

_____

ESSENTIAL QUESTION

How did the Church influence political and cultural changes in medieval Europe?

As you gather evidence to answer the Essential Question, think about:

- how the Church exercised political power during the Middle Ages.
- the impact of new religious orders on medieval Europe.
- how the Church impacted the daily lives of everyday people.

1B **HISTORY** Use the graphic organizer to explain how the Investiture Controversy was resolved at the Concordat of Worms.

Role of King in Appointing Bishops	Role of Church in Appointing Bishops

My Notes

_____

_____

_____

_____

_____

_____

_____

2 **EXPLAINING ISSUES** How did Pope Innocent III use interdicts to exert political power over secular rulers?

_____

_____

_____

_____

_____

3 CONTRASTING How might the new monastic orders of Cistercians, Franciscans, and Dominicans have been more effective than Benedictine monks in combating heresy?

_____

_____

_____

4 ANALYZING INDIVIDUALS Why is Hildegard of Bingen an important figure in medieval church history? In what way does she symbolize changes that were occurring in religious orders during the Middle Ages?

_____

_____

_____

_____

_____

5 EVALUATING INFORMATION How did the Church respond to people suspected of heresy? Do you think the Church's reaction was legitimate? Why or why not?

_____

_____

_____

_____

_____

_____

6 DESCRIBING What were some ways people in medieval Europe practiced their Christian faith?

_____

_____

_____

_____

_____

_____

Testament of Francis of Assisi

How did the Church influence political and cultural changes in medieval Europe?

DIRECTIONS: Read the excerpt. Then respond to the questions that follow.

EXPLORE THE CONTEXT: Francis of Assisi was born in 1181 to a wealthy Italian family. As a young man, he underwent a spiritual conversion that ultimately led him to take a vow of poverty. He begged for food while wandering the region near his birthplace of Assisi, preaching to a growing number of followers. The Franciscans, as they became known, lived among the people calling for a return to the simplicity of the early Church. Shortly before his death in 1226, Francis dictated what is known as his "Testament" (a statement of belief), in which he restated his views about the proper Christian life.

PRIMARY SOURCE: TESTAMENT

" The Lord gave to me, Brother Francis, thus to begin to do penance; for when I was in sin it seemed to me very bitter to see lepers, and the Lord Himself led me amongst them and I showed mercy to them. And when I left them, that which had seemed to me bitter was changed for me into sweetness of body and soul. And afterwards I remained a little and I left the world. And the Lord gave me so much faith in churches that I would simply pray and say thus: "We adore Thee Lord Jesus Christ here and in all Thy churches which are in the whole world, and we bless Thee because by Thy holy cross Thou hast redeemed the world."

. . .

And when the Lord gave me some brothers, no one showed me what I ought to do, but the Most High Himself revealed to me that I should live according to the form of the holy Gospel. And I caused it to be written in few words and simply, and the Lord Pope confirmed it for me. And those who came to take this life upon themselves gave to the poor all that they might have and they were content with one tunic, patched within and without, by those who wished, with a cord and breeches, and we wished for no more.

. . .

The Lord revealed to me this salutation, that we should say: "The Lord give thee peace." Let the brothers take care not to receive on any account churches, poor dwelling-places, and all other things that are constructed for them, unless they are as is becoming the holy poverty which we have promised in the Rule, always dwelling there as strangers and pilgrims. "

—St. Francis of Assisi (c. 1226)

VOCABULARY

penance: the act of doing a good deed to make up for a wrong one

redeemed: saved from sin

confirmed: approved

breeches: trousers ending above the knee

salutation: greeting

1 **ANALYZING INDIVIDUALS** According to Francis, what did God ask him to do to make up for his earlier, sinful lifestyle? How did this affect Francis's thinking?

_____

_____

_____

2 **INFERRING** What can you infer about social conditions in medieval Europe from this excerpt from the Testament of Francis?

_____

_____

_____

3 **DRAWING CONCLUSIONS** Many large, ornate cathedrals have been built in the name of Francis. What do you believe he would have thought about that? Explain your answer.

_____

_____

_____

_____

_____

4 **ANALYZING EVENTS** Why do you think the Church made Francis of Assisi a saint just two years after his death?

_____

_____

_____

_____

_____

5 **HISTORY** Assess the impact of Francis of Assis on the people and traditions of the Church.

_____

_____

_____

_____

ESSENTIAL QUESTION

How did the Church influence political and cultural changes in medieval Europe?

Decree Forbidding Lay Investiture

DIRECTIONS: Read the decree. Then respond to the questions that follow.

EXPLORE THE CONTEXT: The Investiture Controversy was a conflict that began in the eleventh century between Holy Roman Emperor Henry IV and Pope Gregory VII over who would control appointments of bishops (investiture). In November 1078, Gregory announced in the following decree that members of the clergy were forbidden from accepting investiture from lay people.

PRIMARY SOURCE: PAPAL DECREE

1. Decree of Nov. 19th, 1078, forbidding lay Investiture. Inasmuch as we have learned that, contrary to the establishments of the holy fathers, the investiture with churches is, in many places, performed by lay persons; and that from this cause many disturbances arise in the church by which the Christian religion is trodden under foot: we decree that no one of the clergy shall receive the investiture with a bishopric or abbey or church from the hand of an emperor or king or of any lay person, male or female. But if he shall presume to do so he shall clearly know that such investiture is bereft of apostolic authority, and that he himself shall lie under excommunication until fitting satisfaction shall have been rendered.

    —Pope Gregory VII (1078)

VOCABULARY

decree: ruling, judgment

contrary to: against

holy fathers: ancient and influential Christian theologians and writers

lay person: someone who is not a member of the clergy

trodden: trampled, stepped upon

bereft: lacking, without

excommunication: the act of expelling someone from the Church

satisfaction: an act of atonement assigned by a priest to make up for a sin.

rendered: carried out

1 EXPLAINING ISSUES What reasons does Gregory give for opposing the practice of lay investiture?

_____

_____

_____

_____

_____

_____

_____

_____

2 SUMMARIZING What is the punishment for a cleric who accepts a church office from a lay person?

_____

_____

_____

3 ANALYZING INDIVIDUALS Based on this decree, what do you think the relationship between Henry IV and Gregory VII was like? Explain your answer.

_____

_____

_____

_____

4 CIVICS Why do you think both kings and popes wanted the power to appoint bishops? What does the Investiture Controversy say about the relationship between church and state in medieval Europe?

_____

_____

_____

_____

_____

_____

5 COMPARING AND CONTRASTING TEXTS Compare the Decree Forbidding Lay Investiture with the Testament of Francis of Assisi. How is Gregory's vision of the Church different from that of Francis's?

_____

_____

_____

_____

_____

The Crusades

DIRECTIONS: Search for evidence in the lesson to help you answer the following questions.

1 **EXPLAINING ISSUES** Why did Europeans begin the Crusades?

_____

_____

_____

_____

_____

2 **ANALYZING EVENTS** Why do you think the crusaders established four separate states in the East? How did this impact the European economy?

_____

_____

_____

_____

_____

3 **DESCRIBING** Who was Saladin? Describe his role in the Third Crusade.

_____

_____

_____

_____

_____

ESSENTIAL QUESTION

How did the Church influence political and cultural changes in medieval Europe?

As you gather evidence to answer the Essential Question, think about:

- factors that led to the Crusades.
- who benefited because of the Crusades, and who did not.
- what the consequences of the Crusades were.

My Notes

_____

_____

_____

_____

_____

_____

_____

4 **IDENTIFYING CONNECTIONS** How did the economic success of Italian port cities during the Crusades impact the sacking of Constantinople in 1204?

_____

_____

_____

_____

5 **EVALUATING EVIDENCE** Why do you think the crusaders were ultimately unsuccessful?

_____

_____

_____

6A **IDENTIFYING CAUSES** How did the Crusades lead to the breakdown of the feudal system in Europe?

_____

_____

_____

_____

_____

6B **HISTORY** Use the graphic organizer to identify the major effects of the Crusades.

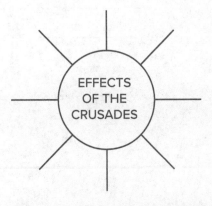

EFFECTS OF THE CRUSADES

Forgiveness of Sins

ESSENTIAL QUESTION

How did the Church influence political and cultural changes in medieval Europe?

DIRECTIONS: Read the excerpt. Then respond to the questions that follow.

EXPLORE THE CONTEXT: As early as the eighth century, Muslim armies from Spain periodically attempted to cross the Pyrenees Mountains into present-day France. There they encountered resistance from the Franks, Germanic peoples who controlled large portions of western Europe. In this excerpt, Pope Leo IV encourages the Frankish army to fight the Spanish Muslims, hoping to prevent their further spread into Christian territories.

PRIMARY SOURCE: PAPAL STATEMENT

> ❝ Now we hope that none of you will be slain, but we wish you to know that the kingdom of heaven will be given as a reward to those who shall be killed in this war. For the Omnipotent knows that they lost their lives fighting for the truth of the faith, for the preservation of their country, and the defense of the Christians. And therefore God will give them the reward which we have named. ❞
>
> —from *Forgiveness of Sins for Those Who Die in Battle with the Heathen* (847)

VOCABULARY

omnipotent: all-powerful; in this case, God

heathen: any non-Christian person

1 **DETERMINING POINT OF VIEW** Describe Pope Leo's point of view toward the Frankish soldiers and toward the Muslims. How do you know?

_____

_____

_____

_____

_____

_____

2 **ANALYZING TEXT** What reasons does the pope give to convince the Frankish soldiers to fight the Muslims? Do you think this language motivated the Franks to take up arms?

_____

_____

_____

_____

_____

_____

3 **COMPARING AND CONTRASTING TEXTS** How does this passage by Pope Leo compare to Pope Urban II's later speech at the Council of Clermont in 1095 regarding the Crusades?

_____

_____

_____

_____

4 **PREDICTING** Do you think Pope Leo would have supported the Crusades? Explain your reasons.

_____

_____

_____

_____

5 **HISTORY** Pope Leo made this statement almost 50 years after an earlier pope had crowned Frankish king Charlemagne emperor of the Romans. After Charlemagne's death in 814, his empire quickly began to weaken. Given this background, what do you think Pope Leo was trying to achieve?

_____

_____

_____

_____

ESSENTIAL QUESTION

How did the Church influence political and cultural changes in medieval Europe?

Crusaders

DIRECTIONS: Study the image. Then respond to the questions that follow.

EXPLORE THE CONTEXT: The *Chroniques de France* is a compilation of the history of France, composed by monks at the abbey of St. Denis in the late thirteenth century. The royal volume describes French history from the Fall of Troy through the death of King Louis IX (Saint Louis). Subsequent events were added to later volumes. This illustration depicts Louis IX setting out on the Seventh Crusade in 1248. Louis's army was defeated by a Muslim army in Egypt in 1250. He died in 1270 on a later Crusade to Tunisia.

PRIMARY SOURCE: ILLUMINATED MANUSCRIPT PAGE

—from *Chroniques de France*

1 **INTEGRATING VISUAL INFORMATION** Which figure in this illustration is King Louis? How do you know? Who are the people to the left of the illustration? What do they appear to be doing?

_____

_____

_____

_____

2 **INFERRING** What can you infer about the character of Louis IX? What do you think his relationship was with the Church?

_____

_____

_____

_____

_____

_____

3 **DRAWING CONCLUSIONS** Louis was defeated in his first Crusade to Egypt and died in his second Crusade to Tunisia. How are these facts compatible with the way he is depicted in this illustration?

_____

_____

_____

_____

_____

4 HISTORY What do you think was King Louis's attitude toward French Jews? Explain your answer.

_____

_____

_____

_____

_____

_____

_____

_____

ESSENTIAL QUESTION

How did both innovations and disruptive forces affect people during the Middle Ages?

As you gather evidence to answer the Essential Question, think about:

- the characteristics of Gothic architecture.
- how the university system began to develop in the Middle Ages.
- what types of literature flourished during the Middle Ages.

My Notes

_____

_____

_____

_____

_____

_____

_____

Culture of the Middle Ages

DIRECTIONS: Search for evidence in the lesson to help you answer the following questions.

1 **EVALUATING** How did the development of ribbed vaults, pointed arches, and flying buttresses in Gothic churches enhance the experience of worshippers?

_____

_____

_____

_____

_____

_____

_____

2A **COMPARING AND CONTRASTING** Use the graphic organizer to compare and contrast medieval universities with modern universities.

Medieval vs. Modern Universities	
Similarities	**Differences**

2B **EXPLAINING ISSUES** How did medieval university students apply scholasticism to their studies? In what way does scholasticism continue to impact education today?

_____

_____

_____

_____

_____

3 **HISTORY** Why might some medieval Church officials have disapproved of the ideas of Thomas Aquinas?

_____

_____

_____

4 **DESCRIBING** What were some popular subjects for medieval writers?

_____

_____

_____

5 **ANALYZING CHANGE** Why were epics and romances written in the vernacular rather than in Latin?

_____

_____

_____

6 **DRAWING CONCLUSIONS** Should historians consider the work of Geoffrey Chaucer to be a reliable representation of life in medieval England? What impact do you think Chaucer had on the development of English?

_____

_____

_____

_____

ESSENTIAL QUESTION

How did both innovations and disruptive forces affect people during the Middle Ages?

Founding of the University of Heidelberg

DIRECTIONS: Read the excerpt. Then respond to the questions that follow.

EXPLORE THE CONTEXT: After the death of Pope Gregory XI, the European Church divided into two hostile factions. With the Great Schism of 1378, two popes were elected: one residing in Avignon, France, and the other in Rome. The German Church, along with German royalty, sided with Rome. This forced German students to leave the renowned University of Paris, which sided with the French pope. Rupert I approached the Roman pope, Urban VI, for permission to establish a university. Rupert founded the University of Heidelberg in 1386 with the blessing of Pope Urban VI.

VOCABULARY

theology or *divinity*: religious studies

faculties: groups of departments at a university

canon law: laws of the Catholic Church

civil law: laws of the state

disposed: arranged

subservient: submissive, obedient

PRIMARY SOURCE: DECLARATION

66 We, Rupert the elder, by the grace of God Count Palatine of the Rhine, elector of the Holy Empire and duke of Bavaria—lest we seem to abuse the privilege conceded to us by the apostolic see [the pope] of founding a place of study at Heidelberg like to that at Paris, and lest, for this reason, being subjected to the divine judgment, we should merit to be deprived of the privilege granted,—do decree . . . that the university of Heidelberg shall be ruled, disposed and regulated according to the modes and matters accustomed to be observed in the university of Paris. Also that, as a handmaid of the Parisian institution—a worthy one, let us hope,—the latter's steps shall be imitated in every way possible; so that, namely, there shall be four faculties in it: the first, of sacred theology or divinity; the second, of canon and civil law, which, by reason of their similarity, we think best to comprise under one faculty; the third, of medicine; the fourth, of liberal arts—of the threefold philosophy, namely, primal, natural and moral, three mutually subservient daughters. 99

— from *The Foundation of the University of Heidelberg* (1386)

Henderson, Ernest F., Tr. 1896. Select Historical Documents of the Middle Ages. London: George Bell and Sons.

1 **SUMMARIZING** Which subjects were to be taught at the University of Heidelberg? Which school served as a model for the University of Heidelberg?

_____

_____

_____

_____

2 **INFERRING** What can be inferred about the University of Paris from this declaration?

_____

_____

_____

_____

3 **ANALYZING IDEAS** What evidence can you find of the influence of scholasticism in this declaration? What does Rupert mean by calling primal, natural, and moral philosophy "three mutually subservient daughters"?

_____

_____

_____

_____

_____

_____

4 **HISTORY** How do you think the establishment of the University of Heidelberg impacted intellectual life in Germany?

_____

_____

_____

_____

_____

ESSENTIAL QUESTION

How did both innovations and disruptive forces affect people during the Middle Ages?

Romanesque and Gothic Architecture

DIRECTIONS: Examine the images. Then respond to the questions.

EXPLORE THE CONTEXT: Medieval churches were typically built in either the earlier Romanesque or later Gothic style. Romanesque churches were stocky and heavy-looking, with thick walls, round arches, and small windows. Low and imposing, they typically lacked elaborate exterior decoration. Gothic churches, by contrast, were slender and tall, with pointed arches, multiple stained glass windows, and intricate exterior decoration. Pictured below are Fontenay Abbey, founded in France in 1118, and Notre Dame de Paris, completed in 1345.

PRIMARY SOURCE: ARCHITECTURE

1 **DIFFERENTIATING** Which building is in the Romanesque style and which is in the Gothic style? How do you know?

_____

_____

_____

_____

_____

_____

2 **CONTRASTING** What do you think the interior of each building is like? Explain.

_____

_____

_____

_____

3 ECONOMICS Which structure do you think cost more to build? Why do you think so?

_____

_____

_____

_____

_____

4 **DRAWING CONCLUSIONS** Do you think the Romanesque and Gothic styles invite different types of spiritual or religious experiences among worshippers? Why or why not?

_____

_____

_____

_____

_____

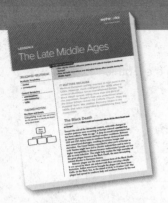

ESSENTIAL QUESTION

How did both innovations and disruptive forces affect people during the Middle Ages?

As you gather evidence to answer the Essential Question, think about:

- how the Black Death affected medieval Europe.
- why the Hundred Years' War was so consequential.
- why some European monarchies during the 1400s changed while others did not.

My Notes

_____

_____

_____

_____

_____

_____

_____

The Late Middle Ages

DIRECTIONS: Search for evidence in the lesson to help you answer the following questions.

1 **DESCRIBING** What was the Black Death? Which parts of Europe were especially affected by the Black Death? Why?

_____

_____

_____

_____

_____

2 **IDENTIFYING CONNECTIONS** How was the Black Death made even worse by the Great Famine of the early 1300s?

_____

_____

_____

_____

_____

3 **ECONOMICS** How did the Black Death impact the economy of Europe? How did it help weaken the feudal system?

_____

_____

_____

_____

_____

_____

4 EXPLAINING ISSUES Why did anti-Semitism increase as a result of the Black Death?

_____

_____

_____

5 DETERMINING CENTRAL IDEAS What was the Great Schism? What challenges did it create for the Church?

_____

_____

_____

_____

_____

_____

6A ANALYZING EVENTS What was the cause of the Hundred Years' War? How did the English use weapons technology and tactics to their advantage at the beginning of the war?

_____

_____

_____

_____

6B SUMMARIZING Use the graphic organizer to summarize conditions in Europe by the late 1400s.

France	England	Spain	Central and Eastern Europe

How did both innovations and disruptive forces affect people during the Middle Ages?

The Black Death

DIRECTIONS: Read the excerpt. Then respond to the questions that follow.

EXPLORE THE CONTEXT: Writing several hundred years before the outbreak of the Black Death in Europe, ancient historian Procopius describes a similar plague that devastated parts of the Eastern Roman Empire in the 6th century. Termed the Justinian Plague, this disease—like the Black Plague—spread along trade routes. The large city of Byzantium (Constantinople) was an ideal breeding ground for the disease.

PRIMARY SOURCE: BOOK EXCERPT

> And in the second year it reached Byzantium in the middle of spring, where it happened that I was staying at that time . . . . they were taken in the following manner. They had a sudden fever, some when just roused from sleep, others while walking about, and others while otherwise engaged, without any regard to what they were doing. And the body showed no change from its previous color, nor was it hot as might be expected when attacked by a fever, nor indeed did any inflammation set in, but the fever was of such a languid sort from its commencement and up till evening that neither to the sick themselves nor to a physician who touched them would it afford any suspicion of danger. It was natural, therefore, that not one of those who had contracted the disease expected to die from it. But on the same day in some cases, in others on the following day, and in the rest not many days later, a bubonic swelling developed; and this took place not only in the particular part of the body which is called boubon, that is, "below the abdomen," but also inside the armpit, and in some cases also beside the ears, and at different points on the thighs. . . .

Death came in some cases immediately, in others after many days; and with some the body broke out with black pustules about as large as a lentil and these did not survive even one day, but all succumbed immediately. With many also a vomiting of blood ensued without visible cause and straightway brought death. Moreover I am able to declare this, that the most illustrious physicians predicted that many would die, who unexpectedly escaped entirely from suffering shortly afterwards, and that they declared that many would be saved, who were destined to be carried off almost immediately. So it was that in this disease there was no cause which came within the province of human reasoning; for in all cases the issue tended to be something unaccountable. . . .

Indeed the whole matter may be stated thus, that no device was discovered by man to save himself, so that either by taking precautions he should not suffer, or that when the malady had assailed him he should get the better of it; but suffering came without warning and recovery was due to no external cause. . . .

VOCABULARY

languid: lazy, relaxed

commencement: beginning

pustules: boils

malady: sickness

During that time it seemed no easy thing to see any man in the streets of Byzantium, but all who had the good fortune to be in health were sitting in their houses, either attending the sick or mourning the dead. And if one did succeed in meeting a man going out, he was carrying one of the dead. And work of every description ceased, and all the trades were abandoned by the artisans, and all other work as well, such as each had in hand. Indeed in a city which was simply abounding in all good things starvation almost absolute was running riot. Certainly it seemed a difficult and very notable thing to have a sufficiency of bread or of anything else; so that with some of the sick it appeared that the end of life came about sooner than it should have come by reason of the lack of the necessities of life. 🙳

— Procopius, *History of the Wars, Books I and II* (542)

1 ANALYZING INFORMATION What was the first sign that one had been infected by the plague? In what way might this have made the disease especially difficult to control?

_____

_____

_____

_____

2 DESCRIBING What are the most notable symptoms of the disease, as described by Procopius?

_____

_____

_____

_____

3 EVALUATING EVIDENCE In what ways did the plague baffle physicians of the day?

_____

_____

_____

_____

4 ECONOMY How does Procopius describe the economy of Byzantium during the Black Death? Cite evidence from the text in your answer.

_____

_____

_____

_____

ESSENTIAL QUESTION

How did both innovations and disruptive forces affect people during the Middle Ages?

John Wyclif on the Corruption of Friars

DIRECTIONS: Read the excerpt. Then respond to the questions that follow.

EXPLORE THE CONTEXT: John Wyclif (ca. 1330–1384) was an English priest and reformer. He criticized the honored status of the clergy, the veneration of saints, and the very existence of the papacy. He also helped translate the Bible into Middle English, believing that the Bible alone is the only reliable source of information about God. Wyclif had a particular animosity toward monasticism, as illustrated in the following excerpt.

PRIMARY SOURCE: RELIGIOUS TREATISE

Also friars feign them as hypocrites, to keep straitly the Gospel and poverty of Christ and his apostles; and yet they are most contrary to Christ and his apostles, in hypocrisy, pride, and covetousness. For they show more holiness in bodily habit, and other signs, than did Christ and his apostles, and for their singular habit or holiness, they presume to be even with prelates and lords, and more worthy than other clerks; and in covetousness they can never make an end, but by begging, by queething [bequeathing], by burying, by salaries, and trentals [thirty masses], and by shriving [confessing], by absolutions and other false means, cry ever after worldly goods, where Christ used none of all these; and thus for this stinking covetousness, they worship the fiend as their God.

. . .

Also friars beg without need for their own rich sect, and not for their poor bed-ridden men that may not go and have no man to send for their lifelode [livelyhood]; but rather draw rich men's alms from such poor men. And therefore charity is outlawed among them, and so is God: and leasings [lies], and covetousness and fiends be inhabited among them; for they deceive men in their alms to make costly houses, not to harbour poor men, but lords and mighty men; and teach men to suffer God's temple, that be poor men, to perish for default; and thus they be traitors to God, and his rich people whom they deceive in their alms, and manquellers [murderers] of poor men, whose lifelode they take away from them by false leasings, and therefore they be irregular before God, and despise him, and harm the people when they say mass or matins in this cursed life, as Holy Writ teaches, and Austin and Gregory declare fully.

—Tracts and Treaties of John Wyclif

VOCABULARY

feign: to pretend

covetousness: greed

prelates: bishops or other high church officials

Austin and Gregory: Saint Austin and Pope Gregory, who sent Austin to England as a missionary

1 **DETERMINING POINT OF VIEW** What is Wyclif's general attitude toward friars? Provide examples from the text to support your answer.

_____

_____

_____

_____

_____

2 **IDENTIFYING BIAS** In what way might Wyclif's description of friars be biased?

_____

_____

_____

3 **PREDICTING** How do you think the Church reacted to Wyclif's teachings?

_____

_____

_____

_____

4 **UNDERSTANDING CONTEXT** What do you think Wyclif means by calling the friars "murderers of poor men"?

_____

_____

5 **HISTORY** What is Wyclif's legacy in the history of Christianity? Explain your answer.

_____

_____

_____

_____

_____

ESSENTIAL QUESTIONS

How did the Church influence political and cultural changes in medieval Europe?

How did both innovations and disruptive forces affect people during the Middle Ages?

My Notes

_____

_____

_____

_____

_____

_____

_____

_____

_____

_____

_____

_____

① Think About It

Review the supporting questions you developed at the beginning of the chapter. Review the evidence you gathered in the chapter. Were you able to answer each Supporting Question? If there was not enough evidence to answer your Supporting Questions, what additional evidence do you need to consider?

_____

_____

_____

_____

② Organize Your Evidence

Complete the chart below with information you learned about developments related to the medieval Church and developments related to political, intellectual, and artistic life in medieval Europe.

RELIGIOUS DEVELOPMENTS OF THE MIDDLE AGES
RELIGIOUS DEVELOPMENTS OF THE MIDDLE AGES
CULTURAL DEVELOPMENTS OF THE MIDDLE AGES

③ Talk About It

In the space below, write about how religion influenced the daily lives of people in the Middle Ages. In what ways did this change from 1000s to the end of the 1400s? Describe some specific examples.

_____

_____

_____

④ Write About It

Work in small groups. With your group, consider the items you identified in your charts as you talk about which events were most important in the development of medieval Europe. Take notes on your discussion below.

_____

_____

_____

_____

⑤ Connect to the Essential Question

You are a university student in medieval Europe. As you begin your studies, you decide to keep a diary to record your observations of how the arts, ideas, and politics of the Middle Ages reflect your beliefs and those of your fellow students. Make at least ten diary entries in which you discuss various aspects of literature, art, theology, and political news you encounter—as well as your studies at the university. In your entries, talk about why these things are happening and how they relate to commonly held beliefs of the time.

_____

_____

_____

_____

_____

_____

CITIZENSHIP
TAKE ACTION

The relationships between citizens and their government have changed greatly over time. By the end of the Middle Ages, great political and social changes were happening across Europe, and the roles of both rulers and subjects began to change. The feudal system was beginning to break down, stronger nation-states were developing, and thriving trade fueled the growth of cities and towns. Monarchs in France and England, in particular, increasingly relied on the support of the middle class as well as the nobility.

DIRECTIONS: What do you think is the proper relationship between a government and its people? Contact some representatives from your local government (such as city council members, congressional representatives, and so forth) and put the question to them. Summarize their responses and compare them to your own views.

_____

_____

_____

_____

_____

_____

_____

_____

_____

_____

_____

_____

Kingdoms and States of Medieval Africa, 500–1500

ESSENTIAL QUESTION

How does geography affect society, culture, and trade?

Think about what you already know about Africa. How do you think geography might have affected its society, culture, and trade?

TALK ABOUT IT

With a partner, discuss the kinds of information you would need to know to answer the Essential Question as it relates to Africa. For example, one question might be: How does geography vary throughout Africa? Another might be: What different societies and cultures developed throughout Africa?

DIRECTIONS: Now write down three additional questions that will help you explain how geography affected society, culture, and trade in Africa.

MY RESEARCH QUESTIONS

Supporting Question 1:

_____

_____

_____

Supporting Question 2:

_____

_____

_____

Supporting Question 3:

_____

_____

_____

African Society and Culture

DIRECTIONS: Search for evidence in the lesson to help you answer the following questions.

1 **CONTRASTING** How is the terrain of East Africa different from the rest of Africa?

_____

_____

_____

ESSENTIAL QUESTION

How does geography affect society, culture, and trade?

As you gather evidence to answer the Essential Question, think about:

- how geography varies in the different parts of Africa.
- how various African societies are similar and how they differ.
- how trade brought new religious beliefs to West and East Africa.

2 **GEOGRAPHY** Complete the chart below to identify Africa's climate zones and how they affect agriculture in those areas.

Location	Climate Zone	Description	Agriculture
Northern coast/ southern tip			
Below northern coast/above southern tip		Arid	Little or no farming
Along Equator			
North and south of rain forest			

My Notes

_____

_____

_____

_____

_____

_____

3 **DESCRIBING** What characteristics did Early African societies have in common?

_____

_____

_____

_____

_____

_____

4 **CONTRASTING** How did the roles of men and women differ in African society?

_____

_____

_____

_____

_____

5 **SUMMARIZING** What religious beliefs did most African societies share?

_____

_____

_____

_____

_____

6 **IDENTIFYING EFFECTS** How did trade affect religion in West and East Africa?

_____

_____

_____

_____

_____

7 **IDENTIFYING CONNECTIONS** How were the arts and religion connected in early African societies?

_____

_____

_____

_____

_____

ESSENTIAL QUESTION

How does geography affect society, culture, and trade?

VOCABULARY

thrush: a type of songbird

sultan: the king of a Muslim country

pempi: a platform with three steps

Ibn Battuta on Griots

DIRECTIONS: Read the excerpt. Then respond to the questions that follow.

EXPLORE THE CONTEXT: The famous Moroccan traveler Ibn Battuta spent a year in the Mali Empire. In this excerpt from his book *Rihlah (Travels)*, Battuta describes a festival in which poets, or griots, performed for Mansa Sulaymān, whom Battuta refers to as the "sultan." Mansa Sulaymān was the successor to Mansa Magha, who ruled after Mansa Musa. "Dugha," who is mentioned in this excerpt, was the sultan's interpreter.

PRIMARY SOURCE: BOOK EXCERPT

"On feast-days, after Dugha has finished his display, the poets come in. Each of them is inside a figure resembling a thrush, made of feathers, and provided with a wooden head with a red beak, to look like a thrush's head. They stand in front of the sultan in this . . . make-up and recite their poems. I was told that their poetry is a kind of sermonizing in which they say to the sultan: 'This pempi which you occupy was that whereon sat this king and that king, and such and such were this one's noble actions and such and such the other's. So do you too do good deeds whose memory will outlive you.' After that the chief of the poets mounts the steps of the pempi and lays his head on the sultan's lap, then climbs to the top of the pempi and lays his head first on the sultan's right shoulder and then on his left, speaking all the while in their tongue, and finally he comes down again. I was told this practice is a very old custom among them, prior to the introduction of Islam, and that they have kept it up. "

—from Ibn Battuta, *Travels in Asia and Africa, 1325–1354*

1 **DRAWING CONCLUSIONS** Based on the definition of a thrush, why might the poets have been dressed like thrushes?

_____

_____

_____

_____

_____

_____

2 HISTORY Although Battuta describes the poetry as a "kind of sermonizing," how does the subject of the poetry relate to what you know about the tradition of the griots?

_____

_____

_____

_____

_____

_____

_____

3 **ANALYZING TEXT** Why would the sultan likely have enjoyed the poets' recitations?

_____

_____

_____

_____

_____

_____

_____

4 **DRAWING CONCLUSIONS** Based on the actions of the chief of the poets, what purpose does the _pempi_ seem to serve?

_____

_____

_____

_____

_____

_____

ESSENTIAL QUESTION
How does geography affect society, culture, and trade?

West African Ceremonial Masks

DIRECTIONS: Study the images. Then respond to the questions that follow.

EXPLORE THE CONTEXT: African artists made remarkable masks using various media, including wood, ivory, bronze, and iron. The masks often represented ancestors, spirits, or gods and were believed to have spiritual powers. The first mask on the left below was likely created in the 16th century for the king of Benin, in what is now Nigeria. It is believed that it portrayed the king's mother and would have been worn as a pendant around his neck to honor her. The second mask was created sometime before 1880 in the Bamum kingdom, in what is now Cameroon. Masks like this one, with beads and cowrie shells, are under the authority of the Fon, or king, and are only displayed on special occasions, such as the funerals of important people. The third mask was created in the kingdom of Benin in the 18th or 19th century. Made of bronze and iron, it illustrates the impressive metalwork created by the Benin artists.

PRIMARY SOURCE: SCULPTURE

—photographs of West African ceremonial masks

1 **DESCRIBING** What different materials may have been used to create the masks?

_____

_____

_____

2 COMPARING What elements do the three masks have in common?

_____

_____

_____

_____

_____

3 HISTORY The tiara and collar on the first mask feature Portuguese faces. What does including Portuguese faces in a ceremonial mask indicate about how the Portuguese were viewed by the kingdom of Benin at this time?

_____

_____

_____

_____

4 INFERRING The headdress at the top of the second mask features the image of a spider, a symbol of wisdom. Why would this image likely have been added to the mask?

_____

_____

_____

_____

5 DRAWING CONCLUSIONS The collar on the third mask contains a row of mudfish designs. Because they live both in the water and on land, mudfish were seen as living in two worlds, the human and the divine. Based on this fact and other elements of the mask, whom do you think this mask might have portrayed?

_____

_____

_____

_____

_____

ESSENTIAL QUESTION

How does geography affect society, culture, and trade?

As you gather evidence to answer the Essential Question, think about:

- how Ghana had an abundance of gold, which it traded for goods brought by Muslim merchants from North Africa.

- how the Berbers and their camel caravans were crucial in trade across the Sahara.

- how the kingdom of Songhai rose to power because it was located along major trade routes.

- how the sea trade along the East African coast brought cultural influences from Muslim traders and settlers.

My Notes

_____

_____

_____

_____

_____

_____

_____

Kingdoms and States of Africa

DIRECTIONS: Search for evidence in the lesson to help you answer the following questions.

1 **SUMMARIZING** Complete the chart below to describe the kingdoms of Ghana, Mali, and Songhai as described in the student text.

Kingdom	GHANA	MALI	SONGHAI
Location			
Time Period			
Famous Rulers	N/A		
Economy			

2 **ANALYZING EVENTS** Why were the Berbers crucial to the trans-Saharan trade?

_____

_____

_____

3 **IDENTIFYING EFFECTS** Mansa Mūsā was a devout Muslim. How did this affect the city of Timbuktu?

_____

_____

_____

_____

4 **IDENTIFYING EFFECTS** What were some of the effects of the Bantu migration on East Africa?

_____

_____

_____

_____

5 GEOGRAPHY How was the development of the Swahili language and culture related to East Africa's location?

_____

_____

_____

_____

_____

_____

6 **CONTRASTING** How was government in southern Africa before the 11th century different from government in northern Africa?

_____

_____

_____

7 GEOGRAPHY How did Zimbabwe's location help it become the wealthiest and most powerful state in southern Africa?

_____

_____

_____

_____

Equestrian Figure from Mali Empire

DIRECTIONS: Study the image. Then respond to the questions that follow.

EXPLORE THE CONTEXT: The image below is a terra-cotta sculpture, created between 1200 and 1400 C.E. and found near the city of Djenne. This city became an important stop in the trans-Sahara trade route. The Mali warrior is depicted dressed in military gear and astride a horse. Some Arabic documents note that Mansa Musa had a cavalry of more than 100,000 during his reign in the early 1300s C.E. Horses were not native animals to Africa and required tremendous care and maintenance.

PRIMARY SOURCE: SCULPTURE

1 **INFERRING** If you had not read Explore the Context, how might you guess that the man in the sculpture is a warrior?

_____

_____

_____

_____

2 **DRAWING CONCLUSIONS** What does the fact that the sculpture depicts a warrior tell the viewer about Mali?

_____

_____

_____

_____

3 **ECONOMICS** Since horses are not native to Africa, what does including a horse in this sculpture tell us about Mali's economy?

_____

_____

_____

_____

4 **EVALUATING** Why is it remarkable that the sculpture is in such good condition?

_____

_____

_____

_____

ESSENTIAL QUESTION

How does geography affect society, culture, and trade?

Rituals and Beliefs of the Nyakyusa

DIRECTIONS: Read the excerpt. Then respond to the questions that follow.

EXPLORE THE CONTEXT: The Nyakyusa were a Bantu-speaking people who lived in the area north of Tanzania, in the Ngonde plain. Monica Wilson records the rituals and beliefs of this people in the following excerpt focused on the ruler called King Kyungu.

VOCABULARY

precautions: safety measures

nasal: having to do with the nose

beforehand: in advance

SECONDARY SOURCE: ANTHROPOLOGICAL STUDY

❝Great precautions were taken to preserve his health. He lived in a separate house with his powerful medicines . . . When the Kyungu did fall ill he was smothered by the nobles who lived around him at Mbande, and buried in great secrecy, with a score or more of living persons—slaves—in the grave beneath him, and one or two wives and the sons of commoners above. And in the midst of all this slaughter the nobles brought a sheep to look into the grave that the dead Kyungu might be gentle (mololo) like the sheep! The living Kyungu was thought to create food and rain, and his breath and the growing parts of his body—his hair and nails and the constantly replaced mucus of his nose—were believed to be magically connected with the fertility of the Ngonde plain. When he was killed his nostrils were stopped so that he was buried 'with the breath in his body'; while portions of his hair and nails and of his nasal mucus were taken from him beforehand and buried by the nobles of Ngonde in the black mud near the river. This was 'to defend the country against hunger, to close up the land, to keep it rich and heavy and fertile as it was when he himself lived in it.' ❞

—Monica Wilson, *Communal Rituals of the Nyakyusa*, 1970

1 **ANALYZING CENTRAL IDEAS** Why was the Kyungu's health so important to the Nyakyusa?

_____

_____

_____

2 **IDENTIFYING CONNECTIONS** Why did the Nyakyusa nobles take portions of the Kyungu's hair, nails, and nasal mucus before he was killed?

_____

_____

_____

_____

3 **INFERRING** Why might the nobles have wanted to ensure that the dead Kyungu would be gentle like a sheep?

_____

_____

_____

_____

4 **DRAWING CONCLUSIONS** Based on their actions, what beliefs about the afterlife did the Nyakyusa have?

_____

_____

_____

_____

5 **ECONOMICS** How does what you have read about the economy of the Bantu-speaking people help explain the actions of the Nyakyusa nobles?

_____

_____

_____

ESSENTIAL QUESTION

How does geography affect society, culture, and trade?

My Notes

_____

_____

_____

_____

_____

_____

_____

_____

_____

_____

_____

_____

_____

1 Think About It

Review the supporting questions you developed at the beginning of the chapter and the evidence you gathered. Were you able to answer each supporting question? If not, what additional evidence do you think you need to consider?

_____

_____

_____

_____

2 Organize Your Evidence

Complete the chart below with information you learned about how geography affected society, culture, and trade in medieval Africa.

Geography's Effect on Society, Culture, and Trade in:	
West Africa	
East Africa	
South Africa	

3 Talk About It

Work in a small group. With your group, compare the charts you created in the Organize Your Evidence activity. Did you all identify the same effects? If not, add information from your group members to your chart. Then talk about the geography of different parts of Africa. How did the effects of geography vary from one part of Africa to another? Take notes about your discussion below.

_____

_____

_____

_____

_____

4 Write About It

Using information from your chart and the discussion with your small group, focus on a particular part of Africa. Write a paragraph answering the Essential Question for that part of Africa.

_____

_____

_____

_____

_____

5 Connect to the Essential Question

Plan, create, and present a multimedia presentation that helps answer the Essential Question: *How does geography affect society, culture, and trade?* Your multimedia presentation should show how geography affected these three aspects of life in medieval Africa. Include maps to illustrate the different features of the geography of Africa and images to show the effects on society, culture, and trade. Add narration to explain the connections between geography and these effects. Before presenting to your class, ask one or more of your peers to watch your presentation, and incorporate their feedback into your final presentation.

CITIZENSHIP
TAKE ACTION

MAKE CONNECTIONS   As you have read, griots were a special class of storytellers in Africa. They served as oral historians who kept the people's history alive. Today, storytelling and oral history continue to play an important role, not only in Africa, but in the United States as well. One organization in the United States that promotes the recording and sharing of oral histories is StoryCorps. This organization's mission is "to preserve and share humanity's stories in order to build connections and create a more just and compassionate world." StoryCorps accomplishes this mission through the recording of interviews, which are then preserved at the American Folklife Center at the Library of Congress. Their website, storycorps.org, provides resources that people can use to record and preserve the stories of people in their own communities.

DIRECTIONS: Using the resources on the StoryCorps website, https://storycorps.org, conduct an interview with an older person in your community. The StoryCorps website provides sample questions that you can use, or you can write your own. If technology allows, you may want to consider downloading the free StoryCorps mobile app, which allows you to record interviews and then upload them to the Library of Congress.

In the space below, write the questions you plan to ask in your interview. Then, after you have conducted the interview, write a brief summary of the interview and what you learned from the experience.

Pre-Columbian America

ESSENTIAL QUESTIONS

In what ways were civilizations in early Mesoamerica and South America complex?

How were civilizations in early Mesoamerica and South America influenced by previous cultures?

Think about how a culture's location affects how sophisticated it is. How could a civilization that is physically isolated develop a sophisticated culture? How did the Olmec and Chavin civilizations affect Mesoamerica and South America?

TALK ABOUT IT

With a partner, discuss the sort of information that could help you answer these questions. For example, you may wish to ask: How did the Olmec farm, worship gods, and build structures that were similar to the Mayans?

DIRECTIONS: Now write down three additional questions that will help you explain how early cultures influenced Mesoamerica and South America. For example, you might ask, "What can we learn from the ruins left by Maya and Aztec cultures?"

MY RESEARCH QUESTIONS

Supporting Question 1:

_____

_____

Supporting Question 2:

_____

_____

Supporting Question 3:

_____

_____

ESSENTIAL QUESTIONS

In what ways were civilizations in early Mesoamerica and South America complex?

How were civilizations in early Mesoamerica and South America influenced by previous cultures?

As you gather evidence to answer the Essential Question, think about:

- how early peoples in eastern North America shifted to full-time farming and how their cultures were influenced by their surrounding environments.
- how Mayans created ways to measure time and record history.
- how the Aztec established a monarchy and hierarchy, ruling much of the area that is modern-day Mexico.

My Notes

_____

_____

_____

_____

_____

The Peoples of North America and Mesoamerica

DIRECTIONS: Search for evidence in the lesson to help you answer the following questions.

1 **COMPARING AND CONTRASTING** How did the lifestyles of most Plains Indians differ from the Anasazi?

_____

_____

_____

2 **SUMMARIZING** Use the following chart to identify important characteristics of the Mayan civilization.

Maya	

3 **IDENTIFYING CAUSES** What are some theories about what caused the Mayan civilization to decline?

_____

_____

_____

4 ANALYZING TEXT How was the Mayan calendar developed?

_____

_____

_____

_____

_____

_____

5 INFERRING Based on what is known about the decline of the Toltec civilization, what conclusion can be drawn about how their metalworking was utilized?

_____

_____

6 DRAWING CONCLUSIONS How did the Aztec nobility rely on the rest of the population?

_____

_____

_____

Diego de Landa on Maya Civilization

ESSENTIAL QUESTIONS

In what ways were civilizations in early Mesoamerica and South America complex?

How were civilizations in early Mesoamerica and South America influenced by previous cultures?

VOCABULARY

inclined: of a mind

reckoning: calculating

sacraments: rituals

omens: signs

divinations: predictions

antiquities: history

esteem: honor

DIRECTIONS: Read the excerpt. Then respond to the questions that follow.

EXPLORE THE CONTEXT: Diego de Landa was a Franciscan monk sent to the Yucatán in A.D. 1549. His task was to convert the Maya to Catholicism. He learned a great deal about Maya culture and recorded it in many books. This passage is an excerpt from one of those books.

PRIMARY SOURCE: BOOK

❝ [The high priests] taught the sons of the other priests, and the second sons of the chiefs, who were brought to them very young for this purpose, if they found them inclined toward this office. The sciences which they taught were the reckoning of the years, months and days, the festivals and ceremonies, the administration of their sacraments, the omens of the days, their methods of divination and prophecies, events, remedies for sicknesses, antiquities, and the art of reading and writing by their letters and the characters wherewith they wrote, and by pictures that illustrated the writings. They wrote their books on a long sheet doubled in folds, which was then enclosed between two boards finely ornamented; the writing was on one side and the other, according to the folds. The paper they made from the roots of a tree, and gave it a white finish excellent for writing upon. Some of the principal lords were learned in these sciences, from interest, and for the greater esteem they enjoyed thereby; yet they did not make use of them in public. ❞

—Diego de Landa, *Yucatan Before and After the Conquest*

1 **UNDERSTANDING CONTEXT** Why did Diego de Landa go into such detail about the way the books were folded and the Mayans tracked their time?

_____

_____

_____

_____

2 **INTERPRETING** What evidence shows that Mayan society held religion in high regard?

_____

_____

_____

3 **DRAWING CONCLUSIONS** What information about the Mayan people is missing from de Landa's excerpt?

_____

_____

_____

_____

4 HISTORY **INFERRING** Why do you think the Franciscans sent de Landa to convert Mayans to Catholicism in the first place?

_____

_____

_____

5 **DRAWING CONCLUSIONS** What does the title of de Landa's book _Before and After the Conquest_ reveal about de Landa's work?

_____

_____

_____

_____

ESSENTIAL QUESTIONS

In what ways were civilizations in early Mesoamerica and South America complex?

How were civilizations in early Mesoamerica and South America influenced by previous cultures?

Mayan Temples

DIRECTIONS: Study the image. Then respond to the questions that follow.

EXPLORE THE CONTEXT: The photo shows an aerial, wide angle view of the main plaza of the Temple of the Jaguar, Tikal National Park, Petén Region, Guatemala.

PRIMARY SOURCE: PHOTO

—Mayan Temples at Tikal National Park, Guatemala

1 **INTEGRATING VISUAL INFORMATION** What does the placement of the structures in the picture explain about their function?

_____

_____

_____

_____

_____

_____

2 INTERPRETING In addition to the material used to build the structures, what can be revealed about the shape of the structures, given the technology of the time?

_____

_____

_____

_____

_____

3 `HISTORY` **IDENTIFYING PERSPECTIVES** What makes the ruins a tourist attraction?

_____

_____

_____

4 DRAWING CONCLUSIONS What do you think European explorers thought about the pyramids when they saw them for the first time?

_____

_____

_____

_____

5 EVALUATING INFORMATION What kind of work do you think it took to build the pyramids, and who did the work?

_____

_____

_____

_____

_____

_____

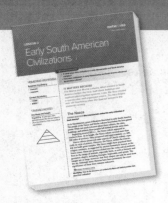

ESSENTIAL QUESTIONS

In what ways were civilizations in early Mesoamerica and South America complex?

How were civilizations in early Mesoamerica and South America influenced by previous cultures?

As you gather evidence to answer the Essential Question, think about:

- how the Nazca culture in Peru preserved some aspects of the Chavin culture and how the Moche civilization developed near modern-day Equador.

- how the Inca Empire had a highly structured political system and society.

- how the Inca carried out complex engineering projects and kept detailed records without a writing system.

My Notes

Early South American Civilizations

DIRECTIONS: Search for evidence in the lesson to help you answer the following questions.

1 **COMPARING AND CONTRASTING** How did the Moche and Inca systems of written language compare?

_____

_____

_____

2 **SUMMARIZING** Use the following chart to identify important characteristics of the Inca Empire.

Government organization:	Architecture:
The Inca	
Cultural Events:	Writing System:

3 **UNDERSTANDING CONTEXT** Why can't anthropologists agree on the significance of the Nazca lines?

_____

_____

_____

_____

4 **ANALYZING INFORMATION** What have historians learned about the Moche by looking at their pottery?

_____

_____

5 **ANALYZING CENTRAL IDEAS** What were the engineering systems of the Incas like and why were these systems significant?

_____

_____

_____

_____

6 **DRAWING CONCLUSIONS** Why were the _quipu_ an important record keeping system for the Inca?

_____

_____

A Conqueror's View of the Inca

ESSENTIAL QUESTIONS

In what ways were civilizations in early Mesoamerica and South America complex?

How were civilizations in early Mesoamerica and South America influenced by previous cultures?

DIRECTIONS: Read the excerpt. Then respond to the questions that follow.

EXPLORE THE CONTEXT: Pedro de Cieza de Léon was a Spanish conquistador who interviewed native people in the Andean region of what is now Peru. This excerpt gives us a view into the Inca system of record keeping and governance.

PRIMARY SOURCE: FIRST-HAND ACCOUNT

66 [I]n the time of the Kings Incas, orders were given throughout all the towns and provinces of Peru, that the principal lords and their lieutenants should take note, each year, of the men and women who had died, and also of the births. For as well for the assessment of tribute, as for calculating the number of men that could be called upon to serve as soldiers, and for the defence of the villages, such information was needed. This was easily done, because each province, at the end of the year, was ordered to set down in the quipus, by means of the knots, all the men who had died in it during the year, as well as all who were born. In the beginning of the following year, the quipus were taken to Cuzco, where an account was made of the births and deaths throughout the empire. These returns were prepared with great care and accuracy, and without any fraud or deceit. When the returns had been made up, the lord and his officers knew what people were poor, the number of widows, whether they were able to pay tribute, how many men could be taken for soldiers and many other facts which were considered, among these people, to be of great importance. As this empire was of such vast extent, . . . there were a great number of storehouses for provisions and other necessaries for a campaign, and for the equipment of soldiers, if there was a war these great resources were used where the camps were formed, without touching the supplies of allies, or drawing upon the stores of different villages. If there was no war, all the great store of provisions was divided amongst the poor and the widows. 99

—Pedro de Cieza de Léon, *The Second Part of the Chronicle of Peru,* 1540

fraud: deception

deceit: dishonesty

extent: size

allies: individuals associated by a common goal or purpose

provisions: supplies of food and resources

1 UNDERSTANDING CONTEXT Why did Pedro de Cieza de Léon go into such detail about the way the quipu system was used by the Inca?

_____

_____

_____

_____

_____

2 ANALYZING TEXT Why were the quipus taken to Cuzco?

_____

_____

_____

3 EVALUATING EVIDENCE What evidence does de Léon give to indicate that the Inca had a strong military?

_____

_____

_____

4 INFERRING How might the quipu indicate the number of people who could or could not pay their tribute?

_____

_____

_____

5 DRAWING CONCLUSIONS Although the quipu system was efficient and complex, why did most civilizations that came after develop a written language?

_____

_____

_____

ESSENTIAL QUESTIONS

In what ways were civilizations in early Mesoamerica and South America complex?

How were civilizations in early Mesoamerica and South America influenced by previous cultures?

Nazca Lines

DIRECTIONS: Study the image. Then respond to the questions that follow.

EXPLORE THE CONTEXT: The photo shows an aerial view of Nazca Lines in the desert of Peru. Pedro de Cieza de León was the first known to have written about the geoglyphs, which he mistook for trail markers when he explored Peru. Pilots first discovered them from the air in the 1920s. In 2018, drone technology helped Peruvian archaeologists discover and map more than 50 new geoglyphs in the desert. The Nazca people are believed to have created 'The Monkey' between 200 B.C. and A.D. 700.

PRIMARY SOURCE: PHOTO

—"The Monkey" Nazca Lines in the desert of Peru

1 **INTEGRATING VISUAL INFORMATION** What features of "The Monkey" geoglyph likely required the most planning, and why?

_____

_____

_____

_____

2 **INTERPRETING** What is a possible reason for the lines leading up to the monkey?

_____

_____

_____

3 GEOGRAPHY **IDENTIFYING EFFECTS** How does its desert location help preserve the geoglyph?

_____

_____

_____

4 **MAKING CONNECTIONS** The Nasca Lines are only partially visible from nearby mountains. What does this add to theories about what why lines were made?

_____

_____

_____

_____

5 **DRAWING CONCLUSIONS** Many geometric shapes such as the triangles below the monkey are located across the Peruvian desert. What are some possible purposes for those lines?

_____

_____

_____

_____

_____

ESSENTIAL QUESTIONS

In what ways were civilizations in early Mesoamerica and South America complex?

How were civilizations in early Mesoamerica and South America influenced by previous cultures?

My Notes

_____

_____

_____

_____

_____

_____

_____

_____

_____

_____

_____

_____

_____

1 Think About It

As you read the chapter, you gathered evidence to help you answer the Supporting Questions. Were you able to answer each Supporting Question? If not, what additional evidence do you think you need to gather to prepare your answers?

_____

_____

_____

_____

2 Organize Your Evidence

Complete the chart below with information you learned about ways the civilizations of the Maya, Aztec, and Inca were considered complex.

Maya	Aztec	Inca

3 Talk About It

Work in small groups. With your group, discuss at least one way the Mayans were influenced by the Olmec civilization before them.

_____

_____

_____

_____

_____

4 Write About It

Choose one of the civilizations discussed in the chapter and explain how geography and the environment affected the culture of the people.

_____

_____

_____

_____

_____

5 Connect to the Essential Question

Work in groups to prepare a visual essay about one of the civilizations from the chapter. The visuals should guide the viewer to understand the connection to each Essential Question of the chapter.

_____

_____

_____

_____

_____

_____

_____

_____

CITIZENSHIP
TAKE ACTION

MAKE CONNECTIONS Not everyone is aware of the influence that early civilizations have had on our modern culture. Information about history is not often presented in a format that reaches people today. Popular culture that incorporates historic information, such as films or music that reference the past, has a chance of teaching people about past cultures.

DIRECTIONS: Work in groups to write and film a short movie about the Nazca lines. Include details about how they were discovered, what they could mean, and why experts cannot reach a conclusion about their use. The film can be a documentary or a drama.

_____

_____

_____

_____

_____

_____

_____

_____

_____

_____

_____

_____

_____

_____

_____

_____

_____

CHAPTER 15

The Renaissance in Europe

ESSENTIAL QUESTIONS

How can trade lead to economic prosperity and political power?

How can ideas be reflected in art, sculpture, and architecture?

Think about what you have already learned about life in Europe during the Middle Ages. Note that trade with other civilizations to the east was bringing a revival of interest in the achievements of the ancient world. Much of the knowledge of these achievements had been lost when the Roman Empire collapsed. Beginning in the 1300s, however, Italian merchants began importing ideas as well as goods from as far away as China and India. By the 1400s, these ideas were revolutionizing European life.

TALK ABOUT IT

With a partner, discuss the sort of information you would need to know to answer these questions. For example, one question might be: How did the profitable trade between Italy and India bolster the power of the ruling families of Italian cities?

DIRECTIONS: Now write down three additional questions that will help you evaluate how trade led to economic prosperity and political power in Renaissance Europe. This prosperity, in turn, allowed leaders to sponsor artists, sculptors, and architects. For example, you might ask, "How did Renaissance sculpture reflect the ideals of ancient civilizations, most notably Greece and Rome?

MY RESEARCH QUESTIONS

Supporting Question 1:

_____

_____

Supporting Question 2:

_____

_____

Supporting Question 3:

_____

_____

The Italian States

DIRECTIONS: Search for evidence in the lesson to help you answer the following questions.

1 **DESCRIBING** Use the web diagram below to identify the major characteristics of the Italian Renaissance.

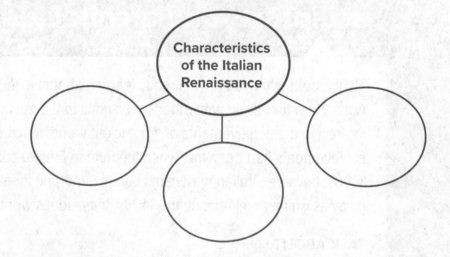

ESSENTIAL QUESTION

How can trade lead to economic prosperity and political power?

As you gather evidence to answer the Essential Question, think about:

- the renewed interest in the individual in Italy in the 1300s.
- the roles that independent Italian city-states played in Italian politics.
- how Machiavelli viewed political power.

2 HISTORY What role did the emerging city-states of Milan, Venice, Florence, Naples, and Rome play in Italian politics during the Renaissance?

_____

_____

_____

_____

_____

_____

_____

_____

_____

_____

My Notes

_____

_____

_____

_____

_____

_____

3 **EVALUATING** How did the growth of powerful monarchies in France and Spain lead to war in Italy?

_____

_____

_____

_____

_____

4 **ECONOMICS** What impact did the concentration of political power in the Italian city-states have on the economy of Italy as a whole?

_____

_____

_____

_____

_____

5 **ANALYZING INDIVIDUALS** How did Machiavelli's views on government affect the growth and power of the Italian city-states?

_____

_____

_____

_____

_____

6 **SUMMARIZING** How did the peasants and townspeople of the period help make the Renaissance achievements possible?

_____

_____

_____

_____

ESSENTIAL QUESTION

How can trade lead to economic prosperity and political power?

How to Gain a Ruler's Favor

DIRECTIONS: Read the excerpt. Then respond to the questions that follow.

EXPLORE THE CONTEXT: Lorenzo de' Medici was one of the most influential people in Italy's history. Rather than governing Italy as an all-powerful ruler, de' Medici surrounded himself with others who could assist him in his governance. Niccolò Machiavelli dedicated his political treatise on power, *The Prince*, to de' Medici's grandson and ruler at the time, Lorenzo di Piero de' Medici. Machiavelli believed that, when necessary, rulers should ignore Christian principles if following them would be perceived as a weakness or lead the ruler to lose power.

PRIMARY SOURCE: BOOK

“ Those who wish to acquire favor with a ruler most often approach him with those among their possessions that are most valuable in their eyes, or that they are confident will give him pleasure. So rulers are often given horses, armor, cloth of gold, precious stones, and similar ornaments that are thought worthy of their social eminence. Since I want to offer myself to your Magnificence, along with something that will symbolize my desire to give you obedient service, I have found nothing among my possessions that I value more, or would put a higher price upon, than an understanding of the deeds of great men, acquired through a lengthy experience of contemporary politics and through an uninterrupted study of the classics. Since I have long thought about and studied the question of what makes for greatness, and have now summarized my conclusions on the subject in a little book, it is this I send your Magnificence. **”**

—from Niccolò Machiavelli, *The Prince,* 1513

VOCABULARY

favor: approval, support

eminence: importance, reputation

symbolize: represent

contemporary: modern-day

the classics: classic literature

summarized: to give a short report on a subject

1 CITING TEXT EVIDENCE What gift does Machiavelli propose to give the ruler? Cite text evidence to support your answer.

_____

_____

_____

_____

_____

2 HISTORY Think of the time in which Machiavelli lived and wrote. It was the height of the Renaissance in which Italians had rediscovered the creative energy of the ancient Greeks and Romans. Many of the Greek city-states had established democracies. Rome had started out as a republic but had abandoned that form in favor of an emperor. Would Machiavelli have favored democracies or empires with absolute rulers? Give reasons to support your answer.

_____

_____

_____

_____

3 DETERMINING CENTRAL IDEAS Why should people present the ruler with lavish gifts?

_____

_____

_____

4 ANALYZING POINTS OF VIEW Why is Machiavelli offering the ruler a book rather than precious stones or other valuable merchandise?

_____

_____

_____

5 IDENTIFYING CONNECTIONS Think of governments around the world today that you study or read about in the media. Do any of these governments follow the principles that Machiavelli discussed? Give examples to support your answer.

_____

_____

_____

_____

_____

The Book of the Courtier

DIRECTIONS: Read the excerpt. Then respond to the questions that follow.

EXPLORE THE CONTEXT: The Italian Baldassare Castiglione was born near Mantua, Italy, at the height of the creativity of the Renaissance in 1478. He spent his life in government service, both to city-states and to the pope. In 1528, he published his most famous work, *The Book of the Courtier*. It provides a discussion about the qualities that make a person an ideal courtier. As with many works of the Renaissance, the book imitates the style and tone of ancient writers such as Plato and Cicero.

PRIMARY SOURCE: BOOK

❝ I do not deny that the same virtues may rule the low-born and the noble: but (not to repeat what we have said already or the many other arguments that could be adduced in praise of noble birth, which is honoured always and by everyone, it being reasonable that good should beget good), since we have to form a Courtier without flaw and endowed with every praiseworthy quality, it seems to me necessary to make him nobly born, as well for many other reasons as for universal opinion, which is at once disposed in favour of noble birth. For if there be two Courtiers who have as yet given no impression of themselves by good or evil acts, as soon as the one is known to have been born a gentleman and the other not, he who is low-born will be far less esteemed by everyone than he who is high-born, and will need, much effort and time to make upon men's minds that good impression which the other will have achieved in a moment and merely by being a gentleman. And how important these impressions are, everyone can easily understand: for in our own case we have seen men present themselves in this house, who, being silly and awkward in the extreme, yet had throughout Italy the reputation of very great Courtiers; and although they were detected and recognized at last, still they imposed upon us for many days, and maintained in our minds that opinion of them which they first found impressed there, although they conducted themselves after the slightness of their worth. We have seen others, held at first in small esteem, then admirably successful at the last. ❞

—Castiglione, *The Book of the Courtier,* 1528

VOCABULARY

adduced: cited as evidence

beget: give rise to; bring about

flaw: a mistake or shortcoming

Copyright © McGraw-Hill Education   Castiglione, Baldassare. 1903. *The Book of the Courtier.* Translated by Leonard Eckstein Opdycke. New York: Charles Scribner's Sons.

1 **CITING TEXT EVIDENCE** Does Castiglione believe that a peasant can rise socially and lead a virtuous life or service to the government? Cite specific text evidence to support your answer.

_____

_____

2 **CONTRASTING** The United States has what is known as a meritocracy. Under such a system, people are free to choose jobs best suited to them. Even if someone is born poor, there are no formal barriers that prevent the person from working hard in school, getting a good education, and then getting a high-paying or highly satisfying job. American employers, including the government, hire people based on their abilities and education, not on the social status of their parents. Contrast the meritocracy that we enjoy with the system described by Castiglione. Which affords the individual the most opportunities? Cite evidence to support your answer.

_____

_____

_____

_____

_____

_____

3 **ANALYZING IDEAS** According to Castiglione, what immediate advantages do nobles have?

_____

_____

_____

4 **CIVICS** Presented with two courtiers who behave exactly the same, even though one is low-born, which one does Castiglione think society and the government should view as more valuable? Why?

_____

_____

_____

5 **SUMMARIZING** What is Castiglione's stated purpose in the excerpt?

_____

_____

Ideas and Art of the Renaissance

DIRECTIONS: Search for evidence in the lesson to help you answer the following questions.

ESSENTIAL QUESTION

How can ideas be reflected in art, sculpture, and architecture?

As you gather evidence to answer the Essential Questions, think about:

- the renewed interest in the individual in Italy in the 1300s.
- the creativity of Italian painters, sculptors, and architects.
- how the Northern Renaissance differed from the Italian Renaissance.

① DESCRIBING Use the web diagram below to identify the major characteristics of humanism.

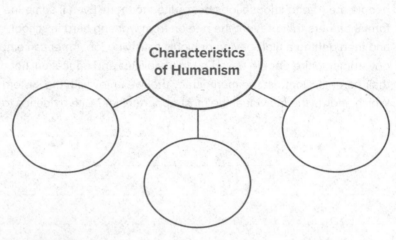

Characteristics of Humanism

② HISTORY How was Petrarch able to ensure that Renaissance ideas spread from Italy throughout Europe in a relatively short time?

_____

_____

_____

_____

③ DETERMINING CENTRAL IDEAS How did new technologies contribute to a rise in literacy?

_____

_____

_____

_____

_____

_____

My Notes

_____

_____

_____

_____

_____

_____

_____

4 **IDENTIFYING EFFECTS** What impact did the liberal studies that became the core of humanist schools have on the students who attended them?

_____

_____

_____

_____

_____

5 **COMPARING AND CONTRASTING** How was the art of the Renaissance the same as the art of medieval Europe? How was it different?

_____

_____

_____

_____

_____

_____

_____

6 **CONTRASTING** How did the art of the Northern Renaissance differ from its Italian counterpart?

_____

_____

_____

_____

_____

_____

_____

Leonardo da Vinci: Renaissance Man

DIRECTIONS: Study the image. Then answer the questions that follow.

EXPLORE THE CONTEXT: Leonardo da Vinci, the Renaissance artist famed for paintings such as the Mona Lisa and The Last Supper, was also an accomplished scientist. In his notebooks, the two fields often overlap, such as in the following illustrations of the human foot and arm. Da Vinci was most likely the first scholar and artist to make such detailed anatomical studies. He accompanied these illustrations with notes; however, it is difficult to read this writing normally, as it is backwards. The reader can only view it "normally" by holding it to a mirror.

PRIMARY SOURCE: NOTEBOOK

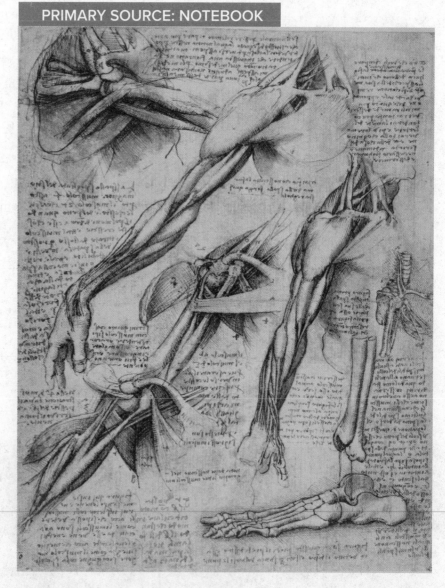

Copyright © McGraw-Hill Education   ©akg-images/Superstock

1 **DESCRIBING** What is the subject of these sketches?

_____

_____

2 **INTERPRETING** What do these sketches tell us about the human figure in da Vinci's art?

_____

_____

_____

3 **DRAWING CONCLUSIONS** Why might da Vinci have used writing that could only be read by looking in a mirror?

_____

_____

_____

4A **IDENTIFYING CONNECTIONS** How do da Vinci's sketches exemplify Renaissance ideals?

_____

_____

_____

_____

4B **HISTORY** In what sense do da Vinci's illustrations connect larger social movements?

_____

_____

_____

_____

ESSENTIAL QUESTION

How can ideas be reflected in art, culture, and architecture?

Madonna and Child

DIRECTIONS: Study the paintings. Then respond to the questions that follow.

EXPLORE THE CONTEXT: One of the great Renaissance legacies was the tremendous outpouring of the arts, particularly painting. The two paintings below provide two examples of that art. While both paintings are of the Madonna and the baby Jesus, the painters used different techniques to show their subject. The painting on the left, "Madonna and Child," is from the Northern Renaissance. It was painted by Robert Campin, one of the earliest and greatest of the Flemish painters. The painting on the right, "Madonna and Child Enthroned," is the work of the great Italian master, Raffaello Sanzio, often known simply as Raphael.

PRIMARY SOURCE: PAINTINGS

1 **ANALYZING CENTRAL IDEAS** What is the major purpose of each painting?

_____

_____

2 **CONTRASTING** How are the settings for the two paintings different?

_____

_____

_____

3 **INTERPRETING** Who does Raphael have looking down on Mary? Why do you think the artist chose this type of presentation?

_____

_____

_____

4 HISTORY How do you know that both artists believe that Mary and Jesus are holy?

_____

_____

5 **SUMMARIZING** Flemish artists were known for including everyday objects in their paintings. What objects does Campin use here?

_____

_____

6 **INTEGRATING VISUAL INFORMATION** What elements of Campin's painting could not have been historically accurate? Give reasons to support your answer.

_____

_____

_____

_____

7 **ANALYZING STRUCTURE** Campin shows only Mary and Jesus, while Raphael shows a variety of men and women, along with another child in his work. Who do you suppose these other people were? Why are they included here?

_____

_____

_____

_____

ESSENTIAL QUESTIONS

How can trade lead to economic prosperity and political power?

How can ideas be reflected in art, sculpture, and architecture?

My Notes

_____

_____

_____

_____

_____

_____

_____

_____

_____

_____

_____

_____

_____

_____

_____

_____

_____

1 Think About It

Review the supporting questions you developed at the beginning of the chapter. Review the evidence on the economic, political, and artistic achievements of the European Renaissance that you studied in the chapter. Also make certain that you have information on the impact that trade had on the people of the time. Do you have enough information on how this trade brought a renewed interest in studying the cultures of Greece and Rome as well as their legacies? Then review the information that you gathered on the great artistic achievements of the Renaissance, including painting, sculpture, and architecture. Were you able to answer each Supporting Question? If there was not enough evidence to answer your Supporting Questions, what additional evidence do you think you need to consider?

_____

_____

_____

2 Organize Your Evidence

Complete the web diagram below with information you learned about how the economic prosperity and political power that trade brought to Renaissance Europe and how this prosperity helped fund developments in art, sculpture, and architecture. Include each figure's name and major contribution.

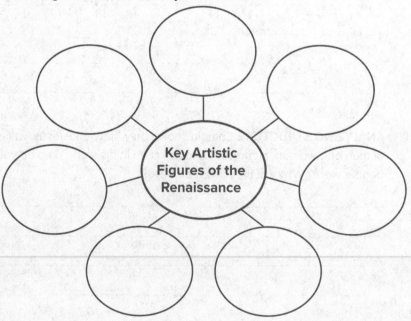

Key Artistic Figures of the Renaissance

3 Write About It

The creative burst that gripped the city-states of Italy in the 1400s and 1500s owed its origins to an increase in trade with societies of the Middle East and of Asia. As stable rulers took power in Italian city-states, they sought to enrich their own coffers. Trade provided one such way of doing so. Leaders funded voyages to the East where they purchased goods that could be sold at a profit to people in Italy. The traders then used their profits to fund even more expeditions that purchased even more goods. Use what you have learned to construct a time line of the major economic and political developments that helped make the Renaissance a reality.

_____

_____

4 Talk About It

Work in small groups. With your group, choose one of the artists, sculptors, or architects explored in the text to study in more detail. You may also choose to use Internet or print resources to find information on someone who is not mentioned in the text but whose work you admire. Try to find some biographical information on your subject, along with a list of three or four of your subject's major works. Where are these works today? Are they in museums where the public can enjoy them or are they in private collections where only a chosen few may see them? Or perhaps they have been lost to history. Then use what you learn to create a multimedia presentation that links the past—as noted in your text and in some of your research—with the present—what your sources teach you. If possible, try to include some video as part of your presentation.

_____

_____

5 Connect to the Essential Question

Think about what you have learned about the Renaissance, both its causes and its effects. Note that the explosion of prosperity that resulted from increased trade gave people a living and then some leisure time in which to pursue artistic endeavors. During a relatively short period, Europeans rediscovered the achievements of the ancient Greeks and Romans and went on to create unprecedented masterpieces in painting, sculpture, and architecture. Now think of life in your community today. Does your community include an art museum that showcases artists from throughout history? If so, try to arrange a visit to find information on the artists featured. Then compare what you see with what you know about art during the Renaissance. What similarities can you find? What differences do you see? You might also check whether your community includes retail stores that sell artwork. Visit one of these galleries and make the same comparisons with the works for sale with those you have learned about from the Renaissance. You might choose to do the same for sculpture or for architecture. Use what you learn as the basis for an illustrated informational essay in which you compare modern art or the art that you have seen in a local museum to Renaissance art.

_____

CITIZENSHIP
TAKE ACTION

MAKE CONNECTIONS During the Renaissance leaders of Italian city-states vied with each other to make their city the most glorious and prosperous in the region. Part of this effort included sponsoring artists to create paintings, statues, or buildings that glorified the city and its achievements. Many of these works of art were based on classical models that the people of the Renaissance had rediscovered. Painters, however, worked in a new medium—oil on canvas—that had not existed during the classical period. Artists today continue to refine the technique, often using acrylic rather than oil, and sometimes producing serigraphs. This process, also called silkscreening, involves pressing ink through a fine screen onto paper. A stencil of the image the artist has drawn is placed on a tight screen with paper below it. Ink is then spread on top and forced through the screen. The process allows the artist to apply a variety of colors and to produce quantities of the work. Usually the artist then signs each print and numbers it. The process can also be used with oil paints and with canvas.

Think about your own community and the artists who work there. Select one and contact him or her either by telephone or email. Ask if it would be possible for you to visit the artist's studio to learn what techniques he or she uses and what medium he or she prefers when producing art. Explain to the artist that you are studying a chapter on the Renaissance in your history class and that you are working to compare the techniques that modern artists use in comparison with those that Renaissance artists used. You might even ask the artist whether they believe that they owe any of their art techniques to the Renaissance masters. Invite the artist to visit your classroom and to present examples of their art to the class, while explaining the technique used in creating the art. Then work with the artist as well as with other members of your class to address the question of how art helps enrich the lives of the people of your community. Are there any public parks that include works of art? If so, what purpose do they serve? Why should the government support artists who produce these works? Use what you learn as the basis for a community education pamphlet in which you encourage the local government to fund more public art projects. Perhaps the artist you invited to address the class would be willing to provide illustrations that would make your pamphlet more appealing.

The Reformation in Europe

ESSENTIAL QUESTIONS

What conditions can encourage the desire for reform?

How can reform influence society and beliefs?

Think about what you have already learned about life in Europe during the Renaissance. The Papal States, centered in Rome, controlled immense wealth. Many Europeans, however, believed that the Church had become more concerned with worldly rather than spiritual affairs. They sought to reform some of the practices of the Renaissance Church. Instead, they split from the Roman Catholic Church, forming a variety of new Christian denominations.

TALK ABOUT IT

With a partner, discuss the sort of information you would need to know to answer these questions. For example, one question might be: How did the Roman Catholic Church of the Renaissance splinter into a variety of denominations?

DIRECTIONS: Now write down three additional questions that will help you evaluate how the Reformation transformed Europe. This transformation, in turn, led to an unprecedented period of religious turmoil in Europe. For example, you might ask, "What were the major denominations that arose in Europe after Martin Luther made his Ninety-five Theses public?

MY RESEARCH QUESTIONS

Supporting Question 1:

_____

Supporting Question 2:

_____

Supporting Question 3:

_____

The Protestant Reformation

DIRECTIONS: Search for evidence in the lesson to help you answer the following questions.

1 DESCRIBING What is the relationship of Christian humanism to reform of the Catholic Church?

_____
_____
_____
_____
_____

2 ANALYZING INDIVIDUALS What role did the teachings of Desiderius Erasmus have on the Reformation?

_____
_____
_____
_____
_____
_____
_____

3 EXPLAINING ISSUES Use the table below to explain why reformers thought each listed practice of the Renaissance Church needed to be reformed.

Issue	Why It Needed to Be Reformed
salvation	
indulgence	
veneration of relics	

ESSENTIAL QUESTION

What conditions can encourage the desire for reform?

As you gather evidence to answer the Essential Question, think about:

- practices of the Renaissance Church that reformers targeted.
- Martin Luther's ideas for reforming the Church.
- the role of politics in the German Reformation.

My Notes

_____
_____
_____
_____
_____
_____
_____

4 **IDENTIFYING EFFECTS** How did Martin Luther's idea of justification by faith alone lead to a break with the Catholic Church?

_____

_____

_____

_____

_____

_____

_____

5 **CIVICS** How did the Reformation in Northern Europe, particularly in Germany, become a political movement?

_____

_____

_____

_____

_____

_____

_____

_____

6 **IDENTIFYIING EFFECTS** What impact did the Peace of Augsburg have on life in the German states?

_____

_____

_____

_____

_____

_____

Criticism of the Catholic Church

ESSENTIAL QUESTION

What conditions can encourage the desire for reform?

DIRECTIONS: Read the excerpt. Then respond to the questions that follow.

EXPLORE THE CONTEXT: Desiderius Erasmus was a priest, humanist, and dedicated scholar who found himself caught between the Church and the spirit of the Reformation. Erasmus used much of what he learned from the Italian humanists and developed a critical study of the Greek New Testament as well as of the Church Fathers. He was also very interested in education, and his writings on the subject helped solidify the new humanist emphasis on studying the classics as part of a worthwhile education. A prolific writer, Erasmus wrote to people at all levels within the Church, including the following letter to the Bishop of Augsburg, in Germany.

PRIMARY SOURCE: LETTER

❝The state of the Church distracts me. My own conscience is easy; I was alone in saying from the first that the disorder must be encountered in its germs; I was too true a prophet; the play, which opened with universal hand clapping, is ending as I foresaw that it must. The kings are fighting among themselves for objects of their own. The monks instead of looking for a reign of Christ, want only to reign themselves. The theologians curse Luther and in cursing him curse the truth delivered by Christ and the Apostles and . . . alienate with their foul speeches many who would have returned to the Church or but for them would have never left it. No fact is plainer than that this tempest has been sent from heaven by God's anger, as the frogs and locusts and the rest were sent on the Egyptians; but no one remembers his own faults, and each blames the other. It is easy to see who sowed the seed and who ripened the crop. ❞

—Erasmus to the Bishop of Augsburg, August 26, 1528 in *Life and Letters of Erasmus: Lectures Delivered at Oxford 1893–4*

VOCABULARY

encountered: come across; met with

universal: worldwide

theologians: people who study God and religion

alienate: turn away

1 HISTORY What wars is Erasmus referencing in his letter to the bishop?

_____

_____

_____

_____

2 EVALUATING EVIDENCE What does Erasmus mean when he writes that "the state of the Church distracts me"?

_____

_____

_____

3 DETERMINING CENTRAL IDEAS What central idea is Erasmus communicating to the bishop?

_____

_____

_____

4 DETERMINING POINT OF VIEW Why does Erasmus write that "his own conscience is easy"?

_____

_____

_____

5 IDENTIFYING BIAS How does Erasmus view monks and theologians?

_____

_____

_____

6 IDENTIFYING CONNECTIONS History is filled with stories of wars over religion. Here Erasmus is talking about the religious wars between Lutherans and Catholics during the Reformation. Why do you think people are willing to go to war over religious beliefs?

_____

_____

_____

The Ninety-five Theses

Copyright © McGraw-Hill Education   Luther, Martin. Harvard Classics Vol. 36 : The Prince, Utopia, Ninety-Five Theses. Edited by Eliot, Charles W. New York: P F Collier & Son Company. 1910.

ESSENTIAL QUESTION

What conditions can encourage the desire for reform?

DIRECTIONS: Read the excerpt. Then respond to the questions that follow.

EXPLORE THE CONTEXT: Until 1517, Martin Luther was an obscure German monk. That year Luther published his Ninety-five Theses in which he attacked the Catholic Church's practice of selling indulgences that would forgive the buyer's sins and ensure entry into heaven. The Theses had two major points. First, he believed that the Bible was the basis of all religious authority in Christianity. Second, people enter heaven only by what they believe—their faith—not by what they have done in life—their deeds. The Theses marked the beginning of the Reformation and the split in Christianity, between Roman Catholics on one side and Protestants on the other. The divide continues today.

PRIMARY SOURCE: PETITION

VOCABULARY

disputation: debate or argument

penitence: action of showing sorrow and regret

indulgences: forgiveness of sins

elucidating: making clear

avarice: greed

❝Disputation of Dr. Martin Luther Concerning Penitence and Indulgences IN the desire and with the purpose of elucidating the truth, a disputation will be held on the underwritten propositions at Wittenberg, under the presidency of the Reverend Father Martin Luther, Monk of the Order of St. Augustine, Master of Arts and of Sacred Theology, and ordinary Reader of the same in that place. He therefore asks those who cannot be present and discuss the subject with us orally, to do so by letter in their absence. In the name of our Lord Jesus Christ. Amen.

27. They preach man, who say that the soul flies out of purgatory as soon as the money thrown into the chest rattles.

28. It is certain that, when the money rattles in the chest, avarice and gain may be increased, but the suffrage of the Church depends on the will of God alone.
. . .

32. Those who believe that, through letters of pardon, they are made sure of their own salvation, will be eternally [punished] along with their teachers.
. . .

35. They preach no Christian doctrine, who teach that contrition is not necessary for those who buy souls out of purgatory or buy confessional licences.

36. Every Christian who feels true compunction has of right plenary remission of pain and guilt, even without letters of pardon.

37. Every true Christian, whether living or dead, has a share in all the benefits of Christ and of the Church given him by God, even without letters of pardon.
. . .

40. True contrition seeks and loves punishment; while the ampleness of pardons relaxes it, and causes men to hate it, or at least gives occasion for them to do so.
. . .

43. Christians should be taught that he who gives to a poor man, or lends to a needy man, does better than if he bought pardons.

... *continued*

44. Because, by a work of charity, charity increases and the man becomes better; while, by means of pardons, he does not become better, but only freer from punishment

45. Christians should be taught that he who sees any one in need, and passing him by, gives money for pardons, is not purchasing for himself the indulgences of the Pope, but the anger of God. **"**

—Martin Luther, Ninety-Five Theses

1 **CITING TEXT EVIDENCE** What does Martin Luther state will happen to people who believe that the indulgence they purchased will get them into heaven? Cite evidence from the text to support your answer.

_____

_____

2 **ANALYZING** What does Martin Luther believe is the only way to get out of purgatory and into heaven?

_____

_____

3 **HISTORY** Martin Luther posted his Ninety-five Theses in 1517. Copies of the Theses were quickly printed and distributed throughout Europe. How might the Reformation have been different if there had been no printing press at the time?

_____

_____

_____

_____

4 **IDENTIFYING** How do some of the theses seem to conflict with the idea of justification by faith alone?

_____

_____

5 **ANALYZING** What does Luther think is a better use of the money spent on indulgences?

_____

_____

ESSENTIAL QUESTION

How can reform influence society and beliefs?

As you gather evidence to answer the Essential Question, think about:

- the major elements of Swiss Protestantism.
- the role that King Henry VIII played in establishing the Church of England.
- the Anabaptists and their role during the Reformation.
- how the Reformation changed European society.
- how the Reformation forced changes within the Catholic Church.

My Notes

_____

_____

_____

_____

_____

_____

The Spread of Protestantism

DIRECTIONS: Search for evidence in the lesson to help you answer the following questions.

1 **DESCRIBING** How did disagreement about specific Christian rites lead to a division in Protestantism and the growth of Calvinism?

_____

_____

_____

_____

_____

_____

_____

2 **CONTRASTING** How was the Reformation in England different from the Reformation in other parts of Europe?

_____

_____

_____

_____

_____

_____

_____

3 **CIVICS** What were the main beliefs of the Anabaptists?

_____

_____

_____

_____

_____

4 **DETERMINING POINT OF VIEW** Use the table below to list the Protestant views on education, the family, women, and anti-Semitism.

Issue	Protestant Views on its Role
Education	
Family	
Women	
Anti-Semitism	

5 **IDENTIFYING EFFECTS** How did the Roman Catholic Church respond to the Reformation?

_____

_____

_____

_____

_____

_____

6 **ANALYZING INDIVIDUALS** Why were Ignatius of Loyola and Teresa of Avila so important to the Counter-Reformation?

_____

_____

_____

_____

_____

_____

_____

_____

How can reform influence society and beliefs?

The Necessity of Reforming the Church

DIRECTIONS: Read the excerpt. Then respond to the questions that follow.

EXPLORE THE CONTEXT: John Calvin became one of the preeminent Protestant theologians of his time. His writings had a tremendous impact on the Reformation. Calvin believed that the Bible was the word of God handed down to humans. He also believed in predestination, in which God chooses who will enter Heaven based on grace alone. Calvin spent most of his adult life in Germany and in Switzerland where he used Protestant principles to set up the government of Geneva. Once in power, Calvin allowed for no dissenters in Geneva. In his first five years as leader of the city, 58 people were executed and 76 exiled because they did not agree with Calvin's theological beliefs.

PRIMARY SOURCE: PAMPHLET

❝ And, first, the pastoral office itself, as instituted by Christ, has long been in desuetude. His object in appointing bishops and pastors, or whatever the name be by which they are called, certainly was, as Paul declares, that they might edify the church with sound doctrine. According to this view, no man is a true pastor of the church who does not perform the office of teaching. But, in the present day, almost all those who have the name of pastors have left that work to others. Scarcely one in a hundred of the bishops will be found who ever mounts the pulpit in order to teach. And no wonder; for bishoprics have degenerated into secular principalities. Pastors of inferior rank, again, either think that they fulfill their office by frivolous performances altogether alien from the command of Christ, or, after the example of the bishops, throw even this part of the duty on the shoulders of others. Hence the letting of sacerdotal offices is not less common than the letting of farms. What would we more? The spiritual government which Christ recommended has totally disappeared, and a new and mongrel species of government has been introduced, which, under whatever name it may pass current, has no more resemblance to the former than the world has to the kingdom of Christ.

If it be objected, that the fault of those who neglect their duty ought not to be imputed to the order, I answer, first, that the evil is of such general prevalence, that it may be regarded as the common rule; and, secondly, that, were we to assume that all the bishops, and all the presbyters under them, reside each in his particular station, and do what in the present day is regarded as professional duty, they would never fulfill the true institution of Christ. They would sing or mutter in the church, exhibit themselves in theatrical vestments, and go through numerous ceremonies, but they would seldom, if ever, teach. According to the precept of Christ, however, no man can claim for himself the office of bishop or pastor who does not feed his flock with the word of the Lord.

VOCABULARY

desuetude: state of disuse

edify: instruct or improve morally

sacerdotal: relating to priests

imputed: ascribe to someone

presbyters: elder or minister

turpitude: depravity or wickedness

. . . continued

Then while those who preside in the church ought to excel others, and shine by the example of a holier life, how well do those who hold the office in the present day correspond in this respect to their vocation! At a time when the corruption of the world is at its height, there is no order more addicted to all kinds of wickedness. I wish that by their innocence they would refute what I say. How gladly would I at once retract. But their turpitude stands exposed to the eyes of all exposed their insatiable avarice and rapacity exposed their intolerable pride and cruelty. The noise of indecent revelry and dancing, the rage of gaming, and entertainments, abounding in all kinds of intemperance, are in their houses only ordinary occurrences, while they glory in their luxurious delicacies, as if they were distinguished virtues. **"**

—John Calvin, "The Necessity of Reforming the Church"

1 DETERMINING POINT OF VIEW What does Calvin believe is the main duty of priests and of bishops?

_____

_____

2 IDENTIFYING BIAS What does Calvin think about the current generation of clergy in the Roman Catholic Church?

_____

_____

3 DETERMINING CENTRAL IDEAS What is the central idea in the excerpt?

_____

_____

4 EVALUATING EVIDENCE Recall what you have learned about the role that Martin Luther played in the Reformation. Reread the excerpt from Martin Luther that you studied at the beginning of the chapter. How do Calvin's arguments about the Church in this excerpt compare to Luther's arguments in the Ninety-Five Theses?

_____

_____

_____

5 CIVICS This pamphlet was written several years before John Calvin became leader of the Geneva government. What in the excerpt provides a preview of how he would govern the city?

_____

_____

_____

How can reform influence society and beliefs?

The Council of Trent

DIRECTIONS: Read the excerpt. Then respond to the questions that follow.

EXPLORE THE CONTEXT: The Council of Trent was a meeting of Roman Catholic Church leaders that held three sessions between 1545 and 1563. As a direct response to the tumult of the Reformation, the Council issued decrees designed to reform the Church and define its doctrines. Despite the lengthy periods between sessions, the Council did much to counter the Reformation and bring people back to Catholicism. This excerpt, written in 1546, is from an early meeting of the Council.

PRIMARY SOURCE: RELIGIOUS DECREE

❝ On Preachers of the word of God, and on Questors of alms.

But whereas the preaching of the Gospel is no less necessary to the Christian commonwealth than the reading thereof; and whereas this is the chief duty of bishops; the same holy synod hath resolved and decreed, that all bishops, archbishops, primates, and all other prelates of the churches be bound personally, if they be not lawfully hindered, to reach the holy Gospel of Jesus Christ. But if it should happen that the bishops and others aforesaid, be hindered by lawful impediment, they shall be bound, according to the form prescribed by the general council, to appoint fit men to discharge wholesomely this office of preaching. But if any one disdain to execute this, let him be subjected to strict punishment.

Archpriests also, curates, and all those who in any manner soever hold any parochial or other churches, which have the cure of souls, shall, at least on the Lord's days and solemn feasts, either personally, or, if they be lawfully hindered, by others who are competent, feed the people committed to them, with wholesome words, according to their own capacity, and that of their [congregations]; by teaching the things which it is necessary for all to know unto salvation, and by announcing to them with briefness and simplicity of discourse the vices which they must needs avoid, and the virtues which they must follow after, that they may escape everlasting punishment, and obtain the glory of heaven. And if any one of them neglect to discharge this duty, even though he may plead, on whatsoever ground, that he is exempt from the jurisdiction of the bishop, and even though the churches may be, in what manner soever, said to be exempted, or perhaps annexed or united to a monastery that is even out of the diocese, let not the watchful pastoral care of the bishops be wanting, provided [those churches] really be within their diocese ; lest that word be fulfilled ; The young children have asked for bread, and there was none to break it unto them. Wherefore, if, after having been admonished by the bishop, they shall neglect this their duty for the space of three months, let them be compelled by ecclesiastical censures, or otherwise, according to the discretion of the said bishop; in such wise that even, if this

VOCABULARY

disputation: debate or argument

penitence: action of showing sorrow and regret

indulgences: forgiveness of sins

elucidating: making clear

avarice: greed

. . . continued

seem to him expedient, some fair remuneration be paid, out of the fruits of the benefices, to another person to discharge that office, until the principal himself, coming to his right senses, shall fulfil his own duty . . . But if, which heaven avert, a preacher should spread errors, or scandals, amongst the people, even though he preach in a monastery of his own, or of another order, let the bishop interdict his preaching:. But if he preach heresies, let him proceed against him according to the appointment of the law, or the custom of the place, even though the said preacher should plead that he is exempted by a general or special privilege: in which case the bishop shall proceed by apostolic authority, and as the delegate of the Apostolic See. But let bishops be careful, that no preacher be harassed, either by false accusations, or in any other way calumniously; or have any just cause of complaint against them. . . . **"**

—Canons and Decrees of the Council of Trent

1 **CITING TEXT EVIDENCE** How does this text counter Calvin's criticism that the Catholic clergy has abandoned teaching in favor of pursuing worldly goods? Cite supporting text evidence.

2 **ANALYZING** What does the Council state is the main duty of the prelates during worship services?

3 **HISTORY** The decrees of the Council of Trent did much to reform the practices that had led to the Reformation. How were bishops to deal with priests who taught heresy?

4 **CONTRASTING** How is the Council of Trent's concept of salvation different from Luther's?

5 **IDENTIFYING CONNECTIONS** How do the doctrines presented in the excerpt differ from the basic teachings of the Calvinists that were gaining power in Switzerland around this time?

ESSENTIAL QUESTIONS

What conditions can encourage the desire for reform?

How can reform influence society and beliefs?

My Notes

_____

_____

_____

_____

_____

_____

_____

_____

_____

_____

_____

_____

_____

1 Think About It

Review the supporting questions you developed at the beginning of the chapter. Review the evidence you gathered on the desire for reform of the Catholic Church and the conditions in the Renaissance Church led people to advocate reforms. Then review the information you gathered on how the Reformation affected European society and the Catholic Church. Were you able to answer each Supporting Question? If there was not enough evidence to answer your Supporting Questions, what additional evidence do you think you need to consider?

_____

_____

_____

_____

2 Organize Your Evidence

Complete the web diagram below with information you learned about the major figures of the Reformation and how the Catholic Church responded to the changes.

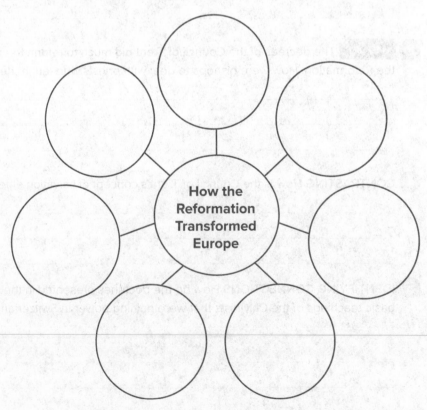

How the Reformation Transformed Europe

❸ Write About It

The Reformation transformed both the social and political order in what had been a religiously unified Europe. The abuses of the Renaissance Church led people to urge reforms. These reformers believed that the Catholic Church had become corrupt. At first they did not want to separate from the Church. They simply wanted to change some of its practices. Instead, Protestantism was born. Choose one of the leaders of the Reformation that you read about in the chapter. Then use Internet or print resources to learn more about the person's life and role in the Reformation. Use what you learn to write a short biography that concentrates on the person's role in the Reformation.

_____

_____

❹ Talk About It

Work in small groups. With your group, choose one of the denominations, including the Roman Catholic Church, explored in the chapter. Use Internet and print resources to study it in more detail or another denomination not mentioned in the chapter but that you know has churches nearby. Try to find specific information on the doctrines of the denomination today as well as number of members, whether the denomination is gaining or losing members, and a list of the nearest churches that belong to the denomination. Has the denomination gone through any changes in doctrine over the last twenty years? If so, what impact have they had on the denomination? Then use what you learn to create a multimedia presentation that links the past—as noted in the chapter and in your research—with the present—what your sources revealed. If possible, try to include some video as part of your presentation.

❺ Connect to the Essential Question

Think about what you have learned about the Reformation, both its causes and its results. Note that the explosion of creativity and wealth of the Renaissance affected the Roman Catholic Church as well as the people of Italy in general. Many people of the time believed that the Church had become corrupt. They pointed to the selling of indulgences that guaranteed the buyer a road to heaven as a prime example. These reformers wanted the Church to return to its roots—that of providing the people with spiritual guidance during this life and a path to salvation in the afterlife. Once started, however, the movement gathered supporters and leaders with amazing speed. Soon Europe was split into Protestant and Catholic regions. Wars erupted between the two sides that settled none of the major religious issues. Work with a partner and choose one of the leaders of the Reformation discussed in the chapter, or do research about other Reformation leaders not mentioned but who played a role in the Reformation. With your partner develop a 5-minute interview for a cable news program. One of you will play the reporter; the other will play the Reformation figure. The purpose of the interview is to show your viewers the motives behind the historical figure's actions. Why did the person take the actions he or she did?

What was the purpose? Did the results surprise the person? Does the subject have any regrets or wish that events had turned out differently? Given the chance, would the subject change anything? If so, what? If not, why not?

CITIZENSHIP
TAKE ACTION

MAKE CONNECTIONS Before 1517, Europe had two major Christian denominations, the Roman Catholic Church and the Eastern Orthodox Church. Martin Luther unintentionally changed all that when he posted his Ninety-five Theses in Germany. Before the century was out, several different versions of Protestantism had become the dominant form of worship for Christians in many parts of Europe. And the growth of denominations did not stop with the 1500s. Even today, new churches catering to specific demographic groups are organized in communities throughout the world. At the same time, some older denominations lose members and close churches because of lack of support. Christianity, like all religions, continues to grow, change, and adapt.

DIRECTIONS: Think about your own community and the churches, temples, and mosques that form a part of it. Choose one of these to learn more about. If possible, choose one that you do not attend so you can learn new information about another form of worship. Arrange to visit the church, temple, or mosque and speak with one of the staff members about their doctrines and beliefs. Use what you learn to design a Facebook page that details the institution, the service schedules, and basic beliefs. Be certain to illustrate your Facebook page.

_____

_____

_____

_____

_____

_____

_____

_____

_____

The Age of Exploration, 1500–1800

ESSENTIAL QUESTION

What are the effects of political and economic expansion?

Think about how European expansion resulted in the movement of goods, people, and ideas. How did peoples from Latin American colonies interact with each other? What natural resources and products came from the colonies of Portugal and Spain?

TALK ABOUT IT

With a partner, discuss the sort of information that could help you answer these questions. For example, you may wish to ask: Why did European nations undertake voyages of discovery?

DIRECTIONS: Now write down three additional questions that will help you explain the effects of political and economic expansion during the age of Exploration. For example, you might ask, "What regions were involved in the Columbian Exchange and the slave trade?"

MY RESEARCH QUESTIONS

Supporting Question 1:

_____

_____

Supporting Question 2:

_____

_____

Supporting Question 3:

_____

_____

European Exploration and Expansion

DIRECTIONS: Search for evidence in the lesson to help you answer the following questions.

ESSENTIAL QUESTION

What are the effects of political and economic expansion?

As you gather evidence to answer the Essential Question, think about:

- what ideas and intentions motivated European expansion.
- why Portuguese and Spanish explorers sailed west across the Atlantic Ocean.
- why the Aztec and Inca could not fight off European conquistadors.
- how rival nations began to challenge the Portuguese and the Spanish.

My Notes

_____

_____

_____

_____

_____

_____

_____

1 **ECONOMICS** What economic motivations did Europeans have for exploring other regions?

_____

_____

_____

2 **SUMMARIZING** Complete the chart below to identify characteristics of the Spanish conquests.

	Hernán Cortés	Francisco Pizarro
Area conquered		
Technology used		
How gained victory		

3 **ANALYZING CHANGE** Why was it significant that the Portuguese gained control of the spice trade in the 1500s?

_____

_____

_____

4 **DRAWING CONCLUSIONS** How was Ferdinand Magellan's voyage both a success and a failure?

_____

_____

_____

5 **COMPARING AND CONTRASTING** How were the explorations of John Cabot and Pedro Cabral alike and different?

_____

_____

_____

6 **IDENTIFYING EFFECTS** What was one unintended and devastating effect of the Spanish conquest of the Aztec and the Inca?

_____

_____

_____

ESSENTIAL QUESTION

What are the effects of political and economic expansion?

VOCABULARY

unendurable: not able to tolerate

comrades: members of the same group

defiled: ruined, made filthy

obliged: felt the responsibility to do it

gaunt: bony, thin

famished: starving

rigging: the lines and wires that support the masts on sailing vessels

pretense: to act as if something were true; pretending

singed: charred, scorched, blackened

Magellan's Voyage

DIRECTIONS: Read the excerpt. Then respond to the questions that follow.

EXPLORE THE CONTEXT: *Magellan; or, The First Voyage Round the World,* by George M. Towle, was written as one in a series of history books. The story provides insights into what early explorers encountered in their quest to discover unknown lands and seas.

SECONDARY SOURCE: BOOK EXCERPT

66 What made the heat still more unendurable, the supply of fresh water was now almost exhausted; what remained had become so filthy and nauseous that the wanderers could not drink it without shuddering, and it often made them ill. Then Magellan was grief-stricken to be forced to reduce the rations of his brave and suffering comrades. The only food left consisted of course biscuit and these were, as one who was on board says, 'reduced to powder, and full of worms.' They had been gnawed and defiled by rats, and were scarcely eatable. But even such food was a rich and rare luxury compared to that to which the poor fellows were at last reduced. In no long time not a biscuit, not a crumb remained. Then they were obliged to do the very thing that Magellan had spoken of, when he said he would go forward, 'even if they had to eat the leather off the yards.' This miserable apology for food was now, indeed, all that was left. The gaunt and famished sailors tore off the ox-hides under the main yard, which had been placed there to protect the rigging from the strain of the yard. The leather was so tough that the hungry teeth could make no impression upon it. They attached pieces of it to strong cords, and let them trail in the sea for four or five days. When they were thus soaked through, the sailors made a poor pretense of cooking the leather. They placed it over the fire, until it was singed, and then ate it greedily. 99

—from *Magellan; or, The First Voyage Round the World,* 1879

1 **ANALYZING EVENTS** Even though the excerpt describes the hardships faced by the crew, how does it also appeal to a sense of adventure?

_____

_____

_____

_____

2 **INTERPRETING** What does the author mean by a "poor pretense" of cooking the leather?

_____

_____

_____

_____

_____

3 **DETERMINING POINT OF VIEW** How does the author convey Magellan's feelings about the ordeal his crew was experiencing?

_____

_____

_____

_____

_____

4 HISTORY How does this account compare to the accounts of European explorers we usually hear about?

_____

_____

_____

_____

_____

5 **DRAWING CONCLUSIONS** What does the title of Towle's book _Magellan; or, The First Voyage Round the World_ imply about Magellan's role in the voyage? Do you agree?

_____

_____

_____

_____

_____

_____

Copyright © McGraw-Hill Education   Richman, Irving Berdine. 1919. The Spanish Conquerers: A Chronicle of the Dawn of Empire Overseas. New Haven: Yale University Press.

ESSENTIAL QUESTION

What are the effects of political and economic expansion?

VOCABULARY

grave: serious or solemn

Grijalva: another explorer (from Cuba) who visited the coast of Mexico

expedition: journey

raiment: clothing

sway: to have power over something or someone

adduced: confirmed

visage: the appearance or expression of a person's face

bestriding: putting a leg on either side of something, such as a horse

A Chronicle of the Spanish Conqueror Cortés

DIRECTIONS: Read the excerpt. Then respond to the questions that follow.

EXPLORE THE CONTEXT: The excerpt jumps into a description of the conflict between Spanish explorer Hernán Cortés and the Aztec ruler, Montezuma II. Based on an Aztec legend, a God who opposed human sacrifice said he would someday return. Because of this, Montezuma did not act aggressively toward Cortés when the Spanish landed.

SECONDARY SOURCE: BOOK

" In the mind of Montezuma, meanwhile, the grave question has been: Can these Spaniards, these strangers of the sunrise, be gods? When Grijalva's expedition appeared off the coast in 1518, it had been reported to Tenochtitlan that in the 'waters of heaven,' as the open sea was called, 'floating towers' had appeared, from which had descended beings with white faces and hands, with beards and long hair, and wearing raiment of brilliant colors and 'round headcoverings.' Could these beings be priests or heralds of the Fair God Quetzalcoatl, come, according to the Maya-Nahua tradition, to resume sway over his people? Before proof could be adduced, Grijalva had departed; and then, shortly, had come swift messengers with news of Cortés and with pictures of his 'floating towers' and of his fair-visaged, yet bearded attendants, handling the thunder and bestriding fierce creatures . . . "

—from *The Spanish Conquerors, a Chronicle of the Dawn of Empire Overseas,* 1919

1 **INTERPRETING** What did the Aztec see when they referred to "waters of heaven" and "floating towers"?

_____

_____

2 IDENTIFYING PERSPECTIVES How did Aztec religious beliefs put them in danger when the Spaniards arrived?

_____

_____

_____

_____

_____

3 HISTORY What does the text say happened before the witnesses could confirm who those in the first ships were?

_____

_____

_____

_____

4 MAKING CONNECTIONS Why is the description "fair-visaged, yet bearded attendants" considered a contradiction and a curiosity to the Aztec?

_____

_____

_____

_____

5 DRAWING CONCLUSIONS What does the passage suggest about the Aztec civilization, which had lasted more than 200 years?

_____

_____

_____

_____

_____

_____

The First Global Economic Systems

DIRECTIONS: Search for evidence in the lesson to help you answer the following questions.

ESSENTIAL QUESTION

What are the effects of political and economic expansion?

As you gather evidence to answer the Essential Question, think about:

- how a world economy arose from trade, exploration, colonization, and new financial practices.
- how the Columbian Exchange transformed economies and lifestyles.
- how the Dutch, English, and French expanded into Asia for economic gain.
- how European expansion into Africa led to the Atlantic slave trade.

1 ECONOMICS What economic opportunities were revealed by European exploration for new trade routes?

_____

_____

_____

2 **SUMMARIZING** Use the chart below to identify important characteristics of the Columbian Exchange.

Columbian Exchange

My Notes

_____

_____

_____

_____

_____

_____

_____

3 **CITING TEXT EVIDENCE** What are two examples given of positive effects of newly introduced plants and animals in the Columbian Exchange?

_____

_____

_____

_____

_____

4 **ANALYZING CHANGE** How did European expansion lead to an increase in the slave trade?

_____

_____

_____

_____

5 **INFERRING** How did the triangular trade and the Columbian Exchange change civilizations around the world?

_____

_____

_____

_____

6 **DRAWING CONCLUSIONS** How did the slave trade affect communities in Africa?

_____

_____

_____

ESSENTIAL QUESTION

What are the effects of political and economic expansion?

The History of Smallpox

DIRECTIONS: Read the excerpt and answer the questions that follow.

EXPLORE THE CONTEXT: The author of this account draws from various primary sources to describe the history of smallpox. The disease is first recorded as appearing in Asia and Africa and eventually moving into Europe and the Americas. He details the treatments, and as an early proponent of vaccination, describes the discovery and use of smallpox inoculations.

SECONDARY SOURCE: BOOK

"The Spaniards who landed on that coast pretended to be civilized, the standard of Christ was borne before them, and they proclaimed themselves the propagators of his benevolent doctrines. How they practised his precepts may be judged of by the consequence of their arrival.

It is computed that Hispaniola then contained a million of [Native Americans]; in reducing them to Christianity and slavery, immense numbers were massacred by fire arms and blood hounds; when resistance ceased, the wretched [Native Americans] having excessive tasks imposed upon them, and being forced to work in the mines, were consumed with labor and famine; and the remainder . . . were totally extinguished by the Measles and Small Pox.

. . .

Before the fleet sailed [from Cuba] the Small Pox reached the island, and an infected [African] slave was embarked. Although the Spaniards were perfectly acquainted with the Small Pox, yet they suffered this slave, when covered with pustules, to be landed with the troops at Zempoalla, where the [Native Americans] were both ignorant of the contagious nature of the disease, and of any means of mitigating its violence.

They soon caught the infection, which spread through Mexico, and occasioned such desolation, that in a very short time three millions and a half of people were destroyed, in that kingdom alone; the Emperor Quetlavaca, brother and successor to Montezuma, was among the victims. "

—from *The History of the Small Pox,* James Moore, 1815

VOCABULARY

propagators: those who promote and spread ideas

benevolent: characterized by doing good

precepts: rules or principles

Hispaniola: Caribbean island colonized by Spaniards

pustules: blisters containing pus

mitigating: making less severe

1 HISTORY What does the first paragraph explain about Hispaniola?

_____

_____

_____

2 ANALYZING POINT OF VIEW What opinion does the author seem to have about the natives of Hispaniola?

_____

_____

_____

3 INFERRING What does the author's mention of the landing at Zempoalla suggest about human health and the spread of disease?

_____

_____

_____

_____

_____

4 ANALYZING IDEAS How does mentioning that Montezuma's brother was a victim of smallpox help or hurt the author's claim about the disease?

_____

_____

_____

5 IDENTIFYING CONNECTIONS How do you think a modern-day health professional could use the message of this excerpt to make a case about the spread of disease?

_____

_____

_____

_____

ESSENTIAL QUESTION

What are the effects of political and economic expansion?

VOCABULARY

countenances: facial expressions

pestilential: causing contagious epidemic disease

copious: abundant

improvident avarice: short-sighted greed

galling: very irritating

fetters: pair of chained rings attached to ankles

Horrors of a Slave Ship

DIRECTIONS: Read the excerpt. Then respond to the questions that follow.

EXPLORE THE CONTEXT: Olaudah Equiano's autobiography describes his early life in West Africa, his capture at age 11, and the sea voyage that brought him to slavery in the West Indies and eventually Virginia. He traveled widely with the sea captain who purchased him and received some education. Later he was able to buy his freedom, and he became a dedicated abolitionist.

PRIMARY SOURCE: AUTOBIOGRAPHY

"The first object which saluted my eyes when I arrived on the coast was the sea, and a slave ship, which was then riding at anchor, and waiting for its cargo. These filled me with astonishment, which was soon converted into terror when I was carried on board. I was immediately handled and tossed up to see if I were sound by some of the crew; and I was now persuaded that I had gotten into a world of bad spirits, and that they were going to kill me. . . . Indeed such were the horrors of my views and fears at the moment, that, if ten thousand worlds had been my own, I would have freely parted with them all to have exchanged my condition with that of the meanest [enslaved person] in my own country. When I looked round the ship too and saw a large furnace or copper boiling, and a multitude of [Africans] of every description chained together, every one of their countenances expressing dejection and sorrow, I no longer doubted of my fate; and, quite overpowered with horror and anguish, I fell motionless on the deck and fainted . . . At last, when the ship we were in had got in all her cargo, they made ready with many fearful noises, and we were all put under deck, so that we could not see how they managed the vessel. But this disappointment was the least of my sorrow. The stench of the hold while we were on the coast was so intolerably loathsome, that it was dangerous to remain there for any time, and some of us had been permitted to stay on the deck for the fresh air; but now that the whole ship's cargo were confined together, it became absolutely pestilential. The closeness of the place, and the heat of the climate, added to the number in the ship, which was so crowded that each had scarcely room to turn himself, almost suffocated us. This produced copious perspirations, so that the air soon became unfit for respiration, from a variety of loathsome smells, and brought on a sickness among the slaves, of which many died, thus falling victims to the improvident avarice, as I may call it, of their purchasers. This wretched situation was again aggravated by the galling of the chains, now become insupportable; and the filth of the necessary tubs, into which the children often fell, and were almost suffocated. The shrieks of the women, and the groans of the dying, rendered the whole a scene of horror almost inconceivable. Happily perhaps for myself I was soon reduced so low here that it was thought necessary to keep me almost always on deck; and from my extreme youth I was not put in fetters. In this situation I expected every hour to share the fate of my companions, some of whom were almost daily brought upon deck at the point of death, which I began to hope would soon put an end to my miseries. **99**

—*The Interesting Narrative of the Life of Olaudah Equiano*, Olaudah Equiano, 1789

1 ANALYZING INDIVIDUALS Reflecting on his experience, what are some of his own emotions that you think Olaudah Equiano hopes to communicate to the reader?

_____

_____

_____

2 INTERPRETING Why does Equiano refer to the slave purchasers as having "improvident avarice"?

_____

_____

_____

3 HISTORY What text evidence shows that the enslaved people were kidnapped and had no warning or knowledge that they were being sent into a life of slavery?

_____

_____

_____

4 ANALYZING POINT OF VIEW To what does the author partly attribute his ability to survive the ship's voyage?

_____

_____

_____

5 ANALYZING IDEAS During the journey, what did Equiano think might have helped him out of his situation, and why?

_____

_____

ESSENTIAL QUESTION

What are the effects of political and economic expansion?

As you gather evidence to answer the Essential Question, think about:

- how Europeans established new social and political structures in Latin America.
- how the Portuguese and Spanish benefited economically from their Latin American colonies.
- how the Portuguese and Spanish governed their Latin American colonies.

My Notes

_____

_____

_____

_____

_____

_____

_____

_____

Colonial Latin America

DIRECTIONS: Search for evidence in the lesson to help you answer the following questions.

1 **IDENTIFYING EFFECTS** What were the economic and environmental effects of resource extraction and farming by the Portuguese and Spanish?

_____

_____

_____

_____

_____

2 **SUMMARIZING** Use the following chart to describe the social classes of colonial Latin America.

Peninsulares:

⬇

Creoles:

⬇

Mestizos and mulattoes:

⬇

Africans and conquered Native Americans:

3 **EVALUATING INFORMATION** What role did the Spanish *encomienda* system play in the lives of Native Americans?

_____

_____

_____

_____

4 **IDENTIFYING EFFECTS** What were three benefits the missions in Latin America provided for the Catholic Church?

_____

_____

_____

5 **SUMMARIZING** What role did women play in the religious life of colonial Latin America?

_____

_____

_____

6 **DRAWING CONCLUSIONS** How do you think outsiders who came to Latin American colonies could fit in to the social structure?

_____

_____

_____

ESSENTIAL QUESTION

What are the effects of political and economic expansion?

Letter from Lope de Aguirre to the King of Spain

DIRECTIONS: Read the excerpt. Then respond to the questions that follow.

EXPLORE THE CONTEXT: The following is an excerpt from a letter written in 1561 from Spanish conquistador Lope de Aguirre to the King of Spain, Philip II. In his letter, de Aguirre defies the monarchy and declares an independent state of Peru as his own kingdom. In this excerpt, he expresses his opinions about the missions. Not long after the letter was written, royal troops captured and executed de Aguirre.

PRIMARY SOURCE: LETTER

66 But the corruption of morals among monks is so great in this land, that it is necessary to chastise it severely. There is not an ecclesiastic here, who does not think himself higher than the governor of a province. I beg of thee, O great king, not to believe what the monks tell thee in Spain. They are always talking of the sacrifices they make, as well as of the hard and bitter life they lead in America. Be assured that when they shed tears there, in thy royal presence, it is that here they may be the more powerful. Wouldst thou know the life which they lead here? They are engaged in trade, striving for benefices, selling the sacraments of the church for a price, enemies of the poor, avaricious, gluttonous, and proud to that degree that, at the least, every friar pretends to rule and govern all these lands. They never desire to preach to any poor [Native American], yet they are possessed of the best estates. The life they lead is surely a hard one, for does not each of them, as a penance, have a dozen girls, and as many boys, who catch fish, kill partridges, and gather fruit for them. Remedy this, O king and lord, or else, I swear to thee, on the faith of a Christian, that heaven will punish thee, and great scandals will follow. I say this to let thee know the truth, though neither I, nor my companions, either desire or hope for thy mercy. 99

—*from* Letter from Lope de Aguirre to the King of Spain, 1561

VOCABULARY

chastise: to criticize severely

ecclesiastic: member of the clergy

benefices: a position given to clergy with guaranteed property or income

avaricious: greedy

gluttonous: tending to eat excessively

penance: punishment imposed after repenting a sin

Copyright © McGraw-Hill Education   Simón, Pedro. 1856. "Letter from Lope de Aguirre to the King." In *Search of El Dorado and Omagua in 1560-1.* Translated by William Bollaert. London: Hakluyt Society.

1 HISTORY   What is the historical context of de Aguirre's letter to the king?

_____

_____

_____

2 **ANALYZING POINT OF VIEW** What corruption does de Aguirre see that he believes the king does not understand?

_____

_____

_____

3 **INFERRING** In what way does de Aguirre think the monks fool the king?

_____

_____

_____

_____

4 **ANALYZING IDEAS** How does de Aguirre try to get the king to take action to change the missions system?

_____

_____

_____

5 **DRAWING CONCLUSIONS** After de Aguirre's death, he became an antihero in literature and cinema. What do you think was so fascinating about a person like him?

_____

_____

_____

_____

ESSENTIAL QUESTION

What are the effects of political and economic expansion?

VOCABULARY

dost: does (archaic)

erring: straying (archaic)

astray: off the correct path

Excerpt from *The Divine Narcissus*

DIRECTIONS: Read the excerpt. Then respond to the questions that follow.

EXPLORE THE CONTEXT: The following poem is from a play written in 1689 by renowned Mexican nun, poet, and scholar, Juana Ines de la Cruz, who became the unofficial poet of the Spanish court. The play is an allegory with a religious theme. The "divine Narcissus" represents Christ. The poem expresses a shepherd's appeal to a sheep lost from the flock.

PRIMARY SOURCE: POEM

from "The Divine Narcissus"

66 O my lost lamb,
Thy master all forgetting,
Whither dost erring go?
Behold how now divided
From me, thou partest from thy life!

In my tender kindness
Thou seest how always loving
I guard thee watchfully,
I free thee of all danger,
And that I give my life for thee.

Behold how that my beauty
Is of all things beloved,
And is of all things sought,
And by all creatures praised.
Still dost thou choose from me to go astray.

I go to seek thee yet,
Although thou art as lost;
But for thee now my life
I cannot still lay down
That once I wished to lose to find my sheep. 99

—*from* "The Divine Narcissus," by Juana Ines de la Cruz

1 **ANALYZING IDEAS** Based on de la Cruz's life, what do you think is her purpose for writing the play and the poem?

_____

_____

_____

2 **INTERPRETING** The poem introduces the play, and the first scene begins with human sacrifice, based on the belief that in return the harvest will succeed. What does this suggest about de la Cruz's understanding of the Aztec religion and the people she is helping convert?

_____

_____

_____

_____

3 **HISTORY** What does the poem reveal about the role of women in colonial Latin America?

_____

_____

_____

4 **ANALYZING POINT OF VIEW** How do you think laborers who saw the play that mixed themes of Aztec and Christian religions might view its message?

_____

_____

_____

_____

5 **IDENTIFYING PERSPECTIVES** How would you describe the general mood of the poem?

_____

_____

_____

_____

ESSENTIAL QUESTIONS

What are the effects of political and economic expansion?

My Notes

_____

_____

_____

_____

_____

_____

_____

_____

_____

_____

_____

_____

1 Think About It

Review the Supporting Questions you developed at the beginning of the chapter. Review the evidence you gathered in the chapter. Were you able to answer each Supporting Question? If there was not enough evidence to answer your Supporting questions, what additional evidence do you think you need to consider?

_____

_____

_____

_____

2 Organize Your Evidence

Complete the chart below with information you learned about political and economic expansion of European empires.

Political Expansion	Economic Expansion

3 Talk About It

Work in small groups. With your group, give one example of political expansion during the 1500s, and talk about how it changed the indigenous peoples, their customs, and their social structure.

_____

_____

_____

_____

_____

_____

4 Write About It

Choose an example of one nation's economic expansion during the 1500s. Then write a feature article explaining its origins, its progression, and its benefits to the nation. Include any unanticipated problems that arose as well as unanticipated effects.

_____

_____

_____

_____

_____

_____

5 Connect to the Essential Question

Work in groups to create a poster of a world map that shows one of the trade routes discussed in the chapter. The routes shown on the maps should guide the viewer to understand the connection to the chapter's Essential Question. Include a map key and captions to explain the routes and their economic impact.

_____

_____

_____

_____

_____

_____

CITIZENSHIP
TAKE ACTION

MAKE CONNECTIONS News editorials can teach the public a lot about an issue, including how our political and economic systems were developed. Editorials present an argument with a clear point of view, but they use facts and research to support a position and strengthen the call to action. For example, an editorial about present-day global trade might provide context by including information about early global economic systems and compare the effects trade growth has on various parts of the world.

DIRECTIONS: Write an editorial about an issue of your choice related to a topic in the chapter. Include facts and details from the chapter that will defend your point of view about the issue. If possible, publish the article with a school or local newspaper or website.

_____

_____

_____

_____

_____

_____

_____

_____

_____

_____

_____

_____

_____

_____

Conflict and Absolutism in Europe

ESSENTIAL QUESTION
What effect might social, economic, and religious conflicts have on a country?

Think about how this question might relate to the government, religion, and conflicts in sixteenth-century Spain, England, and France.

TALK ABOUT IT

Discuss with a partner what information you would need to know to answer this question. For example, one question might be, "What were the conflicts about in sixteenth-century Spain, England, and France?" Another might be, "In which countries during this period did the ruler hold absolute power?"

DIRECTIONS: Now write down three additional questions that you need to answer to be able to describe the conflicts in sixteenth-century Spain, England, and France.

MY RESEARCH QUESTIONS

Supporting Question 1:

_____

_____

_____

_____

Supporting Question 2:

_____

_____

_____

Supporting Question 3:

_____

_____

_____

Europe in Crisis

DIRECTIONS Search for evidence in the lesson to help you answer the following questions.

ESSENTIAL QUESTION

What effect might social, economic, and religious conflicts have on a country?

As you gather evidence to answer the Essential Question, think about:

- the Edict of Nantes as an effective solution to the wars in France.
- why Philip II of Spain had trouble controlling part of his empire.
- how Elizabeth I managed England's foreign policy.

1 **DETERMINING CONTEXT** Why did the witchcraft trials of this era gradually fade away?

_____

_____

_____

_____

2 ECONOMICS Spain experienced an economic slowdown in the early sixteenth century. Fill in the graphic organizer to show why the Spanish economy faltered.

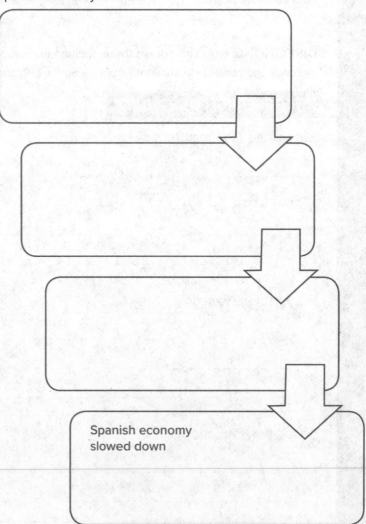

Spanish economy slowed down

My Notes

_____

_____

_____

_____

_____

_____

_____

3 IDENTIFYING CONNECTIONS All the major powers in Europe, except England, were involved in the Thirty Years' War. The war began as a religious dispute but later shifted to political conflict. How and why did this happen?

_____

_____

_____

_____

4 UNDERSTANDING CONTEXT Given the context of Europe at this time, how did the Edict of Nantes prevent further conflict between Catholics and Protestants in France?

_____

_____

_____

5 SUMMARIZING Use the graphic organizer to summarize reasons for the defeat of the Spanish Armada in 1588.

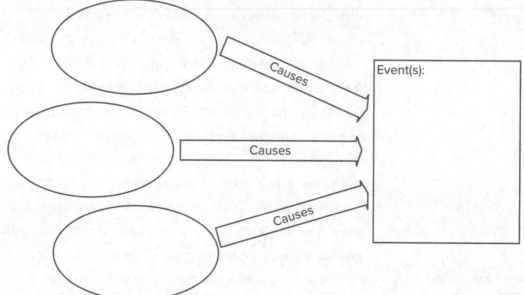

6 EXPLAINING EFFECTS During the French Wars of Religion, Catholicism was the official state religion in France. Huguenots represented only about 7 percent of the French population. Huguenots, however, made up 40–50 percent of French nobility. The king persecuted Protestants throughout France, yet he had little success in suppressing Protestantism. Explain why this was the case.

_____

_____

_____

ESSENTIAL QUESTION

What effect might social, economic, and religious conflicts have on a country?

Witches in 17th-Century England

DIRECTIONS: Read the excerpt and answer the following questions.

EXPLORE THE CONTEXT: *The Wonderfull Discoverie of Witches in the Countie of Lancaster* was written by Thomas Potts in 1613. This was a period of intense fear of witches and witchcraft that resulted in innumerable trials of men and women suspected of being witches. Unmarried poor women over age 50 were most often accused, but men were accused as well. The "trial" often amounted to torturing the alleged witches at length until they confessed to whatever evil activity they had been accused. Lancashire is a county in the northwestern part of England marked by hills and moorland (open, sometimes barren land that is unusable for farming).

PRIMARY SOURCE: BOOK

❝ In the early part of the seventeenth century, the inhabitants of this district must have been, with few exceptions, a wretchedly poor and uncultivated race, having little communication with the occupants of the more fertile regions around them, and in whose minds superstition, even yet unextinguished, must have had absolute and uncontrollable domination. Under the disenchanting influence of steam, manufactures, and projected rail-roads, still much of the old character of its population remains. . . . The 'parting genius' of superstition still clings to the hoary hill tops and rugged slopes and mossy water sides, along which the old forest stretched its length, and the voices of ancestral tradition are still heard to speak from the depth of its quiet hollows, and along the course of its gurgling streams. He who visits Pendle will yet find that charms are generally resorted to amongst the lower classes; that there are hares which, in their persuasion, never can be caught, and which survive only to baffle and confound the huntsman; that each small hamlet has its peculiar and gifted personage, whom it is dangerous to offend; that the wise man and wise woman (the white witches of our ancestors) still continue their investigations of truth, undisturbed by the rural police or the progress of the schoolmaster; that each locality has its haunted house; that apparitions still walk their ghostly rounds—and little would his reputation for piety avail that clergyman in the eyes of his parishioners who should refuse to lay those 'extravagant and erring spirits,' when requested, by those due liturgic ceremonies which the orthodoxy of tradition requires. ❞

—Thomas Potts, *The Wonderfull Discoverie of Witches in the Countie of Lancaster,* 1613

VOCABULARY

apparition: ghostly figure

avail: help

disenchanting: freeing from illusion; bringing back to reality

erring: making a mistake

hamlet: small village

hares: rabbits

hoary: ancient

liturgic: relating to religious ceremony

piety: religious devotion

uncultivated: lacking in refinement

1A GEOGRAPHY According to its title, Thomas Potts's book is about the discovery of witches in Lancaster County. Why do you think he described the area in such detail?

_____

_____

_____

_____

1B INFERRING Besides the fact that the author thinks it is a likely place to find witches, what can you infer about the area?

_____

_____

_____

2 DETERMINING MEANING Think about the adjectives and adverbs Potts uses to describe this area of Lancashire. Give a few examples of these words and explain why he chose them.

_____

_____

_____

_____

3 IDENTIFYING EFFECTS What effect do you think the witchcraft trials had on England?

_____

_____

4 IDENTIFYING CAUSES Why did witchcraft trials dwindle in frequency and finally fade away?

_____

_____

_____

5 IDENTIFYING PERSPECTIVES From what perspective is Potts writing? How can you tell?

_____

_____

ESSENTIAL QUESTION

What effect might social, economic, and religious conflicts have on a country?

"The Bloody Project"

DIRECTIONS: Read the excerpt closely and answer the questions that follow.

EXPLORE THE CONTEXT: In 1648 when England was torn by conflict, the pamphlet "The Bloody Project" was published. "W. P. Gent" is probably a pen name for William Walwyn, an Englishman who was involved in radical local politics. Walwyn was a Leveler, a political faction in England active in the mid-1600s. Some of the causes championed by the Levelers included religious toleration, law reform, equality before the law, and universal male suffrage. After a period of brief influence in the New Model Army, leading Levelers were arrested and imprisoned, and their popularity waned.

PRIMARY SOURCE: PAMPHLET

66 Can there be a more bloody Project than to engage men to kill one another, and yet no just cause declared? Therefore I advise all men that would be esteemed Religious or Rational, really to consider what may be done for the future that is conducible to the Peace of the Nation; If the Peace of the Nation cannot be secured without the Restauration of the King, let it be done speedily and honorably, and provide against his misgovernment for the future; let his powers be declared and limited by Law.

If the Peace of the Nation cannot be secured by the continuance of this Parliament, let a Period be set for the dissolution thereof, but first make certain provision for the successive calling, electing and sitting of Parliaments for the future; let their Priviledges be declared and power limited, as to what they are empowered and what not; for doubtless in Parliament rightly constituted consists the Freedom of a Nation: And in all things do as you would be done unto, seek peace with all men.

But above all things, abandon your former actings for a King against a Parliament, or an Army against both; for the Presbyterians against the Independents, etc. for in so doing you do but put a Sword into your enemies hands to destroy you, for hitherto, which of them soever were in power, they played the Tyrants and oppressed, and so it will ever be, when Parties are supported: Therefore if you engage at all, do it by Lawful Authority, let your Cause be declared, and just also, and let it be for the good of the whole Nation, without which you will not only hazard being Slaves, but also contract upon yourselves and Posterities the guilt of Murderers. Vale. 99

—W. P. Gent, *The Bloody Project*, 1648

VOCABULARY

Restauration: restoration; putting something back in place

dissolution: dissolving or dismantling an organization or governing body

hitherto: up to this point

vale: very old-fashioned synonym for "goodbye" or "farewell"

1A **DETERMINING CENTRAL IDEAS** What is the main idea of this pamphlet?

_____

_____

1B **UNDERSTANDING CONTEXT** Why was this main idea important to the author? In what context was this text written?

_____

_____

_____

2 **CIVICS** Give one or more examples of how the author says people should apply values and democratic principles in this excerpt.

_____

_____

_____

_____

3 **EVALUATING** The English Civil War started in 1642 and continued for almost a decade. What were some of the war's effects on England?

_____

_____

4 **DISTINGUISHING FACT FROM OPINION** Is the excerpt factual or is the author stating his opinions? Explain your answer.

_____

_____

5 **DETERMINING MEANING** Do you think this pamphlet is persuasive? Why or why not?

_____

_____

_____

_____

_____

War and Revolution in England

DIRECTIONS Search for evidence in the lesson to help you answer the following questions.

1 SUMMARIZING Use the graphic organizer to summarize Locke's conception of people's "natural rights."

Locke's Natural Rights of All People

2 IDENTIFYING CONNECTIONS List three things that enabled Cromwell and his New Model Army to seize control of England.

_____

_____

_____

_____

_____

_____

_____

3 INTERPRETING Why was Philip II of Spain known as "the most Catholic king"?

_____

_____

_____

_____

_____

ESSENTIAL QUESTION

What effect might social, economic, and religious conflicts have on a country?

As you gather evidence to answer the Essential Question, think about:

- the conflict between Parliament and the king.
- the conflicts between Catholics and Protestants.
- the new visions of society proposed by Hobbes and Locke.

My Notes

_____

_____

_____

_____

_____

_____

_____

4 **ANALYZING TEXTS** Why was the Restoration period named the way it was? What was restored?

_____

_____

_____

_____

5 **COMPARE AND CONTRAST** Reread the section of this lesson that discusses Hobbes's _Leviathan_ and Locke's _Two Treatises of Government._ Fill in the Venn diagram to illustrate how Locke's and Hobbes's ideas differed and how they shared certain aspects.

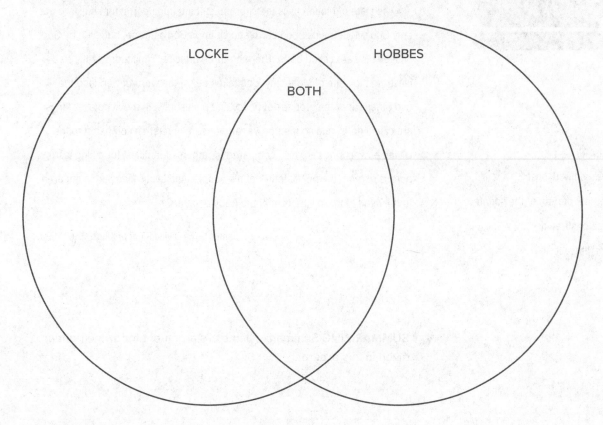

LOCKE   HOBBES

BOTH

6 CIVICS   Is the Divine Right of Kings compatible with democracy?

_____

_____

_____

_____

ESSENTIAL QUESTION

What effect might social, economic, and religious conflicts have on a country?

The Divine Right of Kings

DIRECTIONS: Read the following excerpt and answer the questions that follow.

INTRODUCTION: James I was king of England from 1603 to 1625, the year he died. As the excerpt shows, he was convinced that kings were appointed to the throne by God and, as such, were free to do as they wished.

PRIMARY SOURCE: TEXT

66 The state of Monarchy is the supremest thing upon earth; for kings are not only God's lieutenants upon earth and sit upon God's throne, but even by God himself they are called gods. There be three principal similitudes that illustrate the state of Monarchy: one taken out of the word of God, and the two other out of the grounds of policy and philosophy. In the Scriptures kings are called gods, and so their power after a certain relation compared to the Divine power. Kings are also compared to fathers of families; for a king is truly *parens patriae*, the politic father of his people. And lastly, kings are compared to the head of this microcosm of the body of man. 99

—James I, The Divine Right of Kings, 1597–1598

VOCABULARY

similitudes: comparisons

parens patriae: partent of the country

politic: wise or shrewd

microcosm: little world

1A **SUMMARIZING** Summarize James I's argument for divine right as given in this excerpt.

_____

_____

_____

_____

_____

_____

_____

_____

Copyright © McGraw-Hill Education   James I. 1610. The King's Speech to Parliament. Reprinted by Tanner, J. R. 1960. Constitutional Documents of the Reign of James I - A.D. 1603–1625. Cambridge University Press.

1B **EVALUATING** Evaluate James I's argument and explain why it is convincing or unconvincing.

_____

_____

_____

_____

_____

2 **CIVICS** Do you agree with James I that the leader of a country should be considered the "parent of the country"? What values does this idea promote?

_____

_____

_____

_____

_____

3 **INFERRING** What can you infer about James I from his belief in the divine right of kings?

_____

_____

_____

_____

4 **ANALYZING TEXT** Does James make a good case for divine right? Why or why not?

_____

_____

_____

_____

_____

Copyright © McGraw-Hill Education   English Parliament. 1628. The Petition of Right. Reprinted by Hume, David. 1872. The Student's Hume: A History of England From the Earliest Times to the Revolution in 1688. New York: Harper & Brothers Publishers.

ESSENTIAL QUESTION

What effect might social, economic, and religious conflicts have on a country?

VOCABULARY

tallage: tax

divers: various; some

writs of habeas corpus: orders for a legal inquiry to determine whether a person has been lawfully or unlawfully imprisoned

sojourn: temporary stay

vexation: annoyance

The Petition of Right

DIRECTIONS: Read the following excerpt and answer the questions that follow.

INTRODUCTION: Parliament delivered the Petition of Right to Charles I in 1628. Parliament was reacting to a series of illegal actions by the king, such as arbitrarily imposing a tax on the English people because England's funds were being depleted by war. The petition comprised a list of demands for certain rights and liberties for English citizens. The petition is excerpted below.

PRIMARY SOURCE: PETITION EXCERPT

" To the King's Most Excellent Majesty,

Humbly show unto our Sovereign Lord the King, . . . that whereas it is declared and enacted . . . that no tallage or aid shall be laid or levied by the king or his heirs in this realm, . . . it is declared and enacted, that from thenceforth no person should be compelled to make any loans to the king against his will, because such loans were against reason and the franchise of the land. . . .

III. And whereas also by the statute called 'The Great Charter of the Liberties of England,' it is declared and enacted, that no freeman may be taken or imprisoned . . . or be outlawed or exiled, or in any manner destroyed, but by the lawful judgment of his peers, or by the law of the land.

IV. And in the eight-and-twentieth year of the reign of King Edward III, it was declared and enacted by authority of parliament, that no man, . . . should be put out of his land or tenements, . . . nor disinherited nor put to death without being brought to answer by due process of law.

V. Nevertheless, . . . divers of your subjects have of late been imprisoned without any cause showed; and when for their deliverance they were brought before your justices by your Majesty's writs of habeas corpus, . . . no cause was certified, . . . yet [they] were returned back to several prisons, without being charged with anything. . . .

VI. And whereas of late great companies of soldiers and mariners have been dispersed into divers counties of the realm, and the inhabitants against their wills have been compelled to receive them into their houses, and there to suffer them to sojourn against the laws and customs of this realm, and to the great grievance and vexation of the people. . . .

XI. All which they most humbly pray of your most excellent Majesty as their rights and liberties, according to the laws and statutes of this realm; . . . shall not be drawn hereafter into consequence or example; and that your Majesty would be also graciously pleased, for the further comfort and safety of your people, to declare your royal will and pleasure, that in the things aforesaid all your officers and ministers shall serve you according to the laws and statutes of this realm. "

—The Petition of Right, 1628

1 **SUMMARIZING** Briefly summarize the demands Parliament makes in the excerpt.

_____

_____

_____

_____

2 **ANALYZING CHANGE** What was one effect of the Petition of Right?

_____

_____

_____

3 CIVICS Compare the demands in the petition of right with those in the U.S. Bill of Rights. Are there similar ideas in these two documents? How do these ideas promote democratic ideals? Support your answer with information from the text and from the excerpt.

_____

_____

_____

4 **IDENTIFYING CONNECTIONS** In what way did the Petition of Right affect U.S. history?

_____

_____

5A **ANALYZING TEXT** Describe the tone of the petition and explain your answer.

_____

_____

5B **DETERMINING POINT OF VIEW** Based on your answer in 5A, what result did Parliament likely intend the Petition of Right to achieve?

_____

_____

_____

Absolutism in Europe

DIRECTIONS: Search for evidence in the lesson to help you answer the following questions.

1 **EXPLAINING EFFECTS** Show how Louis XIV strengthened his power by filling in the graphic organizer.

	EFFECT: STRENGTHENED ROYAL POWER
CAUSE:	
CAUSE:	
CAUSE:	
CAUSE:	

ESSENTIAL QUESTION

What effect might social, economic, and religious conflicts have on a country?

As you gather evidence to answer the Essential Question, think about:

- how Peter the Great made Russia a world power.
- why the Austrian Empire was not a centralized absolutist empire.
- why Philip IV's attempt to centralize power in Spain failed.

2 **SPATIAL THINKING** The Austrian Empire included Austria, the Czech Republic, Hungary, Croatia, Transylvania, and Slavonia. It was never a centralized empire. Use the map in your textbook to explain why.

_____

_____

_____

_____

My Notes

_____

_____

_____

_____

_____

_____

_____

_____

3 **DETERMINING CONTEXT** Explain why Philip IV's attempt to centralize power in Spain ultimately failed.

_____

_____

_____

_____

_____

4 RELATING EVENTS Describe how the rulers of the Spanish, Austrian, and Russian Empires attempted to solve conflicts.

_____

_____

_____

_____

_____

5 HISTORY In 1689 the absolutist Peter the Great became czar. He visited the West and returned to Russia determined to "westernize" his empire. What was the result of his visit to the West?

_____

_____

_____

_____

_____

_____

6 UNDERSTANDING CAUSES Use the graphic organizer to show examples of what Peter the Great did that resulted in Russia becoming a world power.

Cause 1		Cause 2

Effects

Cause 3		Cause 4

ESSENTIAL QUESTION

What effect might social, economic, and religious conflicts have on a country?

The Hall of Mirrors at the Palace of Versailles

DIRECTIONS: Reread the section of this lesson that discusses absolutism in the reign of Louis XIV. Then read the introduction, study the image, and answer the questions that follow.

EXPLORE THE CONTEXT: The palace of Versailles is Louis XIV's monument to himself. The palace and grounds comprise almost 2,000 acres. The oldest part of the building dates from 1623, when it was used as a hunting lodge. Louis XIV began expanding it in 1661, and construction continued for more than 50 years. The Hall of Mirrors covers almost 100,000 square feet (about 9,000 sq. m). It has 17 mirrored arches with 21 mirrors each, which reflect the 17 windows in the hall. Other materials used include marble and gilded bronze. Today the palace is open to the public as a museum. Its worth is estimated at $50 billion.

PRIMARY SOURCE: PHOTOGRAPH

1 **DESCRIBING** In your own words, describe the palace of Versailles and the effect it was intended to have.

_____

_____

_____

2 **DRAWING CONCLUSIONS** Louis XIV was an absolutist ruler who successfully managed conflicts in France during his reign. Explain how the Hall of Mirrors is a good illustration of the concept of absolutism.

_____

_____

_____

3 ECONOMICS What does the palace of Versailles suggest about the state of the French economy and Louis's economic priorities at the time of the palace's construction?

_____

_____

_____

_____

4 **INFERRING** What can you infer about Louis XIV from the image of his palace?

_____

_____

_____

5A **IDENTIFYING EFFECTS** In your opinion, what effects could the palace of Versailles have had on French citizenry?

_____

_____

5B **IDENTIFYING CAUSES** What does the construction of the palace of Versailles tell you about Louis' priorities as King?

_____

_____

ESSENTIAL QUESTION

What effect might social, economic, and religious conflicts have on a country?

Peter the Great, Czar of Russia

DIRECTIONS: Read the text and answer the questions that follow.

EXPLORE THE CONTEXT: Peter the Great became Czar of Russia in 1682 when he was ten years old. He ruled jointly with his brother, Ivan V, until 1696. He embarked upon a career of military expansion and modernization of Russia based on his understanding of developed western European states. He visited England in 1698 while trying to create a European alliance to oppose the Ottoman Empire. The following is a description of Peter by Bishop Burnet, an English bishop who spent time with Peter in 1698.

PRIMARY SOURCE: TEXT

❝He is a man of a very hot temper, soon inflamed and very brutal in his passion. He raises his natural heat by drinking much brandy, which he rectifies himself with great application. . . .

He is mechanically turned, and seems designed by nature rather to be a ship carpenter than a great prince. This was his chief study and exercise while he stayed here. He wrought much with his own hands and made all about him work at the models of ships. He told me he designed a great fleet at Azuph [i.e. Azov] and with it to attack the Turkish empire. But he did not seem capable of conducting so great a design, though his conduct in his wars since this has discovered a greater genius in him than appeared at this time. . . .

After I had seen him often, and had conversed much with him, I could not but adore the depth of the providence of God that had raised up such a furious man to so absolute an authority over so great a part of the world . . .

He went from hence to the court of Vienna, where he purposed to have stayed some time, but he was called home sooner than he had intended upon a discovery, or a suspicion, of intrigues managed by his sister. The strangers, to whom he trusted most, were so true to him that those designs were crushed before he came back. But on this occasion he let loose his fury on all whom he suspected. Some hundreds of them were hanged all around Moskow, and it was said that he cut off many heads with his own hand; and so far was he from relenting or showing any sort of tenderness that he seemed delighted with it. How long he is to be the scourge of that nation God only knows. ❞

—Bishop Burnet, *Impressions of Peter the Great*, 1898

VOCABULARY

rectifies: to purify an alcohol

providence: divine guidance or planning

intrigues: plots to overthrow a ruler

scourge: a tool used to punish

1 **SUMMARIZING** What impression does the text give you of the personality and priorities of Peter the Great?

_____

_____

2 **UNDERSTANDING CONTEXT** Do you think the author approves of Peter? Why, or why not?

_____

_____

_____

3 **COMPARING AND CONTRASTING** What opinion might the author of this text have about the Divine Right of Kings? How can you tell?

_____

_____

_____

_____

_____

4 **UNDERSTANDING CONTEXT** The text describes a rebellion against Peter. How does this, and Peter's reaction, suggest the kind of ruler Peter was and the sort he aspired to be?

_____

_____

_____

5 CIVICS Consider the text's description of Peter the Great. In a democratic society, citizens choose their rulers based on their values, their judgment of a candidate's behavior, and the policies they prefer. How might a democratic society have viewed Peter the Great?

_____

_____

_____

_____

ESSENTIAL QUESTION

What effect might social, economic, and religious conflicts have on a country?

As you gather evidence to answer the Essential Question, think about:

- how Mannerism and baroque styles of art might have grown out of the widespread conflicts in Europe.

- why Shakespeare's plays were so popular.

- how Cervantes' novel *Don Quixote* might have reflected this tumultuous era in Spanish history.

My Notes

_____

_____

_____

_____

_____

_____

_____

European Culture After the Renaissance

DIRECTIONS Search for evidence in the lesson to help you answer the following questions.

1 **HISTORY** Your textbook says, "In El Greco's paintings, the figures are elongated or contorted and he sometimes used unusual shades of yellow and green against an eerie background of stormy grays." Why do you think El Greco painted this way?

_____

_____

_____

2 **DETERMINING CONTEXT** Explain how the plays of Shakespeare and other Elizabethan dramatists appealed to such a wide variety of audiences.

_____

_____

_____

3 **INFERRING** What does the popularity of the works of Cervantes and Vega tell us about Spanish culture during this period?

_____

_____

_____

_____

_____

4 DESCRIBING Fill in the chart with specific qualities of the Mannerist painters and the baroque painters that you learned about in your textbook.

Mannerist	Baroque

5 DRAWING CONCLUSIONS Based on what you have learned about these two schools of art, what conclusions can you draw about both styles?

_____

_____

_____

6 DIFFERENTIATING Based on what you have learned about these two schools of art, in what ways do they differ?

_____

_____

_____

_____

_____

_____

ESSENTIAL QUESTION

What effect might social, economic, and religious conflicts have on a country?

Witches in *Macbeth*

DIRECTIONS: Read the excerpt from *Macbeth*. Then respond to the questions that follow.

EXPLORE THE CONTEXT: *Macbeth*, first staged more than 400 years ago, is one of Shakespeare's most popular plays. It is a tragedy about the negative effects of ambition on those who seek political power. Other themes include guilt and revenge. The excerpt below concerns the "Three Weird Sisters"—witches who prophesy that Macbeth will soon become king. In this scene, the sisters are cooking something in a cauldron that involves some strange ingredients.

PRIMARY SOURCE: PLAY

First Witch

Round about the cauldron go;

In the poison'd entrails throw.

Toad, that under cold stone

Days and nights has thirty-one

Swelter'd venom sleeping got,

Boil thou first i' the charmed pot.

ALL

Double, double toil and trouble;

Fire burn, and cauldron bubble.

Second Witch

Fillet of a fenny snake,

In the cauldron boil and bake;

Eye of newt and toe of frog,

Wool of bat and tongue of dog,

Adder's fork and blind-worm's sting,

Lizard's leg and owlet's wing,

For a charm of powerful trouble,

Like a hell-broth boil and bubble.

ALL

Double, double toil and trouble;

Fire burn and cauldron bubble.

Third Witch

Scale of dragon, tooth of wolf,

Witches' mummy, maw and gulf

Of the ravin'd salt-sea shark,

Root of hemlock digg'd i' the dark,. . .

ALL

Double, double toil and trouble;

Fire burn and cauldron bubble.

Second Witch

Cool it with a baboon's blood,

Then the charm is firm and good.

—William Shakespeare, *Macbeth*, 1623

VOCABULARY

cauldron: very large cooking pot

entrails: guts; intestines

newt: a small salamander

adder: type of snake

maw: large, gaping hole, usually of a mouth

gulf: a deep hole or chasm

1 **DESCRIBING** The witches seem to be making soup. Describe some of the ingredients given in the excerpt.

_____

_____

2 **DRAWING CONCLUSIONS** Do you think the witches are just cooking up a nutritious soup? Why or why not?

_____

_____

3 **HISTORY** How does this text contribute to our understanding of beliefs about witchcraft in Shakespeare's time?

_____

_____

_____

_____

4 **UNDERSTANDING CONTEXT** Based on the reading in your textbook, do you think the audience in Shakespeare's time would believe in witches?

_____

_____

5 **DETERMINING MEANING** What kind of feeling or tone has Shakespeare set in the scene? How did he achieve this?

_____

_____

_____

_____

6 **INFERRING** What can you infer about the three witches? Cite words from the primary source to support your answer.

_____

_____

Artemisia Gentileschi, Baroque Painter

ESSENTIAL QUESTION

What effect might social, economic, and religious conflicts have on a country?

DIRECTIONS: Look at the painting and answer the questions.

INTRODUCTION: Artemisia Gentileschi was a baroque painter in Italy in the early seventeenth century. Because female painters were not well respected at that time, she is lesser known than some of her contemporaries. She was rediscovered in the late twentieth century and is now considered an outstanding painter of the baroque era. She is especially admired for her vivid and lifelike depictions of female figures, often depicted as strong and capable, in contrast to trends at the time.

PRIMARY SOURCE: PAINTING

1 DESCRIBING What aspects of this painting immediately strike you as noteworthy or important?

_____

_____

_____

2 **INFERRING** What can you infer about Clio, the woman in the painting?

_____

_____

_____

3 **EXPLAINING ISSUES** Gentileschi was not respected as a painter because she was a woman. She was known for painting portraits of strong, confident women. How might these two things be related?

_____

_____

_____

4 **IDENTIFYING BIAS** In the previous question, you learned that Gentileschi was often overlooked due to her gender, and her talent was ignored. Do you identify this as bias? Why or why not?

_____

_____

_____

5 **COMPARING AND CONTRASTING** Imagine if Gentileschi were alive today. Do you think she would be routinely overlooked as a woman painter the same way she was in her lifetime? Why or why not?

_____

_____

_____

6 **CIVICS** Although Gentileschi was subject to sexism in the seventeenth century, she persevered. Now she is part of the pantheon of great women artists. How might this story be relevant to modern people?

_____

_____

_____

_____

ESSENTIAL QUESTION

What effect might social, economic, and religious conflicts have on a country?

My Notes

_____

_____

_____

_____

_____

_____

_____

_____

_____

_____

_____

_____

_____

_____

_____

_____

1 Think About It

Review the supporting questions you developed at the beginning of the chapter. Review the evidence you gathered in the chapter. Were you able to answer each Supporting Question? If there was not enough evidence to answer your Supporting Questions, what additional evidence do you think you need to consider?

_____

_____

2 Organize Your Evidence

Complete the chart below to organize what you feel is the most significant information you learned about the conflicts in Europe in Chapter 2. A few answers are provided to get you started.

ENGLAND	FRANCE	SPAIN
Religion	Religion	Religion
Witchcraft trials	Louis XIV absolutist	Huge empire

③ Write About It

Gather and organize what you learned in the chapter, then make notes that will help you in the following project. You can use the chart from Organize Your Evidence to help in your organization. Then write a short essay addressing the Essential Question for this chapter.

_____

_____

_____

_____

_____

_____

_____

_____

_____

④ Connect to the Essential Question

Imagine you are a reporter from the twenty-first century assigned to travel back in time to the seventeenth century and interview Louis XIV, the king of France. What questions will you ask? What will you do if he refuses to answer or ignores a question? Use what you have learned in this chapter, as well as independent research, to write an interview article with the absolutist who called himself the Sun King. Include visual aids like portraits and photographs to accompany your article, and present the article on a mocked-up newspaper page.

CITIZENSHIP
TAKING ACTION

MAKE CONNECTIONS Conflicts always have an effect on a society or community, no matter how small the community. For instance, perhaps some people in your town want to widen a street to improve traffic flow, while others want to add a bike lane to the street instead. Or maybe a "big box" store wants to build an outlet on the outskirts of town. Some residents may oppose it because they are afraid a large store might put small local stores out of business, but others might want the big box store because they believe it will offer lower prices.

DIRECTIONS: Research a current conflict in your community. Then decide which side you support and create a pamphlet to educate your neighbors about the issue. Remember to make your pamphlet colorful and easy to understand so that people will want to read it. Write the pamphlet as persuasively as possible to win over people to your side. When your pamphlet is finished, make copies and hand them out to your classmates, teachers, and neighbors. You can even mail it to your elected officials.

_____

_____

_____

_____

_____

_____

_____

_____

_____

_____

_____

The Muslim Empires

ESSENTIAL QUESTIONS

What factors help unify an empire?

How can the creation of a new empire impact the people and culture of a region?

Think about the different factors that helped unify each of the three Muslim empires. What did they have in common? What did each take from the peoples they conquered?

TALK ABOUT IT

With a partner, discuss what you would need to know to answer these questions. For example, one question might be, "How did conquest affect people's belief systems in the three Muslim empires?"

DIRECTIONS: Now write down three additional questions that will help you understand the lasting effects the expansion of empires have on a region's people, culture, and way of life. For example, you might ask, "What factors influenced the status of women in the Ṣafavid Empire? How did the Moguls bring together Persian and Indian influences in art?"

MY RESEARCH QUESTIONS

Supporting Question 1:

_____

_____

Supporting Question 2:

_____

_____

Supporting Question 3:

_____

_____

_____

ESSENTIAL QUESTION

How can the creation of a new empire impact the people and culture of a region?

As you gather evidence to answer the Essential Question, think about:

- how the Ottomans built their empire.
- what life was like under Ottoman rule.

My Notes

_____

_____

_____

_____

_____

_____

_____

The Rise and Expansion of the Ottoman Empire

DIRECTIONS: Search for evidence in the lesson to help you answer the following questions.

1 **IDENTIFYING CAUSES** What were the keys to the Ottomans' success in toppling the Byzantine Empire?

_____

_____

_____

_____

_____

_____

2 **ANALYZING EVENTS** Why was the Ottomans' capture of Constantinople important? From there, where did the empire expand? How did this impact the Muslim world?

_____

_____

_____

_____

_____

_____

_____

_____

_____

3 **DESCRIBING** What were the Ottoman sultan's powers? How was the empire administered?

_____

_____

_____

_____

_____

4 **CONSTRUCTING HYPOTHESES** Why do you think the Ottomans were tolerant of other religions and cultures?

_____

_____

5A **DESCRIBING** Use the graphic organizer to identify the four main occupational groups in the Ottoman Empire and state a fact about each.

Occupational Group	Description

5B **EXPLAINING ISSUES** Discuss the status of women in the Ottoman Empire. Why was their status different than that of women in other Muslim regions?

_____

_____

_____

_____

_____

6 **SUMMARIZING** What were some of the artistic achievements of the Ottoman Empire? What is considered their most important artistic contribution? Who was Sinan and what is notable about his work?

_____

_____

_____

_____

_____

Copyright © McGraw-Hill Education   De Lamartine, Alphonse Marie Louis. Reprinted 1914 by Eva March Tappan. "The Surrender of Rhodes." In The World's Story in Fourteen Volumes With Illustrations. Volume VI - Russia, Austria-Hungary, the Balkan States, and Turkey. Boston and New York: Houghton Mifflin Company, 1522.

ESSENTIAL QUESTION

How can the creation of a new empire impact the people and culture of a region?

Süleyman Conquers Rhodes

DIRECTIONS: Read the excerpt. Then respond to the questions that follow.

EXPLORE THE CONTEXT: The Siege of Rhodes, led by Ottoman sultan Süleyman, occurred between June and December of 1522. Ottoman capture of this Greek island just off the coast of modern-day Turkey secured Ottoman control of the Mediterranean. Süleyman led a navy of over 300 ships along with 75,000 troops against the Knights of Rhodes. Despite the knights' bravery, their Grand Master, Phillippe Villers de L'Isle-Adam, surrendered to Süleyman in December 1522. This excerpt is from a 19th century French poet and historian's work, *History of Turkey.*

SECONDARY SOURCE: BOOKISTA

❝ L'Isle-Adam returned to the city, as admired by the vanquisher as by the vanquished. The day following [Süleyman], dressed as a common . . . cavalryman . . . and attended by only two pages in the same costume, mounted horse and came to visit, under guaranty of truce, the city which he was going at last to possess. He entered at the hour of the repast of the knights of the palace of the grand master, and the hall wherein these monk-warriors messed in common. He asked to see L'Isle-Adam, through one of his pages who spoke Greek. L'Isle-Adam, recognizing the sultan, received him as guest and not as sovereign. The young man and the old man conversed a long time on the terrace of the palace, which commands a view of the city, of the sea, and of Asia Minor, encircled like a garden by the snow-capped mountains of Cilicia. The sultan, penetrated with esteem for the hero of Rhodes, proposed to him a longer delay, and easier conditions for the evacuation of the island. The grand master made him a present of four magnificent cups of gold enriched with topazes, which decorated the treasury of the order. [Süleyman] was affected to tears on contemplating the preparations for eternal exile which the victory and the capitulation imposed upon these aged officers of Rhodes, of whom this island was become the country. "It is not without sorrow and shame," said he to his pages in remounting his horse, "that I force this venerable Christian to abandon in his gray hairs his home and his possessions. ❞

—from *History of Turkey,* by Alphonse de Lamartine, 1854

VOCABULARY

page: a young boy in training for knighthood

repast: meal

messed in common: took meals together

capitulation: surrender

1 **DETERMINING POINT OF VIEW** What is the writer's point of view in this selection? How do you know?

_____

_____

_____

_____

_____

_____

2 **CITING TEXT EVIDENCE** According to this account, what terms did the Ottomans offer the defeated inhabitants of Rhodes? Cite text evidence to support your answer.

_____

_____

_____

_____

3 **DISTINGUISHING FACT FROM OPINION** How much of this account is factual and how much is the writer's speculation? Explain your answer.

_____

_____

_____

_____

_____

_____

4 CIVICS What qualities of a good leader are evident in this passage? Consider both Süleyman and L'Isle-Adam in your answer.

_____

_____

5 **ANALYZING POINTS OF VIEW** Even during his lifetime, Süleyman was referred to by westerners as "the Magnificent." How does this explain the way de Lamartine talks about him in this passage?

_____

_____

_____

ESSENTIAL QUESTION

How can the creation of a new empire impact the people and culture of a region?

Ottoman and Byzantine Architecture

DIRECTIONS: Study the photographs. Then respond to the questions that follow.

EXPLORE THE CONTEXT: Ottoman architectural styles borrowed extensively from Iranian and Islamic Mamluk traditions as well as earlier Byzantine architecture. Hagia Sophia, commissioned by Byzantine emperor Justinian and finished in 537, is considered the best example of Byzantine architecture in the world. Originally a Christian cathedral, Hagia Sophia was converted to a mosque after the Ottoman capture of Constantinople in 1453. Selimiye Mosque, finished in 1575, is widely considered the masterpiece of the great Ottoman architect, Sinan. Constructed during the reign of Süleyman, its tall, slender minarets and large central dome is typical of Ottoman architecture.

PRIMARY SOURCE: OTTOMAN AND BYZANTINE ARCHITECTURE

Hagia Sophia, Istanbul, Turkey

Selimiye Mosque, Edirne, Turkey

1 DRAWING CONCLUSIONS What do these structures tell you about the importance of religion in the Ottoman Empire? Explain.

_____

_____

_____

_____

2 **EVALUATING** What can we learn about Ottoman attitudes toward non-Islamic cultures from these photos?

_____

_____

_____

_____

_____

_____

_____

_____

3 **HISTORY** Explain how these pictures symbolize the end of the Byzantine Empire and setbacks for Christianity.

_____

_____

_____

_____

_____

_____

_____

4 **UNDERSTANDING CHANGE** What evidence can you find suggesting that the Ottomans made architectural changes to Hagia Sophia?

_____

_____

_____

_____

_____

_____

_____

ESSENTIAL QUESTION

How can the creation of a new empire impact the people and culture of a region?

As you gather evidence to answer the Essential Question, think about:

- the factors that led to the weakening of the Ottoman Empire.
- why there were tensions between the Ottomans and the Ṣafavids.
- what life was like under the Ṣafavids.

My Notes

The Ottomans and the Ṣafavids

DIRECTIONS: Search for evidence in the lesson to help you answer the following questions.

1A **DIFFERENTIATING** Why did Europeans refer to Süleyman as "the Magnificent"? Why did his own subjects call him "Lawgiver"?

1B **UNDERSTANDING CHANGE** Use the graphic organizer to identify changes within the Ottoman Empire that contributed to its disintegration. Rank the changes in order of importance.

2 **EXPLAINING ISSUES** How did religion bring the Şafavids in conflict with the Ottomans? How did the Ottomans finally respond?

_____

_____

_____

3 **COMPARING AND CONTRASTING** What was the status of women in the Şafavid Empire? How did this compare with their status in the Ottoman Empire?

_____

_____

_____

_____

4 **DESCRIBING** Describe the culture of Şafavid Persia.

_____

_____

_____

_____

_____

_____

5 **ANALYZING EVENTS** Why were the Şafavids less prosperous traders than the Ottomans?

_____

_____

_____

6 **EVALUATING** Based on what you read in the text, which Şafavid ruler do you believe accomplished the most during his rule, Shāh Esmā'īl or Shāh 'Abbās? Explain.

_____

_____

_____

ESSENTIAL QUESTION

How can the creation of a new empire impact the people and culture of a region?

Ottoman Janissaries

DIRECTIONS: Study the drawing. Then respond to the questions that follow.

EXPLORE THE CONTEXT: The Janissaries were the elite soldiers of the Ottoman Empire. As the empire grew, the sultans came to rely on the Janissaries' prowess to win many of their battles. Early on, the janissaries were boys enslaved from the Christian parts of the Ottoman Empire and trained as soldiers loyal only to the sultan. By the 18th century, this method of recruitment had been abolished. By this time, too, the corps had gained great prestige and wealth. With loosening of recruitment and training requirements, the corps slowly lost its military skill. Its frequent revolts against the state and growing military ineffectiveness caused the Ottoman sultan Mahmud II to disband the corps in 1826. This drawing by Arif Mehmed Pasha is from a collection he published in 1863 detailing the clothes worn by Ottoman officials.

SECONDARY SOURCE: DRAWING

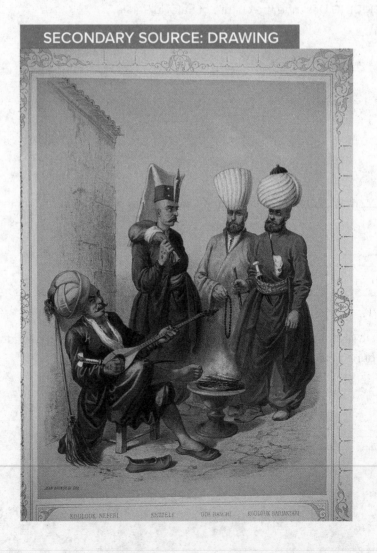

1 **INTEGRATING VISUAL INFORMATION** What impression of the janissaries is presented in this drawing?

_____

_____

_____

_____

_____

2 **DRAWING CONCLUSIONS** Can this drawing be trusted to give an accurate depiction of the Janissaries? Why or why not?

_____

_____

_____

_____

_____

_____

3 HISTORY How does this drawing suggest that the Janissaries' importance as soldiers had waned by the late 18th century?

_____

_____

_____

_____

_____

4 **PREDICTING** How might a drawing or painting of Janissaries from the 1500s look different than the one created by Arif Mehmed Pasha?

_____

_____

_____

_____

ESSENTIAL QUESTION

How can the creation of a new empire impact the people and culture of a region?

Ṣafavid Soldiers

DIRECTIONS: Study the following painting. Then respond to the questions that follow.

EXPLORE THE CONTEXT: The Ṣafavid Empire relied on a strong military force to conquer new territory and put down internal uprisings. The painting below, c. 1600, shows how these elite Persian soldiers were equipped.

PRIMARY SOURCE: PAINTING

1 **DESCRIBING** Describe how this Şafavid soldier is equipped for battle. What does this suggest about the nature of combat he might have experienced?

_____

_____

_____

_____

2 **HISTORY** How does this painting suggest that the Şafavids used new technologies to help them expand their empire?

_____

_____

_____

_____

3 **CONSTRASTING** How does this image of a Şafavid soldier contrast with Arif Mehmed Pasha's drawing of the Janissaries?

_____

_____

_____

_____

4 **DRAWING CONCLUSIONS** What place do you think soldiers held in the social hierarchy of Şafavid society? Explain your answer.

_____

_____

_____

_____

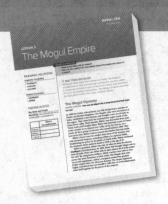

ESSENTIAL QUESTION

What factors help unify an empire?

As you gather evidence to answer the Essential Question, think about:

- who the Moguls were and how they built their empire.

- what life was like under Mogul rule.

- why the Mogul Empire went into decline.

The Mogul Empire

DIRECTIONS: Search for evidence in the lesson to help you answer the following questions.

1 **DETERMINING CENTRAL IDEAS** Who were the Moguls? How did early Mogul rulers such as Bābur and Akbar establish a new dynasty on the Indian subcontinent?

_____

_____

_____

_____

2 **EXPLAINING ISSUES** What was Akbar's policy toward religion? How was this policy expressed in practical terms? Why do you think he adopted this stance?

_____

_____

_____

_____

_____

_____

3A **SUMMARIZING** In the graphic organizer, summarize the key details about the reign of each of the six great Mogul emperors.

Name of Ruler	Notable Achievements
Bābur	
Akbar	
Jahāngīr	
Shāh Jahān	
Aurangzeb	

3B **ANALYZING CHANGE** What conclusions can you draw about the history of the Mogul Empire from the information you compiled in the graphic organizer?

_____

_____

_____

_____

_____

4 **HISTORY** How did the clash of religious cultures in Mogul India impact the lives of women?

_____

_____

_____

_____

_____

_____

5 **IDENTIFYING CONNECTIONS** How does the Taj Mahal represent the blending of cultures present in Mogul India? How do you think such massive building projects might have hastened the decline of the Mogul Empire?

_____

_____

_____

_____

_____

6 **IDENTIFYING CAUSES** How did the arrival of Europeans on the Indian subcontinent contribute to the end of the Mogul Empire?

_____

_____

_____

_____

_____

ESSENTIAL QUESTION

What factors help unify an empire?

Guru Gobind Singh

DIRECTIONS: Study the painting. Then respond to the questions that follow.

EXPLORE THE CONTEXT: This painting, created in the 1830s, depicts Guru Gobind Singh with fellow Sikhs. Guru Gobind Singh helped shape Sikhism by naming the holy book, the Guru Granth Sahib, as his successor. He also established the Khalsa, a community of initiated Sikhs. The signs of the Khalsa (commonly known as the "Five Ks") are Kesh (uncut hair covered by a turban); Kanga (hair comb); Kirpan (short sword); Kara (metal bracelet); and Kachera (traditional underwear).

SECONDARY SOURCE: PAINTING

1 **INTEGRATING VISUAL INFORMATION** Which figure in the painting is Guru Gobind Singh? How do you know?

_____

_____

_____

_____

_____

2 **DESCRIBING** What personal qualities does Guru Gobind Singh display in this image? Explain your answer.

_____

_____

_____

_____

_____

3 GEOGRAPHY What do you notice about the appearance of each figure in this painting? Why do you think they are all unshaven?

_____

_____

_____

_____

_____

4 **COMPARING AND CONTRASTING** How does this image of the guru compare to portrayals of other religious figures you have seen?

_____

_____

_____

_____

_____

ESSENTIAL QUESTION

What factors help unify an empire?

VOCABULARY

consternation: alarm, worry

striking: remarkable

arrayed: dressed

obeisance: deferential respect

The Death of Mogul Emperor Humayun

DIRECTIONS: Read the excerpt. Then respond to the questions that follow.

EXPLORE THE CONTEXT: Seydi Ali Reis served as an admiral in the Ottoman navy in the 16th century. The excerpt is from an account of his travels throughout Asia and the Middle East. In this section, he describes how the Mogul court reacted to the death of their emperor, Humayun, the son of the emperor Bābur and father of the emperor Akbar.

PRIMARY SOURCE: TRAVELOGUE

❝ . . . the Khans and Sultans were in the greatest consternation; they did not know how to act. I tried to encourage them and told them how at the death of Sultan Selim the situation was saved by the wisdom of Piri Pasha, who managed to prevent the news of his death from being noised abroad. I suggested that, by taking similar measures, they might keep the Sovereign's death a secret until the Prince should return. This advice was followed. The divan (council of State) met as usual, the nobles were summoned, and a public announcement was made that the Emperor intended to visit his country-seat, and would go there on horseback. Soon after, however, it was announced that on account of the unfavorable weather the trip had to be abandoned. On the next day a public audience was announced, but as the astrologers did not prophesy favorably for it, this also had to be given up. All this, however, somewhat alarmed the army, and on the Tuesday it was thought advisable to give them a sight of their monarch. A man called Molla Bi, who bore a striking resemblance to the late Emperor only somewhat slighter of stature, was arrayed in the imperial robes and placed on a throne specially erected for the purpose in the large entrance hall. His face and eyes were veiled. The Chamberlain Khoshhal Bey stood behind, and the first Secretary in front of him, while many officers and dignitaries as well as the people from the riverside, on seeing their Sovereign made joyful obeisance to the sound of festive music. The physicians were handsomely rewarded and the recovery of the monarch was universally credited. ❞

—from *The Travels and Adventures of the Turkish Admiral Sidi Ali Reis*, by Seydi Ali Reis, 1899

1 **SUMMARIZING** Summarize the events as described by Seydi Ali Reis.

_____

_____

_____

_____

_____

2 **INFERRING** Why do you think court officials were especially eager to keep Humayun's death a secret from the army?

_____

_____

_____

3 CIVICS What does this excerpt tell us about the government of the Mogul Empire during the reign of Humayun?

_____

_____

_____

_____

_____

4 **ANALYZING SOURCES** Do you think this story is true? What does it tell us about how Seydi Ali Reis wanted to be seen by his readers?

_____

_____

_____

_____

5 **IDENTIFYING PERSPECTIVES** How would you characterize Seydi Ali Reis's attitude toward the Mogul court? Explain.

_____

_____

_____

ESSENTIAL QUESTIONS

What factors help unify an empire?

How can the creation of a new empire impact the people and culture of a region?

My Notes

_____

_____

_____

_____

_____

_____

_____

_____

_____

_____

_____

_____

① Think About It

Review the supporting questions you developed at the beginning of the chapter. Review the evidence you gathered in the chapter. Were you able to answer each Supporting Question? If there was not enough evidence to answer your Supporting Questions, what additional evidence do you need to consider?

_____

_____

_____

_____

② Organize Your Evidence

Complete the chart below with information you learned about the three Muslim empires, with special emphasis on the cultures and unique characteristics of each.

Ottoman Empire	Ṣafavid Empire	Mogul Empire

3 Write About It

In the space below, identify one factor that helped unify each of the three Muslim empires. Then identify a factor for each empire that created disunity.

_____

_____

_____

_____

4 Talk About It

Work in small groups. With your group, consider the items you identified in your charts as you talk about the characteristics of each Muslim empire. Think about why the cultures developed as they did. Take notes on your discussion below.

_____

_____

_____

5 Connect to the Essential Question

You are a merchant who has come to the Ottoman Empire, the Ṣafavid Empire, or the Mogul Empire to trade. Write an account of your travels throughout the empire you have chosen to trade with. What goods are trading for in the empire? How is the society organized? What types of arts and architecture is found in the society you've chosen to write about? Organize the information into a pamphlet to inform other merchants about the potential for trade in the empire you chose.

_____

_____

_____

_____

_____

_____

_____

_____

_____

CITIZENSHIP
TAKE ACTION

MAKE CONNECTIONS New architectural styles flourished in the Muslim Empires. The Ottomans built magnificent mosques with large domes framed with minarets showing the importance of Islam to the empire. The Moguls blended Persian and Indian influences together to create a new architectural style best reflected by the Taj Mahal. These buildings often reflected the piety and power of the ruler at the time. In the United States, many of our important government buildings like the Capitol Building are built in a neoclassical style. These buildings, similar in style to ancient Greek or Roman architecture, bring to mind the earliest republics that the founders hoped to emulate.

DIRECTIONS: Research government buildings in your state or town. How did they chose the designs for these buildings? What were the architects hoping to achieve with the style that they used? Invite a guest speaker from the local historical society to discuss the history of the government buildings in your area with your class.

_____

_____

_____

_____

_____

_____

_____

_____

_____

_____

_____

_____

_____

_____

_____

The East Asian World

ESSENTIAL QUESTIONS

What factors help unify a kingdom or dynasty?

How can external forces influence a kingdom or dynasty?

Think about what you have already learned about life in China under the Sui, Tang, and Song dynasties. Note that under the only female ruler, Empress Wu, the Tang dynasty and the civilian bureaucracy were both strengthened. In Japan, major cultural, political, and social institutions evolved, including the rise of the samurai. Beginning in the 1600s, the Ming dynasty began a new era of power in China. Then the Qing dynasty continued to build power. Meanwhile, powerful rulers arose in Japan, Korea, and Southeast Asia.

TALK ABOUT IT

With a partner, discuss the sort of information you would need to know to answer these questions. For example, one question might be: What factors helped unify China, Japan, Korea, and Southeast Asia?

DIRECTIONS: Now write down three additional questions that will help you evaluate the factors and external forces that helped unify China, Japan, Korea, and Southeast Asia, and how external forces influenced developments there. For example, you might ask, "How was the Yi dynasty able to remain in control of Korea for five centuries"?

MY RESEARCH QUESTIONS

Supporting Question? 1:

_____

Supporting Question 2:

_____

Supporting Question 3:

_____

The Ming and Qing Dynasties

DIRECTIONS: Search for evidence in the lesson to help you answer the following questions.

ESSENTIAL QUESTIONS

What factors help unify a kingdom or dynasty?

How can external forces influence a kingdom or dynasty?

As you gather evidence to answer the Essential Questions, think about:

- the factors that allowed the Ming Dynasty to unify China.
- how the Qing dynasty maintained control of China.
- the influence that European traders had on China.

My Notes

_____

_____

_____

_____

_____

_____

1 **EVALUATING INFORMATION** How did China flourish politically and culturally during the Ming dynasty?

_____

_____

_____

_____

_____

_____

_____

2 **EVALUATING EVIDENCE** How were the Qing, only the second non-Chinese dynasty, able to successfully rule such a vast empire?

_____

_____

_____

_____

_____

_____

3 **INTEGRATING INFORMATION** How did Chinese architecture, decorative arts, and literature reflect the power of the Ming and the Qing dynasties?

_____

_____

_____

_____

_____

4 **CONTRASTING** Use the following web diagram to contrast the Chinese and European methods of conducting trade.

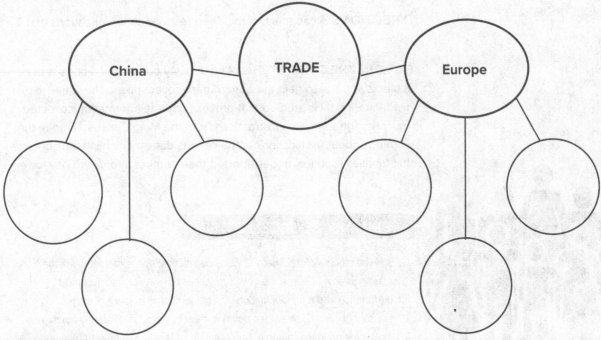

5 ECONOMICS Describe the major components of the Chinese economy under the Ming and Qing dynasties.

_____
_____
_____
_____

_____
_____

6 **ANALYZING STRUCTURE** How was Chinese society organized during the Ming and Qing dynasties? How did this provide the empire with stability?

_____
_____
_____
_____
_____
_____

ESSENTIAL QUESTION

What factors help unify a kingdom or dynasty?

The Ming Census

DIRECTIONS: Read the excerpt. Then respond to the questions that follow.

EXPLORE THE CONTEXT: The Ming dynasty conducted a census of its subjects in order to help the government collect taxes. The Chinese historian Ping-ti Ho studied that process and the information collected. This passage translates instructions from the Ming Census. Despite the warnings about falsifications in the census data, many historians believe that families routinely underreported their number in order to pay lower taxes.

PRIMARY SOURCE: LETTER

66 The officials of the Board of Revenue will take notice that although the country is now at peace the government has not yet secured accurate information about the population . . . The number of persons of each household must all be written down without falsification. Since my powerful troops are no longer going out on campaigns, they are to be sent to every county, in order to make a household-to-household check of the returns. If it is discovered in the course of checking that some local officials have falsified the returns, those officials are to be decapitated. Any common people who hide from the census will be punished according to the law and will be drafted into the army. 99

—Ping-ti Ho, *Studies on the Population of China, 1368–1953*

VOCABULARY

revenue: income, usually taxes

secured: acquired

falsification: misrepresentation, deception

1 **HISTORY** Why did the government want the people to be counted?

_____

_____

_____

_____

_____

_____

_____

Copyright © McGraw-Hill Education   Ho, Ping-ti. 1959, 2013. Studies on the Population of China, 1368-1953. Volume 4. Cambridge, Massachusetts: Harvard University Press.

2 **SUMMARIZING** Was this letter written during a period of war or peace? How do you know?

_____

_____

3 **DETERMINING CENTRAL IDEAS** What is the central idea of this letter of instructions?

_____

_____

_____

_____

4 **INFERRING** What can you infer about how earlier censuses had been conducted? Give reasons to support your answer.

_____

_____

_____

_____

_____

_____

5 **IDENTIFYING CONNECTIONS** The United States Constitution specifically states that the people must be counted every 10 years. What is the purpose of the American census? How is it different from that of the Ming census? How do the penalties for underreporting numbers in the American census compare with those of the Ming census? Why do you think this is so?

_____

_____

_____

_____

_____

_____

_____

ESSENTIAL QUESTION
What factors help unify a kingdom or dynasty?

Dream of the Red Chamber

DIRECTIONS: Read the excerpt. Then respond to the questions that follow.

EXPLORE THE CONTEXT: The novel became a key literary form in Ming and Qing China. *Dream of the Red Chamber,* often considered the best Chinese novel ever written, was first published in the mid-1700s. The author, Cao Zhan, also called Cao Xueqin, wrote the story of the Jia family and the love between Lin Daiyu and her cousin Baoyu. The author was also an expert storyteller, as illustrated by the excerpt here that examines Chinese legends of the goddess of works.

PRIMARY SOURCE: NOVEL

❝ The Empress Nü Wo, (the goddess of works,) in fashioning blocks of stones, for the repair of the heavens, prepared . . . 36,501 blocks of rough stone. . . . Of these stones, the Empress Wo only used 36,500; so that one single block remained over and above, without being turned to any account. This was cast down the Ch'ing Keng peak. This stone, strange to say, after having undergone a process of refinement, attained a nature of efficiency, and could, by its innate powers, set itself into motion and was able to expand and to contract.

When it became aware that the whole number of blocks had been made use of to repair the heavens, that it alone had been destitute of the necessary properties and had been unfit to attain selection, it forthwith felt within itself vexation and shame, and day and night, it gave way to anguish and sorrow.

One day, while it lamented its lot, it suddenly caught sight, at a great distance, of a Buddhist bonze and of a Taoist priest coming towards that direction. . . . But on noticing the block newly-polished and brilliantly clear, which had moreover contracted in dimensions, and become no larger than the pendant of a fan, they were greatly filled with admiration. The Buddhist priest picked it up, and laid it in the palm of his hand.

"Your appearance," he said laughingly, "may well declare you to be a supernatural object, but as you lack any inherent quality it is necessary to inscribe a few characters on you, so that every one who shall see you may at once recognise you to be a remarkable thing. And subsequently, when you will be taken into a country where honour and affluence will reign, into a family cultured in mind and of official status, in a land where flowers and trees shall flourish with luxuriance, in a town of refinement, renown and glory; when you once will have been there . . . "

The stone listened with intense delight. ❞

—*Dream of the Red Chamber*

VOCABULARY

cast: thrown

innate: inborn

destitute: found lacking

forthwith: quickly

vexation: anger

bonze: priest

Copyright © McGraw-Hill Education · Xueqin, Cao. The Dream of the Red Chamber. H. Bencraft Joly, Tr., Hongkong: Kelly & Walsh, 1892.

1 **CITING TEXT EVIDENCE** Why is the stone so upset? Cite evidence from the text to support your answer.

_____

_____

2 **ANALYZING EVIDENCE** What powers does the stone possess?

_____

_____

3 HISTORY Traditionally, academics considered that the modern novel originated with Samuel Richardson, with his 1740 publication of _Pamela_. The novel _Dream of the Red Chamber_ was probably written around the same time as Richardson's work, yet few westerners study it in detail or even know of its existence. Why do you think this is so? Provide reasons to support your answer.

_____

_____

_____

_____

4 **ANALYZING TEXT** In what ways does the author give the stone human characteristics?

_____

_____

5 **EVALUATING TEXT EVIDENCE** How doe the writer show his respect for the Buddhist and Taoist religions in this excerpt? Provide evidence to support your answer.

_____

_____

_____

_____

_____

_____

The Reunification of Japan

DIRECTIONS Search for evidence in the lesson to help you answer the following questions.

1 **ANALYZING** What powerful political figures played pivotal roles in reunifying Japan? Explain the role that each played.

_____

_____

_____

_____

_____

_____

_____

_____

ESSENTIAL QUESTIONS

What factors help unify a kingdom or dynasty?

How can external forces influence a kingdom or dynasty?

As you gather evidence to answer the Essential Questions, think about:

- political changes that happened after the reunification of Japan.
- the role Europeans played in the newly unified Japan.
- achievements of the Tokugawa Era.

2 **IDENTIFYING EFFECTS** What policies did the new rulers of Japan institute toward the Europeans? What was the result of these policies?

_____

_____

_____

_____

_____

3 **ECONOMICS** Use the table below to list the achievements that the Tokugawa made in trade and industry.

Issue	Tokugawa Achievements
trade	
industry	

My Notes

_____

_____

_____

_____

_____

_____

4 **SUMMARIZING** What artistic achievements were made in Tokugawa Japan?

_____

_____

_____

_____

_____

5 **ANALYZING STRUCTURE** What type of social system developed in Tokugawa Japan? What conditions allowed it to develop?

_____

_____

_____

_____

_____

_____

_____

_____

_____

_____

_____

_____

_____

6 **ANALYZING INDIVIDUALS** How were the Tokugawa rulers able to control all of Japan?

_____

_____

_____

_____

_____

ESSENTIAL QUESTION

How can external forces influence a kingdom or dynasty?

The Expulsion of the Jesuits

DIRECTIONS: Read the excerpt. Then respond to the questions that follow.

EXPLORE THE CONTEXT: Jesuit missionaries had converted thousands of Japanese to Christianity, starting in 1549 when Francis Xavier arrived in Japan. They had even converted some of the daimyo. However, some of the Jesuits destroyed local shrines, and in 1587 the shogun Hideyoshi issued an edict prohibiting Christian activities in Japan.

SECONDARY SOURCE: HISTORIAN'S ACCOUNT

"1. Japan is the country of gods, but has been receiving false teachings from Christian countries. This cannot be tolerated any further.

2. The [missionaries] approach people in provinces and districts to make them their followers, and let them destroy shrines and temples. This is an unheard of outrage. When a vassal receives a province, a district, a village, or another form of a fief, he must consider it as a property entrusted to him on a temporary basis. He must follow the laws of this country, and abide by their intent. However, some vassals illegally [commend part of their fiefs to the church]. This is a culpable offense.

3. The padres, by their special knowledge [in the sciences and medicine], feel that they can at will entice people to become their believers. In doing so they commit the illegal act of destroying the teachings of Buddha prevailing in Japan. These padres cannot be permitted to remain in Japan. They must prepare to leave the country within twenty days of the issuance of this notice.

4. The black [Portuguese and Spanish] ships come to Japan to engage in trade. Thus the matter is a separate one. They can continue to engage in trade.

5. Hereafter, anyone who does not hinder the teachings of the Buddha, whether he be a merchant or not, may come and go freely from Christian countries to Japan. **"**

Fifteenth year of Tenshō [1587], sixth month, 19th day

— Japan: A Documentary History, Volume 1, The Dawn of History to the Late Tokugawa Period by David J. Lu

VOCABULARY

vassal: holder of land in a feudal system

fief: estate in a feudal system

culpable: deserving blame

padres: missionaries, in this case Jesuit missionaries

1 **DETERMINING POINT OF VIEW** What attitude does Hideyoshi have toward the Christians who have come to Japan?

Lu, David J. Japan - A Documentary History. Volume I. London and New York: Routledge. 2015.

2 **IDENTIFYING BIAS** What led Hideyoshi to issue this edict?

_____

_____

_____

_____

_____

3 **DETERMINING CENTRAL IDEAS** What is the Japanese idea regarding property ownership? Why is it so important in this excerpt?

_____

_____

_____

_____

_____

4 **COMPARING AND CONTRASTING** Recall what you have learned about the policies that Chinese leaders adopted when European Christian missionaries tried to win converts in China. How were the policies of the Tokugawa similar to those of the Chinese? How were they different?

_____

_____

_____

_____

_____

5 **ECONOMICS** How do you account for the fact that the Tokugawa rulers were only forcing out the missionaries who had been trying to convert the Japanese people to Christianity?

_____

_____

_____

_____

_____

_____

*What factors help unify a
kingdom or dynasty?*

Samurai and Daimyo

DIRECTIONS: Study the photograph. Then respond to the questions
that follow.

EXPLORE THE CONTEXT: This photograph shows a man standing, facing
right, and a man wearing a sword kneeling before him, facing left, holding
another sword as though offering it to the man standing in front of him. It is
believed to depict a samurai kneeling before a daimyo around 1877.

PRIMARY SOURCE: PHOTOGRAPH

1 **DESCRIBING** What role did the Daimyo play in feudal Japan before the Tokugawa Era? How did their role change under the Tokugawa?

_____

_____

_____

2 **ANALYZING** What does the photograph tell you about the relationship between the samurai and the daimyo?

_____

_____

_____

3 **ECONOMICS** In Tokugawa Japan, the shogun was supreme ruler below the emperor and was responsible for distributing the national rice crop. How would such a role help ensure the loyalty of both the daimyo and the samurai such as the ones shown in the photograph?

_____

_____

_____

_____

_____

4 **INFERRING** What can you infer the daimyo and the samurai relied upon to defeat their enemies in combat?

_____

_____

_____

_____

ESSENTIAL QUESTIONS

What factors help unify a kingdom or dynasty?

How can external forces influence a kingdom or dynasty?

As you gather evidence to answer the Essential Questions, think about:

- how geography affected the development and growth of civilization in Korea.

- how the Yi dynasty united Korea.

- the stability of Southeast Asia at the beginning of the sixteenth century.

- the impact of Islam on Southeast Asia.

- the influence of Europeans in Southeast Asia.

My Notes

_____

_____

_____

_____

_____

_____

_____

_____

The Kingdoms of Korea and Southeast Asia

DIRECTIONS: Search for evidence in this lesson to help you answer the following questions.

1 EXPLAINING What was a major literary legacy of the Korean civilization?

_____

_____

_____

_____

2 GEOGRAPHY How did geography affect the history of Korea?

_____

_____

_____

_____

3 DESCRIBING How were the Yi able to maintain control over Korea for five centuries?

_____

_____

_____

_____

4 ECONOMICS How did the trade with Islamic states affect the people of the Malay Peninsula and the Indonesian archipelago?

_____

_____

_____

_____

_____

5 IDENTIFYING CAUSES Use the web diagram below to list the factors that led the Koreans to limit contact with foreign countries and the impact that these policies had on Korea.

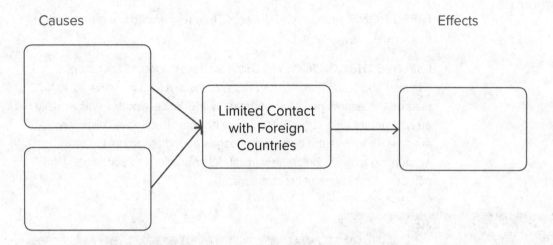

Causes

Effects

Limited Contact with Foreign Countries

6 ANALYZING STRUCTURE What type of social and governmental systems developed in Southeast Asian civilizations? What conditions allowed them to develop? What conditions ended them?

_____

_____

_____

_____

_____

_____

_____

_____

_____

_____

_____

_____

ESSENTIAL QUESTION

How can external forces influence a kingdom or dynasty?

Dutch Traders

DIRECTIONS: Study the engraving. Then respond to the questions that follow.

EXPLORE THE CONTEXT: The Dutch engravers Pieter Serwouters (Flemish, 1586–1657) and Dirck Pietersz. Voscuyl (Dutch, active 1614–1622), created the engraving below in the early 1600s. Serwouters was actually an accountant for a large Dutch firm of his time. But he was also very creative. To relieve the boredom of pages of endless figures in his accounting ledgers, he created insightful engravings to accompany the numbers. This is one of his creations.

PRIMARY SOURCE: ENGRAVING

—Rijksmuseum, Amsterdam

1 DETERMINING POINT OF VIEW How does Serwouters portray the Dutch traders in relation to the Asians with whom they are trading?

_____

_____

_____

2 IDENTIFYING BIAS What bias does Serwouters show in the engraving? Explain your answer.

_____

_____

_____

_____

3 DETERMINING CENTRAL IDEAS What is the central idea that Serwouters is presenting in the engraving?

_____

_____

_____

_____

4 ECONOMICS How did trade with the Europeans benefit both the Asians and the Europeans.

_____

_____

_____

5 INTERPRETING Who do you think is the person in the heavens holding the tablets? Give reasons to support your answer.

_____

_____

_____

_____

ESSENTIAL QUESTIONS

What factors help unify a kingdom or dynasty?

How can external forces influence a kingdom or dynasty?

The Travels of Ibn Battuta

DIRECTIONS: Read the excerpt. Then respond to the questions that follow.

EXPLORE THE CONTEXT: Ibn Battuta began travelling in 1325 at the age of 20. His first journey was his Hajj, or pilgrimage to Mecca, required of all devout Muslims. But unlike most Muslim travelers, Battuta simply kept travelling, covering about 75,000 miles and about 44 countries, most of which were Muslim. Toward the end of his life Ibn Battuta dictated the story of his travels so there would be a historic record of where he went and what he saw. While some of the stories describe places or people who did not actually exist, the stories still give us a valuable record of what life was like in the Muslim world at this time. The following excerpt is his account of meeting the king of Java, an island in the Indonesian archipelago.

PRIMARY SOURCE: NARRATED ACCOUNT

66 The King of 'Mul Java is an infidel. I was introduced to him without his palace; he was then sitting on the bare ground, and his nobles were standing before him. His troops are presented before him on foot, no one in these parts having a horse except the King, for they ride on elephants generally. The King, on this occasion, called me to him, and I went. He then ordered a carpet to be spread for me to sit upon. I said to his interpreter, how can I sit upon a carpet, while the Sultan sits upon the ground? He answered: This is his custom, and he practices it for the sake of humility: but you are a guest; and, besides, you come from a great Prince. It is, therefore, right that you should be distinguished. I then sat, . . . 99

——*The Travels of Ibn Battuta*

VOCABULARY

infidel: nonbeliever

interpreter: person who translates languages

sultan: Muslim king

1 **CITING TEXT EVIDENCE** How do you know that Java was not a Muslim country at this time? Cite text evidence to support your answer.

_____

_____

_____

_____

_____

Batuta, Ibn. Translated by The Rev. Samuel Lee. The Travels of Ibn Batuta. London: The Oriental Translation Committee. 1829.

2 **ANALYZING** What does the excerpt show about what the people of Southeast Asia thought about having guests? Give reasons to support your answer.

_____

_____

_____

3 **HISTORY** Today 85 percent of the people who live on Java, the most populous island in the world, are Muslim. Detail how Islam spread to the island. Which religion remained the dominant religion in mainland Southeast Asia?

_____

_____

_____

_____

4 **CONTRASTING** How is the reception that the Javanese king gives Ibn Battuta different from the reception given to outsiders in Korea, Japan, and China that you studied earlier?

_____

_____

_____

_____

5 **IDENTIFYING CONNECTIONS** The excerpt notes that everyone except the king rides on elephants. This practice has been common in Southeast Asia for centuries. However, today there is a growing movement to protect elephants. As urban development and industry have continued to use more land in Southeast Asia, the habitat available for elephants has shrunk. Governments in the region are now investigating ways to conserve these natural habitats by prohibiting development in certain areas. Do you agree or disagree with this approach to conservation? Provide reasons to support your answer.

_____

_____

_____

_____

_____

ESSENTIAL QUESTIONS

What factors help unify a kingdom or dynasty?

How can external forces influence a kingdom or dynasty?

My Notes

_____

_____

_____

_____

_____

_____

_____

_____

_____

_____

_____

_____

1 Think About It

Review the supporting questions you developed at the beginning of the chapter. Review the evidence you gathered in the chapter. Were you able to answer each Supporting Question? If there was not enough evidence to answer your Supporting Questions, what additional evidence do you think you need to consider?

_____

_____

_____

_____

2 Organize Your Evidence

Complete the table below with each society's major accomplishments and their relationship with foreigners.

Civilization/Dynasty	Accomplishments	Relationships With Other Cultures
China: Ming dynasty		
China: Qing dynasty		
Japan: Tokugawa Era		
Korea: Yi dynasty		

Civilization/Dynasty	Accomplishments	Relationships With Other Cultures
Burma and Thailand		
Vietnam		
Melaka		

3 Write About It

Theater was a part of literature that flourished in both China and Japan during the period you have just studied. Use Internet and print resources to learn more about Japanese kabuki theater or Chinese theater during this time. Use what you learn to write a scene for a play. Include a storyline similar to one that would have been presented at the time. If possible, craft costumes authentic to the period and perform the scene for the class.

4 Connect to the Essential Question

For each society in the chapter, think about the factors that enabled the rulers to unify their kingdom or empire and to rule it effectively. Next, choose one of the present-day nations located in the territory that was once ruled by one of the dynasties or kings mentioned in the chapter. Take the role of a citizen of that modern nation. You are its delegate to the United Nations committee that is studying worldwide educational systems. Tomorrow you are going to address the committee on the need for students throughout the world to study your nation's history. What can students learn from your nation's history? What accomplishments did your nation achieve that people need to be aware of? What relevance does this history have to people living elsewhere? Use your textbook, Internet, and print resources to gather information. You will have five minutes for your speech, so make your points clearly and concisely. If possible, have the rest of the class play the roles of committee members and make your speech to them.

CITIZENSHIP
TAKE ACTION

MAKE CONNECTIONS Between 1400 and 1800, the Europeans were launching their voyages of discovery as they ventured away from their shores in search of riches from East Asian societies. The interactions between the cultures of East Asia and the Europeans took a variety of forms. Sometimes it was peaceful trade. At other times zealous Christian missionaries, hoping to save people's eternal souls, tried to convince local people to abandon their local religions and accept Christianity. More often than not, the rulers of the affected nations banished the missionaries and sometimes the traders as well. Nevertheless, contact among all the societies you studied in the chapter continued. Through the centuries that contact has increased to the point that today we can instant message almost anyone, anywhere.

DIRECTIONS: Think about your own community and the people living in it. It may include immigrants from a variety of countries, including many from East Asia. After five years in the United States immigrants who meet certain requirements are allowed to become citizens of the United States. One of the requirements to achieve this citizenship is to take a citizenship test, which shows that the immigrant has mastered our concept of a constitutional government. You have decided to become a tutor to help one of these immigrants study for the citizenship test. Choose a topic in American government that your student will need to master for the test. For example, you might choose how a bill becomes a law, the civil service system, or the powers of the Supreme Court. You can use Internet or print resources to find other topics that the citizenship test covers. Then develop a lesson plan for the topic. How do you plan to teach the concept? What resources will you need to include? Be certain that your lesson plan includes objectives that the student needs to master after studying the lesson as well as a short quiz of four multiple-choice questions that you can use to assess your student's mastery of the concept.

The Enlightenment and Revolutions

ESSENTIAL QUESTION

Why do new ideas often spark change?

Think about how new ideas about science, philosophy, art, and politics arose during the sixteenth to eighteenth centuries and how those ideas led to radical changes around the world.

TALK ABOUT IT

With a partner, discuss the sort of information you would need to discover to explain how new ideas in science, art, philosophy, and politics led to radical changes during the sixteenth to eighteenth centuries. How do new ideas change the world around us? How do new ideas generate more new ideas?

DIRECTIONS: Now write down three additional questions that will help you explain how new ideas emerged in the sixteenth to eighteenth centuries and how those ideas changed the world in which people lived. For example, you might ask "What new ideas arose in science in the sixteenth century? How did these changes affect the world?"

MY RESEARCH QUESTIONS

Supporting Question 1:

_____

_____

Supporting Question 2:

_____

_____

Supporting Question 3:

_____

_____

ESSENTIAL QUESTION

Why do new ideas often spark change?

As you gather evidence to answer the Essential Question, think about:

- how scientific discoveries lead to new ways of thinking about the world.

- how new ideas arise, are promoted, and sometimes opposed.

- how new ways of thinking about the world can lead to changes and revolutions in world affairs and people's daily lives.

My Notes

_____

_____

_____

_____

_____

_____

The Scientific Revolution

DIRECTIONS: Search for evidence in the lesson to help you answer the following questions.

1 **SUMMARIZING** Use the graphic organizer below to analyze new ideas and discoveries in science during the Scientific Revolution. The first two have been done for you.

Major Discoveries of the Scientific Revolution

Scientist	Discovery	Impact or Consequences
Nicolaus Copernicus	The earth revolves around the sun	Proposed a model of the universe based on observation; demonstrated that the Earth was not the center of the universe
Johannes Kepler	Demonstrated that planets move in elliptical orbits	Disproved the Ptolemaic model of the universe

2 **IDENTIFYING CONNECTIONS** How did new ideas about astronomy develop during this period?

_____

_____

_____

_____

3 **EXPLAINING CAUSES** Which new technologies and techniques led to the wave of scientific discoveries during this period?

_____

_____

_____

4 **RELATING EVENTS** How were the philosophical ideas of Descartes and Bacon influenced by the Scientific Revolution?

_____

_____

_____

_____

5 GEOGRAPHY What cultural factors in Europe at the time were the early scientists challenging? Why were these factors specific to Europe?

_____

_____

_____

_____

6 **EXPLAINING CAUSE AND EFFECT** Use the flow chart below to graphically organize how successive scientists and discoveries improved our understanding of the universe. The first step has been provided for you.

Copernicus theorizes that the Earth revolves around the Sun.	→		→		→		→	

ESSENTIAL QUESTION

Why do new ideas often spark change?

Sixteenth-Century Illlustration of a Human Brain

DIRECTIONS: Use the image to answer the questions.

EXPLORE THE CONTEXT: Before the work of Andreas Vesalius, doctors used descriptions of the human body taken from classical doctors and writers like Galen. Many of Galen's ideas about the body were incorrect. Vesalius demonstrated that dissection and description of human bodies was necessary to form a more complete understanding of how the body worked. Manuals based on Vesalius's work were illustrated with detailed anatomical drawings to teach new doctors the basics of human anatomy.

PRIMARY SOURCE: ENGRAVING

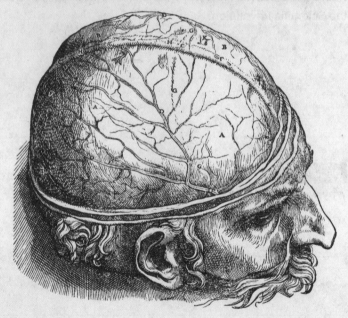

PRIMA SEPTIMI LIBRI FIGVRA·

PRIMAE FIGVRAE, EIVSDEMQVE CHARACTERVM INDEX.

1 **INTEGRATING INFORMATION** What does this image demonstrate about the skill of doctors and artists in this time?

_____

_____

_____

2 UNDERSTANDING CHANGE How does this image indicate that ideas about medicine and science were changing during this period?

_____

_____

_____

3 UNDERSTANDING CONTEXT How much work has gone into the production of this image? Why might that slow the spread of knowledge of this kind?

_____

_____

_____

4 EXPLAINING EFFECTS How might the production and spread of images like this have changed the way medicine was practiced?

_____

_____

_____

5 CIVICS How might an image such as this, published in a manual, have affected public understanding of medicine for the better?

_____

_____

_____

6 EVALUATING Does this image remind you of modern-day medical technology? How does this image compare to modern images?

_____

_____

_____

ESSENTIAL QUESTION
Why do new ideas often spark change?

Papal Condemnation of Galileo

DIRECTIONS: Use the text to answer the questions.

EXPLORE THE CONTEXT: Galileo Galilei was a brilliant scientist and inventor who was born in Pisa, Italy, in 1564. In the early years of the seventeenth century, Galileo began to use a telescope to observe stars, planets, and other celestial objects. He published his findings in a series of books. Galileo demonstrated that his observations supported the Copernican, heliocentric theory of the universe. His ideas brought him into conflict with the Catholic Church, which taught a geocentric model of the universe as a matter of doctrine. After Galileo disobeyed an earlier condemnation and published his book, *Dialogue Concerning the Two Chief World System*s, he was tried and found guilty of spreading heretical ideas in 1633 and placed under house arrest.

PRIMARY SOURCE: JUDGMENT

66 Whereas you, Galileo, son of the late Vincenzio Galilei, of Florence, aged 70 years, were denounced, in 1615, to this Holy Office, for holding as true a false doctrine taught by many, namely, that the sun is immovable in the center of the world, and that the earth moves, and also with a diurnal motion; also for having pupils whom you instructed in the same opinions; - also for maintaining a correspondence on the same with some German mathematicians; also for publishing certain letters on the sun-spots, in which you developed the same doctrine as true; also for answering the objections which were continually produced from the Holy Scriptures, by glozing the said Scriptures according to your own meaning; and whereas thereupon was produced the copy of a writing, in form of a letter, professedly written by you to a person formerly your pupil, in which, following the hypothesis of Copernicus, you include several propositions contrary to the true sense and authority of the Holy Scriptures . . . 99

—Excerpt from the Papal condemnation of Galileo, 1633

VOCABULARY

denounced: to be publicly declared to be wrong

doctrine: an idea approved by the church

correspondence: to exchange communications

glozing: to make a comment or interpretation

hypothesis: theory

1 **DETERMINING CENTRAL IDEAS** Why did the Church condemn Galileo? What were his crimes?

_____

_____

2 **CITING TEXT EVIDENCE** How can you tell that this was not Galileo's first trial?

_____

3 **DETERMINING POINT OF VIEW** Why do you think the work of Galileo and his colleagues was viewed as dangerous or threatening by the Church?

_____

_____

_____

_____

4 **DETERMINING CONTEXT** How can this source help us to understand the development of a "scientific community" during Galileo's time?

_____

_____

_____

5 CIVICS Do authorities have a right to suppress radical ideas that they view as dangerous or challenging to their authority? What rights should people like Galileo have?

_____

_____

_____

_____

6 **EVALUATING** Looking back from a modern perspective, was the Church's condemnation of Galileo successful? Explain your reasoning.

_____

_____

_____

The Ideas of the Enlightenment

DIRECTIONS Search for evidence in the lesson to help you answer the following questions.

ESSENTIAL QUESTION

Why do new ideas often spark change?

As you gather evidence to answer the Essential Question, think about:

- how scientific discoveries lead to new ways of thinking about the world.
- how scientists, philosophers, and other thinkers try to change the world.
- how new ideas in science and philosophy are reflected in art, music, and culture.

1 **EXPLAINING CAUSE AND EFFECT** Use the graphic organizer below to identify scientific ideas which inspired Enlightenment thinkers and the theories and ideas which arose from these inspirations. The first one has been done for you.

The Influence of Science on the Enlightenment

Scientific Idea or Discovery	Impact on the Enlightenment
Laws of Gravity	Rational inquiry; observation; model of the universe as a machine

2 **IDENTIFYING CONNECTIONS** In what way might the deism championed by Voltaire be compared to the model of the universe proposed by Copernicus and Newton?

_____

_____

_____

_____

_____

_____

My Notes

_____

_____

_____

_____

_____

_____

3 EXPLAINING CAUSE AND EFFECT How did new technology influence the rise and spread of Enlightenment ideas? How did this influence the ideas of the Enlightenment?

_____

_____

_____

_____

4 SUMMARIZING Use the Venn diagram below to identify different aspects of Enlightenment ideas and organize them into the categories Arts and Culture; Science and Philosophy; and Politics and Rights. Two examples have been provided for you.

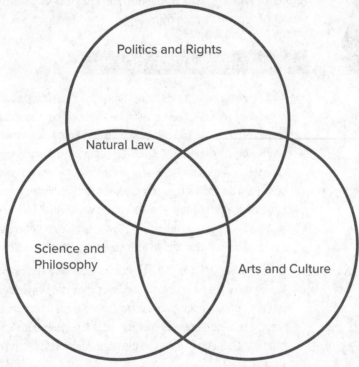

5 GEOGRAPHY What impression does the information presented in this lesson give you about the culture of Europe during this period?

_____

_____

_____

_____

_____

_____

ESSENTIAL QUESTION
Why do new ideas often spark change?

Vindication of the Rights of Woman

DIRECTIONS: Use the text to answer the questions.

EXPLORE THE CONTEXT: Mary Wollstonecraft was an English writer and women's rights advocate who was born in 1759. She was a well-educated and skilled writer, and she used her talents to argue powerfully against monarchy and tyranny and for the rights of ordinary people, especially women. She lived, worked, and corresponded with a variety of radical thinkers, including Thomas Paine and her husband, the anarchist philosopher William Godwin. Her most famous book, *A Vindication of the Rights of Woman*, was published in 1792. It is considered one of the first works of feminist philosophy.

PRIMARY SOURCE: BOOK

❝Let us examine this question. Rousseau declares, that a woman should never, for a moment feel herself independent, that she should be governed by fear to exercise her NATURAL cunning . . . in order to render her a more alluring object of desire, a SWEETER companion to man, whenever he chooses to relax himself. He carries the arguments, which he pretends to draw from the indications of nature, still further, and insinuates that truth and fortitude the corner stones of all human virtue, shall be cultivated with certain restrictions, because with respect to the female character, obedience is the grand lesson which ought to be impressed with unrelenting rigor.

What nonsense! When will a great man arise with sufficient strength of mind to puff away the fumes which pride and sensuality have thus spread over the subject! If women are by nature inferior to men, their virtues must be the same in quality, if not in degree, or virtue is a relative idea; consequently, their conduct should be founded on the same principles, and have the same aim. ❞

—Mary Wollstoncraft, *A Vindication of the Rights of Woman*, 1792

VOCABULARY
alluring: attractive

insinuates: suggests

cultivated: grown *in a deliberate manner*

rigor: inflexible; unyielding

consequently: as *a result*

1 **DETERMINING CENTRAL IDEAS** To what argument is Mary Wollstonecraft responding? What does she think of it?

_____

_____

_____

_____

_____

2 **UNDERSTANDING CONTEXT** How does this source help us to understand the intellectual culture of the Enlightenment?

_____

_____

_____

3 **DETERMINING POINT OF VIEW** Was Rousseau's or Wollstonecraft's position more common at that time? How can you tell?

_____

_____

_____

4 **EXPLAINING CAUSE AND EFFECT** How had the circumstances of women changed to allow Wollstonecraft to write her text? What changes would she like to see as a result?

_____

_____

_____

_____

5 **IDENTIFYING CONNECTIONS** Consider the quotation from Locke in the Lesson Opener. How are Locke's ideas and Wollstonecraft's ideas related?

_____

_____

_____

6 **CIVICS** Consider the line, "their conduct should be founded on the same principles, and have the same aim." In what way was this a radical idea at the time? Is there any sense in which it is still a radical idea today?

_____

_____

_____

_____

ESSENTIAL QUESTION

Why do new ideas often spark change?

Eighteenth-Century Button Makers

DIRECTIONS: Use the text to answer the questions..

EXPLORE THE CONTEXT: Initially, Denis Diderot had not been commissioned to write an encyclopedia but rather to translate the *Cyclopedia* of Englishman Ephraim Chambers into French. Diderot wanted his encyclopedia to contain information on every form of human endeavor and understanding. He hoped his encyclopedia would transform thinking and education by providing information on every conceivable subject. The following image shows the processes and tools used in button-making. The ideas of the Enlightenment and the technology of industry greatly influenced one another.

PRIMARY SOURCE: PAMPHLET

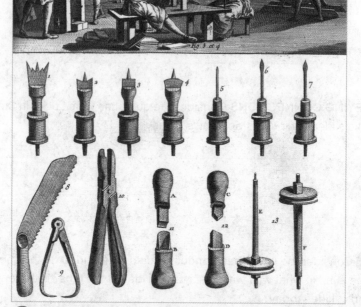

1 **INTEGRATING INFORMATION** How does this image support the lesson's claims about the ideas of the Enlightenment?

_____

_____

_____

2 **UNDERSTANDING CONTEXT** Why might the artist have viewed this image as interesting enough to publish? What does this tell you about the influences on Enlightenment thinkers?

_____

_____

_____

_____

3 **IDENTIFYING CONNECTIONS** Both this image and Wollstonecraft's text can be said to be attempting to "change the general way of thinking." Why is this the case? How do these sources differ in that aim?

_____

_____

_____

_____

4 **DETERMINING CONTEXT** Many of the ideas of the Enlightenment were philosophical, consisting of ideas about politics, morality, the nature of knowledge, and religion. How does this source differ? What extra element does it add to our understanding of the Enlightenment?

_____

_____

_____

5 **ECONOMICS** What can this image tell us about the economy of the 18th century? What does it not show us? What consequences might we expect from the popularization of images like this?

_____

_____

_____

_____

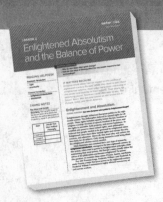

Enlightened Absolutism and the Balance of Power

ESSENTIAL QUESTION

Why do new ideas often spark change?

As you gather evidence to answer the Essential Question, think about:

- how new ideas influence political changes.

- how authorities react to challenges to their power and authority.

- how conflicts between peoples and nations arise.

- how new ideas can be interpreted differently by people with different backgrounds, needs, and agendas.

DIRECTIONS Search for evidence in the lesson to help you answer the following questions.

1 SUMMARIZING Use the graphic organizer below to summarize the different aspects of enlightened absolutism.

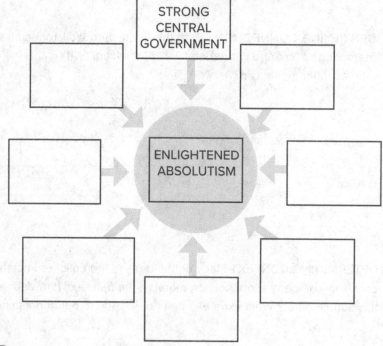

2 DETERMINING CONTEXT Why did some European monarchs try to adopt Enlightenment ideals?

_____

_____

_____

3 SUMMARIZING Did European monarchs agree with all of the proposals of Enlightenment thinkers? Why?

_____

_____

_____

_____

My Notes

_____

_____

_____

_____

_____

_____

_____

4 CIVICS In what ways did European monarchs disappoint the philosophes and other Enlightenment figures? How did they disappoint democratic reformers?

_____

_____

_____

_____

5 **CITING TEXT EVIDENCE** What evidence does the text offer that European monarchs were pursuing policies based on a rational assessment of political realities?

_____

_____

_____

6 **COMPARING AND CONTRASTING** Use the following chart to compare the values and policies of European monarchies during the eighteenth century with values and policies of the modern-day American government. Assess whether those policies are based on Enlightenment values.

Eighteenth-Century Policy	Modern Policy	Eighteenth-century policy based on Enlightenment values?	Modern policy based on Enlightenment values?
Farming is carried out by serfs on behalf of aristocrats.	Farming is carried out by private citizens for profit.	No	Yes

Frederick II on Government

Frederick II. 1777. Essay on the Forms of Government. Translated 1916 by Barker, J. Ellis. The Foundations of Germany. New York: E. P. Dutton.

ESSENTIAL QUESTION

Why do new ideas often spark change?

DIRECTIONS: Use the text to answer the questions.

EXPLORE THE CONTEXT: Frederick II of Prussia, or Frederick the Great, ruled Prussia from 1740 to 1786. He presided over an expansion of Prussia's military power and cultural prestige. He is considered an enlightened despot because while he exercised absolute authority, he tempered his use of power by patronage of arts and culture and limited social reforms. He wrote a treatise on politics, *Essay on the Forms of Government*, as a justification of his rule and as a manual for his successors.

PRIMARY SOURCE: POLITICAL TREATISE

66 Princes, sovereigns, and kings have not been given supreme authority in order to live in luxurious self-indulgence and debauchery. They have not been elevated by their fellow-men to enable them to strut about and to insult with their pride the simple-mannered, the poor, and the suffering. They have not been placed at the head of the State to keep around themselves a crowd of idle loafers whose uselessness drives them towards vice. The bad administration which may be found in monarchies springs from many different causes, but their principal cause lies in the character of the sovereign. A ruler addicted to women will become a tool of his mistresses and favorites, and these will abuse their power and commit wrongs of every kind, will protect vice, sell offices, and perpetrate every infamy. . . .

. . . If we wish to elevate monarchical above republican government, the duty of sovereigns is clear. They must be active, hard-working, upright and honest, and concentrate all their strength upon filling their office worthily. . . .

Rulers should always remind themselves that they are men like the least of their subjects. The sovereign is the foremost judge, general, financier, and minister of his country, not merely for the sake of his prestige. Therefore, he should perform with care the duties connected with these offices. He is merely the principal servant of the State. Hence, he must act with honesty, wisdom, and complete disinterestedness in such a way that he can render an account of his stewardship to the citizens at any moment. Consequently, he is guilty if he wastes the money of the people, the taxes which they have paid, in luxury, pomp, and debauchery. He who should improve the morals of the people, be the guardian of the law, and improve their education should not pervert them by his bad example. 99

—Frederick II of Prussia, *Essay on the Forms of Government,* 1777

VOCABULARY

debauchery: excess

loafers: lazy people

vice: wickedness

disinterestedness: not taking *sides*

pomp: ceremony and grandeur

1 **DETERMINING CENTRAL IDEAS** Using this passage, what does Frederick II seem to think is the most important duty of a monarch?

_____

_____

_____

2 **DETERMINING CONTEXT** Consider the following line: "if we wish to elevate monarchical above republican government, the duty of sovereigns is clear." Why does Frederick II include this line? What ideas have prompted this statement?

_____

_____

_____

_____

3 **UNDERSTANDING CONTEXT** Using your answer from Question 2, explain the relationship between Frederick II's ideas about government with those of Enlightenment thinkers.

_____

_____

_____

4 **CITING TEXT EVIDENCE** How can you tell that Frederick II is conscious of the lives of common people? Cite evidence to support your answer.

_____

_____

5 **INTERPRETING** Why might Frederick II's ideas on government be a form of social contract?

_____

_____

_____

6 **CIVICS** Could Frederick II's ideas still function as a guide to political office-holders in the modern era? Explain your answer.

_____

_____

Description of Empress Maria Theresa

DIRECTIONS: Use the text to answer the questions.

EXPLORE THE CONTEXT: Luise Gottsched was a writer, translator, poet, and playwright who lived in Prussia in the mid-eighteenth century. She is renowned as one of the foremost authors of comedies from this period. In the following letter, she described a visit she and her husband made to the court of Empress Maria Theresa of Austria. Maria Theresa faced the difficult task of maintaining absolute rule in a state that was fractured by linguistic and cultural differences. Despite this, she was able to turn around the fortunes of the Austrian Empire and create a state that was the envy of Europe.

PRIMARY SOURCE: LETTER

66 About eleven o'clock, a man-servant, dressed in gorgeous livery, came and told us to follow him. He led us through a great many frescoed corridors and splendid rooms into a small apartment which was made even smaller by a Spanish screen placed across it. We were told to wait there. In a few moments, the Mistress of Ceremonies came. She was very gracious to us. In a little while, her Majesty entered followed by the three princesses. My husband and myself each sank upon the left knee and kissed the noblest, the most beautiful hand that has ever wielded a scepter. The Empress gently bade us rise. Her face and her gracious manner banished all the timidity and embarrassment we naturally felt in the presence of so exalted and beautiful a figure as hers. Our fear was changed to love and confidence. Her Majesty told my husband that she was afraid to speak German before the Master of that language. 'Our Austrian dialect is very bad, they say,' she added. To which my man answered that, fourteen years before, when he listened to her address at the opening of the Landtag, he had been struck by the beauty and purity of her German. She spoke, on that occasion, he said, like a goddess.

Then the Empress laughed merrily, saying, ''Tis lucky I was not aware of your presence or I should have been so frightened that I should have stopped short in my speech.' She asked me how it happened that I became so learned a woman. I replied, 'I wished to become worthy of the honor that has this day befallen me in meeting your Majesty. This will forever be a red-letter day in my life.'

Her Majesty said, 'You are too modest. I well know that the most learned woman in Germany stands before me.' My answer to that was, 'According to my opinion, the most learned woman, not of Germany only, but of all Europe, stands before me as Empress.' Her Majesty shook her head. 'Ah, no,' she said, 'my familiar acquaintance with that woman forces me to say you are mistaken.' 99

—Luise Gottsched, letter describing Empress Maria Theresa, 28 September, 1749

VOCABULARY

frescoed: walls decorated with painted plaster

timidity: shyness

befallen: happened to

1 **DETERMINING CENTRAL IDEAS** What is the main impression that Luise Gottsched had of Maria Theresa and her court?

_____

_____

2 **IDENTIFYING CONNECTIONS** Does Maria Theresa's court appear to have adopted the ideas of Enlightenment thinkers?

_____

_____

3 **INTEGRATING INFORMATION** Using the evidence presented in this source and Frederick II's essay, do you think that Frederick II and Maria Theresa would agree about the role of the monarch?

_____

_____

_____

4 **INTERPRETING** How might Mary Wollstonecraft have criticized the meeting between Luise Gottsched and Empress Maria Theresa?

_____

_____

5 **CITING TEXT EVIDENCE** How can you tell that the idea of women's education surprises the Empress? Cite evidence to support your answer.

_____

_____

6 **CIVICS** Does Maria Theresa's meeting with Luise Gottsched conform to democratic values? What are the democratic and undemocratic aspects of the meeting?

_____

_____

_____

_____

The American Revolution

DIRECTIONS Search for evidence in the lesson to help you answer the following questions.

1 **SUMMARIZING** Use the graphic organizer below to summarize the different factors and ideas which led to the American Revolution.

ESSENTIAL QUESTION

Why do new ideas often spark change?

As you gather evidence to answer the Essential Question, think about:

- how long term factors and short term triggers combine to create changes.
- how the ideas of the Enlightenment influenced the American Revolution.
- how conflict can lead to change.

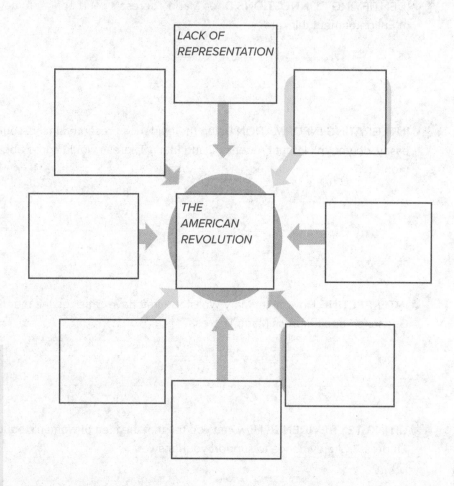

My Notes

_____

_____

_____

_____

_____

_____

_____

_____

2 **UNDERSTANDING CONTEXT** Could the American Revolution have been prevented if Britain had decided not to impose the Stamp Act?

_____

_____

_____

_____

_____

_____

3 **UNDERSTANDING CHANGE** How had new ideas changed Britain's form of government? How did these changes contrast with the changes brought about by the American Revolution?

_____

_____

_____

_____

4 **GEOGRAPHY** How did the cities of Charleston, Boston, and New York help to create the situation that would become the American Revolution?

_____

_____

_____

5 **DETERMINING MEANING** Why is _Common Sense_ an apt name for Thomas Paine's pamphlet?

_____

_____

6 **EXPLAINING CAUSE AND EFFECT** Use the flow chart below to graphically organize a logical sequence of events and ideas to show how the Declaration of Independence arose from the ideas of the Enlightenment.

Newton describes laws of gravity and nature	→		→		→		→	

ESSENTIAL QUESTION

Why do new ideas often spark change?

Declaration of Rights and Grievances

DIRECTIONS: Use the text to answer the questions.

EXPLORE THE CONTEXT: The First Congress of the American colonies is also known as the Stamp Act Congress. It was called in order to create and present a united petition to the government of Great Britain in protest of the imposition of the Stamp Act. Representatives from the colonies of Massachusetts, Rhode Island, Connecticut, New York, New Jersey, Pennsylvania, Delaware, Maryland, and South Carolina attended. In the petition, the congress laid out the grievances of the colonies and explained why they thought the Stamp Act should be abolished.

PRIMARY SOURCE: PETITION

"The Members of this Congress, sincerely devoted, with the warmest Sentiments of Affection and Duty to his Majesty's Person and Government, inviolably attached to the present happy Establishment of the Protestant Succession, and with Minds deeply impressed by a Sense of the present and impending Misfortunes of the *British* colonies on this Continent; having considered as maturely as Time will permit, the Circumstances of the said Colonies, esteem it our indispensable Duty, to make the following Declarations of our humble Opinion, respecting the most Essential Rights and Liberties of the Colonists, and of the Grievances under which they labour, by Reason of several late Acts of Parliament.

I. That his Majesty's Subjects in these Colonies, owe the same Allegiance to the Crown of *Great-Britain*, that is owing from his Subjects born within the Realm, and all due Subordination to that August Body the Parliament of *Great-Britain*.

II. That his Majesty's Liege Subjects in these Colonies, are entitled to all the inherent Rights and Liberties of his Natural Born Subjects, within the Kingdom of Great-Britain.

III. That it is inseparably essential to the Freedom of a People, and the undoubted right of *Englishmen*, that no Taxes be imposed on them, but with their own Consent, given personally, or by their Representatives.

IV. That the People of these Colonies are not, and from their local Circumstances, cannot be, Represented in the House of Commons in *Great-Britain*.

V. That the only Representatives of the People of these Colonies, are Persons chosen therein by themselves, and that no Taxes have ever been, or can Constitutionally imposed on them, but by their respective Legislature...."

—First Congress of the American Colonies, The Declaration of Rights and Grievances, 1765

VOCABULARY

impending: forthcoming

grievances: grudges; problems

allegiance: loyalty

subordination: to submit to a rule

1 **CITING TEXT EVIDENCE** What are the ideals and values which underpin the case made by the colonies in this petition?

_____

_____

2 **DETERMINING CENTRAL IDEAS** Do the colonies accept the British government as legitimate?

_____

_____

_____

3 **ANALYZING TEXT PRESENTATION** What is the structure of this text? Why has this structure been used? What is the effect?

_____

_____

_____

4 **INTEGRATING INFORMATION** How does the tone of this source compare to that of Luise Gottsched's account of her meeting with Empress Maria Theresa, an Analyze the Source from Lesson 3? Cite evidence to support your answer.

_____

_____

_____

5 **IDENTIFYING CONNECTIONS** What other texts can you connect to this document? How was this document influenced by earlier ideas, and how did it influence later ideas?

_____

_____

_____

_____

6 **CIVICS** How effective do you think a petition can be as a means of seeking change? What circumstances need to exist for a petition to be effective?

_____

_____

ESSENTIAL QUESTION

Why do new ideas often spark change?

Taxation in the New United States

DIRECTIONS: Use the text to answer the questions.

EXPLORE THE CONTEXT: The Federalist Papers were a series of articles written by Alexander Hamilton, James Madison, and John Jay published anonymously. They were intended to make the argument for a strong federal government during the time in which the Constitution of the United States was still being debated. Here Hamilton, addresses the need for the federal government to possess powers of taxation, contentious because the American Revolution had been prompted by a series of tax revolts.

PRIMARY SOURCE: ARTICLE

IT HAS been already observed that the federal government ought to possess the power of providing for the support of the national forces; in which proposition was intended to be included the expense of raising troops, of building and equipping fleets, and all other expenses in any wise connected with military arrangements and operations. But these are not the only objects to which the jurisdiction of the Union, in respect to revenue, must necessarily be empowered to extend. It must embrace a provision for the support of the national civil list; for the payment of the national debts contracted, or that may be contracted; and, in general, for all those matters which will call for disbursements out of the national treasury. The conclusion is, that there must be interwoven, in the frame of the government, a general power of taxation, in one shape or another.

Money is, with propriety, considered as the vital principle of the body politic; as that which sustains its life and motion, and enables it to perform its most essential functions. A complete power, therefore, to procure a regular and adequate supply of it, as far as the resources of the community will permit, may be regarded as an indispensable ingredient in every constitution. From a deficiency in this particular, one of two evils must ensue; either the people must be subjected to continual plunder, as a substitute for a more eligible mode of supplying the public wants, or the government must sink into a fatal atrophy, and, in a short course of time, perish.

In the Ottoman or Turkish empire, the sovereign, though in other respects absolute master of the lives and fortunes of his subjects, has no right to impose a new tax. The consequence is that he permits the bashaws or governors of provinces to pillage the people without mercy; and, in turn, squeezes out of them the sums of which he stands in need, to satisfy his own exigencies and those of the state. In America, from a like cause, the government of the Union has gradually dwindled into a state of decay, approaching nearly to annihilation. Who can doubt, that the happiness of the people in both countries would be promoted by competent authorities in the proper hands, to provide the revenues which the necessities of the public might require? **"**

—Federalist #30, The New York Packet, December 28, 1787

VOCABULARY

jurisdiction: authority

revenue: income from taxes

propriety: good manners

atrophy: to grow weaker

bashaw: a ranking officer in the Ottoman Empire

dwindled: to grow smaller

Exigencies: needs

Hamilton, Alexander. 1787. Federalist Paper No. 30, Concerning the General Power of Taxation. From the New York Packet, Friday, December 28, 1787.

1. **IDENTIFYING CONNECTIONS** In what sense can this source be said to advocate a rational view of the world? Explain your answer.

_____

_____

2. **CITING TEXT EVIDENCE** How has Hamilton been influenced by the new ideas about economics which were developing at the time? Cite evidence to support your answer.

_____

3. **ANALYZING TEXT PRESENTATION** How does Hamilton structure his argument in order to make it appealing to the Americans who would be reading his article?

_____

_____

_____

4. **UNDERSTANDING CONTEXT** What does the publication of this article in a newspaper suggest about the audience to which it is aimed? What does this imply about American society?

_____

_____

_____

5. **IDENTIFYING CONNECTIONS** How are the Federalist Papers related to texts like _A Vindication of the Rights of Woman_? Cite some other texts which are related in the same way.

_____

_____

6. **ECONOMICS** Are you persuaded by Hamilton's argument? Are there arguments against Hamilton's proposals?

_____

_____

_____

ESSENTIAL QUESTION

Why do new ideas often spark change?

My Notes

_____

_____

_____

_____

_____

_____

_____

_____

_____

_____

_____

_____

1 Think About It

Review the supporting questions you developed at the beginning of the chapter. Review the evidence you gathered in the chapter. Were you able to answer each Supporting Question?

_____

_____

_____

2 Organize Your Evidence

Complete the chart below with information you learned about new ideas that arose in the sixteenth to eighteenth centuries, the changes that resulted from these ideas, and the consequences of these changes (including the rise of further new ideas).

NEW IDEA	CHANGES	CONSEQUENCES

3 Talk About It

Work in a small group. With your group, discuss the ideas, changes, and consequences that you have identified and noted down in your charts. Did you all pick the same ideas and changes? Do you disagree on the consequences of those changes? Overall, which idea do you think was the most crucial in leading to change in this period? Why?

4 Write About It

Following your discussion in the Talk About It Activity, write about two examples of changes that came about in this period because of new ideas. Describe how different ideas were combined by people with different goals and interests to create those changes.

_____

_____

_____

_____

_____

5 Connect to the Essential Question

Following your work in the Talk About It activity, choose the ideas, changes, and consequences you identified as the most vital during this period. Plan, create, and present a multimedia presentation, including images, music, and animations if available, in which you describe the mix of ideas and innovations which led to those changes. Ask for peers to comment on your plan, and integrate their feedback into your presentation. Be sure to present information in a logical chain of cause and effect but also consider the ways that ideas are built upon one another and reinterpreted by different people with different motives. Ensure your presentation is both engaging and informative.

CITIZENSHIP
TAKING ACTION

The pace of change today can be difficult to keep up with. Just as in the past, it is sometimes hard to see what the consequences of new ideas and technologies will be. Not all changes are for the better. The personal computer, the internet, and robotic automation have changed the American workplace very rapidly. Some have benefited from the increased flexibility and viability of working from home, and businesses benefit from the productivity gains of automation and information technology. Recently, the internet has allowed activists in countries like Tunisia and Egypt to coordinate and successfully change their governments, but it has also created an information overload so massive that people sometimes have trouble distinguishing fact from fiction.

Organize a debate in your school about the ways that new ideas are set to change our world in the near future. If you are able, identify community leaders, businesspeople, or academics from your local area to come and present an argument at your debate. Try to include people who have a mixture of opinions about different ideas and changes that are likely to arise, as well as differences of opinion on whether those changes will be positive or negative.

As part of your debate, invite your classmates to prepare and ask questions of the speakers to further refine their arguments. Take notes during the debate. After the debate, work in small groups to analyze the arguments and perspectives you have heard. Write a three-paragraph summary of the information you have gained from the debate, outlining the ideas and changes you think are most likely to occur, as well as what you think of the likely consequences.

_____

_____

_____

_____

_____

_____

_____

The French Revolution and Napoleon

ESSENTIAL QUESTION

What causes revolution?

Think about how this question might relate to the political, economic, and social events and circumstances that could cause a revolution.

TALK ABOUT IT

Discuss with a partner what information you would need to know to answer this question. For example, one question might be, "What type of political, economic, and social changes could lead to a revolution?" Another might be, "How did these changes affect the French?"

DIRECTIONS: Now write down three additional questions that you need to answer to be able to explain what events and circumstances occurred to cause the French Revolution.

MY RESEARCH QUESTIONS

Supporting Question 1:

_____

_____

_____

_____

Supporting Question 2:

_____

_____

_____

Supporting Question 3:

_____

_____

The French Revolution Begins

DIRECTIONS: Search for evidence in the lesson to help you answer the following questions.

1 **ECONOMICS** Use the graphic organizer to compare the three estates.

Estate	Population	Place in Society
First or		
Second or		
Third or		

ESSENTIAL QUESTION

What causes revolution?

As you gather evidence to answer the Essential Question, think about:

- the types of events and circumstances that can lead to a revolution.
- the economic conditions in France before the French Revolution.
- the political conditions before the French Revolution.

My Notes

_____

_____

_____

_____

_____

_____

_____

2 **IDENTIFYING CONNECTIONS** Who was in the Third Estate? How was the Third Estate affected economically by the Revolution?

_____

_____

_____

_____

_____

_____

_____

_____

3 EXPLAINING CAUSES How did the Estates-General reflect the nature of power in France?

_____

_____

_____

4 UNDERSTANDING CONTEXT Why did France's budget go into crisis?

_____

_____

_____

_____

5 SUMMARIZING Complete the chart by filling in the causes and effects that led to the French Revolution.

Cause	Effect
Inequality within the three estates	
Bad harvest	
Failed attempt to change the Estates-General voting	

6 EXPLAINING EFFECTS Why did the Third Estate revolt?

_____

_____

_____

ESSENTIAL QUESTION

What causes revolution?

A Budget Fit for a King

DIRECTIONS: Read the excerpt. Then respond to the questions that follow.

EXPLORE THE CONTEXT: *The Livre Rouge (Red Register)* was Louis XVI's personal account book. The "livre" was the name given to the primary unit of money in France at the time. In 1790 the National Assembly demanded that it be published to make the spending of French royalty more transparent. To better understand the value of the figures given, multiply each by 13. That will give you the equivalent value in current U.S. dollars.

PRIMARY SOURCE: KING'S ACCOUNT BOOK

" Summary of the Livre Rouge

The total amount entered in the Red Book from May 19th 1774 to August 16th 1789 is 227,983,716 livres, 10 sous and one denier.

This sum can be broken down under several headings:

To the king's brothers: 28,364,211 livres

Gifts, gratuities: 6,174,793 livres

Pensions, salaries: 2,221,541 livres

Charity: 254,000 livres

Indemnities, advances, loans: 15,254,106 livres

Acquisitions, exchanges: 20,868,821 livres

Financial transactions: 5,825,000 livres

Foreign affairs, postal costs: 135,804,891 livres

Various expenses: 1,794,600 livres

Personal expenses of the king and queen: 11,423,750 livres. "

Source— *Livre Rouge*, released by the National Assembly, 1790

VOCABULARY

livre: former unit of money that equaled one pound of silver, which currently equals around $236 in U.S. dollars

sou: bronze coin that was worth a small amount of money

gratuities: gifts of money

indemnities: protection or security against damage or loss

acquisitions: act of gaining possession

1 **ANALYZING INFORMATION** What information is conveyed about the king's spending?

_____

_____

_____

_____

2A ECONOMICS How much did spending differ between Louis XVI's personal expenses and donations to charity?

_____

_____

_____

2B What might this tell you about Louis XVI's opinion of donating to charity?

_____

_____

_____

_____

3 **IDENTIFYING EFFECTS** How does the _Livre Rouge_ reflect the financial situation between Louis XVI and the peasants?

_____

_____

_____

_____

4 **UNDERSTANDING EFFECTS** How do you think the publication of the _Livre Rouge_ affected the common people of France?

_____

_____

_____

_____

5 **DRAWING CONCLUSIONS** What can you conclude about the publication of the _Livre Rouge_ with regard to the French Revolution?

_____

_____

Life in the French Countryside Pre-Revolution

DIRECTIONS: Read the excerpt. Then respond to the questions that follow.

EXPLORE THE CONTEXT: Arthur Young was a prominent English writer on agriculture who is also known for his social and political observations. He happened to be in France during the early part of the French Revolution. Young provides a snapshot of poverty in France in stark contrast with the lavish spending recorded in the *Livre Rouge*. In the excerpt below, he reports on the conditions in early July 1789 in his book *Travels in France*.

PRIMARY SOURCE: BOOK

"(June 10th)

Everything conspires to render the present period in France critical: the want of bread is terrible: accounts arrive every moment from the provinces of riots and disturbances, and calling in the military, to preserve the peace of the markets. The prices reported are the same as I found at Abbeville and Amiens 5 [sous] a pound for white bread, and 3 1/2 [sous] to 4 [sous] for the common sort, eaten by the poor: these rates are beyond their faculties, and occasion great misery. . . . It appears plain to me, that the violent friends of the commons are not displeased at the high price of corn, which seconds their views greatly, and makes any appeal to the common feeling of the people more easy, and much more to their purpose than if the price was low. **"**

Source— Arthur Young, *Travels in France*, 1792

VOCABULARY

revolutionaries: people who start or carry out revolution

violent friends of the commons: revolutionaries

seconds: supports or affirms

1 **EVALUATING TEXT EVIDENCE** What does Arthur Young's account of the conditions in France before the French Revolution reveal?

_____

_____

_____

_____

2 **UNDERSTANDING CHANGE** How does Young explain the effects of the price of bread?

_____

_____

_____

_____

3 **DETERMINING MEANING** What does Young mean when he writes that the revolutionaries were not displeased with the price of corn?

_____

_____

_____

_____

_____

4 **DISTINGUISHING FACT FROM OPINION** Is the _Livre Rouge_ fact or opinion? What about Young's excerpt?

_____

_____

_____

_____

5 **CIVICS** Does Young apply values and democratic principles in this excerpt? Explain why or why not.

_____

_____

_____

_____

6 **DRAWING CONCLUSIONS** Based on the information in the introduction to the excerpt and the excerpt itself, is it reasonable to conclude that Young is sympathetic to the common people in France?

_____

_____

_____

Radical Revolution and Reaction

DIRECTIONS Search for evidence in the lesson to help you answer the following questions.

ESSENTIAL QUESTION

What causes revolution?

As you gather evidence to answer the Essential Question, think about:

- how political movements can lead to a revolution.
- the economic factors that caused the Radical Revolution.
- how the events during and after the Terror led to the overthrow of the French government.

1 **COMPARE AND CONTRAST** What type of decisions did the National Convention make after the French Revolution? How are those different from the decisions the Estates-General made at the meeting before the French Revolution?

_____

_____

_____

_____

_____

2 **IDENTIFYING CONNECTIONS** Describe the crisis that formed after Louis XVI's death.

_____

_____

_____

_____

_____

3 **HISTORY** How did de-Christianization affect France?

_____

_____

_____

_____

_____

My Notes

_____

_____

_____

_____

_____

_____

_____

4 **EXPLAINING ISSUES** Use the chart to list the Committee of Public Safety's adopted policies. Include the effects of the policies or why they failed.

Adopted policy	Effect/why it failed

5 **SUMMARIZING** In the chart below, list the characteristics of the new constitution.

The Council	The Council of Elders	The Directory

6 **EXPLAINING ISSUES** What was the criteria to be an elector or qualified voter?

_____

_____

ESSENTIAL QUESTION
What causes revolution?

The Law of Suspects

DIRECTIONS: Read the excerpt and respond to the following questions.

EXPLORE THE CONTEXT: The French National Convention passed the Law of Suspects in September 1793. This law ordered the arrest of people suspected of opposing the revolution. It tended to target former nobles, émigrés, removed or suspended officials, and those suspected of treason and hoarding goods. The "Great Terror" started soon after these laws were passed.

PRIMARY SOURCE: POLICY

1. Immediately after the publication of this decree, all suspects found on the territory of the Republic and who are still at liberty will be arrested.

2. Suspects are:

   i. Those who, either by their conduct or their relationships, by their conversation or by their writing, are show to be partisans of tyranny and federalism and enemies of liberty;

   ii. Those who cannot justify, under the provisions of the law of 21 March last, their means of existence and the performance of their civic duties;

   iii. Those [who] who have been refused certificates of civic responsibility;

   iv. Public officials suspended or deprived of their functions by the National Convention or its agents, and not since reinstated, especially those who have been, or ought to be, dismissed by the law of 12 August last;

   v. Those former nobles, including husbands, wives, fathers, mothers, sons or daughters, brothers or sisters, and agents of emigres, who have not constantly manifested their loyalty to the Revolution;

   vi. Those who have emigrated during the interval between the 1 July 1789 and the publication of the law of 8 April 1792, although they may have returned to France during the period of delay fixed by the law or before.

The *comites de surveillance* [Surveillance Committees] established under the law of 21 March last, or those substituting for them, are empowered by the decrees of the representatives of the people. . . and are charged with drawing up, in each local district, a list of suspects, of issuing arrest warrants against them, and of affixing seals to their private paper. . .

Source— The Law of Suspects passed by National Convention, September 1793

VOCABULARY

tyranny: dictatorship

decree: an order by a legal authority

émigrés: someone who has left the country for political reasons

emigrated: left one's country to settle in another one

Donnachie, Ian and Lavin, Carmen. 2003. From Enlightenment to Romanticism - Anthology I. Manchester and New York: Manchester University Press.

1 **SUMMARIZING** Who is considered a suspect in this law?

_____

_____

_____

2 **EVALUATING TEXT EVIDENCE** What do you think the law means when it says "those former nobles, together with husbands, wives, fathers, mothers, sons or daughters, brothers or sisters, and agents of the émigrés, who have not constantly demonstrated their devotion to the Revolution"?

_____

_____

3 **DETERMINING POINT OF VIEW** Based on what you have read in your textbook and in the Law of Suspects, what is the point of view of the National Convention that passed these laws?

_____

_____

4 CIVICS Based on the law, what system was put in place to enforce this law?

_____

_____

5 **ANALYZING INFORMATION SOURCES** Why would the National Convention include in the Law of Suspects those who move to another country from July 1, 1789, to March 30, 1793?

_____

_____

6 **PREDICTING** How do you think this law affected the country?

_____

_____

_____

ESSENTIAL QUESTION
What causes revolution?

Robespierre Justifies Terror

DIRECTIONS: Use the image to answer the questions below.

EXPLORE THE CONTEXT: Maximilien Robespierre (1758–1794) was president of the Jacobin Club and of the Committee of Public Safety, elected by the National Convention, which effectively governed France during the radical phase of the revolution. The National Convention was effectively a dictatorship, which Robespierre believed was necessary to safeguard the revolution from within and without. Here in a speech on February 5, 1794, Robespierre justifies the use of terror.

PRIMARY SOURCE: SPEECH

66 . . . The two opposing spirits that have been represented in a struggle to rule nature might be said to be fighting in this great period of human history to fix irrevocably the world's destinies, and France is the scene of this fearful combat. Without, all the tyrants encircle you; within, all tyranny's friends conspire; they will conspire until hope is wrested from crime. We must smother the internal and external enemies of the Republic or perish with it; now in this situation, the first maxim of your policy ought to be to lead the people by reason and the people's enemies by terror.

If the spring of popular government in time of peace is virtue, the springs of popular government in revolution are at once virtue and terror: virtue, without which terror is fatal; terror, without which virtue is powerless. Terror is nothing other than justice, prompt, severe, inflexible; it is therefore an emanation of virtue; it is not so much a special principle as it is a consequence of the general principle of democracy applied to our country's most urgent needs. . . .

Society owes protection only to peaceable citizens; the only citizens in the Republic are the republicans. For it, the royalists, the conspirators are only strangers or, rather, enemies. This terrible war waged by liberty against tyranny—is it not indivisible? Are the enemies within not the allies of the enemies without? The assassins who tear our country apart, the intriguers who buy the consciences that hold the people's mandate; the traitors who sell them; the mercenary pamphleteers hired to dishonor the people's cause, to kill public virtue, to stir up the fire of civil discord, and to prepare political counterrevolution by moral counterrevolution—are all those men less guilty or less dangerous than the tyrants whom they serve? 99

Source— Maximilien Robespierre, "On the Moral and Political Principles of Domestic Policy," February 5, 1794.

VOCABULARY

irrevocably: beyond any doubt

virtue: honor; integrity

emanation: feeling; mood

mercenary: greedy; selfish

1 **DETERMINING CENTRAL IDEAS** Why did Maximilien Robespierre give this speech?

_____

_____

_____

2 **INTERPRETING** What does this speech reveal about the enforcement of the Law of Suspects?

_____

_____

_____

3 **UNDERSTANDING CONTEXT** What does Robespierre mean when he says, "Society owes protection only to peaceable citizens; the only citizens in the Republic are the republicans. For it, the royalists, the conspirators are only strangers or, rather, enemies"?

_____

_____

_____

_____

4 **IDENTIFYING BIAS** Could Robespierre have been biased about this topic? How is your opinion supported in his speech?

_____

_____

_____

5 **CIVICS** What was Robespierre's idea to enforce support for the Republic?

_____

_____

6 **PREDICTING** Do you think this speech will allow more executions of those against the revolution?

_____

_____

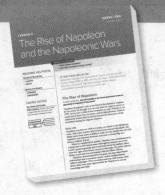

ESSENTIAL QUESTION

What causes revolution?

As you gather evidence to answer the Essential Question, think about:

- how Napoleon was able to take power.
- how Napoleon spread the principles of the Revolution.
- why Napoleon was defeated

My Notes

_____

_____

_____

_____

_____

_____

_____

The Rise of Napoleon and the Napoleonic Wars

DIRECTIONS Search for evidence in the lesson to help you answer the following questions.

1 **HISTORY** Why was Napoleon considered a child of the revolution?

_____

_____

_____

_____

2 **SPATIAL THINKING** Why did Napoleon suggest striking Britain through Egypt in 1789?

_____

_____

_____

_____

_____

3 **DETERMINING CONTEXT** How did Napoleon use his military background to gain power?

_____

_____

_____

_____

_____

_____

4 **RELATING EVENTS** Fill in the chart below to show the chain of events that led to Napoleon's making peace with the Catholic Church.

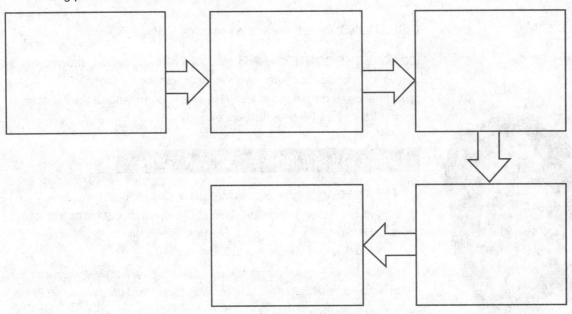

5 **EXPLAINING EFFECTS** Using the chart below, list some of the principles of the Civil Code or Napoleonic Code.

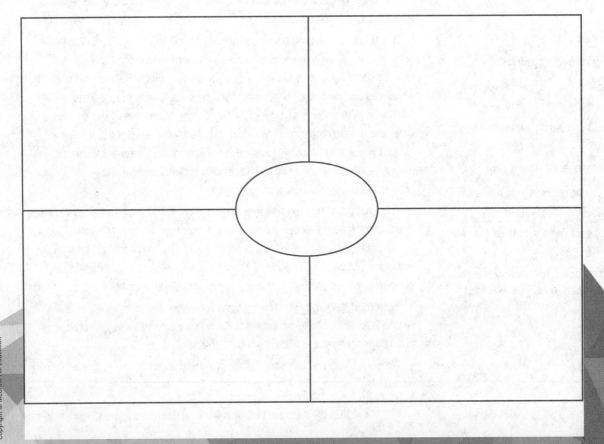

ESSENTIAL QUESTION
What causes revolution?

Young Napoleon's Speech in Italy

DIRECTIONS: Read the following passage. Answer the questions below.

EXPLORE THE CONTEXT: Napoleon, then a young officer, showed his genius for propaganda and psychological warfare through this proclamation to his troops in 1796. He was in command of the French army in Italy when he gave this speech.

PRIMARY SOURCE: PROCLAMATION

"In a fortnight you have won six victories, taken twenty-one standards, fifty-five pieces of artillery, several strong positions, and conquered the richest part of Piedmont [a region in northern Italy]; you have captured 15,000 prisoners and killed or wounded more than 10,000 men. . . .

You have won battles without cannon, crossed rivers without bridges, made forced marches without shoes, camped without brandy and often without bread. Soldiers of liberty, only republican phalanxes could have endured what you have endured. Soldiers, you have our thanks! The grateful Patrie will owe its prosperity to you. . . .

The two armies which but recently attacked you with audacity are fleeing before you in terror; the wicked men who laughed at your misery and rejoiced at the thought of the triumphs of your enemies are confounded and trembling.

But, soldiers, as yet you have done nothing compared with what remains to be done. . . . Undoubtedly the greatest obstacles have been overcome; but you still have battles to fight, cities to capture, rivers to cross. Is there one among you whose courage is abating? No. . . . All of you are consumed with a desire to extend the glory of the French people; all of you long to humiliate those arrogant kings who dare to contemplate placing us in fetters; all of you desire to dictate a glorious peace, one which will indemnify the Patrie for the immense sacrifices it has made; all of you wish to be able to say with pride as you return to your villages, "I was with the victorious army of Italy!"

Friends, I promise you this conquest; but there is one condition you must swear to fulfill—to respect the people whom you liberate, to repress the horrible pillaging committed by scoundrels incited by our enemies. Otherwise you would not be the liberators of the people; you would be their scourge. . . . Plunderers will be shot without mercy; already, several have been. . . .

Peoples of Italy, the French army comes to break your chains; the French people is the friend of all peoples; approach it with confidence; your property, your religion, and your customs will be respected.

We are waging war as generous enemies, and we wish only to crush the tyrants who enslave you. "

Source— Napoleon Bonaparte's proclamation to his troops in Italy, 1796

VOCABULARY

phalanxes: units of troops in close array

prosperity: state of being successful; thriving

indemnify: to compensate for damage or loss sustained

victorious: conquering; triumphant

pillaging: seizing ruthlessly, as money or goods, by open violence, as in war

liberators: people who set others free, as from imprisonment

plunderers: people who steal goods or valuables by open force, as in war

1 **DESCRIBING** Briefly describe what Napoleon is trying to convey in his speech.

_____

_____

_____

_____

2 **ANALYZING TEXT** Why do you think Napoleon used these tactics in his speech?

_____

_____

_____

3 **CITING TEXT EVIDENCE** How can you tell that Napoleon was using propaganda in his speech?

_____

_____

_____

4 CIVICS Do authorities have a right to use propaganda to their advantage?

_____

_____

_____

_____

5 **ANALYZING CHANGE** What is happening at the beginning of the excerpt that shows Napoleon's position has become less secure.

_____

_____

_____

6 **SUMMARIZING** In your own words, summarize Napoleon's proclamation.

_____

_____

_____

_____

ESSENTIAL QUESTION

What causes revolution?

Madame de Staël on Napoleon

DIRECTIONS: Read the excerpt, then answer the questions that follow.

EXPLORE THE CONTEXT: Anne-Louise Germaine de Staël, or Madame de Staël, was one of Napoleon's chief opponents in the literary world. She was a witty conversationalist and took an active interest in politics. Both sought the limelight and were often at odds. He finally exiled her in 1803.

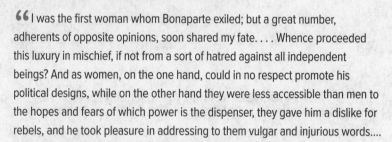

PRIMARY SOURCE: SPEECH

“ I was the first woman whom Bonaparte exiled; but a great number, adherents of opposite opinions, soon shared my fate. . . . Whence proceeded this luxury in mischief, if not from a sort of hatred against all independent beings? And as women, on the one hand, could in no respect promote his political designs, while on the other hand they were less accessible than men to the hopes and fears of which power is the dispenser, they gave him a dislike for rebels, and he took pleasure in addressing to them vulgar and injurious words....

Had Bonaparte been satisfied with acting the proud part of a great general and first magistrate of the republic, he would have soared in all the height of his genius far above the small but pointed shafts of drawing-room wit. But when he entertained the design of becoming an upstart king, a citizen gentleman upon the throne, he exposed himself as a fine aim to the mockery of fashion; and to restrain it, as he has done, he was obliged to have recourse to terror and the employment of spies. Bonaparte wished me to praise him in my writings, not assuredly that any additional praise would have been remarked in the fumes of the incense which surrounded him; but he was vexed that I should be the only writer of reputation in France who had published books during his reign without making any mention of his gigantic existence, . . . Till then my disgrace had consisted merely in my removal from Paris; but from that time I was forbidden to travel and was threatened with imprisonment for the remainder of my days. The contagion of exile, the noble invention of the Roman emperors, was the most cruel aggravation of this punishment. They who came to see the banished exposed themselves to banishment in their turn; the greater part of the Frenchmen with whom I was acquainted avoided me, as if I had been tainted with a pestilence. This appeared to me like a comedy when the pain it gave was not extreme; and as travelers under quarantine mischievously throw their handkerchiefs to the passersby, to compel them to share in the wearisome sameness of their confinement, so when I happened to meet a man of Bonaparte's court in the streets of Geneva I was tempted to terrify him by my polite attentions. ”

Source— Germaine de Staël,
from *Considerations on the Principal Events of the French Revolution*, 1796

VOCABULARY

exile: to prohibited someone from staying in or returning to his or her country

injurious: doing or involving injury or wrong, as to another

magistrate: civil officer charged with the administration of the law

vex: to torment; trouble; distress; plague; worry

pestilence: something that is considered harmful, destructive, or evil

1 CIVICS What values and democratic principles is Madame de Staël questioning in this passage?

_____

_____

_____

_____

2 UNDERSTANDING CONTEXT What was happening with women's rights in France during Napoleon's reign?

_____

_____

_____

3 RELATING EVENTS How does this passage help us understand how women were treated?

_____

_____

_____

4 EVALUATING Does de Staël feel her exile was justified?

_____

_____

_____

5 EVALUATING EVIDENCE Based on the excerpt, do you think de Staël's exile did anything to make her less outspoken?

_____

_____

6 DRAWING CONCLUSIONS What can you conclude about Napoleon's attitude toward women after reading this excerpt?

_____

_____

_____

The Fall of Napoleon and the European Reaction

DIRECTIONS Search for evidence in the lesson to help you answer the following questions.

ESSENTIAL QUESTION

What causes revolution?

As you gather evidence to answer the Essential Question, think about:

- how Napoleon's control started a revolution.
- how the revolution affected Napoleon's reign.
- how the revolution changed society.

1 **DESCRIBING** What was the French Grand Army doing in 1812?

_____

_____

_____

_____

_____

_____

_____

_____

2 **HISTORY** Fill in the cause-and-effect chart with the events that led to Napoleon's exile to Elba.

			Napoleon exiled to Elba

My Notes

_____

_____

_____

_____

_____

_____

3 UNDERSTANDING CONTEXT What was the state of the French government during Napoleon's exile?

_____

_____

_____

_____

_____

4 CAUSE AND EFFECT Use the chart below to fill in the causes and effects of the defeat of Napoleon.

Cause	Effect
European rulers restore the old order	
	Conservatism was put in place
	Military force used to crush revolutions in Spain and Italy
Conservative governments worked to maintain the old order	

5 DIFFERENTIATING What is the difference between liberalism and nationalism?

_____

_____

_____

_____

ESSENTIAL QUESTION
What causes revolution?

The Congress of Vienna

DIRECTIONS: Use the images to answer the questions below.

EXPLORE THE CONTEXT: Prince Klemens von Metternich, sitting in the center, was the Austrian foreign minister. He was the most influential figure at the Congress of Vienna, a meeting with Great Britain, Austria, Prussia, and Russia in 1814. The Congress of Vienna was a meeting of ambassadors to arrange a final peace settlement after Napoleon was defeated.

PRIMARY SOURCE: IMAGE

1 **UNDERSTANDING CHANGE** Why was the Congress of Vienna held?

_____

_____

_____

_____

2A **EXPLAINING ISSUES** What role did Metternich play at the Congress of Vienna?

_____

_____

_____

2B **INTEGRATING VISUAL INFORMATION** What in this image shows that these are important, powerful men?

_____

_____

3 **UNDERSTANDING CONTEXT** What political philosophy did Metternich and others at the congress follow?

_____

_____

_____

4 **IDENTIFYING CONNECTIONS** Explain why these conservative leaders felt the need to gather and discuss the future of Europe at this time.

_____

_____

_____

5 **INTERPRETING** What was the principle of legitimacy? Why did Metternich subscribe to it?

_____

_____

_____

6 **HISTORY** Based on what you have learned so far, do you predict that the Congress of Vienna will make lasting changes in Europe?

_____

_____

_____

ESSENTIAL QUESTION

What causes revolution?

Napoleon in Exile

DIRECTIONS: Use the image to answer the questions below.

EXPLORE THE CONTEXT: This satirical cartoon of Napoleon, entitled "The Journey of a Modern Hero to the Island of Elba," was printed in 1814 after his first defeat by a coalition of European states, including Great Britain and Prussia. Satirical cartoons were used as a form of expression not just against Napoleon but many political figures, past and present. Many cartoons use exaggeration, and in cartoons, Napoleon was often portrayed as a brat or as very short.

PRIMARY SOURCE: IMAGE

① **DESCRIBING** What does the cartoon show?

_____

_____

_____

_____

2 **UNDERSTANDING CONTEXT** Why would the artist create a satirical cartoon about Napoleon?

_____

_____

_____

_____

3 **HISTORY** What important things were going on at the time that relate to the cartoon? How does this information help you understand the cartoon?

_____

_____

_____

_____

_____

4 **DRAWING CONCLUSIONS** Do you think people were pleased with the depiction of Napoleon based on this cartoon? Explain your reasoning.

_____

_____

_____

_____

_____

5 **INTERPRETING** Why is Napoleon in a "sad position"?

_____

_____

6 **ANALYZING POINT OF VIEW** What was the cartoonist's viewpoint of Napoleon, based on his depiction here?

_____

_____

_____

ESSENTIAL QUESTION

What causes revolution?

My Notes

_____

_____

_____

_____

_____

_____

_____

_____

_____

_____

_____

_____

_____

1 Think About It

Review the supporting questions you developed at the beginning of the chapter. Review the evidence you gathered in the chapter. Were you able to answer each Supporting Question? If there was not enough evidence to answer your Supporting Questions, what additional evidence might you need to consider?

_____

_____

_____

2 Organize Your Evidence

Complete the chart below to organize the causes and effects of significant events during the French Revolution to the downfall of Napoleon in the chapter.

EVENT	CAUSE(S)	EFFECT(S)
French economy is in crisis		Louis XVI was forced to call a meeting of the Estates-General.
	Power vacuum after execution of king; Austria, Prussia, Spain, Portugal, Britain, and the Dutch Republic took up arms against France	
		Adoption of a new calendar
Coup d'état		
		Catholic Church not an enemy of the French government anymore

3 Talk About It

Work in a small group. With your group, discuss the major causes of the French Revolution. How did those causes lead to the later effects? Did others see the same causal relations? Did anyone identify a relationship that you had not noticed before? Did you find yourself objecting to anyone's claim of a causal relation between events?

4 Connect to the Essential Question

Create a multimedia time line of the events that led to the French Revolution and the aftermath. Include images and text from people (both leaders and ordinary people, if possible) as well as political, economic, and social reasons that you think contributed to the revolution. Be sure to present information in a logical chain of cause and effect and show how these events built upon each other.

CITIZENSHIP
TAKE ACTION

MAKE CONNECTIONS As emperor, Napoleon required all manuscripts to be reviewed by the government before being published, a practice known as censorship. Censorship is closely related to attempts to ban books, which sometimes happens in the modern United States. People tend to have strong opinions about banning books. Attempting to ban books is something that requires civic participation, or participation in the governance of your community.

Think of your favorite book, or one you have read recently, and imagine that people in your community have called for it to be banned. Write a letter to a government official in which you explain why you think the book should not be banned. For a stronger argument, you will need to support your opinion with evidence, which means you will need to do research about recent attempts to ban books in the United States. When doing research online, be sure to use credible sources. Ask your teacher if you are not sure whether a source is credible.

_____

_____

_____

_____

_____

_____

_____

_____

_____

_____

Industrialization and Nationalism

ESSENTIAL QUESTION

How does revolution bring about political and economic change?

Think about the different kinds of revolutionary changes that came about in the nineteenth century. Notice how significant changes can have a variety of consequences that can continue to drive ongoing upheaval and instability.

TALK ABOUT IT

Discuss with a partner what information you would need to know to explain how a revolutionary approach to something—meaning a radically new and different way of handling something—can cause changes in other areas. For example, one question might be, "What factors led to the Industrial Revolution?"

DIRECTIONS: Now write down three additional questions that you need to answer to be able to describe how political and economic consequences can come about in response to revolutionary changes.

MY RESEARCH QUESTIONS

Supporting Question 1:

_____

_____

Supporting Question 2:

_____

_____

Supporting Question 3:

_____

_____

ESSENTIAL QUESTION

How does revolution bring about political and economic change?

As you gather evidence to answer the Essential Question, think about:

- what changes occurred in the labor market.
- how the labor market changed in response to technological advances.
- how labor market changes caused social changes.

My Notes

_____

_____

_____

_____

_____

_____

_____

_____

The Industrial Revolution

DIRECTIONS Search for evidence in the lesson to help you answer the following questions.

1 ECONOMICS Use the graphic organizer to compare industrial activity before and after the revolution in manufacturing (iron and cloth) and distribution (rail).

Industry	Pre-revolution	Post-revolution
Iron (tons produced)		
Cotton cloth (tons of cotton imported for weaving into cloth)		
Railroad transport (miles of track)		

2 **IDENTIFYING CONNECTIONS** How did the use of steam engines affect the manufacturing and distribution of products such as iron and cotton cloth?

_____

_____

_____

_____

3 **RELATING EVENTS** How did the Industrial Revolution cause population migrations?

_____

_____

_____

_____

_____

_____

4 **COMPARING AND CONTRASTING** What factors made the process of industrialization slower in France and Germany than in Great Britain?

_____

_____

_____

_____

5A **SUMMARIZING** The Industrial Revolution caused a change in how the merchant middle class viewed and treated workers. In the table below, compare how merchants and factory owners did business.

	Merchants	Factory Owners
What was owned by the person running the business?		
In what way was safety an issue for workers?		
How were workers hired and how did the work pay?		

5B **SUMMARIZING** How did the new working class of the Industrial Revolution differ from the working classes of the earlier, farm-based economy?

_____

_____

_____

6 **DETERMINING CONTEXT** How did the Industrial Revolution give rise to the welfare state?

_____

_____

_____

_____

_____

The Wealth of Nations

ESSENTIAL QUESTION

How does revolution bring about political and economic change?

DIRECTIONS: Read the excerpt and answer the following questions.

EXPLORE THE CONTEXT: *The Wealth of Nations* was written in 1776 by Adam Smith (1723–1790), a philosopher and economic theorist from Scotland. Smith wanted to discuss the "commerce society" as he saw it. He thought that the way a society made its profits had important implications for the people, including moral implications. At this time concern grew over the need for affordable food for a growing but impoverished population. Smith highlights the important role that the potato—a new crop brought from the Americas—could play in Britain. He shows the economic benefit of the potato and proposes it could become the fuel for the nation's peasant workers.

PRIMARY SOURCE: BOOK

66 The food produced by a field of potatoes is not inferior in quantity to that produced by a field of rice, and much superior to what is produced by a field of wheat. Twelve thousand weight of potatoes from an acre of land is not a greater produce than two thousand weight of wheat. The food or solid nourishment, indeed, which can be drawn from each of those two plants, is not altogether in proportion to their weight, on account of the watery nature of potatoes. Allowing, however, half the weight of this root to go to water, a very large allowance, such an acre of potatoes will still produce six thousand weight of solid nourishment, three times the quantity produced by the acre of wheat. An acre of potatoes is cultivated with less expense than an acre of wheat; the fallow, which generally precedes the sowing of wheat, more than compensating the hoeing and other extraordinary culture which is always given to potatoes. Should this root ever become in any part of Europe, like rice in some rice countries, the common and favorite vegetable food of the people, so as to occupy the same proportion of the lands in tillage which wheat and other sorts of grain for human food do at present, the same quantity of cultivated land would maintain a much greater number of people, and the laborers being generally fed with potatoes, a greater surplus would remain after replacing all the stock and maintaining all the labor employed in cultivation. A greater share of this surplus, too, would belong to the landlord. Population would increase, and rents would rise much beyond what they are at present. 99

—Adam Smith, from *The Wealth of Nations*, 1776

VOCABULARY

fallow: farmland left unplanted so it can recov[er] its fertility

culture: farming techniques

rents: the farmer's payment to landowners fo[r] use of the land

Smith, Adam. 1776. An Inquiry into the Nature and Causes of the Wealth of Nations, Volume 1. London: W. Strahan and T. Cadell.

1 **ANALYZING THEMES** What is Smith's purpose in comparing wheat and potatoes in this passage?

_____

_____

2 **EVALUATING EVIDENCE** What reasoning does Smith use to persuade his reader that potatoes are a superior crop?

_____

_____

_____

3 **INFERRING** What other kinds of arguments might a person use to persuade farmers to grow a different food crop?

_____

_____

_____

4 **ANALYZING SOURCES** How does Smith anticipate and answer to potential objections to his proposal?

_____

_____

_____

5 **ANALYZING CENTRAL IDEAS** What is needed in order for Smith's proposed change in crops to succeed?

_____

_____

_____

6 **HISTORY** What is Smith's perspective? What is his relationship to farming?

_____

_____

_____

ESSENTIAL QUESTION

How does revolution bring about political and economic change?

Letters from England from Don Manuel Alvarez Espriella

DIRECTIONS: Read the excerpt and answer the following questions.

EXPLORE THE CONTEXT: Robert Southey published *Letters from England* pseudonymously under the name Don Manuel Alvarez Espriella. This satirical passage describes a conversation between a fictional Spanish tourist (Espriella) and a gentleman in Manchester giving him a tour of the cotton factories there. It shows how many people were sometimes blind to or willfully ignorant of the destructive impact it had on those employed by the factories.

PRIMARY SOURCE: BOOK

❝ Mr.— remarked that nothing could be so beneficial to a country as manufacture. 'You see these children, sir,' said he. 'In most parts of England poor children are a burthen to their parents and to the parish; here the parish, which would else have to support them, is rid of all expense; they get their bread almost as soon as they can run about, and by the time they are seven or eight years old bring in money. There is no idleness among us: they come at five in the morning; we allow them half an hour for breakfast, and an hour for dinner; they leave work at six, and another set relieves them for the night; the wheels never stand still.'

I was looking, while he spoke, at the unnatural dexterity with which the fingers of these little creatures were playing in the machinery. . . .

'We are well off for hands in Manchester,' said Mr.—; 'manufacturers are favourable to population, the poor are not afraid of having a family here, the parishes therefore have always plenty to apprentice, and we take them as fast as they can supply us. In new manufacturing towns they find it difficult to get a supply. Their only method is to send people round the country to get children from their parents. Women usually undertake this business; they promise the parents to provide for the children; one party is glad to be eased of a burden; and it answers well to the other to find the young ones in food, lodging and clothes, and receive their wages.' 'But if these children should be ill-used', said I. 'Sir,' he replied, 'it never can be the interest of the women to use them ill, nor of the manufacturers to permit it.'

It would have been in vain to argue had I been disposed to it. Mr.— was a man of humane and kindly nature, who would not himself use any thing cruelly, and judged of others by his own feelings. I thought of the cities in Arabian romance, where all the inhabitants were enchanted: here Commerce is the Queen witch, and I had no talisman strong enough to disenchant those who were daily drinking of the golden cup of her charms. ❞

Source— Don Manuel Alvarez, from *Letters from England,* 1807

VOCABULARY

manufacture: factory production of goods, as opposed to production by hand

burthen: cost

parish: a district governed by the landowner

get: earn

dexterity: skill using the hands

consumption: tuberculosis, an infection usually in the lungs, that killed many until a vaccination was discovered in 1921

apprentice: train

talisman: magical object

commerce: business

Nicholas, Mrs. A. H. 1836. The Republic of Letters; A Republication of Standard Literature. Vol. VI. New York: George Dearborn, Publisher.

1 **INTERPRETING** According to the passage, what were the working conditions in British factories of the time?

_____

_____

2 **INFERRING** What does the Englishman think of the working conditions in the factories?

_____

_____

_____

_____

3 **ANALYZING POINT OF VIEW** What does the Spanish tourist think of the working conditions in the factories?

_____

_____

_____

_____

4 **DETERMINING CONTEXT** If Southey's goal is ultimately to spark reform in factory working conditions, why do you think he chose to write a story from the perspective of a Spanish tourist instead of writing from the perspective of the worker or writing a nonfiction essay about these conditions?

_____

_____

_____

_____

5 **HISTORY** What does the passage tell us about how the revolution in technology brought about economic change in Britain?

_____

_____

_____

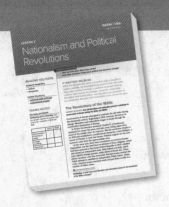

ESSENTIAL QUESTION

How does revolution bring about political and economic change?

As you gather evidence to answer the Essential Question, think about:

- the different goals of revolutionary groups in different regions.
- how the old economic and political conditions led to calls for revolutionary change.
- why some revolutions failed to create lasting change.

My Notes

_____

_____

_____

_____

_____

_____

Nationalism and Political Revolutions

DIRECTIONS Search for evidence in the lesson to help you answer the following questions.

1 **ANALYZING ISSUES** Which political revolutions of 1830 were successful, and which were not?

_____

_____

_____

_____

_____

_____

2 **COMPARE AND CONTRAST** How did liberalism and nationalism cause people to rebel against government?

_____

_____

_____

_____

_____

_____

_____

3 CIVICS **ANALYZING CHANGE** What new freedoms and rights were sought by those fighting for liberalism?

_____

_____

_____

_____

_____

_____

4 UNDERSTANDING CAUSE AND EFFECT Use the graphic organizers to examine the causes and outcomes of these European political revolutions of 1848.

AUSTRIAN EMPIRE

What revolutionary political changes did the rebels seek?	→	What was the outcome?

FRANCE

What revolutionary political changes did the rebels seek?	→	What was the outcome?

GERMAN CONFEDERATION

What revolutionary political changes did the rebels seek?	→	What was the outcome?
		The elected monarch refused to accept the crown granted by popular vote.
The 38 separate states proposed a unified Germany under a parliamentary system.		

5 IDENTIFYING EFFECTS How did nationalism—which drove Hungary to demand its own parliamentary self-rule from the Austrian Empire—finally lead to the failure of Hungary to adequately govern itself?

_____

_____

_____

ESSENTIAL QUESTION

How does revolution bring about political and economic change?

An Eyewitness Account of a Battle in the French Revolution of 1848

DIRECTIONS: Read the excerpt and answer the following questions.

EXPLORE THE CONTEXT: Alphonse de Lamartine (1790–1869) was a politically involved writer. In 1851 he published *History of the French Revolution of 1848*. Lamartine played an important role in helping to create the Second French Republic. He championed personal liberties and issues of the poor. He was known for calling on the French to retain their tricolored flag instead of adopting a red flag for the new Republic. In this excerpt, he offers an eyewitness view of a battle in the French Revolution of 1848.

PRIMARY SOURCE: EXCERPT

" At dawn the routes which led to the gates of Paris were covered with columns of cavalry, infantry and artillery, which the commands of government had collected. These troops were imposing, obedient, well-disciplined, but sad and silent. The sadness of civil war clouded their brows. They took successively their position on the principal streets branching off from the quarters which pour forth the population of Paris. The multitude did not fight en masse upon any point. Dispersed and floating bands disarmed only isolated stations, broke open the armorers' shops, and fired invisible shots upon the troops. The barricades, starting from the centre of the church Saint Mary, were raised, branching out and gradually multiplying almost under the feet of the army. Hardly were they reared when they were abandoned. The troops had only stones to contend with,—It was a silent battle, whose progress was felt without hearing the noise.

The National Guard, assembled by a tardy call, collected legion by legion. It remained neutral, and confined itself to interposing between the troops and the people, and demanding with loud voice the dismissal of the ministers, and reform. It thus served as a shield to the revolution.... "

—Alphonse de Lamartine, *History of the Revolution of 1848*, 1849

VOCABULARY

artillery: large weapons such as cannons

en masse: as a group; all together

armorers: sellers or makers of weapons or armor

1A **ANALYZE THE TEXT** The narrative in this excerpt is somewhat vague. To whom is Alphonese de Lamartine referring when he describes "troops [who] were imposing, obedient, well-disciplined"?

_____

1B To whom is Lamartine referring when he writes "the multitude"?

_____

_____

_____

2 **INTERPRETING** The National Guard is called "neutral," but Lamartine also says they demanded reform. How do you interpret this?

_____

_____

3 HISTORY Does Lamartine reveal any bias in this excerpt? How can you tell?

_____

_____

4 **DRAWING CONCLUSIONS** What can you conclude Lamartine means when he says the troops "had only stones to contend with"?

_____

_____

5 **DETERMINING MEANING** What does the line "The sadness of civil war clouded their brows" mean?

_____

_____

6 **SUMMARIZING** In your own words, summarize the excerpt.

_____

_____

_____

_____

_____

ESSENTIAL QUESTION

How does revolution bring about political and economic change?

An Exile Writes of Italy From France

DIRECTIONS: Read the excerpt and answer the following questions.

EXPLORE THE CONTEXT: The author of this letter, Giuseppe Mazzini, was an Italian journalist and political activist. He had already been imprisoned by the Austrians following the 1830s rebellion, and upon release he was exiled from his home county. His notoriety enabled him to launch a political organization he called "Young Italy" from his new home in France. In this letter he declares the principles of this new political organization and the changes sought in Italy.

PRIMARY SOURCE: ESSAY

"Young Italy is a brotherhood of Italians who believe in a law of *Progress* and *Duty*, and are convinced that Italy is destined to become one nation. . .

Young Italy is Republican and Unitarian. Republican—because theoretically every nation is destined, by the law of God and humanity, to form a free and equal community of brothers; and the republican is the only form of government that insures this future.

Because all true sovereignty resides essentially in the nation, the sole progressive and continuous interpreter of the supreme moral law. . . .

Because both history and the nature of things teach us that elective monarchy tends to generate anarchy; and hereditary monarchy tends to generate despotism. . . .

Young Italy is *Unitarian*— Because, without unity, there is no true nation. Because without unity, there is no real strength; and Italy, surrounded as she is by powerful, united, and jealous nations, has need of strength before all things. . . .

Without unity of religious belief, and unity of social pact; without unity of civil, political, and penal legislation, there is no true nation. . . .

The means by which Young Italy proposes to reach its aim are—education and insurrection, to be adopted simultaneously, and made to harmonize with each other.

Education must ever be directed to teach by example, word, and pen, the necessity of insurrection. Insurrection, whenever it can be realised, must be so conducted as to render it a means of national education. . . .

Young Italy draws a distinction between the period of insurrection, and that of revolution. The revolution begins as soon as the insurrection is triumphant. . . .

The colors of Young Italy are *white, red,* and *green*. The banner of Young Italy will display these colours, and bear on the one side the words—*Liberty, Equality, Humanity*; and on the other—*Unity, Independence.* "

Source— Giuseppe Mazzini, *General Instructions for the Members of Young Italy,* 1832

VOCABULARY

republican: representative government selected by those governed

unitarian: uniting all of Italy

sovereignty: authority to govern

despotism: rule by an all-powerful leader who enforces cruelty or oppression

elective monarchy: rule by a king or queen who is chosen by the people

social pact: the organization of society so that citizens feel their government's authority over them is legitimate and worthy to uphold

penal legislation: the creation of laws governing the punishment of criminals

insurrection: violent uprising against a government by its own people

1. **INTERPRETING TEXT** How would the republican form of government advocated by Mazzini allow Italians to "form a free and equal community of brothers," as opposed to being ruled by Austria?

_____

_____

_____

2. **DETERMINING MEANING** How would "unity of religious belief, and unity of social pact" help create the new Italian state Mazzini proposes?

_____

_____

_____

3. **INFERRING** Why does Mazzini believe Italy "has need of strength before all things"?

_____

_____

_____

4. **CIVICS** Mazzini says the purpose of education is to teach the necessity of insurrection, and in turn he sees insurrection as a means to educate people. How could insurrection—successful or unsuccessful—teach people that more insurrection is needed?

_____

_____

_____

5. **DETERMINING MEANING** What do you think Mazzini means when he says, "The revolution begins as soon as the insurrection is triumphant"?

_____

_____

_____

6. **ANALYZING STRUCTURE** Why do you think Mazzini placed the words _Liberty, Equality,_ and _Humanity_ on one side of the new banner of Young Italy and the words _Unity_ and _Independence_ on the other?

_____

_____

_____

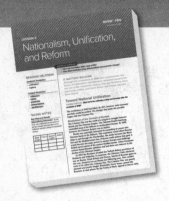

ESSENTIAL QUESTION

How does revolution bring about political and economic change?

As you gather evidence to answer the Essential Question, think about:

- the effects of the Crimean War.
- the different types of change that occurred in nineteenth century Britain.
- the growing divisions in the United States.

My Notes

_____

_____

_____

_____

_____

_____

_____

_____

Nationalism, Unification, and Reform

DIRECTIONS Search for evidence in the lesson to help you answer the following questions.

1A **UNDERSTANDING CONTEXT** Why was Russia interested in fighting the Ottoman Empire for control of the Balkans?

_____

_____

_____

1B **UNDERSTANDING CONTEXT** Why were Great Britain and France interested in helping defeat Russia in its attempt?

_____

_____

_____

2 Complete the chart below on the Crimean War.

CAUSE AND EFFECT: CRIMEAN WAR

Cause	Effect
	Austria refused military support to Russia
Russian forces were overpowered.	

3 **DESCRIBING** How did the Kingdom of Piedmont in northern Italy defeat Austria and gain control of unification efforts across Italy?

_____

_____

_____

_____

4 ANALYZING EFFECTS Louis-Napoleon was elected the new Emperor of France by a nearly unanimous vote. What measures did he take to satisfy the revolutionary need for liberalism in government, and how did they fail?

_____

_____

_____

_____

_____

_____

5 IDENTIFYING STEPS Use the graphic organizer to show why the governments of Austria and Russia could no longer deny the calls of revolutionaries for radical changes, how they attempted to satisfy the revolutionaries, and what the outcomes of those strategies were.

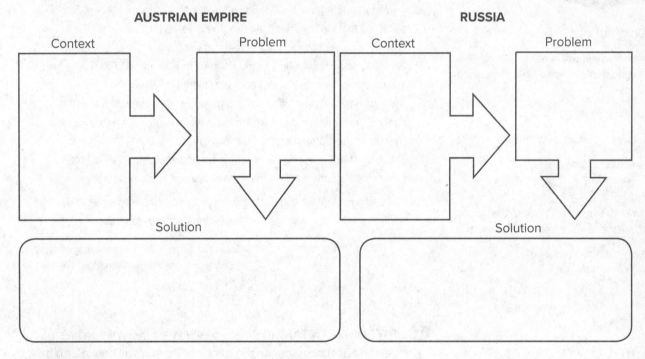

AUSTRIAN EMPIRE

Context · Problem · Solution

RUSSIA

Context · Problem · Solution

6 CIVICS COMPARING What struggles in America resulted from the attempt to embody both the liberalism and the nationalism of its Constitution?

_____

_____

_____

_____

Wilhelm I, First German Emperor

For the "Fatherland and Everlasting Peace". Reported in The New York Herald. January 21, 1871.

ESSENTIAL QUESTION

How does revolution bring about political and economic change?

DIRECTIONS: Read the excerpt and answer the following questions.

EXPLORE THE CONTEXT: Wilhelm I, King of Prussia, took the new title German Emperor after his army defeated France under the strategic leadership of Otto von Bismarck. Bismarck eliminated the threats posed by France and Austria, paving the way for the many kingdoms of Germany to unify. The German empire was a federal monarchy, with kings holding a degree of power over their individual states while the King of Prussia had a permanent constitutional appointment to the supreme position of President of the Confederation.

PRIMARY SOURCE: DOCUMENT

The Emperor Proclaims His New Dignity and Patriotic Resolution

> In consequence of the appeal of the German Princes and of the free towns for us to restore the German empire, after a lapse of sixty years, we announce that we consider it our duty to the Fatherland to accept the imperial dignity. Henceforth we and our successors will bring to the title of Emperor of Germany the hope that God will vouchsafe a blissful future to the Fatherland, and that under our auspices its ancient splendor may be restored. We partake of the dignity conscious of our duty to preserver with German fidelity the rights of the empire and of its members to maintain peace and to support and strengthen the independence of Germany, in the hope that the German people will reap in lasting peace within our boundaries the fruits of their bloody battles and be safe against the renewal of French attacks.
>
> God God grant that we and our successors may protect the empire, not by warlike conquests, but by works of peace, freedom and civilization. 99

—Speech of Kaiser Wilhelm I upon being declared emperor of the Second German Empire, 1866

VOCABULARY

empire: extensive group of states, kingdoms, etc. ruled by one supreme leader

summons: call

imperial: relating to an empire

propitious: favorable

ardent: passionate

Kaiser: German for "caesar," the name given to the emperor

König: German for "king"

1 **DETERMINING MEANING** What does Wilhelm mean when he says, "we and our successors on the throne of Prussia will henceforth bear the imperial title in all our relations and in all the business of the German Empire."

_____

_____

_____

_____

2 **DETERMINING MEANING** What does Wilhelm mean by pledging to carry out the duties of "protecting, with German loyalty, the rights of the Empire and of its members" as well as "protecting the independence of Germany . . . depends in its turn upon the united strength of the people."

_____

_____

_____

3 **UNDERSTANDING CONTEXT** Why might it be difficult for the emperor to balance protecting both the empire's constituent kingdoms as well as the unified empire itself?

_____

_____

_____

_____

4 **ANALYZING EFFECTS** How did nationalism help unify Germany?

_____

_____

_____

5 **PREDICTING** How could nationalism cause problems for the newly established German empire if it were to take root in the kingdoms?

_____

_____

_____

_____

6 **ECONOMICS** What economic outcome does Wilhelm hope will result from the unification of the German kingdoms?

_____

_____

_____

_____

ESSENTIAL QUESTION

How does revolution bring about political and economic change?

A Warning to the New Czar: "Tsaricide is Popular in Russia"

DIRECTIONS Read the excerpt and answer the following questions.

EXPLORE THE CONTEXT: Czar Alexander II had just been assassinated, and this letter from the Executive Committee of the Revolutionary Committee to his heir, Czar Alexander III, advises him on dealing with the revolutionary spirit in Russia. The czar did not follow the Committee's advice, instead maintaining repressive measures against the people.

PRIMARY SOURCE: LETTER

"Your Majesty:

. . . A dispassionate glance at the grievous decade through which we have just passed will enable us to forecast accurately the future progress of the revolutionary movement. . . . [It] will continue to grow and extend; deeds of a terroristic nature will increase in frequency and intensity. . . . and the idea of revolution -- of its possibility and inevitability -- will establish itself in Russia more and more firmly. . . .

. . . . Whatever may be the intentions of the Tsar, the actions of the government have nothing in common with the popular welfare or popular aspirations. . . . [T]he masses of the people are in a state of pauperism and ruin; are subjected to the most humiliating surveillance, even at their own domestic hearths. . . .

These are the reasons why the Russian government exerts no moral influence and has no support among the people. . . . These are the reasons why even such a deed as killing a Tsar excites in the minds of a majority of the people only gladness and sympathy. Yes, your Majesty! Do not be deceived by the reports of flatterers and sycophants; Tsaricide is popular in Russia.

From such a state of affairs there can be only two modes of escape: either a revolution, . . . or a voluntary turning of the supreme power to the people. In the interest of our native land, . . . in the hope of averting the terrible miseries that always accompany revolution, [we approach] your Majesty with the advice to take the second course. Be assured, so soon as the supreme power ceases to rule arbitrarily, so soon as it firmly resolves to accede to the demands of the people's conscience and consciousness, you may, without fear, discharge the spies that disgrace the administration, send your guards back to their barracks, and burn the scaffolds that are demoralizing the people. . . .

And now, your Majesty, decide! Before you are two courses, and you are to make your choice between them. We can only trust that your intelligence and conscience may suggest to you the only decision that is compatible with the welfare of Russia, with your own dignity, and with your duty to your native land."

—Letter of the Revolutionary Committee to Alexander III, 1881

VOCABULARY

tsar: also "czar"; Russian emperor

aspirations: hopes

pauperism: poverty

hearth: fireplace/cooking area

sycophants: those who give excessive yet false support

tsaricide: murder of the Russian emperor

_____. 1881. Letter of the Revolutionary Committee to Alexander II. Reprinted 1909 by Robinson, James Harvey and Beard, Charles A. Readings in Modern European History. Boston: Ginn and Company.

1. **DETERMINING CENTRAL IDEAS** Why did the committee advise the czar that "the Russian government exerts no moral influence and has no support among the people"?

_____

_____

2. **SUMMARIZING** What two potential outcomes did the committee see in Russia's near future?

_____

_____

_____

3. **DETERMINING CENTRAL IDEAS** What action did the committee want new Czar Alexander III to take?

_____

4. **ANALYZING IDEAS** Why does the committee tell the new emperor that "Tsaricide is popular in Russia"?

_____

_____

_____

5. **DETERMINING MEANING** Why does the committee tell Czar Alexander III that if he would allow the people to play a role in their own government, he could then "discharge the spies that disgrace the administration, send your guards back to their barracks, and burn the scaffolds that are demoralizing the people"?

_____

_____

_____

6. **HISTORY** How would you characterize the relationship between the Russian czar and the people of his empire?

_____

_____

_____

_____

Nation Building in Latin America

DIRECTIONS Search for evidence in the lesson to help you answer the following questions.

1A **DESCRIBING** Who were the creoles and the *peninsulares* of Latin America?

_____

_____

_____

_____

_____

1B **DETERMINING CENTRAL IDEAS** What were the political leanings of creoles and *peninsulares*?

_____

_____

_____

_____

_____

2 **RELATING EVENTS** Use the graphic organizer to create a time line showing the dates independence was achieved by at least five different Latin American countries.

LATIN AMERICAN INDEPENDENCE

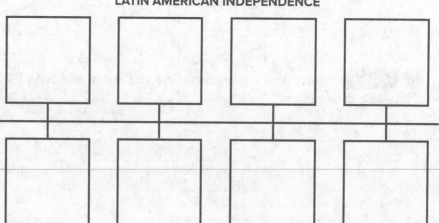

ESSENTIAL QUESTION

How does revolution bring about political and economic change?

As you gather evidence to answer the Essential Question, think about:

- what changed after Latin America's revolutionary rebellions.
- what stayed the same after Latin America's rebellions.
- the leaders of the revolts and their motivations.

My Notes

_____

_____

_____

_____

_____

_____

_____

3 **EVALUATING TEXT EVIDENCE** Who were José de San Martín of Argentina and Simon Bolivár of Venezuela?

_____

_____

_____

4A `HISTORY` How did the major powers of Europe react to the Latin American countries' independence from Spanish and Portugal?

_____

_____

_____

_____

4B How did the United States react to the successful independence movements in Latin America?

_____

_____

_____

5 **INTEGRATING INFORMATION** How did Texas become independent from Mexico and eventually gain statehood in the United States?

_____

_____

_____

6 **UNDERSTANDING CHANGE** What changes followed the revolutions for independence in Latin America?

_____

_____

_____

_____

_____

ESSENTIAL QUESTION

How does revolution bring about political and economic change?

The Execution of Pedro Murillo, Revolutionary

DIRECTIONS Read the excerpt and answer the following questions.

EXPLORE THE CONTEXT: In 1809 the La Paz Revolution declared independence from Spanish authorities and set Bolivia on a course of national independence. Pedro Domingo Murillo led the revolt and became president of the self-appointed military governing body, the *Junta Tuitiva*. Royalist forces captured him in 1810, and he was hanged with other revolutionaries. He is famous for saying these words: "Compatriots, I die, but tyrants won't be able to extinguish the torch I ignited. Long live freedom!" Joaquin Pinto painted the execution of Murillo.

PRIMARY SOURCE: PAINTING

VOCABULARY

compatriots: fellow citizens

1 ANALYZING Why do you think the painter included two representations of its subject, Pedro Murillo?

_____

_____

_____

_____

_____

2 ANALYZING SOURCES How do you think it would change the painting if Pinto had chosen to paint just one image of Murillo, either standing tall or being executed?

_____

_____

_____

_____

_____

3 INTERPRETING What do the famous words of Murillo add to the painting: "Compatriots, I die, but tyrants won't be able to extinguish the torch I ignited. Long live freedom!"?

_____

_____

_____

_____

_____

4 DESCRIBING The painter chose to depict the fallen hero holding the ignited torch referenced in the quotation. What are the characteristics of a torch, and what is Murillo saying about this quest by comparing it with a torch that burns on and on?

_____

_____

_____

5 EVALUATING Does the painting succeed in conveying the feeling of rebellion?

_____

_____

_____

6 HISTORY Does the painter support the revolution? Why or why not, and how can you tell?

_____

_____

ESSENTIAL QUESTION

How does revolution bring about political and economic change?

Father Miguel Hidalgo Proclaims an End To Slavery in Mexico

DIRECTIONS Read the excerpt and answer the following questions.

EXPLORE THE CONTEXT: Father Miguel Hidalgo is considered the father of the Mexican Revolution. He led an attack against the Spanish, but his forces were not equipped to overcome them. Hidalgo was sentenced to death for his role in the battle. Elite creoles and *peninsulares* joined Hidalgo's forces, and later managed to overthrow the Spanish rule and appoint their own monarch to govern Mexico.

PRIMARY SOURCE: PROCLAMATION

❝ [A] warning to all slaveholders: that immediately upon receiving this official notice, they must liberate [their slaves], giving to each one necessary documents with proper inserts, so that they may appear in court, give testimony, enter contracts and deal in all matters executing business that any other free person would conduct, and that those known to be slaveholders that do not thus release their slaves will suffer, without excuse, the death penalty and the confiscation of their properties.

This order equally is now imposed upon all, so hereafter no one shall purchase nor sell any slave, nor must the scribes, whether on paper or in person, extend current deeds related to this kind of contract, under penalty of suspension of office and of the confiscation of their goods if they do not carry forth [this edict] with humanity and mercy. It is also the desire of His Excellency that all payment of taxes placed upon the various castes be abolished forever, whatever has been the charge, so that no judge or tax collector may charge this tax, nor must the poor who were charged them pay them. And I hereby warn all administrators of the customs houses, tax collectors and toll booth attendants, that the native people will not be charged for their right to scrape the *maguey* plants nor for the fruit of the *pulque*, for they are poor people for whom what they earn is barely enough for the maintenance and subsistence of their families. Nor should they be taxed for their sugar cane brandy more than one peso for each barrel that leaves their factories for the capital, and this for a single time, so that having to pass the barrels from one area to others, they will not be demanded anything else. Thus with only the first peso charged to them, the account will be satisfied. . . . And so that this notice reaches all, and that no one alleges that he is ignorant, I order this edict to be published in Vallodolid on the 19th of Oct, of 1810. . . . ❞

Source— Miguel Hidalgo, from "Edict Against Slavery," 1810

VOCABULARY

scribe: one who keeps the official records of civil matters and government business

caste: social groups divided according to the relative privilege of their members

customs house: place where people paid tax on certain types of items they are transporting

maguey: the agave plant, native in Mexico

pulque: an alcoholic beverage made by fermenting maguey

peso: unit of money in Mexico

1 **ANALYZING TEXT** What action does the edict demand from slaveholders in Mexico?

_____

_____

2 CIVICS **APPLYING VALUES AND DEMOCRATIC PRINCIPLES** What penalty will slaveholders face if they fail to comply with the edict?

_____

_____

3 **SUMMARIZING** Make a list of the types of taxes that the edict reduced or eliminated.

_____

_____

_____

4 **INTERPRETING** Why might "his Excellency" have chosen to proclaim the end of slavery in the same edict used to proclaim the end of or reduction of certain taxes?

_____

_____

_____

5 **COMPARING AND CONTRASTING** This edict was proclaimed a few weeks after Hidalgo's failed attempt at leading a revolt against the Spanish. Can you see the edict drawing on any revolutionary political ideas that were also seen in the European revolutions?

_____

_____

_____

_____

6 **INTERPRETING** What does this edict tell us about the lives of enslaved and free people in Mexico?

_____

_____

_____

_____

Romanticism and Realism

DIRECTIONS Search for evidence in the lesson to help you answer the following questions.

1 **UNDERSTANDING CONTEXT** What did the adherents of romanticism object to about the Enlightenment?

_____

_____

_____

_____

2 **SUMMARIZING** What was the attitude of the romantics toward the Industrial Revolution?

_____

_____

_____

3 **DETERMINING CENTRAL IDEAS** Use the graphic organizer to list central themes found in romantic art, music, and literature

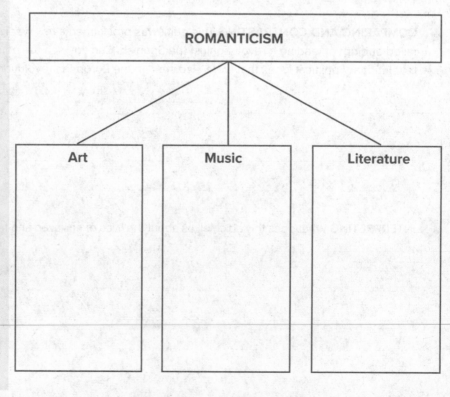

ESSENTIAL QUESTION

How does revolution bring about political and economic change?

As you gather evidence to answer the Essential Question, think about:

- romanticism and realism as two different ways of looking at the world.

- the different views of the role of the artist in romanticism and realism

- the heightened interest in scientific research as a result of the Industrial Revolution.

My Notes

_____

_____

_____

_____

_____

_____

_____

4 **IDENTIFYING CONNECTIONS** Darwin's claim that humans evolved from an earlier animal form was very controversial in his time. How did this theory in turn affect other ideas that people had about human origins?

_____

_____

_____

_____

5 **DETERMINING CONTEXT** Explain how the Scientific Revolution relates to the increasing secularization of the nineteenth century.

_____

_____

_____

_____

_____

_____

6 **HISTORY** Where romanticism placed emphasis on art as an expression of the artist's unique vision, realism led artists to see their art as a depiction of observable truths, almost scientific in its accuracy. How did artists of both approaches convey their concern at the negative effects of the Industrial Revolution?

_____

_____

_____

_____

_____

_____

A Romantic View of Nature

ESSENTIAL QUESTION

How does revolution bring about political and economic change?

VOCABULARY

germ: starting point

hamlet: village

league: approximately three miles

abode: home

massed: put together

o'er: over

tract: parcel of land

unremitting: never-ending

plough: farm tool used to ready soil for plantir

hence: therefore

keel: lower part of a ship, used to refer to the whole ship

sound: body of water connected to a larger bc of water

to and fro: back and forth

indignant: angry

bane: curse

DIRECTIONS: Read the excerpt and answer the following questions.

EXPLORE THE CONTEXT: William Wordsworth (1770–1850) was a romantic English poet. He valued nature and the artist's imagination as the source of inspiration. Wordsworth lived in a remote region and famously spent long hours trekking across the countryside with his sister, Dorothy. His poem, "The Excursion," from the period of British romanticism provides a critical response to the impact of the Industrial Revolution on countryside he so enjoyed.

PRIMARY SOURCE: POEM

66 Meanwhile, at social Industry's command,
How quick, how vast an increase! From the germ
Of some poor Hamlet, rapidly produced
Here a huge Town, continuous and compact,
Hiding the face of earth for leagues -- and there,
Where not a Habitation stood before,
The Abodes of men irregularly massed
Like trees in forests -- spread through spacious tracts,
O'er which the smoke of unremitting fires
Hangs permanent, and plentiful as wreaths
Of vapour glittering in the morning sun.
And, wheresoe'er the Traveller turns his steps,
He sees the barren wilderness erased,
Or disappearing; triumph that proclaims
How much the mild Directress of the plough
Owes to alliance with these new-born Arts!
-- Hence is the wide Sea peopled, -- hence the Shores
Of Britain are resorted to by Ships
Freighted from every climate of the world
With the world's choicest produce. Hence that sum
Of Keels that rest within her crowded ports,
Or ride at anchor in her sounds and bays;
That animating spectacle of Sails
Which through her inland regions, to and fro
Pass with the respirations of the tide,
Perpetual, multitudinous! . . .
. . . I grieve, when on the darker side
Of this great change I look; and there behold. . .
Such outrage done to Nature as compels
The indignant Power to justify herself;
Yea, to avenge her violated rights.
For England's bane. . . . 99

—William Wordsworth, "The Excursion," 1814

1A DESCRIBING How does Wordsworth describe the village?

_____

_____

_____

_____

1B INTERPRETING TEXT Based on Wordsworth's description, how do you think he feels about the villages growing up around factories?

_____

_____

_____

_____

2 COMPARING What comparison is the poet making when he states: "the smoke of unremitting fires / Hangs permanent, and plentiful as wreaths / Of vapour glittering in the morning sun"?

_____

_____

3 ANALYZING TEXT How does the poet seem to feel about the ships he sees? Circle any words or phrases in the poem that help you draw your conclusion.

_____

_____

4 EVALUATING How does the poet seem to feel about the changes he discusses?

_____

_____

_____

5 HISTORY Review the attributes of romanticism and explain how Wordsworth's poem typifies that artistic movement.

_____

_____

_____

_____

Charles Dickens's *Oliver Twist*

DIRECTIONS: Read the excerpt and answer the following questions.

EXPLORE THE CONTEXT: Charles Dickens (1812–1870) was an English novelist and social critic. Dickens published much of his work in serial form, printed in installments by magazines over a period of time. Literacy became more common during Dickens's career, and the new class of readers waited anxiously for the next installment of their favorite stories. His writing style exemplifies realism in literature. The stories are meant to reflect life as it was actually lived, rather than any idealized or romanticized representation of life. Dickens's descriptions of poverty are particularly vivid. Dickens used the engagement and interest of readers in the characters to turn attention toward significant social problems of his time.

PRIMARY SOURCE: BOOK

> "The houses on either side were high and large, but very old; and tenanted by people of the poorest class, as their neglected appearances would have sufficiently denoted without the concurrent testimony afforded by the squalid look of the few men and women who, with folded arms and bodies half doubled, occasionally skulked along. A great many of the tenements had shop-fronts; but they were fast closed, and mouldering away: only the upper rooms being inhabited. Others which had become insecure from age and decay, were prevented from falling into the street by huge beams of wood which were reared against the walls, and firmly planted in the road; but even these crazy dens seemed to have been selected as the nightly haunts of some houseless wretches, for many of the rough boards which supplied the place of door and window, were wrenched from their positions to afford an aperture wide enough for the passage of a human body. The kennel was stagnant and filthy; the very rats that here and there lay putrefying in its rottenness, were hideous with famine. "
>
> —Charles Dickens, *Oliver Twist*, 1837

VOCABULARY

denoted: indicated

squalid: shabby, filthy

skulked: walked as if trying to remain hidden

tenement: slum

mouldering: decaying

tottering: swaying

aperture: opening

putrefying: decomposing

kennel: shelter

1 ANALYZING TEXT How do Dickens's word choices illustrate the subject matter?

_____

_____

_____

2 INTERPRETING Paraphrase Dickens's comment that "even these crazy dens seemed to have been selected as the nightly haunts of some houseless wretches."

_____

_____

3 UNDERSTANDING CONTEXT Why do you think Dickens included the rats in his description of the buildings?

_____

_____

_____

_____

_____

_____

4 EVALUATING EVIDENCE What are the attributes of realism? How does this passage illustrate some of those elements?

_____

_____

_____

_____

5 GEOGRAPHY What is your impression of the neighborhood given the descriptions of closed shops and buildings propped up with beams?

_____

_____

_____

_____

6 IDENTIFYING PERSPECTIVES Imagine someone is telling you about this area using the description in this excerpt. Do you think the person is a local resident or an outsider?

_____

ESSENTIAL QUESTION

How does revolution bring about political and economic change?

My Notes

_____

_____

_____

_____

_____

_____

_____

_____

_____

_____

_____

_____

_____

_____

_____

1 **Think About It**

Write the supporting questions you developed at the beginning of the chapter. Review the evidence you gathered in the chapter. Were you able to answer each Supporting Question? If there was not enough evidence to answer your Supporting Questions, what additional evidence do you think you need to consider?

_____

_____

_____

2 **Organize Your Evidence**

Complete the chart below on revolutionary activity from the chapter.

REVOLUTIONS OF EUROPE

Year	Country	Describe the Revolutionary Activity
1804	England	Richard Trevithick's new steam locomotive hauls cargo and passengers
	France	
1833		
		The new constitutional monarch Louis-Philippe of France is overthrown. The Second French Republic is launched, with a legislature and a monarch elected by popular vote of all French men. They elected Charles Louis Napoleon Bonaparte.
1850		
	Russia	
		Charles Darwin publishes *On the Origin of Species by Means of Natural Selection*, causing controversy among those who felt his theory was contrary to their religious beliefs.
	France	

③ Talk About It

Work in a small group. With your group, discuss which later events can be seen as effects or reactions to earlier events. Did others see the same causal relations? Did anyone identify a relationship that you had not noticed before? Did you find yourself objecting to anyone's claim of a causal relation between events?

④ Write About It

Following your discussion in the Talk About It activity, write about two shifts you have identified as resulting from revolutionary changes of some type. Explain each initial revolutionary event and how it led to more changes.

_____

_____

_____

_____

_____

⑤ Connect to the Essential Question

Make a poster showing a time line of major events and changes that took place in a particular country, empire, or region during the nineteenth century. Use different colored writing or boxes around the writing to indicate the kind of change—political, technological, social, economic, or other type of change discussed in the chapter. Be sure to include a key on the poster that explains what each color means. When one change seems to lead to or result in another change, offer an explanation for the connection.

CITIZENSHIP
TAKING ACTION

MAKE CONNECTIONS   We continue to experience a stream of medical, scientific, and technological advances that affect our social, political, and economic lives. At the same time, there are still calls for self-rule around the globe, and governments continue to rely on military force to achieve political ends. Research a modern example of either a revolutionary new development or a region undergoing a revolutionary struggle for political authority and create a presentation to introduce your classmates to the region or issue undergoing change and the resulting struggles and conflicts. Are there resolutions on the horizon? Your presentation should include visual aids to help your audience grasp the issues.

Mass Society and Democracy

ESSENTIAL QUESTION

How are political and social structures influenced by economic changes?

A second Industrial Revolution happened during the late nineteenth and early twentieth centuries and shaped most of modern society. What innovations were created during this time? How did these advancements affect the political and social structures in Europe and in the North America?

TALK ABOUT IT

With a partner, discuss the sort of information you would need to discover how technological innovations played a role in the political, social, and economic changes during the late nineteenth and early twentieth centuries. For example, you might ask, "What contributed to the demand for higher standards of living?"

DIRECTIONS: Now write down three additional questions that will help you explain how these innovations influenced the political and social structures during this time.

MY RESEARCH QUESTIONS

Supporting Question 1:

_____

_____

Supporting Question 2:

_____

_____

Supporting Question 3:

_____

_____

ESSENTIAL QUESTION

How are political and social structures influenced by economic changes?

As you gather evidence to answer the Essential Question, think about:

- how innovations in technology and science can impact economies.
- how innovations in modes of production impacted the lives of factory workers.
- political and social theories that developed in response to innovations in industrialization.

My Notes

_____

_____

_____

_____

_____

_____

The Growth of Industrial Prosperity

DIRECTIONS Search for evidence in the lesson to help you answer the following questions.

1A **IDENTIFYING EFFECTS** How did the Bessemer process, the internal combustion engine, and electricity revolutionize modes of transportation and industry in Europe?

_____

_____

_____

_____

_____

_____

_____

1B **RELATING EVENTS** How did these changes impact the economy? How did they affect the allocation of wealth throughout Europe?

_____

_____

_____

_____

2 **IDENTIFYING CONNECTIONS** How did industrialization contribute to the formation of socialist political parties and trade unions?

_____

_____

_____

_____

3 **EXPLAINING CAUSE AND EFFECTS** In the graphic organizer below, describe how different innovations in factory efficiency impacted production. Then describe how those changes impacted the lives of factory workers.

CAUSE in TECHNOLOGY	EFFECT in WORKING CONDITIONS
Electricity:	Longer hours of production:
Assembly Line:	Repetition:
Mass Production:	Dangerous Conditions for Workers:

4A CIVICS How might industrialization and mass production in Europe at this time have led to social theories, such as Marxism?

_____

_____

_____

4B **INTERPRETING CHARTS** Use the Venn diagram below to compare and contrast similarities and differences between pure Marxists and revisionists.

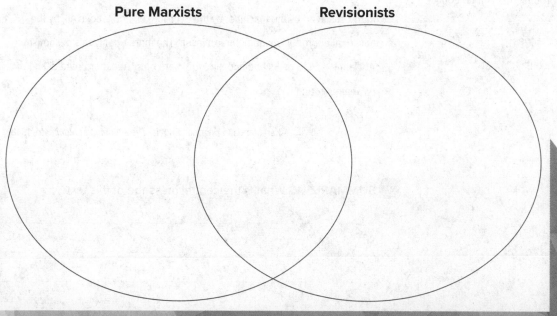

Pure Marxists   Revisionists

How are political and social structures influenced by economic changes?

The Communist Manifesto

DIRECTIONS: Use the text to answer the questions.

EXPLORE THE CONTEXT: *The Communist Manifesto* is an 1848 political pamphlet by German philosophers Karl Marx and Friedrich Engels. Both philosophers were appalled at the horrible conditions in the industrial factories and blamed industrial capitalism for the conditions. The manifesto briefly summarizes their views on history, society, and economy, and outlines the manner in which they believed socialism would come to supplant capitalism.

PRIMARY SOURCE: MANIFESTO

❝In proportion as the bourgeoisie, i.e., capital, is developed, in the same proportion is the proletariat, the modern working class, developed, a class of labourers, who live only so long as they find work, and who find work only so long as their labour increases capital. These labourers, who must sell themselves piecemeal, are a commodity, like every other article of commerce, and are consequently exposed to all the vicissitudes of competition, to all the fluctuations of the market. . . . Modern industry has converted the little workshop of the patriarchal master into the great factory of the industrial capitalist. Masses of labourers, crowded into the factory, are organised like soldiers. As privates of the industrial army they are placed under the command of a perfect hierarchy of officers and sergeants. Not only are they slaves of the bourgeois class, and of the bourgeois State, they are daily and hourly enslaved by the machine, by the over-looker, and, above all, by the individual bourgeois manufacturer himself. The more openly this despotism proclaims gain to be its end and aim, the more petty, the more hateful and the more embittering it is.❞

—Karl Marx and Friedrich Engels, *The Communist Manifesto*, 1848

VOCABULARY

piecemeal: piece by piece

commodity: product that can be bought and sold

vicissitudes: changes

despotism: absolute control

1 **SUMMARIZING** What is the central message of this text?

_____

_____

2 ECONOMICS According to the text, how might "consumer culture" have changed conditions for the working class?

_____

_____

_____

_____

3 **ANALYZING** The text argues that the working conditions of the proletariat are a form of slavery. What evidence does the text provide for this conclusion?

_____

_____

_____

_____

4 **INFERRING** What insight into class struggle and tension does this text provide?

_____

_____

_____

_____

5 **PREDICTING** How might the ideas of Marxist theory have posed a threat to social and political structures during this time?

_____

_____

_____

_____

6 **RELATING EVENTS** In what way do you think Marxism influenced the formation of trade unions?

_____

_____

_____

_____

ESSENTIAL QUESTION

How are political and social structures influenced by economic changes?

VOCABULARY

bobbins: a spool

digress: break from main topic

hitherto: until now

Factory Labor in New England

DIRECTIONS: Use the text to answer the questions.

EXPLORE THE CONTEXT: During the Second Industrial Revolution, the mill girls were workers who came to work in industrial corporations in Lowell, Massachusetts. As a child, author Harriet Robinson (1825–1911) worked as a "bobbin doffer," removing the cylinder that held thread, in a Massachusetts cotton mill. She was involved in a worker's strike and later became a writer and poet. She was also active in the early women's suffrage movement, but died before women secured the vote in the United States.

PRIMARY SOURCE: ARTICLE

❝The early mill-girls were of different ages. Some (like the writer) were not over ten years old; a few were in middle life, but the majority were between the ages of sixteen and twenty-five. The very young girls were called "doffers." They "doffed," or took off, the full bobbins from the spinning-frames, and replaced them with empty ones. These mites worked about fifteen minutes every hour and the rest of the time was their own. When the overseer was kind they were allowed to read, knit or go outside the mill-yard to play. They were paid two dollars a week. The working hours of all the girls extended from five o'clock in the morning until seven in the evening, with one half-hour each, for breakfast and dinner. Even the doffers were forced to be on duty nearly fourteen hours a day. This was the greatest hardship in the lives of these children. Several years later a ten-hour law was passed, but not until long after some of these little doffers were old enough to appear before the legislative committee on the subject, and plead, by their presence, for a reductions of the hours of labor. Those of the mill-girls who had homes generally worked from eight to ten months in the year; the rest of the time was spent with parents or friends. A few taught school during the summer months. Their life in the factory was made pleasant to them. In those days there was no need of advocating the doctrine of the proper relation between employer and employed. Help was too valuable to be ill-treated. . . The most prevailing incentive to labor was to secure the means of education for some male member in the family. To make a gentleman of a brother or a son, to give him a college education, was the dominant thought in the minds of a great many of the better class of mill-girls. I have known more than one to give every cent of her wages, month after month, to her brother, that he might get the education necessary to enter some profession. I have known a mother to work years in this way for her boy. I have known women to educate young men by their earnings, who were not sons or relatives. There were many men now living who were helped to an education by the wages of the early mill-girls. It is well to digress here a little, and speak of the influence the possession of money had on the characters of some of these women. We can hardly realize what a change the cotton factory made in the status of the working women. Hitherto woman had always been a money saving rather than a money earning, member of the community. Her labor could command but small return. If she worked out as servant, or "help," her wages were from 50 cents to $1.00 a week; or, if she went from house to house by the day to spin and weave, or do tailoress work, she could get but 75 cents a week and her meals. As teacher, her services were not in demand, and the arts, the professions, and even the trades and industries, were nearly all closed to her. **"**

Source— Harriet H. Robinson, "Early Factory Labor in New England," 1888

1 **DESCRIBING** What kind of document is this? What is it about? In which period was it written?

_____

2 **DETERMINING CONTEXT** How might this account have affected public understanding of the conditions of workers during this time?

_____

_____

3 **CONTRASTING** How might the formation of trade unions have had an impact on the labor conditions faced by the mill girls? How do the lives of women today differ from the mill girls?

_____

_____

_____

_____

_____

4 HISTORY How did Harriet Jane Hanson Robinson's account of the mill girls differ from Marx's _The Communist Manifesto_? How were they similar?

_____

_____

_____

_____

_____

The Emergence of Mass Society

DIRECTIONS Search for evidence in the lesson to help you answer the following questions.

ESSENTIAL QUESTION

How are political and social structures influenced by economic changes?

1A **IDENTIFYING CAUSES** What caused the housing and public sanitation issues in cities?

_____

_____

_____

_____

_____

As you gather evidence to answer the Essential Question, think about:

- how cities adjusted to urban growth.
- how urban growth affected social structures.
- the challenges of rapid social change.

1B **ANALYZING CHANGE** Use the chart below to describe how the government addressed these issues.

Solution	How It Helped
Boards of Health	
Sewer System	
Heaters	

My Notes

_____

_____

_____

_____

_____

_____

2 CIVICS Use the chart below to describe the social structure that developed during the nineteenth century.

Class	Characteristics
New Elite	
Diverse Middle Class	
Working Class	

3 EVALUATING What were some of the benefits of the Second Industrial Revolution?

_____

_____

_____

4A IDENTIFYING PERSPECTIVES Did the rural working class see the benefits of the innovations? Explain your answer.

_____

_____

_____

4B INFERRING How did Samuel Smiles address inequality and poverty in his book, *Self-Help*?

_____

_____

_____

_____

An American Magnate on Wealth

Copyright © McGraw-Hill Education   Carnegie, Andrew. 1889. "Wealth". Reprinted in The North American Review Volume 0148 Issue 391 (June 1889). Ithaca, New York: Cornell University Library.

ESSENTIAL QUESTION

How are political and social structures influenced by economic changes?

VOCABULARY

magnate: a wealthy and influential person, especially in business

Inestimable: valuable

benefactions: contributions

unostentatious: humble

brethren: brothers

DIRECTIONS: Use the text to answer the questions.

EXPLORE THE CONTEXT: Andrew Carnegie was an American steel magnate noted for his wealth and dedication to philanthropy. He regularly wrote about political and social issues. In 1889 he penned the article "Wealth" for the *North American Review* to outline what he believed was the social responsibility of the extremely wealthy. It inspired others to follow in philanthropy.

PRIMARY SOURCE: ARTICLE

❝Poor and restricted are our opportunities in this life; narrow our horizon; our best work most imperfect; but rich men should be thankful for one inestimable boon. They have it in their power during their lives to busy themselves in organizing benefactions from which the masses of their fellows will derive lasting advantage, and thus dignify their own lives. The highest life is probably to be reached, not by such imitation of the life of Christ as Count Tolstoi gives us, but, while animated by Christ's spirit, by recognizing the changed conditions of this age, and adopting modes of expressing this spirit suitable to the changed conditions under which we live; still laboring for the good of our fellows, which was the essence of his life and teaching, but laboring in a different manner.

This, then, is held to be the duty of the man of Wealth: First, to set an example of modest, unostentatious living, shunning display or extravagance; to provide moderately for the legitimate wants of those dependent upon him; and after doing so to consider all surplus revenues which come to him simply as trust funds, which he is called upon to administer, and strictly bound as a matter of duty to administer in the manner which, in his judgment, is best calculated to produce the most beneficial results for the community—the man of wealth thus becoming the mere agent and trustee for his poorer brethren, bringing to their service his superior wisdom, experience and ability to administer, doing for them better than they would or could do for themselves. ❞

—Andrew Carnegie "Wealth," *The North American Review*, 1889

1 **SUMMARIZING** What does Carnegie write is the duty of the extremely wealthy?

_____

_____

_____

2 **IDENTIFYING CONNECTIONS** Why might this editorial have been important at the time that it was published?

_____

_____

_____

3 ECONOMICS What was Carnegie's economic status when he wrote this editorial? Why would knowing this be important for this passage?

_____

_____

_____

4 **ASSESSING** What does Carnegie mean when he writes, "The highest life is probably to be reached, not by such imitation of the life of Christ as Count Tolstoi gives us, but, while animated by Christ's spirit. . . "

_____

_____

_____

5 **UNDERSTANDING CONTEXT** Based on what you have read in the textbook, what kind of impact might this editorial have if the rich followed Samuel Smiles's advice?

_____

_____

6 **PREDICTING** Based on what you have read, how might rich men have reacted to this editorial?

_____

_____

_____

ESSENTIAL QUESTION
How are political and social structures influenced by economic changes?

On Emigrating From Poland to the United States

DIRECTIONS: Use the source to answer the questions.

EXPLORE THE CONTEXT: Immigration to the United States increased during the industrial era. Many came from central, eastern, and southern Europe, China, and Japan. The excerpt below is from the *Ellis Island Collection of Oral Histories,* a collection of 2,000 interviews from immigrants who came through Ellis Island, a location used to process many immigrants entering New York Harbor. In it, Morris Abraham Schneider recounts his 1920 journey at age 10 on a steamship from Poland.

PRIMARY SOURCE: ORAL HISTORY

VOCABULARY

steerage: part of the ship for those with the cheapest tickets

cavernous: huge, spacious

vermin: an unpleasant or harmful animal that is usually hard to control, such as mice, flies, lice and bedbugs

❝When we got on the Rotterdam, we had a field day. One, I was never on ship before and it was absolutely, I was awed by it. It was overwhelming. All the people and boarding the ship, it was all a brand new experience. We left Rotterdam, we set sail and about a half hour after the ship started my sister got very sea sick. It took us fourteen days to cross the Atlantic and in the entire crossing, she was in steerage, and the only time she came up for a breath of fresh air was just about a half hour before we saw the Statue of Liberty. Now the experience of the ship, being young was an adventure in that particular situation, because we were on the lowest level of the ship. We couldn't go aboard. Some kids were more adventurous. My brother and I, we would sneak aboard, we were always chased. And we saw some people who traveled maybe in first or second class and we looked upon them as royalty, but we were confined primarily to steerage.

Steerage was one huge place. It was the lowest deck. The stench, it was the summer, in August, the humidity, the heat, having no air conditioning, having cooling facilities, it was very hot, compounded by the fact that there must have been anywhere from two to three hundred people in that huge cavernous area. The body smells, the body odors, the lack of sanitation, the lack of any kind of facilities, washing, there was no such thing as washing or bathing. The stench, the vermin, it was rat infested. But, being children, I guess, had its advantages, in this case because we always tried to get out of there. We tried to go, get out of the steerage, get out of the babble of voices, get out of the heat and the stench and get on the main deck. We all were permitted to stay there for a little while but we were constantly chased. But the crossing went for us, for me in particular, went very quickly. ❞

Source—US National Parks Service, "Ellis Island Collection of Oral Histories: Morris Abraham Schneider," November 17, 1991

Sigrist, Jr., Paul. 1991. Interview of Morris Abraham Schneider. Interview date November 17, 1991. Ellis Island Collection: EI-116.

1 **SUMMARIZING** How would you describe Morris Abraham Schneider's trip to the United States? Where did he come from? Who did he travel with? How long did it take?

_____

_____

2 **CITING TEXT EVIDENCE** How does Schneider describe steerage?

_____

_____

_____

_____

3 **UNDERSTANDING CONTEXT** From what you read in the textbook, why would someone like Schneider travel under these conditions to the United States?

_____

_____

_____

_____

4 **DETERMINING MEANING** What does Schneider mean when he writes, "My brother and I, we would sneak aboard, we were always chased."

_____

_____

_____

5 **ASSESSING** How does Schneider refer to his youth throughout the passage?

_____

_____

6 HISTORY What does the text say about the class tension on the steamship?

_____

_____

ESSENTIAL QUESTION

How are political and social structures influenced by economic changes?

As you gather evidence to answer the Essential Question, think about:

- how the rise of political democracy had an impact on European politics.

- how might the rise of political democracy have threatened existing empires in Western Europe.

- how the working class influenced political change.

My Notes

The National State and Democracy

DIRECTIONS Search for evidence in the lesson to help you answer the following questions.

1 **ANALYZING CHANGE** Explain how political developments in Western Europe differed from the politics of Central and Eastern Europe?

_____

_____

_____

_____

_____

_____

_____

2 **CIVICS** What factors might have influenced political differences between Western Europe and Central and Eastern Europe?

_____

_____

_____

_____

_____

_____

3 **ANALYZING CHANGE** How did the shift from an agricultural economy to an industrial economy in the United States affect the lives of Americans?

_____

_____

_____

4 **EXPLAINING CAUSE & EFFECT** Use the chart to explain how socialist uprisings created change during the rule of Czar Nicholas II.

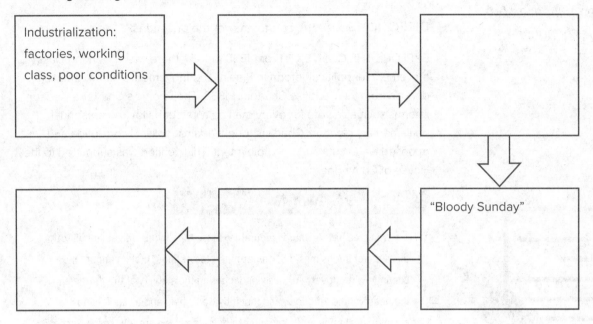

Industrialization: factories, working class, poor conditions →

→ ↓

"Bloody Sunday"

← ←

5 **EVALUATING** Consider the protests for democratic social reform in Russia. Now consider protests for social reform today. Use the graphic organizer to illustrate how protests have the power to create social change.

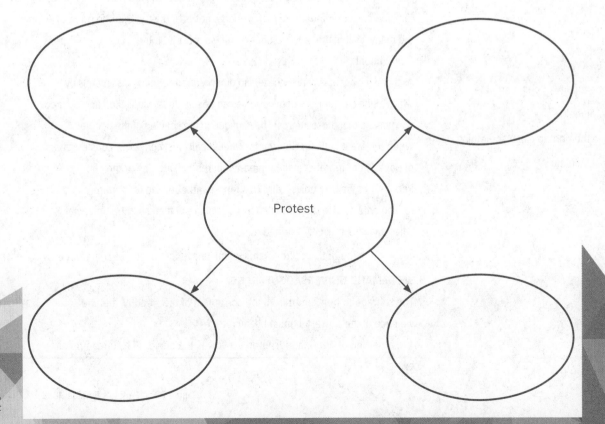

Protest

ESSENTIAL QUESTION

How are political and social structures influenced by economic changes?

VOCABULARY

humility: the quality of being humble

vindicated: upheld

entitle: give the right to claim something

implicitly: absolutely

The Chartists

DIRECTIONS: Use the text to answer the questions.

EXPLORE THE CONTEXT: From 1838 to 1857, there was a working-class movement for political reform in Britain. The movement's name, Chartism, derived from the People's Charter of 1838. The People's Charter asked for reforms such as a vote for every man on a secret ballot and an annual parliamentary election. Chartists fought against political corruption and opposed wage cuts and unemployment. This petition was submitted to the House of Commons.

PRIMARY SOURCE: CHARTER

66 We come before your Honourable House to tell you, with all humility, that this state of things must not be permitted to continue; that it cannot long continue without very seriously endangering the stability of the throne and the peace of the kingdom; and that if by God's help and all lawful and constitutional appliances, an end can be put to it, we are fully resolved that it shall speedily come to an end.

We tell your Honourable House that the capital of the master must no longer be deprived of its due reward; that the laws which make food dear, and those which by making money scarce, make labour cheap, must be abolished; that taxation must be made to fall on property, not on industry; that the good of the many, as it is the only legitimate end, so must it be the sole study of the Government.

As a preliminary essential to these and other requisite changes; as means by which alone the interests of the people can be effectually vindicated and secured, we demand that those interests be confided to the keeping of the people.

When the State calls for defenders, when it calls for money, no consideration of poverty or ignorance can be pleaded in refusal or delay of the call.

Required as we are, universally, to support and obey the laws, nature and reason entitle us to demand, that in the making of the laws, the universal voice shall be implicitly listened to.

We perform the duties of freemen; we must have the privileges of freemen.

WE DEMAND UNIVERSAL SUFFRAGE.

The suffrage to be exempt from the corruption of the wealthy, and the violence of the powerful, must be secret.

The assertion of our right necessarily involves the power of its uncontrolled exercise. 99

Source— The People's Petition, 1838

1 **ANALYZING PERSPECTIVE** What type of document is this? To whom is this document directed?

_____

_____

2 **ANALYZING INFORMATION** What type of social reform does this document address?

_____

_____

_____

3 **DESCRIBING** Based on the document, how might one describe the political conditions of the working class during this time?

_____

_____

_____

4 **INTERPRETING** What is meant by "the good of the many, as it is the only legitimate end, so must it be the sole study of the Government"?

_____

_____

_____

5 CIVICS According to this document, explain how the wealthy had a major influence on politics in Britain?

_____

_____

_____

_____

6 **IDENTIFYING CONNECTIONS** Apart from working class laborers, who else would have benefitted from universal suffrage?

_____

_____

The Bagdad Railway

ESSENTIAL QUESTION

How are political and social structures influenced by economic changes?

DIRECTIONS: Use the text to answer the questions.

EXPLORE THE CONTEXT: The Berlin-Baghdad Railway, also known as the "Bagdad Railway", was built from 1903 to 1940 as a way to connect Berlin with Baghdad, then part of the Ottoman Empire. The Germans wanted to establish a port in the Persian Gulf, but the 1,000-mile rail line was never in operation. Had it ever been in operation, Germans would have had access to oil fields in Mesopotamia and a connection to the port of Basra on the Persian Gulf.

PRIMARY SOURCE: BOOK

66 That a commercial revolution of the nineteenth century should revive the old avenues of trade with the East was a matter of the utmost importance to all mankind. To the Western World the expansion of European commerce and the extension of Occidental civilization were incalculable, but certain, benefits. Statesmen and soldiers, merchants and missionaries alike might hail the new rail- ways and steamship lines as entitled to a place among the foremost achievements of the age of steel and steam. To the East, also, closer contacts with the West held out high hopes for an economic and cultural renaissance of the former great civilizations of the Orient. Alas, however, the reopening of the medieval trade-routes served to create new arenas of imperial friction, to heighten existing international rivalries, and to widen the gulf of suspicion and hate already hindering cordial relationships between the peoples of Europe and the peoples of Asia. Economic rivalries, military alliances, national pride, strategic maneuvers, religious fanaticism, racial prejudices, secret diplomacy, predatory imperialism these and other formidable obstacles blocked the road to peaceful progress and promoted wars and rumors of wars. The purchase of the Suez Canal by Disraeli was but the first step in the acquisition of Egypt, an imperial experiment which cost Great Britain thousands of lives, which more than once brought the empire to the verge of war with France, and which colored the whole character of British diplomacy in the Middle East for forty years. No sooner was the Trans-Siberian Railway completed than it involved Russia in a war with Japan. So it was destined to be with the Bagdad Railway. Itself a project of great promise for the economic and political regeneration of the Near East, it became the source of bitter international rivalries which contributed to the outbreak of the Great War. It is one of the tragedies of the nineteenth and twentieth centuries that the Trans-Siberian Railway, the Suez Canal, and the Bagdad Railway potent instruments of civilization for the promotion of peaceful progress and material prosperity could not have been constructed without occasioning imperial friction, political intrigues, military alliances, and armed conflict. 99

Source— Edward Mead Earle, *Turkey, the Great Powers, and the Bagdad Railway: A Study in Imperialism*, 1924

VOCABULARY

incalculable: too great to be calculated

fanaticism: excessive notions on a subject

Disraeli: Benjamin Disraeli, former British prime minister

acquisition: gaining; procuring

regeneration: rebirth; transformation

potent: powerful; strong

Earle, Edward Mead. 1924. Turkey, the Great Powers, and the Bagdad Railway - A Study in Imperialism. New York: J. J. Little & Ives Company.

1 **ANALYZING** The construction of the Berlin-Baghdad Railway was intended to reopen old trade routes, create economic regeneration in the Near East, and ease political tensions. Based on source, was this a success?

_____

_____

_____

2 **EVALUATING EVIDENCE** What are some reasons the railway was not successful?

_____

_____

3 **INTERPRETING** How would you interpret the hope that the railway would restore "economic and cultural renaissance of the former great civilizations" in relation to the Ottoman Empire?

_____

_____

4 **INFERRING** Why was the Ottoman Empire in a state of decline during this time?

_____

_____

_____

5 ECONOMICS How might the construction of the railway have made an impact on the destiny of the Ottoman Empire?

_____

_____

_____

6 **COMPARING AND CONTRASTING** The Ottoman Empire began to fall apart in the late 1800s. Meanwhile, how were Western Europe and North America faring during this time?

_____

_____

_____

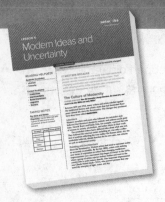

Modern Ideas and Uncertainty

DIRECTIONS Search for evidence in the lesson to help you answer the following questions.

1 **ANALYZING CHANGE** How did art, music, and literature change during the Second Industrial Revolution?

_____

_____

_____

_____

_____

_____

_____

_____

_____

_____

2 **IDENTIFYING CAUSES** How do you think architecture was influenced by the Second Industrial Revolution?

_____

_____

_____

_____

_____

_____

3 **IDENTIFYING CONNECTIONS** What are the connections between Social Darwinism and the growth of nationalism in many countries?

_____

_____

_____

_____

_____

_____

ESSENTIAL QUESTION

How are political and social structures influenced by economic changes?

As you gather evidence to answer the Essential Question, think about:

- how the politics of the Second Industrial Revolution influenced art, music, and architecture.

- how literature serves as a vehicle for social change.

- how might innovations in science have changed the way people perceived the universe.

My Notes

_____

_____

_____

_____

_____

_____

4 **COMPARE AND CONTRAST** Use the Venn diagram below to compare and contrast the artistic movements of Impressionism and Post-Impressionism.

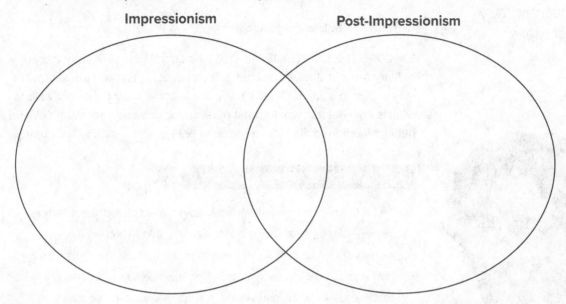

Impressionism   Post-Impressionism

5 **DESCRIBING** Use the organizer below to describe the innovations of the following historical figures.

George Eastman	
Marie Curie	
Albert Einstein	
Sigmund Freud	

6 **SUMMARIZING** What do you think would have happened to human perception without innovations brought on by the Second Industrial Revolution?

_____

_____

_____

ESSENTIAL QUESTION

How are political and social structures influenced by economic changes?

VOCABULARY

Gentiles: people who are not Jewish

obstinacy: stubbornness

Polotzk: a historical city in what is now Belarus

synagogue: a place where Jewish congregation meet

rubles: Russian monetary unit

shanty: shack

vigilant: watchful

The Promised Land

DIRECTIONS: Use the text to answer the questions.

EXPLORE THE CONTEXT: *The Promised Land* is the 1912 autobiography of Mary Antin. Antin was an immigration rights activist and the second of six children in a Jewish family. Her book tells the story of her early life in what is now Belarus amid czarist persecution of Jewish communities and her immigration to the United States in 1894. It sold over 85,000 copies.

PRIMARY SOURCE: BOOK

The Gentiles used to wonder at us because we cared so much about religious things — about food and Sabbath and teaching the children Hebrew. They were angry with us for our obstinacy, as they called it, and mocked us and ridiculed the most sacred things. There were wise Gentiles who understood. These were educated people, like Fedora Pavlovna, who made friends with their Jewish neighbors. They were always respectful and openly admired some of our ways. But most of the Gentiles were ignorant. . .There was one thing, however, the Gentiles always understood, and that was money. They would take any kind of bribe, at any time. They expected it. Peace cost so much a year, in Polotzk. If you did not keep on good terms with your Gentile neighbors, they had a hundred ways of molesting you. If you chased their pigs when they came rooting up your garden, or objected to their children maltreating your children, they might complain against you to the police, stuffing their case with false accusations and false witnesses. If you had not made friends with the police, the case might go to court; and there you lost before the trial was called unless the judge had reason to befriend you. . . .

[T]he Czar was always sending us commands,—you shall not do this and you shall not do that,—till there was very little left that we might honestly do, except pay tribute and die.

. . . The flag [for the Czar's birthday] must show from every house, or the owner will be dragged to to police station, to pay a fine of twenty-five rubles. What happened to the old woman who lives in that tumble-down shanty over the way? . . . The old woman had no flag, and no money. She hoped the policeman would not notice her miserable hut. But he did, the vigilant one, and he went up and kicked the door open with his great boot, and he took the last pillow from the bed, and sold it, and he hoisted a flag above the rotten roof. . . .

Source— Mary Antin, *The Promised Land,* 1912

Copyright © McGraw-Hill Education   Antin, Antin, Mary. 1912. The Promised Land. Boston: Houghton Mifflin Company.

1 SUMMARIZING What is Antin describing in this passage?

_____

_____

_____

2 CITING TEXT EVIDENCE How was Antin antagonized?

_____

_____

_____

3 ANALYZING TEXT What does Antin mean when she writes, "Peace cost so much a year, in Polotzk."

_____

_____

_____

4 IDENTIFYING BIAS What was the criteria for Antin to call someone a wise Gentile?

_____

_____

_____

5 CIVICS What is Antin's purpose in writing about policeman's actions to the old woman?

_____

_____

_____

_____

6 EVALUATING Does Antin feel these actions towards Jews were justified?

_____

_____

ESSENTIAL QUESTION

How are political and social structures influenced by economic changes?

A New Kind of Painting

DIRECTIONS: Use the image to answer the questions.

EXPLORE THE CONTEXT: Mary Cassatt was born in 1844 into an upper middle class family in Pennsylvania. Her family's wealth allowed her to travel the world and study art in Paris, where she became an influential impressionist. Her work is noted for its use of color and pattern and for its subject matter depicting quiet, domestic, and feminine spaces largely ignored by her male counterparts.

PRIMARY SOURCE: PAINTING

1 ANALYZING SOURCES Why does this image fall into the impressionism movement?

_____

_____

_____

_____

2A DESCRIBING What does the image show?

_____

_____

2B COMPARING How does this image differ from the painting styles that came before it?

_____

_____

_____

3 UNDERSTANDING CONTEXT Why is this scene an example of impressionism?

_____

_____

_____

_____

4 GEOGRAPHY What was happening in the world at the time that might relate to the subject of this painting?

_____

_____

5 IDENTIFYING BIAS What does this painting reveal about Cassatt's individual point of view?

_____

_____

_____

_____

6 INTEGRATING VISUAL INFORMATION Why was Cassatt's painting style considered "feminine"?

_____

_____

ESSENTIAL QUESTIONS

How are political and social structures influenced by economic changes?

My Notes

_____

_____

_____

_____

_____

_____

_____

_____

_____

_____

_____

_____

_____

_____

1 Think About It

Review the supporting questions you developed at the beginning of the chapter. Review the evidence you gathered in the chapter. Were you able to answer each Supporting Question? If there was not enough evidence to answer your Supporting Questions, what additional evidence do you think you need to consider?

_____

_____

2 Organize Your Evidence

Complete the chart below with information you learned about the economic changes during the Second Industrial Revolution and how it played a role in politics, society, and culture.

Economic Changes	Politics	Society & Culture

3 Talk About It

Work in a small group. With your group, discuss the ideas, changes, and consequences that you have identified and noted down in your charts. Compare your charts. Did you all pick the same ideas and changes? Do you disagree on the consequences of those changes? Overall, which idea do you think was the most crucial in leading to change in this period? Why?

4 Write About It

Write about two examples of changes that came about in this period because of new ideas. Describe how different ideas were combined by people with different goals and interests to create those changes.

_____

_____

_____

_____

_____

_____

_____

_____

_____

5 Connect to the Essential Question

Create a visual essay of the different artistic movements that were borne out of the Second Industrial Revolution. Your presentation should include references to impressionism, abstract painting, and changes in architecture. Define impressionism, abstract painting, and the architecture that developed during this time and include examples that show the characteristics. Connect these styles to the political and technological situation during the Second Industrial Revolution. Ensure that your presentation is accurate, engaging, and informative.

TAKING ACTION

MAKE CONNECTIONS Between 1880 and 1920, over 20 million immigrants came to the United States, mostly from Europe, China, and Japan. These immigrants left their homes to escape poverty, war, religious persecution, or restrictions on their social class. Some came to the country with special skillsets they use to find work while others learned a trade at a job. Immigrants from countries around the globe continue to make this move to the United States today.

DIRECTIONS: Find and interview an immigrant who came to the United States. Speak with them and learn why they came to the United States. What motivated them to make the move? What was the trip like? With whom did they come? How did they decide where to go? What was the immigration process like? What are they doing now?

After conducting this interview, use the information to create a multimedia presentation about the immigrant you interviewed. Introduce them to the class with visuals such as photographs and video.

_____

_____

_____

_____

_____

_____

_____

_____

_____

_____

_____

The Reach of Imperialism

ESSENTIAL QUESTION

What are the causes and effects of imperialism?

Toward the end of the nineteenth century, industrialized nations began an intense race to acquire colonies throughout Africa and Asia. Consider the factors that led to Western expansion and the effects of imperialism.

TALK ABOUT IT

With a partner, discuss the sort of information you would need to discover to explain why the late nineteenth century gave rise to a new form of imperialism. Consider the economic, political, and social factors that led to the rise of imperialism. For example, you might ask: "What motivated European powers to acquire foreign land? How did colonization impact the colonized?"

DIRECTIONS: Now write down three additional questions that will help you explain the causes and effects of imperialism.

MY RESEARCH QUESTIONS

Supporting Question 1:

_____

_____

Supporting Question 2:

_____

_____

Supporting Question 3:

_____

_____

Colonial Rule in Southeast Asia

DIRECTIONS Search for evidence in the lesson to help you answer the following questions.

1A IDENTIFYING CAUSES How did capitalism play a role in Western expansion?

_____

_____

_____

_____

ESSENTIAL QUESTION

What are the causes and effects of imperialism?

As you gather evidence to answer the Essential Question, think about:

- factors that led to the rise of imperialism.
- how imperialism is tied to racism and Social Darwinism.
- how colonization led to resistance and war.

1B IDENTIFYING CONNECTIONS How did economic motivations create international rivalries between imperial powers?

_____

_____

_____

_____

2 INFERRING How did Social Darwinism, racism, and religion lead to the rise of new imperialism? Use the chart below to organize this information.

Ideas	Factors leading to the rise of new imperialism
Social Darwinism	
Racism	
Religion	

My Notes

_____

_____

_____

_____

_____

_____

_____

3 **DIFFERENTIATING** Explain the different motives Great Britain, France, and the United States had for establishing control over specific places in Southeast Asia.

_____

_____

_____

_____

_____

_____

_____

4 **DIFFERENTIATING** What is the difference between direct rule and indirect rule?

_____

_____

_____

_____

_____

_____

_____

_____

_____

5 **HISTORY** Describe the different colonial rebellions throughout Southeast Asia.

_____

_____

_____

_____

_____

_____

_____

ESSENTIAL QUESTION

What are the causes and effects of imperialism?

Perry Arrives in Japan

DIRECTIONS: Use the image to answer the questions.

EXPLORE THE CONTEXT: U.S. president Millard Fillmore assigned Commodore Matthew Perry on a mission in 1852 to force the Japanese ports to open to American trade. When Perry arrived in the fortified harbor of Uraga in Japan, he ordered his ships to steam towards Edo. In an attempt to Japan, he refused to leave. He demanded a representive be sent to receive a letter from Fillmore, requesting a trade agreement. Perry made it clear that if no one was sent for the letter, he would deliver it forcibly. This anonymous print depicts the arrival of Perry's ship into the bay. The style of vivid paints on woodblock prints was popular during the Edo era.

PRIMARY SOURCE: WOODBLOCK PRINT

1 IDENTIFYING What was the subject of this print and what is its significance?

_____

_____

2 INTERPRETING What scene does this woodblock print depict?

_____

_____

_____

3A DRAWING CONCLUSIONS In addition to depicting a historical scene, how else does the image depict broader social change of the period?

_____

_____

_____

_____

3B INFERRING What does this print tell us about America's status as a global power during this time?

_____

_____

_____

4 IDENTIFYING CONNECTIONS How is this style of art connected to the Edo period?

_____

_____

5 CIVICS How could this print be interpreted as a political statement?

_____

_____

_____

_____

ESSENTIAL QUESTION

What are the causes and effects of imperialism?

VOCABULARY

subjugation: enslavement

sovereignty: supreme power or authority

cessation: ending or being brought to an end

heresy: blasphemy

abhor: to hate or be disgusted by something or someone

grievous: severe or seriously bad

Platform of the American Anti-Imperialist League

DIRECTIONS: Use the text to answer the questions.

EXPLORE THE CONTEXT: The American Anti-Imperialist League was established on June 15, 1898, as a way to battle the annexation of the Philippines by the United States. The League was against expansion and used public meetings, lectures, and the printed word to spread its message against imperialism. They argued that the United States's expanding on economic or humanitarian grounds would result in abandoning the ideals of self-government and non-intervention.

PRIMARY SOURCE: POLITICAL PLATFORM

66 We hold that the policy known as imperialism is hostile to liberty and tends toward militarism, an evil from which it has been our glory to be free. We regret that it has become necessary in the land of Washington and Lincoln to reaffirm that all men, of whatever race or color, are entitled to life, liberty and the pursuit of happiness. We maintain that governments derive their just powers from the consent of the governed. We insist that the subjugation of any people is "criminal aggression" and open disloyalty to the distinctive principles of our Government.

We earnestly condemn the policy of the present National Administration in the Philippines. It seeks to extinguish the spirit of 1776 in those islands. We deplore the sacrifice of our soldiers and sailors, whose bravery deserves admiration even in an unjust war. We denounce the slaughter of the Filipinos as a needless horror. We protest against the extension of American sovereignty by Spanish methods.

We demand the immediate cessation of the war against liberty, begun by Spain and continued by us. We urge that Congress be promptly convened to announce to the Filipinos our purpose to concede to them the independence for which they have so long fought and which of right is theirs.

The United States has always protested against the doctrine of international law which permits the subjugation of the weak by the strong. A self-governing state cannot accept sovereignty over an unwilling people. The United States cannot act upon the ancient heresy that might makes right.

Imperialists assume that with the destruction of self-government in the Philippines by American hands, all opposition here will cease. This is a grievous error. Much as we abhor the war of "criminal aggression" in the Philippines, greatly as we regret that the blood of the Filipinos is on American hands, we more deeply resent the betrayal of American institutions at home. The real firing line is not in the suburbs of Manila. The foe is of our own household. The attempt of 1861 was to divide the country. That of 1899 is to destroy its fundamental principles and noblest ideals. 99

Source— "Patriotic Eloquence relating to the Spanish-American War and its Issues," compiled by Robert I. Fulton and Thomas C. Trueblood, 1900

1 **ANALYZING** Is the text arguing for or against imperialism? Explain your answer.

_____

_____

_____

2 **IDENTIFYING CONNECTIONS** Does this text demonstrate that American colonization of the Philippines was an example of direct rule or indirect rule? Explain your answer.

_____

_____

_____

3 **COMPARING AND CONTRASTING** How does the Anti-Imperialist League document make connections between American imperialism and the American institution of government?

_____

_____

_____

_____

4 **IDENTIFYING BIAS** How might the platform of the American Anti-Imperialist League demonstrate political bias?

_____

_____

5A **UNDERSTANDING CONTEXT** What events led to the formation of the American Anti-Imperialist League and the publication of the source above?

_____

_____

5B **CIVICS** What was the purpose of the American Anti-Imperialist League?

_____

_____

Empire Building in Africa

DIRECTIONS Search for evidence in the lesson to help you answer the following questions.

1A **IDENTIFYING CAUSES** What caused European imperial powers to take an interest in colonizing Africa after the slave trade ended?

_____

_____

_____

1B **RELATING EVENTS** How did trade continue to have an impact on imperial acquisition?

_____

_____

_____

2 **HISTORY** How did international rivalries affect Europe's colonization of Africa?

_____

_____

_____

_____

_____

3 **ANALYZING INFORMATION** Which territories did Great Britain, France, and Italy acquire? Use the chart below to organize your information.

Great Britain	France	Italy

ESSENTIAL QUESTION

What are the causes and effects of imperialism?

As you gather evidence to answer the Essential Question, think about:

- what motives led European imperial powers to colonize Africa.
- how the continent of Africa was perceived by colonists during this time.
- what circumstances led to the rise of African nationalism.

My Notes

_____

_____

_____

_____

_____

_____

4A **ANALYZING POINTS OF VIEW** How did Europeans view of the people of Africa impact how the colonies were governed?

_____

_____

_____

4B **IDENTIFYING CONNECTIONS** What role did European attitudes toward Africa play in the rise of African nationalism?

_____

_____

_____

_____

_____

5 **EXPLAINING CAUSE & EFFECT** Use the chart below to detail the chain of events that led to the Boer War of 1899.

```
┌─────────────────────────────────────────┐
│                                          │
│                                          │
└─────────────────────────────────────────┘
                    ↓
┌─────────────────────────────────────────┐
│                                          │
│                                          │
└─────────────────────────────────────────┘
                    ↓
┌─────────────────────────────────────────┐
│                                          │
│                                          │
└─────────────────────────────────────────┘
                    ↓
┌─────────────────────────────────────────┐
│                                          │
│                                          │
└─────────────────────────────────────────┘
                    ↓
┌─────────────────────────────────────────┐
│                                          │
│                                          │
└─────────────────────────────────────────┘
```

ESSENTIAL QUESTION

What are the causes and effects of imperialism?

VOCABULARY

odious: very unpleasant

expenditure: amount of money spent

behindhand: unaware of recent events

amply: plentifully

Congo Horrors

DIRECTIONS: Use the text to answer the questions.

EXPLORE THE CONTEXT: Edmund Dene Morel was a British journalist, author, and politician who led a campaign against slavery in the Congo Free State and founded the Congo Reform Association. The "Congo Horrors" occurred from 1885 to 1908 while the Congo Free State was ruled by King Leopold II of Belgium.

PRIMARY SOURCE: BOOK

❝Personally, I had always thought until the early part of 1901, that these mutilations were carried out upon *dead* people only -- natives slain in connection with the odious raids upon villages, for not bringing in a sufficiency of rubber, and that the idea was at once to strike terror into the hearts of other villages, and to justify, in the eyes of the Congo State officer, the expenditure of the cartridges by soldiers whom he had sent out upon the work of slaughter to prove to the satisfaction of their superiors that a village behindhand in its tribute of rubber or food stuffs had been really and effectively wiped out. But it was only towards the end of 1901 that I ascertained, by receiving photographs and letters from the Upper Congo, that mutilations were frequently practised by the Congo soldiery upon the living, upon men, upon women, upon poor little innocent children of tender years. The information I then received has been, alas! but too amply corroborated since from various sources and notably by Mr. Roger Casement. Consul Casement's evidence is abundant and precise. In the Lake Mantumba District he saw two mutilated natives, whose cases authenticated beyond doubt, proved the committal of the deed by Government soldiers "accompanied by white officers." The Government official in this district said men still came to him who had been victims of the practice while the rubber *regime* was in force; in that particular district it seems to have been abandoned a year or two ago; probably owing to the enormous depopulation which had ensued from its application. The Consul was given by the natives the names of six other persons mutilated in a similar way. Many statements were also given to him, and are printed in the report, showing on what a colossal scale these mutilations were carried out, by instructions, in that district. The day he left the Lake five men crossed it from another direction to see him, all being mutilated in the same manner. When informed of the fact by a messenger the Consul was on his return journey and did not therefore meet them. The estimate of a Government officer that 6000 people had been killed or mutilated in six months in the Mamboyo District of the Domaine de la Couronne is referred to in Chapter XIX as is also the sexual mutilations inflicted by the Government soldiers upon the people of L which the Consul obtained from the lips of the refugees from Lake Leopold II.❞

Source— Edmund Dene Morel, *King Leopold's Rule in Africa*, 1905

Morel, Edmund Dene. 1905. King Leopold's Rule in Africa. New York: Funk and Wagnalls Company.

1A DISTINGUISHING FACT FROM OPINION What type of text is the source? Is it opinion based or factual?

_____

_____

1B UNDERSTANDING CONTEXT How are the effects of imperialism conveyed through this passage?

_____

_____

_____

2 ANALYZING INFORMATION What does the reading convey about the conditions faced by the Congolese during this time?

_____

_____

_____

3 IDENTIFYING BIAS From whose perspective was the source written? Does the text support imperialism or is it an anti-imperialist text?

_____

_____

_____

_____

4 HISTORY How might the publication of this text impact public perception of the Congo Free State?

_____

_____

_____

_____

_____

Sauer, J. W. and Theal, Geo. M. 1883. Basutoland Records - Copies of Official Documents of Various Kinds, Accounts of Travellers, &c. Vol II. 1853-1861. Cape Town: W. A. Richards & Sons, Government Printers.

ESSENTIAL QUESTION

What are the causes and effects of imperialism?

VOCABULARY

remonstrated: protest

skirmishes: sporadic fighting

1 UNDERSTANDING CONTEXT

What events were taking place when the source was written?

_____

_____

_____

_____

_____

_____

_____

_____

Letter from the Chief of the Basutos

DIRECTIONS: Use the text to answer the questions.

EXPLORE THE CONTEXT: Moshoeshoe was the chief of the Basotho tribe that lived in what is now South Africa. The tribe lost the western lowlands to the Boers during the Free State-Sotho war in 1868, but Moshoeshoe appealed to Queen Victoria to proclaim Lesotho as a protected territory of Britain. The local chiefs kept power over internal affairs while Britain had control over foreign affairs and the defense of Lesotho. The British supported the process to demarcate the borders of Basutoland.

PRIMARY SOURCE: LETTER

66 In vain I remonstrated. Sir Harry Smith had sent Warden to govern in the Sovereignty. He listened to the Boers, and he proposed that all the land in which those Boers' farms were should be taken from me. I was at that time in trouble, for Sikonyela and the Korannas were tormenting me and my people by stealing and killing; they said openly the Major gave them orders to do so, and I have proof he did so. One day he sent me a map and said, sign that, and I will tell those people (Mantatis and Korannas) to leave off fighting: if you do not sign the map, I cannot help you in any way. I thought the Major was doing very improperly and unjustly. I was told to appeal to the Queen to put an end to this injustice. I did not wish to grieve Her Majesty by causing a war with her people. I was told if I did not sign the map, it would be the beginning of a great war. I signed, but soon after I sent my cry to the Queen. I begged Her to investigate my case and remove "the line," as it was called, by which my land was ruined. I thought justice would soon be done, and Warden put to rights. . . .

I tried my utmost to satisfy them and avert war. I punished thieves, and sent my son Nehemiah and others to watch the part of the country near the Boers, and thus check stealing. In this he was successful, thieving did cease. We were at peace for a time. In the commencement of the present year (1858) my people living near farmers received orders to remove from their places. This again caused the fire to burn, still we tried to keep all quiet, but the Boers went further and further day by day in troubling the Basutos and threatening war. The President (Boshof) spoke of Warden's line, this was as though he had really fired upon us with his guns. Still I tried to avert war.

It was not possible, it was commenced by the Boers in massacring my people of Beersheba, and ruining that station, against the people of which there was not a shadow of a complaint ever brought forward. Poor people, they thought their honesty and love for Christianity would be a shield for them, and that the white people would attack in the first place, if they attacked at all, those who they said were thieves. I ordered my people then all to retreat toward my residence, and let the fury of the Boers be spent upon an empty land; unfortunately some skirmishes took place, some Boers were killed, some of my people also. We need not wonder at this, such is war! But I will speak of many Basutos who were taken prisoners by the Whites and then killed, most cruelly. If you require me to bring forward these cases, I will do so. I will however speak of the horrible doings of the Boers at Morija, they there burnt down the Missionary's house, carried off much goods belonging to the Mission, and pillaged and shamefully defiled the Church Buildings. . . .

Mark X of Moshweshewe, Chief of the Basutos. **"**

Source— Basutoland, "Basutoland Records: Copies of Official Documents of Various Kinds, Accounts of Travellers, &c, Volume 2," 1883

2 **INTERPRETING** What is the author of the source attempting to convey to its recipient?

_____

_____

_____

3 **IDENTIFYING BIAS** Is the source biased against a particular group?

_____

_____

4 **RELATING EVENTS** How does the source relate to imperialism?

_____

_____

5 **HISTORY** What insight does this source provide on the relationship between the colonizer and the colonized in South Africa?

_____

_____

ESSENTIAL QUESTION

What are the causes and effects of imperialism?

As you gather evidence to answer the Essential Question, think about:

- how the British colonial rule affected the Indian people.

- the causes and effects of the Great Rebellion (Sepoy Mutiny).

- the results of the Indian independence movement in the early 1900s.

My Notes

_____

_____

_____

_____

_____

_____

_____

British Rule in India

DIRECTIONS Search for evidence in the lesson to help you answer the following questions.

1A   **HISTORY**   What entity did the British government create to handle British interests in India's political and military affairs?

_____

_____

1B   **CITING TEXT EVIDENCE** Who were the sepoys?

_____

_____

2   **DETERMINING MEANING** Use the chart below to list which groups used the following names for the Great Rebellion.

Term for the revolt	Who used this term?
The Sepoy Mutiny	
The First War of the Independence	
The Great Rebellion	

3 IDENTIFYING CAUSES Use the chart to show the chain of events that led to the Great Rebellion.

> [ ]
>
> ↓
>
> Rumor that the troops' rifle cartridges were greased with cow and pig fat
>
> ↓
>
> [ ]
>
> ↓
>
> [ ]
>
> ↓
>
> A group of sepoys refused to load their rifles.
>
> ↓
>
> [ ]
>
> ↓
>
> [ ]

4 RELATING EVENTS What was the price the Indian people paid for peace and stability brought by British rule?

_____

_____

_____

_____

ESSENTIAL QUESTION

What are the causes and effects of imperialism?

Trade on the East Indian Railway

DIRECTIONS: Use the text to answer the questions.

EXPLORE THE CONTEXT: The British Empire benefited extensively from raw resources extracted from India, including cotton, tea, coffee, sugar, and coal. The introduction of railway systems in India yielded major benefits. Formed in 1845, the British-owned East Indian Railway was the first railway constructed in India. Its lines ran from Calcutta to West Bengal. Initially the company faced major obstacles during its construction, in addition to local resistance towards the project. The East Indian Railway survived initial hardships and became a leading industrial force, dramatically expanded trade and commerce, and employed thousands of people.

PRIMARY SOURCE: BOOK EXCERPT

66 Nothing in the history of the East Indian Railway has been more remarkable than the growth of the coal traffic during the past 15 years. Up to the year 1889 few had recognised its immense possibilities, and there was certainly no idea of a great export - trade setting in, while internal requirements were comparatively small and restricted almost entirely to the needs of railways. There seems to have been at the outset a good deal of prejudice on the part of those who had previously burnt Welsh coal, and particularly on the part of the engineers of the larger steamship companies, against the introduction of Bengal coal in its place ; these prejudices were only overcome by degrees, but once a start had been made the import of coal from the United Kingdom was doomed. In the first half of the year 1885, more than 45,000 tons of Welsh coal were imported into Calcutta, during the first half of 1889 the quantity imported dropped to less than 1,000 tons, and an export trade then started, principally in bunker coal for the use of the steamers of the British India Steam Navigation Company, which extended even more rapidly than the most sanguine anticipated. In 1890 the growth of the export of Bengal coal from Calcutta first attracted serious attention though in proportion to the total downwards traffic the export figures were still comparatively small. Rangoon was the port which at first took the largest quantity. Bombay which is now the largest taker of Bengal coal, adhering very largely to the Welsh product until some years afterwards. 99

Sourece— George Huddleston, *History of the East Indian Railway,* Volume 1, 1906

VOCABULARY

sanguine: optimistic

Rangoon: largest city in Myanmar (formerly Burma)

adhering: to stick to

1 HISTORY What does the source convey about coal traffic from India to Great Britain in the year 1906?

_____

_____

_____

2A EVALUATING EVIDENCE Was the trade of Bengal coal immediately successful?

_____

_____

_____

2B UNDERSTANDING CHANGE What changes that took place in the trade of Bengal coal between 1889 and 1890?

_____

_____

_____

3 INFERRING Why do you think the trade of Bengal coal increased?

_____

_____

_____

4 IDENTIFYING BIAS What prejudices were faced in the early days of the Bengal coal trade?

_____

_____

_____

5 IDENTIFYING CAUSE & EFFECT How might the rise of Bengal coal have had an impact on the coal trade?

_____

_____

_____

Queen Victoria. 1858. "Queen Victoria's Proclamation to the Princes, Chiefs, and People of India." Reprinted 1859 in The History of the Indian Revolt and of the Expeditions to Persia, China, and Japan. 1856-7-8. London: W. and R. Chambers.

ESSENTIAL QUESTION

What are the causes and effects of imperialism?

VOCABULARY

solace: comfort in a time of distress

disclaim: to deny

anywise: in any way

disquieted: to make someone anxious

molested: pester or harass

enjoin: instruct or urge

clemency: mercy

The Empress of India

DIRECTIONS: Use the text to answer the questions.

EXPLORE THE CONTEXT: Queen Victoria ruled the United Kingdom of Great Britain and Ireland from 1837 until her death in 1901. She took the title Empress of India on May 1, 1876, after the East India Company was transferred to the British government by the British Parliament. The people of India became her subjects, and India became the "jewel" in her imperial crown.

PRIMARY SOURCE: PROCLAMATION

66 Proclamation by the Queen in Council, to the princes, chiefs, and people of India" (1858)

Firmly relying ourselves on the truth of Christianity, and acknowledging with gratitude the solace of religion, we disclaim alike the right and desire to impose our convictions on any of our subjects. We declare it to be our royal will and pleasure that none be in anywise favoured, none molested or disquieted, by reason of their religious faith or observances, but that all alike shall enjoy the equal and impartial protection of the law; and we do strictly charge and enjoin all those who may be in authority under us that they abstain from all interference with the religious belief or worship of any of our subjects on pain of our highest displeasure.

And it is our further will that, so far as may be, our subjects, of whatever race or creed, be freely and impartially admitted to offices in our service, the duties of which they may be qualified, by their education, ability, and integrity, duly to discharge.

We know, and respect, the feelings of attachment with which the natives of India regard the lands inherited by them from their ancestors, and we desire to protect them in all rights connected therewith, subject to the equitable demands of the State; and we will that generally, in framing and administering the law, due regard be paid to the ancient rights, usages, and customs of India. . .

Our clemency will be extended to all offenders, save and except those who have been, or shall be, convicted of having directly taken part in the murder of British subjects. With regard to such the demands of justice forbid the exercise of mercy. . . When, by the blessing of Providence, internal tranquility shall be restored, it is our earnest duty to stimulate the peaceful industry of India, to promote works of public utility and improvement, and to administer its government for the benefit of all our subjects resident therein. In their prosperity will be our strength; in their contentment our security, and in their gratitude our best reward. And may the God of all power grant to us, and to those in authority under us, strength to carry out our wishes for the good of our people. 99

Source— Queen Victoria's Proclamation to the Princes, Chiefs, and People of India, 1858

1A **ANALYZING SOURCE** Queen Victoria promises fair treatment of Indians. What does she say will happen to those who had rebelled against unfair treatment?

_____

_____

1B **ANALYZING SOURCE** What is Queen Victoria trying to convey in this proclamation?

_____

_____

_____

2 **HISTORY** Does this proclamation mark a political shift in Indian rule?

_____

_____

_____

3 **UNDERSTANDING CHANGE** How does the source above mark a change in the dynamic between British rule and Indian traditions?

_____

_____

_____

_____

_____

4 **EXPLAINING CAUSE AND EFFECT** Taking into consideration the revolt of 1857, how would this message from Queen Victoria impact cultural tensions between British imperial forces and the people of India?

_____

_____

_____

_____

_____

Imperialism in Latin America

DIRECTIONS Search for evidence in the lesson to help you answer the following questions.

1A **IDENTIFYING CONNECTIONS** What was the relationship between the United States and Latin America during the late 1800s?

_____

_____

_____

_____

_____

_____

_____

1B **INFERRING** What was one motivation for the intervention of the United States in Latin American politics?

_____

_____

_____

_____

_____

2A **DESCRIBING** What is the Roosevelt Corollary to the Monroe Doctrine?

_____

_____

_____

2B **IDENTIFYING CAUSES** What events gave rise to the Roosevelt Corollary to the Monroe Doctrine?

_____

_____

ESSENTIAL QUESTION

What are the causes and effects of imperialism?

As you gather evidence to answer the Essential Question, think about:

- motivations for United States's involvement in Latin America during the 1900s.

- how the United States would benefit from "dollar diplomacy" in Latin America.

- how colonization of Latin America resulted in social change.

My Notes

_____

_____

_____

_____

_____

_____

3 **INTERPRETING** What was the United States's motivation behind "dollar diplomacy"?

_____

_____

_____

4 **ECONOMICS** Using the chart below, organize the pros and cons of "dollar diplomacy" in Latin American development.

Dollar Diplomacy
PROS:
CONS:

5 **IDENTIFYING EFFECTS** What were the effects of the Mexican Revolution?

_____

_____

_____

_____

_____

_____

_____

_____

_____

ESSENTIAL QUESTION

What are the causes and effects of imperialism?

The Plan de Ayla: A Mexican Revolutionary's Plan

DIRECTIONS: Use the image to answer the questions.

EXPLORE THE CONTEXT: Mexican revolutionary Emiliano Zapata wrote the *The Plan de Ayala (Plan of Ayala)* in November 1911 with the help of his mentor and local schoolteacher, Otilio Montaño Sánchez. The plan was written as a response to Franscisco I. Madero, who was unpopular among the liberals and the conservatives. It calls for land reform and freedom from the land that was stolen under Porfirio Díaz, who ruled Mexico from 1877 to 1911. Díaz was forced out of power by Madero.

PRIMARY SOURCE: MANIFESTO

66 Mexicans: consider that the cunning and bad faith of one man is shedding blood in a scandalous manner, because he is incapable of governing; consider that his system of government is choking the fatherland and trampling with the brute force of bayonets on our institutions; and thus, as we raised up our weapons to elevate him to power, we again raise them up against him for defaulting on his promises to the Mexican people and for having betrayed the revolution initiated by him, we are not personalists, we are partisans of principles and not of men! 99

Source— Emiliano Zapata, "Plan de Ayala," 1911

VOCABULARY

bayonet: a weapon with a blade that is attached to a gun muzzle

personalist: an ideal that focuses on individual personality

partisans: a supporter of an ideal or group

1 **SUMMARIZING** What is the main idea of this passage?

_____

_____

_____

_____

_____

_____

2 **CITING TEXT EVIDENCE** What does the text indicate is the reason that Zapata is criticizing Madero?

_____

_____

_____

_____

3 **IDENTIFYING CONNECTIONS** Based on what you know from the textbook, why would Zapata have been critical of Madero?

_____

_____

_____

_____

_____

_____

_____

4 **INFERRING** What does Zapata mean when he says, "we are not personalists, we are partisans of principles and not of men!"?

_____

_____

_____

_____

_____

5 HISTORY How could this plan impact political struggle?

_____

_____

_____

_____

ESSENTIAL QUESTION

What are the causes and effects of imperialism?

Taft's Fourth Address

DIRECTIONS: Use the text to answer the questions.

EXPLORE THE CONTEXT: The term "dollar diplomacy" is most commonly associated with the 27th President of the United States, William Howard Taft. Under Taft's presidency, the United States used its financial power to increase foreign policy by guaranteeing loans to countries from which the United States stood to benefit. The quote below comes from Taft's 1912 "Fourth Annual Message" as president.

PRIMARY SOURCE: PRESIDENTIAL ADDRESS

66 The diplomacy of the present administration has sought to respond to modern ideas of commercial intercourse. This policy has been characterized as substituting dollars for bullets. It is one that appeals alike to idealistic humanitarian sentiments, to the dictates of sound policy and strategy, and to legitimate commercial aims. It is an effort frankly directed to the increase of American trade upon the axiomatic principle that the Government of the United States shall extend all proper support to every legitimate and beneficial American enterprise abroad. How great have been the results of this diplomacy, coupled with the maximum and minimum provision of the tariff law, will be seen by some consideration of the wonderful increase in the export trade of the United States. Because modern diplomacy is commercial, there has been a disposition in some quarters to attribute to it none but materialistic aims. How strikingly erroneous is such an impression may be seen from a study of the results by which the diplomacy of the United States can be judged. 99

Source— William Howard Taft, *"Fourth Annual Message,"* 1912

VOCABULARY

intercourse: interactions between individuals or groups

humanitarian: someone who believes in doing good for all humanity

axiomatic: obvious; self-evident

disposition: state of mind; attitude

1A **SUMMARIZING** What is the Taft administration's diplomatic policy?

_____

_____

_____

_____

_____

Taft, William. 1912. "Fourth Annual Message." Reprinted 1919 in Papers Relating to the Foreign Relations of the United States - With the Annual Message of the President Transmitted to Congress December 3, 1912. Washington: Government Printing Office.

1B **IDENTIFYING CONNECTIONS** According to the text, how has diplomacy under Taft changed from previous administrations? Cite evidence from the text to support your answer.

_____

_____

_____

_____

2 **INTERPRETING** What might critics of the Taft administration's diplomacy have argued?

_____

_____

_____

3 **ECONOMICS** Why would the United States shift from basing its diplomacy on military strength to basing it on economic leverage?

_____

_____

_____

_____

_____

4 **IDENTIFYING BIAS** In what way might Taft's speech be biased? Cite specific evidence from the text to support your answer.

_____

_____

_____

_____

5 **EXPLAINING EFFECTS** How does Taft's diplomacy connect to the United States's policies around imperialism in Latin America?

_____

_____

_____

_____

ESSENTIAL QUESTION

What are the causes and effects of imperialism?

My Notes

_____

_____

_____

_____

_____

_____

_____

_____

_____

_____

_____

_____

_____

1 Think About It

Review the supporting questions you developed at the beginning of the chapter. Review the evidence you gathered in the chapter. Were you able to answer each Supporting Question? If there was not enough evidence to answer your Supporting Questions, what additional evidence do you think you need to consider?

_____

_____

_____

2 Organize Your Evidence

Complete the chart below with information you learned about the effects of imperialism in the following countries.

Africa	India	Latin America

③ Talk About It

Work in a small group. With your group, discuss the motivations, changes, and consequences that you have identified and noted down in your charts. Compare your charts. Did you all pick the same causes and effects? Do you disagree on the consequences of those changes? Overall, which idea do you think were the most crucial events that led to change in this period? Why?

④ Write About It

Following your discussion in the Talk About It activity, write about two examples of change that came about in this period as a result of imperialism. Describe how the rise of western imperialism that led to political and social reform.

_____

_____

_____

_____

_____

⑤ Connect to the Essential Question

Following your work in the previous activities, choose the ideas, changes, and consequences you identified as the most vital during this period. Plan, create, and present a multimedia presentation, including images, music, and animations if available, in which you describe the mix of ideas and innovations which led to those changes. Be sure to present information in a logical chain of cause and effect but also consider the ways that ideas are built upon one another and reinterpreted by different people with different motives. Ensure your presentation is both engaging and informative.

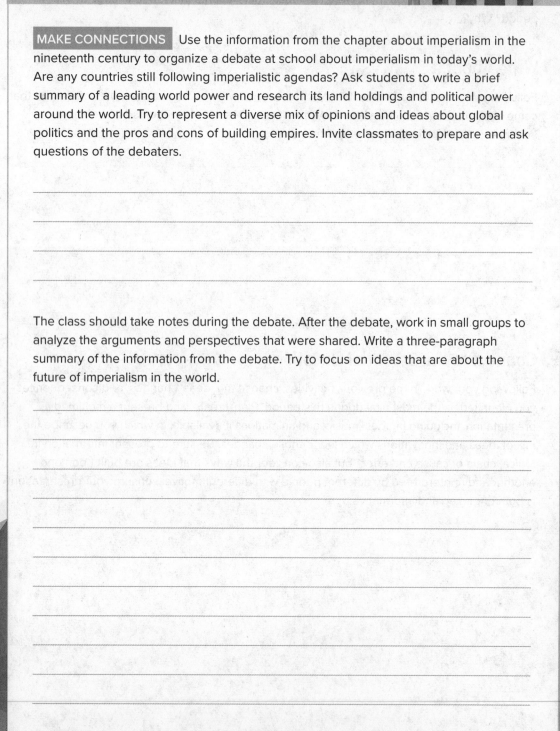

MAKE CONNECTIONS Use the information from the chapter about imperialism in the nineteenth century to organize a debate at school about imperialism in today's world. Are any countries still following imperialistic agendas? Ask students to write a brief summary of a leading world power and research its land holdings and political power around the world. Try to represent a diverse mix of opinions and ideas about global politics and the pros and cons of building empires. Invite classmates to prepare and ask questions of the debaters.

_____

_____

_____

_____

The class should take notes during the debate. After the debate, work in small groups to analyze the arguments and perspectives that were shared. Write a three-paragraph summary of the information from the debate. Try to focus on ideas that are about the future of imperialism in the world.

_____

_____

_____

_____

_____

_____

_____

_____

_____

_____

Challenge and Transition in East Asia

ESSENTIAL QUESTION

How do cultures influence each other?

Think about how the economies and culture of Western nations influenced China during the nineteenth century.

TALK ABOUT IT

With a partner, discuss the sort of information you would need to know to answer this question. For example, you might ask, "What was the current state of politics in China during this time?"

DIRECTIONS: Now write down three additional questions that will help you explain how Chinese culture blended into Western culture during the nineteenth century. For example, you might ask, "What was the current state of politics in China during this time?"

MY RESEARCH QUESTIONS

Supporting Question 1:

_____

_____

Supporting Question 2:

_____

_____

Supporting Question 3:

_____

_____

_____

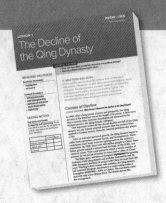

ESSENTIAL QUESTION

How do cultures influence each other?

As you gather evidence to answer the Essential Question, think about:

- how pressure from the West led to the decline of the Qing dynasty.

- how internal corruption and unrest led to the decline of the Qing dynasty.

- the internal response to imperialism in China.

My Notes

_____

_____

_____

_____

_____

_____

_____

_____

The Decline of the Qing Dynasty

DIRECTIONS Search for evidence in the lesson to help you answer the following questions.

1A **EXPLAINING CAUSES** In what way did the West contribute to the collapse of the Qing dynasty?

_____

_____

_____

_____

_____

_____

1B **SUMMARIZING** Use the chart below to list the other factors that caused the collapse of the Qing dynasty.

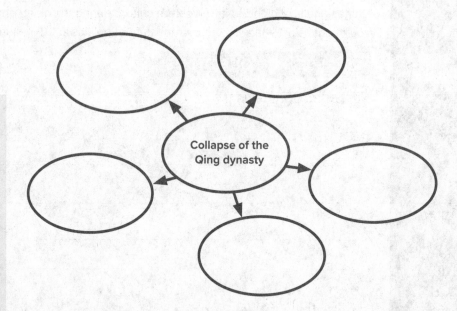

2A `ECONOMICS` How did the trade deficit with China affect Britain?

_____

_____

_____

_____

2B **IDENTIFYING PERSPECTIVES** What was China's reaction to opium? Why?

_____

_____

_____

3 **COMPARING AND CONTRASTING** Use the chart below to list the advantages and disadvantages of the Open Door Policy.

Advantages	Disadvantages

ESSENTIAL QUESTION

How do cultures influence each other?

A Christian Missionary in China

DIRECTIONS: Use the text to answer the questions.

EXPLORE THE CONTEXT: Elijah Coleman Bridgman arrived in China before the Opium War and was the first American Protestant Christian missionary appointed to China. This list was originally written by Reverend Levi Spaulding, another American missionary in Ceylon, now Sri Lanka. Bridgman copied the list into his journal on October 26, 1833.

PRIMARY SOURCE: JOURNAL

QUALIFICATIONS OF A MISSIONARY.

1. *Ardent* Piety.

2. More than a common degree of zeal, but under the control of good common sense, which, by the way, is better than sound learning.

3. Kindness, gentleness, brotherly love.

4. A spirit to be *least of all and last of all* in the field; a spirit to do much and say little.

5. Cheerfulness.

6. *A hasty temper* is bad; *peevishness* is worse.

7. A man must be willing to be called the worst of names, and that to his face, and still be able to keep his temper.

8. He must expect sometimes to be *contradicted* sometimes *blamed*; and this, too, by those whom he must fellowship. 🙴

Source— E. C. Bridgman, from The Pioneer of American Missions in China: The Life and Labors of Elijah Coleman Bridgman, 1864

VOCABULARY

ardent: passionate; enthusiastic

piety: religious devotion

zeal: passion; enthusiasm

peevishness: irritablility; grumpiness

1A DETERMINING CENTRAL IDEAS What is the main idea of these "qualifications"?

_____

_____

_____

_____

1B ANALYZING TEXT PRESENTATION Why would Bridgman italicize certain words?

_____

_____

_____

_____

2A DETERMINING CONTEXT What was going on around the time Bridgman arrived in China?

_____

_____

_____

_____

2B INFERRING Why did Bridgman write this list in his journal?

_____

_____

_____

_____

3 CIVICS Based on this list, why might a missionary have traveled to China, and what might he or she have expected to experience there?

_____

_____

_____

_____

4 DETERMINING MEANING What does Bridgman mean when he writes "A hasty temper is bad; peevishness is worse."

_____

_____

_____

_____

ESSENTIAL QUESTION
How do cultures influence each other?

Hong Xiuquan and the Tai Ping Rebellion

DIRECTIONS: Use the text to answer the questions.

EXPLORE THE CONTEXT: From 1850 to 1864, Chinese peasants led a revolt known as the Tai Ping Rebellion. The rebellion was led by Hong Xiuquan, a Christian convert who styled himself as the younger brother of Jesus. In 1859 when the rebels seized Nanjing, 25,000 men, women, and children were massacred. The revolt continued for 10 years. The document below, written by unknown authors during the Tai Ping Rebellion, shows the influence of Western Christianity.

PRIMARY SOURCE: DOCUMENT

"Throughout the empire the mulberry tree is to be planted close to every wall, so that all women may engage in rearing silkworms, spinning the silk, and making garments. Throughout the empire every family should keep five hens and two sows, which must not be allowed to miss their proper season. At the time of harvest, every sergeant shall direct the corporals to see to it that of the twenty-five families under his charge each individual has a sufficient supply of food, and aside from the new grain each may receive, the remainder must be deposited in the public granary. Of wheat, pulse, hemp; flax, cloth, silk, fowls, dogs, etc., and money, the same is true; for the whole empire is the universal family of our Heavenly Father, the Supreme Lord and Great God. . . . For every twenty-five families there must be established one public granary, and one church where the sergeant must reside. Whenever there are marriages, or births, or funerals, all may go to the public granary; but a limit must be observed, and not a cash be used beyond what is necessary. Thus, every family which celebrates a marriage or a birth will be given one thousand cash and a hundred catties of grain. . . .

In every circle of twenty-five families, the work of the potter, the blacksmith, the carpenter, the mason, and other artisans must all be performed by the corporal and privates; when free from husbandry they are to attend to these matters. Every sergeant, in superintending marriages and funeral events in the twenty-five families, should in every case offer a eucharistic sacrifice to our Heavenly Father, the Supreme Lord and Great God; all corrupt ceremonies of former times are abolished.

In every circle of twenty-five families, all young boys must go to church every day, where the sergeant is to teach them to read the Old Testament and the New Testament, as well as the book of proclamations of the true ordained Sovereign. Every Sabbath the corporals must lead the men and women to the church, where the males and females are to sit in separate rows. There they will listen to sermons, sing praises, and offer sacrifices to our Heavenly Father, the Supreme Lord and Great God. . . ."

Source— Unknown, excerpt from "The Land System of the Heavenly Kingdom," 1853

VOCABULARY

granary: a place to store grain

husbandry: managing crops and animals; farming

eucharistic: holy communion

sovereign: ruler, monarch

Copyright © McGraw-Hill Education Michael, Franz. 1971. The Taiping Rebellion: History and Documents, Vol. 2. Seattle: University of Washington Press.

1 **SUMMARIZING** What is this passage about?

_____

_____

_____

2A **DETERMINING CENTRAL IDEAS** Using this passage, what seems to be the most important duty for the families?

_____

_____

_____

2B **CITING TEXT EVIDENCE** Who is "the empire" in this document?

_____

_____

_____

3A CIVICS What was the political motivation behind this text?

_____

_____

_____

_____

3B **DETERMINING CENTRAL IDEAS** Why would Hong Xuiquan proclaim a new dynasty?

_____

_____

_____

4 **EVALUATING** Was the new dynasty successful? Explain your answer.

_____

_____

_____

_____

Revolution in China

DIRECTIONS Search for evidence in the lesson to help you answer the following questions.

1A **EXPLAINING CAUSES** What social and political factors contributed to the fall of the Qing dynasty?

_____

_____

_____

_____

_____

_____

1B **EXPLAINING EFFECTS** How did the decline of the Qing dynasty give rise to political reform?

_____

_____

_____

2 **ANALYZING INFORMATION** Use the chart below to explain Sun Yat-sen's three-stage reform process.

First Stage	
Second Stage	
Third Stage	

ESSENTIAL QUESTION

How do cultures influence each other?

As you gather evidence to answer the Essential Question, think about:

- the transition from old political structures toward new political structures.

- the modernization of China as a direct result of Western influence.

- major changes in Chinese industry and trade.

My Notes

_____

_____

_____

_____

_____

_____

_____

3 INTERPRETING How might the Revolution of 1911 be perceived as a failure?

_____

_____

_____

_____

_____

_____

_____

_____

_____

4 ECONOMICS What was the impact of westernization on the Chinese economy?

_____

_____

_____

_____

_____

_____

_____

_____

5 IDENTIFYING PERSPECTIVES Explain the struggle between old and new in Chinese culture during this time.

_____

_____

_____

_____

_____

_____

_____

ESSENTIAL QUESTION
How do cultures influence each other?

Chinese Canton Impresses a Briton

DIRECTIONS: Use the text to answer the questions.

EXPLORE THE CONTEXT: Isabella Bird was a British missionary and traveler in the nineteenth century. Bird is best known for having written extensively about her travels throughout the world. Below is an excerpt from her book, *The Golden Chersonese and the Way Thither*, in which she describes her impressions of the city of Canton, a trading outpost in southern China.

PRIMARY SOURCE: BOOK

Canton, January 1, 1879

❝ . . . Many Chinese mansions contain six or seven courtyards, each with its colonnade, drawing, dining, and reception rooms, and at the back of all there is a flower garden adorned with rockeries, fish-ponds, dwarf trees, and miniature pagodas and bridges.

The streets in which the poor dwell are formed of low, small, dark, and dirty houses, of two or three rooms each. The streets of dwellings are as mean and ugly as those of shops are brilliant and picturesque.

This is a meagre outline of what may be called the anatomy of this ancient city, which dates from the fourth century B.C., when it was walled only by a stockade of bamboo and mud, but was known by the name of "the martial city of the south," changed later into "the city of rams." At this date it has probably greater importance than it ever had, and no city but London impresses me so much with the idea of solid wealth and increasing prosperity.

My admiration and amazement never cease. I grudge the hours that I am obliged to spend in sleep; a week has gone like half a day, each hour heightening my impressions of the fascination and interest of Canton, and of the singular force and importance of the Chinese. Canton is intoxicating from its picturesqueness, color, novelty and movement. . . . ❞

Source— Isabella Bird, *The Golden Chersonese and the Way Thither*, 1883

VOCABULARY

colonnade: columns supporting roof

rockeries: heaped arrangement of stones

pagodas: sacred building, usually Hindu or Buddhist

stockade: a barrier, usually in defense against attack or to confine animals

1A ECONOMICS How are the mansions of Canton described in comparison with the poor neighborhoods?

_____

_____

_____

1B **INTERPRETING** What does Isabella Bird indicate about the divide between rich and poor in China during this time?

_____

_____

2 **IDENTIFYING PERSPECTIVES** What is the author's opinion of Canton?

_____

_____

_____

3 **UNDERSTANDING CHANGES** How does Bird illustrate changes within the city of Canton?

_____

_____

_____

_____

4A **PREDICTING** Based on the source, what does Bird predict will happen to China's development?

_____

_____

_____

4B **IDENTIFYING BIAS** How might this text be biased?

_____

_____

_____

_____

ESSENTIAL QUESTION

How do cultures influence each other?

Qing's Failed Attempts at Reform

DIRECTIONS: Use the text to answer the questions.

EXPLORE THE CONTEXT: This excerpt from the *Peking Gazette* was included in a study of the Chinese court authored by Isaac Taylor Headland and published in 1909. Headland taught at Peking University and his wife was the doctor for the Empress Dowager Ci Xi and others royals and high officials. This selection is drawn from the newspaper, which published the new plans for China decreed by Emperor Guang Xu in 1898. These plans formed part of the Hundred Days' Reform Movement, which failed when the Ci Xi took control by means of a coup and had the emperor executed.

PRIMARY SOURCE: BOOK

" The Peking Gazette continued to come daily bringing with it the following twenty-seven decrees in a little more than twice that many days. I will give an epitome of the decrees so that the reader at a glance may see what the emperor undertook to do. . . .

1. The establishment of a university at Beijing.
2. The sending of imperial clansmen to foreign countries to study the forms and conditions of European and American government.
3. The encouragement of the arts, sciences and modern agriculture.
4. The Emperor expressed himself as willing to hear the objections of the conservatives to progress and reform.
5. Abolished the literary essay as a prominent part of the governmental examinations.
6. Censured those who attempted to delay the establishment of the Peking Imperial University.
7. Urged that the Lu-Han railway should be prosecuted with more vigor and expedition.
8. Advised the adoption of Western arms and drill for all the Tartar troops.
9. Ordered the establishment of agricultural schools in all the provinces to teach the farmers improved methods of agriculture.
10. Ordered the introduction of patent and copyright laws. . . .
12. Special rewards were offered to inventors and authors.
13. The officials were ordered to encourage trade and assist merchants.
14. School boards were ordered established in every city in the empire.
15. Bureaus of Mines and Railroads were established.
16. Journalists were encouraged to write on all political subjects.
17. Naval academies and training-ships were ordered. . . .
19. Schools were ordered in connection with all the Chinese legations in foreign countries for the benefit of the children of Chinese in those places.
20. Commercial bureaus were ordered in Shanghai for the encouragement of trade. . . .
25. Schools of instruction in the preparation of tea and silk were ordered established.
26. The slow courier posts were abolished in favor of the Imperial Customs Post.
27. A system of budgets as in Western countries was approved. "

Source— Isaac Taylor Headland, *Court Life in China: The Capital, its Officials and People,* 1909

VOCABULARY

court: the advisors and other functionaries who are found in the company of a monarch

western: relating to Europe and the Americas

1A **SUMMARIZING** What was the emperor's approach to launching the reforms of China?

_____

_____

1B **INFERRING** Why do you think the emperor took this approach to creating reform?

_____

_____

_____

2 **CONSTRUCTING HYPOTHESES** Read the fourth decree and explain its importance.

_____

_____

_____

_____

3 ECONOMICS What economic changes does the emperor seek to implement? Refer to specific decrees in your answer.

_____

_____

_____

_____

_____

4 **EXPLAINING EFFECTS** How does the emperor want China to interact with Western nations?

_____

_____

_____

5 **INTERPRETING** Do you think the emperor shared the views of the radical reformers?

_____

_____

_____

ESSENTIAL QUESTION

How do cultures influence each other?

As you gather evidence to answer the Essential Question, think about:

- how the Japanese responded to Western influences.
- how the Meiji Restoration transformed Japanese culture and politics.
- the cause and effects of Japan's rise as a great world power.

My Notes

_____

_____

_____

_____

_____

_____

The Rise of Modern Japan

DIRECTIONS Search for evidence in the lesson to help you answer the following questions.

1A UNDERSTANDING CHANGE How did Japanese politics shift during the mid-1800s?

_____

_____

_____

_____

1B IDENTIFYING CONNECTIONS How did the West impact the shift in Japanese politics during this time?

_____

_____

_____

_____

_____

2 IDENTIFYING CAUSES Using the chart below, illustrate the chain of events which led to the Meiji Restoration period of Japanese politics.

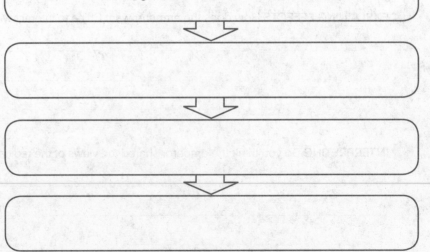

The shogunate's willingness to concede to a U.S. consulate in Japan creates tension among samurai warriors in Satsuma and Choshu.

3A **UNDERSTANDING CHANGE** Explain how the Meiji Restoration changed its perception of Western influence.

_____

_____

_____

3B **EXPLAINING EFFECTS** How did Western influence impact the politics of the Meiji Restoration?

_____

_____

_____

_____

4 CIVICS Use the chart below to identify the differences between the Liberals and the Progressives of the Meiji Restoration.

Progressives	Liberals

5 **IDENTIFYING EFFECTS** How did changes brought on by the Meiji Restoration affect the traditional social system in Japan?

_____

_____

_____

_____

ESSENTIAL QUESTION

How do cultures influence each other?

Political Cartoon of the Russo-Japan War

DIRECTIONS: Use the image to answer the questions.

EXPLORE THE CONTEXT: In the 1800s, Japan was on the rise as an imperialistic power, expanding its territory throughout Asia. This led to competition and rivalry with Russia. In 1904 Japan launched a surprise attack on the Russian naval base at Port Arthur, marking the beginning of the Russo-Japanese War. This cartoon was originally published in the American political journal *Harper's Weekly*, on June 24, 1905, as Russia and Japan contemplated a peace agreement that brought an end to the war.

PRIMARY SOURCE: POLITICAL CARTOON

1 **DESCRIBING** Describe the scene depicted in this cartoon

_____

_____

_____

2 **IDENTIFYING CONNECTIONS** What historical events are referenced in this cartoon?

_____

_____

3 **IDENTIFYING CONTEXT** What does this image say about Japanese and Russian relations during its time?

_____

_____

_____

4 **UNDERSTANDING CONTEXT** How does this cartoon depict the involvement of the United States in the Russo-Japanese conflict?

_____

_____

_____

_____

5 **IDENTIFYING BIAS** How is this image biased?

_____

_____

_____

_____

6 **CIVICS** How does political humor influence public perception?

_____

_____

_____

ESSENTIAL QUESTION
How do cultures influence each other?

VOCABULARY

amity: friendship

paramount: superior; exceeding others

preferential: to give preference to; favor

reciprocally: mutual; shared

Peace in the Russo-Japanese War

DIRECTIONS: Use the text to answer the questions.

EXPLORE THE CONTEXT: The Russo-Japanese War of 1904–1905 was costly both monetarily and in human lives. The Japanese claimed a number of victories, but both countries looked forward to negotiating a peace. U.S. president Theodore Roosevelt mediated a meeting between representatives of the two countries in Portsmouth, New Hampshire, in 1905. Japan accepted a more modest settlement than it had hoped for, and the Treaty of Portsmouth was signed on September 5, 1905.

PRIMARY SOURCE: TREATY

❝ARTICLE I. There shall henceforth be peace and amity between their Majesties the Emperor of Japan and the Emperor of all the Russias, and between their respective States and subjects.

ARTICLE II. The Imperial Russian Government, acknowledging that Japan possesses in Korea paramount political, military and economical interests, engages neither to obstruct nor interfere with measures for guidance, protection and control which the Imperial Government of Japan may find necessary to take in Korea. . . .

ARTICLE III. Japan and Russia mutually engage:

First. — To evacuate completely and simultaneously Manchuria, except the territory affected by the lease of the Liaotung Peninsula, in conformity with the provisions of the additional article I annexed to this treaty, and,

Second. — To restore entirely and completely to the exclusive administration of China all portions of Manchuria now in occupation, or under the control of the Japanese or Russian troops, with the exception of the territory above mentioned.

The Imperial Government of Russia declares that it has not in Manchuria any territorial advantages or preferential or exclusive concessions in the impairment of Chinese sovereignty, or inconsistent with the principle of equal opportunity.

ARTICLE V. The Imperial Russian Government transfers and assigns to the Imperial Government of Japan, with the consent of the Government of China, the lease of Port Arthur, Talien and the adjacent territory and territorial waters, and all rights, privileges and concessions connected with or forming part of such lease, and it also transfers and assigns to the Imperial Government of Japan all public works and properties in the territory affected by the abovementioned lease. . . .

ARTICLE VI. The Imperial Russian Government engages to transfer and assign to the Imperial Government of Japan, without compensation and with the consent of the Chinese Government, the railway between Changchunfu and Kuanchangtsu and Port Arthur, . . .

ARTICLE IX. The Imperial Russian Government cedes to the Imperial Government of Japan in perpetuity and full sovereignty the southern portion of the Island of Saghalin and all the islands adjacent thereto. . . .

ARTICLE XI. Russia engages to arrange with Japan for granting to Japanese subjects rights of fishery along the coasts of the Russian possession in the Japan, Okhotsk and Bering Seas.

Source— *Portsmouth Peace Treaty,* 1905

Tyler, Sydney, 1905. The Japan-Russia War - An Illustrated History of the War in the Far East - The Greatest Conflict of Modern Times. Philadelphia: P. W. Ziegler Co.

1 `HISTORY` What led to the Treaty of Portsmouth?

_____

_____

2 **DETERMINING CENTRAL IDEAS** Based on the excerpt of the Treaty of Portsmouth, who gained more territorial power in East Asia? Explain.

_____

_____

_____

_____

3 **ANALYZING** How did Japan benefit from the Treaty of Portsmouth?

_____

_____

_____

_____

4 **INFERRING** Why did Russia concede so much of its territorial power in East Asia?

_____

_____

5 `HISTORY` How did the events of the Russo-Japanese War, including the terms of the Treaty of Portsmouth, impact the history of Japan as a nation?

_____

_____

6 **INDENTIFYING BIAS** How might the terms of the Treaty of Portsmouth have been seen as unfair?

_____

_____

_____

ESSENTIAL QUESTION

How do cultures influence each other?

My Notes

_____

_____

_____

_____

_____

_____

_____

_____

_____

_____

_____

_____

_____

_____

1 Think About It

Review the supporting questions you developed at the beginning of the chapter. Review the evidence you gathered in the chapter. Were you able to answer each Supporting Question? If there was not enough evidence to answer your Supporting Questions, what additional evidence do you think you need to consider?

_____

_____

_____

2 Organize Your Evidence

Complete the chart below with information you learned about how cultures influence one another and the changes that can result from those influences.

Political influence	
Cultural influence	
Religious influence	
Class influence	

③ Write About It

Work in small groups. With your group, discuss the cultural influences that you have identified and noted in your charts. Compare your charts. Did each member of the group pick the same influences? Describe how the different influences were combined to influence China during the nineteenth century. Explain your answers.

_____

_____

_____

_____

_____

_____

④ Talk About It

Work in small groups. With your group, discuss the potential causes and effects of change throughout East Asia. Compare your charts. Did each member of the group pick the same causes and effects? How did other cultures influence social and political transitions in East Asia? How did culture in East Asia transition from ancient to modern? Were the transitions for the better? Explain your answers.

⑤ Connect to the Essential Question

Create a visual essay that helps to answer the Essential Question: *How do cultures influence each other?* Use the essay as a means of visually illustrating how cultures can influence each other in terms of art, society, and politics. Your visual essay should include relevant images, music, or animation. Essays could be in the form of a drawing, collage, video, or slideshow.

CITIZENSHIP
TAKING ACTION

MAKE CONNECTIONS This chapter covered the struggle between the old and the new that was taking place in China at the turn of the nineteenth century. As countries in East Asia began to modernize their economies as a result of Western influence, so, too, did their cultures begin to modernize. For example, the traditional Confucian ways of China began to disintegrate as a result of younger generations breaking out of those traditions. Does the struggle between new and old still exist? In what ways do earlier generations differ from your generation?

DIRECTIONS: Interview someone from a previous generation, for example, Generation X or a Baby Boomer, and discuss the ways in which your generations are similar or different. Identify some biases you may have towards each other's generations. Identify the positive outcomes that occur as a result of one generation influencing the other. Present the information from your interviews to the class.

_____

_____

_____

_____

_____

_____

_____

_____

_____

_____

_____

World War I and the Russian Revolution

ESSENTIAL QUESTION

Why do politics often lead to war?

Think about political circumstances that lead to war, as well as social and economic factors.

TALK ABOUT IT

Discuss with a partner what type of information you would need in order to understand how political conflicts, national alliances, and imperialistic motivations can lead to war. For example, one question might be, "What were the political conditions before World War I?"

DIRECTIONS: Now write down three additional questions that will help you explain how tension between nations, foreign alliances, imperialism, and nationalism are factors that can pave the way to war.

MY RESEARCH QUESTIONS

Supporting Question 1:

_____

_____

Supporting Question 2:

_____

_____

Supporting Question 3:

_____

_____

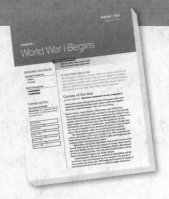

ESSENTIAL QUESTION

Why do politics often lead to war?

As you gather evidence to answer the Essential Question, think about:

- factors that led to the likelihood of World War I.
- how imperialism caused tension among nations.
- the impact of industrialization on modern warfare.

My Notes

World War I Begins

DIRECTIONS Search for evidence in the lesson to help you answer the following questions

1 **IDENTIFYING CONNECTIONS** How did nationalism and militarism contribute to the likelihood of war?

_____

_____

_____

_____

2A **EXPLAINING CAUSES** Explain how the rise of militarization was influenced by competition.

_____

_____

_____

2B **IDENTIFYING CONNECTIONS** Use the chart below to list which rival countries were central to the conflict that led to World War I.

Triple Alliance	Triple Entente

3 **DRAWING CONCLUSIONS** Why did countries form alliances? What was the purpose?

_____

_____

_____

4 **RELATING EVENTS** What series of circumstances pushed European countries towards World War I? Use the flowchart below to organize information.

```
┌─────────────────────────────────────────────┐
│                                             │
└─────────────────────────────────────────────┘
                      ↓
┌─────────────────────────────────────────────┐
│                                             │
└─────────────────────────────────────────────┘
                      ↓
┌─────────────────────────────────────────────┐
│                                             │
└─────────────────────────────────────────────┘
                      ↓
┌─────────────────────────────────────────────┐
│                                             │
└─────────────────────────────────────────────┘
                      ↓
┌─────────────────────────────────────────────┐
│                                             │
└─────────────────────────────────────────────┘
```

5 **HISTORY** Why did the assassination of Archduke Francis Ferdinand in Bosnia cause Germany to get involved?

_____

_____

_____

6 **SUMMARIZING** What were the details of the Schlieffen Plan?

_____

_____

_____

_____

Copyright © McGraw-Hill Education   von Bethmann-Hollweg, Theobald. 1914. Reprinted 2014 by John Hance. Chaos, Confusion, and Political Ignorance – June 28-August 5, 1914: The Untold Truth About the Start of World War II. Trafford Publishing.

ESSENTIAL QUESTION

Why do politics often lead to war?

A "Blank Check" from Germany

DIRECTIONS: Use the text to answer the questions.

EXPLORE THE CONTEXT: After the assassination of the heir to the Hapsburg throne, Archduke Francis Ferdinand, Austria-Hungary sought support for a conflict with Serbia but was concerned about Russian support of Serbia, a fellow Slavic country. Austria-Hungarian Foreign Minister Count Leopold von Berchtold sent a telegraph from Emperor Francis Joseph of Austria-Hungary to Germany. A response from German Imperial Chancellor, Theobald von Bethmann-Hollweg, on behalf of Kaiser Wilhelm II of Germany, is below. In this telegram, Wilhelm II offers his full support to Austria-Hungary in its dealings with Serbia, essentially a "blank check" for war.

PRIMARY SOURCE: TELEGRAM

66 Telegram from the Imperial Chancellor, von Bethmann-Hollweg, to the German Ambassador at Vienna. Tschirschky, July 6, 1914 Berlin, July 6, 1914 Confidential. For Your Excellency's personal information and guidance The Austro-Hungarian Ambassador yesterday delivered to the Emperor a confidential personal letter from the Emperor Francis Joseph, which depicts the present situation from the Austro-Hungarian point of view, and describes the measures which Vienna has in view. A copy is now being forwarded to Your Excellency. I replied to Count Szögyény today on behalf of His Majesty that His Majesty sends his thanks to the Emperor Francis Joseph for his letter and would soon answer it personally. In the meantime His Majesty desires to say that he is not blind to the danger which threatens Austria-Hungary and thus the Triple Alliance as a result of the Russian and Serbian Pan-Slavic agitation. Even though His Majesty is known to feel no unqualified confidence in Bulgaria and her ruler, and naturally inclines more toward our old ally Rumania and her Hohenzollern prince, yet he quite understands that the Emperor Francis Joseph, in view of the attitude of Rumania and of the danger of a new Balkan alliance aimed directly at the Danube Monarchy, is anxious to bring about an understanding between Bulgaria and the Triple alliance [...]. His Majesty will, further more, make an effort at Bucharest, according to the wishes of the Emperor Francis Joseph, to influence King Carol to the fulfilment of the duties of his alliance, to the renunciation of Serbia, and to the suppression of the Rumanian agitations directed against Austria-Hungary. Finally, as far as concerns Serbia, His Majesty, of course, cannot interfere in the dispute now going on between Austria-Hungary and that country, as it is a matter not within his competence. The Emperor Francis Joseph may, however, rest assured that His Majesty will faithfully stand by Austria-Hungary, as is required by the obligations of his alliance and of his ancient friendship. BETHMANN-HOLLWEG **99**

Source— Telegram from the Imperial Chancellor von Bethmann-Hollweg to the German Ambassador at Vienna, July 6, 1914

VOCABULARY

agitation: state of being anxious

renunciation: rejection

competence: efficiency

1 **SUMMARIZING** What is Chancellor von Bethmann-Hollweg communicating with this telegram?

_____

_____

_____

2 **UNDERSTANDING CONTEXT** Why would Germany support Austria-Hungary?

_____

_____

3 **CITING TEXT EVIDENCE** What did it mean when Germany issued Austria-Hungary what was called a "blank check?"

_____

_____

_____

4 **INFERRING** What does Chancellor von Bethmann-Hollweg say regarding Bulgaria?

_____

_____

_____

5 **SUMMARIZING** Based on this telegraph, how were relations between Austria-Hungary and Romania during this time?

_____

_____

_____

_____

6 **HISTORY** Is this telegraph an important World War I document? Why?

_____

_____

_____

ESSENTIAL QUESTION

Why do politics often lead to war?

Austria-Hungary's Ultimatum

DIRECTIONS: Use the text to answer the questions.

EXPLORE THE CONTEXT: On July 22, 1914, one month after the assassination of Archduke Francis Ferdinand, Austria-Hungary issued an ultimatum to Serbia. If the terms of the ultimatum were not agreed upon, Serbia would face military attack. Serbia agreed to all but one of the demands made by Austria-Hungary, thus inciting World War I.

PRIMARY SOURCE: DECLARATION

The Austro-Hungarian Ultimatum to Serbia

❝ This declaration shall be brought to the attention of the Royal army simultaneously by an order of the day from His Majesty the King, and by publication in the official organ of the army.

The Royal Serbian Government will furthermore pledge itself

1. to suppress every publication which shall incite to hatred and contempt of the Monarchy, and the general tendency of which shall be directed against the territorial integrity of the latter;

2. to proceed at once to the dissolution of the Narodna Odbrana to confiscate all of its means of propaganda, and in the same manner to proceed against the other unions and associations in Serbia which occupy themselves with propaganda against Austria-Hungary; the Royal Government will take such measures as are necessary to make sure that the dissolved associations may not continue their activities under other names or in other forms;

3. to eliminate without delay from public instruction in Serbia, everything, whether connected with the teaching corps or with the methods of teaching, that serves or may serve to nourish the propaganda against Austria-Hungary;

4. to remove from the military and administrative service in general all officers and officials who have been guilty of carrying on the propaganda against Austria-Hungary, whose names the Imperial and Royal Government reserves the right to make known to the Royal Government when communicating the material evidence now in its possession;

5. to agree to the cooperation in Serbia of the organs of the Imperial and Royal Government in the suppression of the subversive movement directed against the integrity of the Monarchy; . . .

10. to inform the Imperial and Royal Government without delay of the execution of the measures comprised in the foregoing points.

The Imperial and Royal Government awaits the reply of the Royal Government by Saturday, the twenty-fifth instant, at 6 p.m., at the latest. ❞

Source— Austro-Hungarian Ultimatum to Serbia, 1914

VOCABULARY

ultimatum: final demand

latter: the second person, item, or idea mentioned

dissolution: the ending; conclusion

Narodna Odbrana: Serbian nationalist organization

subversive: troublemaking

1 **DETERMINING CENTRAL IDEAS** What kind of ultimatum was given to Serbia by Austria-Hungary?

_____

_____

_____

2 **UNDERSTANDING CONTEXT** Based on the source, what were relations like between Serbia and Austria-Hungary during this time?

_____

_____

_____

3 **RELATING EVENTS** The source was written on July 22, 1914. Based on your text, what events happened during this time?

_____

_____

4 **INTERPRETING** Does the ultimatum address the assassination of Archduke Ferdinand at the hands of Serbian radicals?

_____

_____

_____

5 **DETERMINING MEANING** What is meant by "cooperation in Serbia of the organs of the Imperial and Royal Government in the suppression of the subversive movement directed against the integrity of the Monarchy"?

_____

_____

6 **HISTORY** How might this be an important historical document?

_____

_____

_____

World War I

DIRECTIONS Search for evidence in the lesson to help you answer the following questions.

1 **DETERMINING MEANING** How does propaganda feed into a war?

_____

_____

_____

_____

_____

_____

_____

2A **RELATING EVENTS** How did the Germans and the French use trenches during the war?

_____

_____

_____

_____

_____

_____

_____

2B **INTERPRETING** Did trench warfare help the troops? Why or why not?

_____

_____

_____

_____

_____

_____

ESSENTIAL QUESTION

Why do politics often lead to war?

As you gather evidence to answer the Essential Question, think about:

- how trench warfare affected the war.
- how the entry of the United States played into the war.
- how and why World War I became a total war.

My Notes

_____

_____

_____

_____

_____

_____

3 ECONOMICS Use the chart below to break down how the governments responded to the long-time war needs.

Need	Solution
More men were needed to continue the war	
Governments needed to expand their power over economies	
	European nations set up planned economies

4A SUMMARIZING What is the Defence of the Realm Act?

_____

_____

_____

_____

4B IDENTIFYING CAUSES What caused the British Parliament to pass the Defence of the Realm Act?

_____

_____

_____

ESSENTIAL QUESTION

Why do politics often lead to war?

VOCABULARY

jurisdiction: area of authority

jeopardize: endanger

The British Defence of the Realm Consolidation Act

DIRECTIONS: Use the text to answer the questions.

EXPLORE THE CONTEXT: After World War I, the British Parliament passed the British Defence of the Realm Consolidation Act as a way to control the growing opposition to the war. Many countries used police powers to stop internal dissent. This act allowed the British government to label protestors as traitors and arrest them, censor newspapers and suspend publications.

PRIMARY SOURCE: LEGAL DOCUMENT

Be it enacted . . . as follows

❝1. (1) His Majesty in Council has power during the continuance of the present war to issue regulations for securing the public safety and the defense of the realm, and as to the powers and duties for that purpose of the Admiralty and Army Council and of the members of His Majesty's forces and other persons acting in his behalf; and may by such regulations authorise the trial by courts-martial, or in the case of minor offenses by courts of summary jurisdiction, and punishment of persons committing offences against the regulations and in particular against any of the provisions of such regulations designed

  (a) to prevent persons communicating with the enemy or obtaining information for that purpose or any purpose calculated to jeopardise the success of the operations of any of His Majesty's forces or the forces of his allies or to assist the enemy; or

  (b) to secure the safety of His Majesty's forces and ships and the safety of any means of communication and of railways, ports, and harbours; or

  (c) to prevent the spread of false reports or reports likely to cause disaffection to His Majesty or to interfere with the success of His Majesty's forces by land or sea or to prejudice His Majesty's relations with foreign powers; or

  (d) to secure the navigation of vessels in accordance with directions given by or under the authority of the Admiralty; or

  (e) otherwise to prevent assistance being given to the enemy or the successful prosecution of the war being endangered. . . .

(3) It shall be lawful for the Admiralty or Army Council

  (a) to require that there shall be placed at their disposal the whole or any part of the output of any factory or workshop in which arms, ammunition, or warlike stores and equipment, or any articles required for the production thereof, are manufactured;

  (b) to take possession of, and use for the purpose of, His Majesty's naval or military service any such factory or workshop or any plant thereof; . . .❞

Source— The British Defence of the Realm Consolidation Act, 1914

_____ 1914. Defence of the Realm Consolidation Act. November 27, 1914. Reprinted 2005 by T. Baty and J. H. Morgan. War: Its Conduct and Legal Results. Clark, New Jersey: The Lawbook Exchange, Ltd.

1 **DETERMINING MEANING** Who is the "Majesty in Council" the document is referring to?

_____

_____

_____

2A **ANALYZING EVENTS** What reasons does the British Parliament give to issue this act?

_____

_____

_____

2B **HISTORY** What was going on when the British Parliament passed this act?

_____

_____

_____

3 **SUMMARIZING** What would happen should someone break one of these laws?

_____

_____

_____

4A **ANALYZING TEXT** What does it mean when the act states that the Admiralty or Army Council are allowed "to require that there shall be placed at their disposal the whole or any part of the output of any factory or workshop in which arms, ammunition, or warlike stores and equipment, or any articles required for the production thereof, are manufactured"?

_____

_____

_____

4B **EXPLAINING EFFECTS** Why would the British Parliament include the text in the previous questions into this act?

_____

_____

ESSENTIAL QUESTION

Why do politics often lead to war?

VOCABULARY

torpedoing: an attack by a torpedo

hitherto: until now

loath: refuse

countenance: appearance

imperative: necessary

Woodrow Wilson on the Sinking of the *Lusitania*

DIRECTIONS: Use the text to answer the questions.

EXPLORE THE CONTEXT: U.S. president Woodrow Wilson sent this letter on May 13, 1915, under the signature of Secretary of State William Jennings Bryan. It was written after the *Lusitania*, owned by the Cunard Line, was sunk by a German U-boat. The ship, known for its speed in crossing the Atlantic, sunk within 20 minutes. Of the 1,959 passengers and crew aboard, 1,198 perished, including 128 Americans.

PRIMARY SOURCE: LETTER

66 . . . In view of recent acts of the German authorities in violation of American rights on the high seas which culminated in the torpedoing and sinking of the British steamship *Lusitania* on May 7, 1915, by which over 100 American citizens lost their lives, it is clearly wise and desirable that the Government of the United States and the Imperial German Government should come to a clear and full understanding as to the grave situation which has resulted. . . .

Recalling the humane and enlightened attitude hitherto assumed by the Imperial German Government in matters of international right, and particularly with regard to the freedom of the seas; having learned to recognize the German views and the German influence in the field of international obligation as always engaged upon the side of justice and humanity; and having understood the instructions of the Imperial German Government to its naval commanders to be upon the same plane of human action prescribed by the naval codes of other nations, the Government of the United States was loath to believe . . . that these acts, so absolutely contrary to the rules, the practices, and the spirit of modern warfare, could have the countenance or sanction of that great Government. . . .

The Government of the United States, therefore, desires to call the attention of the Imperial German Government with the utmost earnestness to the fact that the objection to their present method of attack against the trade of their enemies lies in the practical impossibility of employing submarines in the destruction of commerce without disregarding those rules of fairness, reason, justice, and humanity, which all modern opinion regards as imperative. . . .

The Government and the people of the United States look to the Imperial German Government for just, prompt, and enlightened action in this vital matter with the greater confidence because the United States and Germany are bound together not only for special ties of friendship but also by the explicit stipulations of the treaty of 1828 between the United States and the Kingdom of Prussia. . . . 99

Source— Woodrow Wilson, First Lusitania Note to Germany, 1915

1A **SUMMARIZING** What is this note documenting?

_____

_____

1B **UNDERSTANDING CONTEXT** Why would it be important to write a letter about this event?

_____

_____

_____

_____

2A **IDENTIFYING PERSPECTIVES** What was the U.S. participation with World War I at the time of the letter?

_____

_____

_____

2B **DETERMINING POINT OF VIEW** What was President Wilson's position on joining the war based on this letter?

_____

_____

_____

_____

3 **CITING TEXT EVIDENCE** What treaty did President Wilson mention as a reason to avoid joining the war?

_____

_____

_____

4 HISTORY How could this situation have pushed the U.S. to join World War I?

_____

_____

_____

The Russian Revolution

DIRECTIONS Search for evidence in the lesson to help you answer the following questions.

1 **IDENTIFYING CAUSES** Use the chart below to list the reasons Russia was not prepared for World War I.

Reasons Russia was not prepared for World War I
1
2
3

2A **IDENTIFYING CONNECTIONS** Who was Grigory Rasputin, and how did he affect Czar Nicholas II's power?

_____

_____

_____

_____

2B **RELATING EVENTS** Why was Rasputin assassinated?

_____

_____

_____

ESSENTIAL QUESTION

Why do politics often lead to war?

As you gather evidence to answer the Essential Question, think about:

- what led the people of Russia to revolt during the war.
- what type of actions occurred during the Russian Revolution.
- how the revolution inspired new political movements.

My Notes

_____

_____

_____

_____

_____

_____

_____

3A **ANALYZING INFORMATION** Who were the Bolsheviks?

_____

_____

_____

_____

_____

_____

_____

3B **ANALYZING EVENTS** How did the Bolsheviks overthrow the provisional government?

_____

_____

_____

_____

_____

_____

_____

4 **EXPLAINING ISSUES** What started the civil war in Russia?

_____

_____

_____

_____

_____

_____

_____

ESSENTIAL QUESTION

Why do politics often lead to war?

Street Demonstration in Petrograd

DIRECTIONS: Use the image to answer the questions.

EXPLORE THE CONTEXT: The Russian Revolution was partly fueled by a series of strikes, led by working-class women, in March 1917. The strikes shut down factories throughout Petrograd, the Russian capital, and prompted Czar Nicholas II to step down from power. This did not satisfy the workers. Protests and street demonstrations continued throughout 1917; the protest shown in the photo happened in Petrograd (St. Petersburg) in April 1917.

PRIMARY SOURCE: PHOTO

1 **UNDERSTANDING CONTEXT** What are the reasons people started marching during the Russian Revolution?

_____

_____

_____

_____

2 **IDENTIFYING PERSPECTIVES** Why were the workers unsatisfied with the czar stepping down?

_____

_____

_____

_____

3 **IDETERMINING MEANING** How would the soviet of Petrograd have likely responded to this protest?

_____

_____

_____

_____

4 HISTORY How did the return to Russia of V. I. Lenin affect the protests against the government?

_____

_____

_____

_____

5 **IDENTIFYING EFFECTS** How did the provisional government's decision to stay in World War I change the political climate?

_____

_____

_____

_____

Lenin Establishes the Cheka

Lenin, Vladimir. 1917. Note to F. E. Dzerhinsky With a Draft of a Decree on Fighting Counter-Revolutionaries and Saboteurs. Reprinted 1964 by Yuri Sdobnikov and George Hanna. V. I. Lenin - Collected Works. Volume 26: September 1917-February 1918. Moscow: Progress Publishers.
Copyright © McGraw-Hill Education

ESSENTIAL QUESTION

Why do politics often lead to war?

DIRECTIONS: Use the text to answer the questions.

EXPLORE THE CONTEXT: The Communists gained control of Russia after they won the civil war. They established a policy of war communism that was used to ensure regular supplies for the Red Army. The cheka, a secret Red police, began a Red Terror that aimed at destroying the opposition. This decree established the cheka in a letter from V. I. Lenin to Bolshevik leader Felix Dzerhinsky.

PRIMARY SOURCE: LETTER

❝ON FIGHTING COUNTER-REVOLUTION AND SABOTEURS
The bourgeoisie, the landholders, and all the rich classes are making desperate efforts to undermine the revolution, the aim of which is to safeguard the interests of the workers, the working and exploited masses. The bourgeoisie are prepared to committ the most heinous crimes; they are bribing the outcast and degraded elements of society and plying them with drink to use them in riots. The supporters of the bourgeoisie, particularly among the higher clerical staff, bank officials, and so on, are sabotaging their hard work, and are organising strikes to thwart the government's measures for the realisation of socialist reforms. They have even gone so far as to sabotoge food distribution, thereby menacing millions of people with famine.
Urgent measures are necessary to fight the counter-revolutionaries and saboteurs. In virtue of this, the Concil of People's Commissars decrees. . . .
(1) Persons belonging to the wealthy classes (i.e., with incomes of 500 rubles or more per month, and owners of urban real estate, stocks and shares, or money amounting to over 1,000 rubles), and also all employees of banks, joint-stock companies, state and public institutions, shall within three days present to their house committees written statements in three copies over their own signatures and indicating their address, income, place of employment and their occupation. . . .
(3) Persons guilty of contravening the present law (failing to submit statements, giving false information, etc.) and members of house committees infringing the regulations governing the collection, filing and presentation of these statements to the institutions mentioned above shall be liable to a fine of up to 5,000 rubles for each infringement, or to imprisonment up to one year, or shall be sent to the front, depending on the nature of the offence.
(4) Persons sabotaging the work of, or declining to work in, banks, state and public institutions, joint-stock companies, railways, etc., shall be liable to similar punishment. . . . ❞

Source— Vladimir Lenin, *Collected Works,* vol. 26, 1972

VOCABULARY

bourgeoisie: working class

pogroms: a bloodbath; massacre

partisans: biased; one-sided

commissars: officials in an communist government

decree: act; proclamation

contravening: disobeying

1A SUMMARIZING What rules are stated in the letter?

_____

_____

_____

_____

_____

1B UNDERSTANDING CONTEXT What does Lenin write is the reason for these rules?

_____

_____

_____

2 ECONOMICS How does Lenin believe the wealthy class is undermining the revolution?

_____

_____

_____

3 CITING TEXT EVIDENCE Who does the letter consider the wealthy class?

_____

_____

_____

4 IDENTIFYING BIAS Does this letter reveal bias? Why or why not?

_____

_____

_____

_____

5 INTERPRETING What can be assumed about Dzerhinsky?

_____

_____

_____

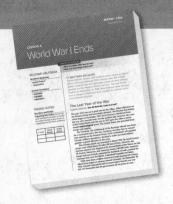

ESSENTIAL QUESTION

Why do politics often lead to war?

As you gather evidence to answer the Essential Question, consider:

- the political and social factors that contributed to the end of World War I.

- how the rise of Communism affected Europe.

- how the rise of Communism influenced the politics of the Central Powers.

My Notes

_____

_____

_____

_____

_____

_____

_____

World War I Ends

DIRECTIONS Search for evidence in the lesson to help you answer the following questions.

1 **UNDERSTANDING CONTEXT** What caused the end of World War I?

_____

_____

_____

2 **IDENTIFYING STEPS** How did German politics change during and after the war? Use the chart below to organize your answers.

Changes in German Politics

3 CIVICS What political reforms developed during and after World War I?

_____

_____

_____

_____

_____

_____

_____

4 **SUMMARIZING** How did U.S. president Woodrow Wilson influence peace negotiations after the war?

_____

_____

_____

_____

5 **IDENTIFYING BIASES** Germany regarded the Treaty of Versailles an "unfair compromise." Why?

_____

_____

_____

_____

_____

_____

6 **EVALUATING** What were some major changes in post–World War I society?

_____

_____

_____

_____

_____

Clemenceau's Opening Address at Versailles

DIRECTIONS: Use the text to answer the questions.

EXPLORE THE CONTEXT: Georges Clemenceau was Prime Minister of France from 1917 to 1920. Clemenceau gave the opening address at the Paris Peace Conference in 1919. During the conference, Clemenceau advocated that reparations be made by Germany for the damage sustained by the allied countries.

PRIMARY SOURCE: SPEECH

" . . . It is a great, splendid, and noble ambition which has come to all of us. It is desirable that success should crown our efforts. This cannot take place unless we all have firmly fixed and clearly determined ideas on what we wish to do.

I said in the chamber a few days ago, and I wish to repeat here, that success is not possible unless we remain firmly united. We have come together as friends; we must leave this hall as friends.

That, gentlemen, is the first thought that comes to me. All else must be subordinated to the necessity of a closer and closer union among the nations which have taken part in this great war and to the necessity of remaining friends. For the league of nations is here. It is yourself. It is for you to make it live and to make it live we must have it really in our hearts.

As I told President Wilson a few days ago, there is no sacrifice that I am not willing to make in order to accomplish this, and I do not doubt that you all have the same sentiment. We will make these sacrifices, but on the condition that we endeavor impartially to conciliate interests apparently contradictory on the higher plane of a greater, happier and better humanity.

That, gentlemen, is what I had to say to you. I am touched beyond words at the evidence of good will and friendship which you show me.

The program of this conference has been laid down by President Wilson. It is no longer the peace of a more or less vast territory, no longer the peace of continents. It is the peace of nations that is to be made. . . . "

Source— Opening Address as Conference President,
Georges Clemenceau, January 18, 1919

VOCABULARY

crown: be triumphant

subordinated: treat something or someone with lesser importance

sentiment: thought; idea

Clemenceau, Georges. 1919. Quoted in The Chicago Daily News Almanac and Yearbook for 1920. Edited by James Langland. Chicago: The Chicago Daily News Company.

Copyright © McGraw-Hill Education

1 **DETERMINING CENTRAL IDEAS** What is Clemenceau expressing in his address?

_____

_____

_____

2 **INTERPRETING** What does Clemenceau mean when he states, "it is no longer the peace of a more or less vast territory, no longer the peace of continents. It is peace of nations that must be made"?

_____

_____

_____

3 **IDENTIFYING CONNECTIONS** Based on information from the chapter, what type influence did Clemenceau have at the Peace Conference?

_____

_____

4 **IDENTIFYING BIAS** What were potential ulterior motivations behind Clemenceau's address?

_____

_____

_____

_____

5 CIVICS How did the peaceful negotiations described by Clemenceau impact politics?

_____

_____

_____

_____

6 **EVALUATING** How did the League of Nations pave the way for present-day international organizations?

_____

ESSENTIAL QUESTION

Why do politics often lead to war?

League of Nations

DIRECTIONS: Use the text to answer the questions.

EXPLORE THE CONTEXT: This is the section of the contract calling for assistance to be given to a member of the League of Nations that experiences aggression from an outside source. It was signed by major Allied governments following WWI, but U.S. president Woodrow Wilson was unable to fulfill his obligation to join because the Senate refused approve the plan. Many Republicans believed that it was better not to become involved in international disputes, and under the U.S. Constitution, the president may not ratify a treaty unless the Senate consents by a two-thirds vote.

PRIMARY SOURCE: LEGAL CONTRACT

❝THE HIGH CONTRACTING PARTIES,

In order to promote international co-operation and to achieve international peace and security

> by the acceptance of obligations not to resort to war,
>
> by the prescription of open, just and honourable relations between nations,
>
> by the firm establishment of the understandings of international law as the actual rule of conduct among Governments, and
>
> by the maintenance of justice and a scrupulous respect for all treaty obligations in the dealings of organised peoples with one another,

Agree to this Covenant of the League of Nations. . . .

ARTICLE 10.

The Members of the League undertake to respect and preserve as against external aggression the territorial integrity and existing political independence of all Members of the League. In case of any such aggression or in case of any threat or danger of such aggression the Council shall advise upon the means by which this obligation shall be fulfilled. ❞

Source— The Covenant of the League of Nations, 1924

VOCABULARY

covenant: contract

scrupulous: diligent

1 **INTERPRETING** When, and in what circumstances, was this document written?

_____

_____

_____

2 **IDENTIFYING CONTEXT** What was the political climate during this time?

_____

_____

_____

3 **SUMMARIZING** What was the purpose of this document?

_____

_____

_____

4 **DETERMINING CENTRAL IDEAS** Article 10 states that members of the League are expected to "preserve as against external aggression the territorial integrity and existing political independence of all Members of the League." What does this mean?

_____

_____

_____

_____

_____

5 **IDENTIFYING CAUSES** In the wake of World War I, why would this type of agreement be necessary?

_____

_____

_____

6 HISTORY How are the alliances of the Triple Entente and the alliances of the League of Nations different? How are they similar?

_____

_____

_____

_____

ESSENTIAL QUESTION

Why do politics often lead to war?

My Notes

_____

_____

_____

_____

_____

_____

_____

_____

_____

_____

_____

_____

_____

_____

_____

1 Think About It

Review the supporting questions you developed at the beginning of the chapter. Review the evidence you gathered in the chapter. Were you able to answer each Supporting Question? If there was not enough evidence to answer your Supporting Questions, what additional evidence do you think you need to consider?

_____

_____

_____

2 Organize Your Evidence

Complete the chart below with information you learned about World War I and the political movements that emerged as a result of the war. Use the chart below to describe each of the political beliefs and ideals.

Political belief or ideal	Description
Militarism	
Industrialization	
Soviets	
Bolsheviks / Communists	

❸ Talk About It

Work in small groups. With your group, discuss the events that occurred during World War I and how the events led to the Russian Revolution. Consider each row on your chart as you talk about which political movements were the most important in motivating Russians to make a change. Compare your charts. Did each member of the group pick the same things? Were the motivations you identified necessary to make a change? Take notes about your discussion below.

❹ Write About It

After your group works on in the Talk About It activity, consider what your group discussed. Specifically, consider how politics, policies, consequences, and contexts were influenced by the political movements during World War I that your group identified and noted down in your charts. Finally, think about the motivations you identified necessary to make a change. Why did you choose them? Are there other factors that you discovered in your small group? Explain your answers.

_____

_____

_____

_____

_____

❺ Connect to the Essential Question

Following your work in the Talk About It and Write About It activities, choose two political events that lead to the Russian Revolution. Then, write an essay describing those two events and why you consider them the most significant in setting Russia on a path to the civil war. Be sure to include historical background and facts as well as your reasoning regarding their significance.

Your essay should include an introduction that sets the stage, providing historical background information necessary for the reader, as well as a thesis statement. The body of the essay should gather and organize information as evidence to support your thesis statement.

CITIZENSHIP
TAKING ACTION

MAKE CONNECTIONS Use what you have learned in the chapter to produce a slideshow presentation comparing World War I to an armed conflict that is currently taking place anywhere in the world. Using images, multimedia, and other sources, demonstrate how political, social, and economic change interacts during war. Include political figures and important events. Title your slideshow something that highlights the theme of your presentation. Then, present your slideshow to the class.

_____

_____

_____

_____

_____

_____

_____

_____

_____

_____

_____

_____

_____

_____

_____

_____

_____

_____

_____

The West Between Wars

ESSENTIAL QUESTION

How might political change impact society?

Think about how the United States and Europe recovered from World War I. Germany's post-war experience was vastly different from that of the United States, which enjoyed the Roaring Twenties. The entire Western world saw major political changes to society and government leading, eventually, to another world war.

TALK ABOUT IT

With a partner, discuss the sort of information you would need to discover how the aftermath of World War I brought about changes in regimes and economies that altered life for many people in Europe. For example, you might ask, "How did the Treaty of Versailles affect the economy of Germany and other countries in Europe?"

DIRECTIONS: Now write down three additional questions that will help you explain the political changes that World War I brought about.

MY RESEARCH QUESTIONS

Supporting Question 1:

_____

_____

Supporting Question 2:

_____

_____

Supporting Question 3:

_____

_____

Instability After World War I

DIRECTIONS Search for evidence in the lesson to help you answer the following questions.

1A **SUMMARIZING** What terms of the Treaty of Versailles became important in the aftermath of World War I?

_____

_____

_____

_____

1B **INTERPRETING** How stable was the peace that resulted from the Treaty of Versailles?

_____

_____

_____

_____

_____

_____

2A **IDETERMINING MEANING** The word "depression" comes from the Latin *deprimere*, which means "to press down." How does the root help you determine the meaning of the word in economic terms?

_____

_____

_____

2B **EXPLAINING CAUSES** What caused the Great Depression in Europe?

_____

_____

_____

_____

ESSENTIAL QUESTION

How might political change impact society?

As you gather evidence to answer the Essential Question, think about:

- how countries on both sides of World War I dealt with the aftermath of the war.
- how the Great Depression came to be.
- how different countries responded to the Great Depression.

My Notes

_____

_____

_____

_____

_____

_____

_____

3 **INTERPRETING** How did each of the following countries respond to the Great Depression?

	Response to the Great Depression
Germany	
France	
Great Britain	
United States	

4 ECONOMICS How did the economic shifts of the Great Depression impact Europe politically? Use the following chart to organize your answers.

Country	Political Changes
France	
United States	
Germany	
Great Britain	

ESSENTIAL QUESTION

How might political change impact society?

VOCABULARY

solemnly: seriously

recourse: something one turns to for protection

renounce: to reject

pacific: peaceful

The Kellogg-Briand Pact

DIRECTIONS: Read the remarks from President Hoover. Then respond to the questions that follow.

EXPLORE THE CONTEXT: The Kellogg-Briand Pact was an international agreement signed in 1928. The countries who signed it initially included Germany, France, and the United States. Many other countries followed suit. If a country decided to go against the treaty, they could possibly go to war. In the remarks below, President of the United States Herbert Hoover comments on the treaty. Hoover served as president after World War I and during the Great Depression. He was largely considered an unpopular president because of his inability to end the depression.

PRIMARY SOURCE: PRESIDENTIAL REMARKS

❝ IN APRIL 1928, as a result of discussions between our Secretary of State of the United States and the Minister of Foreign Affairs of France, the President directed Secretary Kellogg to propose to the nations of the world that they should enter into a binding agreement as follows:

"Article 1—The high contracting parties solemnly declare in the names of their respective peoples that they condemn recourse to war for the solution of international controversies, and renounce it as an instrument of national policy in their relations with one another.

"Article 2—The high contracting parties agree that the settlement or solution of all disputes or conflicts of whatever nature or of whatever origin they may be, which may arise among them, shall never be sought except by pacific means."

That was a proposal to the conscience and idealism of civilized nations. It suggested a new step in international law, rich with meaning, pregnant with new ideas in the conduct of world relations. It represented a platform from which there is instant appeal to the public opinion of the world as to specific acts and deeds. ❞

Source— President Herbert Hoover, "Remarks Upon Proclaiming the Treaty for the Renunciation of War," July 24, 1929

1 **SUMMARIZING** What does the Kellogg-Briand Pact call for?

_____

_____

_____

2 **CITING TEXT EVIDENCE** What is President Hoover's attitude toward the Kellogg-Briand Pact? Cite evidence from the text to support your answer.

_____

_____

_____

3A **ANALYZING TEXT PRESENTATION** What are the main points of Articles 1 and 2?

_____

_____

3B **DETERMINING POINT OF VIEW** What was the author's purpose in arranging Article 1 before Article 2?

_____

_____

_____

4 **DETERMINING CONTEXT** The excerpt of the Kellogg-Briand Pact says nations must seek out peaceful ways to resolve conflict but is not specific. What are some ways a nation might peacefully resolve conflict?

_____

_____

_____

5 **CIVICS** Why do you think Hoover expressed support for the Kellogg-Briand Pact?

_____

_____

_____

_____

6 **IDENTIFYING CAUSES** What does the Kellogg-Briand Pact suggest about the state of mind of the countries who signed it?

_____

_____

ESSENTIAL QUESTION
How might political change impact society?

VOCABULARY

decree: an order issued by an official

admonish: to reprimand or warn

fatherland: a nation of one's "father" or "ancestors"

decisive: determined; certain

objective: independent; unbiased

Hitler Addresses the Reich President

DIRECTIONS: Use the text to answer the questions.

EXPLORE THE CONTEXT: The passage below is part of a mass pamphlet issued by the Nazis after Reich president Hindenburg released the first of a series of emergency decrees on December 1, 1931. These decrees banned political meetings, uniforms, and insignia, among other things, with the hope to reduce public political tension and conflict. Hitler's "open letter" was released twelve days after the fourth emergency decree was issued.

PRIMARY SOURCE: LETTER

" I read the following sentences in your commentary on the Fourth Emergency Decree issued by the Reich President:

"I will continue to resist all efforts by parties to tear apart the German people into two enemy camps in the midst of our spiritual tension and material need. An ancient instinct admonishes all peoples to set aside internal controversies when the fatherland stands at the decisive hour for political action."

Although each of the emergency decrees issued by your government claimed to be at a "decisive moment" of political action, I take it from the extensive introductory speech that this most recent emergency decree is supposed to have even greater significance, since the hour is seen as particularly serious. . . .

In your speech, Mr. Reich Chancellor, you intentionally attack the National Socialist movement, indirectly comparing it to the unity of the rest of the population. Since this attack against a part of the German people includes a reference to me as its leader, I see myself obligated to defend this part of the mass of the people that I lead. . . .

The emergency decree hardly supports an attack against the National Socialist movement since as you yourself grant in your speech, Mr. Reich Chancellor, the economic crisis is at least in part the result of the mistakes of previous governments.

We National Socialists had nothing to do with these governments; in fact we always rejected and fought their mistakes that have finally been recognized.

Political grounds also provide no reason for this attack against the National Socialist movement or me personally. Even if an objective analysis of my opposition had found no justification for our actions, at the very least a sense of political justice . . . would have to conclude that there were other movements and parties within Germany besides the National Socialist Party that at least in part attack the present system and your government very sharply. Although it has a different worldview, the Communist Party, for example, attacks not only the current system, but even the state, indeed the whole order, and with consciously chosen illegal methods. . . . "

Source— Open Letter from Adolf Hitler to the Reich Chancellor, 1932

1 **SUMMARIZING** What are Hitler's goals in this letter? Cite evidence from the text.

_____

_____

_____

_____

2 **DETERMINING MEANING** What does Hitler mean when he writes, "An ancient instinct admonishes all peoples to set aside internal controversies when the fatherland stands at the decisive hour for political action"?

_____

_____

3 ECONOMICS What was the economic condition of Europe when these decrees were published?

_____

_____

4 **IDENTIFYING CAUSES** What political and social factors likely contributed to Reich president Hindenburg's motivations for issuing the emergency decrees?

_____

_____

_____

5 **DETERMINING POINT OF VIEW** How does Hitler contrast the National Socialist Party with the Communist Party? Why does Hitler likely draw this contrast in his letter?

_____

_____

_____

_____

6 HISTORY How do you think the people of Germany felt about the emergency decrees?

_____

_____

_____

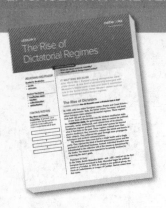

The Rise of Dictatorial Regimes

DIRECTIONS Search for evidence in the lesson to help you answer the following questions.

1A DETERMINING MEANING When you break down the word *totalitarian*, what about that word suggests its meaning?

_____

_____

_____

_____

_____

1B EXPLAINING CAUSE AND EFFECT Given what you know about the aftermath of World War I, why do you think totalitarian governments were on the rise?

_____

_____

_____

_____

_____

_____

_____

2A SUMMARIZING What are some of the strategies totalitarian governments used to maintain power?

_____

_____

_____

_____

_____

_____

ESSENTIAL QUESTION

How might political change impact society?

As you gather evidence to answer the Essential Question, think about:

- what causes instability.
- how economic instability affects other aspects of society.
- how significant changes in government impact life.

My Notes

_____

_____

_____

_____

_____

_____

2B **INTERPRETING** How did Mussolini's totalitarian government compare to Stalin's?

Italy   Both   USSR

3 **DETERMINING CENTRAL IDEAS** How is an authoritarian government different from a totalitarian government?

_____

_____

_____

_____

4 CIVICS What are the similarities and differences between the totalitarian governments of the early 1900s and contemporary democracies? In the bottom of the graphic organizer, write which political structure you agree with most, and explain why.

Similarities	Differences

The Dekulakization of Russia

1931. Progress Report on the Eviction and Relocation of Kulak Families. July 12, 1931. Republished 1997 in Revelations from the Russian Archives. Edited by Diane P. Koenker and Ronald D. Bachman. Washington: Library of Congress.

ESSENTIAL QUESTION

How might political change impact society?

DIRECTIONS: Read the excerpt from the dekulakization files. Then respond to the questions that follow.

EXPLORE THE CONTEXT: Stalin initiated his first Five-Year Plan to transition from an agricultural country to an industrial one. The plan eliminated private farms, and peasants resisted by hoarding crops and killing livestock. From 1929–1932, the USSR launched a violent campaign against richer peasants, called kulaks. The Soviet government deported, arrested, and sometimes executed millions of them. The USSR's goal at the time was to build socialism in the countryside, and the kulaks were seen as a threat to that goal. The text below is an excerpt from a series of declassified and translated Soviet memos.

PRIMARY SOURCE: SOVIET MEMOS

❝DOCUMENT 172 Report on eviction and resettlement of kulaks, July 12 and 14, 1931

II.

PROGRESS OF EVICTION AND RELOCATION

From June I through June 12 of this year we evicted and relocated 134,637 families, including 75,809 families relocated to other regions and 58,828 families relocated within the same region:

A) to Urals:

I) from Ivanovo Industrial Region	3,655 families	18,020 persons to Magnitostroi
2) from Belorussian SSR	4,645 families	20,501 persons to [Magnitostroi]
3) from Ukrainian SSR	31,825 families	131,127 persons to Uralles
4) from North Caucasus krai	15,400 families	71,658 persons to [Uralles]
TOTAL	55,525 families	241,306 persons

The eviction and relocation of kulaks from the Ivanovo Industrial Region, the Belorussian Soviet Socialist Republic, the Ukrainian Soviet Socialist Republic, and North Caucasus krai has been completed. Although all heads of households, i.e., able-bodied men, were completely evicted and relocated, a high dropout rate and high rate of family breakup meant that the numbers of families actually evicted and relocated from the Ivanovo Industrial Region and Belorussian SSR were short of the plan targets by the following amounts:

a) from the Ivanovo Industrial Region	1,345 families
b) from the Belorussian SSR	355 families
TOTAL	1,700 families

On the other hand, the following numbers of families were evicted and relocated over and above the targets from the Ukrainian SSR and North Caucasus Territories:

a) from the Ukrainian SSR	1,825 families
b) from North Caucasus krai	400 families of which 200 were sent to the Uralryb

TOTAL   2,225 families ❞

Source— Declassified Soviet memo on dekulakization, July 1931

VOCABULARY

evicted: forced to leave

krai: border or edge

1A **IDENTIFYING CAUSES** Why did Stalin have the kulaks removed?

_____

_____

_____

1B **DETERMINING CENTRAL IDEAS** How was the removal of the kulaks representative of the kind of government Stalin was seeking to create?

_____

_____

_____

_____

2 **INTERPRETING** Why do you think the Soviet government kept records like this?

_____

_____

_____

3 **IDENTIFYING EFFECTS** How were the kulaks affected by the deportation?

_____

_____

_____

4 **CIVICS** What lessons can be learned from Stalin's deportation tactics here?

_____

_____

_____

5 **IDENTIFYING CONNECTIONS** How is Stalin's policy here an example of political change impacting society?

_____

_____

_____

ESSENTIAL QUESTION

How might political change impact society?

Mussolini Defines *Fascism*

DIRECTIONS: Read the encyclopedia entry by Mussolini. Then respond to the questions that follow.

EXPLORE THE CONTEXT: Benito Mussolini established the first fascist movement in Europe. The word "fascism" comes from *Fascio di Combattimento*, which was Mussolini's political group. Scholars also suggest "fascism" has roots in *fasces*, which was a symbol of bound sticks which meant power in ancient Rome. After the "March on Rome" in 1922, Mussolini came to power in Italy by becoming prime minister. In 1932 Mussolini wrote the entry below for the Italian Encyclopedia.

PRIMARY SOURCE: ENCYCLOPEDIA ENTRY

66 Fascism, the more it considers and observes the future and the development of humanity quite apart from political considerations of the moment, believes neither in the possibility nor the utility of perpetual peace. It thus repudiates the doctrine of Pacifism -- born of a renunciation of the struggle and an act of cowardice in the face of sacrifice. War alone brings up to its highest tension all human energy and puts the stamp of nobility upon the peoples who have courage to meet it. . . .

. . . .The Fascist accepts life and loves it, knowing nothing of and despising suicide: he rather conceives of life as duty and struggle and conquest, but above all for others. . . .

. . . .Fascism [is] the complete opposite of . . . Marxian Socialism, . . . Fascism, now and always, believes in holiness and in heroism; that is to say, in actions influenced by no economic motive, direct or indirect. . . .

After Socialism, Fascism combats the whole complex system of democratic ideology . . . [and] denies that the majority, by the simple fact that it is a majority, can direct human society; . . . it affirms the immutable, beneficial, and fruitful inequality of mankind, which can never be permanently leveled through the mere operation of a mechanical process such as universal suffrage. . . . Fascism denies, in democracy, the absurd conventional untruth of political equality dressed out in the garb of collective irresponsibility, and the myth of "happiness" and indefinite progress. . . .

Fascism conceives of the State as an absolute, in comparison with which all individuals or groups are relative, only to be conceived of in their relation to the State. . . . The Fascist State organizes the nation, but leaves a sufficient margin of liberty to the individual; the latter is deprived of all useless and possibly harmful freedom, but retains what is essential; the deciding power in this question cannot be the individual, but the State alone. . . .

. . . .For Fascism, the growth of empire . . . is an essential manifestation of vitality, and its opposite a sign of decadence. . . . 99

Source— Benito Mussolini, "Fascism," *Italian Encyclopedia,* 1932

VOCABULARY

repudiates: to reject as having no authority

conceives: to create

preponderant: superior

manifestation: state of making something visible or evident

1 **ANALYZING TEXT STRUCTURE** What is the purpose of this encyclopedia entry?

_____

2 **DETERMINING CENTRAL IDEAS** How would you define _fascism_? Cite evidence from the text to support your answer.

_____

_____

_____

_____

_____

3 **IDENTIFYING CONNECTIONS** How does this entry reveal how Mussolini likely felt about the Kellogg-Briggs Pact?

_____

_____

_____

_____

4 **CIVICS** How does fascism compare to democracy? Cite evident from the text.

_____

_____

_____

_____

5 **INTERPRETING** What do you think the Italian people found appealing about fascism?

_____

_____

6 **EXPLAINING EFFECTS** How might fascism have manifested in everyday life?

_____

_____

Hitler and Nazi Germany

DIRECTIONS Search for evidence in the lesson to help you answer the following questions.

1A **UNDERSTANDING CHANGE** What events led up to Hitler's rise to power? Use the time line to list those events in chronological order.

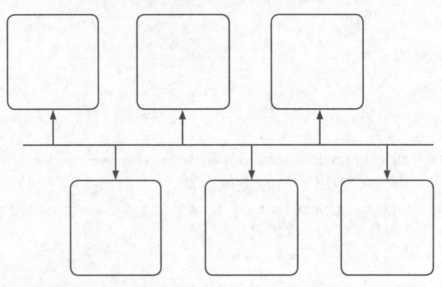

1B **EXPLAINING CAUSES** What factors outside Hitler's ambition and propaganda contributed to his rise to power?

_____

_____

_____

_____

2A **DETERMINING CENTRAL IDEAS** What were Hitler's goals?

_____

_____

_____

_____

_____

ESSENTIAL QUESTION

How might political change impact society?

As you gather evidence to answer the Essential Question, think about:

- how Hitler rose to power.
- how changes in Germany's politics affected different groups of people.
- why Germany was susceptible to a totalitarian regime.

My Notes

_____

_____

_____

_____

_____

_____

2B **IDENTIFYING STEPS** What **steps did Hitler take to achieve his goals?**

_____

_____

_____

_____

_____

3 `ECONOMICS` How did Hitler end the Great Depression in Germany? How does this connect to the strategy of the United States to combat the depression?

_____

_____

_____

_____

4 **EXPLAINING EFFECTS** How did Hitler's political views mean changes to society?

		Impact on Society
Hitler's political views	⇨	

Kristallnacht, the Night of Shattered Glass

DIRECTIONS: Study the photograph of damage from *Kristallnacht.* Then respond to the questions that follow.

EXPLORE THE CONTEXT: On November 9, 1938, the Nazis burned or destroyed a number of Jewish synagogues and stores in Germany, Austria, and the Sudetenland in Czechoslovakia. The night was known as *Kristallnacht,* or the "night of shattered glass." Thirty thousand Jews were forced to leave their homes and sent to concentration camps. The photo below is of a Jewish storefront with damage from the night of *Kristallnacht.* This photograph shows the smashed shop windows the following day.

PRIMARY SOURCE: PHOTOGRAPH

1 **SUMMARIZING** What can you tell about *Kristallnacht* from studying the image?

_____

_____

_____

2 **IDENTIFYING CAUSES** What factors led to Hitler's rise to power? What factors led to his anti-Semitism?

_____

_____

_____

_____

3 **IDENTIFYING CONNECTIONS** How was *Kristallnacht* in line with Hitler's goals?

_____

_____

_____

4 **DETERMINING CENTRAL IDEAS** What political ideology created the circumstances that led to *Kristallnacht*?

_____

_____

_____

5 HISTORY What lessons can we learn from the situation with *Kristallnacht*?

_____

_____

_____

_____

6 **EXPLAINING EFFECTS** What impact did *Kristallnacht* have on the Nazi Party? On the Jewish population?

_____

How might political change impact society?

Jesse Owens in the Berlin Olympics

DIRECTIONS: Study the photograph. Then respond to the questions that follow.

EXPLORE THE CONTEXT: James Cleveland Owens is remembered now as Jesse Owens. He was an African American track and field athlete who won four gold medals in the 1936 Olympic Games. Those Olympics were held in Berlin, and Hitler's intention was to show how superior the Aryan race was. The Berlin Olympics were the first to be televised. Owens became the most popular athlete of the games, and the world was able to watch as he won gold medals in the 100 meters, 200 meters, long jump and 4x100 meter relay.

PRIMARY SOURCE: PHOTOGRAPH

1 **ANALYZING INFORMATION** What is the tone of the image? Based on the tone, who do you think took this picture?

_____

_____

_____

2 **DETERMINING POINT OF VIEW** How might the picture have been different if a German photographer took it?

_____

_____

_____

3 **INTERPRETING** How did Owens disprove Hitler's theory about the superiority of the Aryan race?

_____

_____

_____

4 **IDENTIFYING CONNECTIONS** Why was it important that the 1936 Olympics were televised?

_____

_____

_____

5 CIVICS Many countries spoke vehemently about boycotting the 1936 Olympics but ultimately none did. Do you think the United States should have boycotted the Olympics?

_____

_____

_____

6 **RELATING EVENTS** If the United States had boycotted the Olympics, how might history have changed?

_____

_____

ESSENTIAL QUESTIONS

How might political change impact society?

My Notes

_____

_____

_____

_____

_____

_____

_____

_____

_____

_____

_____

_____

_____

1 Think About It

Review the supporting questions you developed at the beginning of the chapter. Review the evidence you gathered in the chapter. Were you able to answer each Supporting Question? If there was not enough evidence to answer your Supporting Questions, what additional evidence do you think you need to consider?

_____

_____

_____

2 Organize Your Evidence

Complete the chart below with information you learned about the aftermath of World War I and the types of political ideologies and government structures that arose.

Country	Economic changes	Political changes	Social changes
Germany			
Italy			
France			

3 Talk About It

Work in small groups. With your group, discuss how World War I changed Europe and the United States. Think specifically about how political changes affected the way people lived.

4 Write About It

Choose two of the countries mentioned in the chapter and included on your chart. Research both countries further. How were they affected politically and socially after World War I? Write a summary of your research below. Compare it with the paragraphs of your group members.

_____

_____

_____

_____

_____

_____

_____

_____

_____

_____

_____

_____

_____

5 Connect to the Essential Question

Following your work in the Write About It activity, use the research on the countries who were politically and socially affected by World War I and create a poster that compares and contrasts them. Your poster should include a section that answers the Essential Question: _How might political change impact society?_

Your poster should include a mix of text and images. Identify and describe the causal relationship between World War I and many of the political changes that occurred throughout the Western world. Be sure to consider the economic changes that influenced political shifts as well. Prepare to present your poster to the class. Ensure your poster as well as your presentation is accurate, engaging, and informative.

CITIZENSHIP
TAKING ACTION

MAKE CONNECTIONS Much of the study of history is a study of cause and effect. World War I was a significant and traumatic event that had lasting effects throughout the entire world. This chapter focuses on the West and the social, political, and economic impact the had on Europe and the United States. In many cases, the war prompted political leaders to create laws that changed the way people lived. In most cases, the political leaders, including controversial figures, believed they were doing what was best for the country as a whole and its people.

DIRECTIONS: Use the Internet to find an example of a bill put together by a government entity within the United States (state or federal law). Study the way the bill is structured. Most bills begin with a summary at the top and then articles that list the main points of the bill.

Once you have an example bill, decide on a social problem you would like to solve. This may be something in your community or a problem you know exists in the larger world. Use the space below to brainstorm the problem and organize your research. Then, write a bill that you think would help solve that social problem. Remember that bills are supposed to be persuasive. You will have to convince your classmates to vote on your bill.

You will likely need to do research throughout the writing process to double check facts and find statistics to make your bill as persuasive as possible. Be sure all the articles in your bill connect back to the social problem you are attempting to fix. Remember the scope of your bill has to be within what the government can do legally and feasibly.

When your entire class has finished writing bills, you will all pretend to be Congress for a day. You will present your bill to the class, and the class will vote on whether to pass it.

_____

_____

_____

_____

_____

_____

_____

_____

_____

CHAPTER 29

Nationalism Around the World

ESSENTIAL QUESTION

How can political control lead to nationalist movements?

Think about how the end of World War I breathed new life into the colonies' fights for independence. What prompted those fights for independence? What resistance methods did the colonies find most effective? How does the resistance connect to ideas of nationalism?

TALK ABOUT IT

With a partner, discuss the sort of information you would need to discover how political control led to nationalist movements and the effects of those movements. For instance, you might ask, "How did post-World War I independence movements compare to those of previous decades?"

DIRECTIONS: Now write down three additional questions that will help you explain the connections between political control and nationalist movements.

MY RESEARCH QUESTIONS

Supporting Question 1:

_____

_____

Supporting Question 2:

_____

_____

Supporting Question 3:

_____

_____

Copyright © McGraw-Hill Education

Chapter 29

Nationalism in the Middle East

DIRECTIONS Search for evidence in this lesson to help you answer the following questions.

1A **IDENTIFYING CAUSES** What action from the sultan of the Ottoman Empire fostered discontent?

_____

_____

_____

_____

ESSENTIAL QUESTION

How can political control lead to nationalist movements?

As you gather evidence to answer the Essential Question, think about:

- how World War I affected the Ottoman Empire.
- what Arab nationalism looked like.
- how the Israel/Palestine conflict began.

1B **EXPLAINING EFFECTS** How did World War I affect the Ottoman Empire?

Effect

Cause

Effect

Effect

My Notes

_____

_____

_____

_____

_____

_____

_____

2 IDENTIFYING STEPS What were the steps Turkey took toward modernization? Categorize the steps in the graphic organizer below as social, economic, or political.

Step toward Modernization	Category

3A INTERPRETING Why was there a large foreign presence in Persia?

_____

_____

_____

_____

3B IDENTIFYING CONNECTIONS How did the foreign interference in Persia influence nationalists?

_____

_____

_____

_____

4 GEOGRAPHY How did the post–World War I map of the Middle East compare to nationalists' hopes?

_____

_____

_____

_____

Copyright © McGraw-Hill Education   CL-©Source: Library of Congress Prints and Photographs Division [LC-USZ62-77295]; BR-©Everett Historical/Shutterstock

ESSENTIAL QUESTION

How can political control lead to nationalist movements?

Sultan Abdulhamit II and Atatürk

DIRECTIONS: Study the images. Then respond to the questions that follow.

EXPLORE THE CONTEXT: The first photo shows Sultan Abdul Hamid II, one of the last sultans of the Ottoman Empire. The second photo shows Mustafa Kemal Atatürk, the founder of the Republic of Turkey, and its first president

PRIMARY SOURCE: PHOTOS

—photographs of Sultan Abdul Hamid II and Atatürk.

1 **COMPARE AND CONTRAST** How are the portraits of the two leaders similar? How are they different?

_____

_____

_____

2 **INTERPRETING** What does the way the men are dressed tell you about the way Turkey changed after the fall of the Ottoman Empire?

_____

_____

_____

3 **ANALYZING POINT OF VIEW** Keeping dogs as pets is uncommon in traditional Islamic households. What does the photo tell you about the way Turkey changed under Atatürk's reforms?

_____

_____

_____

_____

4 **UNDERSTANDING CONTEXT** What cannot be determined about the rulers by examining the photos?

_____

_____

_____

5 **DRAWING CONCLUSIONS** When he came to power, Mustafa Kemal Atatürk outlawed men from wearing the fez, the brimless hat worn by Sultan Abdul Hamid II in the photo and a part of traditional dress. How do you think this decision affected the citizens of the new nation?

_____

_____

_____

_____

ESSENTIAL QUESTION

How can political control lead to nationalist movements?

The Armenian Genocide

DIRECTIONS: Read the source. Then respond to the questions that follow.

EXPLORE THE CONTEXT: In April of 1915, the Ottoman government began a systematic extermination of its Armenian Christian population. As a result of the genocide, it is estimated that 1.2 million or more Armenians had died by the early 1920s. Horrified by reports of Armenian massacres, U.S. president Woodrow Wilson sent senior officer General James Harbord, of the U.S. Army, to investigate the region and report his findings.

PRIMARY SOURCE: OFFICIAL REPORT

" This mission has had constantly in mind the moral effect to be exercised by its inquiry in the region visited. Very alarming reports had been received from Transcaucasia for several months before its departure from France, particularly as to organized attacks by the Turkish Army impending along the old international border between Turkey and Russia. The itinerary of the mission through Turkey was planned with those reports before it and with the intention of observing as to their truth and if possible to exert a restraining influence. We practically covered the frontier of Turkey from the Black Sea to Persia, and found nothing to justify the reports. The Turkish Army is not massed along the border; their organizations are reduced to skeletons; and the country shows an appalling lack of people, either military or civilian. At every principal town through which we passed the chief of the mission held a conference with the Turkish officials. Inquiry was made as to the Christian Community, some were always interviewed; the interest of America in its own missionaries and in the native Christians was invariably emphasized; the Armenian deportations, the massacres, and the return of the survivors were discussed on each occasion, as well as other matters intended to convince Turkish officials that their country is on trial before the world. The visit of the mission has had a considerable moral effect in securing the safety of Christian lives and property pending action by the peace conference.

We would again point out that if America accepts a mandate for the region visited by this mission, it will undoubtedly do so from a strong sense of international duty, and at the unanimous desire—so expressed at least—of its colleagues in the League of Nations. Accepting this difficult task without previously securing the assurance of conditions would be fatal to success. The United States should make its own conditions as a preliminary to consideration of the subject— certainly before and not after acceptance, for there are a multitude of interests that will conflict with what any American would consider a proper administration of the country. Every possible precaution against international complications should be taken in advance. In our opinion there should be specific pledges in terms of formal agreements with France and England and definite approval from Germany and Russia of the dispositions made of Turkey and Transcaucasia, and a pledge to respect them. "

Source— Conclusion for Conditions in the Near East: Report of the American Military Misson to Armenia, submitted by JAMES G. HARBORD, Major General, United States Army, Chief of Mission, 1920

VOCABULARY

inquiry: investigation

itinerary: plan

exert: apply

invariably: always

trial: determining the guilt or innocence of one accused

mandate: official order

preliminary: introductory

multitude: a large number

dispositions: settlement

1 **SUMMARIZING** What was the purpose of the American military's mission to Armenia?

_____

_____

_____

2 **ANALYZING** What interest would the United States have had in organizing the mission to Armenia?

_____

_____

_____

3 **DETERMINING MEANING** What is meant by Harbord's statement that Turkey was "on trial before the world"?

_____

_____

_____

4 **COMPARING & CONTRASTING** According to this report, how did the Turkish Army fare by the end of the Armenian Genocide?

_____

_____

_____

5 **IDENTIFYING EFFECTS** According to Harbord, how was the mission helpful to the Armenians?

_____

_____

6 **HISTORY** How does Harbord conclude his report? What considerations did the United States have in regards to becoming involved in the Turkish-Armenian War?

_____

_____

_____

_____

Nationalism in Africa and Asia

DIRECTIONS Search for evidence in this lesson to help you answer the following questions.

1A **IDENTIFYING CAUSES** What ideals fueled the African fights for independence?

_____

_____

_____

1B **IDENTIFYING CONNECTIONS** What were the sources for those ideas? Use the graphic organizer to fill the ideals and the sources.

CAUSE & EFFECT
Organizer

> Sources
>
>
>
>
>

> Ideals
>
>
>
>

2A **SUMMARIZING** What was Gandhi's method of reform?

_____

_____

_____

_____

ESSENTIAL QUESTION

How can political control lead to nationalist movements?

As you gather evidence to answer the Essential Question, think about:

- how African nations fought for independence.
- why the Indian independence movement was radical.
- how Japan changed after World War I.

My Notes

_____

_____

_____

_____

_____

2B CIVICS What is one example of Gandhi's civil disobedience?

_____

_____

_____

3 **UNDERSTANDING CONTEXT** What did political control look like in each of the regions listed in the graphic organizer?

Africa	India	Japan

4 **INTERPRETING** What were the goals of the nationalist movements in Africa and Asia? How successful were they in reaching these goals?

_____

_____

_____

_____

_____

ESSENTIAL QUESTION

How can political control lead to nationalist movements?

Presidential Address by Muhammad Ali Jinnah

DIRECTIONS: Read the excerpt from the address. Then respond to the questions that follow.

EXPLORE THE CONTEXT: Muhammad Ali Jinnah was born into British-controlled India, in a part that is now Pakistan. In 1916 he became president of the Muslim League, an organization that fought for the rights of Muslims in a predominantly Hindu society. Jinnah believed that it was possible for Hindus and Muslims to live together in harmony, but after a while he saw the necessity for Muslims to have their own space. He worked with the British to create an independent Pakistan where Indian Muslims could live. He became the first general governor of Pakistan. The address below was given in 1940 and details some of the situations and events leading up to the start of World War II.

PRIMARY SOURCE: PRESIDENTIAL ADDRESS

❝ . . . [T]he Muslim League had all along to face various issues from January 1939 up to the time of the declaration of war. Before the war was declared the greatest danger to the Muslims of India was the possible inauguration of a federal scheme in the central Government. We know what machinations were going on. But the Muslim League was stoutly resisting them in every direction. We felt that we could never accept the dangerous scheme of the central federal Government embodied in the Government of India Act, 1935. I am sure that we have made no small contribution towards persuading the British Government to abandon the scheme of the Central Federal Government. In creating that [state of] mind in the British Government, the Muslim League, I have no doubt, played no small part. You know that the British people are very obdurate people. They are also very conservative; and although they are very clever, they are slow in understanding. After the war was declared, the Viceroy naturally wanted help from the Muslim League. It was only then that he realised that the Muslim League was a power. For it will be remembered that up to the time of the declaration of war, the Viceroy never thought of me, but of Gandhi and Gandhi alone. I have been the leader of an important party in the Legislature for a considerable time, larger than the one I have the honour to lead at present, the Muslim League Party in the Central Legislature. Yet the Viceroy never thought of me. Therefore, when I got this invitation from the Viceroy along with Mr. Gandhi, I wondered within myself why I was so suddenly promoted, and then I concluded that the answer was the 'All-India Muslim League', whose President I happen to be. I believe that was the worst shock that the Congress High Command received, because it challenged their sole authority to speak on behalf of India. And it is quite clear from the attitude of Mr. Gandhi and the High Command that they have not yet recovered from that shock. My point is that I want you to realise the value, the importance, the significance of organising ourselves... ❞

Source— Presidential address by Muhammad Ali Jinnah, March 1940

VOCABULARY

inauguration: a ceremony to induct someone into office

machinations: conspiracy; plot

stoutly: strongly

obdurate: heartless; inhumane

Viceroy: someone acting on behalf of a king or sovereign

1 **SUMMARIZING** What does Jinnah say in this address?

_____

_____

2 **RELATING EVENTS** How does this address relate to the African Independence Movements?

_____

_____

_____

_____

3 **IDENTIFYING CONNECTIONS** How is Jinnah's message similar to Ivan Derer's statement about the Czechs and the Slovaks?

_____

_____

_____

4 HISTORY How does Gandhi's movement relate to Jinnah's?

_____

_____

_____

5 **ANALYZING TEXT STRUCTURE** Who is Jinnah's audience? What information from the text leads you to your conclusion?

_____

_____

_____

6 **CITING TEXT EVIDENCE** What lesson does Jinnah want his audience to take away from his speech? Cite evidence from the text to support your answer.

_____

_____

_____

ESSENTIAL QUESTION

How can political control lead to nationalist movements?

VOCABULARY

brethren: brothers

parcelled: administered

denizens: citizens; occupants

null: invalid

The UNIA's List of Rights for Africans

DIRECTIONS: Read the excerpt from the declaration. Then respond to the questions that follow.

EXPLORE THE CONTEXT: Many African Americans served in World War I, yet at home, they faced intense discrimination, racial violence, and segregation under Jim Crow laws. Marcus Garvey saw and felt their frustration. In Africa, large portions of land were given to white settlers as the black Africans received little to no compensation for it. He used that frustration to draw thousands of African Americans to the Universal Negro Improvement Association (UNIA). The UNIA called for the creation of an independent, black-led nation in Africa. The following document lists the rights Garvey and other members of the UNIA believed all members of his race should have.

PRIMARY SOURCE: DECLARATION OF RIGHTS

❝*Be It Resolved*, That the Negro people of the world. . . , protest against the wrongs and injustices they are suffering at the hands of their white brethren, and state what they deem their fair and just rights, as well as the treatment they propose to demand of all men in the future.

We complain:

1. That nowhere in the world, with few exceptions, are black men accorded equal treatment with white men, although in the same situation and circumstances, but, on the contrary, are discriminated against and denied the common rights due to human beings for no other reason than their race and color.

3. That European nations have parcelled out among them and taken possession of nearly all of the continent of Africa, and the natives are compelled to surrender their lands to aliens and are treated in most instances like slaves.

In order to encourage our race all over the world and to stimulate it to overcome the handicaps and difficulties surrounding it, and to push forward to a higher and grander destiny, we demand and insist on the following Declaration of Rights:

1. Be it known to all men that whereas all men are created equal and entitled to the rights of life, liberty and the pursuit of happiness, and because of this we, the duly elected representatives of the Negro peoples of the world, invoking the aid of the just and Almighty God, do declare all men, women and children of our blood throughout the world free denizens, and do claim them as free citizens of Africa, the Motherland of all Negroes.

3. That we believe the Negro, like any other race, should be governed by the ethics of civilization, and therefore should not be deprived of any of those rights or privileges common to other human beings.

45. Be it further resolved, That we as a race of people declare the League of Nations null and void as far as the Negro is concerned, in that it seeks to deprive Negroes of their liberty.

54. We want all men to know that we shall maintain and contend for the freedom and equality of every man, woman and child of our race, with our lives, our fortunes and our sacred honor.

These rights we believe to be justly ours and proper for the protection of the Negro race at large... ❞

Source— UNIA Declaration of Rights of the Negro Peoples of the World, New York, August 13, 1920

1 **ANALYZING TEXT STRUCTURE** How is this document structured? Why do you think the UNIA chose to structure the document in this way?

_____

_____

2 **SUMMARIZING** What are the UNIA's main complaints, and what rights and ideas do they declare?

_____

_____

_____

_____

3 **EXPLAINING CAUSES** Why does the UNIA believe the League of Nations takes away the rights of Africans?

_____

_____

4 **IDENTIFYING CONNECTIONS** How does the UNIA's declaration connect with the excerpt from _Facing Mount Kenya_ in Chapter 11, Lesson 2?

_____

_____

_____

5 **CITING TEXT EVIDENCE** Who is the intended audience of the declaration? Cite text evidence.

_____

_____

_____

_____

6 **HISTORY** How does the UNIA's declaration connect with Garvey's goal of creating an independent, black-led nation?

_____

_____

Revolutionary Chaos in China

DIRECTIONS Search for evidence in this lesson to help you answer the following questions.

1A **SUMMARIZING** What was the Long March?

_____

_____

_____

_____

1B **IDENTIFYING EFFECTS** What was the impact of the Long March? Use the graphic organizer below to explain your answer.

ESSENTIAL QUESTION

How can political control lead to nationalist movements?

As you gather evidence to answer the Essential Question, think about:

- what factions arose in China.
- how Chiang Kai-shek tried to create a new China.
- whether Chiang Kai-shek was successful in his efforts.

My Notes

_____

_____

_____

_____

_____

_____

Cause

Effect

Effect

Effect

2A **DETERMINING MEANING** What was the "political tutelage" Chiang spoke of?

_____

_____

_____

_____

2B **INTERPRETING** How did Chiang try to modernize China?

_____

_____

_____

_____

3 **ECONOMICS** What economic changes did Chiang make to build a new China?

_____

_____

_____

_____

4 **IDENTIFYING CONNECTIONS** What caused the obstacles to the government Chiang wanted to build?

Chiang's Goals	Obstacles

ESSENTIAL QUESTION

How can political control lead to nationalist movements?

Sun Yat-sen on Reform in China

DIRECTIONS: Read the excerpts from Sun Yat-sen's book. Then respond to the questions that follow.

EXPLORE THE CONTEXT: Sun Yat-sen was the father of modern China. He was born the son of poor farmers. Sun lived in Hawaii for some time and earned a medical degree in Hong Kong. His time in the U.S. created a sense of dissatisfaction with the Chinese government. While he was in Hong Kong, he tried to organize groups to encourage reform. When his attempted coup failed in 1895, he spent time in exile in the U.S., Japan, and Europe. He continued trying to bring reform to China and ultimately became the president in 1923.

PRIMARY SOURCE: BOOK

❝Revelations of Chinese history prove that the Chinese as a people are independent in spirit and in conduct. Coerced into touch with other people, they could at times live in peace with them by maintaining friendly relations and at others assimilate them as the result of propinquity. . . . Nationalistic ideas in China did not come from a foreign source; they were inherited from our remote forefathers. Upon this legacy is based my principle of nationalism, and where necessary, I have developed it and amplified and improved upon it. No vengeance has been inflicted on the Manchus and we have endeavored to live side by side with them on an equal footing. This is our nationalistic policy toward races within our national boundaries. Externally, we should strive to maintain independence in the family of nations, and to spread our indigenous civilization as well as to enrich it by absorbing what is best in world civilization, with the hope that we may forge ahead with other nations towards the goal of ideal brotherhood. . . .

FUNDAMENTALS OF REVOLUTION

It becomes necessary that, apart from destroying enemy influence, those engaged in revolution should take care to develop the constructive ability of the people. A revolutionary program is therefore indispensable.

According to my plan, the progress of our revolution should be regulated and divided into three stages: First, military rule; second, political tutelage; third, constitutional government. The first stage is a period of destruction, during which military rule is installed. . . . The second stage is a transitional period, during which a provisional constitution (not the present. one) will be promulgated. Its object is to build a local self-government system for the development of democracy. . . . The third stage, which marks the completion of national reconstruction, will usher in constitutional government. During this period the self-governing bodies in the various districts should exercise the direct political powers of the people. In district political affairs citizens should have the rights of universal suffrage, initiative, referendum and recall. In national political affairs they should, while directly exercising the right of election, delegate the three other rights to their representatives in the People's Congress. This period of constitutional government marks the completion of national reconstruction and the successful conclusion of the revolution. ❞

Source— Sun Yat-sen, *Fundamentals of National Reconstruction*, 1923

VOCABULARY

conduct: behavior

propinquity: proximity

tutelage: a period of instruction

1 **ANALYZING TEXT PRESENTATION** How is this passage organized? Do you think this kind of organization is efficient?

_____

_____

_____

_____

2 **SUMMARIZING** What are Sun's three stages of revolution?

_____

_____

3 **INTERPRETING** How do Sun's three stages build on each other?

_____

_____

_____

_____

4 **IDENTIFYING CONNECTIONS** How does Sun's _Fundamentals of National Reconstruction_ connect to the quote from Chiang from Chapter 11, Lesson 3?

_____

_____

_____

5 HISTORY How do Sun's ideas about revolution and government compare with those of Mao Zedong? Would they have agreed?

_____

_____

_____

6 **EVALUATING EVIDENCE** Given what you know about nationalist movements, what do you think of Sun's three-stage plan?

_____

_____

_____

ESSENTIAL QUESTION

How can political control lead to nationalist movements?

VOCABULARY

gentry: upper class

autocratic: tyrannical

comrade: member of the Communist party

Report by Mao Zedong

DIRECTIONS: Read the report from Mao Zedong. Then respond to the questions that follow.

EXPLORE THE CONTEXT: Before Mao Zedong rose to power, he was a Hunanese peasant. In 1921 he became one of the founding members of the Chinese Communist Party. Mao could not adopt classical Marxism because it focused on the development of an industrial society and a sense of the value of the industrial workers. In China, the oppressed population were peasants, not industrial workers. Mao worked actively in organizing in rural communities. The following excerpt is a report Mao wrote while investigating a peasant revolt.

PRIMARY SOURCE: REPORT

66 The peasants' revolt disturbed the gentry's sweet dreams. When the news from the countryside reached the cities, it caused immediate uproar among the gentry. Soon after my arrival in Changsha, I met all sorts of people and picked up a good deal of gossip. From the middle social strata upwards to the Kuomintang right-wingers, there was not a single person who did not sum up the whole business in the phrase, "It's terrible!" . . . Even quite progressive people said, "Though terrible, it is inevitable in a revolution." In short, nobody could altogether deny the word "terrible." But, as already mentioned, the fact is that the great peasant masses have risen to fulfill their historic mission and that the forces of rural democracy have risen to overthrow the forces of rural feudalism. The patriarchal-feudal class of local tyrants, evil gentry and lawless landlords has formed the basis of autocratic government for thousands of years and is the cornerstone of imperialism, warlordism and corrupt officialdom. To overthrow these feudal forces is the real objective of the national revolution. In a few months the peasants have accomplished what Dr. Sun Yat sen wanted, but failed, to accomplish in the forty years he devoted to the national revolution. This is a marvellous feat never before achieved, not just in forty, but in thousands of years. It's fine. It is not "terrible" at all. It is anything but "terrible." . . . If your revolutionary viewpoint is firmly established and if you have been to the villages and looked around, you will undoubtedly feel thrilled as never before. Countless thousands of the enslaved-the peasants-are striking down the enemies who battened on their flesh. What the peasants are doing is absolutely right; what they are doing is fine! "It's fine!" is the theory of the peasants and of all other revolutionaries. Every revolutionary comrade should know that the national revolution requires a great change in the countryside. The Revolution of 1911 did not bring about this change, hence its failure. This change is now taking place, and it is an important factor for the completion of the revolution. Every revolutionary comrade must support it, or he will be taking the stand of counter-revolution. 99

Source— Mao Zedong, *Report on an Investigation of the Peasant Movement in Hunan,* 1927

1 **CITING TEXT EVIDENCE** What is Mao's opinion of the peasant revolt? Cite evidence from the text to support your analysis.

_____

_____

_____

2 **INTERPRETING** Mao creates a split between good and evil in his analysis of the revolt. Who is good, and who is evil?

_____

_____

3 **ANALYZING TEXT PRESENTATION** Who is Mao's audience in this report? How do you know?

_____

_____

_____

4 **RELATING EVENTS** How does this report from Mao compare to the previous document by Sun Yat-sen?

_____

_____

_____

5 CIVICS Do you agree with Mao that a revolt is not a "terrible" act?

_____

_____

_____

6 **IDENTIFYING CONNECTIONS** How do Mao's ideas in this passage connect to what you have learned about nationalism?

_____

_____

_____

_____

Nationalism in Latin America

DIRECTIONS Search for evidence in this lesson to help you answer the following questions.

ESSENTIAL QUESTION

How can political control lead to nationalist movements?

As you gather evidence to answer the Essential Question, think about:

- how the United States influenced Latin America.

- what political control and nationalism looked like in Latin America.

- why authoritarian regimes existed in the region.

1A **DETERMINING CENTRAL IDEAS** What was the role of the United States in Latin America in the 1920s and 1930s?

_____

_____

_____

_____

_____

1B **EXPLAINING EFFECTS** What was the effect of the United States's political control and the Great Depression on Latin American countries?

Cause	Effects
United States Political Control	
Great Depression	

2A **SUMMARIZING** What kind of governments were common in Latin America?

_____

_____

_____

My Notes

_____

_____

_____

_____

_____

_____

_____

2B `CIVICS` What specific governments arose in the following countries and what was each government's impact?

Country	Type of Government	Details About Government
Argentina		
Brazil		
Mexico		

3 RELATING EVENTS What are the trends you notice with regard to political control in Latin America?

_____

_____

_____

_____

4 IDENTIFYING CONNECTIONS How did globalization impact culture in Latin America?

_____

_____

_____

ESSENTIAL QUESTION

How can political control lead to nationalist movements?

Mexican President Cárdenas on Oil

DIRECTIONS: Read the speech. Then respond to the questions that follow.

EXPLORE THE CONTEXT: Lázaro Cárdenas was governor of the state of Michoacán from 1928 to 1934, and he was President of Mexico from 1934 to 1940. He bought a new wave of change by fulfilling some of the original goals of the revolution. He distributed 44 million acres of land to landless Mexican peasants, which made him enormously popular. Mexico was known for its large oil reserves, especially in the Gulf of Mexico, and Cárdenas founded a state-controlled oil company named Petróleos Mexicanos (Pemex), which is still a major source of income for the government. The speech below shows a strong sense of nationalism during Cárdenas's leadership.

PRIMARY SOURCE: SPEECH

66 . . . It has been repeated *ad nauseam* that the oil industry has brought additional capital for the development and progress of the country. This assertion is an exaggeration. For many years throughout the major period of their existence, oil companies have enjoyed great privileges for development and expansion, . . . it is these factors of special privilege, together with the prodigious productivity of the oil deposits granted them by the Nation often against public will and law, that represent almost the total amount of this so-called capital.

. . . the oil companies have almost openly encouraged the ambitions of elements discontented with the country's government, every time their interests were affected either by taxation or by the modification of their privileges. . . . They have had money, arms, and munitions for rebellion, . . . money with which to enrich their unconditional defenders. But for the progress of the country, for establishing an economic equilibrium with their workers through a just compensation of labor, for maintaining hygienic conditions in the districts where they themselves operate, or for conserving the vast riches of the natural petroleum gases from destruction, they have neither money, . . . nor the desire to subtract the necessary funds from the volume of their profits. . . .

It is necessary that all groups of the population be imbued with a full optimism and that each citizen, whether in agricultural, industrial, commercial, transportation, or other pursuits, develop a greater activity from this moment on, in order to create new resources which will reveal that the spirit of our people is capable of saving the nation's economy by the efforts of its own citizens.

. . . we wish to state that our petroleum operations will not depart a single inch from the moral solidarity maintained by Mexico with the democratic nations, whom we wish to assure that the expropriation now decreed has as its only purpose the elimination of obstacles erected by groups who do not understand the evolutionary needs of all peoples and who would themselves have no compunction in selling Mexican oil to the highest bidder, without taking into account the consequences of such action to the popular masses and the nations in conflict. 99

Source— Lázaro Cárdenas, Speech to the Nation, March, 18, 1938

VOCABULARY

ad nauseam: something has been repeated so often that it is annoying

prodigious: wonderful; marvelous

hygienic: healthy; sanitary

imbued: to inspire

expropriation: to remove private ownership for public use

decreed: declare; proclaim

compunction: regret; reluctance

1A **SUMMARIZING** What is the topic of this speech by Mexican president Lázaro Cárdenas?

_____

_____

1B **DETERMINING CONTEXT** Based on what you learned in this lesson, why would this be an important topic to discuss?

_____

_____

_____

2A ECONOMICS What does Cárdenas mean when he says the assertion that the oil industry brings in money to the country is an exaggeration?

_____

_____

_____

2B **CITING TEXT EVIDENCE** What does Cárdenas propose as a solution in this speech?

_____

_____

_____

3 **EXPLAINING CAUSE AND EFFECT** How might the two oil companies refusing to pay for labor affect Mexican workers?

_____

_____

_____

4 **INFERRING** Based on this speech, what can be concluded about Cárdenas's position towards the oil industry?

_____

_____

_____

How can political control lead to nationalist movements?

Mexican President Cárdenas Governs

DIRECTIONS: Study the photograph. Then respond to the questions that follow.

EXPLORE THE CONTEXT: While Lázaro Cárdenas was the President of Mexico, the country was known for its large oil reserves, which attracted foreign oil companies, mostly from Britain and the United States. Under the leadership of Cárdenas, the Mexican government used the issue of disputes over workers' wages to take control of the oil fields and property owned by foreign-oil companies. In the photo, Cárdenas, center, is shown at the annual message to the General Congress in September 1938.

PRIMARY SOURCE: PHOTOGRAPH

1 **INFERRING** What were conditions like for factory workers in Mexico during the 1930s?

_____

_____

_____

2 **ANALYZING** In the photograph, Cárdenas stands with the congress, which is generally comprised of the elite in society. What kind of relationship do you think he had with the congress?

_____

_____

_____

_____

3 **HISTORY** What can be assumed by the existence of multiple labor organizations in Mexico during the 1930s? What does it say about the relationship between laborers and the Mexican government?

_____

_____

_____

_____

4 **EVALUATING EVIDENCE** How does Cárdenas's speech to the nation in March of 1938 provide insight into factory conditions?

_____

_____

_____

5 **PREDICTING** Based on what you know about the changes in Mexico during this time, why do you think Cárdenas did not institute a period of tutelage like the plan of Sun Yat-sen in China?

_____

_____

ESSENTIAL QUESTION

How can political control lead to nationalist movements?

My Notes

_____

_____

_____

_____

_____

_____

_____

_____

_____

_____

_____

_____

_____

_____

_____

_____

1 Think About It

Review the supporting questions you developed at the beginning of the chapter. Review the evidence you gathered in the chapter. Were you able to answer each Supporting Question? If there was not enough evidence to answer your Supporting Questions, what additional evidence do you think you need to consider?

_____

_____

_____

_____

2 Organize Your Evidence

Complete the chart below with information you learned about political control and nationalism around the world after World War I.

Region	Political Control	Nationalism
Middle East		
Africa		
Latin America		

3 Talk About It

Work in small groups. With your group, discuss the chart you created in the Organize Your Evidence activity. Compare notes. Add information from your group members to your chart. Did each member of your group choose the same countries? How do your charts differ? Then discuss the following question: What are the connections between the political control column and the nationalism column? Explain your answers.

4 Write About It

Following your discussion in Question 3, write about the nationalism and political control you have identified and noted down in your charts. Describe how nationalism played a role in each country's evolution. Explain your answers.

_____

_____

_____

_____

_____

_____

_____

5 Connect to the Essential Question

Following your work in the Talk About It activity, choose two regions mentioned in the chapter that interest you. Then create a multimedia presentation that helps answer the Essential Question: _How can political control lead to nationalist movements?_ Use information from the two regions you chose.

Include images, text, music, or animation in your presentation. Identify the political climate in both regions and explain its connection to nationalism. Be sure to explain what nationalism is and include specific similarities and differences between the two regions. You may have to do additional research. Your presentation should be informative, accurate, and engaging.

CITIZENSHIP
TAKING ACTION

MAKE CONNECTIONS In the period after World War I, some colonies gained more rights and even independence. Others struggled against Europe and the United States's imperialist desires. Many countries, such as India and several African countries, gained independence in more recent decades. Some parts of the world are still under imperialism. Guam and Puerto Rico, for example, are United States territories. They both have a non-voting presence in Congress.

DIRECTIONS: Use the Internet and library resources to research information about imperialism in the twenty-first century. Try to find at least one primary source, such as a photo, interview, or government document. Once you have organized your research, write an opinion piece about imperialism in the twenty-first century.

Your op-ed should take a clear stance for or against imperialism and include facts to support your opinion. Be sure to include one opposing argument and explain why it did not change your mind. Also, consider the historical context for your conclusions. What political context contributed to the imperialism? What attempts at nationalism or independence has the country taken? Be sure to proofread your op-ed carefully.

World War II and the Holocaust

ESSENTIAL QUESTION

How does war impact society and the environment?

Think about how World War II affected Europe and its population.

TALK ABOUT IT

With a partner, discuss the sort of questions you would need to ask in order to understand the impacts of war. For example, one question might be, "How can government policies affect a society?" Another might be, "How did national borders change as a result of World War II?"

DIRECTIONS: Now write down three additional questions that will help you explain how the Nazis fought two wars during World War II.

MY RESEARCH QUESTIONS

Supporting Question 1:

_____

_____

_____

Supporting Question 2:

_____

_____

_____

Supporting Question 3:

_____

_____

_____

ESSENTIAL QUESTION

How does war impact society and the environment?

As you gather evidence to answer the Essential Question, think about:

- what political events may lead to a war.
- how different ways of thinking can cause a war.
- how economic forces can affect war.

My Notes

_____

_____

_____

_____

_____

_____

World War II Begins

DIRECTIONS Search for evidence in the lesson to help you answer the following questions.

1 **IDENTIFYING PERSPECTIVES** What were Adolf Hitler's beliefs?

_____

_____

_____

_____

_____

_____

_____

2A **SUMMARIZING** How did Hitler violate the Treaty of Versailles?

_____

_____

_____

_____

_____

_____

_____

2B **RELATING EVENTS** What prevented France, Great Britain, and Italy from taking action against Hitler's violation?

_____

_____

_____

_____

_____

_____

_____

_____

_____

3 DESCRIBING Use the chart below to list Germany's alliances.

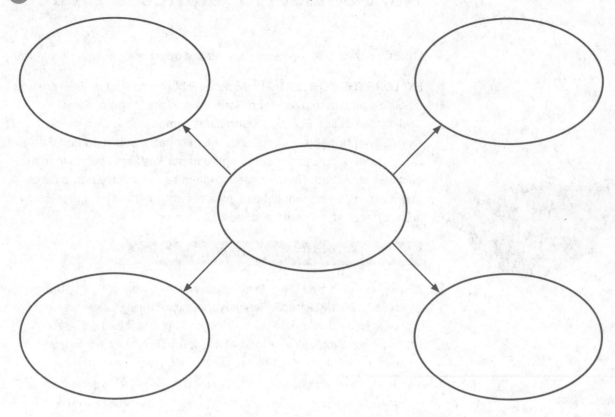

4 HISTORY What was the Nazi-Soviet Nonaggression Pact?

_____

_____

_____

5 DETERMINING CONTEXT What was the dilemma Japan had with the United States? What was Japan's decision?

_____

_____

_____

_____

_____

_____

_____

ESSENTIAL QUESTION

How does war impact society and the environment?

Nazi-Soviet Nonaggression Pact

DIRECTIONS: Use the text to answer the questions.

EXPLORE THE CONTEXT: The Molotov-Ribbentrop Pact of 1939 created a political partnership between Germany and the Union of Soviet Socialist Republics. For this reason it has come to be known as the "Nazi-Soviet Nonaggression Pact." The pact had a public portion that was shared, while another set of agreements was kept secret when the pact was published. The four sections kept secret involve agreements about which country would have influence over certain geographical areas of interest in Poland and the Baltic states.

PRIMARY SOURCE: POLITICAL PACT

❝The Government of the German Reich and The Government of the Union of Soviet Socialist Republics Desirous of strengthening the cause of peace between Germany and the U.S.S.R., and proceeding from the fundamental provisions of the Neutrality Agreement concluded in April, 1926 between Germany and the U.S.S.R., have reached the following Agreement:

Article I. Both High Contracting Parties obligate themselves to desist from any act of violence, any aggressive action, and any attack on each other, either individually or jointly with other Powers.

Article II. Should one of the High Contracting Parties become the object of belligerent action by a third Power, the other High Contracting Party shall in no manner lend its support to this third Power.

Article III. The Governments of the two High Contracting Parties shall in the future maintain continual contact with one another for the purpose of consultation in order to exchange information on problems affecting their common interests.

Article IV. Neither of the two High Contracting Parties shall participate in any grouping of Powers whatsoever that is directly or indirectly aimed at the other party.

Article V. Should disputes or conflicts arise between the High Contracting Parties over problems of one kind or another, both parties shall settle these disputes or conflicts exclusively through friendly exchange of opinion or, if necessary, through the establishment of arbitration commissions.

Article VI. The present Treaty is concluded for a period of ten years, with the proviso that, in so far as one of the High Contracting Parties does not advance it one year prior to the expiration of this period, the validity of this Treaty shall automatically be extended for another five years.

Article VII. The present treaty shall be ratified within the shortest possible time. The ratifications shall be exchanged in Berlin. The Agreement shall enter into force as soon as it is signed.❞

Source— The Molotov-Ribbentrop Pact, 1939

VOCABULARY

belligerent: aggressive; warlike

arbitration: when a neutral party helps negotiate an agreement between opposing forces

proviso: condition

ratified: approved or passed into law

_____. 1939. Treaty of Non-Aggression Between Germany and the Soviet Union, Moscow, 23 August 1939. Reprinted 2001 by J.A.S. Grenville and Bernard Wasserstein. The Major International Treaties of the Twentieth Century - A History and Guide with Texts. Volume One. London: Routledge.

1 **DETERMINING CENTRAL IDEAS** What did each side promise in this pact?

_____

_____

_____

2 **SUMMARIZING** What plans did Hitler ultimately have for the USSR?

_____

_____

_____

3 **INFERRING** Why do you think the Nazis wanted to create this nonaggression pact with the Soviet Union in August 1939? Look at the historical context for the pact.

_____

_____

_____

_____

_____

_____

4A **HISTORY** As mentioned, the pact contained other, secret provisions for how Germany and the Soviet Union would in the future divide control over certain areas of Europe between them. Why do you think the pact contained those additional plans?

_____

_____

_____

_____

_____

4B **CONSTRUCTING HYPOTHESES** Why do you think that the first seven articles were released to the public, while the agreement over territorial control was not?

_____

_____

ESSENTIAL QUESTION

How does war impact society and the environment?

A Japanese Cabinet Minister on Japan and the West

DIRECTIONS: Use the article to answer the questions.

EXPLORE THE CONTEXT: Ryūtarō Nagai (1881–1944), was a politician and cabinet minister in the Empire of Japan. He was noted in his early political career as a champion of universal suffrage, social welfare, labor unions, women's rights, and Pan-Asianism. This selection argues that the United States should support Japan in its efforts to help bring Asian products to world markets. Imperialism is not mentioned directly but may be inferred. The writer addresses himself instead to "great Powers" that he sees "imposing their will upon Asia."

PRIMARY SOURCE: MAGAZINE ARTICLE

" . . . The total land area of the earth is estimated at approximately 50 million square miles, of which some 30 million square miles, or three-fifths, is in the hands of only four great Powers, namely, Britain, France, the Soviet Union, and the United States. Moreover, these four great Powers. . . have veered in the direction of closed economies, closing their doors to outside immigration and raising high tariff walls. America has been very deeply concerned with Japanese activity in Asia, but seems to overlook the fact that Japan has had to follow her present policies for a number of reasons among which not the least important is America's closed door to Asiatic immigration and her closing of markets to Japanese imports. . . all these great Powers have always been imposing their will upon Asia. It is their idea that Asia should not only be for the Asiatics but for all the rest of the world. It is likewise their idea that here in Asia the door should be kept open and opportunity made equal for all peoples. . . . If the peoples of Europe and America have the right to make their own resources inaccessible to others and construct their own self-sufficient economic structures, then the peoples of Asia have the same freedom to exploit their own natural wealth and establish their own self-sufficiency.

If President Roosevelt is truly anxious, as he seems to be, for the peace of East Asia, why will he not co-operate with Japan and eliminate once and for all the menaces to world peace which have arisen from this one-sided attitude of the Powers? Why does he not keep aloof from Britain, France and the Soviet Union who are trying to checkmate Japan in her fight to free the oppressed races of Asia and thus enable them to reconstruct their life on the spirit of justice and the great principle of love and humanity? Japan is animated by the desire to work with other Powers which will respect the independence of all races in Asia and which will work with these races on the principle of equality. With people so disposed, Japan is only too willing to develop the natural wealth of Asia, open up its markets, and construct a new community without oppression or extortion. Japan sincerely believes that it is her duty to build a new Asiatic order in which the peoples of Asia will really enjoy freedom, independence, and peace. . . . "

Source— Nagai Ryūtarō, "Some Questions for President Roosevelt," 1939

VOCABULARY

present: current

menaces: something or someone that causes harm

aloof: distant

disposed: inclined

Copyright © McGraw-Hill Education   Ryutaro, Nagai. 1939. "Some Questions for President Roosevelt". Contemporary Japan, Volume 8, Number 5 (July 1939).

1A **DETERMINING CENTRAL IDEAS** What conflict does the writer discuss?

_____

_____

1B **DETERMINING CONTEXT** What countries were involved in the conflict?

_____

_____

2 **IDENTIFYING CAUSE** What specific policies does Ryūtarō Nagai highlight as the areas of disagreement?

_____

_____

3 **CIVICS** What kind of social conflict does Nagai see behind the problematic policies he is criticizing?

_____

_____

_____

_____

_____

_____

4 **DETERMINING MEANING** What does the writer mean by saying, "Japan is only too willing to develop the natural wealth of Asia, open up its markets, and construct a new community without oppression or extortion. Japan sincerely believes that it is her duty to build a new Asiatic order in which the peoples of Asia will really enjoy freedom, independence, and peace"?

_____

_____

5 **INTERPRETING** What is Nagai specifically asking President Roosevelt to do?

_____

_____

_____

World War II

ESSENTIAL QUESTION

How does war impact society and the environment?

As you gather evidence to answer the Essential Question, think about:

- Germany's early victories and losses during World War II.

- how U.S. involvement changed the war.

- how the Japanese attack on Pearl Harbor affected the American population differently than expected.

My Notes

_____

_____

_____

_____

_____

_____

_____

DIRECTIONS Search for evidence in the lesson to help you answer the following questions.

1 **EVALUATING** Use the chart below to list Hitler's early victories during World War II. What strategy was used in each country?

Countries	Strategy

2A **GEOGRAPHY** What is the Maginot Line?

_____

_____

_____

_____

_____

_____

2B **EVALUATING** Did the Maginot Line work?

_____

_____

_____

_____

_____

3 **IDENTIFYING CAUSES** Why did the United States pass a series of neutrality acts in the 1930s?

_____

_____

_____

_____

_____

4 **ANALYZING INFORMATION** How and why did Hitler shift his strategy to attack Britain? Did it work? Explain your answer.

_____

_____

_____

_____

_____

5 **EXPLAINING EFFECTS** How did Japan's attack on Pearl Harbor backfire?

_____

_____

_____

_____

_____

_____

ESSENTIAL QUESTION

How does war impact society and the environment?

The End of the Nazi-Soviet Nonaggression Pact

DIRECTIONS: Use the statement to answer the questions.

EXPLORE THE CONTEXT: The statement below was delivered by Vyacheslav Molotov, the Foreign Minister of the Soviet Union. Molotov had signed the non-aggression pact with Germany in 1939. On June 22, 1941, Germany launched attacks against the Soviet Union, bombing its cities and attacking its borders. In the face of direct attack just two years after signing a peace contract, Molotov condemns the Nazis for breaking the pact.

PRIMARY SOURCE: POLITICAL STATEMENT

66 Citizens of the Soviet Union.

The Soviet Government and its head, Comrade Stalin, have authorized me to make the following statement:

Today at 4 o'clock a.m., without any claims having been presented to the Soviet Union, without a declaration of war, German troops attacked our country, attacked our borders at many points and bombed from their airplanes our cities. . . .

This unheard of attack upon our country is perfidy unparalleled in the history of civilized nations. The attack on our country was perpetrated despite the fact that a treaty of non-aggression had been signed between the U.S.S.R. and Germany and that the Soviet Government most faithfully abided by all provisions of this treaty. . . .

Entire responsibility for this predatory attack upon the Soviet Union falls fully and completely upon the German Fascist rulers.

At 5:30 a.m. -- that is, after the attack had already been perpetrated, Von der Schulenburg, the German Ambassador in Moscow, on behalf of his government made the statement to me as People's Commissar of Foreign Affairs to the effect that the German Government had decided to launch war against the U.S.S.R. . . .

Likewise a lie and provocation is the whole declaration made today by Hitler, who is trying belatedly to concoct accusations charging the Soviet Union with failure to observe the Soviet-German pact. . . .

This war has been forced upon us, not by the German people, not by German workers, peasants and intellectuals, whose sufferings we well understand, but by the clique of bloodthirsty Fascist rulers of Germany. . . .

The government of the Soviet Union expresses its unshakable confidence that our valiant army and navy and brave falcons of the Soviet Air Force will acquit themselves with honor in performing their duty to the fatherland and to the Soviet people, and will inflict a crushing blow upon the aggressor. . . .

The government calls upon you, citizens of the Soviet Union, to rally still more closely around our glorious Bolshevist party, around our Soviet Government, around our great leader and comrade, Stalin. . . . Victory will be ours. 99

Source— Vyacheslav Molotov's reaction to the German Invasion of 1941

VOCABULARY

perfidy: an act of disloyalty or betrayal

belatedly: late

concoct: create

clique: a small group of people

acquit: to find a person to be innocent of a crime

1A **SUMMARIZING** What was Germany's justification for launching an attack against the Soviet Union?

_____

_____

1B **ANALYZING POINT OF VIEW** What was Foreign Minister Molotov's response to Germany's reasoning?

_____

_____

2 **INFERRING** What additional factors motivated Germany to launch its attack against the Soviet Union?

_____

_____

_____

3 HISTORY How do you think Molotov wants the Soviet people to view the Germans? Why would this be important?

_____

_____

_____

_____

4 **EVALUATING EVIDENCE** Based on Molotov's statement, how did the Soviet Union plan to respond to Germany's attack?

_____

_____

_____

5 **ANALYZING POINT OF VIEW** To whom is this statement directed? What is its purpose?

_____

_____

_____

ESSENTIAL QUESTION

How does war impact society and the environment?

Battle of the Coral Sea

DIRECTIONS: Use the text to answer the questions.

EXPLORE THE CONTEXT: The passage below comes from the staff of General Douglas MacArthur, reporting on the situation in the South Pacific islands. Here they recount the Battle of the Coral Sea. This battle was the first confrontation between aircraft carriers at sea; it took place via the aircraft they carried. The Allied forces had intercepted communications and knew of the Japanese carriers' mission. It was the first time the Allies managed to force the Japanese to turn back.

PRIMARY SOURCE: BOOK

❝ Both sides initiated all-out attacks on 8 May.

About mid-morning, United States carrier planes scored three hits on the *Shokaku* which was forced to retire. At the same time that the *Shokaku* was undergoing attack, planes from the *Shokaku* and *Zuikaku* were attacking the *Lexington* and *Yorktown*. Early in the afternoon the *Lexington*, put out of control by enemy attacks, was abandoned and sunk by its own destroyer escorts. The Yorktown was damaged but remained operational. This exchange terminated one of the most unusual battles in the annals of naval warfare. Not only was it the first engagement between carrier forces in history but surface ships did not exchange a single shot throughout the entire battle.

In addition to reconnaissance and preparatory raids against enemy air installations, land-based aircraft from the SWPA supported the action of the naval forces by flying some forty-five sorties against the enemy fleet. Bad weather intervened, however, and frustrated all attempts to bomb the crippled *Shokaku*, which succeeded in escaping to the sanctuary of Rabaul.

The Battle of the Coral Sea prevented the Japanese from occupying Port Moresby by sea and temporarily delayed their plans to capture Guadalcanal and occupy the Solomons. The race against time by the Allies had now become a split-second effort to develop the northeastern Australia-New Guinea area. The construction of airdromes at Cairns, Cooktown, Coen, Horn Island, and Port Moresby was pushed rapidly, and small garrisons were provided for the airdromes on the York Peninsula and at Port Moresby. On the other hand, the Allied victory was a purely defensive one. Allied forces in the Southwest Pacific were still unable to launch a major offensive. The Japanese had lost an important battle, but the strategic initiative still remained in their hands. ❞

Source— Reports of General MacArthur, "Battle of the Coral Sea," 1966

VOCABULARY

carrier: a military vehicle or ship that transports soldiers

destroyer: a warship

annals: historical records

reconnaissance: a military mission to gather information on an enemy's position and equipment, as well as other points of tactical interest

SWPA: South West Pacific Area

sorties: sudden attacks against an enemy

airdromes: airports on military bases

garrisons: troops guarding a fortress or other military target

1 **SUMMARIZING** What happened during the Battle of the Coral Sea?

_____

_____

_____

2 **EVALUATING TEXT EVIDENCE** Why was the Battle of the Coral Sea an unusual battle in naval history?

_____

_____

_____

3 HISTORY How could the Battle of the Coral Sea be viewed as successful for the United States?

_____

_____

4 **IDENTIFYING CAUSES** What circumstances prevented the United States from destroying the Shokaku?

_____

_____

5 **COMPARING AND CONTRASTING** Evaluate the differences between the Japanese and the United States forces during the Battle of the Coral Sea. Which country had more strategic power?

_____

_____

_____

_____

6 **EVALUATING** How was this battle important within the context of World War II?

_____

_____

_____

The Home Front and Civilians

DIRECTIONS Search for evidence in the lesson to help you answer the following questions.

1 **COMPARING AND CONTRASTING** How was the war front different for the United States compared to its allies?

_____

_____

_____

_____

2 **ECONOMICS** How did the mobilization of the U.S. economy for wartime production affect Americans socially?

_____

_____

_____

_____

_____

_____

_____

3 **SUMMARIZING** How did the United States treat its Japanese and Japanese-American residents and citizens following the Japanese attack on Pearl Harbor?

_____

_____

_____

_____

_____

_____

ESSENTIAL QUESTION

How does war impact society and the environment?

As you gather evidence to answer the Essential Question, think about:

- how a country's war affects its labor pool.
- why a society might be forced to change during a time of war.
- how military tactics might change due to the status of a conflict or the development of new technologies.

My Notes

_____

_____

_____

_____

_____

_____

4 **IDENTIFYING PERSPECTIVES** Compare the roles of women in wartime in the United States, Germany, Japan, and the Soviet Union.

United States	
Soviet Union	
Germany	
Japan	

5 **UNDERSTANDING CONTEXT** How did the bombing campaigns of World War II differ from bombing carried out in earlier conflicts?

_____

_____

_____

6 **DESCRIBING** What changes became necessary for Germany and Japan as they lost their advantage in the war?

_____

_____

_____

ESSENTIAL QUESTION

How does war impact society and the environment?

A Shortage of U.S. Workers

DIRECTIONS: Use the text to answer the questions.

EXPLORE THE CONTEXT: President Roosevelt issued this executive order in 1941 to address the shortage of workers in industries related to the U.S. war effort. The U.S. produced the majority of the military equipment needed for the Allies. In the order, the president addresses the reason for the shortage of labor and proposes a solution.

PRIMARY SOURCE: EXECUTIVE ORDER

    " June 25, 1941

WHEREAS it is the policy of the United States to encourage full participation in the national defense program by all citizens of the United States, regardless of race, creed, color, or national origin, in the firm belief that the democratic way of life within the Nation can be defended successfully only with the help and support of all groups within its borders; and

WHEREAS there is evidence that available and needed workers have been barred from employment in industries engaged in defense production solely because of considerations of race, creed, color, or national origin, to the detriment of workers' morale and of national unity:

NOW, THEREFORE, by virtue of the authority vested in me by the Constitution and the statutes, and as a prerequisite to the successful conduct of our national defense production effort, I do hereby reaffirm the policy of the United States that there shall be no discrimination in the employment of workers in defense industries or government because of race, creed, color, or national origin, and I do hereby declare that it is the duty of employers and of labor organizations, in furtherance of said policy and of this order, to provide for the full and equitable participation of all workers in defense industries, without discrimination because of race, creed, color, or national origin;

And it is hereby ordered as follows:

1. All departments and agencies of the Government of the United States concerned with vocational and training programs for defense production shall take special measures appropriate to assure that such programs are administered without discrimination because of race, creed, color, or national origin;

2. All contracting agencies of the Government of the United States shall include in all defense contracts hereafter negotiated by them a provision obligating the contractor not to discriminate against any worker because of race, creed, color, or national origin;

3. There is established in the Office of Production Management a Committee on Fair Employment Practice . . . The Committee shall receive and investigate complaints of discrimination in violation of the provisions of this order and shall take appropriate steps to redress grievances which it finds to be valid. The Committee shall also recommend to the several departments and agencies of the Government of the United States and to the President all measures which may be deemed by it necessary or proper to effectuate the provisions of this order.

Franklin D. Roosevelt The White House, June 25, 1941. "

Source– Executive Order of President Franklin D. Roosevelt, 1941

VOCABULARY

prerequisite: a necessary requirement before something else can happen

vocational: having to do with a vocation or occupation

1 **SUMMARIZING** What does President Roosevelt aim to achieve with this order?

_____

_____

2A **IDENTIFYING EFFECTS** What are the effects of discrimination in military production and the government that Roosevelt wants to address?

_____

_____

_____

2B **CITING TEXT EVIDENCE** How does Roosevelt propose ending discrimination in military production and the government?

_____

_____

_____

_____

3 **ANALYZING SOURCES** Roosevelt's executive order aims to end discrimination in the workplace based on which traits? Were women included?

_____

_____

_____

4 **EVALUATING** Do you think Roosevelt's order makes a convincing argument for ending discrimination in government and the workplace?

_____

_____

_____

_____

5 **CIVICS** How do you think discrimination against workers may have affected the war?

_____

_____

ESSENTIAL QUESTION

How does war impact society and the environment?

Ration Book Four

DIRECTIONS: Use the text to answer the questions.

EXPLORE THE CONTEXT: Once the United States entered World War II—after the Japanese bombing of Pearl Harbor, Hawaii, in December 1941—it was necessary to limit the consumption of certain products in order to retain enough for the war effort. Automobile tires were the first item to be rationed, with autos themselves rationed next. Various items followed, including metals used in packaging as well as gasoline and many food items. Most of these regulated goods could be purchased only with rationing coupons, which gave the right to purchase the item but did not affect the cost of the item. The coupons were bound into books and distributed to every person in every household in the United States. Retailers were required to personally tear out the coupons from the books as the items were being purchased in order to prevent people from selling the coupons, which was illegal. This selection comes from a radio broadcast in Massachusetts on October 20, 1943.

PRIMARY SOURCE: RADIO ADDRESS

66 War Book Four is really part of an overall program of simplification. During the last few months we have been trying to make some badly needed changes in regulations and procedures as they affect American families, business men, and the local war price and rationing boards. . . .

There are several ways in which war ration book four is going to save us taxpayers time, money and annoyance.

Up to now we have had to issue a new ration book every four or five months. As one book has come off the press, the next one in the series has had to go into production. During the past few weeks you housewives have had to shop with three ration books for each member of the family.

Eventually, war ration book four will be sufficient . . . and that alone will be a blessing for both housewives and retailers.

Some problems still remain to be ironed out, but we are hoping that war book four is going to last for almost two years.

That means an important money-saving for taxpayers. It costs approximately one and a half million dollars to print and distribute each food ration book.

In addition we have had to ask thousands of patriotic school teachers to give millions of man hours of their time to distribute these various books. Under the new plan much of that effort will be saved. . . . 99

Source— Lawrence J. Bresnahan, Director, Massachusetts Office of Price Administration, "Talking about Ration Book Four," October 20, 1943

VOCABULARY

war book: a book of coupons that allowed consumers to purchase certain items that were in demand for the war effort

war price and rationing boards: groups set up to control sales of certain goods by means of setting prices and providing coupons that allowed a person to buy a certain amount of such protected goods

ration: to restrict the sale of certain items to consumers due to limited supplies

housewives: married women responsible for shopping and other domestic duties for their households

1A SUMMARIZING What is Bresnahan's main point in this radio address?

_____

1B IDENTIFYING PERSPECTIVES How does Bresnahan want his listeners to feel about the news he is sharing?

_____

_____

_____

2 UNDERSTANDING CONTEXT What do we learn about the earlier ration books from this address?

_____

_____

_____

3 INFERRING What does the radio address seem to assume is the attitude of American consumers toward the rationing system? Quote from the passage in your answer.

_____

_____

_____

4 ANALYZING INFORMATION What points does Bresnahan mention in support of the new war books?

_____

_____

_____

5 ECONOMICS Why do you think the U.S. government decided to require consumers to use ration coupons to purchase certain items rather than simply take those items out of the public markets?

_____

_____

_____

_____

ESSENTIAL QUESTION

How does war impact society and the environment?

As you gather evidence to answer the Essential Question, think about:

- how the New Order affected Germany and Asia.

- how Adolf Hitler's racism affected Germany.

- how the devastation of the Holocaust affected Europe.

My Notes

_____

_____

_____

_____

_____

_____

_____

_____

The New Order and the Holocaust

DIRECTIONS Search for evidence in the lesson to help you answer the following questions.

1A **DETERMINING CENTRAL IDEAS** What was the goal of Hitler's social engineering project?

_____

_____

_____

_____

_____

1B **SUMMARIZING** What was Hitler's plan for carrying out his social engineering project?

_____

_____

_____

_____

_____

2 **DESCRIBING** What was Hitler's "Final Solution" to what he called the "Jewish problem"?

_____

_____

_____

_____

_____

_____

_____

_____

3 **ANALYZING INFORMATION** Use the chart below to describe the *Einsatzgruppen* and death camps created by Nazi Germany.

	Description
Einsatzgruppen	
Death camps	

4 **EXPLAINING EFFECTS** How many Jews were killed by the Germans?

_____

5 **DETERMINING MEANING** What is the Hebrew word used to describe the mass slaughter of European Jews? What does that term mean when translated into English?

_____
_____
_____
_____
_____

6 ECONOMICS What was the "Greater East Asia Co-Prosperity Sphere," and how did it relate to the war?

_____
_____
_____
_____
_____
_____
_____

ESSENTIAL QUESTION

How does war impact society and the environment?

The U.S. Secretary of the Interior and the Holocaust

DIRECTIONS: Use the text to answer the questions.

EXPLORE THE CONTEXT: This letter from U.S. Secretary of the Interior Oscar Chapman to U.S. Representative from California Will Rogers and his wife represents an initial move within the United States to address the atrocities being committed by the Nazis. Prior to this, there had been some talk of helping Jewish refugees, but a campaign of misinformation from within the government was attempting to prevent the country from becoming involved in the conflict. Chapman's letter is an opening move toward assisting those seeking to escape the Nazis.

PRIMARY SOURCE: LETTER

"Honorable and Mrs. Will Rogers, Jr.,

Room 506 House Office Building,

Washington, D.C.

My dear Mr. and Mrs. Rogers:

A group of interested persons are meeting together next Sunday afternoon, October 24, to discuss some realistic possibilities for combating the deliberate campaign of annihilation which the Germans are now conducting against the Jewish people of Europe. I am sure you agree that this is not just a problem for Jewish people to work out alone, but one of urgent concern for America and all the United Nations.

Mrs. Chapman and I are to be hosts to the group at four o'clock in our apartment at the Westchester and we are particularly anxious for you to be present. You can telephone your response to our apartment, Ordway 2900, or to my office, Republic1820, Extension 704 or 705. The apartment number is 622-B, reached through the second entrance in the building on the right. Sincerely yours,Oscar Chapman "

Source— Letter from Secretary of Interior, 1943

VOCABULARY

deliberate: considered; on purpose

annihilation: to obliterate; to destroy a thing

Chapman, Oscar. 1943. Secretary of Interior on Campaign to Stop German Annihilation of the Jews - The Holocaust - During WWII. October 18, 1943. Reprinted by Shapell Manuscript Foundation website.

1 **SUMMARIZING** What is Chapman saying in this letter?

_____

_____

_____

_____

2A **DETERMINING MEANING** What is the "deliberate campaign of annihilation" against the Jewish people to which Chapman is referring?

_____

2B **DETERMINING CENTRAL IDEAS** What is the Holocaust?

_____

_____

3 **DETERMINING POINT OF VIEW** What does Chapman mean when he writes, "I am sure you agree that this is not just a problem for Jewish people to work out alone, but one of urgent concern for America and all the United Nations"?

_____

_____

_____

_____

_____

4 **CIVICS** How does this letter show the U.S. government applying democratic principles and values?

_____

_____

_____

5 **UNDERSTANDING EFFECTS** What can be predicted with the type of action the United States would take after this meeting?

_____

_____

_____

ESSENTIAL QUESTION

How does war impact society and the environment?

Hungarian Jews Freed From a Nazi Concentration Camp

DIRECTIONS: Use the image to answer the questions.

EXPLORE THE CONTEXT: This photograph shows Hungarian Jews who had been freed from a Nazi concentration camp in Austria. The Nazis killed around six million Jews during the Holocaust. Many Jews died in concentration camps, where they were either worked to death or forced to participate in deadly medical experiments. The U.S. Army provided food and facilities for these malnourished and exhausted victims of World War II.

PRIMARY SOURCE: PHOTOGRAPH

206320

1 **EVALUATING EVIDENCE** What does this photo show about how the Jewish people were treated in the Nazi concentration camps?

_____

_____

_____

2 **EVALUATING** What type of emotion do the men in the photo portray?

_____

_____

_____

3 **ANALYZING VISUALS** What actions are the men in the photograph taking?

_____

_____

_____

4 **CONSTRUCTING HYPOTHESES** Why do you think this photo is important to the history of World War II?

_____

_____

_____

_____

5 **INFERRING** Why did the Allies wait until after the war to acknowledge the full extent of the Holocaust?

_____

_____

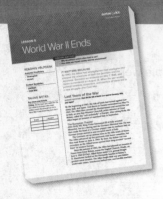

World War II Ends

DIRECTIONS Search for evidence in the lesson to help you answer the following questions.

ESSENTIAL QUESTION

How does war impact society and the environment?

As you gather evidence to answer the Essential Question, think about:

- what ended World War II.
- how the atom bomb played a role in World War II.
- what led to the Cold War.

1   GEOGRAPHY   How did the Allies leverage their geographical position after the Axis powers surrendered to them in Tunisia?

_____

_____

_____

2   GEOGRAPHY   What was the significance of the Allied invasion of the Normandy beaches, known as "D-Day"?

_____

_____

_____

_____

_____

_____

_____

3   INFERRING What was the strategic significance of the Elbe River for Allied troops in Germany?

_____

_____

4   SUMMARIZING Why did the Allies want to take control of Iwo Jima and Okinawa?

_____

_____

_____

My Notes

_____

_____

_____

_____

_____

_____

5 **INFERRING** Why did U.S. president Truman decide to use the atomic bomb against Japan?

_____

_____

_____

_____

6 **COMPARE AND CONTRAST** Fill in the graphic organizer to compare the goals of Stalin and Roosevelt at the Yalta Conference of 1945.

Yalta Conference, 1945

Issue	Roosevelt wanted	Stalin wanted	Outcome
Governments of countries bordering USSR			
Post-war Germany			
War in the Pacific			

ESSENTIAL QUESTION

How does war impact society and the environment?

The Big Three at Yalta

DIRECTIONS: Use the text to answer the questions.

EXPLORE THE CONTEXT: On February 4, 1945, towards the end of World War II, U.S. president Franklin D. Roosevelt, British prime minister Winston Churchill, and Soviet leader Joseph Stalin met in Yalta, a resort city on the northern coast of the Black Sea. This meeting is referred to as the Yalta Conference or the Crimea Conference. The purpose of this meeting was for the great world powers to make decisions regarding the postwar future of the West. The agreement was divided into sections pertaining to several geographic regions.

PRIMARY SOURCE: POLITICAL AGREEMENT

❝AGREEMENT REGARDING JAPAN

The leaders of the three great powers - the Soviet Union, the United States of America and Great Britain - have agreed that in two or three months after Germany has surrendered and the war in Europe is terminated, the Soviet Union shall enter into war against Japan on the side of the Allies on condition that:

1. The status quo in Outer Mongolia (the Mongolian People's Republic) shall be preserved.

2. The former rights of Russia violated by the treacherous attack of Japan in 1904 shall be restored, viz.:

(a) The southern part of Sakhalin as well as the islands adjacent to it shall be returned to the Soviet Union;

(b) The commercial port of Dairen shall be internationalized, the pre-eminent interests of the Soviet Union in this port being safeguarded, and the lease of Port Arthur as a naval base of the U.S.S.R. restored;

(c) The Chinese-Eastern Railroad and the South Manchurian Railroad, which provide an outlet to Dairen, shall be jointly operated by the establishment of a joint Soviet-Chinese company, it being understood that the pre-eminent interests of the Soviet Union shall be safeguarded and that China shall retain sovereignty in Manchuria;

3. The Kurile Islands shall be handed over to the Soviet Union.

It is understood that the agreement concerning Outer Mongolia and the ports and railroads referred to above will require concurrence of Generalissimo Chiang Kai-shek. The President will take measures in order to maintain this concurrence on advice from Marshal Stalin.

The heads of the three great powers have agreed that these claims of the Soviet Union shall be unquestionably fulfilled after Japan has been defeated.

For its part, the Soviet Union expresses it readiness to conclude with the National Government of China a pact of friendship and alliance between the U.S.S.R. and China in order to render assistance to China with its armed forces for the purpose of liberating China from the Japanese yoke.

Joseph Stalin

Franklin D. Roosevelt

Winston S. Churchill **❞**

Source— Crimea Conference, 1945

VOCABULARY

treacherous: disloyal; backstabbing

adjacent: next to something

internationalized: a country under protection of two or more nations

safeguard: buffer; protection

concurrence: simultaneously occurring

1 **SUMMARIZING** Based on the excerpt, what happened at the Yalta Conference?

_____

_____

2 **ANALYZING** Why was participation from the Soviet Union important to Great Britain and the United States?

_____

_____

_____

3 **IDENTIFYING BIAS** Why might an agreement with the Soviet Union have been difficult to achieve?

_____

_____

4 **DESCRIBING** Based on the source, briefly describe the terms of agreement between the Soviet Union and the Allied powers.

_____

_____

_____

5 GEOGRAPHY How did the Yalta Conference impact the Soviet Union's territorial presence in Asia?

_____

_____

_____

6 **EXPLAINING CAUSE AND EFFECT** How did the Yalta Conference set the stage for the Cold War?

_____

_____

_____

Copyright © McGraw-Hill Education   1945. Potsdam Agreement. Reprinted 2003 by Jan Osmanczyk and Anthony Mango. Encyclopedia of the United Nations and International Agreements - Third Edition - Volume 3: N to S. New York: Routledge.

ESSENTIAL QUESTION

How does war impact society and the environment?

The Berlin (Potsdam) Conference

DIRECTIONS: Use the text to answer the questions.

EXPLORE THE CONTEXT: The United States, Great Britain, and the Soviet Union had taken control of Germany and needed a plan for its governance. The Potsdam Agreement between the Allied powers addressed how they would handle post-war Germany to prevent the resurgence of the Nazi party. The agreement, dated August 1, 1945, took place in Potsdam, which borders the German capital city of Berlin. U.S. president Harry Truman, Soviet leader Joseph Stalin, and British prime minister Clement Attlee negotiated these decisions.

PRIMARY SOURCE: POLITICAL AGREEMENT

"II. THE PRINCIPLES TO GOVERN THE TREATMENT OF GERMANY IN THE INITIAL CONTROL PERIOD

1. In accordance with the Agreement on Control Machinery in Germany, supreme authority in Germany is exercised, on instructions from their respective Governments, by the Commanders-in-Chief of the armed forces of the United States of America, the United Kingdom, the Union of Soviet Socialist Republics, and the French Republic, each in his own zone of occupation, and also jointly, in matters affecting Germany as a whole, in their capacity as members of the Control Council.

2. So far as is practicable, there shall be uniformity of treatment of the German population throughout Germany.

3. The purposes . . . by which the Control Council shall be guided are:

(i) The complete disarmament and demilitarization of Germany and the elimination or control of all German industry that could be used for military production. . . .

4. All Nazi laws which provided the basis of the Hitler regime or established discriminations on grounds of race, creed, or political opinion shall be abolished. . . .

5. War criminals and those who have participated in planning or carrying out Nazi enterprises involving or resulting in atrocities or war crimes shall be arrested and brought to judgment. . . .

6. All members of the Nazi Party who have been more than nominal participants in its activities and all other persons hostile to Allied purposes shall be removed from public and semi-public office, and from positions of responsibility in important private undertakings. . . .

7. German education shall be so controlled as completely to eliminate Nazi and militarist doctrines and to make possible the successful development of democratic ideas.

8. The judicial system will be reorganized in accordance with the principles of democracy, of justice under law, and of equal rights for all citizens without distinction of race, nationality or religion. . . ."

Source— Potsdam Agreement, 1945

VOCABULARY

practicable: capable of being practiced or carried out

disarmament: elimination of military weapons

demilitarization: elimination of military forces, troops

1 SUMMARIZING What are the Allied powers trying to accomplish with the agreements in this excerpt from the Potsdam Conference?

_____

_____

1A EXPLAINING CAUSE AND EFFECT How does the plan prevent Nazi ideas from spreading again?

_____

_____

2 CIVICS Why do you think the trio made a plan to reorganize the German legal system?

_____

_____

_____

3 PREDICTING Why did the three powers agree that Nazis would be "removed from public and semi-public office, and from positions of responsibility in important private undertakings"?

_____

_____

_____

4 CONSTRUCTING HYPOTHESES Why do you think the agreement addressed the issue of uniform treatment for all areas and people of Germany?

_____

_____

_____

_____

5 IDENTIFYING CONNECTIONS What major war events happened before and after the Potsdam Conference?

_____

ESSENTIAL QUESTION

How does war impact society and the environment?

My Notes

_____

_____

_____

_____

_____

_____

_____

_____

_____

_____

_____

_____

_____

_____

_____

1 Think About It

Review the supporting questions you developed at the beginning of the chapter. Review the evidence you gathered in the chapter. Were you able to answer each Supporting Question? If there was not enough evidence to answer your Supporting Questions, what additional evidence do you think you need to consider?

_____

_____

2 Organize Your Evidence

Complete the chart below with information you learned about World War II and how it impacted society and the environment.

World War II Cause and Effect Timeline

Cause(s)	Effect(s)
1938–1939: Germany takes the Sudentenland, parts of Czechoslovakia, and invades Poland.	1939:
June 1941: Germany invades the Soviet Union.	1941:
December 1941: Japan bombs U.S. at Pearl Harbor.	December 1941:
1942: The tide turns against the Axis Powers.	1943:
1945: Hitler commits suicide; Mussolini is assassinated; Japan suffers when nuclear bombs are dropped.	1945:

❸ Talk About It

Work in small groups. With your group, discuss the events that occurred during World War II and how they impacted the world when it was over. Consider each row on your chart as you talk about the causes and effects during the six-year war. Take notes about your discussion below.

_____
_____
_____
_____
_____
_____
_____
_____
_____

❹ Connect to the Essential Question

Following your work in the Talk About It activity, create a visual essay that helps answer the Essential Question: _How does war impact society and the environment?_ Use the essay to visually illustrate how World War II impacted different countries and cultures. Your visual essay should include relevant images, drawings, music, or animation. The essay can be in the form of a collage, drawing, video, or slideshow.

_____
_____
_____
_____
_____
_____
_____
_____

TAKE ACTION

MAKE CONNECTIONS After World War II, several books were published about the Holocaust. Holocaust survivor Elie Wiesel wrote about his experience at the concentration camps with his father. He was 16 years old when he was freed. His book *Night* has been translated into 30 languages.

Another famous book was a diary written by Anne Frank. Frank wrote about hiding from the Nazis with her family. The family was captured in 1944 and sent to a concentration camp, where Frank died. She was 15 years old. *The Diary of Anne Frank* was published by her father, who survived the Holocaust, in 1942 and has been published in more than 60 languages.

DIRECTIONS: Choose one of these books and organize a book club at your school. Pick a time to meet—perhaps during class (ask your teacher's permission first), lunch, or after school. Discuss what the book is about. Use the knowledge from your textbook to discuss what was going on during that time. Ask each other what it would be like to experience these situations. The two authors were teenagers when they experienced the Holocaust. How does that change your perspective?

_____

_____

_____

_____

_____

_____

_____

_____

_____

_____

_____

The Cold War

ESSENTIAL QUESTION

How does conflict influence political relationships?

Think about how the Cold War influenced international political relationships.

TALK ABOUT IT

With a partner, discuss the sort of information you would need to discover how the Cold War manifested itself from the end of World War II through the late 1980s and how the Cold War influenced political relationships around the world. For example, you might ask, "How was the Cold War's impact on political relationships different from World War II's?"

DIRECTIONS: Now write down three additional questions that will help you explain how the Cold War influenced political relationships.

MY RESEARCH QUESTIONS

Supporting Question 1:

_____

_____

Supporting Question 2:

_____

_____

Supporting Question 3:

_____

_____

_____

_____

The Cold War Begins

DIRECTIONS Search for evidence in the lesson to help you answer the following questions.

1A **SUMMARIZING** Who were the major players in the Cold War? What disputes signaled the beginning of the Cold War?

_____

_____

_____

_____

1B **EVALUATING EVIDENCE** Read the excerpt from Churchill's speech in Lesson 1. Do you agree with historians that this speech signaled the beginning of the Cold War?

_____

_____

_____

_____

_____

2A **DETERMINING CENTRAL IDEAS** What is the main idea of the Truman Doctrine? The Marshall Plan?

_____

_____

_____

_____

_____

_____

_____

ESSENTIAL QUESTION

How does conflict influence political relationships?

As you gather evidence to answer the Essential Question, think about:

- how World War II shifted the balance of power.
- how the Cold War began and spread.
- what political relationships and alliances emerged during the Cold War.

My Notes

_____

_____

_____

_____

_____

_____

_____

2B IDENTIFYING BIAS What were the major ideas, or assumptions, underlying the Truman Doctrine and the Marshall Plan?

Document	Assumption
Truman Doctrine	
Truman Doctrine	
Truman Doctrine	
Marshall Plan	

3 EXPLAINING CAUSE AND EFFECT What effect did the Cold War have on military and political relationships between countries?

		Effects on Military and Political Relationships
Cause: The Cold War	→	

4 ECONOMICS What impact do you think the new alliances, NATO and the Warsaw Pact, likely had on the economies of the countries involved?

_____

_____

_____

ESSENTIAL QUESTION

How does conflict influence political relationships?

Construction of the Berlin Wall

DIRECTIONS: Study the image. Then respond to the questions that follow.

EXPLORE THE CONTEXT: When the Cold War first started, many people fled from Soviet-ruled East Germany to democratic West Germany by crossing into West Berlin. It was a loophole that allowed people to choose democracy. The Soviet Union responded to this loophole by building a wall that separated East Berlin from West Berlin. The Berlin Wall was both a physical and ideological barrier. It divided the city from 1961 to 1989, when it was demolished. Construction, which is depicted in the image below, began in August 1961 and was officially ordered by the German Democratic Republic. The Berlin Wall was more than just a wall; there were guard posts and trenches to prevent people from crossing.

PRIMARY SOURCE: PHOTOGRAPH

1 **CITING TEXT EVIDENCE** Based on the image, which side is East Berlin? How do you know?

_____

2 **EXPLAINING CAUSE AND EFFECT** What events and factors contributed to the Soviet decision to build the Berlin Wall?

_____

_____

3 **IDENTIFYING CONNECTIONS** How is the construction of the Berlin Wall connected to the events of World War II?

_____

_____

_____

4 **GEOGRAPHY** What impact do you think the Berlin Wall had on the physical space in Berlin?

_____

_____

_____

_____

_____

_____

5 **IDENTIFYING EFFECTS** What do you think was the economic impact of the Berlin Wall?

_____

_____

_____

6 **DETERMINING CONTEXT** What does the image suggest about the political climate in Germany?

_____

_____

_____

_____

ESSENTIAL QUESTION

How does conflict influence political relationships?

Notes Between the United States and the Soviet Union

DIRECTIONS: Read the letters. Then respond to the questions that follow.

EXPLORE THE CONTEXT: By the 1960s, tensions between the United States and the Soviet Union were well-established. Tensions continued to rise when construction on the Berlin Wall began in 1961. In the letters below, the United States addresses the Soviet Union regarding its actions in Berlin.

PRIMARY SOURCE: GOVERNMENT BULLETIN

United States Note to the USSR On Berlin, August 17, 1961

" . . . On August 13, East German authorities put into effect several measures regulating movement at the boundary of the western sectors and the Soviet sector of the city of Berlin. These measures have the effect of limiting . . . passage from the Soviet sector to the western sectors of the city. These measures were accompanied by the closing of the sector boundary by a sizable deployment of police forces and by military detachments brought into Berlin for this purpose.

All this is a flagrant, and particularly serious, violation of the quadripartite status of Berlin. . . . The United States Government has never accepted that limitations can be imposed on freedom of movement within Berlin. The boundary between the Soviet sector and the western sectors of Berlin is not a state frontier. The United States Government considers that the measures which the East German authorities have taken are illegal. . . .

The United States Government expects the Soviet Government to put an end to these illegal measures.

Source—*The Department of State Bulletin*, September 4, 1961

Soviet Reply

. . . The Soviet Government fully understands and supports the actions of the Government of the German Democratic Republic which established effective control on the border with West Berlin in order to bar the way for subversive activity being carried out from West Berlin against the G.D.R. and other countries of the socialist community. . . .

The Government of the U.S.A. attempts in its note to represent its effort to perpetuate the occupation of West Berlin . . . as a concern for the Germans and almost as a concrete expression of the right to self-determination. Such attempts in the final analysis cannot be taken seriously. And if the taking of defensive measures on the G.D.R. border with West Berlin creates certain temporary inconveniences for the city's population, blame for this rests entirely with the occupation authorities and the F.R.G. Government, which have done everything to prevent improvement of the atmosphere in this area in accordance with the legitimate interests of all states. Thus, the protest made in the note of the Government of the U.S.A. is without foundation and is categorically rejected by the Soviet Government. . . . "

Source— *The Department of State Bulletin*, September 4, 1961

VOCABULARY

regulating: controlling

sector: section

flagrant: glaring; obvious

quadripartite: split into four separate parts

unilateral: coming from only one side

1961. Exchange Between U.S. and U.S.S.R. August 17 and 18, 1961. Reprinted July 1962 in The Department of State Bulletin - Volume XLV: Numbers 1149-1174. Washington, D.C.: U.S. Government Printing Office.

1 **DETERMINING CENTRAL IDEAS** What is the main idea of the United States's note to the Soviet Union?

_____

_____

_____

2 **SUMMARIZING** What is the Soviet Union's response to the United States's note?

_____

_____

_____

3 **ANALYZING TEXT STRUCTURE** What is the tone of the note from the United States?

_____

4 **ANALYZING INFORMATION** How are the notes connected to the previous source, the image of construction on the Berlin Wall?

_____

_____

5 **HISTORY** How do these notes illustrate the overarching theme of the Cold War that conflict impacted political relationships?

_____

_____

_____

_____

_____

6 **IDENTIFYING BIAS** How might historians see bias in these notes?

_____

_____

_____

China After World War II

DIRECTIONS Search for evidence in the lesson to help you answer the following questions.

1A SUMMARIZING What was the Great Leap Forward?

_____

_____

1B ECONOMICS Why did Mao initiate the Great Leap Forward?

_____

_____

_____

2A DETERMINING CENTRAL IDEAS What were some of the aspects of society that were affected by Mao's Cultural Revolution?

ESSENTIAL QUESTION

How does conflict influence political relationships?

As you gather evidence to answer the Essential Question, think about:

- how communism changed China.
- why China became involved in the Cold War.
- how the conflict of the Cold War impacted China's political relationships.

My Notes

_____

_____

_____

_____

_____

_____

_____

PERMANENT REVOLUTION

2B **INTERPRETING** How did the Cultural Revolution end?

_____

_____

_____

_____

_____

3 **IDENTIFYING CONNECTIONS** Why did China become involved in the Cold War?

_____

_____

4 **RELATING EVENTS** What was China's role in the Cold War? Use the graphic organizer to describe the three stages of China's development over those decades.

China in the Cold War	
Stage 1: Chinese Communist Party took over	
Stage 2: China allied with the Soviet Union	
Stage 3: China allied with the United States	

ESSENTIAL QUESTION

How does conflict influence political relationships?

Mao's Sixteen Points

DIRECTIONS: Read the excerpt from the manifesto. Then respond to the questions that follow.

EXPLORE THE CONTEXT: The Sixteen Points was a resolution passed by China's Communist Party that established the Cultural Revolution in 1966. According to the Sixteen Points, the "Great Proletarian Cultural Revolution" was "a new stage in the development of the socialist revolution in our country." The resolution established the Red Guard. Even though it encouraged verbal altercations in place of physical fights, the Red Guard often used physical force. The excerpt below is from Mao's Sixteen Points.

PRIMARY SOURCE: BOOK

" . . . Although the bourgeoisie has been overthrown, it is still trying to use the old ideas, culture and customs, and habits of the exploiting classes to corrupt the masses, capture their minds, and endeavor to stage a comeback. The proletariat must do just the opposite: it must meet head-on every challenge of the bourgeoisie in the ideological field and use the new ideas, culture, customs, and habits of the proletariat to change the mental outlook of the whole of society. At present our objective is to struggle against and crush those persons in authority who are taking the capitalist road, to criticize and repudiate the reactionary bourgeois academic "authorities" and the ideology of the bourgeoisie and all other exploiting classes and transform education, literature, and art and all other parts of the superstructure that do not correspond to the socialist economic base, so as to facilitate the consolidation and development of the socialist system. . . .

The masses of the workers, peasants, soldiers, revolutionary intellectuals, and revolutionary cadres form the main force in this Great Cultural Revolution. Large numbers of revolutionary young people, previously unknown, have become courageous and daring pathbreakers. . . . "

Source— Mao Zedong, *The Sixteen Points: Guidelines for the "Great Proletarian Cultural Revolution,"* 1966

VOCABULARY

bourgeois: upper class

proletariat: working class

ideological: related to a set of ideas

repudiate: to reject

1 **INTERPRETING** What is the difference between the proletariat and the bourgeoisie?

_____

_____

_____

_____

2 DETERMINING CENTRAL IDEAS What is the main idea of this excerpt from Mao's Sixteen Points?

_____

_____

_____

_____

3 ANALYZING TEXT STRUCTURE Who is Mao's audience?

_____

_____

_____

4 ANALYZING POINT OF VIEW What is the purpose of these guidelines?

_____

_____

_____

_____

_____

_____

_____

5 CIVICS Do you think a document like the Sixteen Points is an efficient way to motivate and inspire people? Why or why not?

_____

_____

_____

_____

6 CITING TEXT EVIDENCE What phrases and sentences in the text indicate Mao's bias?

_____

_____

_____

_____

ESSENTIAL QUESTION

How does conflict influence political relationships?

Chervonenko's Diary

DIRECTIONS: Read the diary. Then respond to the questions that follow.

EXPLORE THE CONTEXT: Stepan Vasilievich Chervonenko was the ambassador from the Soviet Union to China in the 1960s. He interacted heavily with Deng Xiaoping, who was a major policy maker at the time. Deng Xiaoping took control of China after Mao Zedong's death. He brought the Cultural Revolution to an end in order to pursue more practical reforms. Deng Xiaoping was able to hold a significant amount of power without having an official government position. The excerpt below is from Chervonenko's diary. He recorded a conversation with Deng Xiaoping.

PRIMARY SOURCE: DIARY

" . . . Deng Xiaoping said: "We have a good basis for resolving difficulties— the principles of Marxism-Leninism, the Moscow declaration of 1957 and the Moscow statement of 1960. If only these principles are used as real sources of guidance, and the Declaration and Statement are observed, then there can be no issues which cannot be resolved between the fraternal parties. . . . "

For our part, expressed confidence that the presence of some as-yet unresolved issues between our parties, however significant they might be, does not serve as a barrier to unity between the CPSU and the CCP, and that if the will for close unity were manifested, we could return to a situation that always pleased our people,-a situation of true trust and friendship. . . .

"For us," said Deng Xiaoping, "it is completely clear that the key issue now is agriculture. (In your country, issues of agriculture also occupy an important place, he noted). In past years in the PRC, the city population has grown excessively. For this reason, agriculture, in its present level of development, does not meet the demands of supply such an increased city population. In the course of 1961 alone, the population of the cities alone was reduced by 13 million persons, who returned to the countryside, on the whole to the same places where they had previously lived. A large portion of this number is directed into people's communes, since large capital inputs are needed for the development of state farms. In this year, the re-settlement of another 10 million people from the cities to rural areas is planned. Resettlement to the countryside lessens the problem of supplying the city population. In past years, the development of industry in China took place at high tempos. At the same time, a situation developed where almost in every enterprise the number of workers significantly exceeds the quantity needed for the full use of existing productive capacity. At some enterprises there are as many workers as would be needed only 10 years hence. As a result, an irrational use of labour power is taking place. . . . "

The meeting, which continued all in all for about an hour and a half, took place in an even, calm tone. . . . In parting with us, Deng Xiaoping said: "Your letter calls for solidarity – and that is good. . . . "

Source— Diary of Stepan Vasilievich Chervonenko, March 1, 1962

VOCABULARY

CPSU: Communist Party of the Soviet Union

CCP: Chinese Communist Party

PRC: People's Republic of China

communes: communities where all possessions are shared

capital: money

enterprise: company or place of business

1 **INTERPRETING** Why did Chervonenko write this in his diary?

_____

_____

_____

2 **CITING TEXT EVIDENCE** Based on Chervonenko's diary, how would you describe Deng Xiaoping? Cite evidence from the text to support your answer.

_____

_____

_____

3 **DETERMINING CENTRAL IDEAS** What can you tell from this document about Deng Xiaoping's role in Communist China?

_____

_____

_____

4 **UNDERSTANDING CONTEXT** What does this document indicate about the relations between China and the Soviet Union?

_____

_____

5 **IDENTIFYING CONNECTIONS** How does this document connect to Mao's Sixteen Points?

_____

_____

_____

6 CIVICS What do you think may be included in the diaries of government officials today?

_____

_____

_____

_____

Cold War Conflicts

ESSENTIAL QUESTION

How does conflict influence political relationships?

As you gather evidence to answer the Essential Question, think about:

- how the Cold War impacted political relationships in countries other than the United States and the Soviet Union.
- how proxy wars impact the players involved.
- how the Vietnam War and the Korean War were indicative of larger, ideological conflicts.

My Notes

_____

_____

_____

_____

_____

_____

_____

DIRECTIONS Search for evidence in the lesson to help you answer the following questions.

1A **DETERMINING MEANING** The origin of the word *proxy* is "procuracy," which refers to the office of an official who represents others in a Roman court. Given this definition, how would you define a *proxy war*?

_____

1B **INTERPRETING** Why did the United States and the Soviet Union fight proxy wars instead of fighting each other directly?

_____

_____

_____

2A **SUMMARIZING** What did U.S. President Harry S. Truman say about communism in his inaugural address?

_____

_____

_____

2B **EXPLAINING EFFECTS** How did Truman's comments about communism impact the relationship between the United States and the Soviet Union?

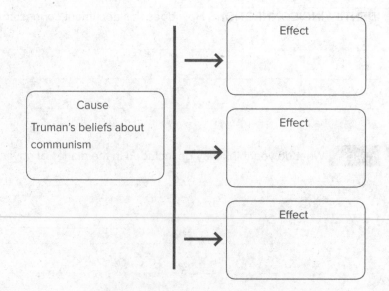

3 IDENTIFYING CONNECTIONS How did nuclear weapons impact political relations during the Cold War?

_____

_____

_____

_____

_____

_____

_____

4 **HISTORY** How was the Vietnam War perceived in the United States? What factors contributed to how the war was perceived?

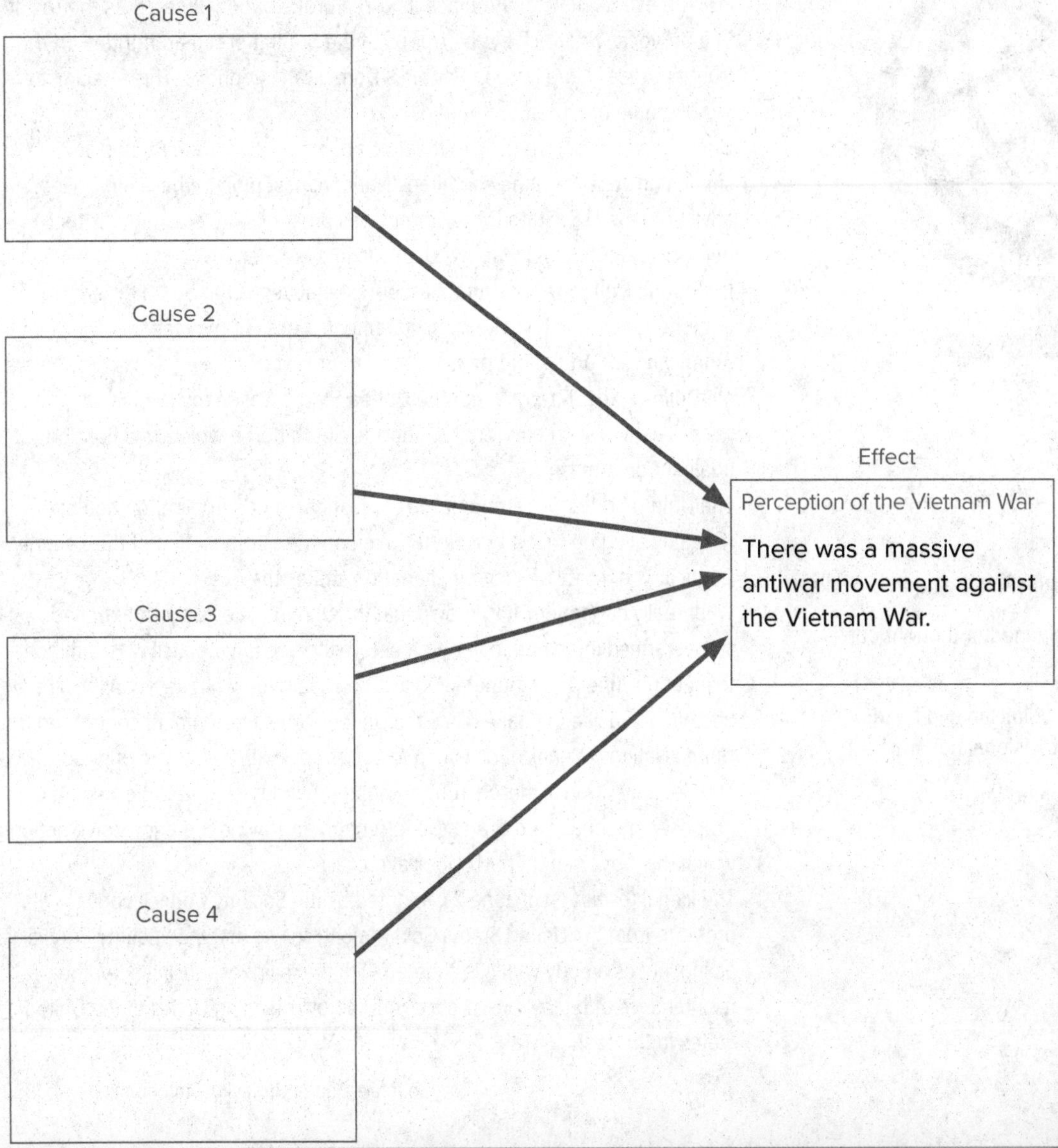

Cause 1

[ ]

Cause 2

[ ]

Cause 3

[ ]

Cause 4

[ ]

Effect

Perception of the Vietnam War

There was a massive antiwar movement against the Vietnam War.

The U.S., U.S.S.R., and Korean War

ESSENTIAL QUESTION
How does conflict influence political relationships?

DIRECTIONS: Read the official statement. Then respond to the questions that follow.

EXPLORE THE CONTEXT: When North Korea invaded South Korea and sparked the Korean War, the United States defended South Korea. The Soviet Union supported North Korea. The Soviets helped North Korea establish a communist government. The United States supported South Korea financially and militarily. Andrei Gromyko, Soviet Minister of Foreign Affairs, made the following statement about Soviet involvement in the Korean War.

PRIMARY SOURCE: OFFICIAL STATEMENT

❝ The events now taking place in Korea broke out on June 25 as the result of a provocative attack by the troops of the South Korean authorities on the frontier areas of the Korean People's Democratic Republic. This attack was the outcome of a premeditated plan. . . .

Only one week before the provocative attack. . ., Syngman Rhee said, in a speech on June 19 in the so-called "National Assembly" where Mr. Dulles, adviser to the U.S. State Department, was present: "If we cannot protect democracy in the cold war, we shall win in a hot war."

It is not difficult to understand that representatives of the South Korean authorities could only make such statements because they felt that they had American support behind them. . . .

Mr. Dulles . . .declared. . . that the United States was ready to give all necessary moral and material support to South Korea which was fighting against Communism.

The United States Government tries to justify armed intervention against Korea by alleging that it was undertaken on the authorisation of the Security Council. The falsity of such an allegation strikes the eye.

What really happened? It is known that the United States Government had started armed intervention in Korea before the Security Council was summoned to meet on June 27, without taking into consideration what decision the Security Council might take. Thus the United States Government confronted the United Nations Organisation with a *fait accompli*, with a violation of peace.

The Security Council merely rubber-stamped and back-dated the resolution proposed by the United States Government, approving the aggressive actions which this Government had undertaken. . . .

The illegal resolution of June 27, adopted by the Security Council under pressure from the United States Government, shows that the Security Council is acting, not as a body which is charged with the main responsibility for the maintenance of peace, but as a tool utilised by the ruling circles of the United States for unleashing war. . . . ❞

Source— Andrei Gromyko, Statement, July 4, 1950

VOCABULARY

provocative: inciting; intending to provoke

premeditated: planned or thought out ahead of time

Syngman Rhee: politician and head of South Korea's provisional government

falsity: state of being false

1 **SUMMARIZING** Describe the differences between a cold war and a hot war.

_____

_____

2 **CITING TEXT EVIDENCE** To what is Gromyko referring when he says, "These facts speak for themselves and need no comment?" Cite evidence from the text to support your answer.

_____

_____

3 **ANALYZING POINT OF VIEW** How does Gromyko's summary of the start of the Korean War differ from the United States's perspective?

_____

_____

_____

_____

_____

4 **DETERMINING MEANING** What is the tone of Gromyko's statement?

_____

_____

5 **COMPARING POINTS OF VIEW** How does the tone of Gromyko's statement compare to Truman's statement on communism in his inaugural address?

_____

_____

_____

_____

6 CIVICS What are some ways countries can solve conflict without military action? Which of these ways is mentioned in Gromyko's statement?

_____

_____

ESSENTIAL QUESTION

How does conflict influence political relationships?

VOCABULARY

assurances: promises

station: to set up

peril: danger

Kennedy's Speech on Cuba

DIRECTIONS: Read the speech. Then respond to the questions that follow.

EXPLORE THE CONTEXT: The Cuban Missile Crisis of October 1962 was the most threatening moment of the Cold War. It was the moment when the Soviet Union and the United States came closest to engaging in nuclear war. After Fidel Castro overthrew the Cuban dictator, the Soviets brought missiles into Cuba and continued to arm the small island despite U.S. president John F. Kennedy's demands to stop. The excerpt below is from Kennedy's speech about the Cuban Missile Crisis.

PRIMARY SOURCE: SPEECH

" . . . Within the past week, unmistakable evidence has established the fact that a series of offensive missile sites is now in preparation on [the island of Cuba]. The purposes of these bases can be none other than to provide a nuclear strike capability against the Western Hemisphere. . .

. . . This action also contradicts the repeated assurances of Soviet spokesmen, both publicly and privately delivered that the arms build-up in Cuba would retain its original defensive character and that the Soviet Union had no need or desire to station strategic missiles on the territory of any other nation. Neither the United States of America nor the world community of nations can tolerate deliberate deception and offensive threats on the part of any nation, large or small. We no longer live in a world where only the actual firing of weapons represents a sufficient challenge to a nation's security to constitute maximum peril. Nuclear weapons are so destructive and ballistic missiles are so swift that any substantially increased possibility of their use or any sudden change in their deployment may well be regarded as a definite threat to peace. For many years both the Soviet Union and the United States, recognizing this fact, have deployed strategic nuclear weapons with great care, never upsetting the precarious status quo which insured that these weapons would not be used in the absence of some vital challenge. . . .

But this secret, swift, and extraordinary build-up of Communist missiles—in an area well known to have a special and historical relationship to the United States and the nations of the Western Hemisphere . . .is a deliberately provocative and unjustified change in the status quo which cannot be accepted by this country if our courage and our commitments are ever to be trusted again by either friend or foe.

The 1930's taught us a clear lesson: aggressive conduct, if allowed to grow unchecked and unchallenged, ultimately leads to war. This nation is opposed to war. We are also true to our word. Our unswerving objective, therefore, must be to prevent the use of these missiles against this or any other country and to secure their withdrawal or elimination from the Western Hemisphere. "

Source— Address on the Cuban Missile Crisis, October 22, 1962

1 DETERMINING CENTRAL IDEAS What is the main idea of Kennedy's speech?

_____

_____

2 CITING TEXT EVIDENCE Who is Kennedy's primary intended audience? Is there a secondary audience for this speech?

_____

_____

_____

_____

3 ANALYZING TEXT STRUCTURE How does Kennedy structure his speech? Describe each of the parts.

_____

_____

4 RELATING EVENTS To what is Kennedy referring when he mentions the 1930s? What effect might this have?

_____

_____

5 HISTORY How does Kennedy evoke the Monroe Doctrine? Cite evidence from the text to support your answer.

_____

_____

_____

_____

6 ASSESSING What was the purpose of Kennedy's speech? Do you think his speech was designed effectively?

_____

_____

_____

ESSENTIAL QUESTION

How does conflict influence political relationships?

My Notes

_____

_____

_____

_____

_____

_____

_____

_____

_____

_____

_____

_____

_____

_____

_____

❶ Think About It

Review the supporting questions you developed at the beginning of the chapter. Review the evidence you gathered in the chapter. Were you able to answer each Supporting Question? If there was not enough evidence to answer your Supporting Questions, what additional evidence do you think you need to consider?

_____

_____

_____

_____

❷ Organize Your Evidence

Complete the chart below with information you learned about the Cold War, specifically how the conflict impacted political relationships across the world.

Country	How Cold War Affected Country
Soviet Union	
United States	
Korea	
China	
Cuba	
Vietnam	

③ Talk About It

Work in small groups. With your group, discuss the effects of the Cold War on various countries. Compare your charts. Did each member of your group choose the same effects?

④ Write About It

Work in small groups. If your group members have different information on their charts, add relevant information to your chart. Then write one small paragraph summarizing how the Cold War impacted political relationships in the countries listed in the chart.

_____

_____

_____

_____

_____

_____

_____

_____

_____

⑤ Connect to the Essential Question

Following your work in the Write About It activity, choose two countries from the chart. Then create a one-act play involving those two countries that answers the Essential Question: _How does conflict influence political relationships?_

Your play should describe the relationship between the two countries. Consider having the United States or the Soviet Union as one of the countries you choose. Your play should last about five minutes and include a script with dialogue and action tags. You should do research to find the names of specific political players, such as ambassadors, to mention in the play. Be sure to include the context of the Cold War and add relevant details that indicate the time period. For instance, the time just after World War II would be different from the 1970s. Your play should be creative, accurate, and engaging.

CITIZENSHIP
TAKING ACTION

MAKE CONNECTIONS   The United States's fear of communism did not completely fade away with the end of the Cold War. In fact, in political elections, a common tactic is for politicians to accuse their opponents of being communist or socialist. This can raise fears in the minds of the American people and influence elections. Contrary to popular belief during the Cold War, many countries have found ways to blend socialism and democracy. They are no longer mutually exclusive.

DIRECTIONS: Begin by researching democratic socialism and countries that use it in their governments. Then write a social media post in which you analyze democratic socialism. Consider the following questions:

For what kind of society does democratic socialism work?
What aspects of socialism already exist in the United States?
Why does the word *socialism* often raise fears?
What are the benefits and drawbacks of socialism?

Remember that people oftentimes read social media posts on their phones, so keep your paragraphs short and your overall post direct. Include at least one link to a relevant source.

_____

_____

_____

_____

_____

_____

_____

_____

_____

_____

Independence and Nationalism in the Developing World

ESSENTIAL QUESTION

How can political change cause conflict?

Think about the challenges new nations in Africa, Latin America, and Asia faced as they shook off colonialism and formed independent nations.

TALK ABOUT IT

With a partner, discuss the sort of information you would need to discover to explain why political change in emerging nations can lead to conflict. What questions would you need to answer in order to explore this topic? For instance, one question might be, "Who determines borders when a new nation forms?"

DIRECTIONS: Now write down three additional questions that will help you explain the kinds of conflict that can surface during times of political change.

MY RESEARCH QUESTIONS

Supporting Question 1:

_____

_____

Supporting Question 2:

_____

_____

_____

Supporting Question 3:

_____

_____

_____

_____

South and Southeast Asia

DIRECTIONS Search for evidence in the lesson to help you answer the following questions.

1 **DESCRIBING** Use the web to record details of the direction in which Jawaharlal Nehru took the new nation of India.

ESSENTIAL QUESTION

How can political change cause conflict?

As you gather evidence to answer the Essential Question, think about:

- methods that nations have used to gain independence.

- the different kinds of governments that have been formed by new nations.

- how changes in new nations lead to conflict.

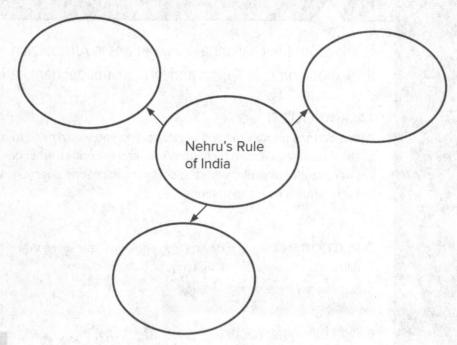

Nehru's Rule of India

My Notes

_____

_____

_____

_____

_____

_____

_____

2 **IDENTIFYING EFFECTS** What events in India have been caused by ethnic and religious conflicts?

_____

_____

_____

_____

_____

_____

_____

3 **EXPLAINING ISSUES** What challenges did the following countries face in the aftermath of gaining their independence?

Country	Challenges
India	
Pakistan	
Indonesia	
Myanmar	

4A **RELATING EVENTS** What characterized the governments of Singapore, Myanmar, and the Philippines in the years after their independence?

_____

_____

4B **DRAWING CONCLUSIONS** Why do military and autocratic regimes often use the tactics of murdering or jailing opponents?

_____

_____

_____

_____

_____

5 CIVICS A new nation needs to first set up its government. Why does this often lead to massive conflict?

_____

_____

_____

_____

_____

_____

ESSENTIAL QUESTION

How can political change cause conflict?

Refugees of the Partition of India and Pakistan

DIRECTIONS: Use the image to answer the questions.

EXPLORE THE CONTEXT: In 1947 India gained independence from England, and leaders had many difficult decisions to make. The majority of India's population practiced the Hindu religion, with Muslims making up a large minority group. Many Muslims feared that their needs would not be met by a government made up of mostly Hindus. As a result, the land was divided into two new nations: India would keep its Hindu majority while two sections to the north would become Muslim-dominated West and East Pakistan. During this division, or partition, two million people migrated to either India or Pakistan. An American photographer took this photograph at a refugee camp in Delhi, India, in 1947, during this migration.

PRIMARY SOURCE: PHOTOGRAPH

1A **IDENTIFYING** What does the photograph show? What emotions might the people be feeling?

_____

_____

1B **INTERPRETING** Why were so many people in South Asia displaced into refugee camps?

_____

_____

_____

_____

_____

2 **DETERMINING POINT OF VIEW** What do you think the photographer wants to communicate with this image?

_____

_____

_____

3 **IDENTIFYING CONNECTIONS** How did the partition reveal the kinds of conflicts that can arise during times of great change?

_____

_____

_____

_____

_____

_____

4 **HISTORY** Many leaders, such as Mohandas Gandhi, were against the idea of partition. How would this photograph have supported their argument?

_____

_____

_____

How can political change cause conflict?

Philippine President Corazon Aquino's Address to the United States Congress

DIRECTIONS: Read the excerpt. Then respond to the questions.

EXPLORE THE CONTEXT: Corazon Aquino became the first female president of the Philippines in February 1986, ending the long dictatorship of Ferdinand Marcos. Her husband, Benigno Aquino, had led the opposition to Marcos's rule but was assassinated in 1983. Protests over his assassination eventually forced Marcos from power. After becoming president, Aquino immediately began democratic reforms, including drafting a new constitution. In this speech before the U.S. Congress in September 1986, Aquino describes her plans for her country.

PRIMARY SOURCE: SPEECH

❝As I came to power peacefully, so shall I keep it. That is my contract with my people and my commitment to God. He had willed that the blood drawn with the lash shall not, in my country, be paid by blood drawn by the sword but by the tearful joy of reconciliation.

We have swept away absolute power by a limited revolution that respected the life and freedom of every Filipino. Now, we are restoring full constitutional government. Again, as we restored democracy by the ways of democracy, so are we completing the constitutional structures of our new democracy under a constitution that already gives full respect to the Bill of Rights. A jealously independent Constitutional Commission is completing its draft which will be submitted later this year to a popular referendum. When it is approved, there will be congressional elections. So within about a year from a peaceful but national upheaval that overturned a dictatorship, we shall have returned to full constitutional government. Given the polarization and breakdown we inherited, this is no small achievement.

My predecessor set aside democracy to save it from a communist insurgency that numbered less than 500. Unhampered by respect for human rights, he went at it hammer and tongs. By the time he fled, that insurgency had grown to more than 16,000. I think there is a lesson here to be learned about trying to stifle a thing with the means by which it grows.

I don't think anybody, in or outside our country, concerned for a democratic and open Philippines, doubts what must be done. Through political initiatives and local reintegration programs, we must seek to bring the insurgents down from the hills and, by economic progress and justice, show them that for which the best intentioned among them fight. ❞

— Corazon C. Aquino, from her address at the Joint Session of the United States Congress, September 18, 1986

VOCABULARY

reconciliation: bringing into agreement or friendliness

polarization: division into opposing groups

insurgency: rebellion against a government

hammer and tongs: violently

reintegration: bringing back into unity

1 **DETERMINING CENTRAL IDEAS** According to Aquino, what was the state of democracy in the Philippines at the time of this speech?

_____

_____

_____

2 **CIVICS** What democratic principles does Aquino emphasize in this excerpt?

_____

_____

3 **DETERMINING MEANING** What do you think Aquino means when she says that "there is a lesson here to be learned about trying to stifle a thing with the means by which it grows"?

_____

_____

4A **IDENTIFYING PERSPECTIVES** Based on this excerpt, how does Aquino think the communist insurgents in her country should be dealt with?

_____

_____

4B **CONTRASTING** How does this differ from the approach of her predecessor?

_____

_____

5 **HISTORY** Later in this speech, Aquino quotes Abraham Lincoln: "With malice towards none, with charity for all, with firmness in the right as God gives us to see the right, let us finish the work we are in, to bind up the nation's wounds, to care for him who shall have borne the battle, and for his widow and for his orphans, to do all which may achieve and cherish a just and lasting peace among ourselves and with all nations." Is the approach to dealing with conflict that Aquino describes in this excerpt similar to what Lincoln expresses in this quote? Explain your answer.

_____

_____

_____

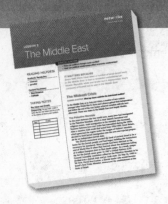

The Middle East

DIRECTIONS Search for evidence in the lesson to help you answer the following questions.

1 **SUMMARIZING** Summarize the major events related to the Israel-Palestinian conflict, leading to 1973.

_____

_____

_____

_____

_____

_____

_____

_____

_____

_____

_____

_____

_____

ESSENTIAL QUESTION

How can political change cause conflict?

As you gather evidence to answer the Essential Question, think about:

- the political, economic, religious, and ethnic roots of conflict in the Middle East.
- how religion has influenced culture in the Middle East.
- tactics used in attempts to reach peace in the Middle East.

My Notes

_____

_____

_____

_____

_____

_____

_____

2 **DETERMINING CENTRAL IDEAS** Explain the purposes of the following agreements.

Agreement	Purpose
Khartoum Resolution	
Camp David Accords	
Oslo Accords	

3 GEOGRAPHY Study the map of Arab-Israel disputes on p. 517 of Chapter 14. The disputed area has religious significance for both Jews and Muslims. What else would make this area valuable for different nations?

_____

_____

4 INTEGRATING INFORMATION In what ways did the United States and the Soviet Union intervene in Afghanistan? How did their strategies reflect their relationships with each other?

_____

_____

_____

_____

_____

_____

5A EXPLAINING CAUSE AND EFFECT How did the Iranian revolution change life in Iran? Use this cause-and-effect chart to organize your answers.

Cause: Iranian Revolution of 1979	→	Effects

5B EXPLAINING ISSUES Most nations in the Middle East, including Iran, have a majority Muslim population. Why has Iran still had conflicts with its neighbors?

_____

_____

_____

_____

_____

ESSENTIAL QUESTION

How can political change cause conflict?

The Iranian Revolution

DIRECTIONS: Use the image to answer the questions.

EXPLORE THE CONTEXT: In the 1970s, under the rule of its monarch, the Shah Reza Shah Pahlavi, Iran raced toward modernization and westernization. Not everyone was happy with the direction in which the country was headed. Ayatollah Ruhollah Khomeini lead the opposition. Conservative Muslims opposed the increasing secularization of the country, and millions still lived in poverty while the shah and his family had lives of extreme privilege and wealth. The shah also made use of a secret police force that jailed, tortured, and even killed his opponents. In the winter of 1978–1979, discontent boiled over, with people marching and rioting in the streets. The shah took a vacation abroad and never returned. In this photograph, protesters march against the shah.

PRIMARY SOURCE: PHOTOGRAPH

1A IDENTIFYING CONNECTIONS What message do these protestors have about the Shah of Iran? What specific arguments do they have against him?

_____

_____

_____

_____

1B **INTERPRETING** After the shah fled the country, he asked for temporary asylum in the United States to receive cancer treatment. The president granted him permission to stay in New York. What opinion would these protestors likely have about the decision of the United States?

_____

_____

_____

2 **COMPARING POINTS OF VIEW** At the time, the American government had a favorable view of the shah, and the Ayatollah Khomeini was considered an enemy. What does this protest tell you about different people's points of view during international conflict?

_____

_____

_____

3 **INFERRING** Some of the protestors are carrying portraits of the Ayatollah Khomeini. What does that tell you about their opinion of him? Why do you think carrying leaders' portraits is a common activity at protests?

_____

_____

_____

4 **DESCRIBING** The _savak_ was the secret police established by the shah of Iran. How were these protestors protecting themselves from the _savak_? What does tell you about the possible consequences of this protest?

_____

_____

_____

5 CIVICS What do you think protestors hope to achieve through marches, signs, and chants?

_____

_____

_____

ESSENTIAL QUESTION

How can political change cause conflict?

Letters Preceding the Camp David Accords

DIRECTIONS: Use the text to answer the questions.

EXPLORE THE CONTEXT: Ever since the creation of the state of Israel, conflict has flared between Arabs and Israelis. In 1978 and 1979, U.S. president Jimmy Carter helped to negotiate the first peace agreement between the neighbors, the Camp David Accords. Israeli prime minister Menachem Begin and Egyptian president Anwar el-Sadat spent 12 days negotiating at Carter's presidential retreat at Camp David, Maryland, before signing the agreement in March 1979. Before the three leaders met, they exchanged letters, including the following.

PRIMARY SOURCE: LETTERS

❝Prime Minister Begin to President Carter

. . . September 17, 1978

Dear Mr. President:

I have the honor to inform you that during two weeks after my return home I will submit a motion before Israel's Parliament (the Knesset) to decide on the following question:

If during the negotiations to conclude a peace treaty between Israel and Egypt all outstanding issues are agreed upon, "are you in favor of the removal of the Israeli settlers from the northern and southern Sinai areas or are you in favor of keeping the aforementioned settlers in those areas?"

The vote, Mr. President, on this issue will be completely free from the usual Parliamentary Party discipline to the effect that although the coalition is being now supported by 70 members out of 120, every member of the Knesset, as I believe, both of the Government and the Opposition benches will be enabled to vote in accordance with his own conscience.

Sincerely yours,

Menachem Begin

President Carter to President Sadat

. . . September 22, 1978

Dear Mr. President:

I transmit herewith a copy of a letter to me from Prime Minister Begin setting forth how he proposes to present the issue of the Sinai settlements to the Knesset for the latter's decision.

In this connection, I understand from your letter that Knesset approval to withdraw all Israeli settlers from Sinai according to a timetable within the period specified for the implementation of the peace treaty is a prerequisite to any negotiations on a peace treaty between Egypt and Israel.

Sincerely,

Jimmy Carter ❞

—Jimmy Carter, *The Camp David Accords - Annex to the Framework Agreements,* 1978

VOCABULARY

discipline: practice

in accordance with: following

prerequisite: something that is required first

void: not valid

Begin, Menachem and Carter, Jimmy. 1978. The Camp David Accords - Annex to the Framework Agreements - Exchanges of Letters. Reprinted by Jimmy Carter Presidential Library & Museum.

1. **DETERMINING CONTEXT** What was the main issue that the three leaders wanted to negotiate?

_____

_____

2. **CIVICS** Negotiations between two sides often make use of a third party, or a person or group who is not directly involved in the problem. Who was the third party in the Camp David Accords? Why is it helpful to have a third party assist with negotiations?

_____

_____

_____

_____

3. **DETERMINING CENTRAL IDEAS** What does el-Sadat consider non-negotiable before the leaders sit down together?

_____

_____

3A. **COMPARING POINTS OF VIEW** How do these letters reveal the differences in the points of view of the Arab and Israel leaders?

_____

_____

_____

_____

4. **IDENTIFYING BIAS** Would you consider Carter's letter biased or unbiased? Explain. Why would it be important for him to keep this tone?

_____

_____

_____

5. **INFERRING** What was going to be special about the way Israel's parliament would determine the vote? What do you think Begin hoped to communicate to el-Sadat with this decision?

_____

_____

_____

_____

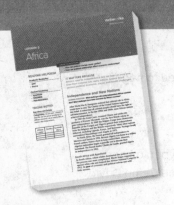

Africa

DIRECTIONS Search for evidence in the lesson to help you answer the following questions.

1 **DESCRIBING** How did the Organization of African Unity (OAU) reflect the philosophy of Pan-Africanism?

_____

_____

_____

_____

_____

2 **COMPARING AND CONTRASTING** How was the African form of socialism unique?

_____

_____

3 **SUMMARIZING** Record details about Joseph Mobutu's rule over Congo.

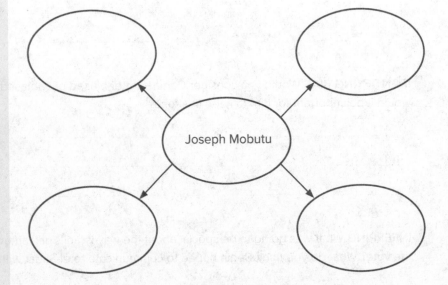

ESSENTIAL QUESTION

How can political change cause conflict?

As you gather evidence to answer the Essential Question, think about:

- how South Africans defeated the practice of apartheid.
- the effects of the Cold War on Africa.
- why many nations embraced the idea of pan-Africanism.

My Notes

_____

_____

_____

_____

_____

_____

_____

4 **ECONOMICS** Most African nations are rich in resources. Why did so many still struggle economically?

_____

_____

_____

_____

_____

5 **SUMMARIZING** Record the events that occurred in Rwanda before and after independence that led to the murder of hundreds of thousands of people.

6 **CITING TEXT EVIDENCE** Cite text evidence to support the idea that Nelson Mandela was a good candidate for the first democratic elections in South Africa.

_____

_____

_____

_____

_____

_____

_____

ESSENTIAL QUESTION

How can political change cause conflict?

South Africa Votes for Mandela

DIRECTIONS: Use the image to answer the questions.

EXPLORE THE CONTEXT: Four years after Nelson Mandela's release from prison, South Africa held its first democratic national elections. The election would mark the final step of the process of ending apartheid. With a parliamentary election system, South Africans would cast a ballot for a party, with the leader of the winning party taking the role of president. Nelson Mandela had returned to the top leadership spot of his original organization, the African National Congress (ANC). On Election Day, April 27, 1994, the ANC won in a landslide, making Mandela the first democratically elected president of South Africa. In this photograph, supporters of Mandela gather with signs to support him in his bid for president.

PRIMARY SOURCE: PHOTOGRAPH

1A **DESCRIBING** What campaign message is Mandela promoting?

_____

_____

1B **DETERMINING CONTEXT** In what ways would that campaign message differ from the policies of South Africa prior to the 1994 election?

_____

_____

_____

2 **DRAWING CONCLUSIONS** What kind of gathering is this? Why do you think so?

_____

_____

_____

3 **DRAWING CONCLUSIONS** Why would Mandela draw massive crowds during his campaign stops?

_____

_____

_____

_____

_____

_____

4 **INFERRING** What unique challenges would Mandela have faced as the winner of this election?

_____

_____

_____

_____

5 CIVICS What purpose do campaign stops with the public serve in the time before an election?

_____

_____

_____

_____

ESSENTIAL QUESTION

How can political change cause conflict?

VOCABULARY

heartening: encouraging

hoisted: raised up

fragmentation: separation

viable: capable of working

I Speak of Freedom

DIRECTIONS: Use the text to answer the questions.

EXPLORE THE CONTEXT: In 1957 the British colony of the Gold Coast gained independence and became the country of Ghana. Its first prime minister, Kwame Nkrumah, had led the fight for independence from Britain. Like Nelson Mandela, he had been imprisoned at times for his resistance to the British. Unlike Mandela, once he became leader of his nation, he ruled in an authoritarian manner. Nkrumah also adopted the philosophy of Pan-Africanism, which he discusses in this excerpt from his book *I Speak of Freedom.*

PRIMARY SOURCE: ESSAY

"... It is clear that we must find an African solution to our problems, and that this can only be found in African unity. Divided we are weak; united, Africa could become one of the greatest forces for good in the world. Although most Africans are poor, our continent is potentially extremely rich. Our mineral resources, which are being exploited with foreign capital only to enrich foreign investors, range from gold and diamonds to uranium and petroleum....Never before have a people had within their grasp so great an opportunity for developing a continent endowed with so much wealth. Individually, the independent states of Africa, some of them potentially rich, others poor, can do little for their people. Together, by mutual help, they can achieve much. But the economic development of the continent must be planned and pursued as a whole. A loose confederation designed only for economic co-operation would not provide the necessary unity of purpose. Only a strong political union can bring about full and effective development of our natural resources for the benefit of our people. The political situation in Africa today is heartening and at the same time disturbing. It is heartening to see so many new flags hoisted in place of the old; it is disturbing to see so many countries of varying sizes and at different levels of development, weak and, in some cases, almost helpless. If this terrible state of fragmentation is allowed to continue it may well be disastrous for us all. There are at present some 28 states in Africa, excluding the Union of South Africa, and those countries not yet free. No less than nine of these states have a population of less than three million. Can we seriously believe that the colonial powers meant these countries to be independent, viable states? The example of South America, which has as much wealth, if not more than North America, and yet remains weak and dependent on outside interests, is one which every African would do well to study. Critics of African unity often refer to the wide differences in culture, language and ideas in various parts of Africa. This is true, but the essential fact remains that we are all Africans, and have a common interest in the independence of Africa. . . . **"**

Source— Kwame Nkrumah, *I Speak of Freedom: A Statement of African Ideology,* 1961

1A **DETERMINING POINT OF VIEW** What was Nkrumah's hope for Africa's future?

_____

_____

1B **UNDERSTANDING CONTEXT** How does this text reflect Nkrumah's support of Pan-Africanism?

_____

_____

1C **EVALUATING ARGUMENTS** What does Nkrumah say to convince readers that Pan-Africanism is a worthy goal?

_____

_____

_____

_____

2 **ANALYZING ISSUES** According to Nkrumah, what was the problem with Africa's natural resources? How might unity among African nations solve this problem?

_____

_____

_____

_____

3 **ANALYZING ISSUES** What does Nkrumah admit is a challenge when it comes to African unity? How does he counter this argument?

_____

_____

_____

_____

4 GEOGRAPHY What geographic obstacles would Nkrumah need to face in order to realize his goal for Africa?

_____

_____

_____

_____

Latin America

DIRECTIONS Search for evidence in the lesson to help you answer the following questions.

1A **EXPLAINING ISSUES** How have South America's natural resources contributed to many countries' unsteady economic conditions?

_____

_____

_____

_____

_____

_____

1B **ECONOMICS** Using Latin American countries as an example, explain how overdependence on other countries can lead to economic instability.

_____

_____

_____

_____

_____

2 **DESCRIBING** Describe how the United States intervened in the affairs of Latin American countries. How was this sometimes harmful?

_____

_____

_____

_____

_____

ESSENTIAL QUESTION

How can political change cause conflict?

As you gather evidence to answer the Essential Question, think about:

- ways that economic problems can lead to political conflict.
- the influence of the Cold War and the rise of Marxism in Latin America.
- how revolutions caused changes throughout Latin America.

My Notes

_____

_____

_____

_____

_____

3 SUMMARIZING Record the events that occurred before, during, and after the Cuban revolution.

Date	Event
1933	
1954	
1959	
1960	

4 COMPARING AND CONTRASTING Compare and contrast the reigns of Augusto Pinochet and Juan Perón.

_____

_____

_____

_____

_____

5 IDENTIFYING EFFECTS What role did Marxism play in the events of the following countries?

Country	Role of Marxism
El Salvador	
Nicaragua	
Colombia	
Chile	

ESSENTIAL QUESTION

How can political change cause conflict?

Billboard in Havana

DIRECTIONS: Use the image to answer the questions.

EXPLORE THE CONTEXT: The relationship between Cuba and the United States has been tense since the 1950s. The U.S. had supported dictator Fulgencio Batista but still recognized the new government of Cuba after the country's revolution. Relations deteriorated soon afterward, however, with the U.S. disapproving of Cuba's communist reforms and close relationship with the Soviet Union. The coast of Florida is only about 100 miles from the island of Cuba. Also, the U.S. has long maintained a naval station and prison at Guantánamo Bay on the island itself, tying the interests of the two countries together. This billboard in Havana, Cuba, translates to "Dear Imperialists: We are not the least bit afraid of you."

PRIMARY SOURCE: PHOTOGRAPH

1A DETERMINING CONTEXT Describe the relationship between Cuba and the United States since 1959.

_____

_____

_____

_____

_____

1B **ANALYZING SOURCES** How does this billboard reflect the relationship between the two countries?

_____

_____

_____

_____

2 **DETERMINING POINT OF VIEW** How has the artist used visuals to communicate his or her point of view?

_____

_____

_____

3 **COMPARING POINTS OF VIEW** What message might an artist on the other side of the conflict want to communicate?

_____

_____

_____

4 **INFERRING** This billboard is located by the building that houses American diplomats in Havana. What is the significance of this location?

_____

_____

_____

5 CIVICS Analyze the effects of using a public billboard in displaying political art. What problems could public political artworks cause?

_____

_____

_____

_____

ESSENTIAL QUESTION

How can political change cause conflict?

Che Guevara on Revolution

DIRECTIONS: Use the text to answer the questions.

EXPLORE THE CONTEXT: Ernesto "Che" Guevara was born in Argentina in 1928. Introduced to the ideas of Marxism, Guevara traveled to Cuba to assist in the communist overthrow of dictator Fulgencio Batista. As one of Fidel Castro's trusted advisors, Guevara remained in Cuba after the revolution to help run the government. In this speech, he addresses a group of medical students and other health-care workers in Havana.

PRIMARY SOURCE: SPEECH

❝Through special circumstances and perhaps also because of my character, after receiving my degree I began to travel through Latin America and I got to know it intimately. Except for Haiti and the Dominican Republic, I have visited—in one way or another—all the other countries of Latin America. In the way I traveled, first as a student and afterward as a doctor, I began to come into close contact with poverty, with hunger, with disease, with the inability to cure a child because of lack of resources, with the numbness that hunger and continued punishment cause until a point is reached where a parent losing a child is an unimportant accident, as often happens among the hard-hit classes of our Latin American homeland. And I began to see that there was something that, at that time, seemed to me almost as important as being a famous researcher or making some substantial contribution to medical science, and it was helping those people.

But I continued being, as all of us always continue being, a child of my environment, and I wanted to help those people through my personal efforts. I had already traveled a lot—I was then in Guatemala....and I had begun to make some notes to guide the conduct of a revolutionary doctor. . . .

However, the aggression came, the aggression unleashed by the United Fruit Company, the State Department, Foster Dulles—in reality, they are all the same thing—and the puppet they put in named Castillo Armas. . . .The aggression was successful, given that the people had not yet reached the level of maturity the Cuban people have today. . . .

Then I realized one fundamental thing: to be a revolutionary doctor or to be a revolutionary, there must first be a revolution. The isolated effort, the individual effort, the purity of ideals, the desire to sacrifice an entire lifetime to the noblest of ideals goes for naught if that effort is made alone, solitary, in some corner of Latin America, fighting against hostile governments and social conditions that do not permit progress. A revolution needs what we have in Cuba: an entire people mobilized, who have learned the use of arms and the practice of combative unity, who know what a weapon is worth and what the people's unity is worth. ❞

Source— Ernesto "Che" Guevara, Speech to Healthcare Workers, Havana, Cuba, August 20, 1960

VOCABULARY

intimately: in a close and detailed way

Foster Dulles: John Foster Dulles, the U.S. Secretary of State from 1953–1959

Castillo Armas: the U.S.-backed ruler of Guatemala, 1954–1957

goes for naught: is a failure

combative: ready to fight

1A **DETERMINING POINT OF VIEW** How did Guevara's background as a medical student affect his perspective of revolutionary causes? How does he direct the content of this speech to his audience?

_____

_____

1B **ANALYZING POINTS OF VIEW** Guevara had grown up in a middle-class family and had the chance to go to university. How did his travels change his point of view of how his fellow Latin Americans lived?

_____

_____

2 **ANALYZING TEXTS** What descriptive language does Guevara use that reveals his opinion of the American government and businesses involved in Latin American disputes?

_____

_____

_____

3 **DETERMINING CENTRAL IDEAS** How did the events in Guatemala change Guevara's goals for himself?

_____

4 **IDENTIFYING CONNECTIONS** How does the message of Guevara's speech connect with the actions of Cuba in other Latin American countries?

_____

_____

_____

5 **HISTORY** Though he was Argentinian by birth, Guevara is a national hero in Cuba. His portrait appears on signs and buildings all over the country. What qualities do you think he had that earned him the respect of so many Cuban people?

_____

_____

_____

_____

ESSENTIAL QUESTION

How can political change cause conflict?

My Notes

_____

_____

_____

_____

_____

_____

_____

_____

_____

_____

_____

_____

_____

_____

_____

_____

1 Think About It

Review the supporting questions you developed at the beginning of the chapter. Review the evidence you gathered in the chapter. Were you able to answer each Supporting Question? If there was not enough evidence to answer your Supporting Questions, what additional evidence do you think you need to consider?

_____

_____

_____

_____

2 Organize Your Evidence

Complete the chart below with information you learned about the kinds of conflicts and challenges that surfaced as new nations emerged in Africa, Asia, and Latin America. Also consider changes that happened as societies and governments responded to these challenges. Choose one nation from each region to examine.

Conflicts, Challenges, and Changes	
South and Southeast Asian Country:	
Middle Eastern Country:	
African Country:	
Latin American Country:	

Copyright © McGraw-Hill Education

③ Talk About It

Work in a small group. With your group, discuss the conflicts, challenges, and changes that you noted in your chart. Compare your charts. If you picked the same country as another group member, did you note the same details in your chart? If you picked different countries, how did the conflicts, challenges, and changes compare among them?

④ Write About It

Following your discussion in the Talk About It activity, write about two countries from the chapter, comparing and contrasting the changes that occurred in the initial years after their independence from colonialism. Analyze how successful the countries were in transitioning to new leadership.

_____

_____

_____

_____

_____

⑤ Connect to the Essential Question

You are an advisor to the leaders of a new country that is setting up a government for the first time. Use what you have learned from the chapter to put together a report, advising the leaders of steps they could take to establish a peaceful, successful country. Point out challenges that they might face and think of possible solutions to those challenges. Use examples from the chapter of countries that were successful and unsuccessful in their leadership. Ensure that your report is well-organized, clear, and informative.

CITIZENSHIP
TAKING ACTION

MAKE CONNECTIONS As you read in the chapter, newly-independent countries faced many challenges when handling the sudden changes in their leadership. People in the countries disagreed about the paths the countries should take, often leading to protests or more serious turmoil. Other countries featured successful negotiations over decisions.

Read about your community or state and find a problem that people disagree about. Research people's opinions on either side of the issue. Choose one side of the issue. Write a persuasive essay trying to get people on the other side of the issue to see your point of view. Remember to be respectful of their views, and support your opinion with facts.

Share your essays in a group. Give each other feedback on how effective your essays are. How do you think people would respond if they saw your essays in a newspaper? What could you do to make the essays more powerful or convincing? What kinds of strategies do you think work best in persuading people or compromising with them?

_____

_____

_____

_____

_____

_____

_____

_____

_____

_____

_____

_____

Life During The Cold War

ESSENTIAL QUESTION

What challenges may countries face as a result of war?

After World War II, the countries of the world adjusted to new governments and new economic realities. In the decades after that conflict, the Cold War shuffled alliances and affected foreign policy for many countries.

TALK ABOUT IT

With a partner, discuss the sort of information you would need to discover to explain the changes countries underwent during the Cold War. What questions would you need to answer in order to explore this topic? For instance, one question might be, "How did alliances shift between World War II and the Cold War?"

DIRECTIONS: Now write down three additional questions that will help you explain the kinds of challenges countries faced as a result of World War II and the Cold War.

MY RESEARCH QUESTIONS

Supporting Question 1:

_____

_____

_____

Supporting Question 2:

_____

_____

_____

Supporting Question 3:

_____

_____

Western Europe and North America

ESSENTIAL QUESTION

What challenges may countries face as a result of war?

As you gather evidence to answer the Essential Question, think about:

- the economic climate in France, Britain, and West Germany in the years after World War II.

- how economic prosperity and the Cold War affected the United States.

- what social changes Americans faced during the 1960s.

My Notes

_____

_____

_____

_____

_____

_____

_____

DIRECTIONS: Search for evidence in the lesson to help you answer the following questions.

1 **COMPARING AND CONTRASTING** Compare the presidencies of Charles de Gaulle and François Mitterrand.

_____

_____

_____

_____

2 **DESCRIBING** What characterized the "economic miracle" during Konrad Adenauer's leadership of West Germany? What would have been surprising about this?

_____

_____

_____

_____

_____

_____

3 **ECONOMICS** How did European countries' formation of the European Economic Community reflect their goals after World War II?

_____

_____

_____

_____

4A **DETERMINING CENTRAL IDEAS** Record ways in which the French and British governments adopted socialist economic policies.

France	Great Britain

4B **UNDERSTANDING CHANGE** Describe how economic policy in Great Britain changed under the leadership of Margaret Thatcher.

_____

_____

_____

5 **SUMMARIZING** Record major economic and political changes that occurred in the United States under the leadership of the following presidents.

President	Changes in the United States
Dwight D. Eisenhower	
Lyndon B. Johnson	
Richard Nixon	
Jimmy Carter	

ESSENTIAL QUESTION

What challenges may countries face as a result of war?

Fallout Shelters

DIRECTIONS: Use the image to answer the questions.

EXPLORE THE CONTEXT: During the 1950s, the United States and the Soviet Union entered into a heightened era of tension. As both countries built their stores of nuclear weapons, the threat of a nuclear war increased. During the presidency of Dwight D. Eisenhower, the Federal Civil Defense Administration distributed information to Americans about what to do in case of a nuclear attack. People were urged to build fallout shelters, underground bunkers that would provide protection from a nuclear bomb's radiation. Fallout is the nuclear material left in the atmosphere after a nuclear blast. Photographs like this one showed kind of shelters homeowners built in their backyards.

PRIMARY SOURCE: PHOTOGRAPH

1 **DETERMINING CONTEXT** What events of the 1950s made it necessary for the U.S. government to distribute information like this image?

_____

_____

_____

2A **RELATING EVENTS** This photograph was taken only about a decade after the end of World War II. How do you think living through that conflict affected how Americans responded to Cold War threats?

_____

_____

_____

2B **INFERRING** At the time, Americans were going through a "Red Scare." How do you think receiving information like this could affect people's opinions on the spread of communism?

_____

_____

_____

_____

3 **DESCRIBING** How does this image show what people would need in order to protect themselves?

_____

_____

_____

4 **DRAWING CONCLUSIONS** How would you describe the mood of the people in the image? Why do you think they are feeling this way?

_____

_____

_____

_____

5 CIVICS Governments often release public service announcements (PSAs) to educate the people about issues, like advice for building a fallout shelter. What do creators of PSAs have to keep in mind as they plan their message?

_____

_____

_____

ESSENTIAL QUESTION

What challenges may countries face as a result of war?

Thatcher on the Soviet Union

DIRECTIONS: Use the text to answer the questions.

EXPLORE THE CONTEXT: In the 1960s and 1970s, two of Great Britain's main parties, the Conservative Party and Labour Party, took power at different times. In 1979, the Conservatives came to power under Prime Minister Margaret Thatcher. This text excerpt is from a speech she gave on the growing threat the Soviet Union presented to Western Europe and the United States.

PRIMARY SOURCE: SPEECH

❝ If we cannot understand why the Russians are rapidly becoming the greatest naval and military power the world has ever seen[,] if we cannot draw the lesson of what they tried to do in Portugal and are now trying to do in Angola[,] then we are destined—in their words—to end up on 'the scrap heap of history'.

We look to our alliance with American and NATO as the main guarantee of our own security and, in the world beyond Europe, the United States is still the prime champion of freedom.

But we are all aware of how the bitter experience of Vietnam has changed the public mood in America. We are also aware of the circumstances that inhibit action by an American president in an election year.

So it is more vital than ever that each and every one of us within NATO should contribute his proper share to the defense of freedom.

Britain, with her world-wide experience of diplomacy and defense, has a special role to play. We in the Conservative Party are determined that Britain should fulfil that role.

We're not harking back to some nostalgic illusion about Britain's role in the past. We're saying—Britain has a part to play now, a part to play for the future.

The advance of Communist power threatens our whole way of life. That advance is not irreversible, providing that we take the necessary measures now. But the longer that we go on running down our means of survival, the harder it will be to catch up.

In other words: the longer Labour remains in Government, the more vulnerable this country will be. . . .

This is not a moment when anyone with the interests of this country at heart should be talking about cutting our defenses.

It is a time when we urgently need to strengthen our defenses.

Of course this places a burden on us. But it is one that we must be willing to bear if we want our freedom to survive.

Throughout our history, we have carried the torch for freedom. Now, as I travel the world, I find people asking again and again, "What has happened to Britain?" They want to know why we are hiding our heads in the sand, why with all our experience, we are not giving a lead. ❞

Source— Margaret Thatcher, Speech at Kensington Town Hall, January 19, 1976

VOCABULARY

opt out: to choose not to participate

inhibit: to prevent

harking back: remembering the past

nostalgic: having happy memories of the past

vulnerable: easy to attack

1 **DETERMINING CONTEXT** According to Thatcher, how was the Cold War threatening Britain?

_____

_____

2A **DETERMINING CENTRAL IDEAS** What was Thatcher proposing as a solution to the problem posed by the Soviet Union?

_____

_____

_____

2B **IDENTIFYING ISSUES** How did Thatcher's goals differ from those of the Labour Party?

_____

_____

3 **HISTORY** NATO (the North Atlantic Treaty Organization) is an alliance of Western European and North American countries that assist each other with security concerns. What role did Thatcher think NATO should play in the Cold War conflict?

_____

_____

4 **EVALUATING ARGUMENTS** How does Thatcher use Britain's past to appeal to her audience?

_____

_____

5 **INFERRING** A newspaper in the Soviet Union called this Thatcher's "Iron Lady" speech. Why do you think they named it that?

_____

_____

_____

_____

_____

_____

ESSENTIAL QUESTION

What challenges may countries face as a result of war?

As you gather evidence to answer the Essential Question, think about:

- how the Soviet Union developed under the reigns of Joseph Stalin, Nikita Khrushchev, and Leonid Brezhnev.
- how Soviet rule influenced Eastern Europe.
- what Eastern Europeans did to rebel against communism.

My Notes

_____

_____

_____

_____

_____

_____

Eastern Europe and The Soviet Union

DIRECTIONS: Search for evidence in the lesson to help you answer the following questions.

1 ECONOMICS How strong was the Soviet Union's postwar economy? Explain.

_____

_____

_____

_____

2 **DETERMINING CENTRAL IDEAS** Complete the web with policies pursued by Nikita Khrushchev as he attempted to de-Stalinize the Soviet Union.

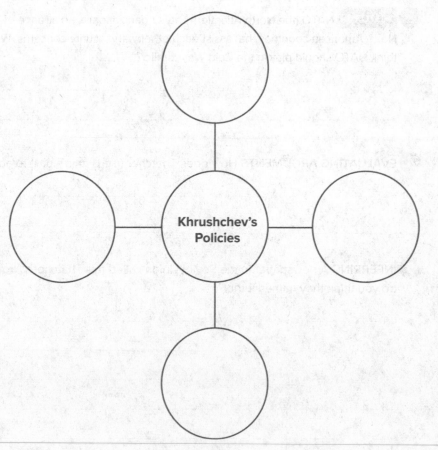

Khrushchev's Policies

3 IDENTIFYING EFFECTS How did the détente between the United States and the Soviet Union affect Soviet citizens' lives?

_____

_____

_____

4 DESCRIBING What major issues plagued the Soviet Union during Leonid Brezhnev's time as general secretary of the Communist Party?

_____

_____

_____

5 EXPLAINING ISSUES Which of the following Eastern European countries did not become a Soviet satellite state? Explain why it was an exception.

East Germany

Romania

Poland

Hungary

Yugoslavia

Czechoslovakia

_____

_____

6 RELATING EVENTS State the major events that led up to the Prague Spring in Czechoslovakia and the events that ended the movement.

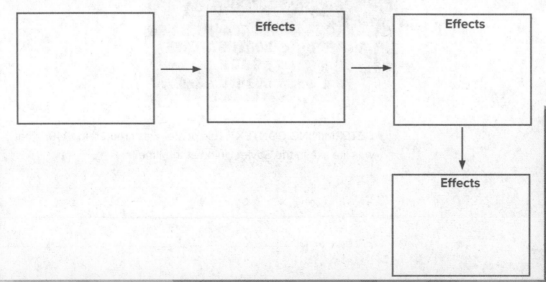

ESSENTIAL QUESTION

What challenges may countries face as a result of war?

Soviet Propaganda

DIRECTIONS: Use the image to answer the questions.

EXPLORE THE CONTEXT: During the Cold War, both the Soviet Union and its foes in the West made use of propaganda. Propaganda is information that is purposely biased in order to promote a certain way of thinking. It can take the form of biased news reports, patriotic rallies, or images that celebrate one way of thinking over another. Many posters produced in the Soviet Union at the time showed positive portrayals of life under Communist rule and negative images of Western leaders. In the poster below, the text reads, "For lasting peace! For people's democracy! Against incendiaries [people who start conflicts] of new war!"

PRIMARY SOURCE: POSTER

1A DETERMINING CONTEXT This poster was created in 1949. What was life like in the Soviet Union at the time?

_____

_____

_____

_____

1B **DETERMINING POINTS OF VIEW** What message does this poster convey about the Soviet Union?

_____

_____

2 **ANALYZING** Describe how the artist has illustrated the Soviet people in the poster. What do you think the artist was trying to communicate about the people? How does that contrast with the reality of the era?

_____

_____

_____

_____

3A **IDENTIFYING BIAS** The people at the bottom right of the poster represent the United Kingdom and the United States. How does the poster show bias against these countries?

_____

_____

3B **ANALYZING** Who is the artist talking about with the word _incendiaries_? What effect would using this word have on the artist's audience?

_____

_____

_____

_____

4 **CIVICS** Why do you think governments make greater use of propaganda during times of conflict?

_____

_____

_____

_____

_____

ESSENTIAL QUESTION

What challenges may countries face as a result of war?

Khrushchev on the Cuban Missile Crisis

DIRECTIONS: Use the text to answer the questions.

EXPLORE THE CONTEXT: A revolution in Cuba in 1959 resulted in the overthrow of President Fulgencio Batista and the establishment of a Communist government, headed by Fidel Castro. As Cuba and the United States ended their relationship and Castro developed ties to the Soviet Union, the American government became concerned. In the spring of 1961, U.S. president John F. Kennedy approved the CIA's secret plan to invade Cuba and overthrow Castro. Known as the Bay of Pigs invasion because of the entry point in a Cuban port of that name, the attack quickly went wrong for the United States. Just two days after American forces landed at the Bay of Pigs on April 17, 1961, the Cubans defeated them. In the telegram below, Soviet premier Nikita Khrushchev sends a message to Kennedy about the invasion.

PRIMARY SOURCE: TELEGRAM

❝ Mr. President, I send you this message in an hour of alarm, fraught with danger for the peace of the whole world. Armed aggression has begun against Cuba. It is a secret to no one that the armed bands invading this country were trained, equipped and armed in the United States of America. The planes which are bombing Cuban cities belong to the United States of America, the bombs they are dropping are being supplied by the American Government. All of this evokes here in the Soviet Union an understandable feeling of indignation on the part of the Soviet Government and the Soviet people. Only recently, in exchanging opinions through our respective representatives, we talked with you about the mutual desire of both sides to put forward joint efforts directed toward improving relations between our countries and eliminating the danger of war. Your statement a few days ago that the USA would not participate in military activities against Cuba created the impression that the top leaders of the United States were taking into account the consequences for general peace and for the USA itself which aggression against Cuba could have. How can what is being done by the United States in reality be understood, when an attack on Cuba has now become a fact?

It is still not late to avoid the irreparable. The Government of the USA still has the possibility of not allowing the flame of war ignited by interventions in Cuba to grow into an incomparable conflagration. I approach you, Mr. President, with an urgent call to put an end to aggression against the Republic of Cuba. Military armament and the world political situation are such at this time that any so-called "little war" can touch off a chain reaction in all parts of the globe. . . . **❞**

Source— Nikita Khrushchev, Telegram to U.S. president John F. Kennedy, April 18, 1961

VOCABULARY

fraught with: filled with (something bad)

evokes: brings to mind

indignation: anger at something unfair

irreparable: unable to be fixed

conflagration: a destructive fire or war

Khrushchev, Nikita. 1961. Telegram From the Embassy in the Soviet Union to the Department of State. Moscow, April 18, 1961. Reprinted 2001 by Thomas Fensch. The Kennedy-Khrushchev Letters. The Woodlands, Texas: New Century Books.

1A **DETERMINING CONTEXT** What characterized Khrushchev's time as head of the Soviet Union?

_____

_____

1B **RELATING EVENTS** How do you think the Bay of Pigs invasion likely affected relations between the United States and Soviet Union?

_____

_____

2 **DETERMINING CENTRAL IDEAS** What does Khrushchev want Kennedy to do?

_____

3 **ANALYZING** What tone do you think Khrushchev takes in this message? What does that tell you about the situation?

_____

_____

4 **DETERMINING CONTEXT** Khrushchev says that "military armament and the world political situation are such at this time that any so-called 'little war' can touch off a chain reaction in all parts of the globe." What does he mean by this statement?

_____

_____

_____

5 GEOGRAPHY Review the location of Cuba on a map. Why was its new Communist government such a major concern for both the United States and the Soviet Union?

_____

_____

_____

_____

_____

The Asian Rim

DIRECTIONS: Search for evidence in the lesson to help you answer the following questions.

1 **IDENTIFYING CAUSES** What factors led to the "Japanese miracle," Japan's massive postwar economic growth?

Causes	Effect
	Japan's dramatic post-war economic recovery

2 **DESCRIBING** Describe how Japan's constitution combined ideas from the U.S. Constitution with some elements of Japan's political past.

_____

_____

_____

_____

_____

3 **CIVICS** How has the national character of Japan affected its society? What do you believe are some characteristics of the United States's national character?

_____

_____

_____

_____

_____

ESSENTIAL QUESTION

What challenges may countries face as a result of war?

As you gather evidence to answer the Essential Question, think about:

- what factors led to great post-war prosperity in Japan.
- why certain countries have been named the "Asian Tigers."
- how China's economy has differed from most of its neighbors'.

My Notes

_____

_____

_____

_____

_____

_____

_____

4A **SUMMARIZING** What do the economies of South Korea, Taiwan, Singapore, and Hong Kong have in common?

_____

_____

4B **INFERRING** Why do you think South Korea, Taiwan, Singapore, and Hong Kong have been given the nickname the "Asian tigers"?

_____

_____

5 **COMPARE AND CONTRAST** Choose two countries from the section "The 'Asian Tigers.'" Compare and contrast their economic focuses as well as their political leadership.

Country: _ _ _ _ _   Country: _ _ _ _ _

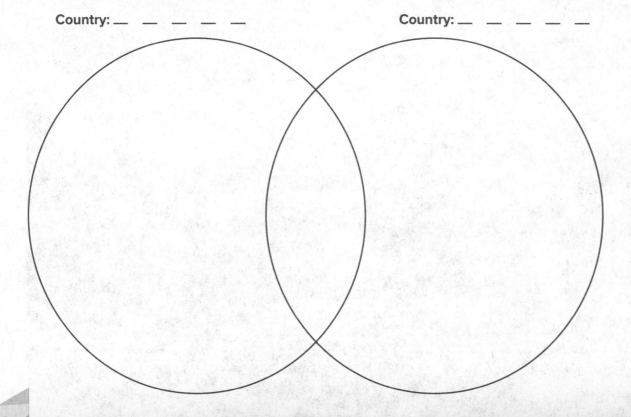

ESSENTIAL QUESTION

What challenges may countries face as a result of war?

Hong Kong's Skyline

DIRECTIONS: Use the image to answer the questions.

EXPLORE THE CONTEXT: Now a territory of China that has some degree of independence, Hong Kong is one of the most densely populated places on Earth. It is also one of the wealthiest, home to some of the world's richest people. Visitors from around the world are impressed with Hong Kong's glittering skyline looming over Victoria Harbor. Another common sight in the harbor are Hong Kong's famous junks, traditional Chinese sailing ships that are still used today.

PRIMARY SOURCE: PHOTOGRAPH

1A **UNDERSTANDING CONTEXT** Why is Hong Kong considered one of the "Asian Tigers"?

_____

_____

1B **INTERPRETING** How does this picture reflect Hong Kong's status as an "Asian Tiger"?

_____

_____

2 **INFERRING** What impression does Hong Kong's skyline make on you? How do you think the people of Hong Kong think of this view of their city?

_____

_____

3 **ANALYZING** Junks are traditional boats that have been used in China and Hong Kong for a long time. What does their presence in the harbor today say about the speed at which Hong Kong has developed?

_____

_____

4 **INFERRING** Junks were once used for trading goods. Today, Hong Kong's junks are used mostly to appeal to tourists going for boat rides. Why do you think the people of Hong Kong want to preserve the use of junks in the harbor?

_____

_____

_____

5 GEOGRAPHY Find Hong Kong and the other "Asian Tiger" countries on a map. What role do you think geography had on their development?

_____

_____

_____

The Constitution of Japan

ESSENTIAL QUESTION

What challenges may countries face as a result of war?

VOCABULARY

Diet: a congress or other legislative meeting

our posterity: future generations of people

striving: working toward

incumbent: necessary for

DIRECTIONS: Use the text to answer the questions.

EXPLORE THE CONTEXT: In the first part of the twentieth century, Japan followed the Meiji Constitution, which had been put in place during the rule of Emperor Meiji, from 1867–1892. Under the Meiji Constitution, a prime minster held some power, but the emperor of Japan was the supreme ruler. Japan's current constitution was drafted in 1946 and adopted as the law of the land in 1947. Below is the first part, or preamble, to the current constitution.

PRIMARY SOURCE: GOVERNMENT DOCUMENT

66 We, the Japanese people, acting through our duly elected representatives in the National Diet, determined that we shall secure for ourselves and our posterity the fruits of peaceful cooperation with all nations and the blessings of liberty throughout this land, and resolved that never again shall we be visited with the horrors of war through the action of government, do proclaim that sovereign power resides with the people and do firmly establish this Constitution. Government is a sacred trust of the people, the authority for which is derived from the people, the powers of which are exercised by the representatives of the people, and the benefits of which are enjoyed by the people. This is a universal principle of mankind upon which this Constitution is founded. We reject and revoke all constitutions, laws, ordinances, and rescripts in conflict herewith.

We, the Japanese people, desire peace for all time and are deeply conscious of the high ideals controlling human relationship, and we have determined to preserve our security and existence, trusting in the justice and faith of the peace-loving peoples of the world. We desire to occupy an honored place in an international society striving for the preservation of peace, and the banishment of tyranny and slavery, oppression and intolerance for all time from the earth. We recognize that all peoples of the world have the right to live in peace, free from fear and want.

We believe that no nation is responsible to itself alone, but that laws of political morality are universal; and that obedience to such laws is incumbent upon all nations who would sustain their own sovereignty and justify their sovereign relationship with other nations.

We, the Japanese people, pledge our national honor to accomplish these high ideals and purposes with all our resources. . . . 99

Source— The Constitution of Japan, 1947

1947. The Constitution of Japan - Effective May 3, 1947. US Department of State - Publication 2836, Far Eastern Series 22.

1 **DETERMINING CONTEXT** What events surrounded the drafting of this constitution? How does that explain why the drafters of the constitution were Americans?

_____

_____

2 **DETERMINING CENTRAL IDEAS** What goals for Japan does the constitution set in place?

_____

_____

3A **DETERMINING CENTRAL IDEAS** According to the writers of this document, what is the relationship between a government and its people?

_____

_____

3B **IDENTIFYING CONNECTIONS** Using your knowledge of the U.S. Constitution, describe how the countries have similar definitions for the role of government.

_____

_____

4 **ANALYZING** Japan had been a fiercely nationalist country during World War II. How does the constitution signal a change from this?

_____

_____

_____

5 **CIVICS** This text is from the preamble, or introduction, to the constitution before the document starts listing specific laws. Why do you think government documents like this often include preambles?

_____

_____

_____

ESSENTIAL QUESTION

What challenges may countries face as a result of war?

My Notes

_____

_____

_____

_____

_____

_____

_____

_____

_____

_____

_____

_____

_____

_____

① Think About It

Review the supporting questions you developed at the beginning of the chapter. Review the evidence you gathered in the chapter. Were you able to answer each Supporting Question? If there was not enough evidence to answer your Supporting Questions, what additional evidence do you think you need to consider?

_____

_____

_____

_____

② Organize Your Evidence

Complete the chart below with information you learned about the kinds of challenges faced by countries worldwide after World War II.

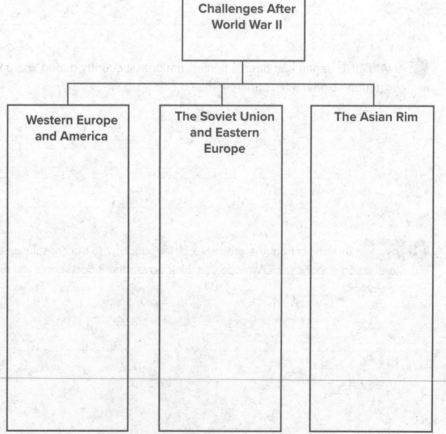

Challenges After World War II

Western Europe and America	The Soviet Union and Eastern Europe	The Asian Rim

③ Talk About It

Work in a small group. With your group, discuss the challenges that you noted in your chart. Compare your charts. What challenges did others note that differ from the ones that you recorded? Which challenges do you think were the most difficult for countries to overcome?

④ Write About It

Following your discussion in the Talk About It activity, write about a problem that either the United States or the Soviet Union faced in the years after World War II. Explain the causes of the problem and then describe what the country did to try to overcome the problem.

_____

_____

_____

_____

_____

⑤ Connect to the Essential Question

You have been tasked by one of the governments mentioned in the chapter to create a public service announcement (PSA) for the people of the country during the Cold War. The PSA is meant to inform people of a problem faced by the country, to give details about the events surrounding the problem, and to keep everyone calm. What information would you want to share with people? How would you use a tone to keep people from panicking about political conflicts? Write a script for a radio PSA meant to educate people about one aspect of life during the Cold War.

CITIZENSHIP
TAKING ACTION

MAKE CONNECTIONS   As you read in the chapter, alliances shifted after World War II. Because some countries developed communist governments and others emerged as capitalist powers, many were at odds with each other. The rivalry between the United States and the Soviet Union dominated much of worldwide relations in the decades after the war. People in each country viewed those in the other with suspicion and hostility. Because of this, there was less motivation to learn about and understand each other's cultures.

Find out about a country that today has a tense relationship with the United States. It could be a country where the United States is occupied in combat or just a country whose government is at odds with ours. Research the history of the country. Find details about how ordinary people live, such as their customs and traditions. Look to understand what makes the country unique rather than focusing on political problems.

Think of a way to present your findings about the country to your classmates. You may want to write a report or create a multimedia presentation. Share the information about your countries with each other. Discuss how learning about a country's culture is helpful when interpreting news about political conflicts with it.

_____

_____

_____

_____

_____

_____

_____

_____

_____

_____

A New Era

ESSENTIAL QUESTION

How can economic and social changes affect a country?

Although the Soviet Union dissolved in 1991, the consequences of the Cold War would affect countries on every continent. Nearly 30 years later, the world faces new economic and social challenges. Consider the factors that created these issues and what people around the world are doing to address them.

TALK ABOUT IT

With a partner, discuss the sort of information you would need to discover to explain how economic and social changes affect a country. Consider the economic and social changes that have occurred in the United States recently. For example, you might ask, "What led to the financial crisis of the late 2000s?" "How did the economy and society change?"

DIRECTIONS: Now write down three additional questions that will help you explain how economic and social changes affect a country.

MY RESEARCH QUESTIONS

Supporting Question 1:

_____

_____

_____

Supporting Question 2:

_____

_____

_____

Supporting Question 3:

_____

End of the Cold War

DIRECTIONS Search for evidence in the lesson to help you answer the following questions.

1A **IDENTIFYING EFFECTS** What factors led to the collapse of the Soviet Union?

_____

_____

_____

_____

_____

_____

1B **RELATING EVENTS** What factors did popular revolutions in 1980s Poland and Czechoslovakia have in common? What factors differed?

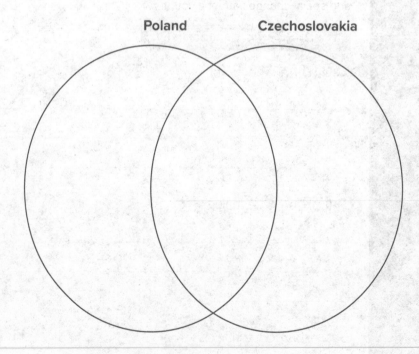

Eastern European Revolutions

ESSENTIAL QUESTION

How can economic and social changes affect a country?

As you gather evidence to answer the Essential Question, think about:

- how the Cold War ended.
- how the end of the Cold War affected post-Soviet countries.
- causes and effects of conflict in the Balkans.

My Notes

_____

_____

_____

_____

_____

_____

_____

_____

2 **INFERRING** How did perestroika and glasnost affect Eastern European political regimes? Complete the chart below to show the effects.

	EFFECTS on EASTERN EUROPEAN COMMUNIST REGIMES
Glasnost	
Perestroika	

3 **DRAWING CONCLUSIONS** What does the term "satellite state" mean in the context of the Soviet Union?

_____

_____

_____

4 **DIFFERENTIATING** What challenges did Boris Yeltsin face? How did these differ from challenges that Vladimir Putin faced?

_____

_____

_____

_____

5 GEOGRAPHY Describe the changes to Yugoslavian geography that occurred during the 1990s.

_____

_____

_____

_____

ESSENTIAL QUESTION

How can economic and social changes affect a country?

Life in a Time of War

DIRECTIONS: Use the image to answer the questions.

EXPLORE THE CONTEXT: From 1992–1995 Sarajevo, the capital of Bosnia-Herzegovina, was under attack by Serbs, who acquired 70 percent of Bosnian territory by 1994. The Serbs followed a policy of ethnic cleansing towards Bosnians, many of whom were Muslim. Despite the violence, the people in the city continued to live their lives. This image, taken in 1993, shows a couple posing on their wedding day next to a car that has been destroyed. The juxtaposition between the happy couple and the shell of a car is striking.

PRIMARY SOURCE: PHOTOGRAPH

1 IDENTIFYING What is the subject of this photograph?

_____

_____

2 INTERPRETING Why is the subject of this photograph significant?

_____

_____

_____

3A DRAWING CONCLUSIONS In addition to illustrating a historical scene, how else does the image inform our understanding of the conflict in Bosnia?

_____

_____

3B INFERRING What does this photograph tell us about the daily life of Bosnians during the war?

_____

_____

4 IDENTIFYING CONNECTIONS Why is it significant that the couple chose to pose next to the car? Explain your answer.

_____

_____

_____

_____

5 GEOGRAPHY Significant Bosnian territory was returned to Bosnians after the war. How does that fact provide a new understanding of this image?

_____

_____

_____

_____

ESSENTIAL QUESTION

How can economic and social changes affect a country?

VOCABULARY

prosperity: wealth

enterprises: businesses or projects

embodiment: the visible form of an idea

crudely: rudimentary

"Tear Down This Wall!"

DIRECTIONS: Use the text to answer the questions.

EXPLORE THE CONTEXT: In 1987 U.S. president Ronald Reagan traveled to West Berlin to celebrate the city's 750th anniversary. There, he gave a speech at the base of the Brandenburg Gate, which was near the Berlin Wall; thus, he could be heard in both East and West Berlin. Also present were Soviet leader Mikhail Gorbachev and Helmut Kohl, Chancellor of West Germany. Reagan's speech was viewed by many as the beginning of the end of the Cold War.

PRIMARY SOURCE: SPEECH

" In the 1950's, Khrushchev predicted: "We will bury you." But in the West today, we see a free world that has achieved a level of prosperity and well-being unprecedented in all human history. In the Communist world, we see failure, technological backwardness, declining standards of health, even want of the most basic kind-too little food. Even today, the Soviet Union still cannot feed itself. After these four decades, then, there stands before the entire world one great and inescapable conclusion: Freedom leads to prosperity. Freedom replaces the ancient hatreds among the nations with comity and peace. Freedom is the victor. And now the Soviets themselves may, in a limited way, be coming to understand the importance of freedom. We hear much from Moscow about a new policy of reform and openness. Some political prisoners have been released. Certain foreign news broadcasts are no longer being jammed. Some economic enterprises have been permitted to operate with greater freedom from state control. Are these the beginnings of profound changes in the Soviet state? Or are they token gestures, intended to raise false hopes in the West, or to strengthen the Soviet system without changing it? We welcome change and openness; for we believe that freedom and security go together, that the advance of human liberty can only strengthen the cause of world peace.

There is one sign the Soviets can make that would be unmistakable, that would advance dramatically the cause of freedom and peace. General Secretary Gorbachev, if you seek peace, if you seek prosperity for the Soviet Union and Eastern Europe, if you seek liberalization: Come here to this gate! Mr. Gorbachev, open this gate! Mr. Gorbachev, tear down this wall! . . .

As I looked out a moment ago from the Reichstag, that embodiment of German unity, I noticed words crudely spray-painted upon the wall, perhaps by a young Berliner, "This wall will fall. Beliefs become reality." Yes, across Europe, this wall will fall. For it cannot withstand faith; it cannot withstand truth. The wall cannot withstand freedom. "

Source— Ronald Reagan, "Remarks on East-West Relations at the Brandenburg Gate in West Berlin," June 12, 1987

1 **ANALYZING** What is Reagan arguing for in this speech? Explain your answer.

_____

_____

2 **IDENTIFYING CONNECTIONS** To what is Reagan referring when he references Moscow's "new policy of reform and openness"?

_____

_____

3A **COMPARING AND CONTRASTING** How does Reagan compare and contrast life in the Soviet Union with life in the "West"? Cite specific examples from the text in your example.

_____

_____

_____

_____

3B **IDENTIFYING BIAS** How might the speaker be demonstrating political bias?

_____

_____

_____

_____

4 **UNDERSTANDING CONTEXT** What occurred in the late 1980s that related to the policies and events mentioned in Reagan's speech?

_____

_____

_____

_____

5 GEOGRAPHY What is the significance of the location of Reagan's speech?

_____

_____

Western Europe and North America

DIRECTIONS: Search for evidence in the lesson to help you answer the following questions.

ESSENTIAL QUESTION

How can economic and social changes affect a country?

As you gather evidence to answer the Essential Question, think about:

- the factors characterizing politics and economics in the United States since the end of the Cold War.
- the factors characterizing politics and economics in Western Europe since the end of the Cold War.
- how the economic and social issues facing United States and Western Europe are similar and different.

1 ECONOMICS Compare and contrast the causes and effects of economic problems that the United States and the European Union faced in the 2000s.

United States	Both Regions	European Union

2 IDENTIFYING CONNECTIONS What characterized attitudes to immigrants in Germany and France in the 2000s? What are possible reasons for these attitudes?

_____

_____

_____

_____

3 IDENTIFYING CAUSES What factors led to the election of American president Barack Obama?

_____

_____

_____

My Notes

_____

_____

_____

_____

_____

_____

4 **EVALUTING EFFECTS** How did the German economy and political apparatus respond to unification? Use the flowchart below to illustrate the process. On each line, describe an effect of the event in the previous line.

   1 East Germany required widespread rebuilding. ⟹

   2 ⟹

   3 ⟹

   4 Social Democrats returned to power in 1995, but failed to address economic problems adequately, leading to increasing attacks on foreigners. ⟹

   5

5A **UNDERSTANDING CONTEXT** What factors allowed for the changing role of NATO?

_____

_____

_____

_____

5B **INFERRING** Why might NATO still be a necessary organization even after the collapse of the Soviet Union?

_____

_____

_____

ESSENTIAL QUESTION

How can economic and social changes affect a country?

The National Debt Clock

DIRECTIONS: Study the image. Then respond to the questions that follow.

EXPLORE THE CONTEXT: The national debt is the total owed by the federal government. This debt is the result of years of deficit spending. Concern about the growing national debt led real estate developer Seymour Durst to create the National Debt Clock in 1989. The purpose of the clock—a digital display that is updated continuously—is to draw attention to how quickly the debt is growing, as well as each family's share of the debt. The clock ran until the year 2000, when budget surpluses had actually reduced the debt. However, by 2002, the federal government was once again running a budget deficit, and the clock was restarted. The National Debt Clock is currently located at One Bryant Park, between 42nd and 43rd Streets in New York City.

PRIMARY SOURCE: PHOTOGRAPH

—photograph of the National Debt Clock

1 **IDENTIFYING CONTEXT** What do you think the people who created the National Debt Clock were hoping it would do?

_____

_____

_____

2 **HISTORY** Why did economic policies in the 1980s likely lead to the creation of the National Debt Clock?

_____

_____

_____

3 **ECONOMICS** The National Debt Clock was able to be turned off in 2000, though it was turned on again in 2002. What does this indicate about the economy at that time?

_____

_____

_____

_____

4 **ANALYZING ISSUES** Why do you think the growing debt is such a concern?

_____

_____

_____

5 **IDENTIFYING CONNECTIONS** If the national debt is such a concern, why has it been so difficult to reduce?

_____

_____

_____

_____

ESSENTIAL QUESTION

How can economic and social changes affect a country?

A Union of European States

DIRECTIONS: Use the text to answer the questions.

EXPLORE THE CONTEXT: The European Community, founded as an economic union in 1958, became a confederation in 1993: the European Union. At the time, the union comprised twelve states but added sixteen more member states by 2013. The European Union adopted a common currency in 2002, known as the euro. In this speech from 2012, the president of the European Council addressed the significance of this union.

PRIMARY SOURCE: SPEECH

" War is as old as Europe. Our continent bears the scars of spears and swords, canons and guns, trenches and tanks, and more. The tragedy of it all resonates in the words of Herodotus, 25 centuries ago: *"In Peace, Sons bury their Fathers. In War, Fathers bury their Sons."* Yet, ... after two terrible wars engulfed the continent and the world with it, ... finally lasting peace came to Europe. In those grey days, its cities were in ruins, the hearts of many still simmering with mourning and resentment. How difficult it then seemed, as Winston Churchill said, *"to regain the simple joys and hopes that make life worth living"*.

As a child born in Belgium just after the war, I heard the stories first-hand. My grandmother spoke about the Great War. In 1940, my father, then seventeen, had to dig his own grave. *He got away; otherwise I would not be here today*.

So what a bold bet it was, for Europe's Founders, to say, yes, we can break this endless cycle of violence, we can stop the logic of vengeance, we can build a brighter future, together. What power of the imagination.
*****

Of course, peace might have come to Europe without the Union. Maybe. We will never know. But it would never have been of the same quality. A lasting peace, not a frosty cease-fire.

To me, what makes it so special, is reconciliation. In politics as in life, reconciliation is the most difficult thing. It goes beyond forgiving and forgetting, or simply turning the page.

To think of what France and Germany had gone through . . ., and then take this step . . . Signing a Treaty of Friendship ... Each time I hear these words – *Freundschaft, Amitié* –, I am moved. They are private words, not for treaties between nations. But the will to not let history repeat itself, to do something radically new, was so strong that new words had to be found. For people Europe was a promise, Europe equalled hope.

When Konrad Adenauer came to Paris to conclude the Coal and Steel Treaty, in 1951, one evening he found a gift waiting at his hotel. It was a war medal, une Croix de Guerre, that had belonged to a French soldier. His daughter, a young student, had left it with a little note for the Chancellor, as a gesture of reconciliation and hope.

I can see many other stirring images before me.

Leaders of six States assembled to open a new future, in Rome, città eterna ... Willy Brandt kneeling down in Warsaw.

The dockers of Gdansk, at the gates of their shipyard.

VOCABULARY

resonate: meet with agreement

reconciliation: the restoration of friendship

materially: regarding wealth or possessions

1 **ANALYZING** How does the speaker characterize the European Union's contribution to peace? Explain your answer.

_____

_____

_____

_____

_____

_____

_____

_____

_____

Mitterrand and Kohl hand in hand.

Two million people linking Tallinn to Riga to Vilnius in a human chain, in 1989.

These moments healed Europe.

But symbolic gestures alone cannot cement peace.

This is where the European Union's "secret weapon" comes into play: an unrivalled way of binding our interests so tightly that war becomes materially impossible. Through constant negotiations, on ever more topics, between ever more countries. It's the golden rule of Jean Monnet: "*Mieux vaut se disputer autour d'une table que sur un champ de bataille*." ("Better fight around a table than on a battle-field.")

If I had to explain it to Alfred Nobel, I would say: not just a peace congress, a perpetual peace congress! . . . "

Source— Herman Van Rompuy, "Nobel Lecture by the European Union," 2012

2 **IDENTIFYING CONNECTIONS** How does this speech characterize post-war Europe?

_____

_____

_____

3 ECONOMICS This speech was given in 2012. What economic context defined the European Union at that time?

_____

_____

_____

4 **DETERMINING MEANING** What is the speaker referring to when he mentions Europe's "secret weapon?"

_____

_____

_____

5 **IDENTIFYING BIAS** How might the speaker be demonstrating political bias?

_____

_____

_____

6 **IDENTIFYING CAUSES** Why might this speech have been appropriate when it was given?

_____

_____

_____

_____

ESSENTIAL QUESTION

How can economic and social changes affect a country?

As you gather evidence to answer the Essential Question, think about:

- political and social changes in China in the late twentieth and early twenty-first centuries.

- cultural and economic changes in Japan since 1990.

- the major economic and social differences between North and South Korea.

- economic and political issues affecting countries in Southeast and South Asia since 1990.

My Notes

_____

_____

_____

_____

_____

_____

_____

Asia and The Pacific

DIRECTIONS: Search for evidence in the lesson to help you answer the following questions.

1 **ECONOMICS** Using the flowchart below, illustrate steps China has taken to participate in world trade since the 1980s. List the steps in the order in which they happened.

1 Tiananmen Square demonstrations lead to the government promotion of rapid economic growth and currying of middle-class urban support through the guarantee of more consumer goods.

2

3

4 China opens a stock market and strengthens international trade relations.

5

6

2 **RELATING EVENTS** How was the development of capitalist practices in China related to the protests in Tiananmen Square?

_____

_____

_____

_____

3 **DRAWING CONCLUSIONS** How did events at Fukushima impact Japan's economy? What were the causes of these events?

_____

_____

_____

_____

4A **IDENTIFYING CONNECTIONS** Contrast the demographic changes that have occurred in China and Japan in since the 1990s.

China	Japan

4B **EVALUTING EFFECTS** How have demographic changes in Japan affected the younger generations?

_____

_____

_____

5 **CONTRASTING** How have the differences in the North Korean and South Korean economies affected their citizens?

_____

_____

_____

_____

_____

_____

_____

ESSENTIAL QUESTION

How can economic and social changes affect a country?

China's Economic Growth

DIRECTIONS: Use the image to answer the questions.

EXPLORE THE CONTEXT: China's promotion of rapid economic growth from the mid-1980s onward has been enormously successful. Manufacturing, particularly the manufacturing of inexpensive consumer goods, as well as the closing of inefficient state enterprises, has contributed to this growth. The below image shows how such policies have affected China's gross domestic product (GDP), a common measure of the wealth that a country produces in a year.

PRIMARY SOURCE: GRAPH

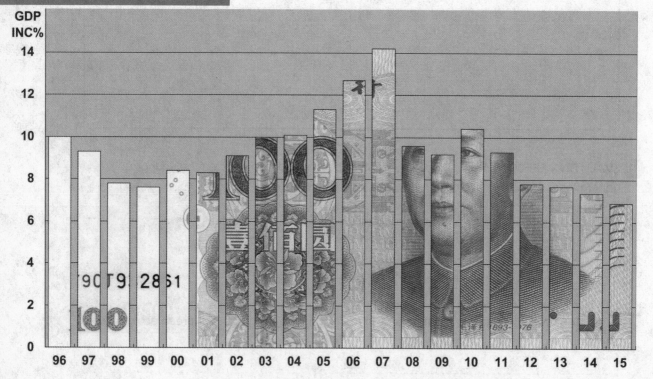

1 **IDENTIFYING** What does the image show, specifically?

_____

_____

2 **INTERPRETING** What trends in China's GDP does the graph indicate?

_____

_____

3A **DRAWING CONCLUSIONS** After 2000, when did China experience the greatest percentage drop in its GDP's growth?

_____

_____

_____

3B **UNDERSTANDING CONTEXT** Why might China have experienced the significant drop in its GDP's growth in the 2000s?

_____

_____

_____

_____

4 **ECONOMICS** What does this graph tell us about the long-term growth of China's economy?

_____

_____

_____

5 **INFERRING** What does data from the most recent years shown on the graph indicate about the growth of China's GDP?

_____

_____

_____

ESSENTIAL QUESTION

How can economic and social changes affect a country?

VOCABULARY

pessimistic: believing the worst about the future

detention: being kept in custody, especially government custody for a political prisoner

The Continued Importance of Tiananmen Square

DIRECTIONS: Use the text to answer the questions.

EXPLORE THE CONTEXT: The image of an anonymous man standing in front of tanks during the Tiananmen Square massacre, on page 601 of the textbook, soon became world famous. The identity of the man, however, has never been revealed. In this 2005 interview, Chinese human rights activist Xiao Qiang discusses the importance of those events and the photograph.

PRIMARY SOURCE: INTERVIEW

❝ [Interviewer] Can you remember your feelings when you first saw photographs of that young man facing a column of tanks?

[Xiao Qiang] The first time I saw that picture on TV was when I was still in America, a Ph.D. student doing a physics experiment in a field. ... I saw what happened on the street with a young man standing in front of tanks. It took a while for that picture to sink in, because hours later I took off on an airplane on my way back to China. I wanted to do something, anything I can, to help my country and my people. [...] That ultimate spirit of freedom will last longer than the strength of tanks and machine guns. . . . Where is Hitler's Nazis? Where is the former Soviet Union? Where is Suharto's Indonesia or Pinochet's Chile? They're all gone, and the Chinese Communist Party and its dictatorship will be gone. The men standing in front of tanks will stay. ... That's what this picture stands for for me. . . .

. . . [You tried to find him.] What do you think might have happened to him?

Every year on that anniversary I get phone calls, interview requests. I have journalists, I have teachers, I have students asking my organization, where is [he]? Who is [he]? How is [he] now? But I don't have that answer. . . . If this man has the guts to stand in front of tanks, I don't think he can be completely silenced about what he has done over the last 17 years if he is a free person. But if he is in detention, given we understand how powerful this symbolic act is, I'm pessimistic about what this brutal regime will do to him these 17 years. I'm pessimistic about if he is still alive. [. . . .]

Just look how hard the Chinese authorities are trying to wipe out this memory. Temporarily they had some success among the Chinese younger generation, among the certain part they can control, but they're trying to make people completely forget what happened, completely forget if ever there [was] a Chinese man [who stood] in front of tanks. But in the long run, they are on the losing side. This memory prevails. The pictures are everywhere – through the Internet, through the satellite TVs. The Chinese have known about their heroes, and this hero will inspire the Chinese again in the future battle for freedom [. . . .] ❞

Source— "PBS Frontline: The Tank Man," 2005

1 **DETERMINING CENTRAL IDEAS** What is the main idea of the text? Explain your answer.

_____

_____

_____

_____

2 **UNDERSTANDING CONTEXT** Why was it important to Xiao Qiang to return to China at such a violent time?

_____

_____

3 **IDENTIFYING CONNECTIONS** Why have people searched so hard to identify the man in front of the tank in the photograph?

_____

_____

_____

_____

4A **INFERRING** What is the irony of how the Chinese government has treated the photograph?

_____

_____

_____

4B **HISTORY** What does Xiao Qiang believe will happen to the Chinese Communist government in the future?

_____

_____

5 **DETERMINING MEANING** What might Xiao Qiang mean when he states that "this hero will inspire the Chinese again"?

_____

_____

Latin America

ESSENTIAL QUESTION

How can economic and social changes affect a country?

As you gather evidence to answer the Essential Question, think about:

- how Mexican politics changed in the 1990s and early 2000s.

- which social and political issues have affected Caribbean and Central American countries since the end of the Cold War.

- how economic factors have influenced South American societies since the end of the Cold War.

My Notes

_____

_____

_____

_____

_____

_____

_____

DIRECTIONS: Search for evidence in the lesson to help you answer the following questions.

1 EXPLAINING CAUSES How did the PRI gain and lose control of the Mexican government? Use the flowchart below to illustrate the process. Place events in the order in which they happened.

1 In 1929 the PRI was founded. ⟹

2 ⟹

3 ⟹

4 Vincente Fox, of the National Action Party, was elected president in 2000.

2 UNDERSTANDING CONTEXT How has the drug trade affected Mexico's society?

_____

_____

_____

_____

3 IDENTIFYING EFFECTS What effect has the drug war had on the drug trade in South and Central America? Why?

_____

_____

_____

_____

_____

4A **RELATING EVENTS** What problems have faced Caribbean and Central American nations since the 1990s? What problems are common to both regions? What issues only affect one or the other? Fill out the Venn diagram below to illustrate these issues.

Recent Problems Facing Caribbean and Central American Nations

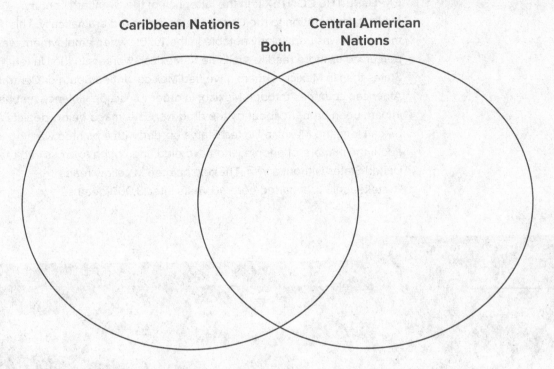

Caribbean Nations

Both

Central American Nations

4B **COMPARING AND CONTRASTING** How do the economies of Haiti and the Dominican Republic compare in terms of their major assets?

_____

_____

_____

_____

_____

5 ECONOMY What has allowed Brazil to strengthen its position as a major country in regional and international economies?

_____

_____

_____

_____

ESSENTIAL QUESTION

How can economic and social changes affect a country?

Mexican Immigration to the U.S.

DIRECTIONS: Use the image to answer the questions.

EXPLORE THE CONTEXT: In the latter half of the twentieth century, Mexican immigration to the United States increased dramatically. This movement was particularly notable in the 1970s, when employment was perceived as more readily available to Mexican workers in the United States than in Mexico. Others have fled Mexico, or fled South or Central American countries through Mexico, in order to escape violence that has, in part, been brought about by the drug war. The image below depicts a fence along the Mexican-United States border, with a painted warning about the number of people who have died attempting to cross into the United States without a visa. The text painted in yellow reads "Gatekeeper . . . it started here. 10 years later, 3,000 deaths."

PRIMARY SOURCE: PHOTOGRAPH

1 **IDENTIFYING** What is the subject of this photograph? What is its significance?

_____

_____

_____

2 **MAKING INFERENCES** The text on the fence refers to Operation Gatekeeper. Based on the image, what do you think Operation Gatekeeper is?

_____

_____

_____

3 **DRAWING CONCLUSIONS** What are the characteristics of this fence? How are they significant?

_____

_____

_____

_____

4A GEOGRAPHY Which side of the fence do you think appears in this photograph? Why?

_____

_____

_____

4B **INFERRING** Who do you think painted this fence? Explain your reasoning.

_____

_____

_____

_____

_____

ESSENTIAL QUESTION

How can economic and social changes affect a country?

VOCABULARY

guerrillas: irregular soldiers who fight by surprise and sabotage rather than traditional warfare

humanitarian demining: the removal of land mines by civilians in peacetime rather than by the military

accords: an official agreement or treaty

1 **ANALYZING** What is the main idea of this text? Explain your answer.

_____

_____

_____

_____

_____

_____

Colombia's Peace Process

DIRECTIONS: Use the text to answer the questions.

EXPLORE THE CONTEXT: On November 30, 2016, the Colombian government signed a peace agreement with the Revolutionary Armed Forces of Colombia (FARC) ending a 60-year guerrilla insurgency. The agreement allowed FARC to form a political party, and required the group to disarm, while the government committed to devote aid to rural areas and families displaced by the upheaval. In this March 2017 report to the Organization of American States, OAS Secretary General Luis Almagro praises the accord while addressing what challenges the people of Colombia will face in implementing the peace.

PRIMARY SOURCE: SPEECH

❝The GS/OAS welcomes the new peace accord reached between the Colombian government and the Fuerzas Armadas Revolucionarias de Colombia – Ejército del Pueblo [Revolutionary Armed Forces of Colombia – People's Army] (FARC-EP) guerrilla movement and encourages Colombia to continue down the path toward achieving a stable and long-lasting peace. Indeed, the Permanent Council has backed the peace process and the conclusion of the armed conflict, having understood the sense of urgency surrounding the current stage of the process.

This enhanced accord will, however, face new challenges that demand greater efforts and a meeting of many more minds in the upcoming phases of the process. One of the most significant challenges, which stems from the referendum's outcome, is the clear need to continue making headway in unifying the Colombian people, by doing everything necessary to strengthen unity and national harmonious coexistence. This demands strength of character and involvement on the part of the political class, society, the people who are demonstrating in the streets, students, victims, and all strata of the country.

Furthermore, the implementation phase, perhaps the most important in the process, will face different challenges in the near future. The changes in the international arena, the election campaign period, legislative development of the agreements, economic constraints, persistence of illegal groups' actions, murders of social leaders, and resistance in the areas that voted against the accords may hinder peace policies from reaching the territories.

Making the mechanisms and components of the accord a reality at the local level in those places hardest hit by the violence is a task that demands decisive and pragmatic measures. Preventing the resurgence of violence in those areas with structural weaknesses or that have not received adequate attention on the part of the State has become an imperative.

In order to effectively respond to stakeholders and the territories, the application of the peace policies provided for under domestic law should be considered without delay. The State has the necessary tools to implement such policies on a whole host of issues, such as humanitarian demining, illicit crop substitution, the surrender of child combatants, and the search for disappeared persons, among others. Such actions would relieve pressure on the process and help to enhance trust between the parties and citizens.

Peace-building requires everyone's involvement, including—as was seen during the referendum—the more than 60% of the electorate that ignored the call to the polls. The Electoral Observation Mission of the OAS, which observed the referendum, reiterated the recommendation in its preliminary report that measures be adopted to increase the exercise of the right to suffrage with the aim of having Colombian citizens fulfill their democratic responsibility. The GS/OAS urges all Colombians to continue working together to achieve transformations that allow for conflict and inequality to be overcome and to bring about the peace that the entire nation needs. **99**

Source— OAS Secretary General Luis Almagro, Twenty-Second Report of the Secretary General,
March 29, 2017

2 **ANALYZING** What change does Almagro consider most vital to a lasting peace? Give an example to support your answer.

_____

_____

_____

3 **DETERMINING MEANING** What does the term "FARC" mean in context?

_____

_____

_____

_____

_____

4 **UNDERSTANDING CONTEXT** Almagro implies that large-scale violence has long been the major impediment to progress and peace. In what forms has this violence taken in Colombia, according to the report?

_____

_____

5 **CIVICS** Along with emphasizing that work toward peace is not finished but just beginning, Almagro also implies a criticism of the Colombian people in the final paragraph. What is that criticism, and what does he propose to address it?

_____

_____

_____

_____

_____

Chapter 34

The Middle East and Africa

DIRECTIONS: Search for evidence in the lesson to help you answer the following questions.

1 **UNDERSTANDING CONTEXT** Why have the Middle East's natural resources been significant in international relations?

_____

_____

_____

_____

_____

_____

2 **RELATING EVENTS** Complete the time line by listing significant developments in Afghanistan and Iraq since the terrorist attacks on September 11, 2001. List the date of each event, and place them in chronological order.

1 2001: The United States invades Afghanistan.

2

3

4 2011: U.S. forces kill Osama bin Laden in Pakistan.

5

6 2013: Violence intensifies in Iraq.

7

8 2014: Elections in Afghanistan have high voter turnout, even among women.

ESSENTIAL QUESTION

How can economic and social changes affect a country?

As you gather evidence to answer the Essential Question, think about:

- the changes that have occurred in the Middle East since the 1990s.
- the causes and effects of the Arab Spring.
- challenges confronting countries in Africa south of the Sahara since the 1990s.

My Notes

_____

_____

_____

_____

_____

_____

3A **UNDERSTANDING CONTEXT** Fill out the comparison chart below to illustrate the causes of revolutions during the Arab Spring in each of the countries listed.

Egypt	Libya	Syria

3B **DRAWING CONCLUSIONS** In what way was the Arab Spring dependent on technology?

_____

_____

_____

4 **INFERRING** What is one significant way in which major social problems have been addressed in sub-Saharan Africa since the 1990s?

_____

_____

_____

5 **HISTORY** How have religious differences contributed to violence in sub-Saharan Africa in the 2000s?

_____

_____

_____

ESSENTIAL QUESTION

How can economic and social changes affect a country?

Progress in Ghana

DIRECTIONS: Use the text to answer the questions.

EXPLORE THE CONTEXT: As many states in Sub-Saharan Africa gained their independence after World War II, there was hope for greater stability in the region. While some of these hopes have become reality, the region still struggles with the legacy of imperialism. U.S. President Barack Obama spoke on this subject in the nation of Ghana in 2009.

PRIMARY SOURCE: SPEECH

66 We must start from the simple premise that Africa's future is up to Africans.

I say this knowing full well the tragic past that has sometimes haunted this part of the world.

. . . . . Here in Ghana, you show us a face of Africa that is too often overlooked by a world that sees only tragedy or a need for charity. The people of Ghana have worked hard to put democracy on a firmer footing, with repeated peaceful transfers of power even in the wake of closely contested elections. (Applause.) And by the way, can I say that for that the minority deserves as much credit as the majority. (Applause.) And with improved governance and an emerging civil society, Ghana's economy has shown impressive rates of growth. (Applause.)

This progress may lack the drama of 20th century liberation struggles, but make no mistake: It will ultimately be more significant. For just as it is important to emerge from the control of other nations, it is even more important to build one's own nation.

So I believe that this moment is just as promising for Ghana and for Africa as the moment when my father came of age and new nations were being born. This is a new moment of great promise. Only this time, we've learned that it will not be giants like Nkrumah and Kenyatta who will determine Africa's future. Instead, it will be you – the men and women in Ghana's parliament – (applause) – the people you represent. It will be the young people brimming with talent and energy and hope who can claim the future that so many in previous generations never realized.

. . . . Now, time and again, Ghanaians have chosen constitutional rule over autocracy, and shown a democratic spirit that allows the energy of your people to break through. (Applause.) We see that in leaders who accept defeat graciously – the fact that President Mills' opponents were standing beside him last night to greet me when I came off the plane spoke volumes about Ghana – (applause); victors who resist calls to wield power against the opposition in unfair ways. We see that spirit in courageous journalists like Anas Aremeyaw Anas, who risked his life to report the truth. We see it in police like Patience Quaye, who helped prosecute the first human trafficker in Ghana. (Applause.) We see it in the young people who are speaking up against patronage, and participating in the political process.

Across Africa, we've seen countless examples of people taking control of their destiny, and making change from the bottom up. We saw it in Kenya, where civil society and business came together to help stop post-election violence.

We saw it in South Africa, where over three-quarters of the country voted in the recent election – the fourth since the end of Apartheid. We saw it in Zimbabwe, where the Election Support Network braved brutal repression to stand up for the principle that a person's vote is their sacred right.

Now, make no mistake: History is on the side of these brave Africans, not with those who use coups or change constitutions to stay in power. (Applause.) Africa doesn't need strongmen, it needs strong institutions. (Applause.) **99**

Source—Barack Obama, "Remarks by the President to the Ghanaian Parliament," July 11, 2009

1 **CITING TEXT EVIDENCE** To what is Obama referring when he references "the tragic past that has sometimes haunted this part of world"?

_____

_____

2 **HISTORY** Who are Nkrumah and Kenyatta? Why does Obama make reference to them in his speech?

_____

_____

3 **COMPARING AND CONTRASTING** What similarities and differences does Obama see between twentieth-century liberation struggles in Africa and nation building in Africa in the twenty-first century?

_____

_____

4 **ANALYZING** What positive political, social, and economic changes are mentioned in the speech? What brought about these changes?

_____

_____

5 **CIVICS** Identify elements of democracy that are mentioned by Obama. Why are these essential to a democratic government?

_____

_____

Copyright © McGraw-Hill Education   Qutait, Tasnim. 2011. Tasnim Qutait's Blog Post on International Intervention. April 5, 2011. Reprinted 2012 in Now That We Have Tasted Hope: Voices From the Arab Spring. San Francisco: A McSweeney's/Byliner Original.

ESSENTIAL QUESTION

How can economic and social changes affect a country?

The Arab Spring in Libya

DIRECTIONS: Use the text to answer the questions.

EXPLORE THE CONTEXT: As part of the Arab Spring, Libyan protesters rose up against then-president Muammar al-Qaddafi's oppressive regime. When Qaddafi's troops used force against the protesters, international organizations stepped in, with the UN authorizing airstrikes that the military alliance NATO then carried out. In this blog post from 2011, Libyan Tasmin Qutait describes why she disagrees with the opinion held by other protesters that these foreign interventions should be seen as an act of imperialism.

PRIMARY SOURCE: BLOG POST

❝ The military intervention in Libya has divided the left into two camps, the pro-interventionists and the anti-imperialists who define it as a military assault equivalent to the war in Iraq. At the center of this division is an apparent contradiction between supporting the people's revolution against autocracy and an anti-imperialist stance which denounces western hypocrisy. As a Libyan, I reject this false contradiction. I see myself as an anti-imperialist, I denounce western double standards, and I supported the revolution and the intervention. I see no need to twist myself into an arguing position where I declare myself to be for the people's revolution, but against the intervention that sustained it. That, to me, would be the contradiction.

. . . We also remember when Gaddafi was lionized by some in the left as an anti-imperialist Nasserite during the 70s and 80s, a time when people were hung in public and Libyans were poisoned against progressive ideas because of the brutality of the regime that pretended to espouse them. . . . We remember when we were the pariah-state, and Libyans were the terrorists after the plutonium. We don't need to be told that this intervention is, as one friend put it, mish ashan sawad eyona—not for the sake of our eyes. . . .

The Libyans dreamed briefly about a revolution like the one in Tunisia or Egypt. One where we could go out and chant "silmiya" [peaceful]. Instead, we had to go from unarmed demonstrations, faced with heavy-caliber weapons to forming a civilian ragtag army, and then Gaddafi's brigades sent that ragtag army into retreat. . . .

We refuse to be puppets to a madman who is not a puppet to the West any longer. We will continue this struggle until we are rid of him, and as the Egyptians and the Tunisians have done before us, we'll continue it after we are rid of him. ❞

Source—"Tasmin Qutait's Blog Post on International Imperialism," in *Now That We Have Tasted Hope: Voices from the Arab Spring,* 2012.

VOCABULARY

imperialism: extending a country's power over another

intervention: one country's interference in another's affairs of state

autocracy: a government in which one person has total control

regime: a government, often authoritarian

lionize: to recognize as important

1 **ANALYZING** How does the author respond to Libyan critics of NATO's intervention in Libya?

_____

_____

_____

2 **IDENTIFYING CONNECTIONS** How does the author describe the changes in Libya's relationship with the international community during her lifetime?

_____

_____

_____

3 **ANALYZING CENTRAL IDEAS** How does the author define her attitude towards the Libyan revolution and towards NATO's intervention?

_____

_____

_____

4 **DETERMINING MEANING** In this context, what does Qutait mean by "We refuse to be puppets?"

_____

_____

_____

5 **IDENTIFYING BIAS** What might the author's motivations for writing this blog post have been?

_____

_____

_____

6 **GEOGRAPHY** What regional influences does Qutait cite as important to the Libyan uprisings?

_____

_____

_____

_____

ESSENTIAL QUESTION

How can economic and social changes affect a country?

My Notes

_____

_____

_____

_____

_____

_____

_____

_____

_____

_____

_____

_____

_____

_____

_____

1 Think About It

Review the supporting questions you developed at the beginning of the chapter and the evidence you gathered. Were you able to answer each Supporting Question? If not, what additional evidence do you think you need to consider?

_____

_____

_____

2 Organize Your Evidence

Complete the chart below with information you learned about the changes in the following countries in the 2000s.

Country	Social Changes	Economic Changes	Effects
United States			
U.S.S.R./ Russia			
Mexico			
China			
Egypt			

❸ Talk About It

Work in a small group. With your group, discuss the effects that you have identified and noted down in your charts. Compare your charts. Did you all pick the same social and economic changes? Do you disagree on the significance or effects of certain social and/or economic changes? Overall, which social or economic changes do you think have been the most significant to all countries on the chart since 1989? Why?

❹ Write About It

Following your discussion in the Talk About It activity, compare and contrast major economic and social changes in two countries from two different continents since 1989 and their effects on various aspects of that country. Use examples and details to justify your argument.

_____

_____

_____

_____

_____

_____

❺ Connect to the Essential Question

Conduct interviews with at least two people who were adults in 1989. The purpose of your interview should be to understand how social and economic changes in the United States have affected individuals, even if they do not themselves make the connection between their opinions or recollections and broader social events. Before you conduct your interviews, make a list of questions you wish to ask. These may be about conflicts, treaties, trends, or other issues you have read about in this chapter. With your subjects' permission, record interviews so you can go back to the information later.

When you have finished your interviews, create a presentation in which you describe the effects that larger social and economic movements had on the individual people you spoke to. Be careful not to make generalizations about all Americans or people of the nationality you interviewed. Connect the reactions of your interviewees to the events, economic and social, that have affected the United States since 1989. Ensure that your presentation is accurate, engaging, true to the interviewee's statements, and informative.

CITIZENSHIP
TAKING ACTION

MAKE CONNECTIONS Use the information from the chapter about social uprisings in the Middle East during the Arab Spring to write a newspaper editorial about the benefits and/or drawbacks of such protests. Working as an editorial board in a small group, each member should examine a different aspect of the Arab Spring protests, including their causes, their spread, their lasting effects, and other issues. Discuss what you have found as a group, trying to represent a diverse mix of opinions and ideas about the aspect of the uprising that you have studied. As a team, come up with the opinion that you wish to present in your editorial and work together to write it. In the editorial, be sure to explain how social and economic changes either led to or stemmed from the Arab Spring, and how they changed the countries affected by the Arab Spring.

Contemporary Global Issues, 1989–Present

ESSENTIAL QUESTION

What influences global political and economic relationships?

Toward the end of the twentieth century, the pace of globalization skyrocketed as communications networks advanced and the Internet came online. This change in speed of development and communications has led to major changes in all aspects of life around the world. This technological advancement created an entirely new landscape for global political, social, and economic relationships while enabling personal participation in the public sphere many new ways.

TALK ABOUT IT

With a partner, discuss the sort of information you would need to discover to explain what influences global political and economic relationships in the modern world. For example you could ask, "Who or what makes and shapes the political and economic news we encounter? Individual people? Nations? Organizations? Institutions?" and "How and why do each of these parties—and others—influence what happens in the world?"

DIRECTIONS: Now write down three additional questions that will help you describe what shapes political and economic relationships in the world.

MY RESEARCH QUESTIONS

Supporting Question 1:

_____

_____

Supporting Question 2:

_____

_____

Supporting Question 3:

_____

Political Challenges In The Modern World

DIRECTIONS: Search for evidence in the lesson to help you answer the following questions.

1 **EVALUATING INFORMATION** How do the agencies of the United Nations work to solve international problems? How effective have these agencies proven to be in avoiding armed conflicts?

_____

_____

_____

_____

_____

2 **DRAWING CONCLUSIONS** What are weapons of mass destruction? How has their existence threatened peaceful resolutions to conflicts in the Middle East during the post–Cold War era?

_____

_____

_____

_____

_____

3 **DESCRIBING** What political challenges do developing nations face today? What have these nations had to do to become more democratic?

_____

_____

_____

_____

_____

ESSENTIAL QUESTION

What influences global political and economic relationships?

As you gather evidence to answer the Essential Question, think about:

- entities that influence relationships between nation states.

- how globalization is tied to social and economic issues.

- how multinational organizations shape public policy.

My Notes

_____

_____

_____

_____

_____

_____

4 CITING TEXT EVIDENCE Choose one of the terrorist organizations discussed in the text. What were the goals of the group? What methods did the group use to achieve these goals? Did the group achieve them?

_____

_____

_____

_____

_____

_____

_____

_____

_____

_____

5 HISTORY Choose one of the regions or nations that has experienced civil war, ethnic cleansing, or genocide in recent years. Then complete the following cause and effect chart for the region or nation you choose. Circle type of issues listed in your chart.

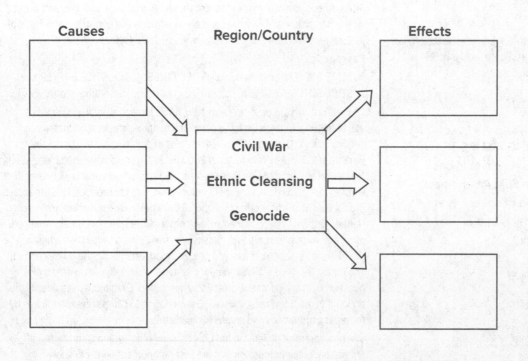

Causes   Region/Country   Effects

Civil War

Ethnic Cleansing

Genocide

ESSENTIAL QUESTION

What influences global political and economic relationships?

VOCABULARY

concurring: a judge's opinion that supports the majority opinion of the court

First Amendment: the text in the U.S. Constitution that guarantees freedoms of speech, religion, press, assembly, and petition of government

dissenting: a judge's opinion that disagrees with the majority opinion of the court

electioneering: to work for the success of a particular candidate, party, ticket, etc., in an election

1 ANALYZING ISSUES The passages reflect opinions about the First Amendment. What type of speech is at issue? Why is that significant?

_____

_____

_____

_____

_____

Citizens United v. FEC

DIRECTIONS: Read the excerpts. Then answer the questions.

EXPLORE THE CONTEXT: In 2007 the non-profit organization Citizens United filed a complaint against the Federal Election Commission (FEC). It alleged the restrictions on political expenditures during an election was a violation of the First Amendment. The Supreme Court, in a 5-4 ruling, agreed.

PRIMARY SOURCE: JUDICIAL OPINIONS

❝ Passage 1:

CHIEF JUSTICE ROBERTS, with whom JUSTICE ALITO joins, concurring.

The Government urges us in this case to uphold a direct prohibition on political speech. It asks us to embrace a theory of the First Amendment that would allow censorship not only of television and radio broadcasts, but of pamphlets, posters, the Internet, and virtually any other medium that corporations and unions might find useful in expressing their views on matters of public concern. Its theory, if accepted, would empower the Government to prohibit newspapers from running editorials or opinion pieces supporting or opposing candidates for office, so long as the newspapers were owned by corporations—as the major ones are. First Amendment rights could be confined to individuals, subverting the vibrant public discourse that is at the foundation of our democracy.

The Court properly rejects that theory, and I join its opinion in full. The First Amendment protects more than just the individual on a soapbox and the lonely pamphleteer. I write separately to address the important principles of judicial restraint and stare decisis implicated in this case. . . .

Passage 2:

JUSTICE STEVENS, with whom JUSTICE GINSBURG, JUSTICE BREYER, and JUSTICE SOTOMAYOR join, concurring in part and dissenting in part.

The real issue in this case concerns how, not if, the appellant may finance its electioneering. Citizens United is a wealthy nonprofit corporation that runs a political action committee (PAC) with millions of dollars in assets. Under the Bipartisan Campaign Reform Act of 2002 (BCRA), it could have used those assets to televise and promote [its broadcast productions] wherever and whenever it wanted to. It also could have spent unrestricted sums to broadcast [its broadcast production] at any time other than the 30 days before the last primary election. Neither Citizens United's nor any other corporation's speech has been "banned," *ante*, at 1. All that the parties dispute is whether Citizens United had a right to use the funds in its general treasury to pay for broadcasts during the 30-day period. The notion that the First Amendment dictates an affirmative answer to that question is, in my judgment, profoundly misguided. Even more misguided is the notion that the Court must rewrite the law relating to campaign expenditures by *for-profit* corporations and unions to decide this case.

The basic premise underlying the Court's ruling is its iteration, and constant reiteration, of the proposition that the First Amendment bars regulatory distinctions based on a speaker's identity, including its "identity" as a corporation. While that glittering generality has rhetorical appeal, it is not a correct statement of the law. Nor does it tell us when a corporation may engage in electioneering that some of its shareholders oppose. It does not even resolve the specific question whether Citizens United may be required to finance some of its messages with the money in its PAC. The conceit that corporations must be treated identically to natural persons in the political sphere is not only inaccurate but also inadequate to justify the Court's disposition of this case. In the context of election to public office, the distinction between corporate and human speakers is significant. Although they make enormous contributions to our society, corporations are not actually members of it. They cannot vote or run for office. Because they may be managed and controlled by nonresidents, their interests may conflict in fundamental respects with the interests of eligible voters. The financial resources, legal structure, and instrumental orientation of corporations raise legitimate concerns about their role in the electoral process.

Our lawmakers have a compelling constitutional basis, if not also a democratic duty, to take measures designed to guard against the potentially deleterious effects of corporate spending in local and national races.

The majority's approach to corporate electioneering marks a dramatic break from our past. Congress has placed special limitations on campaign spending by corporations ever since the passage of the Tillman Act in 1907. . . . **99**

— Excerpt from Supreme Court Case 558 U.S.(2010)

2 **UNDERSTANDING CHANGE** The dissenting opinion claims that this court ruling is a change from long-standing previous policy. How?

_____

_____

3 **CONTRASTING** In the two passages, what are the differing opinions about the status of corporate entities in society?

_____

_____

_____

_____

_____

4 **INFERRING** From his dissenting opinion, why might you infer that Stevens is concerned about corporations? Quote from the passage to support your answer.

_____

_____

_____

5 CIVICS This case was a landmark court case partly because of its interpretation of freedom of speech. Why is this issue considered so important?

_____

_____

Copyright © McGraw-Hill Education 1945. Charter of the United Nations - Chapter VII: Actions with Respect to Threats to the Peace, Breaches of the Peace, and Acts of Aggression. Charter signed June 26, 1945. San Francisco.

ESSENTIAL QUESTION

What influences global political and economic relationships?

VOCABULARY

UN Security Council: one of the six primary organs of the UN, made up of 15 member states, tasked with maintaining international peace and security

aggravation: something that intensifies or worsens a situation

provisional: an arrangement made to address present matters that may be changed later; temporary

The Charter of the United Nations

DIRECTIONS: Use the text to answer the questions.

EXPLORE THE CONTEXT: The United Nations is an international organization that is currently made up of 193 member states. Together, the members work toward achieving global cooperation on economic, human rights, and security issues. The UN Charter is the organization's founding document, which governs its structure and activities. The Charter consists of nineteen chapters, and each chapter is divided into a number of Articles. Chapters I–V outline the organization's purposes, membership, and foundational structure. Chapter VI addresses settlement of disputes. The following excerpt is from Chapter VII, which discusses procedures for establishing responses to threats and acts of aggression.

PRIMARY SOURCE: CHARTER

❝Article 39

The Security Council shall determine the existence of any threat to the peace, breach of the peace, or act of aggression and shall make recommendations, or decide what measures shall be taken in accordance with Articles 41 and 42, to maintain or restore international peace and security.

Article 40

In order to prevent an aggravation of the situation, the Security Council may, before making the recommendations or deciding upon the measures provided for in Article 39, call upon the parties concerned to comply with such provisional measures as it deems necessary or desirable. Such provisional measures shall be without prejudice to the rights, claims, or position of the parties concerned. The Security Council shall duly take account of failure to comply with such provisional measures.

Article 41

The Security Council may decide what measures not involving the use of armed force are to be employed to give effect to its decisions, and it may call upon the Members of the United Nations to apply such measures. These may include complete or partial interruption of economic relations and of rail, sea, air, postal, telegraphic, radio, and other means of communication, and the severance of diplomatic relations.

Article 42

Should the Security Council consider that measures provided for in Article 41 would be inadequate or have proved to be inadequate, it may take such action by air, sea, or land forces as may be necessary to maintain or restore international peace and security. Such action may include demonstrations, blockade, and other operations by air, sea, or land forces of Members of the United Nations. ❞

Source— UN Charter, 1945

1 **DESCRIBING** What is the role of the UN Security Council?

_____

_____

_____

2 **INTERPRETING INTERPRETING** Based on the Charter, interpret the process by which the United Nations works toward conflict resolution in cases of threats or aggressive action.

_____

_____

_____

_____

_____

3 **ANALYZING CONTEXT** How might tension amoung nations on the Security Council influence deliberations?

_____

_____

_____

_____

_____

4 **INFERRING** Can it be inferred that the United Nations employs a measured process? How could the UN alter its approach? Would it be more effective?

_____

_____

_____

_____

5 CIVICS Is the United Nations a higher authority than national governments? Why or why not?

_____

_____

_____

_____

ESSENTIAL QUESTION

What influences global political and economic relationships?

As you gather evidence to answer the Essential Question, think about:

- how the increased pace of globalization has altered how and where poverty occurs.

- how the rise of religious fundamentalism has influenced political activity.

- how the rise of cross-border crimes and terrorism has led to both increased mistrust and increased cooperation.

My Notes

_____

_____

_____

_____

_____

_____

Social Challenges In The Modern World

DIRECTIONS: Search for evidence in the lesson to help you answer the following questions.

1 **ANALYZING ISSUES** Describe the interconnected relationships between gender inequality, poverty, and access to education.

_____

_____

_____

_____

_____

_____

2A **IDENTIFYING** In the space below, describe the impact of migration on world population growth. Then use the table to compare and contrast population-related issues faced by both developing and developed nations.

_____

_____

_____

_____

_____

2B Use the table to compare and contrast population-related issues faced by developing and developed nations.

Developing Nations	
Developed Nations	

3 **MAKING CONNECTIONS** How do you explain the explosion in the number of NGOs over the past century? How is this growth related to globalization?

_____

_____

_____

_____

4 **DRAWING CONCLUSIONS** Why might developing countries be particularly vulnerable to pandemics?

_____

_____

_____

_____

5 **DIFFERENTIATING** How is extreme poverty impacting the overall health and well-being of the population of a developing country?

_____

_____

_____

_____

_____

_____

6 **HISTORY** Consider the United Nations Universal Declaration of Human Rights. How are the tenets of that document implemented and enforced?

_____

_____

_____

_____

What influences global political and economic relationships?

Population Pyramids

DIRECTIONS: Use the following population pyramids to respond to the questions that follow.

EXPLORE THE CONTEXT: A population pyramid is a type of graph that shows the age and gender distribution of a given population. The shape of a population pyramid can provide information about population trends for specific regions. In many developed parts of the world, overall population is declining while the population of older people is growing. By contrast, population pyramids for less developed nations typically show both high birth rates and low life expectancy rates.

PRIMARY SOURCE: POPULATION PYRAMID

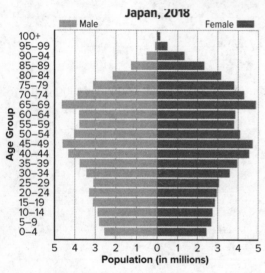

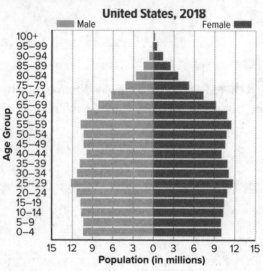

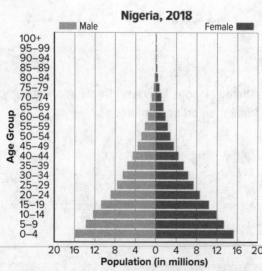

Source: United States Census Bureau.

1 **INFERRING** What are some reasons for the shape of the population pyramid of Japan?

_____

_____

_____

_____

2 **INTERPRETING GRAPHS** Which population pyramid is most typical of a developing nation? Give a reason for your answer.

_____

_____

_____

3 **ANALYZING INFORMATION** Does the shape of the population pyramid of the United States indicate slow, rapid, or negative (little to no) overall population growth? Explain.

_____

_____

4 **DRAWING CONCLUSIONS** Based on the population pyramid of Nigeria, describe what types of programs and services the government should create to meet the needs of its population now and in the next 20 years.

_____

_____

_____

_____

5 GEOGRAPHY Name a country that would have a population structure similar to that of Japan's. Briefly explain your answer.

_____

_____

_____

ESSENTIAL QUESTION

What influences global political and economic relationships?

Malala Speaks to the United Nations

DIRECTIONS: Use the text to answer the questions.

EXPLORE THE CONTEXT: Malala Yousafzai is a young Pakistani woman who was shot in the head by the Taliban on her way from school in 2012. After her recovery, Malala continued her activism work, appearing at the UN General Assembly in July 2013 as a peaceful, nonviolent advocate for the education of young women and children. In 2014 she received the Nobel Peace Prize. In April 2017 she was named the youngest-ever UN Messenger of Peace, the highest honor bestowed by the UN.

PRIMARY SOURCE: EXECUTIVE ORDER

VOCABULARY

Pashtun: a member of a Pashto-speaking people inhabiting southern Afghanistan and northwestern Pakistan

❝So here I stand.... one girl among many.

I speak – not for myself, but for all girls and boys.

I raise up my voice – not so that I can shout, but so that those without a voice can be heard.

Those who have fought for their rights:

Their right to live in peace.

Their right to be treated with dignity.

Their right to equality of opportunity.

Their right to be educated.

Dear Friends, on the 9th of October 2012, the Taliban shot me on the left side of my forehead. They shot my friends too. They thought that the bullets would silence us. But they failed. And then, out of that silence came, thousands of voices. The terrorists thought that they would change our aims and stop our ambitions but nothing changed in my life except this: Weakness, fear and hopelessness died. Strength, power and courage was born. I am the same Malala. My ambitions are the same. My hopes are the same. My dreams are the same.

Dear sisters and brothers, I am not against anyone. . . . I am here to speak up for the right of education of every child. I want education for the sons and the daughters of all the extremists especially the Taliban. . . .

1 ANALYZING Malala makes it clear in her speech that she believes that education is the first step to address numerous global social problems. Why?

The wise saying, "The pen is mightier than sword" was true. The extremists are afraid of books and pens. The power of education frightens them. They are afraid of women. The power of the voice of women frightens them. And that is why they killed 14 innocent medical students in the recent attack in Quetta. And that is why they killed many female teachers and polio workers in Khyber Pukhtoon Khwa and FATA. That is why they are blasting schools every day. Because they were and they are afraid of change, afraid of the equality that we will bring into our society.

I remember that there was a boy in our school who was asked by a journalist, "Why are the Taliban against education?" He answered very simply. By pointing to his book he said, "A Talib doesn't know what is written inside this book." They think that God is a tiny, little conservative being who would send girls to the hell just because of going to school. The terrorists are misusing the name of Islam and Pashtun society for their own personal benefits. Pakistan is peace-loving democratic country. Pashtuns want education for their daughters and sons. And Islam is a religion of peace, humanity and brotherhood. Islam says that it is not only each child's right to get education, rather it is their duty and responsibility.

Honourable Secretary General, peace is necessary for education. In many parts of the world especially Pakistan and Afghanistan; terrorism, wars and conflicts stop children to go to their schools. We are really tired of these wars. Women and children are suffering in many parts of the world in many ways. In India, innocent and poor children are victims of child labour. Many schools have been destroyed in Nigeria. People in Afghanistan have been affected by the hurdles of extremism for decades. Young girls have to do domestic child labour and are forced to get married at early age. Poverty, ignorance, injustice, racism and the deprivation of basic rights are the main problems faced by both men and women **99**

— "Speech to the UN," Malala Yousafzai, July 2013

2 UNDERSTANDING CHANGE What kind of change does Malala say the Taliban fears? Why?

_____

_____

_____

_____

3 UNDERSTANDING CONTEXT Malala is an unusually young person to address the United Nations. Why is this significant, and how might this affect the impact of her position?

_____

_____

4 UNDERSTANDING EFFECTS What impact do you think her speech had on the General Assembly?

_____

_____

5 CIVICS Why is Malala's story particularly compelling? Do you think her experiences, and her subsequent choice to become an education activist, will have an impact? Why or why not?

_____

_____

Global Economies

DIRECTIONS: Search for evidence in the lesson to help you answer the following questions.

1 **DESCRIBING** Use the table below to describe the role that each organization plays in the global economy.

Organization	Role in World Economy
World Bank	
International Monetary Fund	
World Trade Organization	

2 **ANALYZING CHANGE** How have trade agreements changed how business is done around the world?

_____

_____

_____

_____

_____

_____

_____

_____

ESSENTIAL QUESTION

What influences global political and economic relationships?

As you gather evidence to answer the Essential Question, think about:

- factors that drive globalization.
- factors that help to maintain a healthy economy.
- causes and effects of an economic downturn.

My Notes

_____

_____

_____

_____

_____

_____

_____

3 **ANALYZING EFFECTS** What are the economic benefits to the regional union of the European Community (EC), followed by the European Union (EU)?

_____

_____

_____

_____

_____

_____

4 **ANALYZING EFFECTS** What are some of the downsides to globalization?

_____

_____

_____

_____

_____

_____

5A **IDENTIFYING CAUSES** Why did the American housing market collapse in 2008?

_____

_____

_____

_____

5B **IDENTIFYING EFFECTS** What impact did the collapse of the American housing market have on other nations? Why?

_____

_____

_____

_____

Two Financial Crises

ESSENTIAL QUESTION

What influences global political and economic relationships?

VOCABULARY

deflation: reduction of the general level of prices in an economy

aggregate demand: the total amount of goods and services purchased by a population

protectionism: the theory or practice of shielding a country's domestic industries from foreign competition by taxing imports

capital: money invested in a business, or assets used to create goods and services

1 DIFFERENTIATING Why is the comparison between the two crises incomplete?

_____

_____

_____

_____

_____

DIRECTIONS: Use the text to answer the questions.

EXPLORE THE CONTEXT: The Great Depression put the world into a financial freefall which lasted until the end of World War II. Distinct lessons were learned from the Great Depression to better manage such an event in the future. As the Great Recession of 2007–2008 unfolded, the international governments and the financial community followed the lessons from the Great Depression.

PRIMARY SOURCE: REPORT

❝ By now, based on the record of the 1930s as summarized above, a set of policy lessons from the 1930s have emerged fairly well supported by a consensus within the economics profession.

These lessons are highlighted below. . . .

Lesson 1. Maintain the financial system – avoid financial meltdown. The record of the 1930s demonstrates that in case of a financial crisis, the financial system should be supported by government actions in order to prevent a collapse of the credit allocation mechanism and to maintain public confidence in the banking system. The crisis in the US financial system in the early 1930s spread eventually to the real economy, both at home and abroad, contributing to falling output and employment and to deflation, making the crisis in the financial sector deeper via adverse feedback loops.

Lesson 2. Maintain aggregate demand – avoid deflation. The Great Depression shows that it is crucial to support aggregate demand and avoid deflation by means of expansionary monetary and fiscal policies. . . .

Lesson 3. Maintain international trade – avoid protectionism. The Great Depression set off a series of protectionist measures on a global scale. The degree of protectionism was higher than during any other period of modern trade. These measures contributed to the fall in world trade as well as in world production in the early 1930s. The policy lesson from this experience is straightforward: protectionism should be avoided.

Lesson 4. Maintain international finance – avoid capital account restrictions. The Great Depression contributed to a breakdown of the flow of capital across borders, driven by the problems facing the US and European financial systems and the lack of international cooperation. Capital exports declined. Several countries introduced controls of cross-border capital flows. These events made the depression deeper. The policy lesson here is that the free flow of capital should be maintained during the present crisis.

Lesson 5. Maintain internationalism – avoid nationalism. It is proper to view the Great Depression as the end of the first period of globalisation......

2009. Economic Crisis in Europe: Causes, Consequences and Responses. European Commission: Directorate-General for Economic and Financial Affairs.

Have the five lessons above been absorbed into the policy response to the current crisis? While the jury is still out on some of the lessons, the present answer must be a positive one. All of the above lessons from the 1930s seem well learnt today as seen from the following chapters in this report.

The financial sectors in most countries are given strong government support, aggregate demand is maintained through expansionary monetary and fiscal policies, protectionism is so far kept at bay, there has been very little of protectionist revival – far from anything of the scale of the 1930s, the international flow of capital is not hindered by government actions, although criticism has been aimed at the role of global finance in the present crisis, and international cooperation has been strengthened by the present crisis. The present crisis has – in contrast to the 1930s – fostered closer international cooperation. . . .

[T]he EU is now providing a shelter for the forces of depression in Europe. The EU, through its internal market, its single currency and its institutionalised system of economic, social and political cooperation, should be viewed as a construction that incorporates the lessons from the 1930s. Within the EU, the flow of goods and services, of capital and labour remains free – with no discernable interruptions created by the present crisis. This is a remarkable difference to the interwar years that strongly suggests that Europe will manage the present crisis in a much better way than in the 1930s. **”**

"Economic Crisis in Europe: Causes, Consequences, and Responses," 2009

2 **INFERRING** Why does the author emphasizes the importance of a global, or international, outlook?

_____

_____

3 **EVALUATING** What is the role of the European Union in the case of economic crisis?

_____

_____

4 **INFERRING** Who would be acting on the suggestions described?

_____

_____

5 **ECONOMICS** Summarize the economic system being supported in the excerpt.

_____

_____

_____

_____

ESSENTIAL QUESTION
What influences global political and economic relationships?

Anti-Globalization Demonstrations

DIRECTIONS: Use the image to answer the questions.

EXPLORE THE CONTEXT: Demonstrators protested globalization at the G8 Summit, June 9, 2004. The G8 Summit brings together the world's major industrial democracies: Canada, France, Germany, Italy, Japan, Russia, the United Kingdom, and the United States. There are groups of activists in many parts of the world who reject the economic priorities outlined by the major world economies and by multinational organizations like the United Nations.

PRIMARY SOURCE: PHOTOGRAPH

1 IDENTIFYING How are the people in the photograph the same, and how are they different?

_____

_____

_____

_____

2 INFERRING Why do you think the police are at the location and dressed as they are? How might this be interpreted by the demonstrators?

_____

_____

_____

3 DENTIFYING PERSPECTIVES Why do you think demonstrators would come to a G8 economic summit with a banner that says "Kings on tour never mind the poor"?.

_____

_____

_____

_____

4 INFERRING What does this photograph imply about balance of power?

_____

_____

5 UNDERSTANDING EFFECTS Who is the intended audience of the demonstrators? Who is the intended audience of the photograph?

_____

_____

_____

_____

6 CIVICS How could this photograph be interpreted as a political statement?

_____

_____

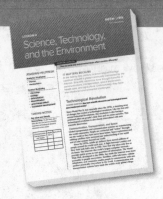

Science, Technology, and the Environment

ESSENTIAL QUESTION

What influences global political and economic relationships?

As you gather evidence to answer the Essential Question, think about:

- factors that contribute to the rapid development of new technology.

- mechanisms that enable technological advancements to gain widespread use.

- barriers to the spread of beneficial technological advancements.

- measures to secure cooperation to address environmental challenges.

DIRECTIONS: Search for evidence in the lesson to help you answer the following questions.

1 **IDENTIFYING STEPS** Use the graphic organizer below to organize the steps of the development of the computer from its origins in World War II to what it is today. Information in two squares has already been added for you.

Development of the Computer

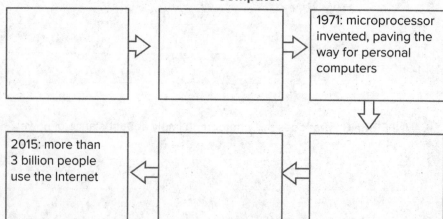

| | | 1971: microprocessor invented, paving the way for personal computers |

| 2015: more than 3 billion people use the Internet | | |

My Notes

_____

_____

_____

_____

_____

_____

_____

2 **ANALYZING** New developments in the field of genetics have enabled advancements in health care and agriculture. While some people hail these advancements as life-saving, others argue that they are dangerous or immoral. Compare and contrast arguments for one of the advancements made.

_____

_____

_____

_____

_____

_____

_____

3 **DIFFERENTIATING** Technological advancements have helped catapult our culture into a new era. Despite this, there are many parts of the world still struggling with access to food, clean water, shelter, and electricity. Can technology be used to improve access to these basic necessities? Why or why not?

_____

_____

_____

_____

_____

_____

4 **UNDERSTANDING CHANGE** The United States has long been considered a world leader on many issues. As environmental challenges are on the rise and the causes and effects of climate change are debated, where does the United States stand as a world leader?

_____

_____

_____

_____

_____

_____

_____

5 CIVICS The world faces many challenges, for which there are a variety of solutions available at the local, national, and international level. Climate change is unique. Why? What are the implications of this?

_____

_____

_____

_____

_____

The Shrinking Aral Sea

DIRECTIONS: Study the image. Then respond to the questions.

EXPLORE THE CONTEXT: Throughout most of history, the Aral Sea in central Asia was the world's fourth largest lake. In recent years, however, the lake has been shrinking at an alarming rate. One of the major causes is the diversion of water from rivers that flow into the Aral Sea. Farmers worked with the Soviet government, which controlled the area at the time, to divert water from rivers in the region to irrigate cotton fields in a desert environment. The satellite pictures below show how much the lake shrank between 1977 and 2009. As the lake shrunk, the climate of the region changed, and the number of deadly sandstorms that spread toxins has increased dramatically. Some residents relocated to other areas. Those who remain suffer high rates of cancer and respiratory diseases caused in large part by the blowing toxins.

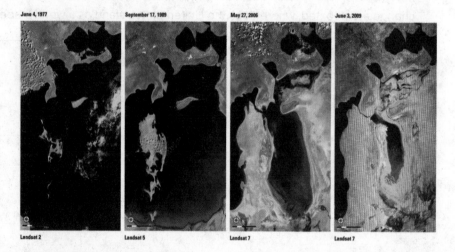

1 ECONOMICS In what ways do you think the vanishing of the sea has affected the economy of the surrounding region?

_____

_____

_____

_____

_____

Copyright © McGraw-Hill Education   Source: Earth Resources Observation and Science (EROS) Center/USGS

2 CIVICS Under Soviet rule, government leaders valued production of exportable goods to be more important than the environment, so they ordered the water be diverted to grow cotton, which could be used at home and sold abroad. The people had no say in these policies and no right to protest them. Could such an environmental disaster occur in the United States?

_____

_____

_____

_____

_____

3 EVALUATING EVIDENCE Why do you think the Soviet government was so committed to diverting the rivers that feed the Aral Sea?

_____

_____

_____

4 CONSTRUCTING HYPOTHESES What ways might the Soviet Union have increased cotton production that would have avoided the destruction of the region around the Aral Sea?

_____

_____

_____

5 ANALING EVENTS Why would saving the Aral Sea have been a long-term benefit for the region?

_____

_____

_____

6 COMPARING AND CONTRASTING The Dead Sea that borders Israel and Jordan is also rapidly disappearing as farmers around the siphon water to irrigate their crops. How might Israel and Jordan work together to save the Dead Sea from the fate of the Aral Sea?

_____

_____

_____

A Declaration of Independence of Cyberspace

ESSENTIAL QUESTION
What influences global political and economic relationships?

VOCABULARY

sovereignty: dominancy; jurisdiction

tyranny: unrestrained exercise of power

solicit: ask

imposition: burden or obligation

1 DETERMINING MEANING

What does Barlow mean when he uses the term *Cyberspace*?

_____

_____

_____

_____

_____

_____

_____

DIRECTIONS: Read the excerpt. Then respond to the questions that follow.

EXPLORE THE CONTEXT: John Perry Barlow (1947–2018) cofounded the Electronic Frontier Foundation and served on the foundation's board from 1990 until his death. Barlow was a fervent believer in the power of the Internet, and he hoped that it would provide a place where people throughout the world could freely exchange ideas. He saw the Internet as a great equalizer where people could share ideas and beliefs in any way they chose without regard to race, social class, religion, education, or wealth.

PRIMARY SOURCE: SPEECH

" Governments of the Industrial World, you weary giants of flesh and steel, I come from Cyberspace, the new home of Mind. On behalf of the future, I ask you of the past to leave us alone. You are not welcome among us. You have no sovereignty where we gather.

We have no elected government, nor are we likely to have one, so I address you with no greater authority than that with which liberty itself always speaks. I declare the global social space we are building to be naturally independent of the tyrannies you seek to impose on us. You have no moral right to rule us nor do you possess any methods of enforcement we have true reason to fear.

Governments derive their just powers from the consent of the governed. You have neither solicited nor received ours. We did not invite you. You do not know us, nor do you know our world. Cyberspace does not lie within your borders. Do not think that you can build it, as though it were a public construction project. You cannot. It is an act of nature and it grows itself through our collective actions.

You have not engaged in our great and gathering conversation, nor did you create the wealth of our marketplaces. You do not know our culture, our ethics, or the unwritten codes that already provide our society more order than could be obtained by any of your impositions.

You claim there are problems among us that you need to solve. You use this claim as an excuse to invade our precincts. Many of these problems don't exist. Where there are real conflicts, where there are wrongs, we will identify them and address them by our means. We are forming our own Social Contract. This governance will arise according to the conditions of our world, not yours. Our world is different. "

— John Perry Barlow, speech at the World Economic Forum, Davos, Switzerland, February 8, 1996

2 **CITING TEXT EVIDENCE** What in the text shows that Barlow is hostile to the government leaders and the governments they represent at the conference?

_____

_____

_____

_____

_____

3 **CIVICS** What does Barlow mean when he refers to the lack of a Social Contract?

_____

_____

_____

_____

_____

4 **IDENTIFYING BIAS** In what ways does Barlow show his anti-government bias?

_____

_____

_____

_____

_____

_____

_____

_____

5 **ANALYZING** According to Barlow, what roles have governments played in the creation and maintenance of Cyberspace?

_____

_____

_____

_____

ESSENTIAL QUESTIONS

What influences global political and economic relationships?

My Notes

_____

_____

_____

_____

_____

_____

_____

_____

_____

_____

_____

_____

_____

_____

1 Think About It

Review the supporting questions you developed at the beginning of the chapter. Review the evidence you gathered in the chapter. Were you able to answer each Supporting Question? If there was not enough evidence to answer your Supporting Questions, what additional evidence do you think you need to consider?

_____

_____

_____

2 Organize Your Evidence

Complete the chart below with information you learned about the factors that influence global political and economic relationships. Be sure to include people and organizations as well as events, developments, and activities. Some items may fit into more than one column.

Political	Social	Economic	Science and Technology

3 Talk About It

Work in a small group. With your group, discuss the motivations, changes, and consequences that you have identified and noted down in your charts. Compare your charts. Did you all pick the same cause and effects? Do you disagree on the consequences of those changes? Overall, which ideas do you think were the most crucial events that led to change in this period? Why?

4 Write About It

Following your discussion in the Talk About It activity, write about two examples of factors that directly influenced global politics or economics. Describe an organization, a development, or an event that changed how people in the world relate.

_____

_____

_____

_____

_____

_____

5 Connect to the Essential Question

Create a website that illustrates, describes, and links to the different factors that can influence global political and economic relationships. Your website should reference governmental organizations, multinational organizations, non-governmental organizations, corporations, financial institutions, and any others you encountered during your inquiry. Your site should include descriptions of all the identified influencers, both positive and negative, and their role in shaping policy or outcomes. When possible, link to websites. Ensure that your presentation is accurate, engaging, and informative.

CITIZENSHIP
TAKING ACTION

MAKE CONNECTIONS Citizens have the power to influence global political and economic relationships; frequently this is accomplished by working with an activist group of some kind—for example, a group actively communicating with legislators to promote policy change, a group working directly on social issues, or a group involved with research or communications to raise awareness of an issue.

Think about an issue about which you feel strongly, and find out what organizations are working for change in that area. Contact their spokesperson or headquarters to find out what you can do to support their work. Outline a plan for taking action.

_____

_____

_____

_____

_____

_____

_____

_____

_____

_____

_____

_____

_____

_____

_____

_____

_____